CW00663071

IRAN AT WAR

1500–1988

DR KAVEH FARROKH

First published in Great Britain in 2011 by Osprey Publishing,
Midland House, West Way, Botley, Oxford, OX2 0PH, UK
44-02 23rd Street, Suite 219, Long Island City, NY 11101, USA

E-mail: info@ospreypublishing.com

A CIP catalogue record for this book is available from the British Library

ISBN: 978 1 84603 491 6

Page layout by Myriam Bell Design, France
Cartography by Peter Bull Art Studio
Index by Michael Parkin
Typeset in Garamond, Futura and Haettenschweiler
Originated by PPS Grasmere Ltd, Leeds, UK
Printed in China through Worldprint Ltd

11 12 13 14 15   10 9 8 7 6 5 4 3 2 1

Osprey Publishing is supporting the Woodland Trust, the UK's leading woodland conservation charity,
by funding the dedication of trees.

www.ospreypublishing.com

Front Cover, top: A rare photograph from 1921, just before the formation of the modern Iranian army, showing
the diversity of the troops. (Author's collection)
Front Cover, bottom: Illustration from *Shahname* of combat between Bijene and Firud from the 16th century.
(Corbis)

Dedication
*To the Spirit of Cyrus the Great whose vision was a major step forward in propelling
forward the concept of human rights and secular rule. I also thank my family and
friends for their support and my loving wife Pari for encouraging me to write this book
on Iran's military history.*

CONTENTS

INTRODUCTION

In essence, *Iran at War* follows on from *Shadows in the Desert: Ancient Persia at War*. Once again, the key question arising is Iran or Persia? As noted in the introductory notes of *Shadows in the Desert*, both are correct. The Greeks referred to the first Iranian Achaemenid Empire as "*Perseeya*" or Persia, a term which then entered the Western and European lexicon. The Iranians refer to themselves as *Eire-An* or *Ir-An* (land of the Aryans); this was in essence a union of Medes, Persians, and the now mostly extinct northern Iranians. The end of the Sassanian Empire in the mid-7th century as a result of the Arabian conquests marks the end of the history of pre-Islamic Iran or Persia. Though it was conquered and its Zoroastrian faith replaced by Islam, Iran's cultural identity endured. It was the Safavids who finally restored a united Iranian realm with frontiers approximating to those seen during the Sassanian era. It important to note that Iran, ever since its formation thousands of years ago, has been a multilingual, multiethnic, and multifaith nation. In Iran's true diverse tradition, the Safavids were an Iranian dynasty but were also Turkic speakers, and much Turkic vocabulary entered the Iranian military lexicon. This is a phenomenon known as the Persianate or Turco-Iranian civilization in which both Iranian and Turkic peoples shared (and continue to share) a mighty and ancient civilizational legacy. Even when Shah Ismail of the Safavids wrote his letter to the Ottoman Sultan Selim Yavuz in Azarbaijani Turkic at the eve of the battle of Chaldiran in 1514, Selim wrote back in Persian!

Readers will note that in Iran's battles throughout the centuries, Kurds, Lurs, northerners, Persians, Azaris, etc often fought side by side in victory or in defeat – their common bond being Iran's ancient history and Persianate culture stretching across the centuries. *Iran at War* offers readers a synopsis of the military history of Iran from the time of the Safavids to the end of the Iran–Iraq War in 1988. Readers will be exposed to Iran's military history during the Safavid, Nader Shah, Zand, Qajar, and Pahlavi eras followed by the onset of the Islamic Republic in 1979 and the Iran–Iraq War. There are numerous chapters that also overlap with complex social and political developments in Iran's history, with notable examples such as the introduction of Shiism in Iran at the time of Shah Ismail, the Mossadegh events of 1953, and the Iranian revolution of 1978–79. Readers with interest in the non-military aspects of these periods are often referred to pertinent works in the references and endnotes.

On a final note, an ancient Iranian axiom describes Iran like the ever-eternal and resilient phoenix or *Simurgh*, rising repeatedly in its history to preserve and defend its integrity, independence, and culture across the centuries. One of the major factors in that resilience has been the tenacity and endurance of Iran's soldiery throughout its history. In victory or in defeat, the Iranian soldier has indeed withstood the test of time.

PART I

THE SAFAVIDS

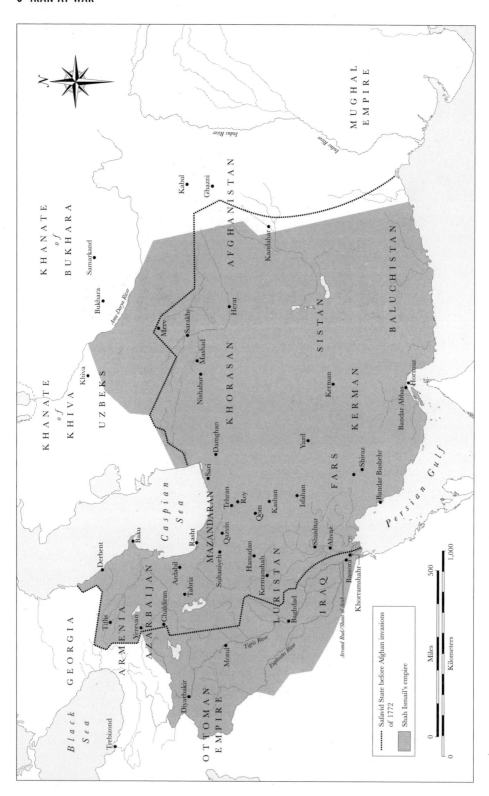

MUGHAL EMPIRE

KHANATE of BUKHARA

Samarkand

Bukhara

Kabul

Ghazni

AFGHANISTAN

KHANATE of KHIVA

Khiva

UZBEKS

Amu-Darya River

Indus River

Merv

Sarakhs

Herat

Kandahar

BALUCHISTAN

Mashad

Nishabur

KHORASAN

SISTAN

KERMAN

Kerman

Hormuz

Bandar Abbas

Damghan

Sari

Yazd

Caspian Sea

Shiraz

FARS

Bandar Bushehr

Rasht

Tehran

Rey

Qom

Kashan

Isfahan

Persian Gulf

Baku

MAZANDARAN

Qazvin

Sultaniyeh

Hamadan

Shushtar

Ahvaz

Derbent

Ardabil

Tabriz

Kermanshah

LURISTAN

Bassora

Khorramshahr

AZARBAIJAN

Chaldiran

Erevan

Baghdad

IRAQ

ARMENIA

GEORGIA

Tiflis

Mosul

Tigris River

Euphrates River

Arvand Rud/Shatt el-Arab

Diyarbakir

Black Sea

Trebizond

OTTOMAN EMPIRE

·········· Safavid State before Afghan invasions of 1772

Shah Ismail's empire

0   500   1,000
Miles

0   Kilometers

N

CHAPTER 1

THE RISE OF THE SAFAVIDS

Preparing the way for the Safavids

The arrival of the Safavids by the early 16th century signaled the rise of the first truly united Iranian empire centuries after the fall of Sassanian Persia to the Arabs in the mid-7th century. The Safavid rise was the consequence of developments during the rule of the Arab Caliphates, the rise of local Iranian dynasties in the Iranian plateau and Central Asia, and the rebellions of Abu-Muslim Khorasani and Babak Khorramdin followed by the Turco-Mongol invasions.

As noted by Ettinghausen, Iran after the Arabo-Islamic conquests "had lost its independence, though not its cultural identity."[1] Iran certainly saw its share of conquerors: the Greeks, the Arabs, the Turks, and the Mongols. Instead of being assimilated and destroyed, the Iranian sense of identity repeatedly rose again, like the *Simurgh* (lit. phoenix) of Iranian mythology.[2] In almost every case, the conquerors were in time conquered by the culture and language of those whom they had vanquished.[3]

Persianate (or Persianized) civilizations are defined as those civilizations variously influenced by the culture and language of post-Islamic Iran and pre-Islamic Persia.[4] Persianate civilizations are not singularly defined as, or confined to, just Persians or wider Iranic peoples such as Kurds, Lurs, etc. In fact many such civilizations were Turkic in origin, notably the Seljuk Turks,[5] Amir Timur (Tamerlane), and his Mughal successors in India;[6] Iranian and Turkic peoples in Central Asia, the Caucasus, and Western Asia, who all share powerful historical bonds in culture, the arts and architecture, music, values, and traditions.[7]

The Persian language and literary tradition spread westwards into Anatolia in the wake of the Mongol invasions of Iran (1219–60).[8] This had a profound impact on the Ottoman Turks of Anatolia. The Turkic Uzbeks of Central Asia, mortal enemies of the Safavids, were (and remain) under heavy Persianate influence. From the eastern fringes of Central Asia to the shores of the Aegean, the powerful legacy of a Turco-Iranian synthesis resonates to this day. The Safavid shahs spoke Azari-Turkish in their court and much Turkic vocabulary entered Iranian military terminology.[9] Turkey today is host to the largest population of West-Iranian speaking Kurds in the Middle East. The Persianate civilization is indeed a phenomenon that transcends race, language, modern political boundaries, and even religion.

Western authors have variously attributed the endurance of Iranian historical and cultural traditions to the "sense of ancient glory, of pride in identity"[10] and "the flexibility and resilience of the Persian character."[11] Part of that flexibility may be the historical Iranian willingness to embrace many of the ways of the conquerors then integrate these into an Iranian cultural milieu.[12]

During the Islamic conquests of Iran (AD 637–651), the Ummayad Caliphate (AD 661–750) had instituted a number of discriminatory anti-Iranian measures. The Persian language and culture was targeted for elimination with Arab sources even reporting of harsh measures taken against

Persian speakers.[13] Despite the efforts of the Caliphate, the culture and language of ancient Persia endured, well into the 13th century. The Caliphate also discriminated against its Iranian converts to Islam. Clawson has noted that despite adopting the Sassanian administrative model of the Iranians to manage their empire, the Arabs implemented a system of "ethnic stratification that discriminated against Iranians."[14] A letter to Ziyad Ibn Abih from Ummayad Caliph Muawiyah (AD 602–680), instructs that Iranians were to be given lower pensions and jobs; discriminated against in prayers when Arabs were present; and forbidden to marry Arab women (Arab men were allowed to marry Iranian women).[15] Muawiyah was very explicit in stating "never treat them [Iranians] as equals of the Arabs."[16] Other discriminatory measures against non-Arabs included declarations that only persons of "pure Arab blood" were worthy to rule in the Caliphate.[17] The succeeding Abbasid Caliphate (AD 750–1258) failed to stem the rising discontent in the Iranian realms. By the early 9th century, much of the Iranian population was growing increasingly resentful and wary of the Caliphate.

In AD 816, Babak Khorramdin (AD 795–838) began a revolt in Iranian Azarbaijan.[18] His objective was to unify the Iranians into a massive revolt against the Caliphate, and his movement made considerable headway. By AD 837, Babak and his followers were in control of much of northwest Iran. The size of his army has been variously described as between 100,000 and 200,000 fighters, which is probably an exaggeration, but it does show that he had much support for his cause.[19] Babak's resistance was ended in 838 when he was defeated by an Iranian general acting on behalf of the Caliphate.[20] The Babak castle in the Kaleybar mountains in the eastern area of Azarbaijan province was evacuated, but Babak was captured and tortured to death by Caliph Al-Mu'tasim (r. AD 833–842). Many of the survivors fled west towards Byzantium, where some took refuge from the caliph's armies by serving the Byzantine army.[21] While the Caliphate had succeeded in militarily defeating an essentially Iranian independence movement, the memories of Babak remained. The survivors of his movement in Iran gradually became absorbed into various Islamic sects.[22] Despite the movement's defeat, the sense of Iranian identity had not been destroyed. It would be in Azarbaijan that the bid to restore Iranian independence would resurface in the person of Shah Ismail and the Safavids.

The poet Ferdowsi (c. AD 935–1020) composed the Iranian epic, the *Shahname* (lit. Book of Kings), around 1000, under the administration of the Ghaznavid dynasty in Central Asia, which was Turkic in origin and Persianate in culture. The *Shahname* promoted the Iranian sense of nationalism by resurrecting pre-Islamic Persia's tales of heroes, myths, and ancient glories. This was to have a major impact upon the political development of contemporary and subsequent Persianate civilizations.[23]

Between 1219 and 1221, the Mongol conqueror Ghenghiz Khan (r. 1206–27) laid waste the mighty Khwarazmian Empire (built on Persian culture) in Central Asia, the city of Herat and much of Khorasan in northeast Iran, and Azarbaijan in Iran's northwest.[24] Large cities were systematically destroyed. In Nishabur, Khorasan, Khwarezm's great city of learning, blood literally poured in the streets. Every man, woman, and child was beheaded and the severed heads neatly piled up into macabre pyramids, around which the Mongols placed the carcasses of cats and dogs.[25] Surviving captives would often be herded outside conquered cities; some would be selected as slaves, the rest executed. Roughly four decades later, Ghenghiz's grandson, Hulagu Khan (r. 1217–65), invaded all of Iran and modern-day Iraq in 1256–60. The Mongol invasion brought killings, plunder, and rape into Iran, spilling west into Mesopotamia. Hulagu's sack of Baghdad in 1258 led to the death of Caliph al-Musra and the abolition of the Abbasid Caliphate.[26] It is estimated that millions of Iranians died during the Mongol invasions, and many more died from starvation following the invasions.[27] Hulagu established his kingdom and that of his descendants, known as the Il-Khanids, in Iran for the next 80 years.[28]

Although the Mongol invasion was terribly destructive, there were some positive consequences.[29] First, Hulagu's territories coincided with those of the former pre-Islamic Persian Empire. After hundreds of years, Iran was more than just a geographical term; it was once again a political entity with no ties to the Caliphate. This laid the basis for the coming of an Iranian state with an indigenous Iranian dynasty. Il-Khanid rulers were tolerant towards religion, meaning that various religious interpretations could thrive, especially Shiism, which would become the official religion of the Safavids.[30] Also, despite Iran's destitute state after the Mongol conquests, Iranian culture thrived during the Il-Khanid era.[31] Despite centuries of foreign rule, a powerful cultural renaissance was taking place, one that would finally find expression in the Safavids.

The military campaigns of yet another conqueror from Central Asia, Amir Timur or Tamerlane (r. 1370–1405), proved as devastating for Iran as those of the Mongols. By the time of Timur's arrival in 1381, Mongol authority had been replaced by a series of petty local dynasties with their own armies. The result was a disunited Iran unable to offer united opposition against Timur's invasions. The brutality of Timur in Iran was legendary, evidenced by, for example, the erection of a gruesome pyramid from the skulls of 70,000 inhabitants of Isfahan who dared to resist him.[32]

Iran's cities at the time of Timur's arrival had witnessed the rise of a number of urban militias, many of them based on the Sufi mystical orders. Among the militias was the mixed Sufi–secular order of the *Sarbedaran* (lit. heads next to the gallows) of Khorasan who were highly effective warriors. These rose in the aftermath of the disintegration of Mongol rule from 1344 until their submission to Timur in the early 1380s. By the time of Timur's arrival, the Mongol-era Jalayerids were still in place in parts of western Iran and Iraq but their strength was waning. In the Anatolian mountains, Kurds and Turcomens often offered stiff resistance against Timur's forces.

Despite his impressive military achievements, Timur failed to nominate an heir. Eventually his successors (known as the post-Timurids) established themselves in eastern Iran, Afghanistan, and much of Central Asia. Among the most impressive of the post-Timurids was Hussein Bayqara of Herat city and province and Khorasan province who became a major patron of Persian arts, language, and literature.[33]

The long-term political consequence of Timur's campaigns in Iran was a power vacuum leading to a civil war between various power centers, particularly the Aq Qoyunlu (1378–1507) and Qara Qoyunlu (1375–1468), Persianate Turcomen confederations of Azerbaijan and Anatolia that had originally arisen in the wake of the collapse of Mongol power.[34] The Aq Qoyunlu strongly and specifically identified themselves with Iran and its culture, citing themselves as Iranian kings.[35]

By 1400, Timur had defeated the Qara Qoyunlu, forcing their leader Qara Yusef to flee to Egypt. After Timur's death, Qara Yusef returned to re-establish the Qara Qoyunlu in Azerbaijan. The Qara Qoyunlu became a significant power, capturing Baghdad four years later, and eventually controlling much of eastern Anatolia, western Iran, northwest Iran, and parts of northern and southwest Iran to the Persian Gulf coast.

Timur had granted the Aq Qoyunlu lands in Diyarbakr in eastern Anatolia in 1402. They were unable to expand their dominations, due to the ascendancy of the Qara Qoyunlu, until Uzun Hassan (1423–78) defeated the Qara Qoyunlu leader, Shah Jahan, in 1467.[36] The Qara Qoyunlu were completely extinguished a year later. The Aq Qoyunlu would prove to be dangerous opponents of the post-Timurids. By 1475–76, Aq Qoyunlu forces also contained native Iranian troops (Kurds, Lurs, and Persians) as well as Arabs.[37]

After the fall of Constantinople to the Ottomans in 1453, European powers were faced with the terrifying prospect of powerful Ottoman armies thrusting into the European continent. Desperate to find ways to curtail the Ottoman threat, the Europeans turned again to the east, hoping to find a new Timur. They found Uzun Hassan (r. 1453–78), one of the most influential leaders of the Aq Qoyunlu. He made an alliance with Emperor David of Trebizond in 1458, but the Ottoman Turks destroyed this kingdom shortly afterwards in 1461.[38] Venetian missions in 1463 and 1471 convinced Uzun Hassan to take military action against the Ottoman Turks.[39] The battles of Arzanjan (1471) and Tercan (1473) followed. At Otluk Beli in the upper Euphrates, Uzun Hassan was decisively defeated by Sultan Mehmed II in August 1473, the Ottoman victory due in large part to their powerful artillery.[40] This explains why a third Venetian mission led by Giosafat Barbaro failed to convince Uzun Hassan to launch another war against the Ottomans, although the Ottomans did not have the capability to overthrow Uzun Hassan.

Azarbaijan: home of the Safavids

Azarbaijan was to become a major bastion against Ottoman Turkish expansion into Iran and the Caucasus. The province and its inhabitants displayed a fierce determination to defend Iran during the Safavid era.[41] In the historical sense, Azarbaijan is confined to the province of that name within the territorial boundaries of northwest Iran, below the Araxes River. The territories in the modern Caucasus within the modern Republic of Azarbaijan above the Araxes River were not known as Azarbaijan until May 27, 1918.[42] Classical sources define the region north of the Araxes River as "Albania" and south of the Araxes as "Media Atropatene" (Iranian Azarbaijan).[43]

The languages in Iranian Azarbaijan were Persian and other Iranian languages, such as Ghilani and Kurdish, until the arrival of Seljuk Turkic invaders in the 11th century AD.[44] The indigenous Iranian culture and Persian language were not destroyed after the Seljuk arrivals, despite the change in language over the ensuing centuries.[45] While the Seljuk invaders were certainly Turkic, they were absorbed by the culture and technology of their Iranian subjects.[46] Kazemzadeh notes that by the early 1200s AD, the Turkic elements in Arran and Azarbaijan were "disappearing rapidly owing to the influence of … Persian civilization."[47] The linguistic Turkification of Albania/Arran and Azarbaijan forcefully began during the Mongol and post-Mongol eras. However, Iranian languages did not disappear, as shown by literature, such as the 14th-century *Nozhat ol Majales* which demonstrates the prevalence of Persian in Azarbaijan and the Caucasus. Literary sources clearly indicate that cities such as Tabriz remained Iranian-speaking for at least four centuries after the Seljuk Turk arrivals. Iranian languages continued to be reported by visitors to the province as late as the 17th century.[48]

The direct ancestor of Shah Ismail I and the Safavids, Sheikh Safi-e-Din Ardabili (c. 1252–1334), was Persian and Kurdish.[49] The 13th-century spiritual leader Sheikh Zahed Gilani (1216–1301) recognized Safi as his successor and gave him the hand of his daughter in marriage.[50] The name "*Safavid*" is derived from the sheikh's name Safi. Sufism and mystical orders have a very long tradition in Iran, with Kurdish orders such as Ahl-e-Haqq or the Yarsean going back into ancient pre-Islamic times.[51] Safi claimed that he was a descendant of Prophet Mohammad through the seventh Imam of the Shiites, Musa al Kazem (d. AD 799).[52] This claim was passed on to Safi's descendants, including the founder of the Safavid dynasty, Shah Ismail.

The Sufi and mystical orders gained much popularity in the aftermath of the Mongol invasions, providing spiritual comfort to the people.[53] It was under these circumstances that Sheikh Safi gained many followers not just in his native city of Ardabil but also in northern Iran and eastern Anatolia. Less known is the role of Sheikh Safi in organizing resistance in Azarbaijan against the Mongol invaders for over three decades (1300–34).[54] At some point between Safi and Ismail, the Safavid line became Shiite. According to Mashkoor, Sheikh Safi and his son Sadreddin were Shafii Sunnis but the Safavids were Shiite from the time of Khajeh Ali.[55] The issue of when the Safavid line became Shiite, however, is strongly debated by Roemer, who argues that no conclusive or direct evidence exists in that regard.[56]

It was during the time of Sheikh Junaid (d. 1460) that the Safavid order changed from a purely mystical movement into one with military and political ambitions.[57] Sheikh Junaid was not only a mystical leader but a warrior whose 5,000 Sufi fighters were deeply motivated by the spiritual beliefs of the Safavid order of Ardabil.[58] They soon acquired a powerful reputation as brave and formidable fighters.[59] There seems to have been a quarrel between Junaid and Jaafar, one of the late Sheikh Ibrahim's brothers. While the succession of leadership was from father to son, Junaid's theological ideas were challenged by Jaafar.[60] The outcome was that Junaid left Ardabil and eventually reached eastern Anatolia. One of his campaigns there was an attempt to capture Trebizond, but he abandoned this upon hearing of the approach of the Ottoman Sultan.[61] In Diyarbakr he forged an alliance with Uzun Hassan of the Aq Qoyunlu. Uzun Hassan married Junaid's sister, Khadija Begum, further strengthening the alliance. Junaid and Uzun Hassan were now firm allies against the Qara Qoyunlu.[62] Uzun Hassan certainly appreciated the presence of Junaid's formidable warriors, who were present at the defeat of the Qara Qoyunlu in 1467.[63]

Junaid was killed in battle against the Shirvans in the Caucasus in 1460.[64] It is not clear whether Junaid was intent on just using Shirvan's territory for passage northwards towards Circassia or whether he also wanted to conquer Shirvan for use as a base for future conquests of Iran. What is certain is that Jaafar and Jahan Shah incited Khalil Sultan Shirvanshah of Shirvan against Junaid.[65]

Despite this major blow, the Safavid lineage endured, with the mantle of leadership passed onto Junaid's son Heidar. He lost no time in cementing the Safavid alliance with the Aq Qoyunlu by marrying Uzun Hassan's daughter, Alamshah Begum.[66] Relations with the house of Aq Qoyunlu cooled considerably after the death of Uzun Hassan as Uzun Hassan's half-Greek son, Yagoub, viewed the presence of a well-equipped and well-trained Safavid force within Aq Qoyunlu domains as a serious threat.[67]

Shortly before his death in 1488, Heidar, inspired by a dream he had had of Imam Ali, ordered his followers to don the 12-gore hat, with each gore representing one of the Imams of Shiite Islam.[68]

Heidar's followers were henceforth known as the *Qizilbash* (Turkic: red-headed ones). Heidar was a remarkable warrior, known for crafting his own armor and swords as well as instituting military drills and martial arts training for his Sufi followers.[69] The Qizilbash were now dedicated religious warriors who spread Shiite Islam by the sword.[70]

Like his father Junaid before him, Heidar led his men into the Caucasus, going as far north as Daghestan and Circassia and even battling the Christian Iranic-speaking Alans (modern Ossetians). The Shirvanshah, Farrokhyashar, allowed passage for Heidar's first two expeditions in 1483 (or 1486) and 1487. The entente soured during Heidar's third campaign in 1488 when he also sacked Shamakhi, the capital of Shirvan. Farrokhyashar sent alarming appeals for assistance to the Aq Qoyunlu leader, Yagoub, who dispatched 4,000 men. It was this force which proved decisive in helping Farrokhyashar defeat Heidar, who was killed at the battle of Tabarasan on July 9, 1488, not far from where Junaid had fallen almost three decades previously.[71] Nevertheless the basis of a powerful Shiite movement based on the Safavid order was already in place. The Safavids had already won converts for their cause in Azarbaijan, the Caucasus, Iran, Iraq, and eastern Anatolia.[72]

CHAPTER 2

SHAH ISMAIL AND THE BATTLE OF CHALDIRAN

Ismail escapes

Heidar was survived by three sons: Ali, Ibrahim, and Ismail (1487–1523). Yagoub imprisoned them all and their mother (his sister) in the fortress of Istakhr in Fars.[1] Ali, the designated successor, was to be later released by another Aq Qoyunlu leader, Rustam, after Yagoub's death. By this time a civil war was raging among the Aq Qoyunlu and Rustam was hoping to capitalize on Ali's ability to mobilize the Safavid order for his benefit. He then re-arrested Ali and his brothers in 1494, alarmed at the rising power of the Safavid house.[2] Ali and his brothers escaped that same year towards Ardabil. Ali was intercepted on his way there and killed in battle with 700 of his warriors.[3] Ali had designated Ismail as his successor and head of the Safavid order.[4] Ismail reached Ardabil but as the Aq Qoyunlu were still in pursuit, his supporters passed him to the safety of Lahijan in Gilan in northern Iran.[5]

A contemporary European portrait of Shah Ismail clearly portrays him with red hair and Indo-European characteristics, showing his part-Kurdish ancestry.[6] Ismail also had Turkmen, Greek, and Georgian[7] ancestry. Considerable effort was put into concealing Ismail's Kurdish origins to present him as a descendant of the family of the Prophet Mohammad.[8] Ismail, like modern Azarbaijanis, was bilingual in both Persian and Azarbaijani-Turkish.[9] He composed many poems in Azarbaijani-Turkish, and his writings in this vernacular did much to contribute to the rise of the Azarbaijani-Turkish language.[10] Nevertheless, Ismail was clear in pointing out his connections to ancient Iran in his poems.[11] In general Ismail seems to have been highly intelligent, generous, a dedicated religious Shiite, and ethically just, caring much for the welfare of his people.[12] Ismail often gave up a significant portion of his share of captured plunder for equitable distribution among his troops and this generosity earned him the fierce loyalty of his troops.[13] Ismail was a strong, formidable, and courageous warrior, highly gifted as an archer. He was also certainly capable of being harsh, showing very little mercy to his opponents and Iran's Sunnis.

In 1499, Ismail, aged 12 or 13, set out with his late father's followers from Gilan towards Ardabil, the spiritual home of the Safavid order.[14] During his trek to Ardabil, Ismail was joined by 1,500 followers of the Safavid order from Syria and Asia Minor.[15] Ardabil's Aq Qoyunlu governor was opposed to Ismail's arrival and forced him to retire to the Talysh area between Gilan and Azarbaijan. The Shirvanshah Farrokhyashar and the Aq Qoyunlu governor both tried to kill or capture Ismail at Talysh during the winter of 1499–1500. Ismail set out again for Ardabil in 1500, but then called out for his followers all over Asia Minor and Syria to join him in Arzanjan. While en route, Ismail was joined by 1,000 Anatolian Turkish or Turcomen Sufis.[16] When Ismail reached Arzanjan in the summer of 1500, he found 7,000 followers from the Turcomen tribes of Afshar, Qajar, Ustajlu, Romlu, Shamlu, Tekellu Varsaq, and Zu ol Qadar already waiting for him. It was most likely at Arzanjan that Ismail began preparing to seize political power in Iran.

As the backbone of Shah Ismail's cavalry, the Turkmen Qizilbash were central to Ismail's early armies.[17] They were organized in units or bands in accordance to their tribe. By the battle of Chaldiran in 1514, they are reported as wearing the best steel armor and mail from Shiraz and powerful shields, with their horses also armored (known as *Badgostvan*). Their weapons included the mace, *Shamshir* curved sword, dagger, lance, and archery equipment.[18] Their helmets were especially robust, designed to provide as much protection possible in close-quarter combat. The Qizilbash also wore the ceremonial 12-gore hats symbolizing the 12 Shiite imams. Their strong loyalty to Ismail and their belief in his invincibility made the Qizilbash especially loyal and steadfast warriors. Ismail was soon joined by Persian, Azarbaijani, Kurdish, and Talysh warriors, especially in the wake of his victories over the Aq Qoyunlu in Iran.[19]

Firearms are thought to have first been introduced to Iran by the Venetians during the Aq Qoyunlu period, specifically at the time of Uzun Hassan (r. 1453–78), as part of an overall strategy of cultivating European relations with the Aq Qoyunlu.[20] Shah Ismail's father Heidar had deployed cannon in his siege of Golestan in 1488.[21] Shah Ismail used artillery in a number of his early campaigns and, on at least one occasion in 1504, muskets. Despite this, the Iranians failed to utilize firearms at the battle of Chaldiran in 1514.

After the great gathering in the summer of 1,500 followers in Arzanjan, Ismail had two choices. He could either take his untested troops into Azarbaijan to confront the Aq Qoyunlu there, or strike into Shirvan in the Caucasus. Shirvan was Ismail's most immediate enemy as both his father Heidar and grandfather Junaid had lost their lives in combat against the Shirvanshahs.

Ismail crossed the Kura River and marched all the way to the port city of Darband on the Caspian.[22] Darband's civilian population evacuated upon his arrival. The local citadel, however, chose to resist. Ismail responded by engaging in a highly effective siege, lasting 20 days. The defenders of Darband defended each of their towers with archery and lances. The Safavids made three unsuccessful attempts to dig mines, then dug a massive hollow below one of the towers, filled it with wood and set it alight. This proved too much for the Darband garrison commander who offered his surrender. Ismail's capture of Darband was of major military benefit for his army. The city offered him much military equipment, especially supplies of the *Jawshan* (shirt-like mail integrated with armored plates) which were immediately distributed to the troops.[23] These were undoubtedly useful to Ismail and his troops when they finally met Farrokhyashar in battle at Golestan in December 1500.[24] The outcome of the battle was a resounding success for Ismail: his army of 7,000 destroyed Farrokhyashar's main army of 27,000, and Farrokhyashar himself was killed.[25] After the battle, Ismail moved south towards the port city of Baku on the Caspian Sea.[26] The city was quickly surrounded and soon submitted to Ismail. He exhumed the bodies of late shirvanshahs and had these burned in retaliation for the deaths of his father and grandfather. Ismail's successes against the shirvanshahs enhanced his prestige and standing among his troops and followers.

Defeat of the Aq Qoyunlu and the capture of Tabriz

Just as Ismail arrived in Arzanjan in 1500, the Aq Qoyunlu reached a compromise to patch up their differences in Iran. Alvand Mirza was to govern Azarbaijan, Arran (modern Republic of Azarbaijan), the Mughan steppe and Diyarbakr in Eastern Anatolia. Murad Mirza was now in charge of the provinces of Fars and Kerman and of the cities and districts of the northwest near Azarbaijan (Zanjan, Hamadan, and Qazvin), the center (Isfahan) Kashan (facing southeast), Rayy (near modern Tehran), and Qom.

Ismail was planning to head back into Iran across the Araxes River for a campaign into Fars province's city of Shiraz, but was distracted by Alvand Mirza's arrival in the Caucasus to confront him. Alvand Mirza brought 30,000 cavalry along with his ally Osman Sultan Torkaman, and 10,000 cavalry from Ganja.[27] These combined to do battle against two of Shah Ismail's top commanders, Ghoraberi-Qajar and Halvachi-Oghlu, who commanded a modest total of just 5,000 cavalry. Ghoraberi Qajar was killed, but Alvand Mirza lost 5,000 of his cavalry. Alvand Mirza, unsatisfied with the outcome, continued to deploy his forces for a showdown against Ismail. This prompted Ismail to move towards Nakhchevan to prepare for Alvand Mirza's arrival.

Shah Ismail arrived at Sharur (near Nakhchevan) with 7,000 troops, nominating Halvachi-Oghlu as his first officer in the theater. In July or August 1501, Alvand Mirza and Halvachi-Oghlu clashed in a bloody battle which lasted from dawn until dusk.[28] Although estimates vary, the *Alam Araye Safavi* reports that up to 18,000 of Alvand Mirza's troops were killed.[29] The battle was decided when Shah Ismail hacked his way with his Shamshir curved sword into Alvand Mirza's ranks to slice off the leg of the enemy standard-bearer.[30] Alvand Mirza and the remainder of his troops fled the field. Ismail's men then raided Alvand Mirza's abandoned camp and each man was rewarded with gold and silver.[31]

After his resounding victory over Alvand Mirza, Ismail entered Tabriz and crowned himself as shah. Despite speaking a Turkic language (as well as Persian), Ismail adopted the Iranian title of *Shah* rather than the Mongol-Turkic *Khan*.[32] Like the ancient Sassanian kings, Shah Ismail was recognized as the shah of the entire Iranian realm.[33] Iranian historiography is clear that the Safavids and Shah Ismail regarded themselves as the heirs of the ancient Persian Empire.[34] As noted by Savory, Ismail had invoked an ancient Iranian tradition of kingship or *Farr* (lit. kingly glory/divine glory) rooted in pre-Islamic times.[35] While it is true that Ismail claimed descent from Prophet Mohammad's lineage,[36] he also claimed to be the descendant of Yazdegird III (r. AD 632–651) the last ruler of Sassanian Persia.[37] Shah Ismail also commissioned a copy of the Iranian epic *Shahname* for his son and successor Tahmasp I (r. 1524–76).[38]

Shah Ismail was also the head of the Safavid sufi-religious order in Ardabil. He was not just the shah of Iran but also the *Pir* (lit. old one/wise one), *Morshed* (lit. spiritual leader), or even *Morshed e Bozong* (lit. grand spiritual leader) to his followers who were known as the *Morid* (lit. follower of the leader), *Ghazi* (lit. warrior) or *Sufi*. The *Moridan* (plural of Morid) were expected to be absolutely loyal to their Morshed, Shah Ismail. Introducing a new Shiite priestly class into Iran was not easy task as the country was predominatly Sunni and had few Shiite clergy. Ismail "imported" Shiite clergy from other countries: one group of Shiite Ulema arrived from modern-day Iraq after Ismail's conquest of Baghdad in 1508 and another group came from Syria.[39] By the latter days of the Safavid dynasty under Shah Sultan Hussein (1694–1722), Shiite scholars arrived from as far away as Lebanon.[40]

Shiism, in combination with a resurgent sense of Iranian nationhood, became a major factor in the motivation of the troops against Ottoman incursions, partly explaining why the Ottomans, the military superpower of the day, failed to conquer Iran. The Europeans, who had a great fear of the mighty Ottoman armies, were quickly drawn to the Safavids. Portuguese admiral Albuquerque even went so far as to claim that Shah Ismail was "a thunderbolt launched by the Almighty for the destruction of Islam."[41] While Albuquerque's statement was certainly misplaced as Ismail greatly revered the Prophet Mohammad and claimed descent from his family, there is no question that Ismail had no love for the Sunni branch of Islam and his determination to eliminate the Sunni creed is well known. He was quick to execute Sunnis who resisted conversion to Shiism, two notable cases occurring in Herat and Baghdad where Sunni theologians, scholars, and even poets were put to the sword.[42] The 16th-century traveler, Ludovico di Varthema, noted Shah Ismail's killings of Sunnis.[43] Ismail was in turn welcomed in cities that had large Shiite populations, notably Kashan and Qom.[44] He also found much support for Shiism in his home province of Azarbaijan, as well as eastern Anatolia.

Although the Qizilbash were Shah Ismail's chief source of military strength, he slowly moved towards building a government apparatus that was more independent of them. Towards the end of his rule, especially after the disastrous battle of Chaldiran in 1514, Ismail promoted more and more Iranian aristocrats into high-level administrative positions.[45] This certainly did not displace the major power centers of the Qizilbash. It would be up to Ismail's successor, Tahmasp I (r. 1524–76), to initiate the recruitment of Caucasians into the army. While the Shiite clergy were certainly influential, Safavid Iran as founded by Shah Ismail cannot be linearly defined as a theocracy.[46]

Shah Ismail secures the Iranian plateau

Shortly after Ismail assumed the Iranian throne, word came to him that a resurgent Alvand Mirza, leading 50,000 fresh troops, was preparing for battle. Two-thirds of Alvand Mirza's army was composed of Ottoman troops furnished by Istanbul. This indicated that the Ottomans were already aware of Ismail's military potential, and were probably worried about his Shiite missionary zeal.

The Aq Qoyunlu, this time led by Morad Mirza, arrived with a force of 30,000, two-thirds of them Ottomans.[47] The battle that took place was notable in that Ismail placed cannon in front of his army. According to the *Alam Araye Safavi*, as soon as Alvand Mirza commenced his cavalry attack "the cannon [from Ismail's army] fired 25 Goolooleh [lit. bullets/cannon balls] killing 7,000 Turkmens and Ottomans."[48] Two of the Ottoman commanders, Osman Pasha and Zal Pasha, were killed during the battle. The total number of Ottoman-Turkmen casualties stood at around 18,000 dead.[49] This battle was especially significant as it proved the effectiveness of cannon against cavalry, especially highly trained Ottoman troops. Despite this success, Ismail didn't permanently incorporate cannon as a regular arm in his forces.

The Aq Qoyunlu, led by Morad Mirza, and their Ottoman allies now raised a new gigantic force of 120,000 troops. Shah Ismail mustered just 12,000 Qizilbash warriors.[50] Battle was joined in the vicinity of Hamadan on June 20, 1503. The Ottoman-Turkmen forces were stationed in seven rows. The battle was hard-fought, but Ismail's daring once again decided the outcome when he led a charge of 2,000 of his best cavalry to slice through the enemy lines. He penetrated as far as the fourth row to slay one of the top Ottoman commanders with his Shamshir sword before returning to his own lines. The shock of this attack caused considerable panic within the Ottoman-Turkmen ranks, leading many to flee the battlefield. The enemy camp was looted and many of the fleeing soldiers were pursued and killed by the Qizilbash. Ismail had prevailed once again and this time up to 40,000 Ottoman and Turkmen warriors had been slain. Ismail's forces engaged in pursuit of the defeated Aq Qoyunlu and their Ottoman allies, following them as far south as Isfahan, where the populace welcomed Ismail. By this time Morad Mirza and 5,000 of his troops had sought sanctuary in the castle of Tabrak. Ismail's troops bored a large hole in the castle's walls then rushed in to slay 3,000 in hand-to-hand combat.

After the capture of Isfahan, many of those Turkmen who had resisted Ismail now came to him in submission. Despite these successes, Ismail still had to face a number of obstinate warriors of the Aq Qoyunlu. These no longer enjoyed Ottoman support, probably because Istanbul was aware of the rising fortunes of Shah Ismail and was reluctant to squander more military resources shoring up the declining political and military fortunes of the Aq Qoyunlu.

The Aq Qoyunlu were not finished as a fighting force in 1503, as Murad was able to raise another 70,000 troops for his cause, forcing Ismail again to mobilize an army of 30,000. They met in a great battle in Fars province. Ismail and his warriors launched cavalry attacks straight into the Aq Qoyunlu lines killing large numbers of the enemy in hand-to-hand fighting using Shamshir swords, lances, and maces. What proved especially decisive was the shattering of the chains fastening the enemy's cannon to its emplacements. Ismail's cavalry hacked the chains using powerful battleaxes, dislodging them from their carriages. Once again Murad fled the field, this time towards Shiraz. In a final showdown in September 1503 Ismail arrived at Shiraz to defeat Murad for the last time. This signaled the end of the ascendancy of the Aq Qoyunlu in Iran.[51]

Ismail's victory at Shiraz finally secured central, western, and southern Iran. Contingents from the entirety of Fars province, Kurdistan and Kermanshah, Yazd and Kerman arrived to offer their allegiance to Shah Ismail. This did not mean that all challenges to Ismail's authority in Iran were over. Kia Hussein Chelavi, the governor of Rustamdar, defied Ismail and rejected his authority. Ismail responded by mobilizing 12,000 troops, which included the Qizilbash, archers, and musketeers. Kia Hussein had engaged in major repairs of fortresses under his jurisdiction, especially those of Gol Khandan, Firuzkuh, and Asta. These measures failed to prevent the arrival of Ismail's army. As soon as the Qizilbash arrived at Rustamdar, a large number of local and Mazandarani warriors simply joined them. Ilyas Beg, one of Shah Ismail's top commanders, pursued Kia Hussein, who had taken refuge in the Iraj castle at Varamin. The Iraj castle was overcome and Kia Hussein was killed but resistance continued. Shah Ismail, who was in Qom at the time, deployed his forces in March 1504 towards the fortress of Gol Khandan. This was decisively overcome, largely through the use of siege equipment, oil-lit projectiles, and artillery firing stone projectiles.[52] The fortress of Firuzkuh was more powerful than Gol Khandan and had been lavishly provisioned to enable it to withstand long sieges. Ismail brought forward his powerful siege engines, battering rams, stone-firing artillery, and glass projectiles filled with flammable oil-based liquids. On the first day of his siege of Firuzkuh, Ismail engaged in psychological warfare. He ordered his drummers and trumpeters to play in unison to demoralize the defenders before bombarding the fortress with artillery for 15 days. This forced the surrender of the garrison and its commander, Ali Kia, by late April 1504. The last fortress was Asta. After a thorough reconnaissance the Qizilbash concluded that besieging Asta with their existing equipment would result in a costly and prolonged operation. The decision was made to cut off the fortress' water supply from the Hableh River. Shah Ismail's troops and engineers managed to divert the river from the fortress, albeit with great effort and difficulty. This soon resulted in a severe water shortage in Asta, forcing its 12,000-man garrison to surrender.[53]

Ismail looks west

Before facing eastern and northeast Iran, Ismail turned his gaze to a traditional base of the Aq Qoyunlu, the province of Diyarbakr in modern-day eastern Turkey. Diyarbakr was an extremely important province as it commanded the defense of Iran's northwest and the Mesopotamian north.[54] The area had been often contested between the Sassanian Empire and the Romano-Byzantines.[55] The region was home to a number of important cities such as Diyarbakr (ancient Amida), Hassankeyf (Hassan Keifa), Mardin, Urfa, Jazira, Uzun, and Sasoun, which boasted very well-built fortresses.[56]

The first city Ismail conquered in eastern Anatolia was Hassankeyf, a formidable city protected by powerful walls approximately 12½–15 miles (20–24km) in diameter. The walls included 360 major towers and small fortresses.[57] The city was held by Ismail's brother-in-law, Sultan Khalil of the Aq Qoyunlu clan. The campaign against the city began with Ismail's dispatch of 10,000 troops under a Qizilbash commander named Ustajlu Mohammad Beg. Sultan Khalil responded by stocking up with a vast amount of supplies to withstand a prolonged siege.

Ustajlu had succeeded in gathering many of the local pro-Qizilbash militias under Ismail's banner. These then tried to fight their way into Hassankeyf's formidable defenses using muskets and traditional arms (especially archery equipment and lances) but no success was achieved. The strength of the city's defenses prompted Ustajlu to use artillery. A four-barreled mortar or artillery piece built during the reign of Sultan Yagoub was brought over from Mardin.[58] Another five-barreled artillery piece, built by an Armenian engineer for Ustajlu, was also brought forward. Most interesting are reports that Ustajlu's forces protected their artillery with a specially built "shield" or timber wall. The "wall" was elevated to allow the artillery to fire and then lowered to protect the artillery pieces.[59] This "fire and shield" system destroyed large numbers of Hassankeyf's powerful defenses and towers. The city finally surrendered after two months. The Safavids wrought terrible vengeance by building ten pyramids of their foes' decapitated heads.[60]

After his successful conquests of eastern Anatolia, the Caucasus and Iran, Ismail thrust towards Mesopotamia and southwest Iran. He began his campaign with the conquest of Mardin in 1507, extinguishing the last bastion of the Aq Qoyunlu in the Middle East.[61] Mosul and Baghdad fell the following year.[62]

A far more serious campaign had to be undertaken in Khuzistan in southwest Iran, home to an extremist Shiite movement, the Mushasha.[63] Ismail had to bring the Mushasha to battle and defeat them. The leader Seyyed Fayyaz was killed but his brother and successor Fallah accepted Safavid suzerainty.

Battles in Central Asia: the Uzbeks

The Uzbeks were still nomads of the steppe when they rose to power in Transoxiana in Central Asia by 1495. Sheibani Khan, the Uzbek leader, was keen to annex the lands of Hussein Bayqara who had died in 1506. Thanks to infighting between the sons of Bayqara, the Uzbeks were able to move into much of Khorasan and occupy the cities of Mashad, Tous, and Herat.[64] This now placed the western part of Khorasan province under threat. It did not take long for the Uzbeks to challenge the newly established Shah Ismail.

In 1507, Sheibani Khan wrote a highly threatening and insulting letter to Ismail demanding that he come to battle.[65] Ismail was too preoccupied at the time with his campaigns in eastern Anatolia, Mesopotamia, and Khuzistan to respond, leaving Sheibani free to roam Iran's northeastern Iranian realms at his leisure. Nevertheless, Ismail had every intention of coming to Khorasan once he had concluded his campaigns to the west. He had also given asylum to Badi ol Zaman, the late Hussein Bayqara's son and heir.[66]

Finally in 1510 Ismail was ready to march northeast. By November of that year he assembled an army of 17,000 troops, from Luristan, Azarbaijan, Arran, Kurdistan, Fars, Kerman, Iraq-Ajam (Hamadan, Qazvin, Zanjan, Isfahan, Qom, Kashan, and Rayy), and Mesopotamia as well as local contingents from Khorasan and the Herat area.[67] The formidable Qizilbash cavalry would again play a pivotal role in the upcoming battle. The Safavid army was outnumbered as Sheibani was able to field 28,000 troops, almost all cavalry.

Ismail's army rapidly liberated Tous and Mashad. As Ismail moved towards Herat, Sheibani fled towards the city of Merv in Central Asia. Sheibani's tactic was an intelligent one. Ismail had not expected to engage in sieges, and hence had not brought much in the way of siege equipment. A means had to be found to bring Sheibani out into the open. Ismail and his Qizilbash commanders adopted Sheibani's literary tactics, and wrote him an insulting letter. They stated that they needed to leave immediately to fight rebels in Azarbaijan and Diyarbakr, and that they would return once the fighting was over. To add to the deception, Ismail ordered his "retreating" army to burn all of their old tents at their encampment. A small force of 300 crack Qizilbash cavalry, led by Amir Beg Muslu, was stationed near the burnt camp.[68]

Safavid spies were highly active and brought up-to-date reports on the Uzbek army and Sheibani's intentions. Sheibani and the Uzbeks, thinking that Ismail was indeed retreating, decided to launch a surprise attack on their opponent's "retreating" army. They reached the burnt-out abandoned camp and found Amir Beg Muslu and his 300 cavalry waiting for them. Muslu engaged in a series of lightning hit-and-run attacks and then feigned retreat. Sheibani and his army took the bait and pursued. But Ismail had prepared a deadly trap.

Ismail had formed his army into a horseshoe shape, and asked Muslu to arrive at their location in the dark of night with the Uzbeks in pursuit. Muslu achieved his task brilliantly: in the darkness of night Muslu led the unsuspecting Uzbeks straight into the ambush.[69] Ismail's troops were equipped with oil-draped torches which were simultaneously lit, just as the war drums and trumpets chorused their message of doom. Ismail unleashed his cavalry from all around the horseshoe into Sheibani and the Uzbeks. Swinging his Shamshir sword, Shah Ismail slew large numbers of Uzbeks during the battle. He soon caught up with Sheibani and killed him as he fled. The total number of Uzbek dead stood at around 10,000.[70] After the battle, Ismail had Sheibani's skull fashioned into a jeweled drinking vessel. There are also accounts that Ismail dismembered Sheibani's hands and legs, sending these to various local governors to affirm that the Uzbek menace had ended.

When Ismail defeated Sheibani and conquered Merv, he also liberated Khadije Khanum, the sister of the post-Timurid prince Zaher e Din Mohjammad Babur (1483–1531). She had been captured by Sheibani and forced to marry him.[71] This inevitably led to an alliance between Babur and Ismail, leading to their military cooperation against the Uzbeks in Transoxiana. Ismail agreed to provide military support for Babur for his claims on Transoxiana on condition that he accepted Shiite Islam.[72] Babur apparently accepted Shiism and even allowed Ismail to exercise his authority over him and his followers.[73] Safavid armies supported Babur's forces in a number of successful battles in 1511–12.[74] Despite this, Babur and his Safavid allies were unable to keep up the momentum of their success; they were finally defeated by an Uzbek army at the fort of Ghujduvan on November 12, 1512.[75] Babur abandoned his claims in Central Asia after eight years, departing to India where he founded the Sunni-Muslim and Persianate Mughal dynasty.[76]

The Uzbeks followed up their success at Ghujduvan by launching a new attack into the Iranian realms in 1512. They sent a powerful force into Khorasan that defeated the local Safavid forces, leading to the occupation of Herat.[77] Ismail, who was in Isfahan, rapidly assembled a new Safavid force which retook Herat.[78] The main Uzbek army remained intact as they had mostly withdrawn upon Ismail's arrival.[79] This set the pattern of Uzbek–Safavid interaction throughout the latter's dynasty: the Uzbeks would launch raids into Iran's northeast whenever they sensed weakness in the Safavid military, then withdraw as soon as a powerful Safavid army arrived to counterattack.

The Portuguese occupy islands in the Persian Gulf

The Persian Gulf has been Iran's major sea outlet since the days of the Achaemenid Empire. By the late Sassanian era the Persian Gulf had become especially vital for Iran's commercial shipping to India, the Pacific, and China.[80] By the early 16th century, the Persian Gulf had become a major center of commercial activity with major outlets at Oman, Muscat, Bahrain, Siraf, Kish and Hormuz. The area was pivotal in the transfer of weaponry, especially archery equipment and swords from Egypt and India.

Europe was to acquire a keen interest in the Persian Gulf. The rise of the powerful Ottoman Empire had cut off all overland trading routes to Iran and India. As Renaissance Europe felt it vital to secure raw materials and new trading markets outside the European continent, another route had to be found to the east. The Ottoman threat was one of the factors that propelled Christopher Columbus' voyage into the Atlantic Ocean. Numerous maritime voyages were made by the European seafarers in search of sea lanes leading to the east. It was the Portuguese who first made a military move into the Persian Gulf, appreciating its potential for trade (especially Persian silk) and its commercial links to the Indian Ocean.

Iran had no navy in the Persian Gulf. This meant that she was at the mercy of any maritime power willing to use force to seize her possessions.[81] This was realized in the person of Alfonso de Albuquerque (1453–1515) who arrived with a powerful Portuguese fleet off the shores of the island of Hormuz in the Persian Gulf in 1507.[82] Albuquerque had undertaken an epic journey around the Cape of Good Hope to reach the Persian Gulf waters. Before proceeding to Hormuz, he occupied a number of locales in the Persian Gulf, including Muscat and the ports of Sohar.[83] Albuquerque's arrival coincided with the Uzbek rampaging of Iran's northeast.

The nominal Iranian ruler of Hormuz was 12-year-old Said e Din, with all matters of policy under the supervision of his vizier, Khajeh Attar. Attar had received plenty of advance warning of Albuquerque's arrival and prepared accordingly. He assembled 400 vessels (most likely large boats or dhows), manned by 2,500 marine fighting men. Defense of the shores and the main town was entrusted to a force of 30,000 men (including 4,000 Safavid troops).[84] When the Portuguese fleet arrived, Albuquerque first engaged in threats and briskly demanded that Hormuz surrender to him. Attar refused. The local nobles were neither as brave nor as defiant as the vizier. The nobles calculated that Ismail was too militarily involved in his battles elsewhere and decided to yield to Albuquerque.[85] Saif e Din became a vassal of the King of Portugal to whom he had to pay an annual tribute.[86]

In response to this takeover, Shah Ismail sent an official to Hormuz to symbolically collect the annual tribute for the Iranian crown. Perplexed at the situation, Saif e Din and his vizier consulted Albuquerque. Albuquerque again responded with threats. He symbolized his resolve by his dispatch of guns, cannon balls, and grenades to the Iranians.[87] He soon regretted this and tried to make amends by sending some precious gifts to the shah. In any event, Albuquerque was not able to retain Hormuz and was forced to leave the island by 1508 when his men grew weary of their stay on the island.

Deteriorating relations with the Ottomans

By 1512, relations between the Ottomans and their Iranian neighbours had been steadily deteriorating for a while. Confrontation was inevitable for three reasons. First, the Ottoman Empire was set on territorial expansion westwards into Europe and eastwards into the Middle East. Eastward expansion would set Istanbul on a collision course with Safavid Iran. Expansion into Europe with an intact Iran on its eastern flank meant that Istanbul always had to contemplate the possibility of a two-front war, and the Europeans were eager to forge alliances with the rulers of Iran against the rising military might of the Ottoman Empire.

The second factor leading the Safavids and the Ottomans towards war was religion. As ardent defenders of the Sunni faith, the Ottomans considered themselves as the seat of the Muslim Caliphate. Iran was now officially a Shiite state, a branch of Islam considered heretical by the orthodox Sunnis of Istanbul. This factor alone was sufficient to rally the Ottoman populace for a holy war against Iran. Ottoman Sultan Selim Yavuz (Turkic: the Grim) (r. 1512–20) was an ardent Sunni. He was resolved to crush Ismail and the Shiites of Anatolia and Iran. The third factor was a derivative of the second – namely the role of pro-Ismail Shiite Qizilbash sympathizers within the Ottoman Empire. These would soon engage in a major rebellion that would shake the Ottoman Empire to its very foundations:

When Ismail had seized the throne of Iran in 1501, he was congratulated by Ottoman Sultan Bayezid II (r. 1481–1512). The latter counselled Ismail to put an end to his destruction of Sunni mosques and graves.[88] Ismail paid little heed to this and continued his quest to expand the Shiite faith at Sunni expense into Ottoman territory. Bayezid II had also been on good terms with Hassan

Khalifa, the pro-Safavid Qizilbash leader in eastern Anatolia.[89] Despite this, relations between the Ottomans and the local Qizilbash were destined to sour.

It was around June 1511 that a major anti-Ottoman rebellion led by the Tekkelu Turcomen led by Shah Qoli broke out in eastern Anatolia.[90] What especially incensed the Sunni leadership of Istanbul was that numbers of the Tekkelu had already joined the Qizilbash of Ardabil in neighbouring Iran. It was clear that the Turcomen were looking eastwards to newly Shiite Iran and its charismatic leader. Many of the Qizilbash had continued to migrate from Anatolia into Iran to join Shah Ismail. This created a mass of fervent religious warriors whom Ismail decided to send back as warriors into the Ottoman regions of Anatolia. A particularly provocative action was Ismail's dispatch of a major expedition led by Ali Khalifa in 1512. This force launched a very damaging offensive deep inside Anatolia, crushing several Ottoman armies.

Selim seized the Ottoman throne in 1513, having fought his father Sultan Bayezid and his brothers for four years in a bitter civil war. From the outset Selim was determined to wreak his vengeance on the Shiite Qizilbash Turkmens of eastern Anatolia and their Safavid patrons in Iran. In a letter to Ismail, Selim accused him of perjury, wrongdoing, and blasphemy.[91] Ismail in turn accused Selim of killing innocent people, violation of sexual mores, and aggression against fellow Muslims.[92]

It is possible that Selim was hoping to provoke Shah Ismail into a face-to-face battle, for by June 1514 Selim had assembled a massive army to attack Iran. He was, however, deeply concerned that the local pro-Iranian Anatolian Qizilbash could harass his army as it marched towards Iran. Selim devised a plan to eliminate them. He sent his officials into the province of Rum in north-central Anatolia to register the names of 40,000 local Qizilbash. Selim then ordered many thousands of them executed or arrested.[93] It is important to note that not all the Qizilbash in Anatolia were Turkmen; there were significant numbers of local Kurds in the movement as well.[94]

Selim also closed the Iranian–Ottoman border to sever the flow of goods between the two states. He wanted to deliver a crippling economic blow to Iran by preventing it from shipping its silk to the west.[95] Conversely, all potential sources of supplies or weapons from the west into Iran were also cut off. This was especially critical as Europe was now unable to send any firearms to Iran through Anatolia.

The battle of Chaldiran

Iran's upcoming contest with the Ottoman Empire was not unlike the wars fought between Partho-Sassanian Persia and the Romano-Byzantine Empire. The only difference was that the resurgent Iranian empire under the Safavids would be facing the Ottoman Turks all along its western, northwest, and Caucasian frontier.[96]

As Sultan Selim marched to war, he was increasingly worried that the Iranian shah would not consent to a set-piece battle. This would then force the Ottoman army to march further east.[97] Such a scenario could prolong the campaign, leading to the unwelcome prospect of having to campaign in eastern Anatolia and northwest Iran during the bitter winter months. Selim's worries appeared to be well-founded. As the Ottoman army marched towards the east, the Safavid governor of Diyarbakr simply evacuated the city. The inhabitants of Diyarbakr then declared their allegiance to Selim who annexed the city on his way towards Azarbaijan.[98]

Mohammad Ustajlu Khan, one of Ismail's most trusted commanders, arrived in Tabriz with alarming news. Ustajlu reported that Selim was now at Erzerum and rapidly moving towards Iran with a huge army. Selim had assembled a massive army variously estimated at between 100,000 and 140,000 men.[99] These included 12,000 Janissaries with firearms,[100] archers and *Sepahi* (royal cavalry guards).[101] Supporting this giant force were 500 cannon.[102] Selim certainly had auxiliary cavalry, but the actual numbers vary according to the sources. Iranian sources variously report the total number of Ottoman cavalry as ranging between 90,000 and 200,000, which is difficult to ascertain.[103] Undoubtedly the most impressive element in the Ottoman army was the Janissaries. Christian boys recruited from the Balkans, they were subjected to very intense military training, constant battle drills, and education and formed into a war-winning arm of the Ottoman military.[104] Selim's subsequent victory had also much to do with logistical planning, especially as he had marched his huge Ottoman army all across Anatolia into Azarbaijan for the decisive contest against Ismail.[105]

Ismail lost no time sending messages for troops to mobilize throughout Iran's cities, tribal regions, and provinces. Some reached Tabriz on time for the battle, but many did not; the forces of Deev Sultan of Balkh reached Azarbaijan after the battle had ended.[106] This meant that the total number of available troops for the upcoming battle was alarmingly low. Primary Iranian sources such as the *Alam Araye Safavi* report 18,000 troops in the Safavid army with the *Habib ol Seyr* citing a total of 12,000 men.[107] In general, it is estimated that the total number of Iranian troops would have numbered around 30,000–40,000 troops, around the backbone of Qizilbash cavalry.[108]

The very large numbers of Ottoman troops, and especially cannon, were a major concern for Ismail.[109] In an emergency military session the Qizilbash chiefs and Shah Ismail unanimously agreed that their only option was to face Selim directly in a set-piece battle.[110] The main problem with this decision was that no solution had been found to neutralize the Ottoman cannon and musketeers. Perhaps Ismail and the Qizilbash chiefs were confident that their cavalry would charge through the Ottoman ranks before Selim's firepower could assert itself on the battlefield.

Ismail and his commanders found a way to turn the size of the Ottoman army against itself. They applied scorched-earth tactics all along the Ottoman advance. This was a highly effective strategy as it left the very large Ottoman army without access to local food or water. Adequate shelter also became a problem as the retreating Safavids destroyed all houses and urban centers along Selim's advance. The scorched-earth tactics put immense pressure on Selim's troops. This situation along with concerns over fighting fellow Muslims led to a near-mutiny among the Ottoman ranks.[111] But the news that Shah Ismail was waiting for the Ottomans at Chaldiran quickly put to rest all dissension.

One of Ismail's major errors before Chaldiran was giving up his mountain base at Khoi.[112] That location would have allowed him a much more effective defense as Selim would have been forced to fight in very difficult geography. Instead Ismail chose to march down to the flat plains of Chaldiran between Khoi and Urumiah (approximately 100 miles (160km) northwest of Tabriz), an ideal location for Ottoman artillery and firearms.[113]

An even greater mistake was Ismail's failure to heed the advice of his two top commanders in the field, Mohammad Beg Ustajlu and Noor Ali Khalifa, who had had experience fighting Ottomans. They urged Ismail to attack immediately before the Turks had time to complete the set up of their cannon and troops.[114] Ustajlu also counseled against frontal attacks due to the strength of Ottoman firepower. But Ismail was swayed by the arguments of another highly influential Qizilbash leader, Durmish Khan Shamlu. The latter counseled that Ismail simply wait until the Ottomans had completed all of their preparations because he thought that a pre-emptive attack before the Ottomans were prepared was "unmanly" and cowardly. Whatever Durmish Khan's motives were, he certainly succeeded in swaying Shah Ismail who then reputedly said "I am not a caravanserai thief... Whatever is decreed by God will occur."[115] So the Ottomans were given ample time to complete the lining up and chaining together of their cannon carriages.[116] The chains would bar Iranian cavalry from dashing through the spaces between the cannon. Mortars were also placed atop each of the cannon carriages.[117] The Ottomans then positioned their 12,000 musket-armed Janissaries behind their cannon.[118] By heeding the advice of Durmish Khan, Ismail had squandered his one chance of minimizing the impact of Ottoman firearms against his forces.[119] Ismail's unfathomable blunder was also perhaps derived from his charismatic overconfidence; he believed himself to be divinely invincible.

Having positioned his forces, Selim selected a hill from which he could observe and direct his forces during the battle. His headquarters were protected by his best men and cannon. Ismail took his position among his troops in the center of the Iranian army, which had no firearm units or cannon. The battle began in the early morning of August 23.[120] The Ottoman cannon immediately opened fire with their large barrels, causing much panic among both Iranian and Ottoman horses.[121]

From the outset the fighting was fierce and bitter. Had Ismail attacked when the Ottomans were still organizing, he might well have broken the Ottoman lines. The *Alam Araye Abbasi* provides a glimpse into the chaos and savagery of the fighting, reporting that when Selim dispatched one of his champions to challenge Ismail in heat of battle, Ismail rode towards the Ottoman, raised his Shamshir sword and cut off his head.[122] Ismail fought beside his troops, but this time the enemy host was too large and well equipped to be overcome by sheer gallantry.

Ismail led the Safavid right flank to attack the Ottoman left flank, killing its commander Hassan Pasha.[123] Despite this terrible blow, the Ottomans did not collapse. Another Ottoman commander, Sinan Pasha, rallied the shaken Ottoman troops, enabling them to stand their ground. Sinan then led a deadly attack with his Balkan or Rumelian troops killing one of Ismail's top commanders, Ustajlu, whose attacking contingents were scattered. Shah Ismail responded by bravely leading charge after charge towards the Ottoman center only to be repelled each time with heavy casualties.[124] The devastating impact of Ottoman firepower has been noted by Iranian sources.[125]

Despite terrible losses, Ismail and his companion Qizilbash cavalry succeeded in reaching the Ottoman front lines a number of times. Using their Shamshir swords, Ismail and the Qizilbash even succeeded in shattering some of the chains linking the Ottoman cannon.[126] But each time they were forced back with heavy losses. Despite this, the Qizilbash attacked once more, forcing many Ottoman troops to fall back to the sanctuary of their cannon and the Janissaries. These actions were certainly brave and impressive, but the Ottoman center remained intact. Sinan then sprang a deadly blow by launching a powerful counterattack from the Ottoman right flank.[127] This attack crashed into Ismail's flank. The impulse of Sinan's attack was so strong that Ottoman troops reached Ismail's camp, capturing plunder and one of his wives.[128] The Iranians now had no choice but to concede defeat. By this stage many of Ismail's top commanders had been killed and Ottoman firearms had taken a terrible toll on Safavid troops. It was clear that no amount of bravery, élan, or dogged determination could overcome the Ottoman juggernaut. Selim though had not escaped unscathed: he had lost a good number of his Albanian, Serbian, and Greek cavalry to the formidable Qizilbash.[129] Still it was Selim who emerged as the undisputed victor at Chaldiran.

Ismail decided to withdraw and yield the field to Selim.[130] He went with a small number of his Qizilbash followers atop a hill and began to sound his *Karney* Sufi flute to signal the retreat. The extent of the catastrophe became evident when only 300 survivors gathered around him.[131] The next day, Selim executed all captured Iranian troop commanders.[132]

Ottoman numerical superiority was definitely a major factor in Ismail's defeat, but Ottoman superiority in artillery and firearms, which enabled them to decimate the Iranian cavalry, was crucial. Ismail had used firearms and artillery in a number of his earlier battles, but at Chaldiran he used neither.[133] He may have chosen not to use them because the Qizilbash viewed firearms with contempt, seeing these as less "manly" than traditional weapons.[134] As noted by Savory, "The inescapable conclusion … is that the Safavids did not use firearms at Chaldiran because they did not choose to use them."[135] A further issue cited by Iranian sources was that no new supplies of European firearms had arrived to Iran prior to Chaldiran.[136] The Portuguese admiral Albuquerque had sought the pope's help to dispatch cannon to Ismail before the battle,[137] but these efforts proved unsuccessful.

Selim captured Tabriz a little over two weeks later on September 5, 1514.[138] The logical course of action would have been to pursue and destroy Shah Ismail, but Selim's generals had other worries. Despite having won the battle at Chaldiran, Selim withdrew from Tabriz just eight days later.[139] Neither he nor his senior commanders wished to spend the bitter winter months in Iran. Ottoman supply lines were overstretched, making them vulnerable to attacks by the local Iranian cavalry in Azarbaijan.[140] The scorched-earth tactics employed in the area ensured that the Ottomans would have no local supplies to sustain them in Azarbaijan.[141] Iranian cavalry could also conduct very costly raids against Ottoman occupation forces; while inside Tabriz the local population was fighting against the Ottoman occupation.[142] These factors combined to dissuade Selim from trying to conquer Iran. As they left Tabriz, the Ottomans did capture Kars to the northwest of Azarbaijan, as well as Nakhchevan, and Yerevan in the Caucasus.[143]

Shortly after Selim departed from Tabriz, Ismail re-entered the city against no opposition. Although Tabriz was once again in Safavid hands, Iran had lost much after Selim's invasion. Much of eastern Anatolia was now detached from Iran. Arzanjan, Diyarbakr, and much of Kurdistan were soon occupied by Istanbul, never to be recovered by the Iranians.[144] These regions were host to a number of Kurdish emirates whose political machinations were similar to the former Aq and Qara Qoyunlu confederations.[145] The Ottomans did little to change the administration of those emirates and even helped strengthen the position of local rulers or "emirs" now under their rule.

The two Kurdish emirates inside Iran, the Ard-Alan and Gowran, were very different from those under Ottoman rule. This was mainly because their rulers were urban and not tribal in origin.[146] For five centuries the Kurdistan region, like Armenia, was caught between the warring Safavid and Ottoman empires, often witnessing devastation and population displacements. Direct rule over the region over an extended period of time was virtually impossible for either empire. As a result both the Safavid and Ottoman empires often exercised their respective authorities through local chiefs. The latter often held the trump card of threatening to switch sides. The power base of these chiefs often derived from their alliances with either the Ottoman or Iranian empires, resulting in the rise of distinct pro-Iranian and pro-Ottoman clans.

Alliances with the West

Albuquerque, still trying to make a good impression on Ismail, sent Miguel Ferreira in 1513 with presents and an amenable message to the shah. Despite these pleasantries, Albuquerque proved his imperialism once more by returning to Hormuz in 1515 with 26 ships and 2,200 soldiers.[147] Iran, reeling from its defeat at Chaldiran a year before, was in no position to fight another major war. Hormuz became a major naval and commercial outpost for the Portuguese Empire. Ismail, who had no navy, had no choice but to comply with what was essentially a *fait accompli*.

Ismail sent his envoy to Albuquerque to propose an agreement: Iran would look the other way at Hormuz if the Portuguese agreed to three specific conditions.[148] The Portuguese were to provide firstly naval transportation for the Safavids for their operations in Bahrain and Qatif in the Persian Gulf and secondly military assistance to the Safavids in their operations at Makran (the coastal strip along Iranian and Pakistani Baluchistan); and most importantly the Portuguese were to forge an alliance with the Iranians against the Ottomans. The third provision was significant as the Iranians expected military support and equipment. The Portuguese acceded to this request by the dispatch to the Iranian army of a number of cannon, muskets, and artillery experts. Despite this agreement, the Safavids did not permanently abandon Hormuz. They had simply entered into an alliance of convenience with a lesser enemy against the Ottomans until circumstances changed.

Shah Ismail made serious efforts to reach out to the Europeans in an endeavor to forge an alliance against the Ottoman Turks. His efforts were reciprocated by King Charles V of Spain, and King Ludwig II of Hungary, who also wanted an Iranian–European alliance against the Ottoman Turks.[149] Both Charles and Ludwig sent their envoys to the Iranian shah.[150]

In 1523, Shah Ismail sent an interesting letter, written in Latin, to Charles V. In it he expressed amazement that the European Christian powers chose to fight each other instead of combining against their common deadly foe, the Ottoman Turks.[151] Ismail urged the Christian powers to set aside their differences and unite against the Ottomans.[152] His letter had clearly demonstrated that he was ready to unite with the Europeans against Istanbul.[153] The letter arrived in Europe just as Ismail died in 1524.

Fortunately for the Ottoman sultans, the vast distances between Iran and Europe (and the primitive state of communications at the time) militated against any coordinated Euro-Iranian military action against them. Nevertheless, the seeds of a European–Iranian alliance had been made. Iran would be heir to European military assistance, a process that would reach its zenith at the time of Shah Abbas I.

The final years of Shah Ismail

After his massive defeat at Chaldiran, Ismail never challenged the Ottomans in open battle again. This did not mean that he completely desisted from militarily opposing Selim. Ismail did send a large Qizilbash force to support the Mamluks against Selim who was moving to conquer Egypt in 1517.[154] Another force of Qizilbash led by the Shamlu and Tekkelu Qizilbash clans was sent by Ismail to fight against Selim's march towards Baghdad, although this particular invasion was abruptly halted after Selim's death in 1520.[155]

The Safavid army was also active in defending its critical northeastern frontiers facing Central Asia. In 1512 the Uzbeks, led by Obeidollah Khan, had launched a new invasion and occupied parts of the province of Herat.[156] The Shamlu Qizilbash warriors again distinguished themselves when Ismail assigned them to defeat and expel the Uzbeks. These campaigns demonstrated that the Safavid army, though battered at Chaldiran, was still intact and highly effective as a fighting force, fully capable of defending the frontiers of the realm.

Chaldiran had certainly resulted in the loss of much territory, but there was another blow to the person of Ismail, one from which he could never recover. Ismail had lost his aura of invincibility, an event which must have shaken his self-confidence. Ismail's sense of dash, boldness, and thirst for battle appear to have subsided after Chaldiran. He was never able to muster the strength to personally lead the Safavid armies into the battlefield.[157] This was a task he entrusted to his commanders. By the last ten years of his life Ismail had increasingly lapsed into a passive state, with a fondness for hunting and pleasurable pursuits.[158] He succumbed to fever and passed away in Tabriz in May 1524.

CHAPTER 3

THE EVOLUTION OF SAFAVID ARMIES (1524–1722)

From Tahmasp I to Mohammad Khodabandeh

The disastrous outcome at Chaldiran in 1514 forced the Safavid leadership to implement reforms for the Iranian army. These were underway during the reign of Ismail's successor, Tahmasp I (r. 1524–76). The Safavid military leadership and Tahmasp realized that the major reasons for the Ottoman army's successes were superb organization, elite units (especially the *Yenicheri* or Janissaries), and firearms.

A glimpse into the state of Iranian armies during the latter years of Tahmasp's reign is provided by a European visitor to Iran, Vincenzo D'Alessandri.[1] Arriving in 1571, D'Alessandri noted that Iran had been divided into five regions.[2] This rationalized the country's defense against attacks by the Ottomans (from the west and northwest), the Uzbeks (northeast), and other potential enemies. These zones were administered by 50 sultans, with each commanding a total of 500–3,000 standing troops. The sultans were capable of raising additional troops from their districts in times of war. Once the sultans had assembled the maximum number of available troops, they would march to a predesignated assembly area to link up with the Shah and the royal guards.

D'Alessandri reports the minimum strength of Iran's cavalry at 60,000 troops, which could be increased in times of war.[3] Iranian cavalry were described as resolute, brave, and highly disciplined in battle. Their primary weapons are described by D'Alessandri as swords (undoubtedly the curved Shamshir), spears, and the musket. Of special interest is D'Alessandri's observation that "Persians are tall and strong ... commonly use swords, lances and guns on the battlefield... Persian Musketeers use their muskets so adeptly ... they will draw the sword at times of necessity ... muskets are slung to the back as to not interfere with the usage of bows and swords ... their horses are very well trained and they have no need to import horses."[4] D'Alessandri's report shows that the Iranians had become highly proficient in the use of firearms before the arrival of the Shirley brothers to Iran during the reign of Shah Abbas I (r. 1587–1629). A major source of firearms instructors for the armies of Tahmasp was the Portuguese.[5]

The rising Iranian proficiency in firearms in concert with their proficiency in close-quarter combat with traditional weapons meant that Iranian troops were capable of facing up to Ottoman troops. This may partly explain why despite their superior numbers, devastating firepower, and high-quality troops the Ottoman Empire proved unable to conquer Iran and overthrow the Safavids.

The pace of the reforms appears to have waned, especially during the latter years of Tahmasp's rule. This was apparently due to the diversion of funds from military affairs towards the coffers of the Safavid royal house. This dealt a heavy blow to the Iranian army. Close to 15,000 unpaid professional troops left Iran to serve in the militaries of India, Central Asia, and the Ottoman Empire.[6] By the time of Tahmasp's death, the state could only afford to field 30,000 cavalry.[7] None would be more disappointed than Iran's potential European allies. On October 7, 1571, they had finally gained an important victory when the combined navies of a number of Christian states (especially Venice and Spain) defeated the Ottomans in the battle of Lepanto. Pope Pius V had then sent a message to Shah Tahmasp I encouraging him to attack the Ottomans and regain his lost territories.[8] Nothing came of this as, according to D'Alessandri, the Shah had become more interested in wealth and women than in fighting the Ottomans.[9]

The state of the army and its reforms reached a new low with the accession of the weak-willed Mohammad Khodabandeh (1578–87). Once again, the Europeans hoped in vain to form a military alliance with the Safavids against the Ottomans. Pope Gregory XIII dispatched Giovanni Battista Vecchietti to obtain information on the state of the Iranian military at the time. Vecchietti reported that Khodabandeh had limited military resources with practically no cannon in service.[10] This is not surprising as this state of affairs was continguous with the latter days of Tahmasp I's reign. Vecchietti also noted that Khodabandeh was a mere puppet of the Turkmen tribal leaders.[11] This was an astute observation as the Qizilbash wielded much power during the reigns of both Tahmasp and Khodabandeh.

Iran, however, was not suffering from any shortage of weapons at this time. According to Mirkhand, workshops across Iran's cities had continued to produce a large number of weapons and deliver these to Safavid arsenals.[12] This would be of great benefit to the revival of the Iranian army after the overthrow of Mohammad Khodabandeh in 1587. When Shah Abbas began to implement his reforms in the 1590s and 1600s, he found that he was able to quickly reconstitute the Iranian army with a large inventory of weapons already stocked in Iran's arsenals.

The Safavid military: organization and units

The Safavid army was to change considerably from its beginnings in the late 15th and early 16th centuries. Many of the units and designations below have their origins in reforms implemented during the reign of Shah Abbas I (1587–1629), with a number of these originating as early as the time of Shah Tahmasp (1524–76).

When Tahmasp I attained the throne in 1524, he pursued his late father's project of forming an elite armed royal guard (Turkic plural *Qoorchilar*, singular *Qoorchi*; original Mongolian term for "archer"). These were drawn from the country's Turkmen warriors, often the Qizilbash. The Qoorchi stood at around 4,500 to 5,000 men by the 1570s.[13] By the end of Shah Abbas I's reign in 1629, these had almost tripled to 12,000 men.[14] Their armaments were a mix of traditional weapons (i.e. curved Shamshir swords, axes, etc.) and muskets. As dedicated royal guards, the Qoorchi were distinct from the main body of Iran's Qizilbash, but would often wear the 12-gore Qizilbash hat in battle. These troops were paid and armed directly by the Safavid royal house, being subject to the direct orders of the king. Qoorchi units at the time of Shah Abbas I were led by Allahverdi Khan (1560–1613), the governor of Fars province. The Qoorchis, whose commander was the *Qoorchi-Bashi*, contained both cavalry and infantry units.[15] By the time of Shah Abbas II in 1642–66, Jean Baptiste Tavernier (1605–89), records a total of 22,000 Qoorchis in military service.[16] The office of the Qoorchi-Bashi was considered one of the most important posts of the Safavid state.[17]

The Qizilbash had been instrumental in bringing Shah Ismail to power. Though formidable warriors, the Qizilbash were highly conservative in their military doctrine. They favoured traditional cavalry and arms while shunning more modern developments in firearms. The Qizilbash were organized around tribal units and provincial contingents led by their respective khans. Every group of a hundred men was led by a *Yuz-Bashi* (Turkic: commander/leader of one hundred).

The khans were represented among the top command echelons of the Safavid army. They had a powerful voice in government and in matters of royal succession. The Qizilbash clans wielded considerable influence in Iran. Their leaders were in key positions of military, economic, and political leadership. Shah Ismail, however, had remained as the undisputed commander-in-chief of the army. In reality, the Qizilbash were the political-military elite that could potentially challenge the Safavid throne. They had very strong tribal loyalties, a factor which could undermine the stability of the state. As lifetime warriors, the Qizilbash looked down on the Iranians who were seen as fit "only" for administrative and bureaucratic duties.

Ismail had soon realized the long-term dangers of the Qizilbash power base within the realm. Although they certainly were excellent warriors, the force was also a double-edged sword, as they could menace the stability and integrity of the realm. As early as 1507, Ismail had appointed an Iranian to the office of the *Vakil* (i.e. viceroy), which was the highest political post in Safavid Iran.[18] The defeat at Chaldiran had certainly shattered Ismail's semi-divine status as the infallible and undefeatable Morshed of his Qizilbash Moridan. While Ismail certainly continued to be respected, the Qizilbash had begun increasingly to act like the feudal-type barons seen in late Parthian times.[19] After Chaldiran, Shah Ismail elevated a number of local Iranian nobles to positions of government but this measure did little to eliminate the primarily Qizilbash influence in the military and government. Ismail's successor Tahmasp I concluded that the only way to reduce Qizilbash influence was to recruit a large new class of *Gholam* (Turkic: slaves/servants) into the military and civilian administration. It would take many more decades before the Turkmens could be significantly displaced from the main levers of power in the government and military, but Tahmasp succeeded in initiating this process.

Caucasian Christians (Georgians, Armenians) and Circassians were brought from the Caucasus to be recruited as the army's *Ghollar*. Like the Christian boys raised as Ottoman Janissaries, the Caucasians were raised and trained as Gholam warriors from an early age. They were proficient in the use of muskets and traditional weapons, notably Shamshir swords, maces, axes, spears, and archery equipment.[20] Gholams could also be placed into various professions to learn various skills and crafts as the state saw fit. Gholam units could be infantry or cavalry, totaling 15,000 men at the time of Shah Abbas I.[21]

It was during the reign of Shah Abbas that Gholam contingents greatly expanded in scope and importance. These, however, never came to threaten or disproportionately influence the political processes of the state. By the reign of Shah Abbas II (1642–66), the total number of Gholam troops stood at 18,000 men.[22] Their numbers remained consistent at 15,000–18,000 men during the reign of Shah Safi II/Suleiman (r. 1666/1668–94).[23] The office of the *Ghollar-Aghassi* (Turkic: General of the Gholams) was second only to that of the Qoorchi-Bashi.[24]

At the beginning of Shah Abbas' reign in 1587, the Qizilbash were able to mobilize up to a maximum of 60,000 troops (almost all cavalry).[25] This was to change as Shah Abbas implemented his reforms, which included promotion of the Gholams. A comparison of the numbers of Qizilbash chiefs in 1578 and 1629 provides a statistical measure of their decline. In a listing of Safavid military commanders in 1576 (last year of Tahmasp I's rule), there are 114 amirs (military commanders) cited of whom almost all are Qizilbash. In contrast, of 90 amirs listed in 1629, only 25 were Qizilbash.[26] The number of Qizilbash warriors was halved by Shah Abbas I to 30,000 troops during his reign.

Another interesting change took place in the armaments of the Qizilbash. These had traditionally been weapons such as swords, mace, lances, and archery equipment. Numbers of Qizilbash also took to wearing light metal helmets in battle.[27] By the time Shah Abbas' reforms had been implemented, numbers of regular Qizilbash troops carried muskets. Top Qizilbash commanders refused to adopt firearms, a testament to their conservative preference for more traditional fighting methods.[28] The reduction of Qizilbash influence removed a chief obstacle against the development of firearm units for the Iranian army.

Regular troops and cavalry numbered at 12,000 and 20,000 respectively under Shah Abbas, and were under the direct command of the shah.[29] The troops were paid and armed directly by the state. The cavalry element was intended to replace the Qizilbash. One of the European translators for the Shirley brothers in Iran wrote later that Shah Abbas I was able to raise a maximum of 100,000 cavalry.[30] This was possible by mobilizing all available units across the country, especially in the tribal and provincial districts. The cavalry in general (regular, provincial, and tribal) were a powerful arm of the Iranian army. European accounts describe regular units deploying a variety of weapons (Shamshir curved swords, spears, archery equipment, firearms etc) with deadly speed and a high level of effectiveness.[31] These are described as being capable of quickly dispersing and coalescing at points of their own choosing during battle.[32]

The *Tofangchilar* (Turkic plural: gunmen/musketeers, singular *Tofangchi*) were the Safavids' formal firearms units. The state of the Tofangchis at the time of Shah Abbas I has been vividly described by the Italian traveler Pietro Della Valle (1586–1652).[33] He noted that the Tofangchis were mainly recruited from the tough and robust Iranian-speaking peasants, in accordance with the advice of the Shirley brothers.[34] This is interesting as the 18th-century Iranian military leader, Nader Shah, was to recruit his musketeers in the same way. The Tofangchis were infantry who used horses for long-distance marches and campaigns.[35] They were able to fire from horseback if necessary. Their units were paid a regular salary throughout the year and expected to report to duty at times of war. Valle was especially impressed by the Tofangchis' ability to set up or leave camp at great speed. They are also described as being able to do so without being detected by the enemy. The Tofangchis were led by commanders known as *Yuz-Bashi*, not unlike the Qizilbash contingents.

Despite their lower social status in comparison to the Qizilbash, the Tofangchis were, according to Valle, among Shah Abbas' favourite units. The best of the Tofangchis came from Iran's northern Mazandaran province.[36] It is not clear how many Tofangchis were in service at the time of Shah Abbas I; estimates vary from 20,000 to 60,000.[37] By the time of Shah Abbas II, these are reported as standing at 40,000–50,000 men.[38] The Tofangchis were noted for maintaining their weapons and uniforms in a high state of cleanliness and preparedness.[39] Tavernier reported the Tofangchis as having a high level of accuracy and agility during the reign of Shah Abbas II. One of their exercises involved a line of ten men aiming their muskets towards a line of ten spears thrust into the ground. Each spear had an apple placed at its top. Every apple would be accurately hit by the Tofangchis from a distance of 100 paces.[40]

The *Jazayerchi* were first introduced during the reign of Shah Abbas II, numbering at 600 troops.[41] These were a new elite troop selected from the most capable and resilient warriors of the realm. They were armed with the larger and heavier hand-held firearm known as the *Jazayer*.[42] This was a much heavier form of musket, which due to its size and weight was fired by placing it on a tripod. For hand-to-hand combat, the Jazayerchis were also armed with Shamshir swords and daggers.[43] The Jazayerchis were to be later increased to 2,000 men.[44]

The *Toopchis* were the artillerymen, manning the cannon units. In overall command of these contingents was the office of the *Toopchi-Bashi* (lit. cannon master/leader).[45] It is difficult to arrive at a consistent estimate of the size of the Safavid artillery corps, which at the time of Shah Abbas I stood at its strongest level. In general, it probably fielded a maximum of 500 cannon and up to 12,000 Toopchis.[46] Cannon were often used in sieges to destroy enemy towers and walls.[47] The Toopchis generally laid sandbags around their artillery nests during siege operations to protect themselves against enemy firearms.[48] The capture of cities and fortresses often entailed the practice of cutting off the besieged locale from all sources of supplies. Western observers note the relative lack of knowledge of the Iranians in their use of cannon in siege warfare.[49] Despite this liability, the Iranians were certainly adept in engineering operations and the digging of tunnels under enemy walls.[50] Excepting perhaps the reforms during the reign of Shah Abbas I, the Iranians never synthesized cannon as an integral part of their weaponry on the battlefield.[51]

This office of the Toopchi-Bashi was of considerable importance during Shah Abbas I's era but had steadily declined by the middle of the 17th century. Tavernier reports on the artillery's low level of efficiency and preparedness; he also notes that numbers of cannon were buried in the grounds of Isfahan.[52] The office of the Toopchi-Bashi was actually temporarily abolished in 1655 (during the reign of Shah Abbas II) due to a combination of financial difficulties, the relatively peaceful state of relations with Iran's neighbours and the low amount of available operational cannon.[53] The generally negative reports of the Iranian artillery continue into the reign of Shah Safi II/Suleiman.[54] By this time the office of the Toopchi-Bashi had been reinstated with a nominal force of 4,000 Toopchis.[55] In practice that force existed mostly on paper, thanks to the consistent overall neglect afforded the artillery arm after the death of Shah Abbas I. Safi II/Suleiman did contemplate a reform of the artillery arm, but the idea was abandoned.[56]

Amiri and Monshi provide a summary of the appropriation of cannon into the Safavid army.[57] The first of these came from battlefield captures of Ottoman and later of Portuguese cannon. The flight of the Ottoman prince Bayezid into Iran (who brought numbers of cannon with him) may also be viewed in this context. The next source of cannon came from the factories established with the assistance of the Shirley brothers during the reign of Shah Abbas I. There were also a number of mobile workshops capable of producing cannon at military camps during campaigns.

Provincial and tribal units were composed of both infantry and cavalry units but were clearly delineated from the regular and standing forces during Shah Abbas' reforms. The costs of maintaining local and tribal units were often incurred by the commanding khans. By the time of Safi II/Suleiman, Iran was (nominally) able to call on an impressive array of provincial contingents supported by local tribal forces from the following locales in the event of an emergency: Kandahar (12,000), Khorasan (20,000), Gilan and Mazandaran (15,000), Darband and Shirvan in the Caucasus (12,000), Azarbaijan (20,000), Yerevan in Armenia (12,000), Luristan (12,000), Susa in the southwest (15,000), south of Iran and Kerman (12,000).[58] Noteworthy were the Qajar tribes who often distinguished themselves as excellent warriors against the Ottomans throughout the Safavid dynasty.[59] These numbers certainly looked impressive on paper, but the reality was that by late Safavid times, the army's state of preparedness and ability to mobilize troops had fallen to dangerously low levels. This was to be disastrously demonstrated when the Afghans succeeded in overthrowing the Safavid dynasty in 1722.

An important Safavid unit contingent was the *Shahsevan* or "Friends of the Shah." These were an all-volunteer national force, mainly composed of Azaris, Kurds, Turkmens, and other tribal-provincial elements. Iranian historians trace their origins to the latter days of Shah Abbas I, numbering up to 120,000 men at that time.[60] Of these 45,000 were permanent troops serving within the elite contingents (Qoorchi and Gholam) and firearm units (Tofangchis and Toopchis). They were also instrumental in reducing the influence of the Qizilbash.[61] The Shahsevan often served as a bulwark of national defense against foreign invasion through Azarbaijan. This was demonstrated two centuries later during the Russian invasions of Iran's khanates in the Caucasus.

The *Yesanchi* were auxiliary units responsible for guarding important buildings and installations. These often cleared the streets for the passage of the shah and his entourage. They were also involved in elaborate ceremonies for visiting ambassadors. One such example occurred when the new ambassadors arriving to Isfahan from the Ottoman Empire, Russia, and Mughal India were greeted with a highly disciplined honor guard of up to 60,000 armed troops lined up on both sides of the road from the shah's palace in Isfahan to the village of Dolatabad.[62] The Yesanchi were also involved in ceremonies and celebrations following battlefield victories.[63]

The *Alamdar* personnel were entrusted with the carrying of flags in battle. The *Alamdar-Bashi* (lit. chief/head banner/flag bearer) had the privilege of bearing the largest and/or most important banners. Iranian flags and banners generally included a number of motifs including those with Qoranic inscriptions, the double-headed Zulfaqar sword of Imam Ali, the names of past fallen warriors, and the Lion and Sun emblem.[64] The Lion and Sun motif would become the major flag of Iran. It can be seen portrayed by Ja'far ibn Mohammad Abū Ma'shar al-Balkhī as early as AD 850, just two centuries after the fall of the Sassanians. The motifs can also be traced back to ancient Iran.[65] Safavid armies used a variety of drums, percussion instruments, and trumpets to build up martial spirit and demoralize the enemy.[66]

The tradition of weapons manufacturing on the Iranian plateau has spanned thousands of years. Iran's military technology has had a symbiotic relationship with developments in Central Asia, China, the Caucasus, the Indian subcontinent, Mesopotamia and Anatolia. The Iranians were especially adept at crafting traditional weapons such as swords, blade weapons, spears, archery equipment, maces, battleaxes, and armor.

Weapons and armor

The *Jabadar-Bashi* ensured that arsenals throughout the country were well-stocked with weapons (traditional weapons, firearms, and gunpowder). The Jabadar-Bashi was also responsible for the supervision of armament production in Iran's factories.[67] At times of war the army would procure its war supplies from the arsenals of those towns and cities closest to the war zone. The army also had a mobile production workshop and repair center to ensure that armaments were always available during campaigns. If defeat was imminent or if a city was about to be captured, the army was obligated to destroy any weapons production equipment that could fall into enemy hands.

The Iranian tradition of forging metals and steel can be traced back to approximately 3000 BC.[68] Persian blades were famous in the West, but mislabeled as "Damascene steel," because they were purchased in the markets of Damascus, where weapons from across the modern-day Middle East were sold.[69] The European error has been noted by Jean Chardin, a French Huguenot jeweler who spent a decade in Iran from 1665.[70] The best-quality steel was in fact from India,[71] but Persian steel was also in high demand and was purchased by foreign buyers from Iran at the time of the Safavids.[72] Persian steel was primarily produced in major cities such as Shiraz, Tabriz, Isfahan, Kerman, Qazvin, Mashad, and Rasht.[73]

The single-edged Iranian curved Shamshir sword was designed for fighting on foot or on horseback. The origin of the Shamshir is debated, but it is certain that this weapon became popular in Iran after the Seljuk, Mongol, and Timurid invasions.[74] By the Safavid era, the curved Shamshir had completely replaced straight swords in Iran. European observers have described the high level of Iranian craftsmanship in the building of swords and blade weapons.[75] The Safavid-era Shamshir gained considerable fame due to its deadly sharpness and its virtually unbreakable blade.[76] As a deadly close-quarter combat weapon the Shamshir was described as "being able to slice the Ottoman Turks in two."[77]

The main Safavid centers for Shamshir sword production were Tabriz, Qom, Isfahan, and Qazvin.[78] Ottoman and Indian sword builders were also to imitate the styles of Assadolah Isfahani and his son Kolbali from the city of Isfahan.[79] In addition, there were many different types of *Khanjar* or daggers being built.[80] Two important centers for producing these daggers were in Kurdistan and Isfahan. There were also cases of Iranian sword-builders imitating Ottoman swords, these being highly valued among the Iranians.

The construction of archery equipment reached a very high level of craftsmanship in Iran during the Safavid era.[81] Archery has a very ancient tradition in Iran, beginning with the earliest Indo-European arrivals to the area.[82] Safavid bows were of the Turco-Persian composite type, built of wood variously combined with sinew, bone, wood, bark, horn, or intestine.[83] There is little doubt of the high quality of Iranian archery equipment. Chardin noted in his travelogues that "Persian bows are the best built in the East."[84]

Arrows could be generally classified as long or short. Long arrows were around 30in (75cm) with shorter arrows acting as darts. The latter could rarely penetrate the opponent's armor, but they were an excellent harassment weapon due to their effectiveness against unprotected horses, unarmored levies, and infantry. Arrows were carried in pouches known as *Tir-Kesh* or *Tir-Dan*. There were at least 12 types of arrowheads including the *Chahar-Par* (four-lobed), and the *Beilak* or *Azar*, which caused severe injuries. There were also a whole class of arrows specifically designed for training purposes and competitive events.

Battleaxes, maces, and spears have a very ancient tradition in Iran. Bronze axe-heads dating at least as far back as the middle to late 3rd millennium BC have been found in Luristan.[85] The ancient Old-Iranian *Avesta* text mentions a weapon known as the "*Chakosh*" which was a double-headed axe thrown at the enemy.[86] The term has undergone many semantic changes such that the term "*Chakosh*" means hammer in modern Persian today. Safavid-era battleaxes were built to a high standard, with the handle of these often having spear-like tips.[87] Tips of spears were built of steel with the shaft being up to 10ft (3m) in length.[88] The mace was also a favourite Safavid weapon, used especially in hand-to-hand combat. Qizilbash warriors used a variant of the mace known as the "*Shesh Par*" (six-sided).[89]

Iran has an ancient tradition of manufacturing armor. Demand for Persian armor over the centuries was prevalent in the Caucasus, the Indian subcontinent, Russia, and Central Asia.[90] The *Zereh* (Iranian mail) consists of a mesh of steel or rings of iron that could be welded, bent, or riveted.[91] The best-quality mail appears to have come from Isfahan and modern Iraq.[92] The *Jawshan,* a shirt-like construction of Zereh integrated with armored plates, appeared almost simultaneously in Iran, the Caucasus, northern India, and Anatolia.[93] Jawshan not only provided excellent protection against arrows, but was also light to wear. There were other types of armor, notably the *Basu-band* used for protecting the forearm and hand in battle.[94] John Cartwright, an English traveler who visited Isfahan in 1603, noted that Iranian mail provided excellent protection against arrows and battleaxes.[95]

The Basu-band was often built for the right hand as the warrior often held the shield with his left hand during battle.[96] The Safavid *Separ* or shield[97] draws from a 4,000-year tradition of shield construction in Iran.[98] Safavid shields were variously built of steel, hide (rhinoceros or elephant), or even tough woods.[99] Safavid shields were circular. Interestingly, small cushions were included inside the Separ to lessen the impact of blows delivered by enemy maces and swords.[100] There was also a four-plated *Chahar-Ayneh* (Persian: four mirrors) that was used for protection of the torso. This was constructed of four rectangular plates: one to protect the chest (*Seeneh-band*), one for the back (*Posht-band*), one *Baghal-band* for the left side of the torso and another *Baghal-band* for the right side.[101] The Chahar-Ayneh was built mainly in cities such as Yazd, Herat, Tabriz, Shiraz, and Isfahan.[102] The Chahar-Ayneh was exported outside of Iran, one prime customer being the Russians.[103]

Safavid *Kolah-Khud* helmets were built of a cone-like dome constructed of hard steel. The neck was protected by mail woven onto the sides and back of the helmet.[104] Prior to wearing the helmet, the warrior would place a seven-layered cloth of silk or felt on his head for additional protection.[105] Helmets and armor protection were also made for the heads of horses.[106]

Reviving the martial arts

The Safavid era witnessed a vigorous revival of the ancient Iranian tradition of martial arts.[107] Chardin reported that "the youth, much like the times of ancient Persia, are introduced to martial exercises."[108] The objective of the Safavids was to inculcate hand-to-hand combat skills, physical strength, and endurance. There was a keen emphasis on cultivating a warrior spirit and high morale, not unlike that seen in the Ottoman Janissaries or *Yenicheri*.

The Pahlavi (Middle Persian) term *Pahlevan* hails back to Partho-Sassanian times. It is a description of a warrior with conviction, courage, generosity, fairness, and mercy in battle, a powerful sense of camaraderie, strict obedience, high standards of culture and moral conduct, who feels an obligation to protect the weak and helpless, who treats non-combatants with generosity.[109] There were a number of training exercises and treatises on warfare for the Pahlevan warriors of the Sassanian era.[110] A unique development from the middle of the Safavid period was the revival of the *Varzesh-e Bastani* (lit. sports of the ancient/Ancient Persia).[111] The Pahlevans also acted as sheriffs or bailiffs in their local area, often patrolling the streets at night to ensure public safety. They became a vital element in Safavid law and order.[112]

Wrestling and hand-to-hand combat training were heavily emphasized. The Safavids placed great stress on face-to-face combat, and specific sword exercises were given for left–right and up–down movements as well as backward slashing actions. The aim of this was to increase strength, stamina, and fencing skills. Stick-fighting, which is still practiced by the Lurs and Bakhtiaris of western Iran to this day, was undertaken with sticks wrapped in wire that weighed up to 20lb (9kg).[113] Other exercises included stretching in order to increase limb flexibility. These training regimens were to yield dramatic results on the battlefield. One case of this occurred in Yerevan in 1604 where after holding out for months, the Ottoman garrison was forced to surrender after just a few hours of hand-to-hand combat.[114] While the Ottomans were among the world's best troops in the use of firearms, the Iranian troops they faced were according to Vecchietti "expert in fighting with sword, lance and bow, and … were greatly superior to the Turks in this."[115]

The exercise venue for wrestling and strength training was the *Zoor-Khaneh* (lit. the house of power). Wrestling in the Safavid era also involved punching, a form of wrestling still seen in Gilan, northern Iran.[116] Training was meant to prepare warriors for facing superior numbers of opponents on the battlefield. The exercise tools of the Varzesh-e Bastani were all derived from weapons.[117] Khorasani has identified six traditional Iranian exercise regimens that survive to this day in Iran's Zoor-Khaneh schools.[118] These are: *Sang*: based on the Separ, equipped with handles and used for "bench press-"type exercises; *Kabade*: a bow of iron or steel with a string of iron-chain, 60in (150cm) in length and around 45lb (20kg); *Takhteh Shena*: a wooden plank 4in (10cm) wide and 3ft (1m) long, used for five types of push-ups, often performed as a group; *Meel*: a wooden mace-like device weighing 25–110lb (11–50kg) and up to 4½ft (1.3m) tall; *Pa Zadan*, a variety of tools used to increase speed and reaction in a series of exercises including stepping exercises and avoidance training; *Charkh*: an ancient exercise of spinning, faster and faster. When the warrior was overwhelmed by superior numbers during battle, he would hold a blade with one or both outstretched hands and "spin and slash" his way out of the impasse.

The Safavids had a variety of other exercises for strength training. One of these involved the throwing spears that were larger and heavier than ordinary combat spears. Constant exercise and training enabled the best warriors to reputedly throw these as far as 600–700ft (180–215m).[119] Safavid troops became very versatile at throwing spears in combat situations.

Training in archery was an ancient Iranian tradition that the Safavids vigorously revived.[120] To ensure that the archer's hands remained steady throughout the process of drawing the bow and releasing arrows, bows of increasing strength and weight would be given to the trainee.[121]

Fighting from horseback had been an essential skill since the Indo-European arrivals into Iran thousands of years before. The Safavids, like all their predecessors in Iran, were keen on developing effective cavalry skills, and polo (usually with 20 players on each side) was a favourite pastime of the Safavids, including Shah Abbas I who participated on a regular basis.[122] One interesting exercise required the rider to shoot an arrow backwards (the Parthian shot) at a cup placed on top of a 120ft (36m) pillar. Accuracy at full gallop was the primary objective. Post-Safavid cavalry became especially adept of delivering the Parthian shot with firearms. There was much emphasis on fluid rider–horse cooperation. Safavid riders were so proficient that they could gallop at full speed, on a loose rein and standing on their stirrups, while in complete control of their mount. Safavid riders could also ride sideways on the saddle to shoot their arrows with deadly accuracy. The best Iranian horses at the time were from the provinces of Luristan, Azarbaijan, and Fars. Arabian horses were also especially prized.

The introduction and development of firearms in Iran

The first systematic effort to train a regular standing force of musketeers began during Tahmasp's reign under Portuguese instructors.[123] Tahmasp and his commanders appreciated the Ottoman proficiency in the use of firearms.[124] In general, the early Safavids relied on foreign deliveries and battlefield captures to maintain a modest force of cannon. During Tahmasp's reign, for example, a defecting Ottoman prince brought high-quality horses (especially Arabians) and 30 cannon to Iran.[125] The Portuguese also provided the Iranians with 200 cannon for use against the Ottomans.[126]

The Ottoman menace during the reign of Mohammad Khodabandeh (1578–87) prompted him to request European assistance. This soon resulted in the arrival of an envoy from Russia's Tsar Ivan IV, with 100 cannon and 500 firearms, to Qazvin.[127] Khodabandeh also made requests to the Grand Duke of Tuscany for Italian artillery instructors. The Pope even offered to supply cannon to the Safavids in 1783.[128]

Shah Abbas I had a keen interest in cannon from the early days of his reign. In a meeting in 1595 with the Russian ambassador in Kashan, Shah Abbas had asked him several questions about Russian cannon.[129] In the same year, Iranian envoys left for Russia to purchase weapons.[130] Three years later, Shah Abbas gained access to European methods of firearms manufacturing. The English brothers Sir Anthony Shirley (c. 1565–1635) and Robert Shirley (c. 1581–1628) arrived in Iran in November 1598.[131] The Shirley mission had been sent by the Earl of Essex to unite Iran with the Europeans against the Ottoman Turks, and facilitate commercial relations between England and Iran.

The Shirleys soon began to introduce European methods of warfare into Iran.[132] One of their chief successes was in helping the Safavids organize their forces into distinct infantry, cavalry, and artillery arms.[133] The Shirleys worked closely with Allahverdi Khan, a major proponent of military reforms.[134] They were also of major assistance in introducing contemporary European methods of mass production for hand-held firearms and artillery in Isfahan.[135] It is estimated that through their efforts, the Shirleys helped the Iranians produce 500 pieces of artillery and 20,000 muskets.[136] The new cannon, in conjunction with those already captured from the Ottomans, gave rise to a highly formidable artillery force.

Despite their achievements, the role of the Shirleys in improving the organization of the Iranian military and firearms production is now believed to have been exaggerated.[137] Chardin provides an astute observation clearly showing that the Iranians were not simply copying European muskets in their factories. He reports for example that "the barrel of the Persian weapon is heavier [than

European counterparts] which makes its range and penetration greater."[138] Another European observer at the time of the Shirleys has stated "I have never seen any gun barrel as well-built as I have seen in Persia."[139] These observations clearly indicate that Iranian engineers had already implemented their own innovations to the musket, probably in accordance with the needs of Safavid military commanders on the Ottoman front. Cannonballs were mainly built in Mazandran. To the Shirleys' credit, the Isfahan firms they designed continued their production into the early Qajar era.[140] Interestingly, the English system for weights, the pound, was used to designate cannonball specifications. For example if a cannonball weighed 80lb (36kg), it would be designated as "*Hashtad Pondi*" (80-pounder) in Persian.[141] The maximum rate of fire for Safavid cannon was approximately one round per minute. Shah Abbas I continued to search for and receive arms from Europe for the Iranian army. As late as the 1610s, he received muskets from Venice and through the East India Company.[142] Iranian cannon were primarily used in sieges against fortresses and cities. They were not thoroughly integrated into Iranian armies on the open battlefield until the reign of Nader Shah (r. 1736–47).

The origins of the *Zanbourak*, essentially a small cannon mounted on a special saddle placed on the back of a camel, are obscure. Some suggest that it was first developed by the Afghans of Kandahar, with others suggesting a Mughal origin.[143] Khorasani explains how the first prototype for this weapon was developed by the Shirley brothers near Lake Van in 1603.[144] This was an especially agile and mobile artillery unit, ideally suited for the vast, rugged, and varied terrain of Iran. The operator of the Zanbourak was known as the *Zanbourakchi*. The Zanbourak was not utilized much by the Safavids. It was certainly used as a major weapon by the Afghans when they invaded Iran in 1722.[145] Nader Shah made full use of this weapon against the Afghans, the Mughals, and the Ottomans. Usage of the weapon became less frequent during the Qajar period and was eventually phased out.

Iran had a number of workshops based in its major urban centers for weapons production. With the arrival of the Shirley brothers, firearms production was also introduced. Factories for the production of both traditional weapons and firearms were soon available in a number of Iran's cities. The quality and workmanship of the products of Iranian weapons factories and workshops were highly praised by European observers during the Safavid era.[146]

After his conquest of Herat, Shah Ismail I encouraged a large number of that city's most talented artisans, artists, ironsmiths, and weapons manufacturers to come to Tabriz in Azarbaijan, where special quarters were constructed for them. This combination of the industrial traditions of Tabriz and Herat resulted in a dramatic improvement in the Iranian weapons production technology. A variety of new types of siege engines were soon invented.[147] These included new designs for stone-throwing artillery engines and launchers for large missiles (arrows/spears). A new type of flammable projectile also appeared, which was essentially hardened glass filled with flammable oils. A fuse on the projectile would be lit before it was shot into enemy ranks. Another interesting weapon was a metallic saucer filled with gunpowder that would explode upon impact. Tabriz-based Heratis are also credited with the design of a new type of metal Tabriz helmet. This was allegedly lightweight yet very robust, especially against arrows and even musket fire, although no samples are known to have been discovered.

Isfahan became a leading center for weapons production during the Safavid era, especially from the time of Shah Abbas I.[148] Traditional weapons were produced, with one entire section of the Aali

Qapu Square dedicated to weapons production.[149] Other sections of Isfahan (e.g. the Bazaar) produced firearms.[150] There were also factories that produced both traditional weapons and firearms. During the reign of Shah Abbas I, one factory housed 200 workers producing cannon, archery equipment, and Shamshir curved swords.[151] Isfahan had also been settled by weapons builders from Mashad, famed for their production of exemplary archery equipment.[152]

A number of other cities such as Shiraz served as leading weapons manufacturing centers. Kermanshah became a leading center, until its destruction by Karim Khan Zand. Major factories were also located in the Caucasus, such as Yerevan, which had a very large weapons production center for the Safavid army against the Ottomans. By the late Safavid era, Qom is also reported as a major center for the manufacture of blades and swords.[153]

Fortifications

There were relatively few fortifications in Safavid Iran compared to Europe. Duri Effendi, an Ottoman ambassador visiting in 1720, noted that Iran had only three major fortresses, Kandahar (facing the Mughals of India), Yerevan (in the Caucasus facing the Ottomans to their east) and Darband (also in the Caucasus).[154] Apart from these, most Iranian cities were not defended by massive fortifications and so were generally unable to withstand armies equipped with artillery. Iranian operations against the Ottomans on the western frontier were often based on mobility, although siege operations would occur (e.g. Sultan Murad IV's successful 1638 siege of Baghdad).

A number of forts built along Iran's frontiers during the reign of Shah Safi II/Suleiman were described as poorly equipped to withstand sieges.[155] This did not mean that the Iranians lacked the knowledge and capability of building effective fortified structures. Chardin's description of Isfahan's Tabrak fortress, for example, reveals that the Iranians were efficient in military fortifications, at least at the time of Shah Abbas II.[156] Tabrak is described as having four major towers, a large ditch, an obstacle up to 30ft (9m) wide, 370 houses (for the troops), a major arsenal, and 40 high-quality cannon seized from the Ottomans and the Portuguese.

Matthee has provided a detailed analysis on the relatively weak state of many Iranian cities with respect to siege warfare by the late 1600s.[157] His survey provides a dismal picture of the defensive walls of major Iranian cities at the time. The walls of Shamakhi (in the Caucasus) and Kashan are described as "badly maintained," and those of Qazvin and Qom as "ruined," with Shiraz, Lar, and Rasht having no walls for defense.[158] Only Darband, Isfahan, and Mashad are identified as having well-maintained walls for defense.[159] The state of Tabriz's walls in the critical province of Azerbaijan is ambiguously described as "Yes/No." With the exception of Yerevan and Darband, virtually all other cities in the Caucasus, northwest Iran and the west (with the likely exception of Kermanshah) were vulnerable to invasion. In the east and northeast, Kandahar and Mashad were the only cities boasting powerful walls capable of withstanding sieges.

Army organization

When war was imminent, the shah would send his messengers to call up all available troops from Iran's cities, provinces, and tribal areas. These would muster in the capital where they were organized by the royal commanders. When mobilization was complete and the army deployed to the critical sector, the commanders and the shah would discuss strategy.[160] However, swift enemy invasions of Iranian territory did not allow the full mobilization of the army in this way. In such critical scenarios, the shah marched as quickly as possible towards threatened sectors with those forces available. Messengers would also be sent throughout the realm for additional troops to join the shah's main army while it was on the march.[161] When all forces finally arrived to join the shah, these would be variously assigned to the standing army's left and right flanks, center, and advance guards.

Scorched-earth tactics were often used against Ottoman armies, notably by Tahmasp and Shah Abbas I. The populations of villages, towns, or even entire cities would be relocated away from the Ottoman path of advance. All buildings and food supplies would be destroyed, and wells poisoned. This ensured that large invading Ottoman armies would be prevented from securing supplies from recently conquered territories. This often wreaked havoc with Ottoman logistics. Invading armies would also be subjected to harassment raids by the Iranian cavalry.[162] If the Ottomans chose to invade with smaller armies instead, they would then risk being outnumbered by hostile Iranian forces.

Spies and informants were an important element of the Safavid military. They were often sent deep inside enemy territory to gain information. Shah Abbas I also introduced the practice of sending spies with emissaries into potentially hostile countries. The spies would quickly relay critical messages through the Iranian postal service, which would rapidly convey these to the high command and even the shah himself.[163] Spying was also applied in battlefield situations. Their main function was to report on the state of both Iranian and enemy front lines and rear echelons.[164] Safavid spies also maintained up-to-date reports on Iran's roads, critical sectors, cities, and garrisons. By the time of Shah Abbas I, the spy network had extended into Iran's cities, villages, and rural areas. The reputation of Shah Abbas I's spies for efficiency gave rise to a number of exaggerated rumors, even that family members in private households suspected each other of being spies for the government![165]

A gradual decline

The Iranians did not place much emphasis on improving their military after Shah Abbas I. Despite this, Safavid armies continued to demonstrate their prowess during the reign of Shah Abbas II (1642–66) by scoring a dramatic victory against the Mughals at Kandahar in 1648–53. The army had (up to this time at least) been kept in constant state of battle-readiness with high numbers of trained troops. This began to change due to perceptions that Iran's territorial integrity was secure against foreign invasions. With the exception of the introduction of the Jazayer troops, Shah Abbas II showed little interest in the Iranian army. Royal troops were to become increasingly demoralized as a result of the increasing corruption from the military administrator's office. Demoralization soon seeped into the lower ranks as the delivery of supplies began to lose consistency. The rot of inefficiency inevitably spread across Iran resulting in a sharp decline in the military effectiveness of provincial contingents.

The artillery arm had begun its deterioration during the reign of Shah Abbas I's successor, Safi I (1629–42). The decline of the artillery was so serious that Safi I had requested assistance from England's King Charles I (1625–49) in rebuilding the Iranian army's Toopchi (artillery) units.[166] The artillery arm continued to decline during the reign of Shah Abbas II.[167] By 1666, Chardin who was present during a military review at the time of Shah Abbas II was blatantly told by an Iranian official that "we have a good army for reviews, but a bad one for war."[168] This seems partly contradictory given Chardin's positive descriptions regarding Iranian training and quality of arms production. It would seem that the military decline was rooted in the inefficiency of upper leadership as well as fiscal mismanagement. These had a profound impact on the Iranian military as a whole. Another observation by contemporary Europeans was the lack of bombs and grenades in the Iranian arsenal.[169]

The situation further deteriorated during the reign of Shah Safi II/Suleiman. Widespread corruption during his reign led to a dangerous slackening in inefficiency. The system of payments to troops became alarmingly deficient.[170] Casualness, dereliction of duty, and the lack of discipline were also evident. Very dangerous was the sense of entitlement that had spread among troops who expected payment but felt little obligation to perform their military duties. The strength of existing military units also fell, with many units now existing only on paper. Perhaps most alarming was the lack of trained troops stationed along Iran's critical frontiers by the late 1670s.[171] The rot which would destroy the military power of the Safavid Empire was now fully in place. The disastrous results of this decline in efficiency would manifest themselves by the early 18th century.

A dangerous vacuum: Iran's lack of a navy

Despite Iran's strides in military developments during Shah Abbas I's reign, especially in firearms production, the Iranians did little to address a serious military problem: they had no navy of their own in the Persian Gulf.[172] The Portuguese had been able to sail into the Persian Gulf in the early 16th century and seize islands for the simple reason that there was no Iranian navy to stop them. Shah Abbas I' successes in ejecting the Portuguese out of islands such as Qeshm and Hormuz owed much to the support of British warships.

Warships in the Persian Gulf belonged to India, the Europeans, and the Arabs (especially Muscat). Iranian ports in the Persian Gulf were often unable to accommodate contemporary war vessels. The Iranians did not build powerful warships in the Persian Gulf, in contrast to the Caspian Sea where the ships were especially sturdy, built of a combination of wood and iron.[173] This meant that Iran remained dangerously vulnerable to the inroads of countries possessing powerful navies, notably the technologically advancing Europeans. For the time being (the Safavid era), relations were certainly constructive between Iran and the West. But with the passage of time, European powers would be inclined to expand their economic and political influence into the Persian Gulf, with little regard for Iran's interests. The long-term dangers of lacking a navy in the Persian Gulf were simply not appreciated by the Safavids. By the early 1700s Iran was already facing a powerful fleet from Muscat but had no naval assets to confront it.

CHAPTER 4

PRESERVING THE EMPIRE (1524–87)

The ascension of Tahmasp I

After Ismail's death in 1524, the powerful Qizilbash, led by Vali Beg Afshar Yuz-Bashi, the leader of the Palace Guard, secured the royal palace and its environs. A royal council composed mainly of the Qizilbash was then formed, resulting in the ascension of 11-year-old Tahmasp I, the son of the late Ismail, to the Iranian throne. After Chaldiran, Ismail had made attempts to curb the Qizilbash Turkmen influence. This process was reversed by Tahmasp's *Atabeg* (Turkic: title of nobility or governor of the state but here meaning tutor), Div Sultan of the Romlu tribe, upon Ismail's death. Div Sultan took over the office *Amir ol Omara* (lit. amir of the amirs). He was to be immediately challenged by another powerful Turkmen tribe of Ustajlu prominent in both Azarbaijan (in the northwest) and Khorasan (in the northeast). Div Sultan managed to retain his post by making compromises with Kopek Sultan (of the Ustajlu) and Chuha Sultan (of the Tekkelu). This resulted in a triumvirate system of rule composed of Div Sultan, Kopek Sultan, and Chuha Sultan. Div Sultan was not content with this state of affairs and sought to eject Kopek Sultan and Chuha Sultan. This led to major battles in the northeast, which soon spread to other parts of Iran.

The fighting resulted in the death of Kopek Sultan and the battering of the Ustajlu tribe. Chuha Sultan then used his guile to incite Tahmasp against his Atabeg, Div Sultan. In the summer of 1527, Tahmasp symbolically shot an arrow towards Div Sultan in the presence of the court, signaling the end of the Atabeg. This was followed by the decline of the Romlu with the Tekkelu gaining ascendancy, but only for three years. The Tekkelu were then challenged in 1531 by Herat's governor, Hussein Khan, leader of the Shamlu tribe. Chuha Sultan was slain with Hossein Khan now assuming his former opponent's position. This success proved ephemeral, as just three years later Hossein Khan was removed from his post and executed. The Turkmen tribal clans behaved like a Praetorian Guard, a situation that was to endure for decades.[1]

The tumultuous state of Turkmen tribal politics proved highly detrimental to the Safavid military in three ways. First, the infighting prevented the Iranians from fully focusing on the rebuilding of their armies. The conflicts also undermined Safavid military efficiency against dangerous invaders such as the Uzbeks and Ottomans. The third problem was that as one clan gained the upper hand, it immediately earned the enmity of the defeated clan(s). The prospect of renewed internecine fighting posed a continual threat for Iran. It was in this context that Tahmasp, like Ismail, looked to counterbalance the power of the Qizilbash, by introducing Gholam units.

Tahmasp's battles with the Uzbeks in Khorasan and the northeast (1524–35)

The Safavids were not just representative of a post-Islamic Iranian cultural revival. They had also inherited the strategic challenges that had troubled their pre-Islamic predecessors, who had faced the Romano-Byzantines to their west and the Turco-Huns to their northeast.[2] By the 1520s the three major empires in Western Asia and the Indian subcontinent were the Ottomans of Anatolia, the Safavids of Iran, and the Mughals of India. The Safavids' greatest military concerns were the Ottomans, followed by the Uzbeks and (to a lesser extent) the Mughals.[3] Like the Sassanian Empire, the Safavids had to contemplate facing enemies on two fronts. Soon after Tahmasp assumed the throne, he was faced with fresh Uzbek attacks from Central Asia along the northeast frontiers. The Safavids never solved the problem of nomadic incursions into Khorasan as the Oxus River was fordable at numerous points, enabling the Uzbeks to launch five invasions between 1524 and 1535.[4]

The first Uzbek attack was somewhat like a large-scale raid, but their ultimate aim was to wrest Khorasan and Herat from the Iranians. The Uzbek attacks were most likely encouraged by the internecine warfare among Iran's Turkmen oligarchy.[5] This is exemplified by a letter written by the Uzbek leader, Obeidollah Khan (the late Sheibani's nephew), to the commander of the Herat garrison being besieged during the winter of 1525–26. Obeidollah noted to Herat's commander that he could expect no help from Tahmasp as the Qizilbash were locked in conflict.[6] He was correct, as Div Sultan of the Romlu could not spare troops to assist Herat due to his military preoccupation with his rivals. Fortunately, Herat held out and Obeidollah Khan withdrew.

Tahmasp succeeded in organizing a military response against the second Uzbek attack in 1528. The Uzbeks had occupied Mashad and Astrabad and were once once again besieging Herat.[7] A very bitter battle occurred at Jaam on September 24, 1528, in which Tahmasp personally took part. The Iranians deployed cannon, using methods learnt from the Ottomans.[8] The Uzbeks mainly relied on their excellent archery skills during the battle. The Iranians then attempted to annihilate the Uzbeks by closing in with "Egyptian swords and large shields."[9] Tahmasp himself charged with 3,000 of his cavalry and struck the Uzbek rear.[10] The Uzbeks were defeated, but the Safavids failed to finish them off and they managed to escape.[11] Tahmasp was unable to continue the fight against the Uzbeks as he was forced to turn west to defeat an Ottoman-linked rebellion at Baghdad led by Zulfaqar Khan Mausillu Torkaman. Baghdad fell to Tahmasp in June 1529 and Mausillu was killed.

Tahmasp's Baghdad adventure gave Obeidollah time to regroup and organize his next attack into Iran. In 1529, the Uzbeks launched their third large-scale attack into Khorasan and the northeast, causing much destruction and hardship.[12] Mashad fell once more with the Uzbeks crushing a Safavid relief force of 3,000 Qizilbash cavalry.[13]

Interestingly, even as Safavid armies had been militarily engaged in northeast Iran, they had also engaged in a number of maneuvers and military reviews in the region. These maneuvers were meant to keep the army in a state of high alert and battle readiness but also to dissuade potential rebels in the area from taking advantage of the Uzbek raids to launch insurrections of their own.[14] These tactics failed to stem the Uzbeks who also succeeded in capturing Herat.[15] The fall of Herat was partly due to the continuing internecine Qizilbash rivalries. Chuha Sultan of the Tekkelu had refused to send military assistance to his rival, Hussein Khan, the commander of Herat. Iranian disunity clearly benefited the Uzbeks, who penetrated as far present-day Damghan.

News of this defeat came as a great shock to the Safavid court, but it was not until the summer of 1530 that Tahmasp marched at the head of a new army against the Uzbeks.[16] As soon as Tahmasp's army arrived, Obeidollah's hand-picked governors took to their heels; Obeidollah himself retreated from Herat. He attempted to recruit more troops in Merv and when this failed he departed for Bukhara. With no Uzbeks to fight, Tahmasp withdrew by November. His army was too large to maintain in the field for an indefinite period without grave supply problems, and, more importantly, Ottoman Sultan Suleiman the Magnificent was now threatening Iran's northern, Caucasian, and western frontiers.

The fourth Uzbek invasion occurred in 1531 and continued for two years.[17] Tahmasp was in Tabriz when the Uzbeks struck, and witnessed the occupation of Khorasan province. This time the Uzbeks reached as far as Rayy in 1533.[18] Herat, which was besieged, was the only locale that held out against the Uzbeks. Then all of sudden, in late October 1533, Obeidollah decided to return to Central Asia.

Tahmasp eventually arrived in Khorasan with his army by December 1533 and spent the winter in Herat to prepare for a massive punitive expedition against the Uzbeks. He finally deployed with his main force towards Balkh by late June 1534 to confront Obeidollah and the Uzbeks. Further military action was then abandoned due to a massive Ottoman invasion of western Iran.

Obeidollah launched the fifth and last of his invasions in 1535. This was largely facilitated by a local revolt against the Qizilbash, who constantly plundered the civilian population. A number of these rebels even made common cause with Obeidollah. Treason by some local citizens delivered Herat into the hands of Obeidollah and his allies. Despite this, Obeidollah was unable to hold on for long. As military discipline plummeted among the Uzbeks, news came that Tahmasp had halted an Ottoman invasion and was marching on Khorasan. Interestingly one of the reasons for Obeidollah's withdrawal was because of his troops' reluctance to fight the Qizilbash.[19] There are reports of Qizilbash warriors crushing the Uzbeks in battle and chasing them back into Central Asia.[20]

Tahmasp's battles with Sultan Suleiman the Magnificent

Even as the Uzbek frontier was temporarily pacified, the Ottoman military machine threatened Iran's western and northwest marches. Suleiman the Magnificent (1520–66), one of the most significant sultans of the Ottoman Empire, was an extremely capable and resourceful military leader. He posed a dangerous military threat to the Europeans, especially as previous Ottoman conquests had already absorbed much of the Balkans, and Serbia in particular.[21] Suleiman had every intention of expanding further into Europe. Belgrade was conquered in August 1521, then in 1526 came Suleiman's great victory against King Louis II of Hungary at the battle of Mohacs. The Hapsburgs retook Hungary, but Suleiman reconquered the country in 1529. Suleiman concluded a ceasefire agreement with the Austrians in January 1533. By 1541, Suleiman's ascendancy over the Europeans was finally secured and Ferdinand and Charles V were forced to conclude unfavourable treaties with Suleiman. While Vienna remained outside the Ottoman orbit despite two sieges, Suleiman's military and political ascendancy in Europe had been firmly established.

The Iranians and the Europeans were both gravely concerned with the powerful Ottoman military machine. One thousand years previously, European Goth chieftains faced with Byzantine armies had sent embassies to King Khosrow I Anushirvan (r. 531–579); and the Europeans now realized how useful the Iranians could be as allies against the Ottomans. The first official contact between Iran and England took place when an envoy of Queen Elizabeth I (1533–1603), Anthony Jenkinson (1529–1610/11), was granted an audience with Shah Tahmasp and the Safavid court in *c.* 1561–62, though this visit failed to achieve any results.[22]

With the cessation of hostilities on his European frontiers, Suleiman turned his gaze eastwards. Suleiman was well aware of the potential danger posed by Iran, especially if it managed to reform and expand its military. Despite their overwhelming victory at Chaldiran, the Ottomans had failed to absorb Iran into their empire. This meant that any Ottoman expansion into Europe had to account for the possibility of Iranian military intervention in the east. Suleiman was intent on achieving complete strategic mastery against the Iranians. Memories of the Qizilbash rebellion in Anatolia, which had shaken the Ottoman Empire to its roots, had certainly not been forgotten either. With Safavid Iran crushed, Istanbul would then be able to focus all of its military might against the Europeans. The elimination of Iran would also allow the Ottomans to conquer the entire Caucasus right up to the Caspian Sea littoral. It was most likely with these objectives in mind that Suleiman launched his three invasions of Iran in 1532, 1548, and 1554, all of which would eventually fail in the face of the Iranians' accomplished scorched-earth tactics and Qizilbash raids, coupled with the bitter winter weather of the Caucasus and northern-northwestern Iran.[23] Suleiman had a keen interest in absorbing Azarbaijan into the Ottoman realm. The loss of this important province would fatally weaken Iran and cut it off from the Caucasus. An opportunity seemed to present itself when Ulama Sultan of the Tekkelu clan, the shah's governor in Azarbaijan, defected to Istanbul (*c.* 1531–32).[24] Ulama Sultan soon discussed Iran's troubles with his Ottoman hosts. He noted the Uzbek invasions and the turbulent tribal forces undermining Iran's stability. Duly impressed, Suleiman soon bestowed the rank of pasha on Ulama Sultan. The sultan then sent him to conquer Bitlis and support the Ottoman invasion of Iran.

Ottoman incursions into Iran began as early as 1532[25] with Ibrahim Pasha, the Ottoman grand vizier, capturing Tabriz on July 15, 1534.[26] Iranian sources report a very large Ottoman force in this operation, this reputedly numbering up to 500,000 troops.[27] By September Suleiman had arrived in Tabriz and from there pushed into Hamadan. Much of Kurdistan was also overrun. The ultimate objective was Baghdad, which fell without resistance to a vast army of 200,000 troops by December 1534.[28] Tahmasp, who was en-route towards Balkh to force a major showdown with the Uzbeks, hurriedly marched his army west towards the Ottoman armies, covering over 1,500 miles (2,400km). As Suleiman entered the Mesopotamian marches, Tahmasp proceeded to deploy his army. The Iranian commanders knew they were not yet ready to tackle the Ottomans in a set-piece battle. Instead they chose to rely on their excellent cavalry to launch lightning raids, harassment, and skirmishes against the lumbering Ottoman supply trains, rear guard formations, and other targets of opportunity.[29] Ottoman supply and communication lines had been stretched to the limit and scorched-earth tactics denied the large forces much-needed supplies.[30] The bitterly cold climate of Azarbaijan also took its toll.

Suleiman then departed for Istanbul. As soon he and his army departed, nearly all of their conquests were repossessed by the Iranians. A vivid example of this is Badran bin Fallah, a Mushasha ruler of Khuzistan, who was forced to acknowledge Suleiman the Magnificent but who sent his son to Tahmasp to confirm his loyalty as soon as Suleiman had departed.[31] Baghdad remained in Ottoman hands, as did the Shiite holy shrines of Karbala and Najaf in southern Iraq. The port city of Basra also surrendered to the Ottomans in 1838, giving them access to the Persian Gulf through the Arvand Rud/Shaat al Arab waterway.[32]

Nevertheless, the Ottomans had failed to destroy Safavid Iran, which still posed a dangerous military threat to their east. By the conclusion of Suleiman's first war with Iran in August 1535, the Ottomans had lost a staggering 50,000 troops, at least a quarter of their original force.[33] The Safavids then constructed a number of fortifications along their borders with the Ottomans.[34]

Eight years later, Suleiman was given another opportunity to strike against the Safavids. Tahmasp's half-brother, Alghas Mirza, arrived in Istanbul to seek asylum.[35] Alghas, who had distinguished himself during the battles against the Uzbeks, had rebelled against Tahmasp once before and been pardoned.[36] Suleiman welcomed Alghas and furnished his "guest" with at least 40,000 cavalry, to be used in an invasion of Iran.[37] The Ottoman force thrust into Marand in Azerbaijan followed by the capture of Tabriz in c. 1548.[38] Alghas then captured Hamadan, following this by attacking Qom and Kashan. He made a determined push towards Isfahan, but it ended in complete disaster due to ferocious resistance from the Safavid army and the local populace.[39] Alghas was then captured by Tahmasp, or else escaped westwards into Ottoman territory.[40] Suleiman's attempt to invade Iran using an allied Safavid claimant had ended in failure.

An interesting account of one of the battles fought near the Euphrates River in Mesopotamia in 1548 is provided by a priest named Juda Thaddaeus Krusinski. Krusinski reports Suleiman arriving with 200,000 troops against Tahmasp's 100,000 troops.[41] Krusinski then adds that Tahmasp "received 10,000 additional soldiers with twenty cannons from the Portuguese."[42] Tahmasp is then described as having participated in a major attack which "with the help of the brave Portuguese defeated the Ottoman Turks completely."[43] The total number of Ottoman losses in the 1548–49 campaign stood at 20,000 troops.[44]

In 1553, Iran launched attacks into the Ottoman Kurdish east. Ismail Mirza (Tahmasp's second son) attacked eastern Anatolia, capturing Akhlar and Arjish. An Ottoman army led by Erzerum's governor, Iskandar Pasha, was then decisively crushed right in front of the city of Erzerum.[45] Three thousand Ottoman troops were killed, and Erzerum was then captured.[46] The Iranian army conducted a number of similar operations, to the consternation of Istanbul.

Suleiman took to the field in May 1554 when he deployed his army from Aleppo for Amida advancing as far as Karabagh in the southern Caucasus, just north of the Araxes above Azarbaijan.[47] This three-month campaign achieved little except the collection of plunder. To their disappointment, the Turks had found the Iranian army unwilling to engage them in a set-piece battle. Instead, the Iranians subjected their Ottoman opponents to constant cavalry raids that harassed and weakened their large army.

Suleiman's territorial gains had come at a heavy price: the Turks had suffered heavy losses and their empire's treasury in Istanbul had been strained.[48] Realizing the futility of continuing, the Ottomans finally decided to end the fighting. This eventually led to the Treaty of Amasiya on May

29, 1555, the first peace treaty between the Ottoman Empire and the Safavids of Iran. While Istanbul could find consolation in the conquest of Baghdad and the Mesopotamian lands, Azarbaijan and other Iranian territories remained in Safavid hands. The Amasiya treaty affirmed the fact that the Ottomans were unable to conquer Iran.

Iran was also desperate for a peace treaty. The country had been badly battered as a result of virtually continuous wars since the days of Ismail. Decades of warfare had resulted in much depopulation and devastation in those provinces bordering the Uzbeks in the northeast and the Ottomans to the west and northwest. Tahmasp and the Safavids had succeeded in keeping the Iranian state intact and were more than capable of resisting Uzbek and Ottoman incursions but they were unable to inflict decisive defeats upon them. It was the appreciation of Ottoman military strength that prompted Tahmasp to move the Safavid capital from Tabriz, relatively close to the Ottoman border, to Qazvin, further inland in Iran.[49]

Like the Safavids, the Ottomans were far from immune from internal dissensions. In 1559, a 10,000-man Ottoman army led by Prince Bayezid, one of Sultan Suleiman's sons, arrived in Iran seeking asylum.[50] Bayezid, his four sons, and their troops were given sanctuary in Qazvin by Tahmasp. Bayezid tried to persuade Tahmasp to provide him with an army to march towards Istanbul.[51] Despite this apparently golden opportunity, Tahmasp remained circumspect, anxious not to disturb the fragile peace. Tahmasp also suspected that Bayezid was plotting against him in Qazvin.[52] Suleiman's threats soon helped Tahmasp make up his mind. He warned Tahmasp that lasting peace was contingent upon the repatriation of Bayezid and his sons.[53] After two years of negotiations, Tahmasp was given gold coins and territorial concessions by Suleiman, resulting in the repatriation of Bayezid and his four sons in 1561.[54] Suleiman then had his son and grandsons put to death. In appreciation for Tahmasp's compliance, Suleiman reaffirmed the terms of the Treaty of Amasiya in 1562.[55]

Tahmasp's battles in the Caucasus

Georgia held a top strategic priority for the Safavids. Tahmasp had launched at least three campaigns there in 1540–54 with Georgian resistance proving fierce. Despite the capture of the Georgian capital Tbilisi by the Qizilbash cavalry, Tahmasp was not always able to maintain control of the region. The Qizilbash in particular suffered high casualties in Georgia, which may explain their subsequent brutality. After the conquest of Tbilisi and Kakheti in Georgia, the Qizilbash rounded up an incredible 200,000 women, girls, and young boys who were then sold into slavery.[56] They also engaged in the systematic destruction of a number of local churches in Georgia.[57] Nevertheless, Tahmasp was finally able to appoint the Bagratid David (brother of King Simon I) as the governor of Georgia. David then came to the Safavid court and converted to Shiite Islam.

The Caucasian Khanate of Shirvan became a part of Iran by 1538, followed shortly later by Baku and Shekki in 1551. Nevertheless the solidification of Iranian influence beyond these khanates thrust the Iranian army into a series of bloody battles. Fighting often involved muskets and close-quarter combat with spears, swords, and other close-quarter weapons.[58] Iranian forces also deployed cannon to batter defiant castles and cities into submission. Fighting was especially intense in the predominantly Sunni Lezgian region. As in Georgia, the Qizilbash cavalry rounded up 100,000 prisoners from the Lezgians who were then brought to Shirvan to be sold as slaves.[59] These rapacious measures proved brazenly inept as they turned local opinion vehemently against the Safavids. The Ottomans became the main beneficiaries of Qizilbash brutality and consistently sought to extend their influence among the Sunni folk of the Caucasus.

These military preoccupations in the Caucasus and distractions to the east, especially Tahmasp's sponsoring Mughal emperor Homayoun's efforts to regain his throne, seriously compromised Safavid efforts at implementing widespread military reforms. Still, enough of these measures were put in place to provide the basis of a new and powerful Safavid military machine under Shah Abbas I.

Tahmasp's legacy and the ephemeral reign of Ismail II

During Tahmasp's final years, a serious rebellion erupted in Gilan. Relations between the Safavids and eastern Gilanis had progressively worsened and the governor appointed to Mazandaran by Tahmasp in 1569 lasted only until 1576.[60] In the mid-1570s, Gilan was overrun by a large force of 20,000 tough Gil and Daylami warriors led by Ahmad Khan Lahejani.[61] Tahmasp assembled an army of 18,000, which thrust into Gilan to engage in heavy fighting, killing at least 1,000 rebels. Fighting subsided somewhat when the rest of the rebels scattered into the northern Iranian forests along the Caspian Sea.[62]

In 1576, Tahmasp's death resulted in a dynastic struggle for succession in which Turkmen tribes played a significant role.[63] Tahmasp's son Ismail II (r. 1576–77) was an excellent warrior who had fought with distinction during Tahmasp's wars against the Ottoman armies of Suleiman. By the age of 19 Ismail II's martial ardour had landed him in command of 8,000 troops.[64] By 1547 he had become the governor of the important khanate of Shirvan.[65] Ismail had led Safavid and local Shirvani warriors into a great victory against vastly superior numbers of Ottoman troops with superior firepower in eastern Anatolia. Duly impressed by his son's achievements, Tahmasp appointed him as the guardian of Khorasan and made him the heir to the Iranian throne. Ismail II, however, then rebelled against his father, who stripped him of his privileges and removed him as heir to the throne.[66] Tahmasp then imprisoned his son in the remote fortress of Qahqaha.[67]

After Tahmasp's death, the two contenders for the throne were Ismail and another of Tahmasp's sons, Prince Haidar.[68] Haidar's support was mainly based on the Ustajlu Turkmen tribe and the Georgian leaders of the Safavid court. Princess Pari Khan Khanum led the pro-Ismail coalition composed of her (Circassian) uncle Shamkhal Sultan and the majority of Turkmen tribes, except the Ustajlu. The issue was decided when 30,000 Qizilbash warriors assembled outside the Qahqaha prison in support of Ismail II.[69] Ismail II then assumed the throne in Qazvin on August 22, 1576. Haidar was arrested and decapitated thereafter by Ismail II's supporters. Ismail then distributed funds from his late father's treasury to reward those troops who had supported him.[70] It is fairly certain that Ismail II's brief 18-month tenure as shah was a bloody episode in Safavid history. Ismail systematically executed nearly all of his brothers, the only one to escape unscathed waas the near-blind Mohammad Khodabandeh, and he most certainly would have been executed had it not been for Ismail's early death.

Lawlessness and banditry had risen alarmingly by the latter years of Tahmasp's rule. Thousands of citizens had been killed by marauding Turkmen warriors in search of plunder. To his credit, Ismail II put a stop to such practices by reestablishing law and order across the country with very stern and severe measures. Perhaps Ismail II's strangest policy was his attempt to re-introduce the Sunni branch of the Muslim faith into Iran.[71] Perhaps he was trying to placate the Ottoman Turks after Suleiman demanded in the Treaty of Amasya that the Iranians stop execrating the Sunni caliphs, Abu Bakr, Omar, and Osman. Domestic factors may also explain Ismail's anti-Shiite policies, aimed at undermining the power of the Shiite clergy in the country; or perhaps they can be explained by Ismail's estranged relationship with his father Tahmasp, his anti-Shiism acting as a rejection of his hated father's legacy. Ismail died in November 1577, under somewhat mysterious circumstances.[72]

Mohammad Khodabandeh: incompetent leadership and heavy losses

Having survived his brother's murder spree, Mohammad Khodabandeh (r. 1578–87) was selected as shah by the Safavid court's council of Qizilbash leaders after Ismail II's death. He arrived to assume the throne in Qazvin on February 11, 1578. Despite their overwhelming power in Iranian politics, the Qizilbash chiefs continued to be unstable, with disastrous consequences for the Iranian state. Their disputes were noticed by the Uzbeks in Central Asia who invaded Khorasan once again just after Khodabandeh had become shah. The Uzbeks overran much of Khorasan, wreaking much destruction but were finally defeated by Mashad's governor, Morteza Qoli Sultan.[73]

From the outset Khodabandeh's rule was perceived as incompetent, a fact that had invited the Uzbek attack and would quickly entice Ottoman invasions to the north and west. Khodabandeh attempted to diffuse potential opposition against him by paying those troops whose pay was in arrears (some had not been paid for 14 years!).[74] He also attempted to win the favour of his subjects by providing lavish grants from the imperial treasury.[75] This measure led to a rapid depletion of state funds and did little to "buy off" potential opposition, would cause problems when the military needed funds to help fend off the Ottoman invasions. Khodabandeh also displayed the despotic practices of his brother, Ismail II, putting Pari Khan Khanum, her uncle Shamkhan Khan and Shah Ismail II's child (Shah Shuja) to death. This action certainly contributed to Iran's dangerous state of political instability. The situation became so desperate that Khodabandeh's queen, Mahd e Olia, was murdered by Qizilbash chiefs in July 1579.[76] Two years later, a rebellion in Khorasan led to that province seceding from the Safavids.[77]

Istanbul was acutely aware of events in Iran. The Kurds of Iran (mainly in western Azerbaijan) and the Caucasian Khanate of Shirvan had erupted in rebellion while Georgia had become split between a pro-Ottoman and pro-Iranian faction. Sultan Murad III (r. 1574–95) saw this as a golden opportunity to attack, in violation of the Amasiya Treaty. The recent Ottoman defeat at the naval battle of Lepanto in 1571 was perhaps another incentive for Istanbul to seek compensation, at Iran's expense.[78]

In 1578, Murad III sent a huge army of between 100,000 and 300,000 troops (including 6,000 musketeers) supported by 600 cannon.[79] Many of these were Istanbul's Crimean Tatar allies who streamed down the Caucasus to support their Ottoman allies against Iran. The Ottomans crushed all Safavid opposition in their wake and captured the Caucasian khanates of Shirvan and Karabakh; much of Georgia was also invaded. This was a catastrophic economic blow to Iran. All Iranian commerce through the Caucasus to the Volga and Eastern Europe was now severed.

The situation deteriorated still further when Azerbaijan was also invaded, an action aided by a number of Kurdish chiefs in the western marches of the province.[80] This crisis prompted

Khodabandeh to dispatch the forces of the Ustajlu governor of Armenia and available Qajar warriors to repel the Ottomans. The Qajars are reported as having fought exceptionally well in hand-to-hand combat with their curved Shamshir swords and spears.[81] Despite their bravery, the Qajars could not throw back the gigantic Ottoman forces arrayed against them. Istanbul continued to hold the initiative as Qajar and other Iranian units were systematically defeated. The bloody nature of the fighting is vividly demonstrated in reports of Ottoman troops building pyramids of skulls from the dead Iranian troops.[82] Prince Hamza Mirza struck back by leading a very successful attack into Shirvan and Karabakh in 1879.[83] The Tatar chief, Adel Giray Khan, was captured by Hamza Mirza and sent to Qazvin. The Ottomans and their Tatar allies had certainly paid a high price for their recent military expedition against Iran; they had lost a total of 20,000 troops.[84]

A new Ottoman force of 260,000 troops arrived to invade Iran in *c.* 1585.[85] Hamza Mirza did his best to assemble troops from Azarbaijan, Fars, western Iran, and Kerman, but his mobilization failed thanks to internal conflicts between Qizilbash chiefs. The failure to form a powerful unified force prompted the Safavids to utilize scorched-earth tactics. Civilians and supplies were completely evacuated from Tabriz, despite opposition from a number of Iranian military leaders. The final decision made was to stand and fight in Tabriz. To that end, Hamza Mirza and his 10,000 cavalry managed to raise 50,000 men from Tabriz. Despite being hopelessly outnumbered, Hamza Mirza's cavalry and the Tabrizi militia took positions along the city's streets and homes. When the Ottomans arrived in Tabriz, they employed their overwhelming firepower (cannon and muskets) to reduce almost of Tabriz's strongholds. Despite their victory, the Ottomans only managed to stay in Tabriz for about 40 days. They were forced to withdraw from the city due to bitter resistance by Tabriz's defenders and most likely by the shortage of supplies. Just as the Ottomans were pulling back from many areas of Azarbaijan, Hamza Mirza, now leading 12,000 cavalry, prepared to strike. Once again, internal conflicts prevented Hamza Mirza from pressing home his attacks, allowing Ottoman forces to withdraw relatively unscathed.

Not all of the Ottomans had withdrawn from Tabriz. An obstinate garrison of Ottoman troops led by the supremely capable Jaafar Pasha continued to occupy the city's citadel. The Tabriz militia had two formidable Tahmasp-era siege guns.[86] Each had barrel length of 5 yards with a bore of 1 yard.[87] When the Tabriz militia brought these guns to reduce the citadel, Jaafar Pasha's men captured one of these by first dispersing the cannon's crew and then lowering ropes to pull the weapon into the citadel.[88] Undeterred, Hamza Mirza had Barkhordar Bashi, an expert Iranian cannon designer build a new cannon for action. Sappers also planned to cut through into the citadel. All of these plans came to naught as another Iranian artillery expert, Qoli Beg Afshar, defected to Jaafar Pasha to reveal Hamza Mirza's strategy. Aware of the direction of the sappers' impending strike, Jaafar Pasha placed his musketeers along their path of advance. As soon as the sappers and troops arrived, Jaafar Pasha's musketeers opened fire and decimated them. The Ottomans had in the meantime sent a relief force led by Farhad Pasha to relieve Jaafar Pasha in the Tabriz citadel. Once again Hamza Mirza did his best to raise troops but only succeeded in mobilizing 10,000 warriors. By this time many of the Qizilbash clans were in open conflict, practically eliminating them as a factor in the war.[89] Given Iran's military and political disarray at this time it is amazing that the country survived as a state. As has often happened in Iran's military history, the rise of a new and brilliant leadership was soon to rescue the country from the brink of disaster.

CHAPTER 5

SHAH ABBAS THE GREAT

The rise of Shah Abbas I

Abbas (1571–1629) was Mohammad Khodabandeh's third son. He was born in Herat during the latter years of his grandfather Tahmasp I's reign. Despite his young age, Abbas had been appointed as the governor of Herat, as it was customary to station a prince of the royal house at that city.[1] When Khodabandeh attained the throne in 1578, his wife Mahd e Olia gained much influence, trying to promote her elder son Hamza instead of Abbas. With the death of Hamza in Karabakh in early December 1586, a number of the Qizilbash looked to Abbas as a possible heir to the Safavid throne.[2]

Morshed Qoli Khan, a powerful Ustajlu Qizilbash leader of Khorasan province, had cultivated close relations with Abbas in Herat. When a new Uzbek invasion again thrust into Khorasan in 1787, Morshed Qoli Khan marched with 16-year-old Abbas to Qazvin to overthrow the reigning Shah. Khodabandeh raised no protest upon Morshed Qoli Khan's arrival in Qazvin. He meekly handed the throne to his son Abbas on October 1, 1587.[3]

The Qizilbash quickly learned that they could not so easily control their new protégé. Abbas I, in contrast to his father, was a strong-willed, resolute, and independent leader. He would curb the influence of the turbulent Qizilbash in the Safavid military and government, reform the military, and regain lost Iranian territories. Known as Shah Abbas the Great, he proved to be the most capable of all Safavid rulers. He was one of Iran's greatest monarchs in history, possibly on a par with the likes of Khosrow I Anushirvan. Shah Abbas was an absolute monarch whose leadership was more secular than religious, and whose rule saw the gradual separation of religious institutions from the political machinations of the state.[4] The theme of patriotism and the preeminence of Iran, already established by Shah Ismail I, became especially prominent under Shah Abbas.[5] The premise of the importance of Iran (and its pre-Islamic past), in contrast to religion, was already in place with the *Shahname*.[6] Despite his secularist tendencies, Shah Abbas was a devout Shiite Muslim. He also had open views towards other religions.[7] Though he could be merciless against Sunni Muslims, as seen by his brutal treatment of Sunnis at Baghdad, which he captured in 1624.

Shah Abbas was a gifted military leader. Like the legendary Shah Ismail I, Abbas joined his troops in battle. In Shah Abbas' view, "the king must live a soldier's life and always move alongside his troops to be able to overcome any difficulties and to be successful at any task."[8] Shah Abbas was very diligent in his constant supervision of military affairs. Every morning after breakfast, he would visit the stables then inspect the weapons factories of Isfahan.[9] He showed great care for the welfare and morale of his troops. In 1606, Allah-Beg Qajar, a most capable military leader, and a number of Qizilbash warriors were severely wounded during an attack against one of Ganja's towers. Shah Abbas ordered the medical tents erected next to the royal tent. The shah would then visit the wounded twice a day, and even help dispense medication.[10]

Shah Abbas relocated the capital from Qazvin to Isfahan in 1598.[11] Qazvin was relatively close to the northwestern borders, which made it vulnerable to Ottoman attacks, whereas placing Iran's political center of gravity at Isfahan would relocate it to Iran's center. Isfahan not only became a major political center, but soon served as the focal point for an important artistic and architectural revival, not unlike that seen in the Sassanid period.[12] This revival can be traced back to Shah Ismail, and by the time of Shah Abbas I Iranian craftsmen and artists were being encouraged to engage in the production of a cornucopia of cloths, ceramics, silks, carpets, porcelain, metal works, and brocades.[13] There was a virtual explosion in calligraphy as well as in the visual arts.[14] Isfahan also spawned a marvel of architectural works during the Safavid era. Shah Abbas I commissioned a vast building program in Isfahan that was largely completed before his death, including the Allahverdi Bridge, the arterial thoroughfares and the great Maidan (lit. the city square) of Isfahan.[15] Examples of religious architecture include the prominent mosques of Masjed Shah and Masjed Sheikh Lotfollah.[16] Shah Abbas' openness to other non-Muslim faiths meant that Christians and Jews were permitted to practice their faiths, and Isfahan witnessed a spike in the building of churches.

Shah Abbas' successful military reforms had a highly beneficial impact on the overall economy. Border areas were now secure with roads safe for travel. Roads had been unsafe since the time of Tahmasp I, making them dangerous for travel and commerce.[17] The securing of the roads ensured a significant increase in commercial activity and trade. Shah Abbas also commissioned the construction of numerous roads and bridges to facilitate movement. Caravanserais, many of which stand today, were also built along the roads. These same road and caravanserai networks served to facilitate the mobility of the army.[18] Shah Abbas' road reforms are reminiscent of the highways of Darius the Great.[19]

The success of the military in repelling foreign invaders, notably the Ottomans and the Uzbeks, allowed for the flourishing of civilian industries, further benefiting the economy. This then resulted in a sharp rise in the living standards of Iranian citizens, even as much of the Islamic world suffered an economic recession.[20] Unfortunately for the people of Iran, Shah Abbas' economic reforms were not destined to last much longer after his rule.

Shah Abbas curbs the power of the Qizilbash

The turbulent power dynamics of the Qizilbash had become a major source of instability inside Iran, and undermined Iran's military performance. Ali Qoli Khan, the leader of the Shamlu tribe, was killed fighting the Uzbeks, with Morshed Qoli Khan of the Ustajlu killed shortly after in combat at Shahrood.[21] This removed potentially dangerous opponents who would most certainly have opposed Abbas' plans to reduce the power and authority of the Qizilbash. He removed a number of Qizilbash commanders from governorship posts and relocated Qizilbash communities into other *Ulka* (lit. tribal districts) held by other Qizilbash tribes.[22] These measures broke down the overall cohesion of the Qizilbash. Shah Abbas also wrested ownership of provincial fiscal affairs away from local Qizilbash chiefs, transferring it to royal control. Provincial revenues would henceforth be collected by the shah's bailiffs or stewards.[23] Many of these newfound funds helped finance the rebuilding of the Iranian army. He continued to bring in recruits from the Caucasus, the Gholams, as introduced under Tahmasp. The Georgians in particular had come to dominate the highest positions in the court, government, and military by the end of his reign.[24]

While Georgia was becoming an increasingly important region for Safavid Iran, the processes of an Iranian–Georgian synthesis had been in place since antiquity.[25] Direct Arab rule in Georgia ended by the 9th century allowing for a vigorous revival of native Georgian independence. Georgia's Christian heritage was revived, but its rejection of Islam did not involve any rejection of its Iranic cultural legacy. This can be attributed to post-Islamic Iranian literature which led to what researchers have characterized as a "cultural synthesis" between Iran and Georgia.[26] Persian literary traditions exerted a mighty influence on Georgia right up to the Russian invasions in the early 19th century AD. Georgian influence in Iran became significant, especially from the 16th century. Many prominent Safavids hailed from a Georgian or part-Georgian background.[27] Two of Tahmasp's sons, Prince Haidar[28] and Prince Mostafa,[29] had Georgian roots. Many Georgians settled in Isfahan, becoming assimilated into the local population.[30] The settling of Georgians in the north (Mazandaran) was especially pronounced. Recent genetic studies indicate that a large proportion of northern Iranians have a proportion of Georgian ancestry.[31] Even as the Safavid Empire was collapsing in 1722, Iranian-Georgians fought against the Afghan invaders at the battles of Golnabad and Fereydunshahr. Georgia remained a crucial region for Iran after the fall of the Safavids.

A case of pragmatism: the Treaty of Istanbul

Shah Abbas had inherited a desperate state when he attained the throne in 1587. Iran was besieged by threats from the Uzbeks in the northeast and the Ottomans to the west and the Caucasus.[32] The army needed time for reforms, retraining and re-equipment. Abbas realized that he could not fight the Uzbeks and Ottomans simultaneously. Compounding this were problems with the Mughals in India and the Portuguese in the Persian Gulf. In response to this seemingly insurmountable geopolitical situation, Shah Abbas adopted a pragmatic approach. He sent Heidar Mirza (son of Hamza Mirza) to sign a humiliating peace treaty with Istanbul. The Peace of Istanbul (March 21, 1590) forced Iran to acknowledge Safavid losses in Azarbaijan (especially the city of Tabriz), Kars (now in Eastern Turkey), the Caucasus (Shirvan, Shamakhi, Nakhchevan, Karabakh, Georgia and its capital Tbilisi), western Iran (Luristan and Kurdistan), and Khuzistan in the southwest.[33] There was also a clause requiring the Safavids to halt the practice of cursing the three caliphs venerated by the Sunnis.[34] The treaty was harsh but it did allow Shah Abbas to crush domestic challenges from rebellious governors at Shiraz and Isfahan.[35] Another advantage of the treaty was that it gave the Iranians time to rebuild their military machine but spared them from having to fight a two-front war. In practice, Shah Abbas wanted a free hand to focus his martial energies against the Uzbeks.[36]

Shah Abbas defeats the Uzbeks

The situation in Iran's northeast had sharply deteriorated. Even as Abbas attained the throne in 1587, the Uzbeks were rampaging all across Iran's Khorasan province. Abbas had taken an army to Khorasan in the late 1580s but did not engage in any set-piece battles against the Uzbeks.[37]

His caution was probably due to the dire state of the Iranian army at the time. Simply put, Iranian forces were as yet incapable of fighting a major battle against the Uzbeks or the Ottomans.

Uzbek forces were led by Abdolmomen Khan, the son of Abdollah Khan. Abdolmomen Khan battered Safavid military forces in Merv, Herat, Nishabur, and Sabzevar. By 1593, Mashad, the provincial capital of Khorasan, was being besieged. In response to these catastrophic events, Shah Abbas attempted a diplomatic solution. He wrote a letter to the Uzbeks requesting that they desist from their attacks and withdraw to their Central Asian homelands. He even courageously offered to settle the issue in a duel with the Uzbek leader, if this would end the violence.[38] The Uzbeks simply ignored all of Shah Abbas' requests. The violence continued with the people of Nishabur being massacred and the inhabitants of Isferain being put to the sword after having killed 4,000 Uzbeks in battle.[39] Soon Sistan province, south of Khorasan, was also swept by the Uzbeks.[40]

The Uzbeks had devised a highly effective and simple strategy against the Safavids: they would invade Iran but would avoid set-piece battles against Safavid armies. Whenever a Safavid army advanced towards them, they would abandon their conquests in Khorasan and retire across the Amu Darya River (the ancient Oxus) to seek refuge in the harsh geography of Transoxania. The Uzbeks would simply wait for the Safavid armies to retire before invading again. Safavid garrisons in cities such as Herat and Mashad would be bottled up while other Uzbek invaders would rampage across Khorasan's countryside.[41] Any Safavid army attempting to pursue the Uzbeks into Transoxiana would do so at its own peril, risking exposed extended communication lines and supply shortages. More ominously, the army would be exposed to the Uzbeks' masterful hit-and-run tactics. These factors had shielded the Uzbeks from having to face the Safavids in their Central Asian homelands.

In a sheer stroke of luck for Abbas, Abdollah Khan's death in 1598 was followed shortly after by the murder of his son Abdolmomen Khan.[42] The decapitation of the Uzbek leadership led to a temporary decrease in the military pressure in the Iranian east, but this did not end the violence. The prospect of plunder in Iran ensured that Uzbek raids and killings continued. However, Uzbek power was fragmenting due to serious dynastic struggles, which gave Abbas a major opportunity to crush the Uzbek menace.

Shah Abbas left Isfahan to battle the Uzbeks on April 9, 1598.[43] In accordance with their primary strategy, the Uzbeks yielded territory and cities to the Safavid army as it advanced. When the Safavids reached Mashad they found the shrine of the eighth Shiite Imam Reza almost completely stripped of its ornaments, including its gold and silver chandeliers. On August 1, 1598, Shah Abbas and the Safavid army left Mashad for Herat, which was under Uzbek occupation. Led by Din Mohammad Khan, the Uzbeks had the option of staying within Herat's formidable fortifications or retiring across the Amu Darya.

Abbas had to lure the Uzbeks out of the safety of Herat, and then intercept them as they attempted to flee into Central Asia. He adopted the successful strategy used by Shah Ismail in 1510. While en-route to Herat, he gave orders for his advance guards to retire from Khorasan. He then announced that his entire army had to withdraw due to a crisis elsewhere in the country.[44] The ruse worked brilliantly. Din Mohammad Khan took the bait. He marched out of Herat with his army into the open plains, believing the danger to be past. He was soon proven wrong. Shah Abbas covered a ten-day journey in just four and a half days, and intercepted the Uzbeks at Rabat e Pariyan on August 9, 1598.

The Uzbeks held a slight numerical advantage of 12,000 men against Shah Abbas' 10,000 troops. The Uzbeks fought well, resulting in a bitter and hard-fought battle. Din Mohammad Khan then led a daring charge with 1,000 of his best, mailed cavalry into the Iranian lines. This caused some initial panic but the royal bodyguards stiffened their resolve after Shah Abbas exhorted them to fight with determination.[45] The royal guards counterattacked against the Uzbek main force. Din Mohammad Khan was wounded by a spear.[46] Uzbek resistance broke down and they began to retreat. But the Safavids were in no mood to show mercy and slaughtered 4,000 fleeing Uzbeks.[47] The remainder escaped into the countryside.[48] The wounded Din Mohammad Khan was killed by local Iranian tribesmen as he retreated. Many of the surviving Uzbeks were then simply massacred with scattered survivors fleeing for their lives across the Amu Darya. Contemporary English accounts report of the heads of 1,700 slain Uzbeks being hanged in Qazvin as evidence of the terrible defeat that Shah Abbas had inflicted on them.[49] The Safavids had liberated not only Mashad and Herat but also the important cities of Balkh, Merv, and Astrabad.[50]

Shah Abbas settled a large number of Kurds into Khorasan to serve as a barrier against future nomadic invasions from Central Asia.[51] Kurdish settlers had first been placed in Khorasan in the reign of Shah Tahmasp during his campaigns against the Ottomans.[52] Many of the wide expanses of Khorasan were lacking in manpower and dangerously exposed to invasions from Central Asia. The formidable Kurdish warriors could absorb the first waves of any invasion, giving time for local garrisons to prepare their defenses and for the main Safavid army to deploy into the region. A total of five Kurdish locales were created in Khorasan.[53]

Despite the success at Rabat e Pariyan and the settling of Kurds in Khorasan, the Uzbeks continued to pose a mortal threat. They invaded once more in 1602–03, this time under the leadership of Baqi Mohammad Khan.[54] The Uzbeks conquered Balkh, defeated local Safavid troops, and captured a large amount of their artillery.[55] Shah Abbas assembled a very large force composed of Ghoorchian royal guards, tribal warriors, 300 cannon, and 1,200 musketeers from western Iran and Khorasan.[56] These deployed to Jijketu and Meymaneh (in modern north Afghanistan) and inflicted a major defeat on the Uzbeks.[57] Shah Abbas then returned with several thousand Uzbek prisoners to Herat. He then went to Badgheis (in modern northwest Afghanistan) and in two months assembled fresh forces to launch a new attack into Jijketu. This battle was distinguished by placing ten musketeers between each pair of cannon; 3,000 musketeers were deployed this way.[58] Shah Abbas' troops also achieved a major coup by capturing a number of Uzbek messengers who soon provided valuable intelligence for the Safavid army. They reported that Baqi Mohammad Khan had assembled 20,000 troops to fight the Safavids.

Shah Abbas decided to first conquer the castle of Andikhod, situated on a vital Safavid supply line. Andikhod had to be taken out before the final showdown with Baqi Mohammad Khan. The Safavid army first drained the surrounding ditch. Sappers and engineers then worked at cleaving through the castle's walls.[59] The Safavids then engaged in an unexpected tactic. At night, they roared their battle trumpets then simultaneously fired all their muskets and 300 cannon.[60] This tactic spread panic among the defenders, many of whom simply abandoned their posts. The defenders then dispatched two emissaries to offer the surrender of Andikhod castle.

With this success Shah Abbas sent a message to Baqi Mohammad Khan to evacuate his recent conquests, notably Balkh. Baqi Mohammad Khan ignored the demands and prepared his 20,000 troops for combat. A bitter battle was fought, and Shah Abbas emerged as the victor. Khorasan province, at the receiving end of Uzbek attacks for so many generations, would now finally witness a period of peace and prosperity. Nevertheless, the Uzbeks were far from finished. The continuing Uzbek threat prompted Shah Abbas to dispatch a contingent of 2,000 Tofangchis to Khorasan as late as 1629.[61]

Shah Abbas defeats the Ottomans

With peace finally restored to the eastern marches and internal security established in the interior, Shah Abbas and the Safavids could finally cast their gaze westward. The Ottomans had taken much territory in the Caucasus and Iran's northwest, west, and southwest.[62] Shah Abbas first proposed an alliance with the Russians against the Ottomans, but this offer was fundamentally rejected.[63] Russian action was limited to small-scale actions along the borders of Daghestan in the northern Caucasus.[64] This meant that Shah Abbas had to face the mighty Ottoman military machine by himself. His advisors urged caution, noting especially Ottoman numerical superiority over Iran.[65] Abbas was encouraged to act by a number of khans from Iran's occupied northwest regions, especially Azarbaijan, who implored him to take action against the Ottomans.[66] A major factor favoring the Safavids was the rule of the Ottoman governor of Baghdad, Uzun Ahmad. He refused to send supplies to the Ottoman garrison at Nahavand in modern-day Iraq, which had been under Ottoman occupation for at least 15 years. The local garrison then engaged in pillages against the local civilian populace to secure its supplies.[67] This resulted in much discontent with many of these locals requesting help from the Safavids. Shah Abbas duly responded by storming and capturing Nihavand.[68] With this action, the shah had thrown down the gauntlet.

The newly reformed Iranian army deployed out of Isfahan on September 14, 1603 towards Azarbaijan. Shah Abbas resorted to guile by deceiving the Ottomans as to his true intentions. He announced that he and his troops were traveling to Mazandaran's forests in the north to engage in a hunting expedition.[69] This is remarkably similar to the ruse used against the Hephthalites (or White Huns) by the Sassanian king Bahram V Gur (r. AD 420–38).[70] Like the Hephthalites centuries before, the Ottomans were taken in. In the meantime orders had been issued to Zolfaqar Khan and Amir Goneh Beg Qajar, the governors of Ardabil and Qazvin respectively, to link up their forces with Shah Abbas' Gholam corps and Ghoorchian royal guards as soon as possible. Abbas' main army reached Tabriz in just 11 days, catching the Ottoman Turks completely unawares. The tactics used by Abbas were brilliant and unorthodox.[71] He selected his top troops to engage in a "commando" operation. They infiltrated Tabriz and slayed a number of Ottoman sentries, without alerting the main garrison. A group of 500 troops then arrived in civilian clothes posing as merchants. These distracted the Ottoman troops from the main Safavid army assembling just outside of Tabriz. With his "Trojan horse" in place in Tabriz, Abbas launched his attack. With many Ottoman sentries already dead at crucial ingress points, Abbas unleashed 6,000 troops to storm into the city. The 500 troops already in Tabriz also began to fight the garrison. After 20 days of combat, the Ottomans surrendered on October 21, 1603.[72]

The liberation of Tabriz, Azarbaijan's chief city, and the place of Shah Ismail's coronation, was of major importance. The victory was a major morale booster for the Iranian army, which had suffered so many defeats at Ottoman hands. The Ottomans in turn had paid dearly for their defeat at Tabriz. In a letter written by Shah Abbas to one of his administration's notables, Jalal e Din Mohammad Akbar, he noted that the Ottomans in Tabriz had "200 cannon, 5,000 musketeers ... supplies lasting for ten years and much equipment for the holding of fortresses."[73] Even more surprising was the joining of many ex-Ottoman troops into the Safavid army. This may be partly explained by the fact that Safavid troops at Shah Abbas' time were paid double the salary and benefits of their counterparts in Ottoman service.[74]

A major factor in the Safavid army's success was the role of local Azarbaijanis in ousting the Ottomans out of Tabriz. Celebrating Tabrizi citizens now took to wearing their 12-gore Safavid hats (outlawed during the occupation), signaling their adherence and loyalty to the Iranian throne and Shiism. Many buildings and houses in the city had been severely damaged during the Ottoman occupation,[75] with many of Tabriz's womenfolk taken at will by the Ottoman troops.[76] Reprisals by Tabriz's citizens were taken against a number of captured Ottoman troops who had committed offenses during the occupation.[77]

After the fall of Tabriz, the Safavid army recaptured Nakhchevan.[78] Shah Abbas sent messages to the remaining Ottoman garrisons in Azarbaijan to surrender.[79] Many did evacuate but instead of marching west into the Ottoman Empire, these coalesced (12,000 in all)[80] in the region of Yerevan, north of the Araxes River.[81] The Ottomans began to organize their defense around three Yerevan fortresses: Koozchi, Yerevan city, and Eshiq. Koozchi was the first to fall, and the most obstinate resistance was offered by the Ottomans in Yerevan city. These held out against besieging Safavid forces for well over six months, into the summer of 1604. The ground was too frozen in winter to allow the Safavids to dig trenches, or dig under the walls, and they had to wait until the thaw.[82]

With fresh supplies, Safavid forces were able to launch a furious assault using cannon and muskets. They also placed explosives under the walls in a number of places. The explosions breached the walls, allowing Iranian assault parties to pour into the fortress.[83] The Ottomans were now forced into close-quarter fighting, in which the Iranians held the advantage. After losing 2,000 of their troops in a few hours, the Ottoman garrison surrendered.[84] With the fall of Yerevan, Eshiq surrendered without a fight. Among the most effective troops during these campaigns were the musketeers of Tabriz.[85]

Shah Abbas was concerned that the formidable Ottomans would quickly re-form to launch a counterattack. He and his top commanders pursued the fleeing Ottoman forces with 20,000 troops.[86] This force finally caught up with a dangerous Ottoman force led by Cheqhal Oghlu at the battle of Ati.[87] Once again the Ottomans were decisively defeated. By this time a large haul of supplies was captured from the Ottoman camps, especially war materiel. Iranian forces also captured important Ottoman documents from the abandoned camp of Cheqhal Oghlu.[88]

The battle for Azarbaijan and the Caucasus was not yet over. Ottoman Sultan Ahmed organized a major Ottoman counteroffensive to crush Shah Abbas' army and retake Tabriz. A very large Ottoman army of 100,000 troops reached Sufiyan (near Tabriz) to confront Shah Abbas leading 62,000 men on November 6, 1605.[89] The Turks resorted to traditional battle tactics by first engaging in a cavalry duel. The aim of this was to draw the Iranian cavalry towards the Ottoman lines and bring them within range of the Ottoman cannon and musketeers.[90] Shah Abbas refused to be swayed by the Ottoman tactics. Instead, he ordered a detachment of Safavid troops to attack the Ottomans from the rear to make them believe that this was where the Iranians were launching their main attack. The Ottomans swung their entire force to their rear, and Shah Abbas struck with his main force of artillery, infantry, and cavalry, completely shattering the Ottoman army.[91] This defeat ensured the Ottomans were ejected from Azarbaijan. The Iranian army was now able to focus on driving out other Ottoman troops still in the Caucasus.

Shah Abbas focused his efforts on Ganja, an important and strategic Caucasian fortress under Ottoman control. Shah Abbas arrived at Ganja in 1606 to make heavy use of trenches, siege works, and cannon fire to subdue its Ottoman garrison. Iranian engineers succeeded in crossing the surrounding ditch and then digging out a large amount of soil from under one of its defensive walls. A large amount of chopped wood was stuffed into the hole and set on fire. This decisively damaged a section of wall, prompting the Ottoman garrison to finally surrender. When Safavid forces entered the city they obliged its citizens to tabulate their names on a royal registry. The aim of this was to identify those Iranian collaborators who had cooperated with the Ottomans during their occupation. Up to 2,500 Iranian "fifth-column" collaborators were identified and put to death.[92] The Ottoman governor of Ganja, Mohammad Pasha, was handed over by the Safavids to Mazandaran whose citizens had him executed. This was in retribution for Mohammad Pasha's killing of Rustam Sultan, a prominent leader in Mazandaran.

The fall of Ganja posed a major threat to the Ottoman garrison at Shamakhi, capital of the Shirvan khanate. Despite Ottoman attempts to delay the Iranian arrival, the Safavids arrived in early 1606 to besiege Shamakhi castle. They quickly realized this was a tough and obstinate fortress. Its walls and towers were very well built and its surrounding ditch was reported as especially deep.[93] The only way of crossing it was by means of a mechanical bridge that could be retracted into Shamakhi castle.

The assault forces at Shamakhi were divided in two. One flank was to the north of the fortress and the other to its west.[94] The northern flank was led by Allahverdi Khan and the western by Shah Abbas himself, supported by a number of important units such as the Azarbaijani and Kermani detachments. The eastern flank of Shamakhi could not be utilized for the siege as heavy rains had turned the ground there into impassable mud. This meant that heavy equipment such as siege engines, cannon, horses, and pack animals coming in from Shamakhi's east would quickly bog down in the mud. The southern flank of Shamakhi was also left unmanned. The decision to leave the eastern and southern flanks open proved especially hazardous as the Ottomans made sorties from those sectors to launch raids into Safavid positions. But the Ottomans failed to disrupt the Safavid operations' engineering works or the build-up of supplies, which continued unabated through the pouring rain.

The main Safavid strategy was to build a bridge across the ditch surrounding Shamakhi. To protect his engineers against the withering muskets and archery of Shamakhi's defenders, Shah Abbas built a series of "mini-forts," each one surrounded by a ditch. The mini-forts were also a deterrent against Ottoman hit-and-run attacks.

Hossein Qoli Beg Qajar's success in bringing forward heavy siege cannon from Ganja was crucial. The cannon were distributed to the northern and western flanks, where artillery pits stood ready. Soon more troops led by Pir Bodaqh Khan arrived from Tabriz. Just as their military situation was improving, the Safavid troops found their morale severely tested. The first setback was the collapse of a makeshift building, killing a number of personnel. Rumors soon spread that Shah Abbas had been killed in the incident. Shah Abbas put the rumor to rest by appearing among his troops. Another source of anxiety was news of a new Uzbek attack into Khorasan. This prompted a number of troops to consider leaving Shamakhi to fight the Uzbeks in the northeast. Fortunately news soon arrived that the Uzbeks had been quickly crushed by Khorasan's local Safavid forces.

Shah Abbas was finally ready to commence his main effort to capture Shamakhi. On June 27, 1606 his heavy stone-firing cannon pounded the fortress, destroying a number of its towers and structures. Some Iranian engineers managed to land near the fortress and began digging underneath its walls. At this juncture, a number of troops, led by Qaracheqai Beg from Shah Abbas' western flank, stormed and captured one of Shamakhi's critical towers. Soon Zolfaqhar Khan's Azarbaijani troops forced a number of Ottoman troops defending another tower to surrender. The turning point came when 150 Iranian soldiers broke into the fortress. Qaracheqai Beg promptly sent his troops in as reinforcements. Shah Abbas now ordered all troops to converge for the attack. The Ottomans, who were at a disadvantage against Iranian troops in hand-to-hand combat, lost 2,000–3,000 men in the first round of fighting inside the fortress. Iranian fighters then succeeded in opening Shamakhi's gates, allowing the main Safavid force to stream into the city. With the conquest of Shamakhi, the battle for the khanate of Shirvan was finally over.

Despite his victories over the Ottomans, Shah Abbas was acutely aware of their vast military strength and numerical superiority. Istanbul would soon recuperate from its losses to launch yet more counterattacks into Iran's northwest and the Caucasus. Shah Abbas embarked on an expanded scorched-earth program in anticipation of the Ottoman arrival. The entire region between Tabriz and Erzerum in eastern Anatolia was systematically depopulated, with up to 300,000 people, including Kurds, Azaris, and Armenians, resettled, mostly in Iran's interior.[95] Chardin has reported on the destruction of farms and buildings and the poisoning of wells along possible Ottoman invasion routes.[96] Shah Abbas also engaged in a number of military operations in the north of Iran, notably Gilan (1592), Lahijan (1595), and Mazandaran (1596–98), followed by Lar (1601–02).[97] This was part of his overall policy of bringing semi-autonomous provinces under the centralized power of the Safavid state.

The Ottoman army's repeated defeats obliged Istanbul to arrive at a negotiated settlement with Shah Abbas, culminating in the peace treaty of 1612. This forced the Ottomans to renounce their previous Iranian conquests and to recognize the validity of the old Irano-Ottoman frontiers.[98] In a face-saving gesture on Istanbul's behalf, Shah Abbas was to send an annual tribute of 200 camels laden with silk to the Ottoman Sultan.[99]

Shah Abbas was also forced to engage in a number of bruising battles in Georgia in 1614–15 to bring the area under Iranian suzerainty.[100] The fighting here was especially bitter. Iranian sources report the deaths of 70,000 Georgians during the course of the fighting and the rounding up of 130,000 prisoners.[101] The Ottomans, who considered Georgia within their zone of influence, mobilized for another war against Iran. Another pretext for this renewed war was Shah Abbas' failure to send silk to the Sultan as promised in the 1612 treaty.

Resistance in Georgia certainly continued into the 1620s, as Shah Abbas annexed Kakhetia (1620–21) and Meskhetia (1622–24).[102] A rare glimpse into the operations in Meskhetia has been provided by the relatively recent discovery of a gilded bronze winged lion, dated to 1622–23.[103] It bears a striking resemblance to the artistic themes of ancient Medo-Persian Achaemenid or "Persepolis" and Scytho-Sarmatian style arts. No other samples of this type have been discovered in post-Islamic Iran.[104] The mane has a Persian inscription addressed to Khorji Khan (a Georgian general?) from Shah Abbas. Khorji Khan was receiving two winged lions as a royal award for his recent military successes in Georgia.[105] The lions were part of a secret directive to Khorji Khan, who was encamped in the valley of Marktopi.[106] The orders to Khorji Khan were terse and simple: defeat the region's non-compliant Kakhs and then to deport the Kartlians.[107] Khorji Khan was also to behead the Kakh commander, and send his severed head to Shah Abbas. Khorji Khan did not receive the message or awards, as they were intercepted by the Kakh commander who launched his own successful surprise attack. This resulted in the defeat of Safavid troops at Marktopi and the death of Khorji Khan. In the end the Kakhs could not stand against the Safavids, and eventually retreated towards the Ottoman frontier.

The Ottomans finally launched a powerful offensive into the Caucasus in 1616. Pietro Della Valle, an Italian traveler who was in Iran during the time of Shah Abbas, reports the Turkish invasion force at 200,000–300,000 troops.[108] The aim of this force was to capture Yerevan, which was defended by 60,000 Iranian troops.[109] The Ottoman siege of Yerevan was a failure, forcing the Ottomans into a costly withdrawal in 1617.[110] Valle reports that the Iranian Tofangchi musketeers played a key role in repelling the Ottoman assault.[111]

After their defeat at Yerevan, retreating Ottoman troops suffered more losses to the bitter winter cold and the constant attacks of Safavid forces.[112] Despite their recent failure, the Ottomans prepared for another expedition in 1618. This time an Ottoman army of 50,000 troops, led by Khalil Pasha, advanced towards Tabriz in Azerbaijan province.[113] In Ardabil, Shah Abbas sprang an ingenious strategy. He allowed the Ottomans to march into Azerbaijan and seize Tabriz, which was already evacuated. This allowed Shah Abbas to conserve his forces for the counterattack at a time and place of his choosing.

The Ottoman army advanced into Azerbaijan and captured Tabriz with little difficulty. The Ottomans, now probably perceiving themselves as having the upper hand, sent messages to Shah Abbas to yield all territories he had recaptured from Istanbul since 1603. Shah Abbas refused and "officially" declared that he was to set fire to Ardabil before retreating. The Ottomans now walked straight into Shah Abbas' trap: they made the mistake of marching to Ardabil. Shah Abbas was waiting for them with 40,000 troops. The Safavid army set a deadly ambush and inflicted a heavy defeat upon the Ottomans.[114] Peace overtures were now made by the Ottomans. They not only reaffirmed the Iranian conquests but also suffered from the indignity of having the Iranians reduce their tribute to the Sultan to just 100 silk-laden camels.[115] The internal squabbles of the Ottomans had also contributed to their recent military defeats.

Shah Abbas also fought against the Ottomans in the Mesopotamian theater. The Safavid army besieged Baghdad, which fell on January 14, 1624.[116] A major portion of the city's Sunni inhabitants were then brutally massacred, apparently in a bid to "Shia-fy" the city.[117] The fall of Baghdad opened the gate to another string of Ottoman defeats. In the course of 1624, Safavid forces drove Ottoman forces out of Mesopotamia.[118] Kirkuk, Shahrazur, and Mosul in Iraqi Kurdistan all fell, with local Ottoman troops deserting even before the Safavids arrived.[119] The holy Shiite cities of

Najaf and Karbala (modern southern Iraq) were also conquered. So great was the Ottoman disarray that even Diyarbakr in eastern Anatolia fell to the Safavids.[120]

Hafez Ahmad Pasha, now appointed as the commander-in-chief of all Ottoman forces facing Iran, was ordered by Istanbul to eject the Iranians out of Baghdad.[121] He led a powerful army to Baghdad by November 1625. Shah Abbas had sent reinforcements for his Baghdad garrison. Despite this, the Ottomans, who were well-prepared and stocked with supplies, methodically flanked the Baghdad citadel on three sides and occupied the old quarter of the city.

Shah Abbas had also prepared a force to arrive at Baghdad against the Ottoman forces. Hafez Ahmad Pasha had no intention of waiting for Shah Abbas to arrive. He prosecuted his siege with vigor, intending to capture Baghdad before Shah Abbas arrived. In this endeavor, Ottoman forces succeeded in making a breach through one of Baghdad's walls. They then launched assault after assault through that breach, in a desperate bid to break into the city. All of these efforts were repelled by the Iranians, who had expected these tactics and had built a series of inner defense walls. When the Ottomans broke through their breach they were surprised by these defenses and lost 5,000 men before retreating.[122]

Shah Abbas finally reached Baghdad by May 1626, six months into its siege.[123] A frontal assault on Ottoman forces was ruled out as they had dug a wide ditch and placed their cannon and musketeers behind these. The Ottomans were thus able to continue their siege of Baghdad and feel reasonably safe from a frontal Safavid attack. Shah Abbas adapted to this apparent impasse by placing the besiegers themselves under siege. He successfully cut off all of Hafez Ahmad Pasha's major supply routes.[124] In the meantime the Iranian garrison's food supplies in Baghdad were running dangerously low. A raiding party desperately sailed out with boats onto the Tigris River, and were resupplied by the shah's main camp. Hafez Ahmad Pasha's failure to prevent this resupply proved to be a major blunder, as Shah Abbas had succeeded in besieging the Ottomans who were sandwiched between Shah Abbas' relief force and the reinvigorated Baghdad garrison. Hafez Ahmad Pasha was forced to abandon the safety of his defenses to launch a major attack against the waiting Shah Abbas. The Ottomans were badly mauled and suffered heavy losses against the Safavids. With his supplies running out and sickness among his troops, Hafez Ahmad Pasha reluctantly withdrew. Retreating in haste, the Ottomans suffered yet more heavy losses,[125] including the abandonment of several thousand of their sick and wounded troops as well as scores of heavy cannon.[126] Shah Abbas had proved that he was indeed the most successful Safavid monarch and military leader against the Ottomans, a fact duly noticed by the Europeans in the West.

The Persian Gulf: Portuguese ejected from Hormuz

The Portuguese had made powerful inroads into the Persian Gulf area during the reign of Shah Ismail I and a number of strategic islands such as Hormuz had been occupied, fortified, and settled. For over a century the Portuguese had retained control of an important commercial outpost and a critical naval base commanding the travel routes in and out of the Persian Gulf.[127] Shah Abbas had every intention of returning these to Iranian suzerainty.

Harsh Portuguese behavior in Hormuz, Bahrain, and Muscat had resulted in general discontent among the local populace. The Emir of Hormuz soon rebelled, with his warriors killing a number of Portuguese sentries and besieging their fortress. The emir took flight to Qeshm Island when

Portuguese reinforcements arrived at Hormuz. He was killed there, but this failed to end the confrontation between the Portuguese and the islanders.

These events were duly noticed by the British, who by late 1600 had established the East India Company.[128] Richard Steele of the East India Company and a colleague had obtained an important *Farman* or royal edict from Shah Abbas in 1616 known as the *Farman e Abrisham* (lit. royal edict for silk).[129] This obliged Iranian officials to support arriving English traders by allowing them to establish trading posts in the port city of Jask.[130]

These developments were viewed with alarm by the Portuguese whose interests would inevitably clash with those of the English in the Persian Gulf. When English ships led by Edward Connock approached Jask in December 1616, Portuguese ships unsuccessfully attempted to intercept them.[131] After his successful arrival at Jask, Connock set up factories in Isfahan and Shiraz in 1617. The English had scored a major success, as they were now the dominant European power engaged in Iran's silk exports, which stood at an annual total of 4,400,00lbs (2,000,000kg).[132] The English, like the Armenians, were accorded full rights to exercise their Christian faith in Iran. The East India Company's representative in Isfahan was soon regarded as the British ambassador to Iran.

A state of war had existed between Iran and Portugal since the late Allahverdi Khan had ejected the Portuguese from the island of Bahrain in 1601–02.[133] Despite that success, Shah Abbas and his commanders realized that the British world-class fleet was needed to expel the Portuguese from Iran's Persian Gulf islands. After some circumspection, the British agreed to support Shah Abbas with their warships.

After the death of Allahverdi Khan, the governor of Fars province, in 1613, his son Imam-Qoli Khan was appointed as the governor of Fars. Imam-Qoli Khan was then ordered by Shah Abbas to lay claim to Hormuz Island on Iran's behalf. He also demanded the reinstatement of the annual tribute, which had been traditional in the early 1500s, prior to Afonso de Albuquerque's arrival. An all-out war was now inevitable. Imam-Qoli Khan's strategy was to take over the port of Gambroon (renamed Bandar Abbas) and Qeshm Island. The objective was to cut off water and food supplies arriving for the Portuguese in Hormuz.[134] Gambroon was taken but the seven-month effort against Qeshm Island ended in a costly failure.[135] The Portuguese had prevailed at Qeshm Island due to their warships. It was clear that, without British help, the Iranians had little chance of retaking Qeshm or Hormuz.

British warships soon arrived at the port-city of Jask. Imam-Qoli then opened negotiations with the British commander. Two of the British warships were armed with 30 cannon each. The British at first refused to militarily support the Iranians but this attitude soon changed. Imam-Qoli made clear to the British commander the costs of not cooperating with Iran: Shah Abbas would respond by rescinding the favorable commercial privileges of the British.[136] The British agreed to cooperate on four conditions: war booty would be equally split between the Iranians and the British; all Christian prisoners would be handed over to the British; the Iranians would incur half of the costs of the British war effort; and the British East India Company would be exempted from customs fees at the trading post of Gambroon.

The Iranians were now ready to challenge the Portuguese. British ships would escort Iranian troops in boats and support them with naval artillery as they stormed the islands. Operations commenced on January 19, 1622 when a British force of five war vessels and four other ships left Jask.[137] The first military operation was at Qeshm. Iranian troops led by Imam-Qoli Khan landed to confront a fortress manned by just 250 Portuguese and 250 vassal Iranian and Arab troops. Despite the support of ship-based British cannon, the Qeshm fortress held out for six days before capitulating. Captured Iranian and Arab auxiliaries who had fought on behalf of the Portuguese were executed as traitors. The Qeshm fort was now manned by a small contingent of Iranian troops along with four British allies. With Gombroon already in Iranian hands and Qeshm just taken, the Portuguese in Hormuz were clearly doomed.

The British ships and 200 boats set sail towards Hormuz on March 11, 1622.[138] After bitter battles at the shore, the Iranians drove the Portuguese back into their fortress. The fortress, which had large supplies of provisions and water, proved obstinate and held out for 74 days. The issue was finally decided when the Iranians blew up a section of the fortress walls using dynamite. This allowed Iranian troops to storm the fortress, forcing the Portuguese to surrender by May 1622.[139] British naval support had been crucial throughout the Hormuz operations.[140]

After the battle the Iranians handed over their Portuguese prisoners along with their wives and children (3,000 in all) to the British as had been agreed. The Iranians seized much war booty, including 70 cannon, some of which survived in Isfahan's main square as late as 1663. After more than a century, the Iranian flag was flying once more over the island of Hormuz. The Portuguese were to lose more of their Persian Gulf possessions after the reign of Shah Abbas I as they were driven out of Muscat (1650) and Mombasa (1698), by the Arabs of Oman.[141]

The Mughals and the southeast

Iran's powerful neighbour to the east was the Mughal Empire of India. This had been founded in 1526 by Zahir e Din Mohammad Babur (1483–1531), a descendant of Tamerlane. The Mughal Empire and the Iranians had often been allies against the Uzbeks as India's northwest marches were often menaced by the Uzbeks during their invasions of Iran's northeast. Irano-Mughal relations were to sour during Shah Abbas' reign. This conflict was rooted in Mughal emperor Homayoun's (1508–56) granting of Kandahar to Iran in gratitude for Iranian sanctuary from 1540, and Iranian military support for his successful regaining of his throne in 1555.[142] Border areas such as Kandahar first functioned as vassal or buffer mini-states for Iran but this changed in time as these territories became formal Iranian provinces.

Later Mughal emperors were dissatisfied with this arrangement. The Mughals under Homayoun's successor Akbar (r. 1556–1605) took advantage of Iran's vulnerable strategic position in 1590 to seize Kandahar.[143] Shah Abbas' initial strategy had been to recover Kandahar through diplomacy. When this failed, Shah Abbas attacked and retook the city in 1622, during the reign of Mughal emperor Jahangir (r. 1605–27). A major revolt by Mughal prince Khorram (Jahangir's second son), prevented Jahangir from forming an effective military response.[144] Shah Abbas again extended a hand of friendship to Jahangir, stating that he had no further territorial ambitions against India. He also justified his recent action at Kandahar by noting that the city had been legally handed over to Iran by Homayoun. Jahangir was unimpressed but was militarily incapable of ejecting the Iranians from Kandahar.[145] Prior to his recapture of Kandahar, Shah Abbas had also increased Iran's sway in the southeast by his annexation of the Makran region (in modern Pakistani Baluchistan) in 1608–09.[146]

Shah Abbas' later years

Few would dispute Shah Abbas' impressive military, economic, artistic, and architectural achievements. As noted by Singh, "Abbas the Great was the greatest ruler of the Safavid dynasty. He was indeed one of the greatest rulers of the age."[147] His success in cultivating contacts with Europe was especially impressive, as was his establishment of trade with the British East India Company (soon to be followed by the Dutch East India Company). Unfortunately for Iran, the pace of these impressive strides would considerably slow after Shah Abbas' passing in 1629. One of the reasons for this was that Shah Abbas, like all great leaders in history, had his share of vices. Through his reign, he developed an increasing attitude of suspicion. Much of this originated with his fear of vengeance from those disgruntled aristocrats (especially the Qizilbash), whose influence he had curbed.[148] This led him into a constant state of vigilance; he diligently worked to eliminate any possibility of coups against him.

He prohibited all contact between his sons and government courtiers or military leaders.[149] Any violation of this arrangement was met by cruel punishments. Instead, the princes were often sent to the harem, limited to social relationships with eunuchs, harem ladies, and princesses, which did little to train Iran's future leaders in statecraft. Shah Abbas never took any of his sons on military campaigns meaning that his successors were not militarily trained to face external threats. His constant fear of losing his throne provoked the cruel side of his personality. On the mere suspicion of treachery he ordered his son Crown Prince Safi Mirza killed. Despite his remorse, Abbas' suspicions against his kin were never assuaged.[150] A number of other princes were blinded, notably Prince Sultan Mohammad Mirza, Prince Imam Qoli Mirza, and even his grandson Suleiman Mirza (son of Safi Mirza).[151] It is an unfortunate fact that Shah Abbas, who had done so much for Iran, also ensured that his successors would, in the main, be characterized by mediocrity.

CHAPTER 6

THE THREE KINGS AND DECLINE (1629–94)

Centralization of the Safavid state

A distinguishing feature of the three reigns that followed the passing of Shah Abbas – Safi I, Abbas II, and Safi II/Suleiman – was increasing centralization, a policy successfully implemented during Shah Abbas' reign. The once formidable Qizilbash aristocracy had been largely reduced and Qizilbash leaders were not capable of challenging the *Arkan e Dowlat*, or the government's top dignitaries. Government officials now looked increasingly to the throne as the source of power and authority in Iran. The provinces had also been significantly divested of their status as regional power centers; all political authority became increasingly concentrated in the capital city of Isfahan. Local provincial khans or governors were no longer in full control of the revenues of their respective provinces which now fell under Isfahan's administration. The potential for conspiracies continued to exist of course, especially among the court nobles and the royal harem.

However, the seeds were already sown for the final collapse of the Safavid state in the early 18th century. An absolute monarchy with unlimited authority vested in the throne could serve the overall interests of the country well only if highly capable personalities, such as Shah Abbas I, were at the helm. With a less able monarch, the interests of the country could be severely jeopardized. The case of Safi II/Suleiman will later serve to illustrate this point. In fact, all post-1629 Safavid monarchs were ignorant of statecraft when they first assumed the throne, due to their isolated upbringing. At the same time, the court was enjoying increasing decadence and extravagance, especially in the last decade of the 17th century. Safi II/Suleiman for example, often engaged in the pleasures of the harem and drunkenness at the expense of important matters of state. This period also saw the gradual decline of the army's efficiency and striking power. After Shah Abbas the Great, Safavid monarchs failed to realize the importance to Iran of a powerful army. Excessive trust was placed in the Treaty of Zohab (1639) with the Ottomans, preventing the Safavids from taking advantage of geopolitical opportunities to retake lost territories. Despite these weaknesses, Iran's economic state remained robust with its citizens living under relatively good conditions.[1] This had much to do with the economic foundations laid during the reign of Shah Abbas I.

Safi I: territorial losses to the Ottomans and the Treaty of Zohab

When Shah Abbas I died in 1629, he left no brothers or son able to become monarch, and had selected Saam Mirza, son of the late Safi Mirza, to succeed his throne. The grand vizier, Khalifa

Soltan and the Qoorchi-Bashi (commander of the royal guards), Isa Khan, worked hard to facilitate the ascension. Saam Mirza was crowned as Shah Safi on January 28, 1629.

Raised and educated in the harem, Safi I's literacy was rather modest, and he was not gifted with deep intellectual reasoning nor sophisticated decision-making skills.[2] While he was observed to be generous, charming, and warm, he seems also to have been capable of merciless cruelty.[3] Like Shah Abbas I before him, Safi I systematically butchered a large number of the royalty. Unlike his predecessor, he showed only a minimal interest in affairs of state and had little concern for the country's cultural and intellectual development. This thrust the primary burden of stately affairs upon the shoulders of a number of gifted and astute government officials and the harem probably influenced matters of state as well.[4]

Safi I's methodical liquidation of the royalty soon extended to the upper echelons of the state apparatus and the army. A number of top-ranking government officials were simply murdered. One of these was the *Vazir e Azam* (grand vizier) Mirza Talib Urdubadi, murdered in 1634. Imam-Qoli Khan, who had distinguished himself as governor and military commander during Shah Abbas I's reign, was also put to death.[5] Mirza Mohammad Taqhi Etemad ol Dowleh, nicknamed "Saru Taqhi" (lit. Taqhi the fair-haired) was then appointed as grand vizier in 1634. He managed to win the favor of the Shah and secure his influence on the civilian administration and military apparatus. The Vizier was also known for his use of the government's secret services.

Safi's policies of liquidation also damaged the military. Decapitation of important military leaders began in 1630 when the *Sepahsalar e Kol e Sepah* (army commander-in-chief), Zeinal Khan Shamlu, was murdered. Two years later two generals of the Qoorchi royal guards, Cheraqh Khan Zahedi and even Isa Khan (who had helped Safi's ascension), were eliminated. In that same year, Shah Safi I also ordered the killing of the *Ishiq Aghassi Bashi* (lord marshal), Ugurlu Khan Shamlu. These killings did little to raise the military's efficiency, morale, or ability to wage war. These developments were especially dangerous as Iran's neighbors (Ottomans, Uzbeks, Mughals) were keenly observing the country for military weaknesses to exploit. Safi I had virtually guaranteed that Iran would soon be facing new invasions.

The murder of Imam-Qoli Khan soon led to disturbances among the Mushasha Arabs of the Hoveiza area, who acknowledged the Iranian shahs. There were also incursions by the Banu Lam Arabs into the Baghdad area around the time of Shah Safi I's accession. Iran was fortunate that the Arabs did not exploit Iranian military weaknesses and confined their disturbances to their respective regions.[6] The Ottomans on the other hand, were more than willing to take advantage of any situation allowing them to gain Iranian territory.

Sultan Murad IV (r. 1623–40) had the benefit of the services of the highly capable and energetic vizier, Khosrev Pasha, who had every intention of invading Iran. The Peace of Szony between Emperor Ferdinand II (1617–37) and Istanbul had been reaffirmed. This freed Ottoman armies from their military preoccupations in Europe, which allowed Khosrev Pasha to assemble a powerful army by the summer of 1629 to invade Iran. The Ottomans' first thrust was towards Iran's northwest, although Khosrev Pasha's original objective had been Baghdad. Zeinal Khan Shamlu, recently appointed as the army's Sepahsalar, moved his forces to fight the Ottomans at Hamadan.[7] A great battle occurred at Mahidasht on May 4, 1630. This ended in an overwhelming Ottoman victory with Hamadan falling into Ottoman hands. Also captured were the Kurdish areas of northwest Iran and Mosul.[8]

With his victory at Hamadan, Khosrev Pasha embarked on his original objective, Mesopotamia and the city of Baghdad. Safi Qoli Khan, commander of the Iranian garrison at Baghdad, prepared for Khosrev Pasha's arrival. The Ottoman force soon reached Baghdad and began its siege with a furious artillery barrage on November 8, 1630.[9] But repeated Ottoman assaults were thrown back, prompting Khosrev Pasha to withdraw just a few days later.[10] It seems an odd decision, but Khosrev Pasha had good reason to be cautious. Ottoman lines of communication were dangerously exposed to offensives from western Iran, meaning that the Iranians could cut off Khosrev Pasha, isolating him in Mesopotamia. At the very least, the Iranians could engage in their traditional cavalry harassment tactics that would inflict heavy casualties.

As Khosrev Pasha withdrew, Iranian troops quickly crushed all Ottoman garrisons left behind, including the one at Hamadan. Local Kurds who had originally sided with the Ottomans were also subdued. Despite this failure, Istanbul remained confident. The new Ottoman grand vizier, Tabanyasi Mehmed Pasha, was well aware of Iran's internal difficulties and anti-Safavid Georgian resistance in the Caucasus. This ensured the continuation of the war.

The Ottomans scored a great victory at Yerevan in 1631, a battle attended by Sultan Murad IV himself.[11] After this success, the Ottomans advanced to Tabriz, which they plundered and destroyed but did not capture.[12] Ottoman attacks finally resulted in the mobilization of a total of 80,000 Iranian troops, with a large proportion of these being cavalry.[13] One notable contingent was that of Hussein Khan of Luristan who commanded a powerful cavalry force of heavily armored cavalry.[14]

Shah Safi I then participated in a major Safavid counterattack against the Ottomans in the spring of 1632. The Iranians had first completely surrounded Yerevan. Cannon were then positioned in front of each of the city's towers. Ottoman resistance proved fierce. They often launched deadly sorties into Iranian lines and then quickly withdrew into the safety of their fortress. The turning point came when three large cannon finally arrived from Isfahan. These were fundamental in supporting a renewed assault, which finally broke into Yerevan. The Ottoman garrison refused to give up, but after seven hours of hand-to-hand fighting, they were finally forced to surrender.[15] The survivors retreated to the nearby fortress of Narein, but this also fell after seven days.[16]

Iranian offers of peace had been repeatedly rejected by the Ottomans. This was because the Ottomans were still smarting from their defeat at Baghdad in 1624. Istanbul refused to rest until they had driven the Iranians out of Baghdad and Mesopotamia. One notable Ottoman campaign was their launching of 12,000 Greek *Martalos* mountain warriors who invaded Iran in 1635. The Martalos were highly skilled at fighting with both firearms and traditional weapons.[17] Their invasion was a small prelude to the gigantic blow soon to come. In 1638, Sultan Murad IV led a gigantic Ottoman force of 500,000 against Baghdad. The diminutive Iranian garrison of 30,000 fought fiercely but was forced to surrender by late December 1638.[18]

Only 300 Iranians survived the siege and subsequent slaughter of Iranian prisoners by Murad.[19] Then, shortly after the Ottomans had occupied Baghdad, an accidental explosion killed a large number of their troops. Blaming local saboteurs, Murad ordered a massacre, resulting in the deaths of 30,000 civilians.[20] Baghdad and Iraq would remain in Ottoman hands until the later years of the First World War. The Ottomans had prevailed in Mesopotamia just as the Iranians had prevailed in the Caucasus.

The Treaty of Zohab (also known as the Treaty of Qasr e Shirin) was signed on May 17, 1639.[21] Zohab made clear that Iraq was under Ottoman rule but acknowledged the rights of Iranian Shiites to make their annual pilgrimage to the Shiite holy cities of Najaf and Karbala. The Ottomans also acknowledged that Azarbaijan, Rawanduz (in Iraqi Kurdistan), Armenia, and Georgia were under Iran's authority.[22]

Zohab also failed to clearly delineate the border demarcations between Ottoman Mesopotamia and Iran. There was also the contentious issue of Kurds and Arabs now situated on both sides of the ambiguous border. As a result, the treaty had inadvertently set the stage for future friction between the Ottomans and the Iranians. These disputes would be inherited by Iran and the Ottoman Empire's 20th-century Mesopotamian successor: Iraq.

Abbas II: the contest for Kandahar

Shah Safi passed away in 1642 to be succeeded by his ten-year-old son Prince Sultan Mohammad Mirza, who was known as Shah Abbas II (r. 1642–66). Management of the state's affairs was first entrusted to the grand vizier Saru Taqhi Etemad ol Dowleh. Saru Taqhi managed the transition after Safi's death with efficiency. There were hardly any revolts or major challenges against the throne. He did not survive for long as his enemies in the upper nobility had him assassinated in his home on October 1645.

Mirza Mohammad Mehdi was ultimately made grand vizier, but Abbas II was no mere spectator. Unlike his predecessor Safi I, Abbas II was a quick and sharp learner, soon taking a very active role in affairs of state. Abbas II was highly vigilant against corruption at all levels of government and the military and spent several days each week in the dispensation of justice. Much work was also done by Abbas II in suppressing highway banditry. Overall, the Iranian population, especially those of more humble socio-economic backgrounds, were relatively better off than their contemporary counterparts in Europe.[23] In foreign affairs, relations with the Ottomans remained cordial in the overall sense with no wars breaking out. The Treaty of Zohab of 1639 was honored by both sides well up to the end of the Safavid dynasty.

Abbas II had a love for intellectual development. He welcomed learned men, dervishes, scholars, and artists and often organized debates and discussions on numerous topics in the court. Abbas II was especially welcoming to European learned men in his court. Developments in architecture, science, and medicine continued.[24] Shah Abbas II had an almost affable quality, like his predecessors he had a sinister side, having his nephews killed and brothers blinded.[25]

Relations between the Safavids and Mughals had steadily deteriorated during the reign of Safi I. A diagreement between grand vizier Mirza Mohammad Taqhi and the governor of Kandahar over the issue of annual payments had led to the latter's placing his province under Mughal jurisdiction by 1638.[26] The reign of Safi I also witnessed the loss of Iranian influence in the Deccan area of the Indian subcontinent. In 1648, Shah Abbas II initiated the campaign to recapture Kandahar.[27] Safavid forces besieged the city from late 1648 and captured it by February 1649.[28] Artillery apparently played an important role in this operation.[29] Mughal attempts to reconquer Kandahar in 1649 and 1652 were repelled.[30] The most dramatic Mughal effort to retake the city was by another of Shah Jahan's sons, Prince Dara Shikoh. In 1653 a vast Mughal army of

70,000 cavalry and thousands more infantry, archers, and war elephants were led by Dara Shikoh towards Kandahar. Shikoh finally ordered a direct assault against the city on August 21, 1653. The attack was a disastrous failure with 1,000 Mughals being killed and another 1,000 wounded.[31] Just as Mughal forces were withdrawing for the third and final time, the Safavids arranged for a clown and dancing girls to lead a battalion into Kandahar.[32] This was meant to mock the Mughals who had boasted that they would march to Isfahan after capturing Kandahar.[33]

The ascension of Safi II/Suleiman

The passing of Shah Abbas II brought Iran's period of prosperous peace to an end. There were two options for the throne, the seven-year-old Hamza Mirza and the 19-year-old Safi Mirza.[34] At first the choice was the child prince but the leading nobles soon opted for Safi Mirza. He was crowned as Shah Safi II on November 1, 1666. The new Shah suffered from health ailments leading to suggestions by his physician (soon corroborated by a court astrologer) that his poor health and other troubles were all derived from a miscalculation on the horoscope! This led to Safi II being "re-crowned" as Shah Suleiman on March 20, 1668.

The centralization efforts of Suleiman's predecessors had come into full effect and while Suleiman was admired by his subjects, much of his "image" was due to the accomplishments of his predecessors.[35] Suleiman had not been prepared for the mantle of kingship, statesmanship, economic affairs, or military leadership. He had no significant displays of courage, risk-taking, or concerns for his country's well-being. He was generally known to have been lethargic and petulant, with a love for pleasures of the harem, debauchery, and drinking in excess.[36]

Suleiman lacked interest in affairs of state and became increasingly inaccessible to his government officials, choosing to run his country from the harem. His main advisors became his wives and harem eunuchs. Final decisions were conveyed by a harem servant to government officials. This exclusion even extended to the Shah's grand viziers, the *Majlis* (court assembly), and the *Divan* (state council). All government bodies were reduced to a state of obedience towards the harem-based executive body. Even on the rare occasions when the shah was available for consultation, the time limit was brief and the outcome inconclusive. When a European envoy by the name of Ludwig Fabritius managed to gain an audience with the shah in late March 1684, no progress could be made due to the shah's inebriation.[37] Suleiman's lack of leadership led to the rise of corruption, bribery, and favoritism. The overall state of the economy and agriculture inevitably suffered and were in overall decline by the late 17th century.[38] This disastrous state of affairs significantly damaged the army's discipline, efficiency, and fighting capabilities. The Qizilbash's lingering rivalry with other sectors of the army significantly reduced the military's efficiency by the latter days of the Safavids.[39]

Overall, it was fortunate that Shah Suleiman's lack of interest in affairs of state meant there were no major wars during his reign. The Swedes sent a delegation to Suleiman in 1679 to request that he attack the Ottomans who were threatening Swedish possessions south of the Baltic.[40] Suleiman ignored the Swedish request and took no action against Istanbul. Another Swedish request for an Iranian attack against the Ottomans in 1682 was also ignored.[41] Suleiman similarly rejected the appeals of the Holy Roman Emperor Leopold I (1658–1705), John III Subinsky (r. 1676–96) of Poland, and Tsar Alexei (r. 1645–76) of Russia to attack the Ottomans. Suleiman's excuse was that he had to adhere to the 1639 Treaty of Zohab. Suleiman also failed to take advantage of Ottoman weaknesses in Mesopotamia in 1684, 1685, and 1690.[42] Heavy Ottoman military engagements in Europe (Poland, Venice, and Austria) would have significantly limited Istanbul from resisting any Iranian invasion of Mesopotamia.

Shah Suleiman died on July 29, 1694. He had done little to improve the economy, cared little for military affairs, and was indifferent to the long-term security of the country. Barely three decades after Suleiman's death Iran would see major invasions by the armies of the Ottoman Empire and Russia. The catalyst for these future disasters would come from an unexpected direction: the Iranic Afghans from the eastern realms of the empire.

The Central Asian frontier

Iran once again experienced raids from Central Asia upon the arrival of Shah Safi I in 1629, a number of which had been conducted by the Turkmens. These subsided when their leader Isfandyar Khan (1623–42) had "apologized" by handing over his brother Abdol Ghazi to the Safavids in 1630. Far more dangerous were the Uzbeks who continued to pose the greatest threat. In Safi's time they conducted no fewer than 11 raids into Iranian territory with numbers reaching as high as 20,000–30,000.[43] The military pattern was similar to that seen in the past; the Uzbeks would first raid and then pull back into Central Asia.[44]

The crisis prompted Shah Safi I to mobilize the army, especially the Ghoorchis and Tofangchis, against the Uzbeks.[45] Safi I appointed Zaman Beg Tofangchi Aghassi of the Tofangchi corps as the commander of Khorasan province in April 1629. Rustam Beg Sepahsalar, the army commander-in-chief, was assigned to supervise the dispatch of war supplies to Khorasan. With these fresh reinforcements of troops and supplies, Zaman Beg was able to first contain and then defeat the Uzbek invasion forces. Isfahan soon witnessed the arrival of a large number of Uzbek prisoners.[46] Up to 2,000 severed heads of Uzbek warriors were presented to Safi I, and two top Uzbek commanders were also decapitated in Isfahan.[47] Despite these successes, Uzbek raids into Khorasan continued into Shah Abbas II's time. There was at least one case of an Uzbek leader, Mohammad Khan, who sought refuge in Isfahan in 1646 (four years after the ascension of Abbas II).[48] An interesting report by Tavernier at the time of Shah Abbas II describes a number of ships along the Caspian Sea coast being militarily deployed against the Uzbeks.[49]

Uzbek raids were to continue during the reign of Suleiman. Fortunately for Iran, the Uzbek raids at that time resembled acts of pillage and banditry rather than the large-scale invasions of the past. Suleiman also had good relations with the khans of Bukhara and even exchanged embassies with them. As a result, Uzbek raiders entering Iran were not acting under the khans' authority. Another group that sometimes entered Iran through Astrabad was the Kalmucks but these were not a major threat like the Uzbeks. In fact, like the Bukhara khans, the Kalmucks had sent their embassies to Isfahan.

Developments in Georgia

Georgians and Caucasians had been brought into Iran in very large numbers during the reign of Shah Abbas I, although this process had existed in the 1520s–30s. By the time of Safi I, the

Georgians had become a major ethnic group in Iran.[50] King Teimuraz of Kakheti (1589–1663) had been finally defeated in 1634 by Rustam Khan, the ruler of Kartli (1634–58) and the *Vali* (viceroy) of the Safavids. Tbilisi in Georgia was now clearly under the Safavid crown. These successes prompted the nobles of Mingrelia, Guria, and Imeretia to switch their allegiance from Istanbul to the Safavids. Teimuraz, who ousted the Safavid governor of Kakhetia, was later affirmed in his position as lord of Kakhetia, but under Safavid authority. The Safavids supported both Rustam Khan and Teimuraz to ensure that neither gained too much power in Georgia.

Teimuraz, who had at one time asked for help from the Russian Tsar, was defeated by Shah Abbas II in 1659[51] and sent to Astarabad.[52] The Caucasus and Georgia were then relatively tranquil during Suleiman's reign. Kartlia was governed by the Mukhranids who were under Iranian suzerainty. Kakhetia had been governed by Achil Khan, who had followed his father, from 1664. Achil Khan was succeeded by Teimuraz's grandson, Heraclius (Erekli) I in 1675. Shortly after that, all succeeding governors in Kakhetia were Iranians. Meanwhile, large numbers of Georgians had continued to arrive into Iran throughout the 17th century.[53]

The first Russian invasion of Iran

The Russian Cossacks had reached as far as the Terek River in Daghestan by 1600. Relations with Iran were peaceful until they started to build fortifications on the approaches to eastern Georgia, when Shah Abbas I was quick to react. Iranian troops in the Caucasus swiftly attacked, destroying the Russian garrisons and forcing the Cossacks to escape.[54]

The Cossacks, led by Stenka (Stepan) Razin, had engaged in a rebellion and fought battles against the Russian army.[55] Razin, now instigated by Tsar Alexis to turn against Iran,[56] launched a powerful raid into northern Iran in 1664 with 40 ships (each equipped with two cannon), ferrying 6,000 Cossacks.[57] They engaged in a three-day orgy of pillaging, destruction, killings, rape, and the abduction of women.[58] The Cossacks then met their match at the hands of the tough northern Iranian warriors of Rasht and Farah-Abad. The warriors forced the Cossacks to flee to their ships and out of northern Iran.[59] The Romanovs of Russia now did their utmost to limit the damage. They sent a delegation to Isfahan to apologize for the incident and hanged Stenka Razin in Moscow on June 11, 1671.[60]

Cossack raids continued to take place in northern Iran at the time of Suleiman. Numbers of Cossacks even requested to be placed under Iranian jurisdiction. Suleiman, not wanting to provoke a war with Russia, did not accede to those demands.[61]

CHAPTER 7

DOWNFALL, CHAOS, AND OCCUPATION

Last Safavid monarch of Iran: ruling a tottering empire

Shah Suleiman failed to nominate a crown prince before his death in 1694. He reputedly summoned his top advisors around his deathbed during the last hours of his life and provided the dignitaries with two choices for the succession: Prince Sultan Hussein Mirza and Prince Abbas Mirza. The two princes were near opposites in character and temperament. The 26-year old Sultan Hussein Mirza was mild, tranquil, reflective (if not intellectual), ascetic, pious, and religious. According to Suleiman, Sultan Hussein would be a peace-loving shah, seeking tranquility for the realm. Suleiman's other choice, 23-year-old Abbas Mirza, was strong, resolute, bellicose, clear-headed, clever, and ingenious. Suleiman described Abbas as the type of shah who would strengthen and expand the empire.[1] Both princes had been raised in the harem, and neither had had any preparation for statecraft.[2] Sultan Hussein was chosen as shah and crowned on August 6, 1694.[3]

Shah Sultan Hussein was no warrior; he was pious and religious but weak-willed, lacking forcefulness in governmental and military affairs.[4] He soon earned the title *Yakhshidir* (Turkic: very well) as this was his typical response to all matters of state expostulated to him.[5] He quickly fell under the heavy influence of the Mujtahed Mohammad Baqher Majlesi, and soon issued a series of stern religious laws which turned Iran into a repressive theocratic state.[6] Mohammad Baqher Majlesi was a strict Shiite Muslim, who had great antipathy against Sunnis, a factor which explains in part the multitude of revolts that broke out in the empire's Sunni regions, notably those of the Afghans in the northeast, the Shirvanis and Lezgians in the Caucasus, and the Kurds in the west and northwest.[7] Majlesi died in 1699 but his grandson, Mohammad Hussein, continued the "Shia-sizing" policies of his predecessor by persecuting Armenian Christians, Jews, and Zoroastrians.[8] Sultan Hussein supported these policies by issuing an edict demanding that non-Muslims convert to Shiite Islam. In a country characterized by diversity since ancient times, such narrow-minded and bigoted policies could only lead to ruin and disaster. Sultan Hussein also soon adopted the "corrupt" ways of his late father, taking to heavy drinking and becoming ensnared in the pleasures of the harem.[9]

As Sultan Hussein assumed the throne, internal forces were threatening the integrity of the Safavid Empire. Many regional khans and governors were becoming increasingly restive by 1700. Anti-Isfahan regional resentment had increased through the heavy-handed policies of local Safavid governors. Rebellions began to break out among the Lezgians of the Caucasus and the Baluch in the southeastern marches. The Afghan rebellion in Kandahar ultimately proved to be the most disastrous as it led to the toppling of the Safavids.

Central to all of this were the governments of the corrupt and mediocre shahs (Suleiman and Sultan Hussein) whose actions had gone against the interests of the state. Fiscal mismanagement had ensured the sharp decline of the economy and the population's living standards by the late

1600s. Road travel became increasingly unsafe due to banditry and corrupt officials who failed to keep the roads safe. The cumulative impact of all of these liabilities was a government apparatus beset by lethargy, inefficiency, and corruption. The one positive was that the long Ottoman frontier had remained relatively free from wars, excepting border clashes with the Ottomans around Basra in southern Mesopotamia.[10] Axworthy has summed up the situation very well by observing that "Neglect of the interest of the state became the norm."[11]

Trouble began to brew in Iran's Caucasian north when Lezgian tribes attacked Georgia in 1706. This was partly provoked by the self-serving actions of corrupt Iranian officials who had pocketed Isfahan's annual funds earmarked to keep the peace among the Lezgians.[12] The situation further deteriorated when a serious plague broke out out in northwest Iran and the Caucasus by 1717. A Kurdish rebellion in the western marches then sought Ottoman intervention.[13] A serious Lezgian rebellion broke out by 1719 and spread to Shirvan by the summer of 1721.[14] Much of the blame for this rebellion can be placed on the policies of the Safavids. Shiite zealots in Shirvan, for example, had burned Sunni religious books, turned Sunni mosques into stables, and executed local Sunni religious leaders. When the Lezgians attacked Shamakhi on August 15, 1721, local citizens opened the city gates to the rebels. This led to a bloody massacre of local Caucasian Shiites, and the sacking of local Russian trading stations.[15] Local Caucasian Sunnis then appealed to Istanbul for assistance.[16] This was to have disastrous consequences within a few years.

The situation had also deteriorated in the Persian Gulf where Sultan bin Saif II, the leader of Muscat, had taken advantage of Iran's weakness to launch powerful attacks against Iranian islands and Bahrain by the early 1700s.[17] Muscat was now a growing maritime power, thanks to the rising power of its navy.[18] The attacking Muscat fleet had consisted of a ship with 74 cannon, one with 50 cannon, two with 60 cannon, 18 ships carrying 18 cannon each and a number of smaller vessels carrying 4–8 cannon each.[19] The Iranians were desperate to stop the growing power of Muscat which also had ties to the British. A delegation was sent to Louis XIV of France proposing a strengthening of economic ties. In exchange the French would provide naval support against Muscat and even against British warships in the Persian Gulf. Despite an initial treaty being signed in 1708, the French decided against confronting the British and the Muscat navy.[20]

In the late Safavid era, Iran's military was afflicted by demoralization, logistical inefficiency, decline in military training and discipline, and the paucity of heavier firearms. Large number of soldiers and officers deserted, while other officers were more interested in status and wealth than their obligations.[21] Corruption meant that soldiers who did continue to turn up for duty lacked even uniforms or shoes.[22] Since Shah Suleiman's reign, reduced military spending meant that there were few trained troops to guard Iran's critical frontiers.[23] The long process of military neglect of 1629–1722 resulted in a dangerously inefficient army unable to repel the invaders on Iran's borders.

The Afghan rebellion

The territories comprising modern-day Afghanistan (notably Kandahar, Herat, and Kabul) were mainly situated between Safavid Iran and Mughal India. Though the Afghans are of Iranian stock, they, like the majority of Iranic Kurds and Caucasian Lezgians, are predominantly Sunni, with

Shiites being mostly concentrated in modern-day western Afghanistan.[24] The coming Afghan rebellion was to be an especially painful chapter for Iran, one that shook it to the core.

Baluchi tribes in Iran's southeast erupted in rebellion in late 1698/early 1699, and soon launched raids into the Kerman region.[25] Sultan Hussein appointed the Georgian prince, Gorgin Khan, to subdue the rebellion. Gorgin accomplished his task, but concerns of the Baluchi threat prompted him to remain in Kerman. Gorgin was proven right as the Baluchis attacked again in 1704, but this time they struck northeast at Kandahar. Gorgin once again dispersed the Baluchis and rescued Kandahar.

Gorgin, who had already been appointed as the *Beglergegi* or governor of Kandahar province, entered Kandahar city and assumed his post. An excellent soldier, Gorgin was inept as governor. His harsh and strict governance quickly turned the local population against Isfahan. Local Sunni Muslim sensibilities were also offended by the fact that Gorgin's Georgian troops were Christian.[26] The Afghans also resented Gorgin's ban on their raids into Mughal territory. Gorgin was trying to keep the peace with the Mughals, but the Afghans saw this as another example of Isfahan's oppression.

Kandahar's man of influence was Mirvais, a well-known nobleman of the Ghilzai tribe. As resentment against Gorgin and the Georgians grew, Kandahar's residents turned increasingly to Mirvais for leadership. Gorgin mistrusted Mirvais and had him arrested and sent to Isfahan. This action combined with Gorgin's style of governance helped sow the seeds of anger and rebellion among the Ghilzai (and then the Abdali) Afghans.

Gorgin's dispatch of Mirvais to Isfahan was a big mistake. This allowed Mirvais to see how corrupt and rotted the Safavid state had become. Mirvais was also cunning, intelligent, and manipulative, befriending the naïve and gullible shah and earning his trust.[27] He convinced Sultan Hussein to allow him to depart for Mecca in the name of religion. When Mirvais reached Mecca, he obtained a *fatwa* (religious decree) against the Shiite Shah Sultan Hussein.[28]

Mirvais returned to Isfahan, where the shah showered him with titles, before returning to Kandahar. Sultan Hussein had both undermined the authority of his governor Gorgin and taken the first step towards the destruction of the Safavid state. Mirvais, armed with his fatwa, had no difficulty rousing his fellow Ghilzai tribesmen in Kandahar against Isfahan. Mirvais also obtained the support of the Mughals of India.[29] He and the Ghilzai attacked in April 1709, killing Gorgin and nearly all of the shah's Georgian troops in Kandahar.[30] Only a handful of the Georgians managed to escape with great difficulty. The disaster had begun; Kandahar had slipped outside of Isfahan's orbit.

The seriousness of the crisis led Sultan Hussein to assign a new army to crush Mirvais and the Ghilzai rebels. Gorgin Khan's nephew Kaykhosrow Khan Gorji (lit. Georgian) was placed in command. Kaykhosrow, supported by contingents from Khorasan, Herat, and Kerman, led an army of 50,000 troops to besiege Kandahar.[31] The Ghilzai prevailed and Kaykhosrow was killed when he fell off his horse.[32] The Safavid force was completely defeated in October 1711 with the Ghilzai capturing large amounts of weapons, cannon, and horses.[33] This fiasco sent shock waves in Isfahan. The shah now appointed the elderly Mohammad Zaman Khan, the Qoorchi-Bashi, as leader of yet another army to combat the menace of Mirvais. Zaman Khan was accompanied by the contingents of Khorasan and the Qajars of Astarabad and supported by vast stores of supplies and cannon. The force halted at Bastam to gather more recruits, but things began to go terribly wrong. Zaman Khan died of natural causes and the governor of Herat was also killed. The Safavid army, which was barely halfway towards Kandahar, now turned back.[34]

As if the news from the eastern marches was not bad enough, the Uzbeks invaded Khorasan in 1717 as their leader, Shir Ghazi Khan, took advantage of Iran's disarray at Kandahar. Safi Gholi Khan was assigned to command a new army to eliminate the Uzbek threat. He was defeated in his first battle against the Uzbeks but the arrival of the formidable Qajar contingents of Astrabad thoroughly defeated the Uzbeks.[35] Safi Gholi Khan now deployed towards Herat to assemble his army for the big battle against Mirvais. The army was composed of many contingents, including those from Astrabad (the Qajars), Khorasan (including Kurdish warriors), Marv, Nisa, Sarakhs, Abiverd, and Zoor-Abad. When battle was joined with the Ghilzai, the Qajar and Kurdish contingents failed to provide the critical support needed, a major consequence of their animosity against Safi Gholi Khan. The lack of Kurdish and Qajar support led to the disastrous defeat of the Qizilbash contingent, and the slaying of their commander, the son of Safi Gholi Khan.[36] The Ghilzai now launched a major attack into the Safavid lines. Safi Gholi Khan was killed, and the Safavids unraveled. As panic and disorder spread like wildfire through the ranks, the Qajars and the Kurds looted the Safavid camps then headed for home. The other survivors, seeing that all was lost, took to their heels.[37]

As news of the Iranian army's defeats spread throughout the realm, the predominantly Sunni Abdali Afghans of Herat engaged in sporadic revolts, their raids reaching as far as Mashad's environs by 1710.[38] Herat's local Safavid governor responded by imprisoning a number of prominent Abdali khans but was imprisoned in turn by his own troops who had rebelled against him. By 1716 all efforts by Mashad's governor to subdue the Abdali Afghans had also failed.[39]

With Safavid authority ejected from Herat, the Abdalis turned against their traditional enemies, the Ghilzai. Mirvais of the Ghilzai had died in 1715 and had been succeeded by his brother Mir Abdollah who had adopted a conciliatory approach towards Isfahan. Mirvais' son Mahmoud accused his uncle of treason and killed him in 1717.[40] Mahmoud then became the chief of the Ghilzai, determined to finish what his father had started: a holy war against Isfahan. He launched a major offensive towards Isfahan in the summer of 1719.[41] He first pretended that he was attacking the Abdalis in Herat to his north,[42] but instead swung southwest into Seistan and Baluchistan and from there arrived at Kerman.[43] The numbers of Afghans involved in this campaign are difficult to ascertain. Western historians claim 10,000–11,000 Afghans with Iranian primary sources and historians claiming much larger figures at 50,000–100,000![44] Mahmoud decisively defeated the Abdalis in 1720.[45] He sent the severed heads of a number of slain Abdali warriors to Isfahan as an apparent gesture of allegiance to Sultan Hussein. With typical gullibility, the shah bestowed Mahmoud with the honorific title "Hussein Qoli Khan" (lit. the servant of [Shah] Hussein) and appointed him as the governor at Kandahar. This was indeed misguided as Mahmoud had no intention of serving the Safavids.

Despite meeting little resistance, Mahmoud's sojourn in Kerman was a bloody affair; buildings were burnt and the bodies of civilians indiscriminately killed were left in the streets. Iranian and Western sources again diverge as to why Mahmoud left Kerman for Kandahar after nine months. After all, Isfahan had been his final objective. Iranian historiography asserts that Mahmoud's army had been defeated by troops led by Lotfali Khan, the Vali of Fars, forcing Mahmoud and his surviving troops to retreat.[46] Western historians disagree, with Lockhart asserting a rebellion back in Kandahar as the reason for leaving Kerman.[47] After Mahmoud left in mid-1720, the Safavids re-entered Kerman and the new governor-general, Rustam Mohammad Shadlu, proceeded to build up the defenses of Kerman's citadel.[48]

By 1721, Malek Mahmoud Sistani (the former governor of Tun and Tabas) had destroyed Isfahan's authority in the southeast and was launching raids into northeast Iran.[49] Sistani also viewed himself as the heir of the medieval Iranian Saffarid dynasty (AD 861–1003) that had ruled southeast Iran, southwest Afghanistan, and parts of ancient northwest India (now northwest Pakistan).[50] With Iran's situation increasingly unstable, especially in the east, and with the capable Lotfali Khan recently dismissed, Mahmoud decided to strike towards Isfahan once again. This time his army included Baluchis and the Persian-speaking Hazaras of Mongol descent.

On paper, the Iranian army was still impressive. They could theoretically call on a total of 180,000 troops, roughly composed of 120,000 cavalry and 50,000 infantry and 10,000 other troops, including Toopchi artillerymen.[51] Tribal and provincial contingents were (theoretically) able to field well over 100,000 additional troops to support the army in the event of a crisis.[52] But the Safavid army was now a shadow of its former self. The incompetent and lethargic leadership of Sultan Hussein, the Safavid state apparatus, and the military elite ensured that Iran would be unable to mobilize its large pool of troops and tribal contingents. According to Marvi, the Safavids were able to muster a maximum of just 60,000 troops against Mahmoud.[53] These still outnumbered the invading Afghans who (according to Western historians) stood at 10,000–11,000 men.[54] Even this numerical edge meant little as Iranian forces were plagued with numerous problems that drastically reduced their overall military effectiveness.

Mahmoud resumed his march into Iran in the summer of 1721. He reached Kerman by October 22 and placed it under siege.[55] Mahmoud's attempt to storm the citadel frontally was beaten back, thanks to the strengthening of the city's fortifications. Mahmoud lost 1,500 men in the assault. Mahmoud lacked siege cannon, and his heaviest firearms were Zanbourak camel-mounted swivel guns, of no use in siege warfare. The siege dragged on to late January 1722. By this time numbers of Mahmoud's men had deserted and left for Kandahar. A compromise was finally reached in early February: the Kerman citadel agreed to pay off Mahmoud in exchange for his departure from the city. Mahmoud gladly accepted and advanced to Yazd.

The city of Yazd closed its gates as soon as Mahmoud arrived. Yazd proved just as obstinate as Kerman. Afghan attempts to storm Yazd's defenses were beaten back with heavy losses. Once again, Mahmoud's lack of siege artillery and reluctance to lose more men led him to bypass a key city in favor of his ultimate objective, Isfahan. By early March he had arrived near the village of Mohammadabad, 22 miles (36km) northeast of Isfahan.

As the Afghan advanced, the Iranian military leadership provided two proposals to defend against the Afghan invasion. The first, advocated by one of the army's most valuable commanders, Mohammad Gholi Khan Etemad ol Dowleh, was to have the army, supported by local armed citizens, organize a defense inside the city, forcing the Afghans to engage in costly close-quarter urban warfare. In contrast, Seyd Abdollah Moshasha, the Vali of Khuzistan, proposed that the army deploy outside Isfahan to confront the Afghans in the open. Moshasha would personally lead his formidable Khuzistani Arab cavalry during the battle. Moshasha's view prevailed, and attempts were made to raise troops. These did not include the large pool of excellent warriors available throughout Iran's Zoor-Khaneh martial arts schools. Instead, messages were sent to villages and locales near Isfahan promising a six-month tax exemption for all those who volunteered to fight. This resulted in the arrival of a large number of peasants and farmers with little or no training, armed with little more than sticks and clubs. Owing to its pitiful logistics, the state could not provide these men with adequate weapons. The superstitious Sultan Hussein relied on his astrologers to set the actual date of the battle, then ordered that the troops be given traditional Iranian *Ab-Goosht* meat stew, believing that would make them invisible for the upcoming battle![56]

Gholi Khan marched out of Isfahan with 30,000 troops and 24 cannon on March 3, 1722.[57] Accompanying the Iranian artillery was Philippe Colombe, a French artillery expert. Moshasha and his 12,000 Arab cavalry joined Gholi Khan two days later bringing the total number of Safavid troops to either 42,000 or (according to Marvi) 60,000 men.[58] The 10,000–11,000 Afghans were most likely an all-cavalry force.

The Safavids and the Afghans then faced each other on March 8, 1722 at the village of Golnabad. The Iranian army was deployed in four segments. The left flank was led by Ali Mardan Khan Feili (the Vali of Luristan) supported by Alireza Kahkouliyueh's Lur cavalry. Next to him (in the center) was Gholi Khan. Rustam Khan and his 400 Georgian royal palace guards stood to the right of Gholi Khan. Moshasha with his 12,000 Arab cavalry were on the right flank. The cannon were placed in front of Gholi Khan with the bulk of the infantry deployed in the center. While Gholi Khan was nominally in overall command, he and Moshasha did not see eye to eye. This led to serious coordination problems during the battle. In contrast the compact Afghans were characterized by a firm unity of purpose. Mahmoud in overall command led the center, Amanollah Khan the right, with Nasrollah (a Zoroastrian and former outlaw from Seistan) commanding the left. To counterbalance the superior numbers of Iranian troops, Mahmoud, Nasrollah, and Amanollah Khan placed their forces on a hill.

There was a marked difference in the appearance of the opposing armies. The Afghans appeared shabby, humbly dressed, and mob-like in contrast to the professional Safavid troops with their dazzling uniforms and weapons. Comparisons have been drawn between the battle at Golnabad and the battle of Qadissiya fought between the Zoroastrian Sassanians and the Arabo-Muslim forces in AD 637.[59] In both battles, a larger Iranian army faced smaller numbers of highly motivated opponents fired by powerful religious zeal.

Rustam Khan initiated the battle: the Georgians charged into the Afghan left flank. Moshasha and his Arab cavalry on the right flank began to wheel about the Afghan left. The battle could have been won if Gholi Khan had advanced to support the Georgians and the Iranian Arabs. But Gholi Khan stood motionless. Moshasha and the Iranian Arabs brilliantly enveloped the Afghan left, then chose to plunder the Afghan camp rather than slice into Nasrollah's wavering troops.

Ali Mardan Khan and the Lur cavalry now thrust towards the Afghan right. Amanollah Khan's Ghilzai warriors feigned retreat, enticing the Lur cavalry to pursue them. The "escaping" Ghilzai then suddenly parted to the right and left, leaving the Lurs running straight into the path of 100 kneeling camels carrying Zanbourak swiveling light artillery. The zanbouraks quickly opened fire on the Lurs and tore them to pieces. The Ghilzai cavalry then attacked the surviving Lurs and forced them off the battlefield. With this success, Mahmoud moved to eliminate the Iranian artillery. The Ghilzai rushed at the Iranian cannon so quickly that only three of them had time to open fire. Most of the artillerymen, including Philippe Colombe, were killed. Critical was the inaction of Gholi Khan's infantry who failed to protect their artillery comrades against the Afghan cavalry attacks.

Mahmoud now swung his support to Nasrollah, whose lines were being battered by Rustam Khan. Rustam Khan and the Georgians of the royal guard fought bravely but were soon surrounded and outnumbered. Gholi Khan still did nothing; it was as if he and his troops were never there. Rustam Khan fell from his horse while trying to escape, and was killed. The swift and heavy casualties now spread panic among the surviving Safavids. The Safavids had lost 6,000–12,000 men killed and, finally, they simply disintegrated.[60] The Iranian Arabs, seeing that all was lost, abandoned their plunder and fled from the battlefield. Mahmoud's road to Isfahan was open.

News of the Golnabad disaster spread like wildfire in Isfahan, but the Afghans were in no rush to storm the Safavid capital. Mahmoud's troops first buried their 500–600 dead before calmly proceeding towards Isfahan.[61] Three days later Mahmoud arrived and Isfahan was soon surrounded. Mahmoud knew that the only way to capture the capital was to starve it into submission.

The shah and the military leadership realized that the very survival of their country was now at stake. Troops were quickly stationed to guard all towers, gates, ingress points, and all bridges along the Zayende Rud River. This was followed by an emergency session to formulate a strategy on how to defend Isfahan and defeat Mahmoud. Once again, inconsistencies in the leadership bedeviled Safavid military thinking. The nobles and military leaders requested that Gholi Khan deploy out of the city with all available forces to engage and defeat Mahmoud in open battle. Gholi Khan refused, apparently skeptical of his chances for success and aware of the low morale among his troops.[62]

The shah decided to stay in the capital, and appointed Seyd Abdollah as the commander-in-chief of all Safavid forces. It would have been more prudent for the shah to leave before the Afghan noose tightened as he could have raised more troops from the provinces. But the shah rejected this advice and missed the opportunity to evacuate large numbers of civilians out of Isfahan.[63] Sultan Hussein's ineptness thus ensured that Isfahan's civilians would be exposed to terrible suffering, while also putting a heavy strain on the city's dwindling food supplies.

The shah now sent appeals throughout the realm for military assistance. Messages were dispatched to King Vakhtang VI in Georgia and Ali Mardan Khan in Luristan. There was great hope that the Georgians would come to the rescue as the Afghans had a great fear of Georgian troops, especially in close-quarter combat.[64] Some even believed that the Afghans would simply withdraw upon seeing the Georgian troops. The Lurs too were especially fierce fighters and famed for their equestrian skills, martial arts, and proficiency in the use of firearms. Vakhtang VI did not send troops due to his disillusionment with the sorry state of the shah and his government in Isfahan and sympathy with Russia's plans for invasion.[65]

Another problem undermining Isfahan's defense was fifth-columnists who supported Mahmoud's takeover of the capital. These brought up-to-date reports to Mahmoud of Isfahan's deteriorating state, the inner conflicts within the military leadership, and the state of the city's defenses. One report that reached Mahmoud was that the Safavids had hastily buried a number of their cannon as they had retreated back to Isfahan after Golnabad. The Ghilzai soon discovered the buried artillery pieces. The Safavid commanders then devised a "rescue operation" to retrieve the cannon. A raiding party launched a surprise attack and recovered all 24 cannon. These were loaded onto nine wagons and transported back into Isfahan. This action angered Mahmoud who ordered his troops to storm Isfahan's bridges. The key bridges of Allahverdi Khan, Marnan, and Khaju were attacked but each Ghilzai assault was thrown back by deadly cannon fire.

The recent success at the bridges was overshadowed by continuing incompetence and inner conflicts among the leadership. Sultan Hussein further divided his court by removing his son Safi as heir, in favor of his other son, Tahmasp. At this juncture Mahmoud sent an emissary with a white flag into Isfahan to offer his terms for ending the siege. He demanded that the shah offer the hand of one of his daughters in marriage, pay him a huge financial sum, and appoint him as the governor of Kandahar, Khorasan, and Kerman. Predictably, these terms were rejected by Sultan Hussein.

Mahmoud's spy network soon proved its worth. A group of Georgian guards at the Marnan Bridge had taken to excessive drinking and fallen asleep. Mahmoud was informed of this and launched a raiding party, which seized the bridge. The Afghans then broke into the Abbasabad district of Isfahan, tightening the noose around the capital. A number of local citizens did launch successful sorties against the Afghans, but these actions did little to alter the worsening situation. Meanwhile, citizens who tried to flee were mostly captured or killed by the Afghans. People still clung to the hope that the Georgians would come to the rescue, but no help would arrive from the Caucasus.

It was at this juncture that the new crown prince, Tahmasp, managed to escape with 1,000 troops out of Isfahan on June 7/8. The citizenry were certain that Tahmasp would gather fresh troops and return to rescue them. Tahmasp proved to be a major disappointment, wasting precious time by sending messages to provincial chiefs instead of quickly linking up with loyal provincial forces.[66] Tahmasp did finally succeed in raising Bakhtiari, Georgian, Azarbaijani, Luri, Shahsevan, and Qajar warriors as well as troops from other Iranian provinces and tribes, but these arrived too late to save Isfahan.[67]

Warriors from Luristan and Qazvin had attempted to break the siege of Isfahan in May 1722, but Mahmoud had beaten them back. Another rescue attempt was made in June when 8,000 Bakhtiari warriors from western Iran arrived with a large convoy of supplies.[68] These were defeated by just 4,000 Afghans. This was the last sincere attempt to relieve the capital. Another force led by the fickle Malek Mahmoud Sistani arrived in September but was persuaded by Mahmoud to leave without incident. Sistani had been informed that Isfahan was about to fall and that he would become Khorasan's ruler in exchange for his support of Mahmoud. Isfahan was now completely doomed.

The inhabitants of the city did their utmost to fight back, one notable attack killing up to 300 Afghan troops and officers. These efforts however did little to alter the siege. By now the outbreak of famine had also forced many starving citizens to attempt a breakout in search of food and supplies. Mahmoud also destroyed all farms and food sources in the surrounding countryside. Famine soon forced citizens to eat horseflesh and even rats to survive. Starving citizens were dying in Isfahan's streets, among them many of Iran's men of learning and science.[69]

The end of Safavid rule came with great humiliation for Iran. Shah Sultan Hussein rode to Mahmoud's camp at Farahabad and surrendered in October 1722. In an act of indignity, Sultan Hussein removed the Iranian symbol of kingship, the *Jiqqeh*, from his turban and fastened it to Mahmoud's turban. An Afghan force of 3,000, led by Amanollah Khan, rode into Isfahan to formally relieve the Iranian guards there. Mahmoud sat on the Safavid throne and occupied the royal palace. Isfahan's population of over half a million in 1710 had been reduced to barely over 100,000.[70] On November 24, 1722, after the fall of Isfahan and the dethroning of Shah Sultan Hussein, Tahmasp's retinue in Qazvin crowned him as Shah Tahmasp II.[71]

Russia invades Caucasus and northern Iran

Peter the Great (r. 1682–1725) had long harbored territorial ambitions towards Russia's east and south. Peter's plan was to establish a safe route for trade between Russia and India through the Caspian Sea which he planned to militarily dominate. Central to his schemes was the subjugation of Iran as far as (and including) the Persian Gulf. The conquest of Iran would of course mean the domination of Persian silk (especially in Gilan), long coveted by the Russians.[72]

In 1717, Russian statesman and diplomat Artemy Petrovich Volynsky arrived in Isfahan. Officially, Volynsky obtained highly favorable trade concessions from Sultan Hussein, especially when the latter was facing dangerous revolts in his realm. He also obtained information on Iran's state of affairs and ingress routes to India. When Volynsky returned to Russia he provided a detailed account of how badly Iran was deteriorating. Peter was certainly pleased, but he was still engaged in his European wars, especially against Sweden.

Volynsky was appointed as the governor of Astrakhan to keep a close eye on Iran to the south, and continued to collect information about the state of Iran's military communications in its Caucasian and northern provinces as well as the Caspian Sea.[73] Russian military and naval leaders were soon hard at work preparing maps and surveys for the upcoming invasion of Iran.[74] Peter found ready allies within Iran's dominions in the Caucasus, especially Georgia's King Vakhtang who signaled his offer to assist Peter in 1718. The next year, Peter received the allegiance of Shamkhal Adil Gerai of Tarakhi in the northern Caucasus.

Iran's deteriorating political and military situation posed a golden opportunity for Russia. In 1721, as the Afghan attacks into Iran were gaining momentum, the time became ripe for invasion: Peter's peace treaty with the Swedes on August 30 finally freed Russia from its military preoccupations in the north, just as Shamakhi was sacked by the Lezgians.[75] Peter was anxious to move into Iran as soon as possible before the Afghans could advance further into Iran. A bigger worry was Istanbul's ponderings on the Iranian situation and the role the powerful Ottoman army would soon play.

The final trigger for invasion came from Prince Tahmasp, who, during his sojourn in Qazvin, committed a major blunder by appealing to Peter for military assistance.[76] This provided the Russian emperor with the perfect diplomatic pretext to realize his imperial ambitions in Iran. Tahmasp even agreed to yield Shirvan and Daghestan in the Caucasus and the entire northern Iranian rim of Gilan, Mazandaran, and Astrabad.[77] In exchange, Peter would provide military assistance to hoist Tahmasp as Iran's shah and to eject the Afghans from Iran.[78] Not only had

Tahmasp failed to rescue Isfahan, he had also invited the dangerous Russian colossus into the Iranian realm. Iran was about to be carved up like a roast.

The Russian invasion finally began in July 1722, as Isfahan was under siege. A Russian army of 9,000 cavalry and supporting Cossacks led by General Veterani thrust into the Caucasus.[79] Supporting the Russian land offensive was a huge fleet of 274 ships manned by 5,000 sailors[80] led by High Admiral Apraxin. This force was bringing 22,000 infantry veterans of the Swedish wars, 30,000 Tatars, 20,000–22,000 Kalmuks, and 20,000 Cossacks.[81] Apraxin's fleet arrived at Terki, Russian's southernmost possession along the west Caspian coast. From there messages were sent to the governors of Darband, Shamakhi, and Baku to submit to Russia. Darband was occupied in 1722, followed by all other Russian objectives, such as Rasht and Baku, by September 1723.[82] The Russians were certainly not viewed as liberators, as the populace apparently realized that Russian troops had no intention of acting on behalf of Iran. Russian troops engaged in clashes in cities such as Rasht in northern Iran and as noted by Bain, "Baku, which Peter was very anxious to capture … protested that it had always been loyal to the Shah, and could defend itself against rebels, but it was stormed none the less."[83]

The Ottomans invade

Istanbul's strategists realized that Russia's alarming conquests of Iranian territories in the Caucasus posed a threat to the Ottoman Empire's eastern flank. Russia and the Ottomans had battled one another for supremacy in the Black Sea–northwest Caucasus region; their recent bloody contest over the Sea of Azov just one manifestation of that rivalry.[84] Peter's invasion of Iran's Caucasian territories meant that Russian armies would soon be poised to strike into Ottoman Anatolia. As well as defense, Istanbul had of course coveted western Iran, the Caucasus, and especially Iranian Azarbaijan for centuries. With chaos engulfing Iran, Istanbul could now simply march into Iran to take what it perceived as legitimate Ottoman territory.

At this time, the Ottoman Empire was in the throes of its modern reform movement, known as the "Tulip Period" (1718–30), led by Sultan Ahmad III (r. 1703–30) and his grand vizier, Damad Ibrahim Pasha. The vizier realized that the financial costs of reform in combination with popular hostility against the Sultan's court posed a serious threat against the stability of the Ottoman House.[85] The vizier desperately needed a venue to divert rising domestic discontent. An Iranian adventure provided an excellent solution. Istanbul's territorial expansion at Iranian expense was virtually guaranteed given there was no Iranian army to stop them, and plunder and property would go a long way towards servicing Istanbul's costly reforms and maintaining the Sultan's extravagant court.[86] Officially, Istanbul's reasons for invading Iran were to expunge Shiism from Iran and replace it with Sunni Islam; "recover" lost Ottoman territories; and eject the Afghans and Russians from Iranian territory.[87]

Tahmasp sent an envoy, Mortadeh Qoli Beg, to confer with the Ottoman Turks in Istanbul in October 1723. Much like Tahmasp's appeal to Peter of Russia, Qoli Beg implored his Ottoman hosts to help eject the Afghans from Iran and restore the Safavid throne. The Ottomans replied that they would do this on condition that Iran yielded territories such as Azarbaijan and Georgia.[88] By this time, Iran's remaining authority in the Caucasus had fragmented: Vakhtang VI had sent numerous appeals to Russia in the autumn of 1722 to send troops into Georgia, but these never arrived.[89] Vakhtang then began to fight rival Georgian princes, opening the way for an Ottoman invasion of Georgia.

As early as May 1722, Istanbul ordered the governors of its eastern provinces to mobilize troops for an invasion of Iran.[90] The "official" Ottoman announcement came almost a year later in April 1723.[91] By June, the invasion was underway with a total of 30,000 Ottoman troops.[92] As Ottoman troops moved into Iranian territories in the Caucasus and northwest Iran, the dangers of a Turkish–Russian clash became readily apparent. Russia, for example, had been recruiting Cossacks and Circassians just north of the Caucasus, prompting Caucasian Sunnis to appeal to Istanbul for protection.[93] In contrast, the Shiite inhabitants of Azarbaijan province signed a declaration with local Christians as well as those in nearby Ganja and Karabakh stating that they would resist an Ottoman invasion.[94]

British and Austrian ambassadors in Istanbul were collaborating with the "war hawks" in Istanbul in hopes of igniting a Turkish–Russian war.[95] But, thanks to the efforts of the Russian and French embassies in Istanbul, war was averted in favor of negotiations. A formal accord, known as the Treaty of Constantinople, was reached by June 24, 1724. This partitioned Iran between the Russian and Ottoman empires.[96] The Kura River became the boundary between the Ottoman and Russian empires. The Ottomans took over Georgia, Perso-Armenia (including the city of Yerevan), Shirvan, Azarbaijan province, and Hamadan, as well as Kermanshah and Ard-Alan in western Iran. Russia was granted the fertile northern provinces of Gilan, Mazandaran, and Astarabad along the Caspian Sea. Iran had now been stripped of its most productive provinces in northern Iran and the Caucasus as well as western Iran. To add insult to injury, both Ottomans and Russians agreed to recognize the Safavid crown on condition that it acknowledged the partitioning of Iran.[97]

The Turks and Russians were both pleased: Russia was now much closer to the gates of India and the shores of the Persian Gulf, while Ottoman-controlled Iranian territory could now yield funds for the Ottoman court and reforms. The Ottomans were also happy to see many Caucasian Sunnis falling under their orbit. Especially tantalizing was the prospect of a diminished Iran being absorbed into the Sunnism of the Ottoman Empire.

Three Ottoman armies invaded Iran in 1723–25, each commanded by a *Sardar* (Persian: commander). One army deployed towards the Caucasus from Kars and Diyarbakr in June 1724.[98] The attack thrust into Georgia, with Tbilisi and Gori easily falling.[99] The Ottomans were then resisted by a number of Georgian princes who launched guerrilla attacks from local forests and mountains.[100] Iran's remaining Caucasian garrisons put up strong resistance. Aref Ahmad Pasha deployed from Kars with 35,000 troops and heavy siege cannon to besiege Yerevan.[101] After bombarding it with artillery, the Ottomans began mining operations.[102] Explosives were strategically placed, tearing a huge gap in the walls. The Ottomans launched wave after wave of assaults through the gap but Iranian troops beat them back. Ottoman losses were so heavy that at one point they had to request a truce to bury their dead.[103] Eventually, completely cut off and without hope of reinforcement, the gallant Iranian garrison was forced to surrender on September 28, 1724.[104] The four-month siege had come at the heavy price of 20,000 Ottoman dead.[105] Ganja also fell in the same month.[106]

The army led by Abdallah Pasha Kupruluzadeh thrust into Azarbaijan. Kupruluzadeh captured Khoy, Quschi, Tasuj, and Marand in the summer of 1724. Anti-Ottoman sentiments ran high in

Azarbaijan and resistance at Khoy was especially bitter and 8,000 Iranian defenders were killed.[107] Maragha held out for another year before falling to Ottoman troops.[108] With Yerevan finally secured to his north, Kupruluzadeh launched a powerful offensive towards Tabriz. Ottoman-Turkish troops broke through into one of Tabriz's quarters but were quickly bogged down against very bitter Azari resistance. In just one major assault, 4,000 Ottomans were cut off and destroyed.[109] When spies informed Kupruluzadeh of an impending night raid by Iranian troops, he ordered a withdrawal from Tabriz.[110] Undeterred, Kupruluzadeh attacked Tabriz again in July 1725 with 70,000 troops.[111] Prior to this, elite Janissary troops had been forced to reoccupy the cities of Marand and Shabestar and the fort of Diza, thanks to continued local Azari opposition. The bloody fight to enter Tabriz proper began on July 28. The city's citizens fought bitterly for five days and Ottoman soldiers were forced to fight street by street to subdue Tabriz.[112] The Turks and their Tatar allies lost 20,000 men with the Tabrizis suffering 30,000 dead.[113] One account has Kupruluzadeh ordering his troops to loot and pillage Tabriz, while an opposing account describes his gallantry in allowing the defeated Iranian garrison to leave Tabriz with their families and possessions.[114] Ardabil and Urumiah were then conquered,[115] completing the Ottoman conquest of Azarbaijan.

Iran faced yet more disasters further south at the hands of the third Ottoman army which thrust into "Iraq-e-Ajam" (non-Arab Iraq, a region just east of Iranian Kurdistan and southwest of Azarbaijan near modern Hamadan). The Ottoman garrisons of Baghdad, Van, and Shahrazur coalesced to push into western Iran, supported by a very large number of Ottoman-Kurdish contingents.[116] Luristan fell first in September 1723, thanks in part to the assistance of local Sunnis who opposed the Safavids.[117] Kermanshah in Iranian Kurdistan fell by mid-October.[118] Ottoman forces then arrived near Hamadan on June 29, 1724.[119] The city featured well-built towers, walls, and fortifications, obliging the Ottomans to dig trenches for their troops. Attempts were made to set fire to the city's towers. Hamadan's garrison launched attacks but pulled back after losing 5,000 men.[120] Ottoman engineers succeeded in blowing up a number of mines, creating a wide gap in one of Hamadan's walls.[121] Ottoman troops then rushed through this opening but met bitter resistance.[122] The Ottomans then built powerful wooden canopies to protect their trenches against Iranian attacks.[123] The Hamadan garrison responded by hurling oil-lit torches at the defenses to set them on fire. The Ottomans ingeniously defeated these efforts by using special hooks to capture and discard torches that landed on their canopies.[124]

In contrast to the Ottomans, the Iranians had no cannon at Hamadan. They turned to a French Carmelite, Jean Joseph, to help them build one cannon.[125] Joseph refused at first explaining that he lacked expertise but after desperate pleas, Joseph built one cannon. The cannon exploded, which actually shocked the Ottoman Turks and caused them to pull back.[126] It was around this time that Tahmasp sent a section of his troops to assist Hamadan but these were defeated and forced to retreat.[127] Ottoman mining efforts finally allowed Turkish troops to pour into Hamadan. The bitter hand-to-hand combat finally ended on September 1, 1724. The Turkish commander, Ahmad Pasha, displayed his gallantry by providing safe passage to the Iranian garrison and any local citizens wishing to leave. With Hamadan secured, the Ottomans captured Nahavand, Borujerd, and the entire province of Luristan. Borujerd subsequently revolted against the Ottomans and had to be put down. Ard-Alan was also been occupied. Western Iran was now an Ottoman possession.

The Afghan–Ottoman treaty

The Ottoman vizier, Damad Ibrahim, had refused at first to accept the ambassadors of Ashraf who had replaced Mahmoud as the leader of the Ghilzai in Iran. Ashraf responded by launching a major attack against Ottoman troops stationed around Hamadan in January 1726.[128] The Afghans achieved military success, prompting Ashraf to renew his efforts for political recognition from the Ottomans. Damad Ibrahim responded positively when Ashraf offered to support the spread of Sunni Islam in Iran: by October 1727 a formal peace treaty had been signed between the Ottomans and the Afghans at Hamadan.[129] The Afghans ceded the border areas they had captured from the Ottomans and retired into Iran's interior.[130] In return, the Ottomans formally recognized Ashraf and the Afghans as the rulers of Iran.[131] Iranian national honor suffered yet another blow as Tahmasp II had not even been a factor during the Afghan–Ottoman talks. The partitioning of Iran was now complete: the Ottomans occupied much of western Iran, the western Caucasus, and Azarbaijan; the Russians occupied northern Iran, Baku, and the Caspian rim of the Caucasus; and the Afghans possessed Iran's east, interior, and south. Iran had ceased to exist as an independent state.

PART II
NADER SHAH

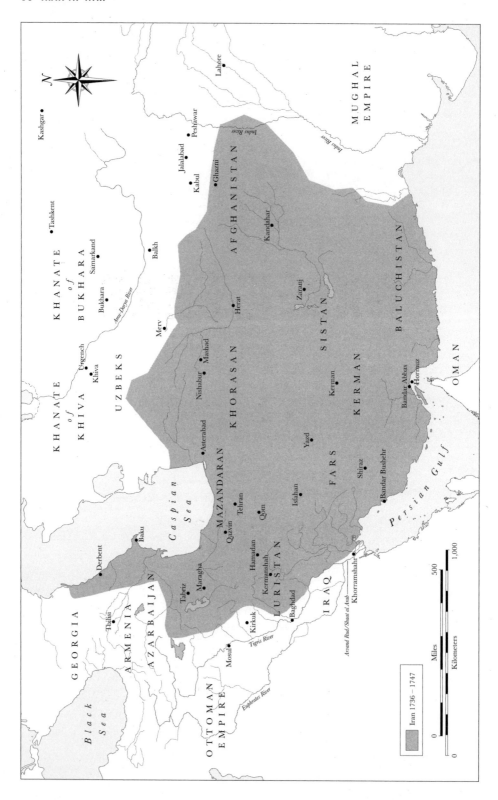

Map legend:

Iran 1736 – 1747

Miles: 0 ... 500 ... 1,000
Kilometers: 0 ...

Labels on map:

Kashgar

MUGHAL EMPIRE

Lahore

Peshawar
Jalalabad
Kabul
Ghazni

AFGHANISTAN

Indus River

Tashkent

KHANATE of BUKHARA

Samarkand
Bukhara

Balkh

Amu Darya River

KHANATE of KHIVA

Urgench
Khiva

UZBEKS

Merv

Kandahar

Herat

Zaranj

SISTAN

BALUCHISTAN

Nishabur
Mashad

KHORASAN

Kerman

KERMAN

Bandar Abbas
Hormuz

OMAN

Asterabad

Caspian Sea

Yazd

FARS

Shiraz
Bandar Bushehr

Persian Gulf

MAZANDARAN

Tehran
Qom
Qazvin

Isfahan

Baku
Derbent

Hamadan
Kermanshah
Maragha
Tabriz

LURISTAN

Baghdad

IRAQ

Khorramshahr
Arvand Rud/Shatt al Arab

GEORGIA
Tbilisi

ARMENIA

AZARBAIJAN

Black Sea

Kirkuk
Mosul

Tigris River

OTTOMAN EMPIRE

Euphrates River

CHAPTER 8

THE RISE OF NADER KHAN (1736–47)

Nader Qoli was born in Dastgerd in early August 1698, just four years after the ascension of Shah Sultan Hussein.[1] He was 24 when the Ghilzai Afghans sacked Isfahan and overthrew the Safavids. His father, Imam Qoli, was of humble peasant origins, variously earning his living as a herdsman and sheepskin coat maker.[2] He died when Nader was still a child. Nader, which means "the rare one," was very much a man of the horse, sword, bow, and lance, hunting dangerous wild animals from a young age.[3] Nader hailed from the Qaralkhlu branch of the Afshar Turkmen clan.[4] The Afshars had provided significant military support for the Safavid dynasty since the days of Ismail I.[5] Nader displayed his military talents very early. He was about 14 or 15 when he joined the militia of Baba Ali Beg Kuse Ahmadlu of the Afshar tribe, the governor of the city of Abivard in northern Khorasan.[6] He first served as a Tofangchi.[7] Despite his talents with traditional weapons, Nader very quickly learned to appreciate the importance of the musket and the centrality of firearms in any military force. It was not long before his talents propelled him to a very high position under Ahmadlu.

The weakening of Safavid rule and its military in the early 18th century enabled a revival in the power of the Afghan tribes. The Abdalis rebelled against Isfahan in 1711. The Safavid government in Isfahan made repeated and unsuccessful attempts to defeat the rebels. In 1716, Ahmadlu and 500 troops were part of a government contingent sent to suppress the Abdalis. Nader was left behind as Ahmadlu's governor at Abivard. The mission failed and Ahmadlu was killed in the fighting. The governorship was assumed by Ahmadlu's brother Qorban Ali. Nader conducted further successful campaigns against Turkmen raiders during Qorban Ali's tenure. Qorban Ali soon died, probably from disease or perhaps even murdered by Nader.[8] Nader then became deputy to Hassan Ali Khan, the new governor sent from Isfahan. Nader got his first experience fighting the Afghans during one of the failed Safavid campaigns to retake Herat. During the fighting, Nader witnessed the ineptitude of the Safavid military, especially in their use of firearms. The cannon had been misplaced so that they fired into the Iranian formations, wreaking havoc among the troops; the distraught commander lost his nerve and blew himself up on a powder keg. The Abdalis broke the Iranian lines, resulting in a complete disaster. Nader and his men escaped from the debacle.

Nader strengthened his military position by capturing Kalat in 1720, a rising plateau situated between Abivard and Mashad. Nader now controlled the land around northern Khorasan and could extend his power south of Abivard.

Rebellions had sprung up throughout Khorasan by the early 1720s with many attempting to set up their own independent fiefdoms. Mashad, the provincial capital, was taken over by rebels. At this juncture Malek Mahmoud Sistani arrived from Isfahan. He had reached an accord with the Afghans in 1722 to recognize their authority in exchange for his becoming the ruler of Khorasan. Sistani crushed the rebels in Mashad and took the city. Nader was not yet strong enough to suppress the widespread rebellion across the province but he was formidable and even Sistani had no wish to quarrel with him.[9]

Free from the need to confront Sistani, Nader set out to crush his enemies. Those who opposed him were mercilessly crushed and those who submitted treated honorably. Nader eagerly accepted defeated foes and their troops as long as they pledged their loyalty to him. He was joined by a number of large contingents, including the Mongol-descended Tahmasp Khan Jalayer and his troops, who were entrusted with guarding Kalat.

Sistani must have realized that by failing to confront Nader he had allowed him to grow in strength. Nader was soon confident enough to challenge Sistani in Mashad. Nader's small army of 1,200 was well equipped with Zanbourak camel-mounted guns and cannon.[10] He successfully raided Mashad's environs against Sistani's much larger forces.[11] Nader was not yet attempting to overthrow Sistani, but he had proved how formidable he had become. His fame grew further, and he received requests for assistance, such as from the city of Merv, which asked for his help in dealing with Turkmen raiders. With each appeal and response, Nader's prestige soared higher and attracted more and more fighters into his army. Sistani's days in Khorasan were numbered.

Prince Tahmasp II and the rise of Nader Khan

Prince Tahmasp II had been crowned as Shah Tahmasp II at Qazvin in October 1722 after his father's surrender to Mahmoud, leader of the Afghans besieging Isfahan.[12] After the fall of Isfahan, Mahmoud sent a force under Amanollah Khan to capture Qazvin, Golpayegan, and Kashan. In December, Qazvin fell and Tahmasp was driven out. The Afghans' brutal treatment of civilians in Qazvin resulted in a major uprising by January 1723, with 4,000–12,000 Afghans killed. Amanollah Khan escaped with a few survivors, after having been surrounded for three days. The sight of the defeated remnants of Amanollah Khan's force arriving at Isfahan was a major blow to Mahmoud's prestige.

After his expulsion from Qazvin, Tahmasp and his followers fled to Azerbaijan. But he couldn't stay there long as the Ottomans were invading. Tahmasp received appeals from Tabriz, the Caucasus, northwest and western Iran for assistance against the Ottomans, but he could not do anything, and the regions had no choice but to surrender to the Ottomans.[13] Tahmasp then appears to have been intercepted by the Afghans near Tehran, where he was severely defeated and very nearly captured.[14] Tahmasp made it to the north, finally reaching Astrabad. He obtained military support from the local Qajar tribe led by Fathali Khan, who had a long history of distinguished military service under the Safavids.

By 1725 Mahmoud's authority was weakening; he was opposed by the Iranian people and losing favor with his troops. His cousin Ashraf was increasingly popular with the Afghan troops so Mahmoud imprisoned him, further undermining his credibility. In early February 1725 Mahmoud heard that Sultan Hussein's son, Safi Mirza, had escaped. He gathered the male Safavid nobles in the courtyard of the Safavid palace, their hands tied behind their backs. One by one, he put them to the sword. Sultan Hussein had been spared, but could finally bear the executions no longer and rushed into the courtyard from his chambers to protect two of his remaining young sons. The former king was wounded, but the children were spared. However all Sultan Hussein's uncles, brothers and other kinsmen were dead. Iranian historians estimate that between 150 and 300 nobles were massacred by Mahmoud in that macabre episode.[15]

After the massacre, Mahmoud forced the surrender of Shiraz and advanced as far as Bandar Abbas on the Persian Gulf. But on April 22, 1725, Amanollah Khan and a number of the Ghilzai warriors released Ashraf from his prison in Isfahan. Ashraf, Amanollah Khan, and hundreds of other Ghilzai warriors poured into the palace. After overcoming Mahmoud's guards, they captured Mahmoud, who died just days later.[16] Ashraf was declared shah on April 26, 1725. To the Iranians not much had changed, their tyrant had simply been replaced with another.

Ever since he had arrived at Fathali Khan Qajar's camp at Astrabad, Tahmasp had been itching to march on Isfahan.[17] Fathali Khan was more circumspect. He knew their forces were not strong enough yet to launch a direct assault on Isfahan.[18] Fathali decided that their martial energies were to be directed in nearby Khorasan, especially against Malek Mahmoud Sistani in Mashad.[19]

Nader had scored a major victory in 1726 by finally defeating the Chameshgazak Kurds and taking their main base at Khabooshan in Khorasan. This was a notable success as Nader gained more high-quality Kurdish warriors into his army and was soon launching attacks as far east as the environs of Herat. Duly impressed, Tahmasp sent a message to Nader inviting him to join forces to retake Mashad.[20] Nader accepted and received Tahmasp with great honor at Khabooshan, leading the Safavids to bestow the honorary title of "Tahmasp Qoli Khan" (Servant of the Shah Tahmasp) upon him.[21] Nader was now a figure of national importance.

Ever since Tahmasp had been given sanctuary in Astrabad by Fathali Khan Qajar, relations between the pair had been tense. Fathali had in fact clashed with Tahmasp as he had arrived in Mazandaran, but later came to him in submission.[22] Fathali, however, showed very little respect and was able to maintain his domination of Tahmasp so long as there were no other domineering personalities. But Fathali would soon meet his match in Nader.[23]

The defeat of Malek Mahmoud Sistani

Tahmasp requested that Nader assemble as many forces as he could muster to assist in the capture of Mashad and ousting of Malek Mahmoud Sistani. Leading 30,000 troops, Nader arrived with Tahmasp and Fathali to besiege Mashad by late September.[24] Fathali led fewer than 2,000 cavalry and Tahmasp's forces were virtually negligible. The military initiative was held by Nader; Tahmasp, and even Fathali, were of secondary military importance. As the siege was being implemented, Fathali made contact with Sistani in Mashad.[25]

Nader intercepted Fathali's letter to Sistani on October 10, 1726 and presented it to Tahmasp, who ordered Fathali arrested. One account states that Nader urged that Fathali be sent to Kalat first, perhaps fearing that a quick execution would lead to the departure of the Qajars.[26] Tahmasp pretended to agree but had Fathali beheaded the next day. Fortunately for Nader, a Qajar rival of Fathali took over command of the Qajar contingent, the army remained intact, and the siege continued.

After the death of Fathali, Malek Mahmoud Sistani launched a raid apparently under the impression that Fathali's death had weakened the besieging forces. The force, which included Sistani's artillery, was completely defeated by Nader's well-trained forces. A number of officers, including the artillery master, were killed, and the force was driven back into Mashad. But what finally led to the fall of Sistani was betrayal by Pir Mohammad, his commander-in-chief. In secret correspondence with Nader, he assured him that he would open one of the city gates.[27] He was as good as his word, and with his help, Nader's troops poured into the city on the night of November 10–11, 1726. Failing to eject the invaders, Sistani decided to make his last stand at the citadel, but soon surrendered to Nader. He was treated with generosity by Nader, and allowed to retire as a religious man. The following year Sistani was found to be in contact with Turkmen, and Nader had him executed.

The defeat of Malek Mahmoud Sistani and the capture of Mashad greatly enhanced Nader Khan's prestige.[28] Following this success Nader tamed the rest of Khorasan by 1727 to help restore political homogeneity to that province. Nader's main challenge was the Kurds of Khabooshan who were finally subdued with some heavy fighting. The other khans of the province were successively brought into line, and with each success Nader's military base grew progressively larger and stronger.

CHAPTER 9

THE NEW IRANIAN ARMY (1726–47)

Before Nader could take on the formidable Afghans he had to rebuild the Iranian army. This was no easy task given the terrible defeats that Iranian troops had suffered in 1722. Iranian morale had been badly shaken as the Afghans had worsted the Iranians in almost every battle and put them to flight. Nader's ability to revive the lost martial ardor of the Iranians, badly shaken by the Afghan, Ottoman, and Russian invasions, was nothing short of a miracle. He is described by Iranian sources as a savior of the Iranian nation. He set the standard of soldierly virtue by personally leading his men into battle, regardless of danger; one sees parallels with Iranian monarchs such as Shah Ismail I or Khosrow I Anushirvan. Despite his demands for absolute military discipline, Nader shared with his officers a profound sense of camaraderie.

Before any battles could begin, Nader began restoring Iranian morale by instituting vigorous training in martial arts and firearms and the implementation of strict discipline. It was here that Nader demonstrated his genius: his alchemy of military genius and charisma combined to produce some of the most spectacular armies seen in Iran's military history.

Military revolution in the east: firearms come of age

Muskets and artillery had been deployed during the Safavid era, but it was during Nader Shah's time that a veritable revolution took place in Iran to parallel European developments in the deployment of firepower.[1] Nader realized the potential of disciplined bodies of infantry acting together in the massed and accurate firing of musketry. His *Jazayerchiha* musketeers would be his "anchor" on the battlefield. They were placed on an intense training and drill regimen lasting at least three hours a day.[2] The musketeers were well protected, and artillery was often placed to their front to act as a barrier against cavalry attacks. The cavalry were trained as intensely, especially in the art of massed coordination of attacks, feigned retreats, and counterattacks. The promotion of officers according to merit ensured that the leadership of the army was entrusted to a new generation of capable and daring officers. The overall result of Nader's intense training, emphasis on firepower, and a new professional officer corps was the rise of a new army characterized by combat efficiency discipline, and fluidity of command. Nader Shah's military genius transformed the Iranian army into a world-class combined arms war machine that was soon to earn the respect of Afghans, Mughals, Ottomans, and Russians alike.

The Jazayerchiha had been formed during the Safavid era and continued to be a vital component of the Iranian army during Nader's time. They were a vital segment of the infantry in supporting the cavalry strikes and defending against enemy (infantry and cavalry) strikes. The Jazayerchiha were armed with big musket-type guns known as *Chakhmaghi* [flintlock] characterized as having "long and heavy barrels necessitating the need to mount them on tripods when firing in combat."[3] The tripods ensured accuracy of fire during combat as the Chakhmaghi could weigh in at approximately 40lbs (18kg).[4] The Jazayerchiha were led by a commander known as the *Jazayerchi-Bashi*. Each Jazayerchi-Bashi commanded a total of 20,000 Jazayerchis.[5] The Jazayerchis campaigning in Ottoman Mesopotamia in early 1733 are reported to have worn belts of gold and silver and felt hats known as *Kacheh Papagh*, featuring the Pahlavi medallion.[6]

The *Gharachoorlooha* fired their muskets after the Jazayerchiha. Their muskets were lighter than those of the Jazayerchiha. They loaded gunpowder by means of a horn, enabling them to measure the gunpowder and control the range of the shot.[7] Contemporary European musketeers used paper cartridges containing a standard amount of gunpowder and bullet, making their fire less accurate than that of their Persian and Ottoman counterparts. Their accuracy came at a steep price, as reloading took longer than it did the Europeans.[8] Nader appears to have ameliorated this by training the Persian musketeers to engage in line firing.

Persian and Ottoman muskets were generally heavier than those seen in Europe. They were able to fire larger bullets at longer ranges, being especially effective against cavalry attacks. Unlike Europeans, Iranian musketeers did not deploy bayonets, but were able to fight at close quarters if necessary.[9] Western sources also report on the rigorous training of Iranian musketeers who had developed high capabilities for firing accurately and en masse.[10]

Nader impressed a number of effective reforms on the Iranian infantry especially after his defeats at the hands of Osman Pasha's forces in July 1733.[11] Nader's reforms resulted in dramatic improvements to the overall efficiency, organization, mobility, and striking power of the revitalized Iranian army.[12] The infantry were now subdivided into three distinct segments: The Jazayerchiha, Gharachoorlooha, and the *Piyadegan*.[13] Nader instilled a professional *esprit de corps* by introducing a uniform for the entire infantry force of blue tunics and crimson trousers. Each soldier's rank was displayed on his headgear.

After the Afghan victories of 1722, Nader was aware of the dangers of tough enemy infantry. Traditional infantry were crucial in defending against enemy infantry attacks. Likewise, effective infantry were needed for offensive purposes such as engaging enemy formations face-to-face, as a follow-up to musket and artillery salvoes as well as mopping-up operations. The corps that was entrusted with such duties since Safavid times was now known as the Piyadegan.

The Piyadegan were exclusively armed with spears and traditional infantry weapons such as swords, daggers, maces, and axes. The Piyadegan were effective follow-up forces that would deploy into the enemy positions after the strikes of the artillery, Jazayerchiha, Gharachoorlooha, and cavalry. These warriors were in the tradition of Iran's ancient martial arts, and their highly developed hand-to-hand fighting methods originated in the Zoor-Khaneh. The Piyadegan were also proficient in archery, enabling them to support the strikes of the artillery and Jazayerchiha and defend against infantry and cavalry strikes. When the battle opened the Piyadegan stood in ranks to the rear of the Jazayerchiha and Gharachoorlooha to allow their salvoes to be delivered.[14] They would then be deployed as strategy or battlefield circumstances dictated.

The cavalry had held a most esteemed position in the Iranian army since the days of the ancient Medes and the Persians, and still formed a major component of the Iranian army.[15] Nader placed a heavy emphasis on the proper care of horses.[16] He introduced the revolutionary concept whereby the state paid for a cavalryman's horse.[17] State sponsorship of equestrian expenses helped remove the reluctance of many cavalrymen to risk their mounts in battle.

The most prestigious cavalry units were Nader's own personal guard, known as the *Savaran e Saltanati* (the royal cavalry) and the *Savaran e Sepah e Khorasan* (the cavalry of the army of Khorasan).[18] There was also a core personal guard of 3,000 men known as the *Gholaman* or *Bandegan-e-Shah* (lit. servants of the Shah).[19] There was a heavy cavalry arm intended for close-quarter combat, protected with armor of mail and plate and spiked helmets designed to deflect downward saber strokes.[20]

The royal cavalry was responsible for the protection of Nader Shah and his clan and was an important nucleus of the army's strike forces. As an elite cavalry unit, the Savaran e Saltanati often led the first cavalry charges in combat, fronted by Nader himself. Recruitment was drawn from the Afshar, Jalayerid, and Qajar clans as well as the Shahsevan of Azarbaijan and the Bakhtiari-Lurs of western Iran. The selection of young men from each clan was made on the basis of bravery and skill in combat. These were then furnished with the finest horses in the Iranian realm. There were a total of 20,000 Savaran e Saltanati[21] organized into 20 *Fowj*.[22] The Savaran e Saltanati was also known as the *Qizilbash e Naderi* [Turkic: the red heads of Nader]. Their headgear, indicative of the cavalryman's elite status, was a red four-pointed hat of Nader's design, often adorned with white (or other color) ribbons.

Many of Nader's best cavalry came from Khorasan. The Savaran e Sepah e Khorasan was recruited from the Baluchis and Afghans towards eastern and southeastern Iran, Uzbeks and Turkmen in Central Asia and the Kurds of northeast Iran. These provided effective support to the Savaran e Saltanati and repeatedly proved crucial to Nader's battlefield victories. These also wore a tall pointed hat, known as the *Kulah e Naderi* (the hat of Nader), which often had a sheepskin or goatskin ribbon wrapped around it.[23] The Savaran e Sepah e Khorasan grew to 70,000 men and their conduct so impressed Nader that numbers of them were inducted into the Savaran e Saltanati.[24] Cavalrymen were generally armed with a curved sword, axe, a single or pair of matchlock muskets (either tucked into the belt or carried in pouches woven onto the saddle), and sometimes archery equipment and spears.[25] Muskets had become one of the standard weapons of the cavalry by 1736.[26] Nader placed a heavy emphasis on rigorous training in rapid flanking movements and maneuver.[27]

Nader's army had ample supplies of modern artillery but these were often not used in Nader's deep strike missions into enemy territory. This was due to Nader's preference for rapid maneuver and flanking with his entire army. Heavy artillery was used in terrain where transportation and deployment were possible, but Nader's preference was for lighter and more portable artillery amenable to rapid transportation and deployment anywhere, in support of the attacking cavalry and infantry. The artillery corps was commanded by the *Toopchi-Bashi*.

The strategic preference for rapid maneuver explains the popularity of the Zanbourak in Nader Shah's armies. These were led by the *Zanbourak-Bashi*.[28] When Nader Shah engaged in attacking enemy positions, the Zanbourak camel corps would deploy as far forward as possible due to the very short range and inaccuracy of the weapon. The Zanbourak more than made up for their inaccuracy by creating panic and disorder among enemy troops. They were highly effective in Nader's campaigns in Afghanistan, Central Asia, and India, though possibly less so against the well-trained troops of the Ottoman Empire.

Other units of importance in Nader's army were the *Nasghchiyan*, *Shaterha*, *Gheravalan*, and *Parchamdaran*. The Nasghchiyan were of paramount importance as they ensured the maintenance of military discipline within the various units of the army.[29] The Shaterha were essentially armed advance guards moving ahead of the main army to ensure the smooth procession of the shah or the high commanders. Another important unit was the Gheravalan, armed sentries who guarded military camps when the army was at rest.[30] The Parchamdaran (lit. flag bearers), numbering no more than 1,000 men, carried the army battle standards, royal insignia, and the Iranian flag to battle.[31] There were also a number of European advisors in the engineering corps. These proved their worth numerous times by building bridges over difficult waterways and mountain passes during Nader's campaigns.[32] The *Charkhchian* were, as in the Safavid era, responsible for the advance guards of the army.

Organization and command

After the fall of the Safavids, the Iranian army had fractured into disorganized parts across the country. Nader's genius was in reintegrating those pieces into a new, unified army under his command.[33] While the overall structure of Nader Shah's army was not altogether different from its Safavid predecessor, it also acted as the country's government. Much of the command structure and Turkic-style terminology of the Safavids was retained.

Nader assigned the defense of Iran into five *Urdu* (Turkic: military camp) zones, which was somewhat reminiscent of Khosrow I's 6th-century system of regional defense.[34] The first Urdu was Khorasan, responsible for the defense of the Central Asian and eastern frontiers. Khorasan was also the gateway to the eastern Afghan marches, Central Asia, and India. The second Urdu was in the Caucasus, responsible for safeguarding Iran's commercial links with the steppes and Eastern Europe as well as defense against the Ottoman and Russian empires. The third Urdu was in Kermanshah, vital for its war industries as well as its proximity to the Ottoman-Mesopotamian heartland. The fourth Urdu was stationed in Fars to enable rapid deployment to western Iran, southwest Iran and south towards the Persian Gulf. The fifth Urdu was based at Kandahar, monitoring the Afghans and providing the Iranian army with a base of operations against the Indian subcontinent.

Each sector or Urdu was commanded by a *Beglarbegi*. Overseeing the Beglarbegis was Nader Shah and his trusted inner circle known as the *Valian*. These were primarily Nader's sons, nephews, and other trusted family and clan members. Following the Valian and Beglarbegis came the khans who often held the titles of *Beg* or *Sultan*. A group of the khans was entrusted with leading the various branches of the army. Three khans were responsible for supplies and inventory: the *Mostofi ol Mamalek* was responsible for accounting the costs of the military campaigns of the Iranian army; the *Nazer-e Bebotat* oversaw the purchase and acquisition of supplies for the army; while the office of the *Divan Begi* was responsible for legal affairs as well as monetary issues of individual troops and officers.

Taheri's study of original Iranian sources concludes that the army of Nader Shah totaled 200,000 fighting troops including 50,000 Afghans, 20,000 Afshars, 6,000 Baluchis, 6000 Turkmen, and 6,000 Uzbek warriors.[35] Venetian accounts describe the backbone of the Iranian army as being drawn from Iran's tribal warriors and provincial towns, these being recruited in a quota system in accordance with each area's population.[36]

According to Marvi[37] the hierarchical system of ranks in ascending order was as follows: the *Ghazi* (the regular soldier), *Oon Bashi* (leader of 10 *Ghazi*), *Yooz Bashi* (leader of 100 troops or 10 *Oon Bashi*), *Meen Bashi* (commanding a *Fowj* of 1,000 or 10 *Yooz Bashi*). There were also the

Sarkheylan, the *Sarkardegan*, and the *Sardaran* (these were generally the great tribal chieftains, regional leaders and khans). The *Farmande-ye Kol* (the commander-in-chief of the Iranian army) was almost always Nader himself or one of his sons. The *Ghoorchi-Bashi* was, as under the Safavids, the country's minister of defense. The Ghoorchi-bashi attended all important military reviews and ceremonies attended by Nader Shah.

The most "ceremonial" of the military branches, the *Esheek Aghasi* supervised the palace personnel, such as guards and sentries. Also known as *Reesh Sefid Yavalan*, the *Esheek Aghasi* was given a silver ceremonial staff, somewhat reminiscent of Sassanian court traditions. There was also a *Majles-Nevees* (lit. council/meeting writer) who recorded the affairs of Nader's court and affairs. The commander of the royal guards or gholams of the shah was known as the *Ghollar Aghasi*. The *Amir Shekar-Bashi* was responsible for organizing and supervising the royal hunt for Nader and his entourage.

Kermanshah and the armaments industry of Iran

Nader made great efforts to expand and improve Iran's armament industry. The three chief centers for armament production were Kermanshah (western Iran), Isfahan (Iranian plateau), and Merv (Central Asia).

The city of Kermanshah acquired a position of prime importance during the reign of Nader Shah, mainly due to its strategic position, crucial for launching offensives into Ottoman Mesopotamia. The city was a major depot for siege weapons, ready for such offensives. Kermanshah also produced various calibers of high-quality cannon and ammunition. It was for this reason that Kermanshah became known as Iran's "arsenal to the west," a reputation that would last past the reign of Nader Shah.[38] The fortress of Kermanshah, defended by 1,500 cannon, 600 mortars of various types and 8,000 cavalry, protected the city and its facilities against Nader's domestic rivals as well as foreign attacks.

The production plants at Isfahan achieved high volumes of production, such that by 1741, the Iranian army was able to field more than 500 cannon. Merv became one of Iran's chief centers of production for cannonballs and cannon. The city's factories received gunpowder and various explosives and other raw materials from Fars, Khorasan, and Kerman.

Nader Shah also developed the capability of producing heavy weapons in battle theaters, far away from Iran's centers of production. The expansion of the capabilities of the mobile production shops greatly enhanced the striking power and resiliency of the Iranian army.[39]

Tribal elements and defense of frontiers: the case of Khorasan

Nader Shah exhibited a marked preference for ruling the tribes through their own tribal leaders, a policy followed by the Safavids.[40] Nader also continued to resettle tribes to garrison Iran's porous and potentially dangerous frontiers.[41] The forced resettlement of tribes to Khorasan and other frontiers helped protect Iran against foreign invasions, but also ensured that prominent tribes did not become too powerful in their respective domains with the potential to challenge the state. However, resettlements and deportations could lead to resentment, potentially resulting in more rebellions.

Upon his arrival in Mashad on November 11, 1730, while preparing to battle the Abdalis Nader reviewed 50,000–60,000 tribal warriors whom he had recently sent to the northeast.[42] He selected the best fighting young men and recruited these into his army. He also did this with other tribes, ensuring that their martial energies would be utilized by him alone. Many of the tribes had become restless, engaging in rebellion, raids, and plunder and Nader greatly reduced this threat by granting the tribes a major stake in the Iranian army. Warriors were given the prestige of rank and participation in elite units, and were well paid. For the first time in centuries, Iran was able to utilize its pool of martially talented tribal warriors in a single fighting force. This is one of the factors that led to Nader's military successes.

Promotion by merit: rise of a professional officer corps

What made Nader's Iranian army unique both in its own time and compared to previous Iranian (Safavid) armies was the prime importance afforded to military merit, which then led to promotion.[43]

The promotion of warriors according to merit had one transparent consequence: the Iranian army was soon led by officers who were brave, disciplined, loyal, intelligent, and resourceful. The combination of such officers leading a well-trained and well-equipped army meant that Nader Shah's military machine was able to conduct battles effectively against its contemporaries. By the same token, the Iranian army was able to rapidly absorb lessons from setbacks and use these experiences to further enhance its military performance.

Unfortunately for Iran, this officer corps did not last beyond the reign of Nader Shah. Had it remained in place, it could have developed into a strong tradition of officer training that would have at least partially prepared Iran for the challenges it would face from the end of the 18th century.

The professional army: exorbitant costs

The efficiency and striking power of Nader's new Iranian army was indeed impressive. However the constant battles, the need for regular and consistent training, maintenance of lost or damaged military inventory, and a sophisticated logistics system came at a very high price. As Nader transformed the Iranian army into a professional force, the costs of its maintenance increased accordingly.

The backbone of Iran's armies had traditionally been the tribal contingents who had rallied to the royal standard during war and who would return home after the conclusion of the fighting. Nader however wanted a standardized professional force, trained in uniform fashion and militarily unified by a singular training regimen and doctrine. The troops (tribal or urban) had been molded into a single force and Nader wanted them stay on as paid professional troops. This meant that Nader could no longer rely on post-battle plunder to satiate the material appetites of his troops. As noted by Axworthy the new troops "had to be paid well and promptly so that they would not desert."[44] The arbitrary departure of troops would also mean the loss of their accompanying equipment, especially muskets and other war materiel, items that had already cost the state considerable expense.

Measures were set in place to collect state revenues and taxes on a regular basis to service the costs of Nader's army. Nader appointed officials to implement government authority in the cities, mainly for the collection of taxes.[45] The taxes were to prove excessive for the population. The costs of maintaining the army became ever greater as Nader recruited troops from his defeated foes. These had to be re-trained, re-equipped and paid on a regular basis. As the army grew in size and firepower, the economic burden upon the people increased. In tandem with these accompanying social and economic stressors, the Europeans had been able to engage in a number of challenging social, political, and economic reforms.[46] Iran had demonstrated that she was capable of producing armies as effective as those of the Ottomans and the Europeans, however she lacked the economic, political, and social infrastructure necessary to maintain her new professional army.

Iran's first true navy of the post-Islamic era

Since the Safavid era, Iran had faced two distinct maritime threats: from the Caspian Sea to the north and from the Persian Gulf to the south. It was in response to these threats that Nader Shah decided to build the first true Iranian navy in both the Caspian Sea and the Persian Gulf since pre-Islamic times.[47]

The west and north banks of the Caspian Sea could be used by Caucasian raiders such as the Lezgians to land troops into northern Iran, with the Turkomens of Central Asia being able to do the same from the eastern banks of the Caspian. Nader requested ships from the Tsar of Russia for use on the Caspian. The request was rejected outright as a strong Iranian navy in the Caspian Sea was inimical to Russian ambitions.[48] Nader then received assistance from a British national identified as "John Elton" who offered to help Nader establish a powerful Caspian navy.[49] Elton chose Langarood as the headquarters of the fleet, and plans were laid to build large transport ships. A factory was opened in Amol to produce various metals and products such as ammunition for cannon and mortars. Russia was unhappy with these developments and Moscow issued a decree in November 1746 forbidding any British nationals from engaging in any sort of commerce in the Caspian Sea region. This was specifically meant as a protest against Elton and his crew.[50] A number of successful interceptions had been made against piracy directed against Iran's Caspian coastline before Elton's death.[51]

The Persian Gulf coastline to the south was exposed to Arab raids and European ambitions. Nader Shah realized that his forces required modern ships to transport troops across the Persian Gulf to strike at the bases of Arab raiders. A formal request was made to the British authorities of the East India Company to provide a number of ships to assist in the transportation of 5,000 infantry and 1,500 cavalry towards Oman.[52] The British refused, obliging Nader to seek the creation of an indigenous navy for the Persian Gulf.

The government allocated funds for the creation of a small navy and by 1745, 30 small craft equipped with cannon were purchased from Holland and Britain.[53] Nader Shah recruited highly skilled Arab and Indian sailors to man his new ships. The organization of the navy and the planning of its operations were entrusted to Latif Khan. Latif Khan's force first engaged and expelled the Arab raiders who had used Muscat and Oman for piracy and raids against Iranian possessions and settlements along the Persian Gulf coast of Iran. Latif Khan then turned to Kish and expelled other raiders who had come to occupy the island as a base for raids against the Iranian mainland. Mohammad Khan Baluch was captured during operations.[54] These operations were followed by the rehabilitation of the old Portuguese fort at Bushehr which became the headquarters of the new Iranian navy. Latif Khan, who had been promoted as the chief commander of the entire naval force in the Persian Gulf, also purchased a number of Arab-built ships from allied sheikhs in the Persian Gulf.

Despite these successes, raids against the Iranian coast and islands continued. Nader Shah concluded that a larger navy was needed to enforce a more permanent halt to raiding and piracy. For coastal defense, artillery began to be placed in strategic locations such as Bushehr and Bandar Abbas. A mix of Dutch and British companies were contracted to supply more ships to the flotilla. The most powerful of these were two vessels armed with 20 cannon and weighing in at 400 tons each.[55] The reinforced navy first struck at Sheikh Jabarah of Bahrein, who had risen against Nader Shah. Iman Sayf of Muscat then formally requested help against anti-Iranian fighters. Nader dispatched the Iranian navy under the leadership of Mohammad Taqhi Khan towards Muscat. The fleet fired its cannon onto the coasts allowing a force of 5,000 infantry and 1,500 cavalry to land. These forces achieved overwhelming success. This victory allowed Iranian authority to finally be established and a measure of calm to be instilled along the Persian Gulf coastline and on Iranian island possessions. Imam Sayf fell out with Nader Shah after the latter annexed part of Muscat.[56]

Nader Shah then ordered shipbuilding facilities to be built in Bushehr and a naval cannon factory in Gamberon. Plans were for wood to be transported from Iran's forests in the north to the south but transportation problems meant that ships were never built in any numbers.[57] Some progress was made in the production of indigenous naval cannon, but these projects never went beyond the formative stages. After Nader's death, Iran's naval situation in the Persian Gulf steadily declined.

CHAPTER 10

NADER KHAN DEFEATS THE AFGHANS (1727–29)

Iran under the occupying armies

The Ottomans had completed their conquests of western Iran and Azarbaijan by the summer of 1725. Ashraf sent an emissary to the Ottoman Sultan in Istanbul asking that these be transferred to Afghan jurisdiction. The rejection of these demands meant that war was inevitable and conflict began in earnest by May 1726. Ahmad Pasha, Ottoman governor of Baghdad, marched on Isfahan with a huge army of 70,000–80,000 men, though many of them had no wish to fight fellow Sunnis in Ashraf's army.[1] Ashraf arrived to do battle at the head of just 12,000 men.[2] As the Ottomans neared Isfahan, a large reconnaissance party of 6,000 was wiped out by the Ghilzai. Once battle was joined, numbers of Ottoman-Kurdish warriors defected to Ashraf, who then repelled three Ottoman attacks before Ahmad Pasha withdrew to Baghdad.[3] Ahmad Pasha and Ashraf agreed that Ottoman conquests in western and northwest Iran would be recognized in exchange for Ashraf being shah in the rest of Iran.[4] This was a huge blow to Iranian sovereignty as Istanbul was now recognizing an occupier as the shah of Iran. Ashraf's prestige was now at its height, and the Afghan military seemed unassailable after defeating superior numbers of both Iranian and Ottoman troops on the battlefield.

The population of Iran chafed under the heel of the occupying armies. In areas under Ottoman occupation, such as Azarbaijan, houses were destroyed and confiscation of means of livelihood was common.[5] War, famine, and disease had ground the Iranian economy to a virtual halt.[6] Turkish soldiers were allowed to sell Iranian women and children as slaves until this practice was put to an end by an edict from Istanbul on December 5, 1725.[7]

Conditions were even worse in those areas under Afghan occupation.[8] After many of the Safavid nobility, and the last shah, were put to death, Ashraf introduced a "race law" which assigned Iranians as the lowest of all races.[9] The Ottoman ambassador in Isfahan, Mohammad Rashid, observed that Iranian citizens were dying of starvation and were in constant fear of arbitrary execution or (at best) having their houses robbed, sacked, and burned by the Afghans.[10] Ashraf failed to realize that such harsh policies would eventually lead to a devastating backlash against the Afghans.

Defeat of the Abdalis and the submission of Herat

By the end of 1726, Mashad had been liberated, with Fathali Khan Qajar no longer alive to pose a challenge against Nader's rising military authority. Nader was now the commander-in-chief of the new Iranian army, with Tahmasp and his own royal troops playing a supportive or secondary military role. Nader knew that he had to clear Iran of the occupying Afghans before he could take on the Ottomans and Russians to the northwest and west of Iran. Nader's strategy was to crush first the Abdalis, then the more powerful Ghilzai, followed by the Ottomans and Russians. While the Abdalis were weaker than the Ghilzai, they were still a powerful and dangerous force. As long as their military power remained unchecked, they would always have the potential to storm into Khorasan, especially if Nader became involved in wars against the Ottomans to the west.

After rebuilding the Iranian army, Nader and Tahmasp set out in the summer of 1727 with 8,000 troops on a dual task: to subdue Hussein Sultan of Sistan, and crush the Abdali Afghans in Sangan Khaf and Behdadin. The Sistani chief and Sangan Khaf Abdalis were both subdued easily, while the Abdalis in Behdadin resisted for two days before submitting. The peace did not last, as the Abdalis in Sangan Khaf revolted in Nader's rear, prompting him to secure additional artillery from Mashad. An Abdali appeal for help resulted in 20,000 Abdali troops marching from Afghanistan towards Sangan.

Nader and Tahmasp reached Sangan Khaf before the Abdali reinforcements could arrive. Sangan Khaf was pummelled by Iranian artillery and finally forced to surrender after Nader's cavalry charge captured a crucial bridge leading into the city.[11]

Shortly after Sangan Khaf was destroyed, an Afghan army of 7,000–8,000 Abdalis arrived.[12] Nader Khan organized his forces for battle and took up position in the center.[13] Tahmasp stood separately with his troops, which included 2,000 musketeers. The battle was especially bloody and at one point, one of the flanks of the Iranian army buckled under Afghan pressure, but the situation was rescued by an attack by 1,000 royal troops led by Tahmasp, which killed 500 Afghans. While this action was decisively won by the Iranians, the Afghans refused to give up. There were further bloody clashes over the next four days, until the Abdalis retreated in haste, abandoning equipment to the Iranians.[14]

Despite the victories at Sangan and the securing of Khorasan, Nader felt that he had to break the nucleus of Abdali power to his rear before any attempts could be made to liberate Isfahan. It was agreed that Tahmasp would proceed from Nishabur with Nader marching out of Mashad. The two forces would then link up at Sultanabad to make their strike against the Abdalis at Herat. Intrigue and court politics ensured that the plan would go awry almost at the outset. Tahmasp's court ministers persuaded him to go to Mazandaran in the north instead of joining Nader. Tahmasp then suggested to Nader that he proceed against the Abdalis by himself.[15] There were also reports that Tahmasp was attacking Nader's allies and ordering that Nader's commands were to be ignored.[16] This was unacceptable to Nader, who returned to Mashad. It was now clear that before any new campaigns could be launched against the Afghans, the issue of authority between Tahmasp and Nader had to be settled.

As Nader marched with his forces to confront Tahmasp, the latter retreated to the city of Sabzevar. Nader forced Tahmasp to surrender on December 23, 1727 after subjecting Sabzevar to heavy artillery fire. The issue of Nader's authority was now settled. Tahmasp became basically a figurehead shah in exile with the real military power resting with Nader. Nader in turn realized that Tahmasp, as a prince of the Safavid house, was a valuable asset in rallying the loyalty of the Iranian populace to his quest to liberate Iran from its foreign occupiers.

What exactly occurred next varies a little according to the source. The Russian ambassador to Iran at the time, Avramov, claimed that Nader and Tahmasp had joined forces to campaign unsuccessfully against 200,000 Abdalis at Herat in the summer of 1728.[17] The Abdalis however were under no illusions and realized that Nader's army would return to battle them and, in preparation, they buried their differences. Zulfaqhar Khan became the governor of Farah with Allahyar Khan assuming the governorship of Herat. He commanded the bulk of Abdali troops, ready for the inevitable showdown at Herat. Before Nader could undertake any massive campaign against the Abdalis, he cleared Mazandaran and Astarabad of rebels in late 1728. The rebels were allegedly pro-Tahmasp, though the latter denied any connection. Nader of course distrusted Tahmasp's claim, but for now retained him as shah.

The Iranian army led by Nader and accompanied by Tahmasp finally set out from Mashad towards Herat on May 4, 1729. The showdown was to occur near a fort named Kafar Qaleh (now Islam Qaleh) about 62 miles (100km) west of Herat. For the Iranians, the upcoming battle was of great military and psychological importance, for at the same place, just a decade previously, Mohammad Zaman Khan (Zulfaqhar's Khan's father) had crushed the Safavid forces of Safi Qoli Khan.

Nader surrounded his troops with artillery, with the cavalry stationed on one flank. This would allow Nader to wield his cavalry as a single mobile strike force as well as a "fire brigade" in case things went wrong on the flanks of the infantry. The Abdalis launched the first major strike and forced back the Iranian musketeers but were then crushed by Nader's cavalry charge.[18]

The Abdalis retreated in haste across the Hari-Rud River, taking up positions at Kusuya, 75 miles (120km) north of Herat. Nader pursued and another showdown ensued with the Abdalis at Kusuya. Nader was victorious and the Abdalis broken. This time they retired so hurriedly that they abandoned weapons, tents, ammunition baggage, and artillery.[19] The Abdalis fell back in tatters to Herat, but before long they reorganized to fight against the advancing armies of Nader. The Abdalis marched to Ribat e Parian, roughly 8 miles (12km) north of the Hari-Rud River and 19 miles (30km) northwest of Herat. The outcome of the day-long battle was yet another defeat for the Abdalis who left at least 1,000 dead as they retreated.[20]

Allahyar Khan, realizing that he could not hold out in Herat against Nader, offered peace terms. Nader's response was that Allahyar Khan and his commanders had to come to the Iranian camp and offer their peace proposals personally. Just as Allahyar Khan was deciding to offer his submission to Nader he got word that Zulfaqhar Khan was marching from Farah to assist him.[21] Zulfaqhar Khan arrived with the main body of his forces at Shakiban, roughly 30 miles (50km) west of Herat.

Nader sent a portion of his forces to find and destroy Zulfaqhar Khan at Shakiban but he managed to avoid them. Allahyar Khan then attacked Nader and his main force just as Zulfaqhar Khan attacked the forces that had been sent against him. Nader sent a relief force to hold off Zulfaqhar while he and his main force fended off the Abdalis of Allahyar Khan. The battles lasted into the next day, with Nader triumphant against both Allahyar Khan and Zulfaqhar Khan.

Realizing that all was lost, the Abdalis offered peace proposals to Nader who once again demanded that they come to him and offer their obeisance in person. The Abdali chiefs then complied by coming to Nader bearing gifts and their submission. The Abdalis declared their allegiance to Iran and promised to join the Iranian army to partake in future battles against their historical rivals, the Ghilzai.[22] Nader and Tahmasp treated the Abdalis generously and accepted their offer. Allahyar Khan was made the governor of Herat on behalf of Tahmasp. Having successfully defeated the Abdalis, Nader and Tahmasp departed for Mashad, which they reached on July 1, 1729.[23]

Defeat of the Ghilzai and the liberation of Isfahan

The Iranians had learnt the importance of coordinating and pooling their forces as a requisite for military success.[24] In contrast, the Ghilzai had become dangerously overconfident in their capabilities and equally contemptuous of their adversaries. Ashraf reputedly boasted that he was more than happy to have Tahmasp come to Isfahan as this would save him the effort of having to hunt him down in the mountains. The Ghilzai warriors of Ashraf called Tahmasp "*Sag-Zadeh*" (lit: son of a dog).

Despite his bravado, Ashraf finally realized that a mortal threat did indeed exist against his rule, especially when he got news of Nader's successes at Herat in May 1729.[25] Alarmed at the prospect of a Tahmasp–Nader advance towards Isfahan, Ashraf sent troops to reinforce his forces in Qazvin. He then set out from Isfahan with 30,000 troops on August 2, 1729, soon arriving in Tehran.[26] From here he awaited the arrival of reinforcements before marching to Sangan.[27]

It was not until September 12, 1729 that Tahmasp and Nader began their advance towards the former Safavid capital, going through Nishabur and Sabzevar. Ashraf, now leading 40,000, was besieging Semnan further to the west in early September.[28] When he learned of Nader's army deploying towards Isfahan, Ashraf left behind a portion of his forces to continue besieging Semnan and marched to confront the Iranian army. The advance guard of the Ghilzai army led by Mohammad Saidal Khan tried to attack Nader's forces and capture their artillery at Bastam. They were decisively defeated, forcing them to flee as far as Mehmandoost village, about 14 miles (23km) northeast of Damghan.[29] This engagement presaged what would soon befall the Ghilzai. Ashraf, realizing the gravity of the danger facing him, decided to join his defeated advance guard at Mehmandoost to make his stand there.

Nader and Tahmasp lost no time in catching up with Ashraf. They arrived at the Mehmandoost River (east of Mehmandoost village) to begin their first set-piece battle against the Ghilzai. Estimates of Ashraf's army range from 25,000 to 50,000.[30] Another source reports Ashraf placing 20,000 men at the left and another 20,000 at the right flanks with 3,000 of his best troops in the center.[31]

The battle was joined on September 29, 1729.[32] Just as battle began the Iranians began to withdraw left towards the base of the Tal hills. The Ghilzai, thinking they had won and were pursuing a terrified enemy, engaged in pursuit. The Iranian "retreat" was protected by Nader's highly effective rearguard which kept the Ghilzai at a distance with musket and arrow fire. Nadir kept his army very organized and placed his assets accordingly. The "retreating troops" were assembled as one compact body at the base of the hills with the cannon and camel-mounted zanbouraks being placed on the slopes of the hill. Strict orders were given for the infantry musketeers and artillerymen to hold their fire until the Afghans came into close range.[33] The infantry were ordered to calmly stand their ground and not move unless ordered by Nader.[34]

The Ghilzai mounted the traditional Afghan assault of attacking in three thrusts simultaneously, lunging towards the Iranian center and flanks.[35] Nader now ordered his artillery to open fire against the middle Ghilzai thrust. This ripped through the packed Ghilzai ranks, killing up to 400 in the first volleys, and killing a number of Ashraf's top commanders right in front of him.[36] The Afghan cavalry attacks on the Iranian left and right fared no better. The Iranian musketeers held their fire until the Afghan horsemen were closing in, then opened fire with devastating fury and precision, cutting down hundreds of the attackers.[37] As the Afghans tumbled onto the ground, their comrades crashed into them from behind, causing further casualties and chaos. Ashraf tried his best to reorganize, but again and again Iranian cannon and musketeers discharged their deadly fire. With what appeared to be pinpoint precision, Iranian artillery also blasted away at the Afghans' Zanbourak camel-mounted swivel-guns with Ashraf's standard bearer also being torn to pieces by the Iranian guns.[38]

With the Ghilzai attacks crushed, Nader ordered his musketeers and Jazayerchis to advance into the heart of Ashraf's camp.[39] These and the Qizilbash cavalry ripped into the remnants of the Ghilzai artillery, ripping to shreds all opposition.[40] Nader's infantry rolled all the way into the Ghilzai center, with much close-quarter fighting taking place with swords and lances.[41] Realizing that they had lost, Ashraf and his remaining warriors had to flee. One estimate placed Iranian losses at 4,000 with the Afghans having suffered at least three times that number.[42]

Tahmasp's differences with Nader had once again surfaced after Mehmandoost but an understanding was reached allowing for the march to Isfahan to resume. Ashraf and the battered remnants of his army had fallen back to Varamin and asked for all remaining Afghan troops in Tehran to join him. With these reinforcements Ashraf deployed east of Varamin to set up an ambush at the Khwar pass. Ashraf knew that the Iranian army would have to pass Khwar and it was here where he hoped to turn the tide. However Nader discovered Ashraf's plans and sent a group of his musketeers to fall upon Ashraf to the rear while he attacked frontally. This pincer action caught Ashraf by surprise, crushing his forces once again. As Ashraf and his Ghilzai fled, they abandoned large stores of supplies and cannon to Nader.[43] With this new disaster, Ashraf had no choice but to flee to Isfahan to make his stand there.

Nader had in the meantime convinced Tahmasp to go to Tehran.[44] This was a wise move as it secured this important town, now evacuated by the Afghans, for the reviving Iranian kingdom. It also got Tahmasp "out of the way" and allowed Nader to fully concentrate his attention on finishing off the Afghans. Ashraf, realizing that his position in Iran was in jeopardy, sent frantic appeals to the Ottomans for help. Ahmad Pasha of Baghdad obliged, sending up to a brigade of Ottoman artillerymen to assist the Ghilzai in Isfahan.[45] This would indicate that Ashraf's artillery losses at Mihmandoost and the Khwar Pass had been heavy. It is also possible that Ashraf was worried abou the poor performance of his artillery in relation to Nader and was hoping that his Ottoman allies could help even the odds. Ashraf left Isfahan with these combined Ghilzai–Ottoman forces towards Moorcheh-khor village about 43 miles (70km) northwest of Isfahan. But before leaving, Ashraf behaved with special brutality against Isfahan's population.[46]

Nader had been marching towards Isfahan through the longer route of Kashan-Natanz, more suitable for transport than the mountain route.[47] As Nader approached Moorcheh-khor, he decided to pretend that he was marching straight to Isfahan. There was good reason not to attack Ashraf directly at Moorcheh-khor as his defensive positions there were formidable. By "pretending" to march directly on Isfahan, Nader was hoping to lure Ashraf out.[48] But Ashraf decided to stay put and decided to imitate Nader's tactics.[49] He assembled his army in a single body, instead of the traditional three-part Afghan method of attack. Like Nader he placed his infantry in the center, cavalry on the flanks. Ashraf deployed the 250 pieces of Ottoman artillery that he had captured from Ahmad Pasha in 1726 in a circular manner around his main body of troops, protected by his Jazayerchis and musketeers.[50] What Ashraf failed to realize was that imitation of the new Iranian tactics was far from enough; his troops would need years to develop to the level of Nader's men in training and discipline.

Nader decided to go on the offensive on November 12, 1729 in the vicinity of Moorcheh-khor.[51] He told his troops to obey their commanders, with the cavalry given specific orders not to dismount (to avoid surprise ambushes).[52] The musketeers were placed at the front lines.[53] These moved forward as they had at Mehmandoost, firing volley after volley into the Ghilzai, who were taking cover in trenches. It is estimated that up to 7,000–8,000 Afghans may have perished in the first hours of fighting due to the relentless fire of Nader's musketeers, Jazayerchis, and artillery.[54] Demonstrations by the Afghan horsemen at the Iranian flanks and rear proved ineffectual. The Iranian infantry now stormed into the trenches, routing the Ghilzai. Ashraf's center collapsed with Nader's men capturing much artillery, crushing the Afghan musketeers and Jazayerchis. Among the prisoners were the Ottoman artillerymen sent by Ahmad Pasha.[55] Nader pardoned them and sent them home.

With the battle at Moorcheh-khor lost, Ashraf and his men retreated into Isfahan. He did not stay there for long, retreating to Shiraz on November 13, 1729, just one day after the battle of Moorcheh-khor.[56] As Nader and his troops entered Isfahan three days later, they were greeted by a jubilant populace thankful to see the hated Ashraf ejected for good.[57] Nader secured the royal palace and sent messages to Tahmasp to come to Isfahan to assume the throne. Nader ordered all hiding Afghans who had behaved brutally to be brought forward and executed. Tahmasp entered Isfahan on December 9, and sat on the imperial throne in the Safavid tradition.[58] The restoration of the Safavid House was to prove ephemeral.

Nader consolidates his political power

Tahmasp wanted Ashraf to be hunted down as soon as possible, but Nader insisted on resting and refitting his troops first, a prudent move which would pay dividends. But Nader was also in no hurry to finish off Ashraf, as he wanted to wrest as much political power as possible from Tahmasp first. Tahmasp had already bestowed the titles "*Tahmasp Qoli Beg*" as well as "*Etemad al-Dawla*" to Nader. The latter title signaled the shah's trust (*Etemad*) in Nader. But Nader wanted more than just honorific titles. Before the battle of Mehmandoost, Tahmasp had agreed to grant Nader the fiefdom of the provinces of Mazandaran, Khorasan, and Kerman. Nader now had Tahmasp legally assure this in writing. To further symbolize this, Nader was allowed to wear the *Jiqqeh* on the right side of his head, an emblem of Iranian royalty. Nader now threatened to return to Khorasan (knowing full well that without his help, Tahmasp could do little to repel the Russians, Ottomans, or Ashraf), until Tahmasp and his minsters convinced Nader to stay on as general and complied with his demand that he have the right to collect taxes for his army.[59]

Nader departed Isfahan on December 24, 1729 with an army of 20,000–25,000.[60] He marched to Zarghan (25 miles (40km) northeast of Shiraz) where Ashraf was waiting with 20,000 troops.[61] By the end of battle up to 10,000 of the Ghilzai had been captured.[62] With the destruction of his remaining forces, Ashraf fled once more, even as Afghan nobles pleaded with Nader for mercy. Nader pursued with 500 of his advance guard, and defeated Ashraf's rear guard, but Ashraf had fled all the way to Lar where he imprisoned 25 of the local *Ayyan* (lit. nobles). Nine days later, the Ayyan killed their guards, and took Lar back. Ashraf fled again. The question of Ashraf's demise is debated. One account claims that as he escaped Ashraf was killed and beheaded, with others claiming that he was shot in the head by the forces of his cousin from Kandahar.[63] The Iranians had avenged the defeat of Safi Qoli Khan and Ghilzai authority in Iran had been completely destroyed; however they continued to pose a threat to Iran.[64]

CHAPTER 11

BATTLES WITH THE OTTOMAN EMPIRE AND THE RECONQUEST OF NORTHERN IRAN AND THE CAUCASUS (1730–36)

As soon as Tahmasp II assumed the throne, he demanded that all Ottoman and Russian forces immediately evacuate the occupied territories.[1] Northern Iran and the Caucasus were integral to the cultural, economic, and political integrity of Iran. Azarbaijan was a key province, crucial for any political force wishing to assume power in Iran.

The Ottomans attempted to agree a new settlement, offering to withdraw from all indigenous Iranian territory in Azarbaijan including Tabriz.[2] Western Iran would also be returned including all of Luristan, much of Iranian Kurdistan, and Hamadan in northwest Iran.[3] In return, the vizier demanded that Tahmasp recognize the Ottoman occupation of former Iranian possessions in the Caucasus.[4] Interestingly, the vizier also insisted that Tahmasp recognize Ottoman suzerainty over the Shirvanshah.

Nader Khan considered Ottoman occupation of the Caucasian territories unacceptable and even as diplomatic notes were being exchanged, Nader was moving to eject the Ottomans out of occupied Iranian territory. Tahmasp and Nader must have been aware of the shaky political standing of the vizier, Damad Ibrahim, and Sultan Ahmad III in Istanbul. Shaw speculates that the Iranians may have viewed the conciliatory Ottoman attitude as a sign of Istanbul's internal political disputes.[5]

Nader Khan strikes at the Ottoman Empire

Nader and the Iranian army marched out of Shiraz on March 9, 1730, pausing to celebrate the ancient Nowruz Persian New Year. This was both to thank the troops for their efforts in defeating the Afghans and to prepare them for the greater challenge ahead.[6]

Nader's army first deployed west. He moved his army rapidly through Borujerd in Luristan and from there rapidly reached the town of Nahavand (in today's Hamadan province). The Ottomans, expecting troops of similar caliber to those they had defeated in 1722, were in for a rude shock. In a short but intense engagement, the Ottomans were quickly defeated, forcing them to retreat in haste to the city of Hamadan. As Nader pushed towards Hamadan, he was opposed by another Ottoman army of 30,000 on the steppes near the ancient town of Malayer.

Nader crushed the Ottomans by first engaging in a musketry duel followed by a devastating right-flank thrust and deadly cavalry strikes.[7] The Ottomans, still in shock at seeing such capable Iranian troops, reputedly yelled at each other "Escape! Escape!"[8] Nader took many prisoners, including a number of Ottoman officers, and much loot.

The Ottoman governor of Hamadan, realizing he had no hope of stopping Nader, escaped to Baghdad. Nader entered the city without a fight and liberated up to 10,000 Iranian prisoners. In their haste to flee, the Ottomans committed a major blunder by leaving behind large stores of their excellent artillery and other military equipment.

Kermanshah was a very important city, as its fortifications were a major element in guarding Iran's western frontiers. The city was also home to a thriving industry, especially in the manufacture of weapons. Nader defeated local Ottoman troops and liberated Kermanshah. Soon the entire province had been cleared of Ottoman troops. Nader's first order was for the construction of new fortifications for the city as it stood in the path of any Ottoman invasion coming from Mesopotamia.

Nader and his troops rested for a month in Hamadan before launching the crucial offensive into Azarbaijan province in the northwest. Azarbaijan was especially important as Iran's link to the Caucasus, western Iran, and eastern Anatolia. The Iranian army went forward in mid-July, marching first into western Azarbaijan, securing the frontier marches of Azarbaijan close to the Ottoman frontier in Anatolia.

Nader marched north along the western Iranian frontier and secured Sanandaj in Iranian Kurdistan before entering western Azarbaijan where he defeated Ottoman troops near Mianboab (just south of Lake Urumiah).[9] It would appear that by this time, Ottoman troops had become demoralized by increasing reports of Nader's new Iranian army. There were also reports of mutinies taking place among the Ottomans.

Nader and the Iranian army crushed another Ottoman force near Tabriz in August, with Nader entering the city on August 12. Many of the Ottoman troops trying to flee from Azarbaijan into the safety of Anatolia were hunted down and killed by the Iranian cavalry. Nader captured yet more stores of Ottoman equipment and cannon as well as large numbers of prisoners. Nader was magnanimous and showed no vindictiveness. Many of the senior pashas were released as well as the Ottoman women.

Sultan Ahmad III and Damad Ibrahim responded swiftly: the Iranian ambassador to Istanbul was placed in prison and Ottoman forces were stationed in Van, Kars, and the Caucasus to prepare for the impending Iranian offensives.[10] As Hamadan and Tabriz were cleared of Ottoman troops, the Ottomans were making their own plans to re-enter those cities and lead a major offensive into western Iran. However, the Ottoman survivors of Nader's attacks spread the news of the new Iranian army in Istanbul. This certainly contributed to rising tide of discontent which erupted into open revolt by late September. Both the vizier and the sultan were overthrown.

Nader Khan forced to turn east

After his lightning successes in western Iran and Azarbaijan, Nader was intending to march into the Caucasus to oust the Ottomans there. He was unable to embark on this mission as after just five days in Tabriz, Nader received news that the Abdalis had revolted and taken over Herat. Nader was forced to take his army 1,400 miles (2,250km) east to confront the new Afghan threat.[11]

Hussein Sultan of Kandahar feared facing Nader and intrigued the Abdalis to rebel against Nader. Nader's appointee at Herat, Allahyar Khan, remained loyal, but an Abdali revolt erupted in August 1730 led by Zolfaqhar Khan. Allahyar Khan fled to Mashad, followed by the rebels who made an unsuccessful bid to besiege the city. Nader was insulted by this attack against his power base in Khorasan and was intent on defeating the Abdalis for the final time. It was also crucial that he have the eastern frontier completely pacified to avoid the Iranian army ever fighting on two fronts in the future.

Nader spent the winter of 1730–31 building up his forces and training new troops in preparation for the campaign. Allahyar Khan was sent to the east to help foster opposition against Zolfaqhar Khan. In the midst of these developments, Hussein Sultan continued to assist Zolfaqhar Khan by sending him thousands of Ghilzai warriors. At the same time, he tried to please Nader by releasing two Safavid princesses captured by the Ghilzai in 1722.

By late March 1731, after Nowruz, Nader was ready to confront the Abdalis. He was 6 miles (10km) from Herat by early April and ordered his troops to secure the local villages and castles before the major effort at Herat.[12] Nader solidified his hold on the western approaches to Herat and seized the region of Noghreh, leaving 10,000 men to retain it against possible Afghan attacks. As Nader pushed forward to Herat he beat off yet another Abdali attack. By May 4, the siege of Herat was well underway. Nader was well equipped with cannon and patiently tightened the noose around the city. As the months wore on more and more of Zolfaqhar Khan's Ghilzai allies were killed. All routes into the city were cut and any who dared sortie were killed by Tofangchis and cavalry. The pressure finally forced Zolfaqhar Khan to launch a desperate attack towards Nader's camp on July 22, 1731. Nader quickly responded with deadly effectiveness. He launched a flank attack, leading a frontal cavalry charge himself. Zolfaqhar Khan's attack was torn to bits.

The Abdalis were becoming increasingly demoralized. Saidal Khan had fled and Nader gave them no respite. The Abdalis agreed to submit and requested that Allahyar Khan resume his post. Nader agreed and Zolfaqhar Khan was exiled to Farah. Nader did not march into the city. Despite the apparent peace, the situation remained unstable, especially as stories surfaced of a new 40,000-man force arriving to assist Zolfaqhar Khan. Trying to allay the rising tensions resulting from the rumor, Allahyar Khan himself now broke into rebellion against Nader and even dared to launch attacks against Iranian troops around Herat in September 1731.

Nader responded by resuming the siege. By February 27, 1732, Herat was forced to surrender. Nader was lenient in the treatment of his defeated foes. Allahyar Khan was exiled and Pir Mohammad (Sistani's commander-in-chief at Mashad in 1726) was placed as governor of Herat. Nader's troops calmly entered the city, occupying its main towers and posts, and there was no violence or retribution undertaken against the civilian population. Nader's brother Ibrahim chased Zolfaqhar from Farah, who escaped to his patron Hussein Soltan. Instead of sanctuary Zolfaqar Khan was rewarded with imprisonment.

As before, Nader indicted the defeated warriors of his former adversaries into his own army. The Afghans, after all, were and are among the best fighters in the world. Their inclusion in the Iranian army would make the force even more formidable.

Shah Tahmasp II fails against the Ottomans

The Ottoman situation after Nader's strikes was partly analogous to that of the Byzantine Empire in the early 600s AD. At both times, a dangerous Iranian offensive was conducted just as the government in Constantinople/Istanbul was engaged in political infighting.[13] Istanbul was witnessing the bloodiest revolt in its history, an event known as the Patrona revolt. Once the new sultan, Mahmud I (r. 1730–54), had defeated the rebels, Ottoman authority was re-established in Istanbul and military hostilities resumed against Iran. The new sultan appointed Ali Pasha Hakimoghlu as the *sardar* (commander) of the army facing Iran.

Tahmasp II departed Isfahan with 18,000 men towards Tabriz (end of winter 1731) and appears to have won a victory over an Ottoman force near Yerevan.[14] Hakimoghlu then arrived in the Yerevan theater and thoroughly defeated Tahmasp II in March 1731, resulting in the Iranians losing all of their artillery and a large quantity of supplies.[15] This success allowed Hakimoghlu to project his forces south from Armenia into Azarbaijan, capturing Urumiah on November 15, 1731 and the provincial capital, Tabriz, on December 4, 1731.[16] These victories prompted Sultan Mahmud I to grant Hakimoghlu the coveted title of *Ghazi* (hero) of the empire.

The tactical situation had also deteriorated in the northwest and western parts of Iran. Ahmad Pasha, the Ottoman governor of Baghdad, struck into Iranian Kurdistan and captured Kermanshah by July 30, 1731. A greater disaster was yet to come at Hamadan where Ahmad Pasha completely defeated Tahmasp on September 15, 1731. Hamadan fell just three days later. The Ottoman army was larger than the Iranian army: reputedly 160,000 men faced fewer than 20,000 Iranians and the Iranians were hampered by a critical shortage of supplies.[17] The latter situation may explain why the remaining Iranian artillery pieces and zanbouraks were so ineffective against the Ottomans at Hamadan.[18] Defeated and disgraced on the battlefield, Tahmasp and his battered army retreated in haste back to Isfahan.[19]

A few months later, Ahmad Pasha offered Tahmasp terms for peace. The terms were virtually identical to those originally offered by the former Sultan Ahmad III. The Ottomans offered to hand back western Iran (Hamadan, Kermanshah, Ard-Alan, and Luristan) and Azarbaijan (including Tabriz) in exchange for acknowledging Ottoman rule over the former Iranian territories of the Caucasus. These included Perso-Armenia (including Yerevan), Georgia (the regions of Kartli, Kakheti, and city of Tiflis), Shirvan Nakhchevan, and Ganja (both in modern Republic of Azerbaijan) as well as Daghestan.[20] The areas inhabited by the Hawiza tribe were to be also returned to the Iranians. With respect to the southern front, the Treaty of Qasr-e-Shirin was to remain in place by mutual consent with the Araxes River now forming Iran's northern boundary with the Ottoman Empire.[21]

Tahmasp fully accepted the Ottoman territorial conditions.[22] The Iranians however were far from satisfied with this state of affairs as the situation was now the same as before Tahmasp had demanded the departure of Ottoman troops under Ahmad III. Mahmud I was also unimpressed as he felt Ahmad Pasha had given too much to the Iranians. The sultan was especially displeased with the ceding of Tabriz.[23] By mid-March 1732, Sultan Mahmud I had sacked his grand vizier, Topal Osman Pasha, in favor of his favorite general, Ali Pasha Hakimoghlu.

Nader Khan deposes Shah Tahmasp II

The news of Shah Tahmasp's surrender prompted Nader Khan to march from Herat towards Isfahan. Nader was deeply dismayed at Tahmasp II's disastrous military performance and soft stance in the ensuing negotiations with the Ottomans. Seeing his hard-won gains squandered by Tahmasp's military and political ineptitude, he engaged in two diplomatic maneuvers.[24] He dispatched his own ambassadors to Istanbul to demand revocation of the recent treaty with Tahmasp and that all of Iran's Caucasian possessions be immediately restored. Nader must have anticipated that his demands would be summarily rejected. The Ottomans do not appear to have appreciated his strength, or that their latest military successes were at least partly due to Nader's absence from the battlefield. Nader's second diplomatic action was to write a formal letter to Tahmasp II criticizing him for his treaty with the Ottomans and his lack of concern for the condition of Iranian prisoners in Ottoman territory. He then handed over the command of Khorasan to his brother Ibrahim Khan Zahir o Dowleh and arrived at Isfahan's outskirts with an armed detachment who set up their tents in the city's environs.[25] Thanks to his immense personal popularity, Nader was able to depose Tahmasp II without opposition. Tahmasp II was sent off as a prisoner to Khorasan in the northeast by July 7, 1732.[26] Abbas III, Tahmasp's infant son, was installed as shah with Nader holding the title of *Naeb* (regent) and *Vakil o Dowleh* (prime minister).[27] Nader Khan was now the *de facto* ruler of the realm, having placed his trusted commanders into all key government posts. The stage was now set for another Iranian–Ottoman showdown.

Nader Khan strikes towards Baghdad

The removal of Tahmasp from power allowed the Iranian army to be finally rationalized under the single and effective command of Nader. The Iranian commanders were satisfied to see that the Russians, themselves bitter enemies of the Ottomans, had no intention of opening military actions in the northern Caucasus. Once again Nader sent an embassy to Istanbul to demand the peaceful return of Iran's Caucasian territories. The Ottomans predictably ignored these requests, obliging Nader to mobilize the Iranian army for a new round of combat against the Ottoman Empire.

Nader's military objective was to gain complete control over the entirety of western Iran as well as Ottoman-ruled Iraq, especially Baghdad. Axworthy has suggested that Nader was hoping to then trade Baghdad in exchange for the Ottomans relinquishing their gains in Azarbaijan and the Caucasus.[28] Another possibility was that the fall of Baghdad would lead to wider collapse of Ottoman power in the Mesopotamian theater, allowing the Iranian army to make further territorial gains at Ottoman expense.[29]

Anticipating Nader's intentions in Mesopotamia, the Ottomans quickly deployed their forces into the Kurdish-populated districts of Darna and Shahrazur, apparently with the aim of breaking further into western and possibly northwest Iran. Nader defeated these forces and then cleared Ottoman troops out of Malayir, Hamadan, Nahavand, Sanandaj, and Kermanshah.[30] From Kermanshah, the Iranian army marched into Ottoman territory with 80,000 troops on December 10, 1732, capturing Iraqi Kurdistan.[31]

With a secure platform in Iraqi Kurdistan, Nader deployed south towards Baghdad and easily crushed an Ottoman force on his advance. Ahmad Pasha had constructed a powerful series of defenses to defend Baghdad, especially along the western banks of the Tigris River, fortified with artillery.[32] To cross the Tigris, Nader's engineers and ship builders built 1,000 large boats.[33] These were to be tied together by powerful ropes to form a pontoon bridge, much as the

Achaemenids had done.[34] Forty of Nader's engineers swam across the Tigris to secure the ropes on the western banks, but they were spotted and fired upon.[35] The few survivors swam back in haste towards the eastern bank.

Following this failure, Nader's local Arab allies advised him to select the Yengjeh crossing as the best venue for traversing the Tigris.[36] European expertise, in the person of an Austrian military engineer seconded by the Austro-Hungarian Empire to Nader Khan, was now employed to attempt another crossing of the Tigris.[37] Once again the sturdy palm trees were used to construct planks, which were brought forward by 12,000 cavalry at night in order to conceal their intentions from the Ottomans.[38] The planks were attached to inflated animal skins, to reinforce the buoyancy of the bridge. Nader then crossed the river with 2,500 hand-picked men on February 15, 1733, followed by 1,500 the next day.[39]

To try to confuse the Ottomans, Nader dressed an Iranian officer, Imamverdi Gharakhlu, in his clothes and sat the officer on his command seat in full view.[40] But Ahmad Pasha's scouts however soon learnt that the real Nader had crossed the Tigris. At first the Ottoman troops pulled back.[41] But when the strong current of the Tigris destroyed Nader's bridge leaving Nader and his troops stranded on the western side of the Tigris, Ahmad Pasha dispatched 30,000 troops including artillery, cavalry, and the elite Janissaries to wipe out Nader's bridgehead.[42] The Ottoman troops did their best to assault Nader's bridgehead, forcing the Turkmen and Kurdish contingents to pull back. The Afghan contingents however held out just long enough to allow a fresh contingent of Persian cavalrymen to bolster Nader's defense lines. Nader's troops succeeded in defeating the Ottoman troops and capturing numbers of their artillery by attacking their columns at their flanks.[43] It is not clear why the Ottomans failed to prevail, given their superior numbers. Axworthy suggests the poor terrain may have impeded the Ottomans from deploying their full force in time for battle.[44] Iranian sources however report that Nader's artillery on the eastern bank of the Tigris had opened a massive barrage providing an effective shield against the attacking Ottoman forces.[45] Nader's artillery also rained fire upon Baghdad itself. This meant the Ottomans could not stop additional troops from swimming across the Tigris to reinforce Nader's bridgehead. It is a mystery why Baghdad's artillery did not deliver the effective counterbarrage that later events showed it could produce.

The reinforcements enabled Nader to erect a defensive screen while a pontoon bridge was built. But just as the Iranian army were to cross over in full force, the current snapped the ropes and chains. Enough boats were saved to form a bridge, and 20,000 troops joined Nader and his front-line troops.[46] Ahmad Pasha proved unable at preventing the completion of Nader's bridge as the Iranian artillery at the eastern banks of the Tigris continued their deadly barrage. To make matters worse, one of Nader's naval commanders successfully landed a body of infantry armed with muskets which started to target anyone using Baghdad's gates.

Nader Khan proceeded to completely surround Baghdad. Iranian engineers built a total of 2,700 towers, with each of the towers the distance of a musket shot from the next.[47] The waterways to the city were patrolled by Persian soldiers in boats.[48] The siege proved its effectiveness, especially in its ability to prevent supplies and provisions from entering the city. This prompted Baghdad's citizens to attempt escape from the city.[49] Meanwhile Iranian troops had conquered many of the key towns around Baghdad. Nader even sent troops to Basra far to the south to support anti-Ottoman Arab rebels there.

The Iranian camps besieging Baghdad were elaborate, complete with shops and quarters, totaling 300,000 personnel with just 100,000 of these being combatants (80,000 cavalry and 20,000 infantry and artillery troops).[50] Nader's artillery was not strong enough to enforce an opening for his troops to pour into the city. This was in large part due to Baghdad's powerful artillery which reputedly forced their Iranian counterparts to pull back. This was not a major concern as all Nader had to do was to sit and wait until the city's supplies and provisions ran out, forcing it to surrender. So comfortable and confident were the Iranians that they celebrated the Iranian Nowruz (New Year) on March 21, 1733 in their camps.

According to Matofi, Topal Osman Pasha, governor of Erzerum and now *Saraskar* (lit. head commander) of the Ottoman Empire's eastern armies mobilized 300,000 troops from Istanbul, Damascus, Egypt, Diyarbakr, Van, Tiflis, and Yerevan for the Ottoman counterattack.[51] These numbers are disputed by Axworthy who estimates Osman Pasha's forces at a more modest 80,000 (the core of these being infantry and cavalry from Istanbul) supported with just 60 cannon.[52] Osman Pasha passed Kirkuk and thrust rapidly southwards towards Baghdad.[53]

As the Ottomans arrived at Samarra, Nader dispatched 12,000 of his best musketeers to provide a temporary screen delivering fire barrages against Osman Pasha's troops until the arrival of the main Iranian force from Baghdad.[54] The musketeers were supported by 20,000 Jazayerchis and 30,000 Jawshan-mailed cavalry.[55] In total, Nader assembled 70,000 troops to face Topal Osman, while 12,000 men led by Mohammed Khan Baluch continued the siege of Baghdad.[56]

The battle was finally joined on July 19, 1733. The eruption of the fighting led to ferocious combat in which 30,000 Iranians were killed and 3,000 taken prisoner in exchange for 20,000 Ottoman dead.[57] The Ottoman victory was due to a combination of their excellant musketry, large-caliber cannon, poor Iranian logistics, and the local terrain which impeded the mobility of Nader's cavalry.[58]

Osman Pasha followed up this victory by reaching Baghdad on July 20, 1733. The Ottoman army surprised and routed the remaining Iranian besiegers. The siege of Baghdad, which had come so close to success, was thus broken. Having captured supplies and ammunition from the Iranian camps surrounding Baghdad, the Ottomans also recaptured Kirkuk and Darna. The badly mauled Iranian army had no recourse but to retreat towards their main western bases in Kermanshah and Hamadan.[59]

The state of Ottoman success again proved ephemeral. Nader Khan's resilience and character of leadership did much to rapidly rebuild and reform the Iranian army. Much effort was made to replace losses in weapons, equipment, and transportation.[60] Significant reforms were imparted upon the infantry, including dividing it into Jazayerchiha, Gharachoorlooha, and the Piyadegan (see p.92), especially after their experiences against the Janissaries.[61] Nader Khan also imposed harsh discipline by meting out cruel punishment against those officers who failed his standards of battle.[62] In just 40 days Nader Khan had managed to rebuild the Iranian army; raising 50,000 fresh troops attired with uniforms, as well as 140,000 horses, mules, and camels for transportation.[63] Nader was ready to take on the Ottomans once again.

Nader led his army back towards Baghdad. It was in the Aq Darband Valley region (in the Kirkuk area) on October 26, 1733 that the main battle was fought for the new drive to Baghdad. The Iranian army now faced 100,000 Ottoman troops led by Osman Pasha.[64] The battle was characterized by the heavy use of artillery, muskets, and *Jazayer* heavy muskets. The tide finally turned in the Iranian favor when the Iranians charged through the Ottoman lines. Osman Pasha tried to rally the Ottoman troops but an attack by the Abdalis on the Ottoman flank sealed their fate. The Ottomans were crushed, with 20,000 killed or captured, and Pasha himself killed. Once again, Nader captured vast quantities of abandoned Ottoman equipment, supplies, and cannon.[65] This allowed Nader to march again to Baghdad to besiege it.[66]

Just as success seemed imminent at Baghdad, news reached Nader's camp of rebellions in Iran. This forced him to seek an accommodation with Ahmad Khan Pasha, the governor of Baghdad. The result was the ratification of the Treaty of Baghdad on December 19, 1733. The treaty agreed that the Ottomans were to respect Iran's borders as they were before their invasion of Iran in 1722. To that end Ahmad Pasha gave orders to Ottoman governors of Yerevan, Shirvan, and Georgia to evacuate those territories. Sultan Mahmud, who had not ratified the treaty, countermanded those orders.[67] The treaty also stipulated that the Ottomans not harass Iranian Shiite pilgrims arriving in Karbala and Najaf and that both sides should exchange prisoners and captured cannon. Nader returned to Iran to defeat rebels in Fars, and in western and southern Iraq.[68]

Russia agrees to evacuate occupied territories

Former Shah Tahmasp II convinced the Russians to finally evacuate Iranian territory at Saliyan and the Kura River under an agreement known as the Treaty of Rasht (February 1732).[69] Russian troops remained firmly in place in Baku, Darband, Gilan, and Mazandaran. However Moscow's new empress Anna Ivanovna was aware that Russia was no longer dealing with the ineffectual Shah Tahmasp II. As soon as Nader Khan deposed Tahmasp, Russia worked to reach an understanding with him. Moscow's main concern was to prevent peace between Iran and the Ottomans. Prince Sergei Dmitrievich Golitsyn visited Nader in May 1734 to offer Nader help against the Turks. The offer was spurned by Nader, who was especially angered by the prince's suggestion that Russia's return of Baku and Darband were dependent on Iran's ability to liberate all of its territory from the Turks. He even threatened to strike an alliance with the Ottoman Turks against Russia.[70] Content at seeing a newly reconstituted Iranian army fighting the Ottomans, Russia formally finalized its pledge to return occupied Iranian lands (eastern Transcaucasus, Gilan, Mazandaran) along the southwest and southern Caspian Sea coasts to Iran by 1735.[71] The treaty was formalized at Ganja where the Russians agreed to surrender all of Peter the Great's conquests.[72] Despite having promised to vacate all Iranian territory, numbers of Russian troops are reported to have remained in place, obliging Nader to eject them militarily.[73] After the return of Baku, Darband, Gilan, and Mazandaran to Iran, Russo-Iranian relations were characterized by relative tranquility for the next five decades.[74]

Nader Khan thrusts into the Caucasus

With the revolts suppressed, Nader was able to resume his war with the Ottomans. This time his objective was to the north: Iranian lands in the Caucasus that had been under Ottoman occupation since 1722. The Ottomans in Istanbul were also anxious for a new war as they had already rejected the Treaty of Baghdad. They had sent an envoy to Isfahan to declare to Nader that Abdollah

Koprulu Pasha was the new saraskar legally enabled to make peace with Iran. Nader promptly replied that the Caucasus had to be evacuated. By mid-August, when Nader was in Ardabil preparing for his drive into the Caucasus, he received a new note from Abdollah which asked that the question of repatriating the Caucasus to Iran be deferred for another two years. This was unsatisfactory for Nader, who finalized his preparations to strike.

The first target was the Shirvan Khanate. The Shirvanshah had had considerable difficulty in suppressing Daghestani rebels along the Caspian coast. Taking advantage of this, Nader thrust into Shirvan and captured its local capital Shamakhi in August 1734.[75] Nader's campaign had been greatly facilitated by the assistance provided by local Shiite Qizilbash. The Shirvanshah was fatally vulnerable as the bulk of his army was in fact composed of Shiite Qizilbash troops, all likely to defect to the Iranian army. This may explain why he requested military assistance from the governor of Tiflis and the Crimean Tatars before facing the Iranian army. His efforts proved futile: Nader Khan defeated him twice. The destruction of pro-Ottoman forces allowed Nader Khan to absorb all Shirvan and Daghestan.

Nader then struck towards the western Caucasus and arrived to besiege Ganja on November 3, 1734. The main target was the powerful fortress, garrisoned by 14,000 Ottomans led by Ganjali Pasha. The Ottomans had prepared for the arrival of the Iranian army by accumulating large stocks and the siege of Ganja was to prove to be one of the most difficult battles fought by Nader and his troops.[76]

Ottoman resistance was fierce because they knew that Ganja, along with Yerevan, Kars, and Tbilisi, were strategically crucial for holding the Caucasus. If these fell to Iranian hands then all would be lost. Seeing that the siege of Ganja would not be easily ended, Nader revised his tactics. He left a force there to continue the blockade and then proceeded to blockade Tbilisi (with Georgian assistance), and Yerevan. Koprulu had thus far refused to bring his main forces to battle but with Shamakhi captured and three cities besieged, he now had no choice.

Koprulu moved forward with a massive force of 50,000 cavalry, 30,000 Janissaries, and 40 cannon to face off against 55,000 Iranians at Bhaghavand (north of Yerevan) on June 19, 1735.[77] Cognizant of the power of Ottoman artillery, Nader devised an ingenious stratagem to eliminate these from Koprulu's order of battle. He had 2,000–3,000 Jazayerchis storm a small hill where Koprulu had placed a large concentration of artillery. The Iranians also captured another concentration of Ottoman artillery on Koprulu's left wing. Nader's brilliant strategy not only eliminated the Ottoman artillery but severely damaged Ottoman morale.

Koprulu's troops were exposed to Iranian artillery, supported by up to 500 camel-mounted zanbouraks, which tore havoc into the Ottoman lines. Throughout the battle the Ottoman cannon only managed to fire two or three times before being silenced, whereas the Iranian cannon fired more than 300 cannon balls.[78] As the Ottoman lines began to lose their cohesion, Nader struck with his cavalry in conjunction with an infantry ambush. The Ottoman army was completely defeated and Koprulu was killed.[79] Estimates of Ottoman troops killed and captured range from 20,000 to 50,000.[80]

As the remnants of the Ottoman army retreated, the Iranian army completed its conquest of the Caucasus. Ganja, which had held out so gallantly, finally surrendered to Nader on July 9, 1735. One account states that Nader ordered all of his Jazayerchis, Tofangchis, and cannon to fire simultaneously to distract the Ganja garrison while his elite units stormed through a tunnel into the city.[81] This was followed by the capitulation of Tbilisi on August 2. The last region to be cleared of Ottoman troops was Yerevan, which fell by early October.

The Ottomans now realized that Iran had regained its martial strength and Nader Khan was a military leader to be reckoned with. Sultan Mahmud agreed to make peace and agreed to the terms of the Baghdad Treaty. The Ottomans were also anxious to make peace as they were faced by threats from Russia and Austria.

Nader Khan becomes Nader Shah

Having completely restored Iran's former Caucasian possessions from both Ottoman and Russian occupation, Nader held a council in the Mongol and Turkmen tradition known as the *Qurultai* in the Mughan plains of Iran's Azarbaijan province in January 1736. The Qurultai was attended by Iran's highest noblemen and military leaders. Nader proposed that he should become king instead of the infant Abbas III, a decision which all present accepted. Nader Khan then became Nader Shah on March 8, 1736[82] at Mughan in Azarbaijan. He had arrived there on January 22, 1736, after which he summoned nobleman from across Iran to consult with him regarding the future of the country's government and monarchy.[83] While his nomination as shah of Iran was certainly supported with much enthusiasm, anyone who might have pro-Safavid sympathies certainly did not express them, undoubtedly due to fears of Nader's wrath.

Nader's acceptance of the throne of Iran was on the condition that the Shiite sect of Islam in Iran be replaced with the Sunni doctrine.[84] This demand never took hold in Iran, due to centuries of Safavid rule. But Nader's steadfast loyalty to the historical Iranian state and "his drive to reestablish the glory and the boundaries of the ancient Persian Empire"[85] won him the admiration, loyalty, and respect of his troops and a grateful Iranian populace, relieved to witness the end of years of chaos and foreign invasions. Unfortunately, despite his brilliant military career, Nader proved to be less than talented in the arts of just political governance and economic management.

CHAPTER 12

NADER'S CAMPAIGNS IN INDIA AND CENTRAL ASIA (1737–40)

The conquest of India

By 1736 Nader had successfully defeated all internal challenges towards his rule. However, despite the crushing defeat of Ashraf, the Ghilzai in Afghanistan still remained a threat under Hussein Sultan, Ashraf's cousin.[1] By April 1737 Nader moved his army towards Kandahar in a bid to break Hussein Sultan there.[2] Nader ordered the construction of a new city named Naderabad (lit. Naderville) near Kandahar, essentially an assembly point and army base from which Nader laid siege to Kandahar. The city resisted for nine months, capitulating in January 1738.[3] During the siege Nader dispatched forces to reconquer the Iranian provinces of Baluchistan and Balkh. Nader not only managed to return both provinces to the Iranian orbit, but was able to recruit many excellent Afghan warriors thanks to his lenient treatment of Kandahar after its fall.

With the power of the Ghilzai broken, Nader had eliminated all threats from the east. His army was now at the gates of India. By the early 1700s the late Mughal emperor Alamgir (Aurangzeb) (1658–1707) had pushed the boundaries of Indian authority to include much of the Punjab, Pakistan, and what is now eastern Afghanistan. Nominally, the cities of Kabul, Jalalabad, Lahore, and Peshawar fell within the Mughal orbit, however by the time of Nader's arrival, political authority in the lands bordering Iran were in flux.

It is generally agreed that Nader, flushed with a new round of military successes, cultivated ambitions far beyond Afghanistan, and was looking covetously towards Mughal India and her fabled riches. Lockhart reports that Nader was hoping to use captured Indian wealth to help compensate for the stupendous costs of his relentless military campaigns. Iran's economic state had been desperate since the last days of the Safavids, and Nader's campaigns had depleted the national treasury, and inflicted much hardship upon the civilian population.[4]

In addition, Mohammad Shah of Mughal India had assisted the Afghans in their recent battles against the Iranian army, providing Nader with a useful pretext for invasion.[5] Nader asserted officially that he had no conflict with the Mughals, he merely needed to cross the Mughal frontier to pursue Gilzai fugitives.[6] Mughal India's state of political and military weakness also facilitated the Iranian invasion. Tucker notes that Nader may have been also encouraged to cross the border by the "nefarious intrigue of [Mughal] vassals trying to undermine Mughal authority there."[7] By the early 1700s, Alamgir had instituted a number of strict edicts against his Hindu subjects.[8] The end-result of these efforts was the weakening of the Mughal economy, bureaucratic apparatus, and the military.[9] These factors may explain why since the death of Alamgir in 1707, various regions had become increasingly autonomous despite their nominal loyalty to the Mughal ruler,

Mohammad Shah.[10] To make matters worse, the Hindu lords (the Marathas) were rising in power and began to provide political challenges to the very basis of Muslim ascendancy over the Indian subcontinent.[11] Mughal India's state of political flux certainly would not help her military state, especially against Nader's battle-hardened army. Mughal India was simply too tempting a target for the Iranians: she was vulnerable to invasion and possessed riches that Iran needed.[12]

After the capture of Kandahar, Nader thrust northeast towards Kabul, which fell after a six-day siege in September. Ghazni fell in the same month.[13] Without pausing, Nader's army pushed east to Jalalabad. The march proved to be no easy task as Nader's troops were faced with resistance from local Katoor tribal fighters from the mountains. The Katoors who were defeated after a ferocious battle fled in haste back to their mountain strongholds with Jalalabad falling shortly after to Nader on September 7, 1736.[14] On November 7, 1738 Nader appointed his son Reza Gholi as his viceroy in Iran.[15]

With the fall of Jalalabad, Nader completed his conquest of the eastern Afghan highlands. This set the stage for Nader's major thrust into the Indian subcontinent with 50,000 troops.[16] The Iranian army was soon challenged by a certain Nasser Khan who fought hard to prevent the Iranians from advancing to Peshawar. Nasser Khan received a temporary respite when Nader Shah returned to Iran after Lezgian rebels killed his brother Ibrahim.[17] Nader dispatched a portion of his army to defeat the Lezgian rebels, which obliged him to await reinforcements before thrusting into India. Nader's son Reza Gholi Mirza arrived with a powerful contingent of warriors from eastern Iran and by January 1739 Nader had captured Peshawar and from there proceeded towards Lahore.[18]

The size of Mohammad Shah's Mughal army mobilized against Nader is disputed, with estimates ranging between 100,000 and 1,400,000 fighting men, accompanied by between 100,000 and 1,000,000 non-combatants.[19] The Mughal army was composed of troops from a variety of provinces. Astrabadi reports that part of the Mughal army was composed of "1,500 cannon, 12,000 saf-poozan, 12,000 zanbouraks, 4,000 elephants which entered the battle along with him [Mohammad Shah] who was riding atop a white elephant accompanied by 2,000 Rajas."[20] Hariri reports a total number of 1,400,000 combat troops in Mohammad Shah's army at the eve of the battle of Karenal.[21] Recent Western sources, notably Axworthy, generally agree on the total number of combatants as having been around 300,000, supported by 2,000 war elephants and 3,000 cannon.[22] Axworthy reports that the support personnel numbered a million, which when combined with the total number of combatants gives a total remarkably close to the numbers reported by Hariri.

The Iranians realized that they were facing a foe as formidable as the Ottomans. To gain as much information as possible regarding the Mughal army and its dispositions, Nader is said to have dispatched up to 6,000 Kurdish warriors as spies into India.[23]

Mohammad Shah did not engage in any large-scale battles against Nader's advancing army (estimated at this stage at 50,000–80,000 mostly mounted troops) as it entered deeper inside Mughal territory.[24] Interestingly, the Iranian army also included 7,000 female Turkmen and Kandahari warriors.[25] Iranian–Mughal skirmishes did take place but they were not followed by any decisive set-piece battles. Perhaps the Mughal commanders were content to allow Nader to enter India as far as Delhi in order to deal a single, mortal blow against the Iranian army leaving it trapped deep inside hostile territory.

The vast size of the Mughal support personnel was a major liability, especially against Nader's highly mobile army. This may partly explain why the main Mughal army was so slow in deploying out of Shah Jahan (Delhi) to face Nader. The force lumbered out of the capital on December 12 and by February the next year reached Karenal, a distance of just 62miles (100km).[26] Nader left the bulk of his support retinue with a small guard force at Anbala and arrived at Shahabad, around 43–50 miles (70–80km) from Karenal, by February 19. A Kurdish raiding and reconnaissance party arrived at Karenal and attacked a number of Mughal artillery posts, capturing a number of prisoners. Nader's army then deployed closer to Thanesar. Nader then left his main army to undertake a raiding mission with his Kurdish scouts. He linked up with them at Saraye Azimabad, just 15 miles (25km) from Karenal. The garrison at Saraye Azimabad was subdued with cannon which Nader had brought along with his party.

Nader's army arrived at Karenal and immediately prepared to begin the duel with Mohammad Shah. He allegedly arranged his troops into 72 rows, perhaps in an effort to make his army more compact against Mohammad Shah's larger army.[27] The artillery was placed in line formation in front of the Iranian positions.[28] Nader was apparently concerned by the large size of the Mughal army. Of great concern were the Mughal battle elephants; these were reported to have been trained to attack enemy infantry with sabers grasped in their trunks, and measures were devised to counteract the "saber-elephants."

Mohammad Shah had worked hard preparing for Nader's arrival, but issues with pay, food shortages, and disease breakouts in the Mughal camps seem to have compromised morale.[29] The Mughal army had built strong defensive walls and watchtowers as well as platforms for their artillery. Axworthy however reports the walls as having been built of mud.[30] The Mughals finally commenced the battle by opening up with devastating artillery salvoes, mortars, and volleys of rifle fire. Almost immediately, the right flank of the Iranian army felt the brunt of Mughal firepower.[31] Being close to the capital and their supply dumps, the Mughals had access to vast supplies of weapons and ammunition. To prevent his flanks and positions from collapsing, Nader ensured that troops were brought forward to plug the gaps torn by Mughal firepower and attacks.

A new strategy was needed to break the deadlock. After a few hours, Nader ordered his son, Nasrollah Mirza, to go on the offensive. Nasrollah Mirza led his Azarbaijani, Kurdish, Iraqi, Kuklan, Qajar, Afshar, and Qarachorlu troops straight towards the Mughal lines. The shock of Nasrollah Mirza's strike badly disrupted the order of the Mughal front lines allowing the Iranians to capture a number of Mohammad Shah's royal standards. During the melée one of the top Mughal commanders, Samsam o Dowleh, was killed. Mohammad Shah reportedly panicked, dismounting his white elephant and fleeing the field. Despite their shah's desertion, the other Mughal commanders stood their ground and continued the battle. One of these was Se-adat Khan who ordered the elephant corps to pommel the Iranian positions. Nader had anticipated this move and his gunners, riflemen, and zanbouraks were ready. As the Indian elephants approached, Nader's troops and artillery corps opened fire, wreaking havoc and killing a number of elephants. Many surviving elephants turned back in panic towards the Indian positions, stampeding and killing many Indian troops. The bitter clashes also led to the wounding and capture of Se-adat Khan. This loss may have been a major cause which broke the will of the Mughal army to continue the fight.

Nader, however, is most famous for his ingenious "Camel on Fire" stratagem. Nader, who had anticipated the massive Mughal elephant charge, had ordered that jars stuffed with wood, dry materials, and naphta, and fastened to every Iranian camel.[32] These jars were then set alight.[33] The distraught camels, screaming and agitated, were then released towards the charging Mughal elephants. The strange sight and noise severely frightened the Mughal elephants which immediately panicked, became uncontrollable, and began trampling their Mughal masters.[34] Hanway reports that "at the approach of the camels, the elephants turned about, and put a great part of the Indian army to confusion."[35]

Nader's cavalry and infantry fanned out to destroy the fleeing survivors, killing another 20,000–30,000 Indian troops and taking an unspecified number prisoner.[36] During the course of the battle, the Mughals had lost 300–400 officers, petty sultans, and khans and an approximately equal number had been captured.[37] Despite these terrible losses, Nader had yet to subdue India. Just as the major Mughal force collapsed at Karenal, Mohammad Shah reached Shah Jahan and immediately proceeded to rebuild his forces in the city. According to Iranian sources, he raised a new force of 300,000 troops, mainly by the prodigious expenditure of imperial funds.[38] It was clear that the capture of Shah Jahan would be no easy task. Iranian forces proceeded to besiege the city and were successful in preventing supplies from entering the city.[39]

Mohammad Shah and his commanders decided to offer surrender terms to Nader and end the fighting. All hostilities ceased and Nader entertained Mohammad Shah and the Mughal nobility as honored guests in his camp.[40] Nader sat on the Mughal throne, symbolizing his status as the Shah of India and Iran. Nader had taken the armies of Iran further into the Indian subcontinent than ever before, dwarfing the achievements of the Achaemenids over 2,000 years earlier.[41]

Irrespective of the cordialities and festivities, the Mughals quickly learned that Nader was as merciless at the negotiating table as he was on the battlefield. He demanded and received thousands of camels and elephants loaded with tons of jewels, treasure, and coin, as well as precious national treasures, including the exquisite diamonds Darya-e Noor (The Sea of Light) and Kuh-e Noor (The Mountain of Light).[42] The Iranians also appropriated massive quantities of guns and cannon, 7,000 horses, 10,000 camels, 1,000 elephants, 300 architects and laborers, 200 smiths, 100 masons, 200 merchants, 130 scribes/writers, and 60,000 priceless books.[43] The massive scale of plunder inflicted by the Iranians upon the Indians historically resembled Alexander's plunder of Iran in 323 BC and that of the Arabs at Ctesiphon in AD 637.[44] The massive plunder certainly helped service the costs of the Indian campaign and future battles. Nader was also very generous in the provision of spoils for his officers and troops who had been campaigning for a number of years.

The scale of Nader's appetite for plunder and the rapacity of his demands finally sparked a violent reaction from the Indians. The people of Delhi broke into open rebellion and began attacking Nader's officers in the city.[45] It is estimated that up to 900 Iranian troops and officers perished at the hands of Delhi's citizens.[46] Nader immediately ordered his troops to rampage throughout the city's homes and streets with a free hand. What ensued was nothing less than slaughter in which "rivers of blood flowed."[47] Mohammad Shah and members of the Mughal nobility pleaded to Nader to desist from these actions. The appeal was accepted and the massacre came to an end. Current estimates cite that around 20,000 Delhi citizens perished during Nader's massacre.[48]

Despite having the upper hand, Nader appears to have realized that he and his army could not maintain their occupation of India for long. The Iranian army was simply not large enough to occupy and garrison the Indian subcontinent. In an attempt to forge a political alliance between Iran and India, Nader arranged for his son Nasrollah Mirza to marry one of the nieces of Mohammad Shah. This was followed by Mohammad Shah again assuming the role of emperor of Mughal India. In one of his acts of "gratitude," Mohammad Shah struck coins with Nader's name. In reality, Nader had been afforded a face-saving way of extricating his army from India while he still had the upper hand. After a sojourn of 58 days in Delhi, Nader permanently departed from India.

Nader's Indian adventure had profound consequences for the Indian subcontinent but also for the history of Iran, West Asia, and the rising British Empire (and by implication the West). Nader had delivered a devastating blow against the awesome Mughal military machine and crippled her financial state. This helped create a "window of opportunity" for other world empires, especially those from Europe, to extend their influence into the Indian subcontinent.[49] In particular, the steady growth of British power in India by the late 1700s would have consequences for Iran. Interestingly, Iranian interpretations of Nader's Indian conquest are complex. While Nader's military genius and success in India are appreciated, it is generally acknowledged that these adventures did little to improve the lot of the economy and people of Iran.[50] Nader did little to invest his war spoils into the Iranian economy for the welfare of the people and nation.

Central Asia: showdown with the Uzbeks

Nader headed westwards across Iran towards Ottoman territory (in modern-day Iraq). The city of Kut fell to his forces, resulting in the capture of much plunder. One of the reasons for Nader's success at Kut was the recent increase in the size of his army. When traveling back through Afghanistan, Nader had recruited 40,000 Afghan warriors (mostly Persian-speaking Hazaras of Mongol descent). In the upcoming operations against the Uzbeks, a large number of Caucasian contingents, notably Alans, Armenians, and Lezgians, would fight alongside large contingents of Turkmen, Kurdish, and Indian fighters.[51]

Nader's son Reza Gholi had been campaigning in Iran's northeastern region (especially the Balkh–Andikhui area) in 1737, just as the main Iranian army was starting its push into India. Reza Gholi first advanced to Andikhui in the spring of 1737, which surrendered after six weeks. Next to fall was Balkh. Reza Gholi then pressed on across the Amu Darya River (the Oxus River) with 8,500 troops in August 1737, exactly the opposite of what Nader had wished. Qarshi was besieged, prompting Sultan Abu ol-Fayz Khan Ataligh of Bukhara to attack the small Iranian force. Abu ol-Fayz Khan and his Uzbek warriors first pushed the Iranians back but were then destroyed by Iranian artillery fire. Nader, who was displeased with his son's actions, wrote a letter to Abu ol-Fayz Khan stating that he respected his authority over Bukhara. Reza Gholi's forces then came back across the Amu Darya into Iran. Nader's main reason for accommodating Abu ol-Fayz Khan was that he was focused on his Indian expedition at the time. This attitude would change upon Nader's return from India.

By 1740, Nader was finally ready for his major showdown in Central Asia. The Amu Darya River was a natural obstacle blocking the advance of a large Iranian army towards Bukhara.

Although Reza Gholi's small forces had crossed it in 1737, Nader would require a permanent bridge to sustain the crossing of his much larger army and to keep it supplied from Iran. Such a bridge would also need to be protected against Uzbek attacks. Nader's engineers constructed a bridge in 45 days upon which "two camels could walk beside each other in crossing it."[52] With his links to Iran secured, Nader's army crossed the Amu Darya in August 1740 and proceeded towards Bukhara.[53] The Iranian army arrived intact and encamped near Bukhara. Nader assigned the command of his frontal, left, right, and rear flanks to his most capable and trusted battle-hardened officers. The artillery corps was also assigned their respective commands.

The battle opened on September 22, 1740, with devastating volleys from the Iranian artillery.[54] This almost immediately caused panic among the Uzbek troops who, unaccustomed to artillery, soon lost cohesion.[55] As Abu ol-Fayz Khan's army disintegrated, the Iranian army took possession of much enemy booty.[56] Decisively defeated, Abu ol-Fayz Khan and his military leaders surrendered to Nader by October 1740. The surrender terms were that daily provisions would be afforded for the Iranian army during its sojourn in Turkistan. More significant was the recruiting of 30,000 Uzbek warriors into the Iranian army. In return Nader allowed Abu ol-Fayz Khan to retain his throne in Bukhara. To cement this new alliance Nader married Ataligh's two daughters to his nephew Ali Gholi Khan, and his son Reza Gholi Mirza. Abu ol-Fayz Khan then struck coins with Nader's name on them. With this success, Nader led the Iranian army onto its next conquest in Central Asia.

The Iranian army crossed another major river, the Syr Daria.[57] Ilbares Khan, the ruler of Khwarezm, prepared for battle with Turkmen (e.g. Yamut tribes), Uzbek, and Aral contingents numbering a total of 30,000 cavalry.[58] The lead elements of these soon engaged the forward elements of Nader's army with firearms and lance combat. These proved unable to halt the Iranian army, which soon engaged Ilbares Khan in a full-scale battle. The battle was yet another unqualified success for the Iranian army with Ilbares Khan and his surviving troops fleeing the field.[59] Ilbares and 6,000 Yamut Turkmen warriors regrouped to bar the advance of the Iranian army toward the Fetnak Castle.[60] Nader crushed Ilbares Khan, again fled, and tried to reorganize resistance. With his efforts failing, Ilbares surrendered to Nader at Khiva on November 1740. Unlike the mercy granted to Mohammad Shah and Ataligh, Nader executed Ilbares Khan and 20 of his officers by having their throats cut.[61] Nader then immediately freed Iranian and Russian slaves from captivity. Nader's success in Central Asia was all the more remarkable as it depended on the Iranian army's logistics system successfully supplying the army across 1,900 miles (3,000km) of Central Asian desert.[62]

CHAPTER 13

BATTLES IN THE CAUCASUS AND RENEWED WARS AGAINST THE OTTOMANS (1741–47)

After the successful conclusion of his Central Asian campaigns Nader transferred the Iranian capital from Isfahan to Mashad in northeast Iran's Khorasan province. It was in this area that the "Fort of Nader" or Kelat-e Naderi (also known as Qale Naderi) was built, a site that Nader used to store his vast stock of plunder. In reality, the structure was not strictly a fort but a mountainous region intersected by ravines and gullies to the north of Mashad. Nader built a series of powerful forts at each of the entrances with watchtowers on every critical peak and vantage point.[1] The construction of the defenses took five years, resulting in one of the most formidable fortresses of its time in eastern Iran and Central Asia.[2] Hedayati notes that the Kelat-e Naderi was capable of sustaining 10,000 troops with weapons and supplies against possible long-term sieges.[3] The site was especially strategic as it provided a base in northeast Iran for the pursuit of operations into Central Asia and would remain important over 130 years later.

Thrusting into the North Caucasus: battles in Daghestan

Nader had not forgotten the death of his brother at the hands of the Lezgians in the Caucasus in 1738. Three years later, Nader decided to enter the Caucasus to force the Lezgians to bow to his authority. There was also another reason for Nader's decision to strike into Daghestan. The Ottoman Empire had been suffering from considerable monetary and economic issues, making them reluctant to directly attack Iran.[4] Instead they opted to support the Lezgian guerrillas of Daghestan against Nader Shah and his delegates in the Caucasus.[5] Between April and May 1741, Nader attempted to sway the Lezgians to switch their loyalties to Iran.[6] When his diplomatic efforts failed, Nader decided to impose a military solution upon the Daghestan question.

The Iranian army left Mashad on March 14, 1741, marched across the southern Caspian west towards Azarbaijan and on into the Caucasus.[7] As Nader and his army were passing through the thick forests of Mazandaran in northern Iran, a gunman opened fire in an attempt to assassinate Nader. Almost immediately Nader suspected his first-born son, Reza Gholi, as being behind this plot.[8] The assailant, Nik Qadam, was caught and brought before Nader for interrogation.[9] Nader concluded that Nik Qadam and his son were somehow connected and ordered that his son's eyes be cut out of their sockets. Ever since Nader had assumed the leadership of Iran and her army, he had become increasingly paranoid, probably due to the constant strain of unabated combat, rebellions, and perceived plots against him.[10] Nader's mental state deteriorated further with the departure for pilgrimage of his doctor, Alavi Khan.[11] The terrible blinding of his eldest son must have had a profoundly negative impact upon Nader's already deteriorating mental state.

Nader and his army arrived in Azarbaijan by the summer of 1741 and halted in Ardabil to reorganize and prepare for the thrust into the Caucasus. The army, provided with ample supplies, was reputedly composed of 150,000 men from across Iran and eastern Afghanistan as well as Indian and Uzbek warriors.[12] Nader crossed over into the Caucasus on August 1741.[13] As Nader thrust towards Daghestan, he dispatched a force of 10,000 men to secure Darband which was achieved by October. When Nader reached Daghestan proper he was met with a conciliatory party of many of the local khans. Their submission was accepted by Nader on condition that the khans would offer supplies and foodstuffs for his army during the campaign. Nevertheless, not all of the Lezgian clans refused to submit, which meant that Nader never succeeded in fully asserting his authority upon them.[14]

Renewed war with the Ottoman Empire

After the Mughan assembly in March 1736 when Nader became shah, the Iranians had provided a five-point declaration, one of which was for the Sultan to recognize the Jaafari sect as one of the five branches of the Sunnah in Islam.[15] The recognition would mean that the sultan would also arrange for the provision of a place for the Jaafaris in the holy Ka'ba of Mecca.[16] The sultan, as the leader of the Caliphate and especially the Sunni Ummah, rejected Nader's proposal. Mahmud was actually willing to compromise on some of Nader's religious demands in the interests of preserving the peace, but this would inevitably run contrary to the wishes of the Ulema of Istanbul. They would most likely act to depose the sultan at the slightest hint of his having made any compromise with the Shiites of Iran against whom they had fought for centuries.[17] As Nader threatened war if the Ottoman Empire did not accede to his Jaafari demand, the relative calm that had followed the previous round of Iranian–Ottoman fighting in western Iran was to be shattered once again.

Nader prepared for the new round of combat against the Ottomans by deploying the bulk of his forces to the Kermanshah region in western Iran where he built a very large fortress as a supply base and staging post for the upcoming operations.[18] The total number of fighting troops are said to have totaled 375,000. They were deployed to Leylan and Zohab.[19]

The Ottoman Empire declared war on April 30, 1742. The Ottoman high command made preparations for their army to strike into both western Iran and the Caucasus. Istanbul had genuine fears that Russia would also act against them, which explains why an Ottoman army was sent to Hotin.[20] Contemporary French sources suggest that Nader Shah intended to inflict a major defeat upon the Ottomans and to besiege Istanbul.[21]

As soon as the Iranian army marched across the border on May 29, 1743[22] they began to experience success against the Ottoman forces, resulting in the fall of a number of outposts and castles along the western border. Nader's army then captured Kirkuk with at least 300,000 troops in early August 1743, followed shortly later by Irbil.[23] The most important first strike however was Nader's thrust towards Baghdad. Nader had no intention of investing his forces in an expensive siege. Instead his objective was to ensure that the Baghdad garrison were decisively contained (or exhausted), allowing Nader to focus on the north of the Mesopotamian plains or Iraqi Kurdistan.[24]

After the fall of Kirkuk, the Iranians thrust further into Ottoman (or Iraqi) Kurdistan. Nader detached 12,000 men to defeat the Yezidi Kurds from the mountains of Sinjar, who were led by a chieftain named Yezid.[25] After bitter fighting, Nader's force won the battle, slaying several thousand of their opponents and Yezid.[26] After prevailing in Sinjar, the Iranian army thrust toward the major Ottoman stronghold at Mosul by September 1743.[27] The city was surrounded and besieged. Turkish resistance proved especially fierce resulting in heavy Iranian losses.[28]

There are contradictory accounts as to what happened next. Ottoman sources report that a decisive counterattack defeated Nader's troops and broke the siege.[29] Iranian sources assert that the Ottoman commander of the Mosul garrison, Hussein Pasha, dispatched a negotiating party to Nader bearing gifts and agreeing to submit to his authority.[30] Whatever the truth, it is certain that Nader was not able to stay in one theater too long as prolonged absence from Iran would encourage his increasingly restive subjects to rebel. Nader wanted to exercise mobility in a rapid campaign in which he could conquer as much territory as possible, and thereby bring the Turks to the negotiating table. This is consistent with Iranian historians who maintain that the main reason Nader was anxious for a resolution was the outbreak of rebellions in the Caucasus, Central Asia, and throughout Iran.[31]

Nader's first attempt to take Kars, in July 1744, was repulsed by a vigorous Ottoman defense. This was followed by an attempt against Yerevan, which was defended successfully by the sardar of the eastern Ottoman realms, Yegen Mohammad Pasha.[32] Nevertheless, Nader Shah had been able to successfully block the Ottomans from expanding into Azerbaijan or the Caucasus from their base in Kars.[33]

In August 1745, Nader scored two great victories over the Ottomans. The first occurred near Yerevan on August 9 where a huge Ottoman force of 130,000 troops led by Yegen Pasha fought against a smaller Iranian force of 80,000 troops.[34] Ottoman forces had greatly improved in performance thanks to the efforts of Yegen Pasha, who had worked closely with the French adventurer Bonneval. The Janissaries were able to deploy more flexibly in a coordinated fashion in smaller detachments and their musketry drills and artillery skills had improved considerably. But Nader's troops had also improved, as Nader had placed great emphasis on musketry skills, artillery, and the ability of his troops to move in smaller tactical groups, just like the Ottomans. Nader was also keenly aware of Ottoman skills in firearms. He ordered that his troops simply fire one volley with their muskets and then charge into the Ottoman lines with their shamshirs. This would negate the Ottoman proficiency at musketry and force the Ottomans into hand-to-hand fighting, the Iranians' strength. The battle quickly became an infantry duel with the cavalry of both sides holding back. Seeing that the battle was moving indecisively, Nader donned his armor and led a cavalry charge of 40,000 into the Ottoman flank. The action was hard-fought but beneficial. The Iranian troops were galvanized by the exploits of their leader on the battlefield. This along with Nader's own successes in the field resulted in the fleeing of at least 15,000 irregular Ottoman troops from the field.[35] Cohesion among the Ottoman troops now broke down. By the time the fighting had ended the Ottoman Turks had lost another 20,000 troops.[36]

The Ottomans had been attempting a withdrawal but Nader kept pursuing them and cutting off their source of supplies at Kars. Ten days after Yerevan, the Ottomans suffered an even greater defeat at the battle of Kars. Yegen Mohammad Pasha was slain,[37] with 10,000 Turks killed, 18,000 wounded, and 5000 captured.[38] Iranian casualties totaled 8,000.[39] Iranian artillery had also displayed a remarkable level of efficiency by firing more artillery rounds than their Ottoman counterparts and being more accurate in scoring hits against hostile targets. The Ottomans found some consolation later in the campaigns of Hakimoghlu Ali Pasha, who managed to clear most of eastern Anatolia of Iranian troops by November 1745.[40] Other skirmishes continued into 1747, but it was clear that that Nader Shah held the overall initiative.

The two sides finally came to a negotiated settlement. Nader met Nazif Effendi, the Ottoman envoy, in Saugh Bolaqh, Azarbaijan. Gifts were exchanged, then negotiations began which led to a peace treaty concluded in January 1747.[41]

A brilliant ephemeral glory: Nader Shah and Iran's lost opportunities

Nader Shah had been displeased with the officers of the royal guard and had told one of his Abdali commanders that he suspected the Guards of treachery. Fearing execution, Mohammad Qoli Khan, the leader of the guards, organized a plot to murder Nader. Despite bringing together 70 sympathizers, only three had the resolve to break into Nader Shah's chambers at Fathabad, Khorasan, on the night of June 19, 1747, where they killed Nader with a sword. The assassination of Nader Shah led to political upheaval and chaos, the fragmentation of the military and the resurgence of Afghan campaigns in the eastern realms of Iran.

Were Iran's successes during Nader Shah's reign a "flash in the pan?" Other than from a handful of military experts and historians such as Axworthy, Nader Shah and his exploits have until recently received little attention in the West. This is changing with the arrival of a new stream of western military historians such as Black who observes that "If the Persia of Nader Shah, whose campaigns have indeed received insufficient attention is to be dismissed as of limited long-term significance … then it can be asked why Napoleon is worthy of consideration, as his empire rapidly ended in failure and certainly did not set the geopolitical parameters for the western world."[42]

Iranian historiography has generally focused on the military and economic failures of the Qajars especially with respect to Imperial Russia and Britain. In reality the seeds of Iran's military and economic decline are multi-varied and complex and can be traced as far back as the later days of the Safavids. Nader Shah's military genius saved Iran from being partitioned by Imperial Russia and the Ottoman Empire as well as from raids from Central Asia and Afghanistan.[43] Unfortunately for Iran, Nader failed to transform his military successes into long-term benefits for the country. Napoleon Bonaparte is reputed to have observed the following of Nader Shah's reign: "Nader was a great warrior but lacked the foresight to think of the present state and the future of his country."[44]

In comparison to his Safavid predecessors, Nader's government was essentially a military government, characterized by a militaristic mindset.[45] He tended to rely on a network of spies and *Hamkalaman* (i.e. those with the same word/mindset) to enforce his authority in the provinces.[46] The most notable liability in Nader's system of government was its militaristic nature, which coupled with very harsh measures led to many revolts by the latter days of his rule.

Nader's empire was welded together not only by conquest but by brute force and the imposition of fear. As a strictly militaristic regime, his empire was doomed to fall, as it did shortly after his death. The imposition of harsh punitive measures for actual or perceived transgressions only ensured that the mass of the population would chafe under Nader's rule and take advantage of every opportunity to rebel.

He proved capable of inflicting merciless cruelty upon civilians under his rule, and would crush without remorse any who dared rebel against him.[47] Nader's violence eventually reached into his own household, the blinding of his own son setting the basis for Nader's mental deterioration. He became increasingly paranoid and cruel, and by the end of his life Nader was a much-feared man. His arrival in any city was dreaded as he often engaged in tactics of exhortation, mutilation, and flogging.[48] His policies of forced deportations and resettlements certainly did not endear him to his subjects. Thus towards the end of his life, Nader faced rebellions on every side.

Nader had little interest in the arts, literature, sciences, learning, or architecture. He was at his best in the saddle and the command tent, on the move in battle and at war. This meant that his economic system was geared solely for the oiling of his military machine. The long, costly, and bloody wars exacted a heavy toll on the country's finances and human resources.[49] The revenue was raised by exacting exorbitant taxes on an increasingly destitute population.[50]

Nader's attempts to bridge the Sunni–Shia divide between the Ottoman Turks and the Iranians was notable. But the memories of Ottoman attacks into Iran could not be so easily forgotten. If he had succeeded, both Ottomans and Iranians might have benefited from an alliance against the growing might of imperial Russia. Instead, Ottoman–Iranian relations after Nader benefited the Russians, who took advantage of their animosity to inflict defeats upon each of them during the 19th century. While Nader had rescued Iran from certain fragmentation and absorption, no real basis had been laid at the social, governmental, and economic levels to prepare Iran for its future challenge: the awesome military, political, and economic might of the emerging European powers. This meant that Iran's ability to modernize its military to European levels of efficiency was seriously compromised during and after Nader Shah's tenure. This was in large part due to an economy in shambles and a social structure beset by an antiquated political and educational apparatus.

PART III
THE ZANDS

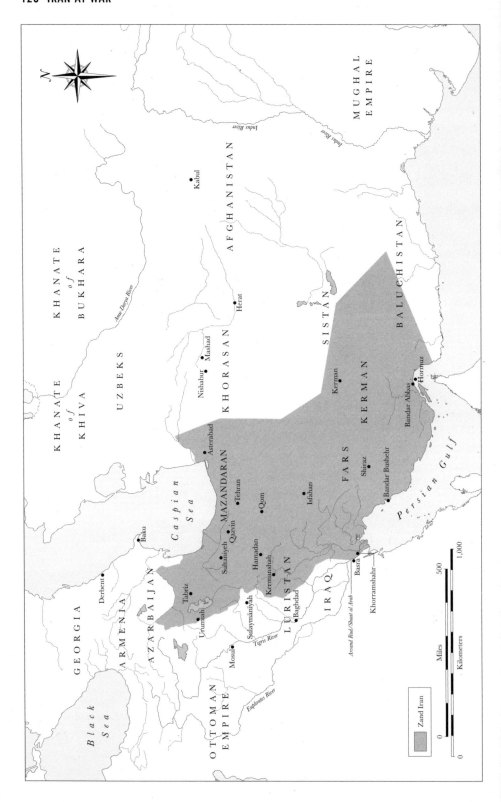

CHAPTER 14

THE RISE OF KARIM KHAN AND THE ZANDS (1747–63)

The Iranian army splinters

Nader Shah's death in 1747 plunged Iran into a dangerous state of civil war, which threatened the country's political stability and territorial integrity. The provinces of Mazandaran and Gilan in the north of Iran soon came under the domination of Mohammad Hassan Khan of the formidable Qajar Turkish tribes. Political chaos also meant that many of Iran's outlying regions (namely the south along the Persian Gulf, and much of western Iran) were increasingly vulnerable to regionalism. A year after Nader Shah's death, his grandson Shahrokh became Shah of Khorasan, and ruled it as a separate state for the next three decades. Seistan and Baluchistan also moved away from the Iranian orbit after the death of Nader Shah.

Nader's favoritism had led to tension within the officer corps of his army. Already on July 2, 1747, the day after Nader's assassination, factions of the army, which was encamped at Khabooshan, began to splinter off.[1] Iran was immediately weakened, less able to defend herself against attack.[2]

The Afghan contingents left for their homes further east into Afghanistan, quickly returning to raiding. The largest of these raids was launched by 100,000 men led by Ahmad Shah Durrani.[3] Afghan contingents in other areas of Iran rose in revolt and violence. Allah Yar Afghan led his 8,000 men in a killing spree in Hamadan in retaliation for the killing of Afghans by the city's citizens a number of years before.[4]

Mohammad Hassan Khan Qajar, the governor of Astrabad, Gorgan, and Mazandaran and commanding 35,000 troops taken mainly from Astrabad and Turkmen from the Yamut and Kuklan clans, would soon become a major contender for political and military supremacy in Iran.[5] However, the most powerful force in Khorasan was that of Sultan Ali Shah, a nephew of the late Nader Shah, who led a force of 75,000 cavalry backed by cannon.[6] Nader Shah's grandson, Shahrokh, commanded a force of 30,000 troops in Khorasan.

Sarafraz Beg Khodabandehlu, an important military leader in northwest Iran, commanded 3,000 shahsevan cavalry and 1,000 warriors from tribes near Hamadan.[7] A more powerful military force stationed in the Hamadan area was the 12,000 cavalry led by Mohammad Ali Khan Taklu.[8] Amir Aslan Khan, a cousin of the late Nader Shah, commanded a crack force of 30,000 Azarbaijani cavalry.

Kurds served in a number of Iranian army units, which at the time of Nader's death were dispersed throughout Iran.[9] Lurs were another important element of Nader Shah's army. Kolbali Khan from Boroujerd in Luristan, for example, commanded 12,000 infantry and cavalry.[10] Another significant faction to splinter off were the Bakhtiari Lurs led by Ali Mardan Khan. These arrived in Mashad to pledge their support for Ali Qoli Khan, a nephew of the late Nader. Ali Qoli Khan had rebelled against his uncle in Khorasan. With the assistance of Ali Mardan Khan, Ali Qoli Khan was enthroned as Adil Shah. The new Shah proved to be a major disappointment, however, as he showed little interest in securing Iran's borders or addressing the rising discontent of the people. Instead of marching into Isfahan, Adil Shah dispatched his brother Ibrahim Mirza to the former Safavid capital and decided to remain in Mashad.[11]

The army in the meantime was growing more restless with Ali Mardan Khan requesting permission to leave with his Bakhtiari Lur warriors towards the southwest. Disregarding the rejection of this request, Ali Mardan Khan decided to proceed, and was pursued by a punitive force which he defeated. Ali Mardan Khan arrived in Isfahan where he found Ibrahim Mirza working to organize an army to dethrone his brother, Adil Shah in Mashad. When his preparations were complete, Ibrahim Mirza placed his viceroy in Isfahan before embarking against his brother in the spring of 1747. The viceroy was Abolfath Khan, a Lur of the Haft-Lang-e Bakhtiari.[12]

The rise of the Lurs

Nader Shah had exiled a number of Lur tribes from the Zagros into Khorasan. One of the most enigmatic Lur tribes to travel back to their homelands after Nader's death was the Zands. Karim Khan (1705–79), who had served as a general during the reign of Nader Shah, led 30–40 families home from Khorasan to Western Iran.[13] He was the son of Itaqh Kahn, one of the Afsharids' most capable warriors, who had won fame for military genius in combat.[14]

The Zands hailed from regions from the Malayir region, specifically the villages of Kamazan and Deh Pari.[15] The ethnicity of the Zands has been variously ascribed to both Lurs and Kurds as the name Zand has appeared in both of the west Iranic peoples. In general, they are agreed to be Lak, or northern Lurs, most likely of Kurdish origin, distinct from Khorramabad's Faili Lurs.[16]

The equestrian skills of the Lurs can be traced as far back as the earliest Indo-Europeans in western Iran.[17] They were highly proficient in cavalry warfare, especially at the feigned retreat, and acted as Iran's first wall of defense against Ottoman invasions of Iran.[18] They regularly harassed the Ottoman garrison at Kermanshah before its expulsion. When Nader Shah had defeated the Zands and resettled them in Khorasan, he utilized these excellent warriors in his subsequent campaigns.

The Lurs and Zands in particular retained many customs of pre-Islamic Iran. Women would fight alongside men in Zand fighting units. There are reports that the wives of Karim Khan and his troops often fought beside them in battle against the Afghans in Nader Shah's time.[19] The Afghans made a point to heap scorn upon the Zand units who defeated them by characterizing their men as "hiding behind their women's skirts."[20]

Despite the importance of Mashad during Nader Shah's reign, political power shifted back west after his death, to Isfahan and then Shiraz. One of the most crucial post-Nader power struggles took place in the late 1740s and early 1750s in the area of Isfahan where three powerful khans, Ali Mardan Khan, Abolfath Khan (governor in Isfahan), and Karim Khan, battled for supremacy. All three were of ancient Lur stock.[21] The most powerful was Abolfath Khan, who commanded 50,000 warriors; Ali Mardan Khan led 20,000 warriors, while Karim Khan had an initial force of 8,000 warriors.[22] The latter's forces later increased to 12,000 men with recruitment from Kamazan and Deh Pari as well as the absorption of troops from defeated rivals.[23]

Karim Khan was accompanied by his ally Zakariya Khan, whose authority extended to the Lur towns of Kazzaz and Borojerd. The latter also had the support of at least 2,000 Qaraquzlu warriors from the Hamadan region.[24] Karim Khan and Zakariya Khan's combined forces thrust towards Golpayegan (in Isfahan province) and captured it after defeating a Bakhtiari-Lur army, thereby securing a strategic juncture on the way to Isfahan. Ali Mardan Khan however took Golpayegan just as Karim Khan went west to face Mehr-Ali Khan Tekkelu of Hamadan.

From Golpayegan, Ali Mardan Khan attempted to capture Isfahan from Abolfath Khan in the spring of 1750 but was soundly beaten by the city's defenders at Murchekhor. Following this setback, Ali Mardan appealed to other khans for help, notably Karim Khan, who agreed to provide support. Strengthened with Karim Khan's troops, Ali Mardan defeated Isfahan's army in May 1750. The city was then breached a few days into its siege with Abolfath Khan preparing a powerful defense of the fortress. Further bloodshed was forestalled after generous terms were offered by the attackers. This brought relief to the suffering populace of Isfahan and the surrounding regions who had endured many depredations during the power contest.

The three khans agreed to place the 17-year-old Abu Torab, a descendant of the Safavids, on the throne as Shah Ismail III by June 29, 1750. In this arrangement, the real power was wielded by Ali Mardan Khan (supported by his Bakhtiari-Lur warriors), who became viceroy, with Karim Khan as the commander of the Iranian army. Abolfath Khan was allowed to keep his post as the governor of Isfahan. It was clear that Shah Ismail III was simply a figurehead to help legitimize the rising power of the Lur khans.

The three-way agreement between the Lur khans failed to endure. Karim Khan returned to his native Luristan and campaigned to expand his influence in western Iran, especially in Kurdistan. In Isfahan, Ali Mardan Khan killed Abolfath Khan, and with the help of Shah Ismail III, conquered the province of Fars and the city of Shiraz. Ali Mardan Khan then made extensive preparations to finish off his remaining rival, Karim Khan. To finance the costs of his upcoming battle with Karim Khan, Ali Mardan Khan imposed heavy taxes on the local populace to reinforce his army.[25] Ali Mardan's augmented forces however were soon badly mauled by musketeers from the village of Khisht in an ambush at the narrow pass of Kotal e Dokhtar. Ali Mardan lost several hundred men as well his recently acquired plunder from Kazerun. As Ali Mardan retreated towards Isfahan, he lost more troops to the incoming winter weather and desertion.

Karim Khan had also prepared for the final showdown. Having secured the allegiance of many powerful clans such as the Bayat and the Khodabandehlu, Karim Khan thrust straight towards Isfahan to battle Ali Mardan Khan. Karim completely defeated Ali Mardan Khan at Chaharmahal in February 1751. Shah Ismail III, now bowing to the inevitable, joined Karim Khan.[26] The bulk of the defeated Bakhtiaris were treated honorably, and Karim Khan secured them as new troops. Ali Mardan, his ally Ismail Khan Faili (the Vali of Luristan), and the remainder of his forces now hastily retreated southwest, into Khuzistan.

The siege of Kermanshah and defeat at Astrabad

Karim Khan's attack on Kermanshah can be traced to his rejection of Hamadan's Mehr-Ali Tekkelu's offer of an alliance after Nader Shah's death. Tekkelu then called in the Vali of the Ard-Alan in

Iranian Kurdistan, Hassan Ali Khan.[27] For a month and a half, the Zand cavalry battled the Ard-Alan Kurds. The Zands were then forced to retire due to a crisis in Golpayegan sometime in April–May 1750. Karim Khan returned to face Mehr-Ali Tekkelu in a final confrontation. The battle resulted in a decisive victory for Karim Khan and the capture of Hamadan. The Ard-Alan however remained at large in the formidable fortress and arsenal of Kermanshah, the strategic lynchpin in western Iran.

The main contenders in the region were Mirza Mohammad Taghi Golestaneh and Abdolali Khan who managed to recruit 6,000 cavalry near Kermanshah.[28] Nader Shah had blinded Hussein Khan Beg Zangeneh of Kermanshah on charges of treason. This did not prevent him from organizing his own army after Nader's death. Zangeneh had recruited warriors from 4,500 infantry and cavalry from clans such as the Zangeneh tribe, and remained a powerful force in the Kermanshah region.[29] These khans were reluctant to pledge their support to other warriors such as Karim Khan while the state of power in Iran was in flux. Zangeneh, for example, had led a determined attack on the Kurdish Zangeneh tribe in 1749 which had been repelled.[30]

A final challenge from Mehr Ali Khan Tekkelu was unsuccessful, and with Tekkelu finally eliminated as a threat, Karim Khan turned his attentions to Kermanshah. Negotiations failed. The Zands ravaged the city of Sanandaj and its neighboring districts in Iranian Kurdistan and then retired to their bases in the Malayir region for the winter. The stage was set for one of Karim Khan's most bloody campaigns.

After his retreat to Khuzistan, Ali Mardan Khan had obtained fresh troops from the vali of Khuzistan, Sheikh Saad of the Al-Kathir Arab tribes. Ali Mardan had also secured the support of Lurs led by Ismail Khan. This new force marched towards Kermanshah in the spring of 1752 and joined its garrison. The Zands, led by Mohammad Khan, launched an attack against Ali Mardan's camp in their drive to besiege Kermanshah, but were repelled with heavy losses. Ali Mardan then deployed into Zand territories, probably hoping to rout the Zands in a decisive showdown. Karim Khan was waiting near Nahavand, however, and once again inflicted a serious defeat upon Ali Mardan Khan in spring or early summer 1752.[31] This time the defeated khan fled westwards into Ottoman territory towards Baghdad. The destruction of Ali Mardan's army allowed the Zands to once again resume their siege of Kermanshah.

Karim Khan was soon challenged by the Qajars based in Astrabad in the north.[32] The Qajars were led by Mohammad Hassan Khan, a son of Fathali Khan Qajar. Mohammad Hassan Khan had successfully expanded Qajar power in northern Iran from Astrabad westwards across Mazandaran, Gilan (including Rasht), and even as far as Qazvin. The Qajars were now serious contenders for the Iranian throne.

Mohammad Hassan Khan marched towards Kermanshah to provide military assistance for its garrison against the Zands, but was resoundedly defeated by Karim Khan.[33] The Qajars soon retired towards Astrabad.[34] Karim Khan, commanding 45,000 men, engaged in pursuit, reached Astrabad and ordered the construction of a large number of trenches and siege works around the city.[35] With the city surrounded, Karim Khan requested a meeting with Mohammad Hassan Khan, but it was refused. Mohammad Hassan Khan's 35,000 troops were mainly from Astrabad, and Turkmen from the Yamut and Kuklan clans.[36] The equipment of Mohammad Hassan Khan's troops was a mixture of traditional weapons and firearms.[37]

As Karim Khan proceeded to deploy more formidable siege engines against Astrabad, Mohammad Hassan Khan had second thoughts. He sent peace offers to Karim Khan which were rejected.[38] Karim Khan proceeded to besiege the city, which experienced an acute shortage of supplies after two months.[39] Mohammad Hassan Khan renewed his earlier offer of "gifts" in exchange for Karim's Khan's departure from Astrabad.[40] Mohammad Hassan Khan also promised Karim Khan that he would suffer a decisive defeat should he reject this offer again.[41]

The Zands however were facing problems of their own. A few nights after the onset of Karim Khan's siege, a number of Qajar warriors secretly left Astrabad to occupy a number strategic positions that could intercept the Zand supply lines. Turkmen warriors also launched consistent hit-and-run raids against the Zands. A set piece battle occured as Mohammad Hassan Khan came out of the city with his troops; the Zand cavalry were then crushed by a rapid Qajar pincer movement.[42] Faced with the prospect of complete destruction, Karim Khan retreated with just 16,000 surviving troops towards Tehran, having lost 12,000 men killed and 15,000 taken prisoner.[43] Shah Ismail III was among those captured.[44]

Despite this victory Mohammad Hassan Khan did not immediately pursue the fleeing Zand army. The Qajar and Turkmen commanders argued that the best course of action was to destroy Karim Khan and the remnants of his army, but Mohammad Hassan Khan sought to reinforce and expand his position in northern Iran and had ambitions to expand his sway to Azerbaijan.

After Astrabad, Karim Khan spent the winter of 1752 in Tehran. After gathering new troops, he moved southwest towards Isfahan by early 1753. By this time, Ali Mardan Khan had once again become a threat, attempting to raise a new army in Luristan with the support of the Ottoman pashas in Baghdad.[45] Suleiman Pasha of Baghdad had helped promote a Safavid pretender by the name of Shah Sultan Hussein II, who was also supported by Ali Mardan Khan. The latter, already reinforced by fresh Lur warriors, had also been assured of aid by Azad Khan. Karim Khan was also concerned with the ongoing siege of Kermanshah, where the Kermanshahis hoped that Ali Mardan Khan would come to their aid. As Ali Mardan Khan marched towards Kermanshah, however, things went wrong. The Safavid pretender proved to be a major disappointment which had a negative impact on Ali Mardan's cause.[46] Karim Khan quickly seized the opportunity against Ali Mardan Khan by marching out of Isfahan towards Kermanshah, which finally capitulated in 1753 after a two-year siege.[47]

Karim Khan easily defeated the remnants of Ali Mardan's forces, who were waiting for support to arrive from Azad Khan. Ali Mardan Khan escaped and then blinded the Safavid pretender, sending him off to Ottoman Iraq. Ali Mardan Khan died at the hands of escaping Zand prisoners in the spring of 1754.[48] His dramatic demise meant that Karim Khan's most dangerous Lur opponents had been eliminated.

The challenge of Azad Khan Afghan

An important force in the Iraq Ajam region was led by another of the late Nader Shah's relations, Ibrahim Khan.[49] Ibrahim had removed his brother Adil Shah from power in Mashad from power and assumed the throne of Iran in Tabriz, Azerbaijan in July 1748. Ibrahim, however, had failed to secure full acceptance as Shah of Iran as many of military leaders and khans preferred Shahrokh in Mashad.[50] Ibrahim Khan was killed by his own officers in September 1748, leading to the election of Shahrokh as Shah in Mashad. With the removal of Ibrahim Khan, Shahrokh was now the ruler of Azarbaijan as well. The situation in Azarbaijan however became more unstable, making it difficult for Shahrokh to maintain his power there.

Control of Azarbaijan slipped into the grasp of Azad Khan in 1749. The latter was an Afghan warlord who had served as a colonel in Nader Shah's army.[51] The situation in Azarbaijan had deteriorated further as the Dumbuli Kurds of the western part of the province had carved their own fiefdoms within the province. Azad Khan was primarily interested in expanding his influence in Iran rather than completely pacifying Azarbaijan. Azad Khan had unsuccessfully attempted to link up with Ali Mardan Khan against Karim Khan in the summer of 1753. Having arrived too late, Azad Khan, who led a numerically smaller force, chose not to engage the victorious Zand army; he retreated and declared that he wished to have no further associations with Ali Mardan and his dubious pretender to the Safavid throne. Karim Khan demanded nothing less than complete submission from the Afghan warlord, who predictably dismissed this demand. Karim Khan's attempt at enforcing his demands by battle ended in complete disaster and Karim ordered his army to retreat to Deh Pari, while he and his brother Sadegh Khan, and half-brother Iskandar Khan, retired to Isfahan and then Shiraz. Apparently, they had decided that the prevailing circumstances militated against theei holding onto Isfahan.

Azad Khan followed up on his success by advancing into the Zand homeland and towards Deh Pari. Using a ruse, Azad Khan captured 15 of Karim Khan's family and other Zand notables based within Deh Pari's fortress, notably Mohammad Khan and Sheikh Ali.[52] The prisoners were then sent towards Urumiah, one of Azad Khan's bastions in Azarbaijan.

Azad Khan now thrust towards undefended Isfahan and easily captured it by October 1753. This was followed by another defeat of Karim Khan by Azad Khan; the Lur warlord then took refuge in the Makhtiari mountains.[53]

By March 1754, Fathali Khan Afshar had been dispatched by Azad Khan with a revitalized army to crush the Zands once and for all. Karim Khan's army had been unable to build a strong cohesive force during the winter and had little hope of standing up to Azad Khan's forces in battle. They fought a desperate rearguard action and escaped through Chamchamal.

Azad Khan put considerable effort into completely annihilating Karim Khan's army. Shiraz fell to Azad Khan in August 1754 and Fathali Afshar cleared Karim Khan's troops out of Kazerun in September. Karim Khan was now being squeezed out of central Iran and his last hope was the Lars, who refused to help. Fortunately for the Zands, Rustam Khan, the leader of Khisht village, came to the rescue; Rustam Khan and Karim Khan joined forces and ambushed Fathali Afshar at Kamarij pass.[54] The Zands chased the remnants of Fathali's army into Shiraz. Realizing the futility of holding onto the city, Azad Khan fled from the city just ten days after the broken troops of Fathali arrived. Karim Khan entered Shiraz on November 29, 1754.

After Chamchamal in March 1754, Karim Khan dispatched Mohammad Khan to proceed towards Kermanshah.[55] The fortress had to be recaptured as it had been forced to pledge its allegiance to Azad Khan. Kermanshah finally fell after heavy use of explosives and bitter hand-to-hand fighting.[56]

After the capture of the fortress, Heidar Khan, a key Zand commander, organized an evacuation from the city and joined Mohammad Khan's army, which had relocated close to the Ottoman border.[57] From here, he would successfully intercept Azad Khan's supply and communications lines to Urumiah. By early 1755 Mohammad Khan had cleared out all of Azad Khan's forces from much of western Iran and captured Valashgerd's formidable Tekkelu fortress. Mohammad Khan had also returned to complete the destruction of Kermanshah's fortress, ensuring that Kermanshah could never become a threat to the Zands again. The artillery was all disassembled, and the pieces tossed into a nearby river. Mohammad Khan then proceeded south to raid Khuzistan for booty, and afterwards marched into Fars province to join Karim Khan.

With the key fortress of Kermanshah destroyed, Karim Khan was ready to push towards Isfahan. Strengthened by the arrival of Mohammad Khan Zand and his troops, the Zands were ready for their next offensive. Karim Khan's first move was to subdue the Lars led by Nasser Khan who had previously refused to assist him. In this instance, Karim Khan was fortunate, as Mohammad Khan Qajar – who had defeated him at Astrabad three years before – was now thrusting his forces against Azad's dominions in Azarbaijan. By November 1755 Azad's forces in Azarbaijan had suffered a decisive defeat at the hands of the Qajars forcing Azad Khan himself to leave Isfahan for Kashan in northwest Iran.[58] Karim Khan then easily took the city of Isfahan on December 17, 1755, having raided Kerman and its environs prior to this. Azad Khan, under pressure from both Mohammad Hassan Khan Qajar and Karim Khan, retreated to Urumiah by the early months of 1756.[59]

Despite their successes in the previous year, the Zands were struggling as their forces were spread thinly across so many theaters. This meant that Karim Khan was not able to quickly bring the full might of his forces to battle in any theater. Especially vulnerable was Isfahan, now held mainly by Arab infantry who had been recruited from Iran's Persian Gulf coastline.[60]

After his campaigns in northern Iran and Azarbaijan, Mohammad Hassan Khan finally decided to gather his forces for a big push towards Isfahan and the southwest. His army now included a good proportion of Astrabadi musketeers. Mohammad Hassan Khan sent a message to Karim Khan to accept Ismail III as the Shah of Iran and to support Qajar forces. Karim Khan's refusal led to a new showdown. The battle was joined at Kazzaz towards the northwest on March 27, 1756 and the Zands were completely defeated.

Karim Khan then came out with the remainder of his troops to make his stand before Isfahan. The two armies met about 9 miles (14km) from Isfahan on April 5, 1756, with Karim Khan defeated again.[61]

Karim Khan and his remaining troops retreated towards Shiraz.[62] Mohammad Hassan Khan and his troops, elated by their second great victory, engaged in pursuit. The Qajars soon reached and surrounded Shiraz, but they lacked proper siege equipment. The Zand gunners proved their devastating accuracy by firing a single cannon shot against one of the tents of the Qajar nobles, killing him and a number of other troops. Mohammad Hassan Khan now sent urgent appeals to Isfahan for siege equipment. But once again the tables turned; Mohammad Hassan Khan received news that Hussein Khan Develu of the Yukhari-Bash faction of the Qajars had seized Astrabad and declared independence. There were also alarming reports that Azad Khan Afghan was now moving his army toward Shiraz. The Qajars abandoned their siege of Shiraz in haste and reached Isfahan after a four-day march.[63] Mohammad Hassan Khan soon decided to abandon his defense of Isfahan, especially given the fact that Azad Khan was accompanied with 40,000 troops.[64] Azad Khan, who was now virtually unopposed, marched back into Isfahan facing no resistance and occupied it once again by mid-August 1756. The Qajars retreated first to Kashan, then to Sari, and from there to Astrabad.[65] Mohammad Hassan Khan was able to come to terms with Hussein Khan Develu thanks to the intercession of the Qajar elders in Astrabad.

Mohammad Hassan Khan set off towards Azarbaijan in 1756 with his Safavid claimant, Shah Ismail III.[66] Azad Khan had meanwhile dispatched 8,000 troops to pursue the Qajars in the north.[67] Mohammad Hassan Khan, who had evidently anticipated this, blocked the Alburz pass with 7,000 troops, forcing the Afghan warlord to go around to Rasht and march eastwards towards the Qajar strongholds by hugging the Caspian Coast along his path of advance.[68] Mohammad Hassan Khan once again outmaneuvered his Afghan adversary. The Qajars rapidly moved from Sari to Amol; it was during this deployment that the Qajars launched a daring nighttime cavalry strike at Lahijan which completely crushed Azad Khan's forces.[69] The city of Rasht, Azad Khan's base of operations, was evacuated by February 1757 and he retreated to Qazvin.[70] Mohammad Hassan Khan, who had now gained the upper hand, kept up the pressure on his Afghan adversary. Firmly ensconced in Rasht and the province of Gilan, the Qajars struck into Azarbaijan.[71] The Qajars reached as far as the Mughan steppes, the Talysh area, and even Astara.[72] Nevertheless Mohammad Hassan Khan did not receive the support that he had been expecting in Azarbaijan in the early months of 1757, and was instead attacked heavily by Qara Khan of Lankaran whose armies were marching from Talysh to Mughan.[73] When the Qajars reached Mughan, only Kazem Khan of Qara-Dagh arrived after one month to lend his support, although some other clans such as numbers of the Shahsevan tribe did join him.[74]

Azad Khan's forces, who had retreated to Urumiah, proved unwilling or incapable of stopping the Qajars, who were gaining ascendancy in Azarbaijan. With Tabriz captured by the Qajars and the situation deteriorating, Azad Khan deployed his main forces (17,000 troops) out of Isfahan on April 15, 1757 to break the Qajar siege of Urumiah.[75] As they moved towards Urumiah, Azad Khan's forces were augmented by a very large number of Kurds, swelling the army to 80,000.[76] Azad Khan also managed to recruit an additional 50,000 troops, these being lavishly equipped with cannon and various firearms.[77] Despite numerical superiority, Azad Khan was crushed, thanks in large part to the devastating effectiveness of the Qajar cannon.[78]

With Azad Khan's main army shattered, the Qajars confidently returned to Urumiah, which fell only a few days later. The fall of Urumiah resulted in the evaporation of what was left of Azad Khan's authority in Azarbaijan. Azad Khan now had no base of support left inside Iran, and fled into Ottoman territory towards Baghdad.[79] With Azad Khan eliminated from Azarbaijan, the Qajars now proceeded to impose their authority in Azarbaijan. By the autumn of 1757, Mohammad Hassan Khan was joined by Kazem Khan of Qara-Dagh for an attack on Panah Khan Javanshir at his fortress at Shusha.[80] The siege of Shusha proved unsuccessful, however, and was abandoned as Mohammad Hassan Khan turned his attention to the south to deal with a resurgent Karim Khan Zand in the Iranian interior.

Karim Khan defeats the Qajars

Just as Urumiah was under siege in Azarbaijan, Karim Khan was actively expanding his authority in the Shiraz region and the outlying regions as far as Khuzistan. By the winter of 1757, Mohammad Hassan Khan had moved out from Azarbaijan through Hamadan and Boroujerd and in a rapid thrust captured Isfahan by December 15.[81] Karim Khan's preoccupation in the Shiraz theater had prevented him from organizing a defense of Isfahan, whose populace was now on the verge of starvation. The Qajars also captured Kerman.[82]

The Qajar army moved towards Shiraz and besieged it by March 1758.[83] The Qajars were now accompanied by a number of allies including Afghans, Uzbeks, and Azarbaijanis.[84] Karim Khan, however, had prepared the city very well, ensuring that supplies of food, ammunition, and weaponry within the city were in abundance while potential sources of food and other resources in the area around the city had been destroyed.[85] The Zands often sortied from the city to briefly engage the Qajars, a tactic which soon resulted in a sharp decrease in the supplies of the Qajar camp. Constant Zand raids also ensured that the Qajar forces were unable to forage over larger areas for supplies.[86] The Qajars not only proved unable to contain the Zand raids, they also ran into difficulties within their own ranks. Mohammad Hassan Khan's Uzbek and Afghan contingents, who had joined the Qajars after Azad Khan's defeats in Gilan, attacked the Qajar forces (July 1758) and then fled, but later joined Karim Khan's forces.[87] The Qajars, now virtually defeated, evacuated the remnants of their battered forces and retreated northwards to Astrabad. As the Qajars travelled north, many of their remaining allies deserted them at Tehran, including Shahbaz Khan of the Dumbuli Kurds, and Fathali Khan Afshar.[88]

Other troubles awaited the Qajars. Hussein Khan of the Qajars, who had been holding Isfahan, had joined Karim Khan, and then rapidly departed to Astrabad to take it over before Mohammad Hassan Khan could arrive. Hussein Khan proceeded to strengthen the city's defenses to hold out against Mohammad Hassan Khan. Karim Khan's hopes that Mohammad Hassan Khan would bog down in front of his home city were dashed as Hussein Khan left Astrabad and fled to Damghan.[89] Evidently, Hussein Khan had a change of heart when Mohammad Hassan Khan's army (with the Safavid claimant Shah Ismail still in tow) arrived at the gates. Nevertheless, Mohammad Hassan Khan's days were numbered, as the Zands had no intention of granting him time or respite for recovery.

Sheikh Ali Khan had been dispatched earlier by Karim Khan with an army towards Mazandaran which captured Sari and successfully linked up with Hussein Khan Qajar. Karim Khan himself arrived in Tehran from Shiraz by December 1758. Mohammad Hassan Khan, realizing the danger of the growing force building up against him, arrived in Mazandaran with 20,000 troops to block the Zand advance at Ashraf (now Behshahr). He was also hoping to crush Sheikh Ali before he could be reinforced by Karim Khan's main army.

At first, the Qajars were successful in blocking off Sheikh Ali at Ashraf. However, the Zands simply bypassed Ashraf and thrust straight towards Astrabad. The Qajars then followed the Zands, resulting in a battle at Kalabad. The Qajars lost that battle forcing Mohammad Hassan Khan to flee into Astrabad. Before emerging from the city to fight Sheikh Ali, Mohammad Hassan Khan massacred many of his potential rivals in the city. Mohammad Hassan Khan finally emerged from the city to fight the Zands on February 14, 1759.[90] The battle ended in a complete rout for Mohammad Hassan Khan who was decapitated in the early stages of the battle.[91] The Zands not only obtained huge plunder from Astrabad, they also captured Shah Ismail III, an especially valuable prize for Karim Khan who at last could convincingly claim that he was the viceroy.

Karim Khan secures Azarbaijan

Azarbaijan was a key area for the control of Iran, so Karim Khan began to militarily invest in securing this crucial province. The key figure in Azarbaijan since 1749 had been Fathali Khan Afshar.[92] Karim Khan set out on an armed reconnaissance mission into Azarbaijan by the spring of 1760.[93] Maragha was secured by the Zands for the time being. However, the capture of Tabriz proved impossible as the city was too well defended by Fathali Khan and the Zands did not have suitable siege equipment. Karim Khan then returned to Tehran before summer, planning to return to Azarbaijan in the following spring. He would not return to that province until the summer of 1762. One reason for the delay may have been Karim Khan's desire to consolidate his political and military position before embarking on the crucial mission of securing Azarbaijan.

In spite of his resounding defeats in 1757, Azad Khan did not become idle. He fled to Baghdad for sanctuary and plotted to retake Azarbaijan from 1758. The Ottoman Suleiman Pasha of Baghdad was supportive of Azad Khan's ambitions as was Georgia's King Heraclius, the latter evidently concerned at the rising power of Karim Khan Zand.[94]

If Azad Khan was hoping to gain the support of his former allies when he entered Azarbaijan, he was sorely disappointed. He was shunned by Shahbaz Khan of the Dombuli Kurds as well as Fathali Khan Afshar (now pledged to Karim Khan), who defeated his advance guard.[95] Fathali then completely destroyed Azad Khan at Maragha in the summer of 1760.[96]

Azad Khan managed to evade capture and fled into Iranian Kurdistan but failed to rally Kurdish support for his failing cause.[97] He then went to Kirkuk in Iraqi (Ottoman) Kurdistan, but his appeals for aid from Suleiman Pasha in Baghdad went unheeded as well.[98] With his prospects virtually hopeless, Azad Khan fled to the Caucasus, going first to Ganja, then Yerevan and finally to Georgia where he obtained sanctuary in the court of King Heraclius in Tbilisi.[99]

Fathali Khan had his own ambitions and was no longer willing to cater to the authority of Karim Khan, forcing the latter to march directly from Tehran into Azarbaijan in 1762. As Karim Khan came close to Qara Chaman (about 80 miles (130km) southeast of Tabriz) in the summer of 1762, he halted and made preparations for battle with Fathali Khan.[100] The battle that ensued was characterized by the heavy use of firepower (especially cannon), hand-to-hand combat, and cavalry duels.[101] Karim Khan prevailed and Fathali's army rapidly disintegrated, his warriors escaping in groups towards the mountains and villages. The Zands hunted down many of their fleeing enemies with muskets, swords, and spears.[102] Shahbaz Khan of the Dumbuli Kurds was captured but Fathali Khan managed to escape and fight another day.[103]

Karim Khan entered Tabriz, but the battle to secure Azarbaijan was far from over as Fathali Khan was still at large. After his defeat at Qara Chaman, Fathali Khan briefly fled into Ottoman territory before returning to Urumiah. Just weeks after Qara Chaman, Karim Khan arrived with a powerful army to place Urumiah under siege.[104]

Fathali Khan and his supporters in Urumiah were hoping that the siege would drag on through the cold Azarbaijani winter. Karim Khan, however, prepared for this and ordered temporary barracks built to provide shelter for his troops against the piercing cold. The Zand army survived the winter, but Urumiah was now desperate. With the city reduced to starvation and with crucial supplies running dangerously low, Fathali Khan was forced to surrender to the Zands in February 1763, thereby ending the seven-month siege.[105]

CHAPTER 15

CONSOLIDATION IN THE INTERIOR AND WESTERN IRAN (1754–79)

Battles in Kerman, Yazd, and against the Lars

Karim Khan's victory over Azad Khan and the Qajars certainly helped secure Iran's northern and northwestern flanks but the Zands also needed to exert their authority over western Iran (especially the Lur tribes), Khuzistan, and the interior (Kerman and Yazd). By the late 1750s, Kerman and Yazd had become practically independent of the central government because of the continuous battles between Qajars, Azad Khan Afghan, and the Zands. As Karim Khan finished his campaigns in the north he proceeded into the interior, the west and Khuzistan, but posed no claims to Shahrokh Khan's Khorasan.

Ever since the Afghan invasions, and even during Nader Shah's reign, Nasser Khan of the Lars had set up his own fiefdom in the province of Lar, regions close to Kerman (Saba), and even as far as the Persian Gulf. This area was dangerously close to Karim Khan's headquarters in Shiraz and simply could not be ignored. Nasser Khan had unsuccessfully attempted to capture Shiraz previously, and assisted the late Mohammad Hassan Khan in attacking Shiraz in 1758. Nasser Khan later successfully imposed himself upon Bandar Abbas, an Iranian port on the Persian Gulf vital for Iran's maritime commerce.

Karim Khan's first confrontation with Nasser Khan occurred in 1755 when he managed to get to within sight of Lur city, which resisted the Zand forces. A truce ensued, but relations remained volatile. The governor of Kerman was also at odds with Nasser Khan. During Karim Khan's battles in Azarbaijan in 1758 a Zand regiment successfully battled against Nasser Khan, but made no attempt to take the fortress at Lar. The final blow came eight years later in 1766 when a Zand army arrived to subdue the fortress at Lar and capture Nasser Khan.[1] The Iranian plateau was now secure for Karim Khan to effectively implement his rule.

Kerman had fallen to Shahrokh Khan after 1747. Shahrokh Khan, however, paid no taxes to the Afsharids in Mashad; his homage was practically nominal. He soon expanded his authority over Abarquh and Yazd, but came into conflict against Momen Khan Bafqi, the previous governor of Kerman, forcing him to seek the military assistance of Nasser Khan of the Lars in 1754. Nasser Khan seemingly obliged by dispatching a force of 8,000 to assist him.[2] Instead of assisting Shahrokh Khan, however, Nasser Khan had his "ally" tied up as soon as he met him. Nasser Khan then demanded a ransom from Kerman, which refused the demand. Nasser Khan marched to Kerman, which repelled all attempts at capture. Shahrokh Khan soon escaped his captors. Seeing the futility of his Kerman adventure, Nasser Khan hastily withdrew.

Shahrokh Khan had difficulties holding onto Yazd, which fell to Taqi Khan Bafqi. By 1758, Karim Khan had had enough and dispatched Zaki Khan to bring Taqi Khan Bafqi to heel. This task was successfully accomplished and Taqi Khan Bafqi was dismissed from his post after being financially penalized by his creditors in the city. Yazd and Kerman soon slipped out of the grasp of the Zands once again. In 1760, the city once again fell to Shahrokh Khan. Karim Khan, by then in Tehran, sent Khoda Morad Khan Zand to secure the entirety of Kerman province once and for all. Fortunately for Khoda Morad Khan, Shahrokh Khan was soon killed in a local rebellion. This failed to translate into a welcome for Khoda Morad Khan whose entrance into Kerman was flatly refused. The standoff was apparently resolved after Khoda Morad Khan negotiated a treaty with the city's new leaders – one which was immediately overturned after Khoda Morad Khan entered the city by October 1760. Khoda Morad Khan's rule did not last long, as in the following March Taqi Khan Bafqi returned. He assembled a group of crack musketeers, scaled the walls of Kerman, and took over the city in a virtual coup d'état.[3] Khoda Morad Khan was killed during the insurrection. Taqi Khan Bafqi soon proved incapable of managing, let alone stabilizing, Kerman province which again fell victim to further disorder. Karim Khan dispatched three expeditions in 1762–65 to capture Kerman but failed against Taqi Khan Bafqi.[4]

The continued success of Taqi Khan Bafqi was a major challenge against the authority of Karim Khan, who by the summer of 1765 was permanently established in Shiraz. A fresh Zand army was dispatched by Ali Khan Shahsevan to take Kerman and put an end to Taqi Khan Bafqi's continued defiance. Ali Khan did well at first and soon drove his adversaries into Kerman city itself. The momentum of the offensive was shattered when one of Taqi Khan Bafqi's expert marksmen shot and killed Shahsevan. Once again the Zand army beat a hasty retreat back towards Shiraz. Undeterred, Karim Khan sent his forces to attack Kerman once again, this time led by Nazar-Ali Khan Zand. When Nazar-Ali Khan Zand reached the city, he engaged in a diplomatic offensive by treating deserters in a benevolent fashion. This may have encouraged others to also desert Taqi Khan Baqfi as the latter's rule had become increasingly unpopular. This time no amount of expert musketry and marksmanship could save Baqfi; the Zand noose around the city ensured that supplies and provisions ran low. By the spring of 1766, Taqi Khan was overthrown by Kerman's disaffected populace who handed their former master to the Zands. When Baqfi was finally brought to Shiraz as a prisoner, he was executed. Kerman's populace could now experience a level of peace and tranquility not seen for years.

More challenges by the Lurs and Khuzistan (1762–65)

Even as Karim was finally putting an end to the insubordination of Kerman, he was also challenged by his fellow Lur kinsmen. The Zands remained loyal to him during his reign with the exception of Zaki Khan, his half-brother and cousin. Zaki Khan may have been disappointed at the lack of appreciation for his role at Qara Chaman in 1762. After that battle, Zaki Khan and his men had left for Tehran and attacked Sheikh Ali's baggage train. Following this, Zaki Khan managed to gain the support of Mohammad Ali Khan Zand against Karim Khan. Zaki Khan and his allies now struck at Isfahan and Kashan, inflicting much hardship upon their respective civilian populations. Zaki Khan was virtually unchallenged while Karim Khan was committed in Azarbaijan. Karim Khan finally intervened in October 1763, nine months after the conclusion of his campaigns in Azarbaijan. Karim Khan assembled an army and deployed out of Ardabil, Azarbaijan, and straight towards Isfahan and Kashan. Zaki Khan and his allies fled to Khuzistan through the Bakhtiari mountain range, where they were joined by numbers of Faili Lurs.[5] His baggage train and a number of hostages had been captured by the advance guard units of Nazar-Ali Khan Zand.[6]

On arrival in Khuzistan, Zaki Khan requested assistance from the vali of Khuzistan, Molla Muttaleb, the sheikh of the Mushasha Shiite Arabs in the province. Muttaleb, who was facing a defiant governor in Dezful, used Zaki Khan's forces to march towards the city in order to gain its submission. The vali was to soon regret his association with Zaki Khan and his dispatch to Dezful. When Zaki Khan approached Dezful he received armed warriors of the Al-Kathir Arab tribe, enemies of Muttaleb, into his forces. Soon Zaki Khan was turned against the vali, resulting in the formation of a three-way entente against Muttaleb: Zaki Khan, the Al-Kathir, and the governor of Dezful.

Mohammad Ali Khan abducted Muttaleb and slaughtered his entire family. The vali was a prisoner of Zaki Khan, and was anxious not be transferred to his sworn enemies, the Al-Kathir. To avoid this, Muttaleb paid Zaki Khan a heavy ransom. Zaki Khan handed Muttaleb over to the Al-Kathir anyway, who predictably executed him. The Al-Kathir then abandoned Zaki Khan. This put Zaki Khan and his forces in a dangerous position as he had betrayed the man who had originally given him sanctuary. With his Khuzistan adventure in tatters, Zaki Khan fled back into the Bakhtiari mountains for sanctuary. Unfortunately, he ran straight into the forces of Nazar-Ali Khan Zand in the early part of 1764.[7] With no options left, Zaki Khan declared his full submission to Karim Khan. The vakil did not seek retribution from the humbled rebel, instead granting him a pardon.

The Bakhtiaris continued to be restless and defiant of the central authorities, even after the defeat of their leader, Ali Mardan Khan. In early 1764, Karim Khan sent an army to Zardeh Kuh to impose his authority. The campaign resulted in the deportation of the Haft-Lang-e Bakhtiari Lurs to the Qom-Varamin region where they were resettled. The Chahar-Lang Bakhtiaris were resettled in Fasa in Fars province. The Zands also recruited 3,000 Bakhtiari warriors into their armies.[8]

The Faili Lurs (to the north of the Bakhtiaris) proved a greater challenge for the Zands. Zaki Khan had recently stirred the Failis in revolt against Karim Khan and they had yet to retract their defiance against the vakil. By early 1765 Karim Khan's armies had successfully entered Khorramabad. Ismail Khan, the leader of the Faili rebellion, fled into Ottoman Iraq. Karim Khan then placed Ismail Khan's brother as leader of the Faili Lurs. Karim Khan then thrust into northern Khuzistan. The initial guard of the Zand army, led by Nazar-Ali Khan Zand, chased the Balu Lam Arab tribe that had assisted Ismail Khan. Following this, a section of the Al-Kathir tribes was attacked. By March 1765, the Zand armies were in control of Dezful and Shushtar. The challenges in Khuzistan and the Persian Gulf, however, were far from over and would require further attention during Karim Khan's reign.

Approximately two months after celebrating Nowruz in Khuzistan (March 21, 1765), Karim Khan and the Zand army marched back to Shiraz. By August 1757, Karim Khan had pacified much of Behbehan and Kuhguliye mountains.[9] When he was in Azarbaijan three years later in 1760, rebellion again broke out in the Kuhguliye region, but the area was pacified by that May.

The government of Karim Khan Zand

Karim Khan entered Shiraz for the final time on July 21, 1765, making it his capital and remaining there until his passing in 1779. Karim Khan had technically become the *Vakil ol Dowleh* of the Shah as early as 1751 when he ejected Ali Mardan Khan from Isfahan. However, it was not until the mid-1760s that Karim Khan was able to completely focus on the business of government and giving the Iranian populace a period of relative peace.[10]

Karim Khan is well known in modern Iranian history as the leader who did not assume the title of "Shah." One factor of course was the lingering halo of the Safavid dynasty and the importance of having at least a symbolic allegiance to the Safavids is clearly demonstrated in the display of Ismail III as a rallying banner, especially in the earlier battles that Karim Khan fought to expand his power base. In practice, Shah Ismail III was placed in the Abadeh fortress where he lived out his days, receiving a regular stipend, provisions, and an annual Nowruz present from the Vakil.

When Karim Khan settled in Shiraz, he changed his title from *Vakil ol Dowleh* to *Vakil ol Raeeyat* (lit. viceroy of the people). Even when Ismail died in 1773, Karim Khan refused to adopt the title of Shah. This was a radical departure for the Iranian state in which the system of government had been based upon the charisma of the Shah and the strong Shia clergy or Ulema.

For three decades, from the early 1720s to the early 1740s, Iran's civilians had suffered horrendously at the hands of invaders, brigands, and pretenders to power. The economy was also adversely affected as a result of the constant wars of Nader Shah. Agriculture too had suffered heavily, especially since the Afghan invasions. The end result was a state of famine, depopulation, and severe economic decline. Care was taken to apply taxes justly, food and supplies were equitably distributed to the populace, with the Vakil taking a personal interest in addressing the concerns of the people.[11] Karim Khan also worked hard to encourage Jewish and Armenian financiers to settle in Iran's cities. Armenians were provided with several villages to resettle around the cities of Isfahan and Shiraz; Shiraz also became the largest center of the Jews in Iran.[12] The quest to build a stronger economy led Karim Khan to invite European and Indian firms to engage in commerce on Iranian soil.[13]

Unlike Nader Shah, Karim Khan did not implement the forced resettlement of rebellious tribal groups. Many of the west Iranic tribes forcibly resettled to Khorasan during Nader Shah's time were allowed to return to their homelands. In general, the vakil would often accept the nomination of chiefs without incident, as long as these did not challenge the authority of the state. The urban areas within tribal territories (e.g. Dezful, Astrabad, Shushtar), were generally administered by a government-appointed tribal leader.

Eliminating the Afghans: the Cyaxares way

The Afghans had threatened Iranian security since their violent eruption into Iran in the 1720s. Once Karim Khan was firmly established in government, he acquiesced to the violent liquidation of the remaining Afghan contingents still in Iranian territory and in the Iranian armies as these were now viewed as a security risk.[14] The reasons for this were related to the tendency of Afghan contingents to revolt and harass the general population in Iran whenever political and military situations availed themselves. This had occurred after the passing of Nader Shah, and under Azad Khan Afghan whose actions in northern Iran and Azarbaijan were still fresh in the minds of the local population.

Karim Khan instituted a very systematic program to eliminate the Afghans.[15] Examples include his invitation of 9,000 high-ranking Afghan officers in Iran for a Nowruz celebration in Tehran; these were then attacked and killed with swords. This event is remarkably similar to the banquet held by the Median king Cyaxares (625–585 BC) in 625, during which he had Scythian nobleman systematically slain.[16] Governors in other regions in Iran also began to liquidate the Afghans in their midst. Zaki Khan engaged in the killing of all Afghan soldiers in the Astrabad region during the Nowruz festivals; reputedly only 200 of their cavalry escaped across the Gorgan River to seek refuge among the Turkmen.[17] Following these events all of the property belonging to the Afghans in Iran was seized by the state and the Afghans ceased to be a threat to the internal security of Iran.[18]

Seeds of the Zand demise: Qajars in northern Iran

Despite vigorous campaigning, Zand authority in northern Iran and Azerbaijan was anything but absolute. The area remained a *de facto* center of the Qajars, despite the defeat of Mohammad Hassan Khan in 1759. When the latter died, most of his nine sons sought refuge in Dasht-e Qipchaq amongst the local Turkmen. From there the Qajars often raided into northern areas through the northeast. During one of these raids, the eldest son, Agha Mohammad Khan Qajar, was captured and sent to Shiraz in 1759 as a hostage. Agha Mohammad Khan's other brothers were variously sent to Qazvin and Shiraz with a further two permitted to remain in Astarabad.[19] While Karim Khan's benevolence towards his defeated foes, notably Agha Mohammad Khan, was certainly remarkable, such policies were fraught with risk. The Qajars were intact and biding their time.

The late Mohammad Hassan Khan's second son, Hussein Qoli, was placed as the governor of Damghan in February 1769. Karim Khan's decision to appoint Hussein Qoli may have been swayed by Agha Mohammad Khan's suggestion that such an appointment would be the best means of ensuring the north's compliance to Shiraz.[20] Hussein Qoli very quickly demonstrated that he was anything but a compliant governor. For eight years after his appointment by Karim Khan, Hussein Qoli built up a powerful base among his Ashaqa-Bash Qajar kinsmen and their respective allies. This was a major challenge against the rival Yukhari-Bash branch of the Qajars, who were supported by the Zands in Shiraz. Hussein Qoli was cunning and intelligent enough to present his actions as an "internecine" conflict rather than a direct challenge to the Zands. Karim Khan's initial reactions towards Hussein Qoli's actions were relatively restrained: three expeditions were sent from Shiraz to restore those Yukhari-Bash leaders displaced by Hussein Qoli. None of these expeditions were aimed at ejecting Hussein Qoli from power; instead Karim Khan was satisfied with receiving "apologies and contrite promises from the young Qajar."[21]

Hussein Qoli's actions finally attracted the military attentions of Zaki Khan. The Qajars were certainly recognized as a force to be reckoned with by the local khans in Mazandaran. Hedayatollah Khan of Gilan (west of nearby Mazandaran province) had been confirmed as the legal governor there by Karim Khan as early as 1763. Nevertheless Hedayatollah Khan's fears of a Qajar revival in the north had led him to seek Russian assistance against the Qajars in 1773.[22] It is interesting that Hedayatollah Khan was more inclined to seek Russian help and that of other local khans than that of Karim Khan. This would suggest that the Gilani leader was not confident in the military supremacy of the vakil at this time.

The catalyst for Zaki Khan's arrival was the obliteration of the Nanmaka castle by Hussein Qoli.[23] Zaki Khan arrived with a force of Lur-Kurd cavalry, and Hussein Qoli retreated to seek refuge among Turkmen allies further to the northeast. He then returned to slay Hassan Khan, who had recently been governor of Astrabad.[24] The governor of Mazandaran, Mohammad Khan Savadkuh, panicked and launched an attack against Astrabad; he also appealed to the Zands for military assistance. Hussein Qoli countered by thrusting past him to capture Sari, Savadkuhi's capital. Savadkuhi was forced into battle, defeated, and killed. Savadkuhi's son, Mehdi Khan, escaped to Shiraz and returned north with Zand forces, but he too was defeated.[25]

The Zands decided to restore their authority once and for all in 1776, and Zaki Khan again entered Mazandaran in force. Zaki Khan then engaged in a brutal campaign against Hussein Qoli's allies, striking at the base of Hussein Qoli's power base. Hussein Qoli made an unsuccessful attempt to capture Astrabad, then went on the run and was soon killed by Turkmen raiders. While order had been seemingly restored, Zaki Khan's brutal measures in the north would not be soon forgotten and the Qajars would rise again.[26]

CHAPTER 16

THE IRANIAN ARMY IN THE ZAND ERA (1747-94)

Zand military organization and leadership

Karim Khan entrusted much of the command of the army to his Lur kinsmen, although the overall command structure remained as it had under the Safavids and Nader Shah.[1] The *Ghoorchi-Bashi*, for example, was still the minister of war, partaking in all important military ceremonies attended by the vakil.

During the "civil war" years, Karim Khan led the Zand armies in person. However, once he had assumed the title of *Vakil ol Raeeyat*, Karim Khan no longer took full command of his armies in the field. Instead he would dispatch another commander, such as his cousin Zaki Khan at Bandar Rig (1768–69), or his brother Sadegh Khan at Basra (1775).[2]

One of the most significant changes to the Iranian army was the reduction in size of the professional army. The vakil ensured that such units received a regular salary, however this did not place an undue burden on other sectors of the economy. The usage of Turkic terminology and systems of organization continued well into the Zand era. It is probable that Karim Khan would have been able to assemble up to a maximum of 200,000 troops (infantry and cavalry).[3] Such numbers, however, were never actually called up in any foreign war or domestic disputes. In the battle for Basra in 1775, the total number of Iranian troops is reported at a maximum of 60,000 troops.[4] The normal complement of the professional army at peacetime stood at around 45,000 men, overwhelmingly of Lur stock: Lurs from western Iran (24,000), Bakhtiari-Lurs (3,000), and other Lur clans (4,000).[5] The non-Lur recruits hailed from Iraq Ajam (12,000), and Fars (6,000).[6] Karim Khan's successors are reported as being able to raise anywhere from 7,000 to 70,000 troops given the resources available to them.[7]

The recruitment of non-regular support troops continued as under the Safavids, summoning khans and leaders from tribes and townships to either assemble at a location, or join the Zands on the move. Nader's system of state sponsorship of weapons and equipment was no longer in place as such tasks were now the responsibility of the recruits and their leaders from the various locales.[8]

Infantry

Since Medo-Achaemenid times, Iranian infantry had traditionally recruited from the Persian peasants of the interior, Kurds of the highlands, or northerners. These were a force to be contended with when they were well trained, armed and led. Iran's best firearms infantry (muskets and Jazayer) at the time of the Zands were Persians from Fars province as well as Garmsir.[9] The Tofangchis were still armed with flint-lock muskets. The Jazayerchis, as before, were led by their respective Jazayerchi-Bashis.

Like the traditional Piyadegan, the Tofangchis were adept at using traditional weapons. Despite being of a "lower" status than the cavalry, positive accounts of their military attributes have been provided. The French traveler and historian Comte de Ferrières-Sauveboeuf, who travelled in Iran in 1782–89, noted that "the [Iranian] infantry has no fear of fatigue, and their simple needs eases the army's provision of supplies for them. A piece of bread, cheese, a little rice, a few dried fruits and some meat is their meal which is transported by mule … at no time at the barracks will one find unnecessary baggage."[10] The Iranian infantry, despite the overall decline in discipline and training in comparison to Nader Shah's time, remained a formidable force on the battlefield.[11]

The Zand savaran

The savaran (cavalry) arm of the Iranian army was the most professional and effective on the battlefield. The Comte de Ferrières-Sauveboeuf noted that "the cavalry of the Persian army are of a very high quality … their horses are capable of climbing high mountains … they do not fear the cold and are capable of traversing long and difficult distances irrespective of rain or snow."[12] This observation is consistent with the fact that the Lurs, the backbone of the Zand army, were mainly cavalrymen, as their Mede and Scythian ancestors had been.[13] The role of the Zand cavalry came to resemble the cavalry in the Partho-Sassanian armies, which often determined the course of the battle.[14] In general, there were three groups of cavalry: *Savaran e Hameeshegi, Savaran e Movaghat,* and *Gard e Saltanati*, as well a number of other mounted units.

The Savaran e Hameeshegi (lit. permanent savaran) were mainly composed of Lurs of the Zand clan. Their firearms were reminiscent of the Nader Shah era and included matchlock and flintlock muskets, and pistols tucked into their belts. Pouches for bullets/ammunition were strapped to the left upper arm, and a sack of gunpowder was strapped to the left side of the belt.[15] The Zand Lur cavalry took great pride in their ability to utilize traditional weapons in battle: Karim Khan himself was well known for his martial skills in sword and spear combat. The Savaran e Hameeshegi were permanently stationed in the capital Shiraz and other key cities such as Tabriz and would immediately deploy to threatened frontiers and battle areas in times of crisis.[16]

The Savaran e Movaghat (lit. temporary savaran) were, like the infantry, recruited from townships and tribal locales at times of war. These acted as a strategic reserve cavalry force supporting the Savaran e Hameeshegi in campaigns. After the conclusion of battles they would disband and return to their homes, apart from a number of the tribal cavalry units which were in fact on constant "standby," often supporting the Gard e Saltanati in garrison duties or the suppression of anti-Zand revolts.[17]

An important elite unit was the Gard e Saltanati (or royal guards), also known as the *Gholam Chakhmaghi*. Their role was the protection of the vakil as well as the senior Zand commanders, and they guarded key positions such as the Arg e Karim Khan.[18] At the core of these royal guards were 1,400 cavalry equipped exclusively with flintlock muskets and high-quality swords.[19] Other units considered elite were the *Yesval* (1,000 troops) who became the vakil's personal guard based in

Shiraz, *Nasghchi* (1,000 troops) responsible for the implementation of laws (similar to bailiffs or court officers), *Faraash* (1,000 troops), *Shater* (300 troops), and *Jarchi* (700 troops).[20]

The Charkhchian were still responsible for the advance guards of the army, but during the Zand era they were also entrusted with two additional tasks: evaluating the geographic characteristics of regions where the army was intending to deploy; and drafting contingency plans against enemy forces and sharing these with the military leadership.[21]

Artillery and firearms

The heavier firearms of the Zand army were reminiscent of the Nader Shah era: cannon, mortars, and zanbouraks. As before, members of the artillery corps were known as the Toopchis with their leaders being the Toopchi-Bashis. The Toopchi-Bashi was often appointed to the post by the vakil and was also referred to as the *Maseer-Atashi* (or director of fire). Members of the zanbourak corps were, as previously, known as zanbouranchis, and led by their respective Zanbourak-Bashis.

The late Nader Shah's emphasis on speed and mobility as well as the lack of suitable roads across difficult terrain and mountainous passes resulted in the primary reliance on the zanbouraks, which often meant that heavier cannon could not accompany the Iranian army in its campaigns. This, however, was not always the case, as evidenced in the case of the battles at Bandar Rig. All in all, by the Zand era, the artillery corps displayed a number of serious shortcomings and did not play a significant role in the Iranian army at the time.[22]

Kermanshah was Iran's major arsenal and fortress facing the vital Ottoman-Mesopotamian theater to the west and its production capabilities were undiminished from Nader Shah's time. But the fortress, production facilities, and ammunition dumps never recovered from the damage they received during Karim Khan's campaign against Kermanshah's Kurdish Kalhor and Zangeneh clans. This was a major blow to the military production capacity of the country as Iran lost a chief weapon production center which would never be adequately replaced.

One of Karim Khan's first edicts when he assumed power in July 1765 was to order the construction of new cannon and mortars; he would later request European assistance in this regard. The camel-mounted zanbourak light cannon and their ordinance had continued to be produced in Iran after Nader Shah's death, but there were serious problems with the heavier calibers of artillery.

Muskets known as the *Tofang e Do Shakh* (gun/musket with two horns) were popular with the Zand tofangchis. These rested on two pods when being fired. Such weapons were mainly manufactured in Shiraz, Kerman, and Lar with the latter two also producing gunpowder. It is not clear whether Iran was able to produce firearms in the same capacity and quality as in Nader Shah's time, when state sponsorship in the domain was regulated, but the loss of Kermanshah's facilities certainly did not help the qualitative and quantitative state of musket production.

Fortresses

Shiraz witnessed much rebuilding during the reign of Karim Khan. Reconstruction was mainly motivated by political and military reasons as the city had undergone multiple sieges during the violent contest for power.[23] The vakil engaged in a major effort to build up the city's battered walls.

William Franklin, who visited Shiraz in 1789, noted: "The fortress of Shiraz is … 25ft [7.5m] in height and 10ft [3m] thick and has eighty towers … around the city is a ditch 60ft [18m] deep and 20ft [6m] wide."[24] The reconstruction project was characterized by the demolition of older structures, reduction of the number of city gates from 12 to six, the amalgamation of a number of quarters, and the construction of 80 round towers along the wall.[25] The Arg-e Karim Khan (citadel of Karim Khan) stands intact today. It was probably built in 1766–67 and became the vakil's living quarters, and later those of the Qajar governors of the city. The Arg had four 40ft (12m)-high walls which were connected by four towers each 46ft (14m) tall, with the entire compound being 13,800ft² (12,800 square metres).[26]

The latent military danger

Few would argue that Karim Khan's focus on implementing just government and humane policies was truly remarkable. On the other hand, Karim Khan failed to adequately address Iran's alarming reduction of military potential, both in quantitative and especially in qualitative terms as well as the centrifugal or regionalist forces (e.g. the Caucasus and especially Georgia) building along the peripheries of the country. Karim Khan was almost the reverse of Nader Shah: the latter put military affairs first at the expense of the populace, while Karim put civil affairs ahead of the military.

While Karim Khan did re-establish a coherent central authority, continual internal conflict in Iran weakened Iran's overall military potential and political strength with respect to its surrounding neighbors. The military reforms that Nader Shah had put in place had not been improved upon and the nucleus of Iran's navy had weakened to such an extent that it led to the overall weakening of Iran's position in the Persian Gulf region and southern coastline. While Karim Khan did show an interest in Iran's military, the dangers of Iran's military disparity against the Europeans do not seem to have preoccupied the Zand leadership. This was mainly because there had been no serious clash of arms with the Europeans that would have demonstrated Iran's growing military weaknesses. Secondly, Iran had to focus on severe domestic economic and political issues before any serious attention could be afforded to military matters. The Iranian army would develop a number of serious weaknesses by the end of the Zand era.[27]

Nader Shah's system of promotion had allowed for the rise of a professional cadre of officers, but this corps dispersed after his death. Lack of state sponsorship for a professional officer corps meant that the rigorous daily training regimen for infantry, cavalry, and artillery of Nader's time fell by the wayside. As a result, the strict discipline and professionalism of battle formations and maneuvers seen during Nader Shah's era was steadily eroded. The military efficiency and training regimens of a unit now depended on the personal knowledge and initiative of its commander. There was no longer a system of standardized military training, or military exercises to ensure flexible coordination between the various arms of the military. The issue was not simply a "Zand problem"; the dispersal of Nader Shah's officers and the loss of the training regimens was a major blow which affected all of Iran's armed elements across the country. For instance, Mohammad Taqi Saravi, a historian of the early Qajar era, has noted the antiquated methods of troop deployment in the battle between Mohammad Hassan Khan and Azad Khan Afghan.[28]

European reports of Zand Iranian cannon were consistently negative. Carsten Niebuhr's description of the Zand artillery concluded: "unfortunately Iranian artillerymen are not familiar with the use of such weapons. One example is the case of the deployment of one of these cannon by Amir Guna Khan at Bandar Rig where lack of familiarity of the use of such cannon resulted in the death of fifty of Guna Khan's Bashis instead of inflicting casualties upon the enemy."[29] The aforementioned Comte de Ferrières-Sauveboeuf observed that "… the Persians do not understand the means to deploy cannon … cannon in their army is more for prestige and decoration rather than a powerful weapon of war…"[30]

These reports lead to the overall conclusion that even though Iranian factories were able to produce fine pieces of cannon, quality in their production was inconsistent. Iranian cannon are described as being "built very badly," with parts of their firing mechanism shattering when jolted on uneven ground or on impact with other heavy objects. Even more alarming were reports that Iranian cannon would actually shatter after firing just a few rounds in battle. However, the accuracy of these reports is now being seriously challenged, especially after recent examinations of late 18th- or early 19th-century artillery presently housed in the Military Museum of Iran.[31] Material and technical analyses of these samples, typical of those produced in the Zand and early Qajar eras, fail to verify the aforementioned negative reports.

Nader Shah had introduced a number of ingenious innovations that had led to dramatic battlefield successes for the Iranian army, but during the Zand era, military doctrines stagnated, particularly siegecraft. Zand siegecraft relied on completely cutting off all means of ingress and egress so that lack of supplies would eventually force the enemy to surrender, as heavy artillery was not available in large numbers. The Zands also emphasized the importance of maintaining vigilance at nightfall and took great pains to keep the siege areas lit by means of devices known as *Kasey-e Boshghabi* (bowl-plates).[32] These techniques were antiquated, and Comte de Ferrières-Sauveboeuf noted that "The siege work done by the Iranian army resembles very much an economic blockade rather than a true military siege."[33] A key liability was that the Iranians had not developed doctrines, like the Ottomans and the Europeans, for maximizing their use of cannon during sieges.

The inability or unwillingness of the Zands to maintain Nader Shah's reforms and address other problems resulted in an alarming decline of the overall military performance of the Iranian army. These developments were particularly dangerous for Iran as European technological progress, growing economic prosperity, and social developments were having a dramatic overall impact upon European military efficiency. By the end of the century, Iranian military organization, doctrine, and weaponry would be dangerously outclassed by Iran's European counterparts.[34]

CHAPTER 17

BATTLES IN THE PERSIAN GULF AND BASRA (1753–79)

One of Nader's Shah's most significant military accomplishments had been the building of a new Iranian navy, but all developments for building up an Iranian navy came to halt during the reign of Karim Khan.[1] One exception was Sheikh Nasser Khan, of the Arab tribe Banu Mazkur, who managed to retain a small number of ships from the Nader Shah era in Iran's favor until his death in 1776, after which his son Sheikh Nasr continued to command the diminutive Iranian "fleet" and supported the Zands against the Ottomans at Basra.[2] The British and the French provided Iran with naval assistance in combat on at least two occasions during the Zand era, but these operations did little to address Iran's serious weaknesses in asserting her authority throughout her southern coastline and island possessions in the Persian Gulf.

This posed problems in policing Iran's southern coastlines and islands, and the protection of maritime commerce in the Persian Gulf. The neglect of the navy, however, was not confined to ships but also extended to port and military and commercial docks. Planning towards the expansion of such facilities was practically non-existent. These factors help explain why so much commerce simply shifted from Bandar Abbas to Ottoman-administered Basra during Karim Khan's reign.

Iran's lack of a navy in the Persian Gulf was to lead to profound geopolitical consequences as Iran faced challenges from the sheikh of Muscat and Arab tribes who were increasingly assertive in the Persian Gulf. Iran also witnessed European ships entering the Persian Gulf, especially those from Britain, Holland, and France.

Decline and anarchy at Bandar Abbas

Bandar Abbas had been Iran's major trading and commercial port for a number of centuries, but when Nader Shah shifted the capital to Mashad in Khorasan, the cities of Kerman and Isfahan, which were linked to Bandar Abbas' port trade, experienced economic decline (although their decline was also linked to the tumultuous years preceding Nader Shah's reign).

Both the Dutch and the British had had their companies based in Bandar Abbas, although this changed as the port's commercial importance steadily declined. It was also difficult to determine who exactly was in charge. The transition from Afsharid rule to Karim Khan had been anything but smooth in the area as the local governor, Molla Ali Shah, and an official by the name of Nasser Khan Lari, fought over the decrepit remnants of Nader Shah's fleet. The Jawasim of Arabia were engaged in these conflicts as well as piracy against commercial shipping. One of the consequences of the decline of Bandar Abbas was the rise in the commercial importance of the port city of Bushehr. By 1765, the British had transferred their East India company headquarters from Bandar Abbas to Bushehr.[3]

While Karim Khan established some semblance of order from the new capital at Shiraz, the situation along the Persian Gulf coastline and the islands remained in flux. At first, Karim Khan had to overcome the opposition of Sheikh Nasser who blocked access to Bushehr. Sheikh Nasser was of the Banu Ma'ain clan, one of the Arab tribes that had become increasingly prominent along Iran's Persian Gulf coastline. In 1753, the sheikh landed a small army at Bahrain with a modest fleet and occupied the archipelago.[4] He would be jailed by Karim Khan two years later, in 1755, and after his release would remain loyal to the Zands for the duration of the vakil's lifetime.

Challenges at Kharq Island and Bandar Rig in the Persian Gulf

The fall of Nader Shah and the disbanding of the nascent navy resulted in the weakening of government authority along Iran's southern coastline from the Arvand Rud/Shaat al-Arab to the Straits of Hormuz. This resulted in the rise of a series of mainly Huwala Arab sheikhs in regions such as the southern Iranian shores and islands such as Qeshm and Qais Hormuz in the Persian Gulf.[5] As they were based on Iranian soil, they were technically obliged to pay tribute to the Iranian central authorities. In practice, this was only done when Iranian authorities enforced the tribute with military might. When armies did arrive, the Arab rulers would simply flee to islands where the Zands could not follow, and return when circumstances improved.[6]

Historically, the income of the Arab rulers was derived from trading, pearl diving, and fishing; however, piracy soon became another favored source of revenue. Port settlements and ships were indiscriminately targeted by both Arabs and Iranians. There were also Arab raiders emanating from the southern Arabian shores of the Persian Gulf. Prominent among these were the Jawasim (or Qhawasim) of Julfar who by the early 1760s had penetrated the island of Qeshm and even landed on the environs of Bandar Abbas.

By the early 1750s, Bandar (port) Rig (roughly 50–53 miles (80–85km) northwest of Bushehr) was being dominated by Mir Nasir Vaghai. The latter's sway nominally extended to Kharq Island. Vaghai however acted independently of the Zands. Adding to this complex power contest was the increasingly assertive presence of the West. European powers had begun to challenge Iranian sovereignty over Kharq and even Bushehr along Iran's Persian Gulf coastline. The British East India Company had settled in Bushehr by 1765 and the Dutch settled on Kharq Island in 1759. Dutch influence in Kharq soon surpassed that of mere commercial enterprise. By 1753 the island had become a virtual fiefdom of Baron Kniphausen and the Dutch. The Ottoman governor of Basra arrested Kniphausen, put him through a trial, imposed a fine, and then had him expelled from Basra. Kniphausen duly returned with a small fleet of three ships from Batavia (modern Jakarta) in the Dutch East Indies (modern Indonesia). From Kharq, Kniphausen blockaded the Arvand Rud/Shaat al Arab waterway's egress into the Persian Gulf. This applied pressure on Basra, forcing its Ottoman authorities to adopt a very accommodating attitude towards Kniphausen.[7]

Kniphausen, however, was more interested in building roots on Kharq Island. The Dutch established a village and a fortress, and soon their presence had become much more than a trading post on Iranian territory. The thriving Dutch colony boasted former Dutch personnel from Bandar Abbas and soon Armenian merchants. The nominal "Iranian" authority in the locale had been practically replaced by the Dutch. The latter argued that Mir Nasir Vaghai had agreed to surrender the island to them, a claim disputed by Vaghai's son, Mir Muhanna, who asserted that the Dutch were in arrears in rent.[8] Citing his father's incapability of realizing the rent claim, Mir Muhanna murdered his father in 1755. In the same year, Mir Muhanna became the dominant ruler at Bandar Rig, militarily defeating the Dutch and destroying their facilities.[9]

Having witnessed the activities of Mir Muhanna, Karim Khan arrived with his forces in Bandar Rig and arrested him and his brother. The brothers were held in Shiraz for a year and released in 1756. Apparently, Karim Khan was confident that they would respect his authority. When the brothers returned to Bandar Rig, they found it already settled by the British. Mir Muhanna killed his brother and completely seized the area. In a repeat of earlier events, Karim Khan arrived at Bandar Rig in 1758 and arrested Mir Muhanna again, only to release him shortly thereafter.[10] Mir Muhanna again proved defiant, prompting Karim Khan to officially demand tribute in 1765. This was backed by an armed force that Karim Khan dispatched to Bandar Rig.[11] When government forces reached Bandar Rig, however, Mir Muhanna and his followers took advantage of the absence of an Iranian navy by sailing to the diminutive island of Kharqu which was adjacent to Kharq Island. While government authority had been finally established on Bandar Rig, Mir Muhanna was still at large. Karim Khan was also unable to enforce Iranian authority upon Kharq Island: Karim Khan had actually demanded tribute from the Dutch, who flatly refused.

Meanwhile, Bushehr, though an Iranian possession, felt the increasing presence of the British East India Company. Paris soon made a move to establish a presence in the Persian Gulf at British expense. A French naval squadron sailed into Bandar Abbas and severely bombarded British assets on October 15, 1759 and took many British prisoners.[12] This event, of course, did not go unnoticed in London. The British greatly valued their growing influence in India and realized the importance of building their commercial and military influence in Iran and the Persian Gulf, whose trade connected them to the Indian Ocean and the commerce of India. The Anglo-French rivalry in the Persian Gulf was simply another arena in the longstanding political and military contest for empire. Eager to damage the interests of their English rivals as much as possible, the French were to support Karim Khan by the late 1760s in his drive to secure Kharq Island. By the mid-1770s, the French were also lending their support to American colonists seeking independence from London in the American Revolutionary War (1775–83). While Britain was to lose her American colonies, she was to greatly compensate for this loss by dramatically increasing her political, economic, and military influence in India and the Persian Gulf by the nineteenth century.

The British, concerned with maintaining their influence in the Persian Gulf, came to Karim Khan for support. Karim Khan provided the British with generous trading rights in Iran.[13] In return, the British were to provide the Iranians with naval assets to help combat challengers such as Mir Muhanna at Kharqu who had by now become a serious liability.[14] For the first time since the time of Shah Abbas, nearly 150 years before, the British were again allying themselves to the Iranians in the Persian Gulf. Sheikh Nasser had one large ship and a number of smaller craft, and with the support of the British launched an operation against Mir Muhanna.[15] The Anglo-Iranian forces were defeated in several battles and the British suffered heavy casualties.[16] More ominous was the inability of the flotilla to prevent Mir Muhanna from launching pirate raids from

Kharqu against commercial shipping. Seeking to protect their maritime interests, the Dutch soon launched a military expedition against Mir Muhanna. The Dutch were defeated, and Mir Muhanna's forces then invaded Kharq and captured its fortress on January 1, 1766.[17] The Dutch commander Van Houting and his entire staff were captured, placed on boats, and dispatched to the Dutch East Indies.[18]

The loss of Kharq was a blow to Dutch prestige, while the British had also been humiliated by Mir Muhanna. They launched yet another unsuccessful attack against Mir Muhanna in 1768[19] who retaliated by seizing a British merchant ship.[20] The immediate consequences for Iran's authority were even more dangerous. Mir Muhanna had captured the most powerful island fort in the Persian Gulf; the island of Bahrain was now under the domination of the Vaghai sheikh; and Karim Khan had simply withdrawn his army from Bandar Rig, practically yielding this locale to Mir Muhanna. When Karim Khan later sent his cousin Zaki Khan to repossess Bandar Rig, the Iranian army was defeated. This force would remain intact, however, and was to eventually retake Bandar Rig.

The French had been observing, undoubtedly with some degree of satisfaction, the trials and tribulations of their British rivals in the Persian Gulf. In 1768, a French delegation arrived to meet Karim Khan in Shiraz. Predictably, they requested commercial rights, especially on Kharq. Karim Khan met these demands on the condition that the French provide military and naval assistance against Mir Muhanna, and also deliver wool for the uniforms of Iranian troops.[21] Thanks to this support, the Zands were now able to prepare for the showdown against Bandar Rig and prepare to land at Kharq.[22] Kharqu was successfully blockaded thanks in large part to the fleet of Sheikh Nasser of Bushehr. Zaki Khan's forces, who had been at large around Bandar Rig, finally achieved success. A key military obstacle was the fortress of Khormoj which featured powerful walls and an effective ditch. The Iranian army operating in that locale consisted of mainly cavalry (5,000 cavalrymen versus just 2,000 infantry), all well supplied with firearms.[23] Georgian and Armenian officers were prominent in this campaign as well.[24] Resistance broke down by early 1769 when revolt among Mir Muhanna's own troops forced him to flee Kharqu. He eventually reached Basra but was executed by the local governor of the city on March 21, 1769.[25] The destruction of Mir Muhanna and his forces meant that Bandar Rig, Kharqu, and Kharq had been restored to Iran. In the end, Karim Khan did not engage in bloody reprisals against the Vaghai Arabs. Instead he allotted the late Mir Muhanna's properties to the former rebels.[26] In another magnanimous gesture, he appointed a Vaghai leader, Hassan Sultan, as the governor of Bandar Rig.[27]

Khuzistan: advent of the Banu Ka'ab

One of the most dangerous tribes to rise and threaten both the Ottoman and Iranian realms was the Banu Ka'ab. Their origins can be traced to 16th-century southern Iraq, from where they initially expanded towards the Khowr Moussa, and later to Dowraqh. Although the Banu Ka'ab had penetrated into Iran's southwest Khuzistan, they were not much of a threat during the reign of Nader Shah. This changed with the latter's death. Sheikh Salman now established Dowraqh as his capital city, and after rebuilding it, renamed it Fallahiya. This development was followed by the expansion of the Banu Ka'ab's authority along the Arvand Rud/Shaat al Arab waterway as well as territories adjacent to its western (Ottoman) and eastern (Iranian) banks. Known as a "triangular empire," which lasted for about three decades, this was roughly 125 miles (200km) along each side.[28] By 1760, the Banu Ka'ab had built a formidable navy which even surpassed that of the pasha of Basra. The Banu Ka'ab were able to freely raid shipping along the Arvand Rud/Shaat al Arab waterway and even land troops that raided trading routes along the Iranian and Ottoman sides of the waterway. Whenever the Ottomans or the Iranians sent retaliatory expeditions against the raiding Banu Ka'ab forces, the latter would prove frustratingly elusive and seemingly melt into the foliage of the marshes. Soon, the Banu Ka'ab became so wealthy that at times they were able to pay off the local Ottoman and Iranian forces to cease operations against them.

The operations of the Banu Ka'ab obliged Karim Khan to shift his attention towards Iran's southwest. The first strike came in 1758 and achieved some limited successes however it was in 1765 that the major operations took place. The British, the Ottomans, and the Iranians effectively coordinated their military actions which resulted in the submission of the Banu Ka'ab sheikh to Karim Khan.[29]

Zaki Khan's bungled operations at Hormuz

Iranian authority in Oman had been steadily declining since Nader Shah's passing. Karim Khan emulated the system of tribute that had been imposed on Oman at the height of Afsharid power. The vakil also demanded that the Omanis return one of the Afsharid warships: the *Rahmani*. The ship had been purchased by the Omanis from the Banu Ma'in Arab tribe, a sale that had not been approved by Karim Khan.

The Imam of Oman categorically rejected Karim Khan's demands, resulting in war. However, Iranian naval and military power were not what they had been. Pirate raids against commercial shipping were to endure for almost the entirety of the Zand dynasty. The most sustained effort was launched in 1773 when Zaki Khan led a flotilla to land an Iranian army on the coasts of Oman, made possible by renewed Iranian authority in Bandar Abbas. Sheikh Abdullah, the leader of the Banu Ma'in tribe, pledged to assist Zaki Khan, offering the hand of his daughter in marriage, and convincing Zaki Khan to go to Hormuz. It was a trap: Zaki Khan was captured and made prisoner. Karim Khan was then obliged to engage in a prisoner swap: Zaki Khan was exchanged for Sheikh Abdullah's son, who had been a hostage in the Zand court at Shiraz.[30]

The end result was that Oman was spared an Iranian invasion and events signaled that Iran was no longer able to assert itself in Oman as previously. This would have serious negative consequences for Iranian economic and political interests in the Persian Gulf. Just as Zaki Khan failed against Oman, the western regions of the Gulf had become a thriving hub of trade backed by a strong navy. Imam Ahmad bin Sa'id of Oman had by the middle of the 18th century built up a powerful navy as well as a strong commercial maritime fleet which ferried goods between India, East Africa, the Red Sea, and the Persian Gulf.[31] By the late 18th and early 19th centuries, Oman had become a major force not only in the Persian Gulf but even in the western regions of the Indian Ocean.[32] By the early 1820s, Oman had built up the most powerful maritime and combat fleet in the Persian Gulf (second only to the British) and captured Bandar Abbas, Qeshm, and Hormuz.[33]

Relations deteriorate with the Ottomans

While most of Karim Khan's efforts were focused on stabilizing his authority within Iran's territorial boundaries and in the Persian Gulf, he did embark on a major war against the Ottoman Empire. Militarily, Karim Khan's upcoming offensives against the Ottomans would be well-timed as the enemy was unprepared to engage in a major war.[34]

The commercial importance of Iran's ports along its southern coastline on the Persian Gulf had been gradually declining. Piracy and raids by Arab tribes on Iran's Persian Gulf coast and islands, and the efforts required to contain and eliminate these were disruptive to Iranian maritime trade. Thus, more and more lucrative Persian Gulf trade shifted west towards the Ottoman port of Basra.[35] This continued even after Karim Khan managed to reinstall much of Iran's authority along her southern coastline. The decision of the British East India Company to shut down operations and factories in Bushehr and relocate its headquarters to Basra in 1769 was also a bitter blow, not only to Bushehr, but to Iran's economy.[36] Meanwhile, Basra's growing wealth and commercial status certainly did not escape the notice of Karim Khan.

Karim Khan was also eager to address the issue of past Ottoman support, through Basra, of the Banu Ka'ab and Oman against him. While the Banu Ka'ab had been subdued, the potential for future Ottoman intervention could not be ruled out. Of special concern were the prospects of Omani–Ottoman cooperation which could prove especially dangerous for Iranian interests in the Persian Gulf. Iran simply did not have the military depth required to indefinitely contain renewed piracy and raids by adventurous Arab tribes from not only Oman but other parts of Arabia.

The Kurdish provinces of Baban and Zohab were of special strategic significance. Not only were these provinces situated in the frontier region between the Iranians and the Ottomans (modern-day Sulaymānīyah province in Iraqi Kurdistan), but these areas also provided access for Iranian armies to rapidly strike towards Baghdad. Karim Khan Zand had been successful in extending Iranian influence into the Baban-Zohab region through the vakil of Iran's Ardalan province. This had been the case ever since the passing of Baghdad's Suleiman Pasha in 1762. This state of affairs however was soon challenged by Omar Pasha who ejected the pro-Iranian Vakil from Baban. In addition to asserting Ottoman influence in Iraqi Kurdistan at Iranian expense, Omar Pasha also instituted a toll on pilgrims traveling towards the Shiite holy centers of Najaf and Karbala. The properties of Iranian pilgrims who had died during the recent Iraqi epidemic were also seized by Ottoman authorities. Iranian protests regarding the agreement made by Nader Shah pertaining to Iranian pilgrims were ignored. This issue tested the prestige of Karim Khan as Iran had practically lost Mashad in Khorasan and its holy Shiite shrine of Imam Reza. The constraints set upon Iran's pilgrims into Iraq by Omar Pasha would inevitably raise questions regarding Karim Khan's ability to safeguard the rights of Iranian pilgrims.

The Iranian army had lost some of its luster after Zaki Khan's bungled operations at Hormuz. It is possible that Karim Khan may have been hoping to divert the martial energies of his restless troops towards a foreign adventure and simultaneously to enhance Iranian military prestige.[37] A military operation against the Ottomans was feasible as Iranian authority in Bandar Rig, Kharq, Khuzistan, and Bandar Abbas along Iran's Persian Gulf coastline had sufficiently stabilized.

Battles with the Ottomans and the capture of Basra

Suleiman Agha, who led the defense of Basra, had thoroughly mobilized and prepared the city to withstand a siege.[38] The Iranian army had also expected a long and drawn-out campaign and ensured a large quantity of supplies would be provided for their troops. Supplies arrived from the provinces of Fars and Khuzistan with two ships also arriving from Iranian ports along the Persian Gulf.[39]

The Iranian campaign against Basra was led by Karim Khan's brother, Sadegh Khan, in April 1775.[40] It is difficult to ascertain exactly how many Iranian troops partook in the offensive. Western and Arab historiography generally agrees that 30,000 Iranians crossed the Arvand Rud/Shaat al Arab waterway, with Iranian sources reporting 60,000 troops.[41] Sadegh Khan first deployed the army to the eastern bank of the Arvand Rud/Shaat al Arab waterway. A large pontoon-bridge of boats was built.[42] The Iranian army then rapidly crossed the Arvand Rud/Shaat al Arab. The Ottomans attempted to halt the arriving Iranian forces with a withering barrage of cannon and artillery fire, but to no avail. A number of Iranian troops were transported across the Arvand Rud/Shaat al Arab waterway by the boats of the Banu Ka'ab Arabs of Khuzistan and the Al-Mazkur Arabs of Bushehr.[43] Many of Suleiman Agha's Arab allies, the Muntafiqh in particular, simply retreated and did not contest the Iranian army as it landed on the western bank.[44] The sheikh of the Al-Mazkur Arabs, Nasser e Din Shah, also assisted Karim Khan in operations along the northern Persian Gulf littoral in 1757–65.[45]

Sadegh Khan very quickly surrounded Basra, which was protected by a series of ditches and moats. Iranian commanders then selected 36 critical points to construct trenches and other siege works against Basra.[46] The onset of the siege was witnessed by the British India Company, trapped in Basra and caught in the crossfire. Led by Henry Moore, the men of the company launched a daring strike against Iranian supply boats, but then decided to completely vacate Basra and departed with their ships towards Bushehr and Bombay.[47] Despite these events, Iran's relations with the British Empire remained constructive overall.

Suleiman Agha sealed the gates of Basra and deployed first-rate Arab sharpshooters from the region to take positions in Basra's towers and fire against Sadegh Khan's troops. Other pro-Ottoman Arab warriors proceeded to raid the Iranian army camps but Sadegh Khan appears to have successfully countered these whilst simultaneously placing more and more heavy cannon around Basra. The main emphasis was on completely sealing off Basra from all outside help and supplies. This soon resulted in serious shortages in the city, leading to famine. Suleiman Agha, however, proved to be a resolute defender. Under his capable leadership, Basra withstood the Iranian siege for a little over a year, buoyed by hopes that a fresh Ottoman army would arrive from Baghdad.[48] This was largely prevented by diversionary Zand attacks into Mesopotamia and eastern Anatolia.[49]

Unable to dispatch resources for the defense of Basra, Omar Pasha sent a request to Imam Ahmad bin Sa'id of Oman for military aid. Imam Ahmad acquiesced by dispatching his son Amir Hillal with a powerful fleet that sailed towards Basra from Muscat.[50] Western sources report the flotilla as comprising 10,000 Omani troops sailing with two large ships and a number of smaller craft, while Iranian sources report 12,000 fighters with 12 supply ships, 100 smaller combat craft, and 100 cannon.[51] As soon as he received news of the incoming Omani expeditionary force, Sadegh Khan sent calls to the Banu Ka'ab in Khuzistan and the governor of Bushehr to block the arrival of the Omani ships. This resulted in the arrival of 3,000 troops and numerous cannon. These forces then installed a powerful iron chain, specifically built for this task in Shiraz, across the Arvand Rud/Shaat al Arab waterway, closing it to marine traffic.[52] Chains were used because Iran simply did not have a navy to enforce a blockade by sea.

The Omani fleet arrived in Basra by October 1776 and realized that their ingress was being blocked by the chain.[53] Ironically, that chain was broken by the Afsharid warship that had become a possession of the Omani navy.[54] The fleet's arrival was also contested by concentrated musket and cannon fire from the coastlines, however the Omanis managed to reach Basra more or less intact. Basra's defenders now erupted in celebrations. The Basra garrison, alongside their Omani allies, then deployed with 12,000 mostly Arab fighters. The battle was over in just a few hours with Sadegh Khan's troops emerging completely victorious.[55]

Soon after the Omanis left, Sadegh Khan's alliance with the local Shiite Khaza'il Arabs greatly assisted the Iranian army in defeating an Ottoman relief force that had finally managed to arrive from Baghdad.[56] The defenders of Basra were now increasingly dispirited and desperate. Their long and heroic resistance was proving to be increasingly futile as all forces coming to their rescue had been crushed. Basra formally surrendered to the Iranian army on either April 16 or 20, 1776.[57] A number of the city's residents then reportedly fled to Baghdad.[58] Negotiations for the surrender had begun earlier on April 5, when Sadegh Khan ordered Iranian troops to transport badly needed food and supplies into Basra.[59] Sadegh Khan stayed in the city for four months then departed for Shiraz, yielding the command of Basra to Mohammad Ali Khan.[60]

Karim Khan failed to translate his military success at Basra into any tangible economic benefits for Iran. It is generally agreed that the governorship of the city by Sadegh Khan was relatively reasonable, but matters deteriorated with the arrival of Mohammad Ali Khan. The latter was known as a tyrannical ruler who seized properties and exacted exorbitant taxes.[61] Nevertheless, there was no religious persecution in the city.[62] Events in Basra deteriorated as the renewed battles in Kurdistan came to an end. Having extracted what he could from Basra, Mohammad Ali Khan now turned to its environs, especially the surrounding towns and tribal areas, such as Al-Zubair which was looted and burnt. Mohammad Ali Khan then overplayed his hand by attacking and robbing the Muntafiqh Arabs in June 1778. The act was especially provocative as Mohammad Ali Khan had earlier pledged the Muntafiqh that he respected their right of safe conduct.[63]

The situation escalated. The Muntafiqh struck back and crushed one of Mohammad Ali Khan's scouting teams in the area. Mohammad Ali Khan then led a powerful punitive force meant to bring the Muntafiqh to heel. The latter, who had been expecting this action, cunningly led Iranian troops into a deadly trap. Led by Sheikh Thamir, the Muntafiqh engaged the Iranian forces to the north of the city in September 1778 and in the ensuing battle virtually wiped out the entire force, including Mohammad Ali Khan.[64] Though victorious, the Muntafiqh did not follow up their success by marching into Basra.

In December 1778, Sadegh Khan arrived in Basra with fresh forces to reinforce its diminished Iranian garrison. The reality for Iran, however, was that holding Basra had now become an economic and military liability. Economically, Basra was no longer a thriving commercial seaport. In fact, Basra had been experiencing economic difficulties as early as 1773, just two years before the Iranian siege.[65] The actions of Mohammad Ali Khan, had done further damage to Basra's economy. Furthermore, Basra was not an important station for caravan trains. Militarily, the holding of Basra was both expensive and risky. It was only a matter of time before the Ottomans would try to retake Basra, and in the meantime the tough and dangerous local Arab tribes had also to be considered. The Iranian army completely evacuated the city and departed east across the Arvand Rud/Shaat al Arab by 1779.[66]

By May 1776, the sultan had declared war against Karim Khan and the Ottomans mobilized their forces to fight in Kurdistan. They were very successful in their first strike, winning a major battle at Marivan against Khosrow Khan of the Ardalan in May 1777. This success proved short-lived as Karim Khan launched a coordinated attack from three sectors and defeated the Ottomans and their Baban allies. This victory ensured the stability of the Kurds of Ardalan. In practice, the state of peace in this region (as in other sectors of the long and porous Ottoman–Iranian border) remained brittle.

CHAPTER 18

DEMISE OF THE ZANDS AND RISE OF THE QAJARS (1779-94)

Political disorder followed the death of Karim Khan in 1779. The relative peace and calm in the country was once again torn asunder by factional differences and civil war due to the inability of the Zands to set aside their differences.[1] There were a number of ephemeral Zand rulers from 1779 to 1794. Karim Khan's adult sons, Abol Fath Khan and Mohammad Ali Khan, have been characterized as "frivolous and incompetent."[2] Ali Morad Khan and Sadegh Khan were also contenders for the throne.

Zaki Khan was quick to try to seize power following Karim Khan's death. In just three days he executed 23 khans, seized their assets, and used these to finance his troops.[3] With these actions Zaki Khan easily dispersed the supporters of Abol Fath Khan. But a few months after his "coup," Zaki Khan was faced with the challenge of Ali Morad Khan, who had been one of Karim Khan's most trusted commanders and had at one time even been trusted by Zaki Khan. Trust now gave way to enmity: Ali Morad Khan had gathered his own support base among a number of commanders and khans and was soon able to create his own private army in Isfahan.[4] Alerted to what was clearly a challenge to his authority in Shiraz, Zaki Khan assembled an army of 20,000 men in haste, without providing them with enough weapons or training.[5] Zaki Khan's army did its utmost to keep its movement secret and managed to arrive close to Isfahan. However soon after its arrival, a group of tribal leaders from the clan of Mafi entered Zaki Khan's tent and shot him. Thus ended the 100-day rule of Zaki Khan; the khans then chose Abol Fath Khan as their leader and marched back to Shiraz.[6]

The reign of Abol Fath Khan proved even more fleeting than that of Zaki Khan. Sadegh Khan allied himself with the disaffected elements of the Zand army to eject Abol Fath Khan in Shiraz after a brief tenure of just 70 days. In the spring of 1780, Sadegh Khan dispatched his son Ali Gholi Khan with 10,000 troops towards Isfahan, which was held by Ali Morad Khan. The latter retaliated by dispatching forces for Taqhi Khan, the governor of Yazd, so that he would deploy to intercept the advance of Ali Gholi Khan. A bitter battle then took place but Taqhi Khan held on and Yazd remained unconquered. Ali Gholi Khan then joined the forces of Hassan Khan, another son of Sadegh Khan, who had arrived from Shiraz, and together they pushed towards Isfahan.

As soon as Sadegh Khan's sons reached Isfahan, one of the city's prominent members, Haji Reza Khan Farahani, simply departed with his warriors. This was a big blow to Ali Morad Khan's ability to defend the city as Haji Reza Khan Farahani had commanded a large body of troops. Ali Morad Khan fled towards Hamadan where he organized a new army and marched back to Isfahan. Upon his arrival a number of troops and their commanders joined Ali Morad Khan. A number of Sadegh Khan's top commanders also defected to Ali Morad Khan. With this expanded and stronger force, Ali Morad Khan punched into Fars province and rushed towards Shiraz.

In Shiraz, Sadegh Khan's situation had badly deteriorated. Fighting had broken out between the city's Lar and Dashtestani units which greatly undermined his ability to defend the city. Ali Morad Khan's siege of Shiraz began in late July or August 1781. Despite his difficulties in maintaining order between the Dashtestanis and the Lars, Sadegh Khan had made thorough preparations for the siege with enough supplies for 18,000 cavalry and 12,000 infantry.[7] Sadegh Khan issued an edict that the families of all men from Shiraz and its environs fighting for Ali Morad Khan would be tortured. To demonstrate his resolve, a number of women and children were brought atop Shiraz's towers and barbarically tortured. This macabre spectacle simply hardened the resolve of the besiegers to bring down Sadegh Khan. Jaafar Khan, another of Sadegh Khan's sons, soon defected to Ali Morad Khan.

Resistance was fierce for at least five months, and the Shiraz garrison would emerge from the city to engage in hit-and-run attacks. But eventually resistance began to slacken as the city's supplies began to run low. By this time winter had set in. Sadegh Khan probably hoped that the bitter cold and weather would undermine his enemies, but Ali Morad Khan simply adopted the same tactics used previously by Nader Shah and Karim Khan: temporary houses were built for the troops as the weather had begun to deteriorate. A wall and towers were then built around the compound, a clear signal to Sadegh Khan that his enemies were determined to stay until Shiraz had fallen to them.

Sadegh Khan dispatched as many raiding parties as he could to destroy the compound but these had no success. The cannon also failed to make an impression. To make matters worse, Shiraz's supplies had reached such low levels by the winter that the local populace was starving. The inhabitants resorted to burning their doors and windows in a desperate bid to get warm. The one secret passage supply route to the city was discovered by Ali Morad Khan's men and cut off. Shiraz was doomed. Starvation was now affecting Sadegh Khan's own troops, a number of whom rebelled. They stormed one of Shiraz's key gates, the Darvazeye Bagh-e Shah, and overcame the guards. The gate was opened and Ali Morad Khan's troops poured into the city in February 1781.[8] They arrested Sadegh Khan in the citadel. He was blinded and then killed a few months later in prison.[9] Ali Morad Khan did not settle in Shiraz. Concerned with the rise of Qajar power in the north, Ali Morad Khan relocated his political and military base to Isfahan.[10] He had defeated his Zand rivals, but would soon be campaigning in Mazandaran against the rising power of Agha Mohammad Khan Qajar.

Zand geopolitical legacy

Karim Khan Zand has been viewed favorably by Iranian historians, and there is much to support the assertion that his system of rule was generally constructive. But Zand rule resulted in a weakening military establishment and a rise in dangers to Iran's geopolitical position, especially her territorial integrity. The vakil's preoccupation with establishing his rule may explain why enough attention was not focused on a number of Iran's key areas along the periphery, notably Khorasan to the northeast, eastern Iran, the Persian Gulf and the Caucasus.

The maximum geographical extent of the Zand administration was approximately half of that during the Safavid era. This was partly due to the virtual breaking off of Khorasan from central authority. One problem of course was that of enforcing Zand authority upon the Qajars in the northeast, a task which Karim Khan only managed with difficulty, and which failed to endure after his passing. This meant that it was difficult to project a politically centralized Iranian authority into Khorasan. While northern Iran was at least nominally under Iranian authority, Khorasan had become a tributary of Ahmad Shah of the Durranis by 1755. There are two recorded contacts between the Zands and the Afsharids.[11] But the real power in Khorasan was Ahmad Shah, and no significant contact is known to have taken place between him and Karim Khan. Karim Khan may have chosen to abandon Khorasan, leaving it as a "buffer" between himself and Ahmad Shah, but he also had a far inferior military to that of Ahmad Shah.[12] It was only after the arrival of Agha Mohammad Khan in Khorasan that this province was again restored to central authority. The provinces in Sistan and Baluchistan became practically autonomous.

As noted, one the greatest military errors during the Zand era was the failure to continue Nader Shah's commissioning of a Persian Gulf navy. This prevented Iran from exerting its authority by sea, especially in protecting its ports and shipping in the Persian Gulf. This was of major consequence as it was during the 18th century that the Arabs of the Persian Gulf managed to gain significant access to the Persian coastline.[13] The motivation propelling the Arab arrival into southern Iran was generally due to the area's better climactic conditions, such as better pasture grounds, date plantations, space, and water supply.[14]

Iranian authority along its coastline during Zand rule declined with even the exercising of authority upon the coastal sheikhdoms of Makran proving tenuous.[15] The Arabs who settled along the Iranian coastline soon developed ambitions to dominate these regions but did cultivate good relations with the local Persian-speakers in their locales.[16] Iranian authorities responded by developing a contractual-type relationship with the Arab immigrants.[17] The latter arrangement secured at least a semblance of Iranian sovereignty over Iran's Persian Gulf coastline, but Iran began to lose its grip over her claimed possessions in the Persian Gulf during the Zand era, notably when the Al-Khalifa family arrived in Bahrain in 1782.[18]

Georgia and much of the Transcaucasia had powerful cultural links with Iran, and the Safavid domains in the Caucasus had included the kingdom of Georgia as well as territories to the south. The collapse of the Safavid dynasty and the invasion of the Caucasus and northern Iran by Peter the Great in the early 1720s had dealt a heavy blow against Iranian authority, especially in the Caucasus. This meant that by the time Karim Khan had established himself in Shiraz in 1765, the Caucasus was only nominally within the Iranian orbit. The closest Karim Khan got to the Caucasus was in Iranian Azarbaijan in 1760–63, but no Zand army actually crossed the Araxes to obtain submission from khanates such as Shirvan. Only Azarbaijan paid taxes regularly and ensured its allegiance during Karim Khan's reign. The Georgian kingdom and Caucasian khanates were now practically autonomous.

When Karim Khan concluded his campaign in Azarbaijan by 1763, Heraclius II of Georgia offered his allegiance to the vakil and was bestowed with the position of *Vali e Gorjestan* (lit. representative of Georgia). The title itself was more symbolic than truly representative of Iranian power in Georgia. In practice, Heraclius had been looking northwards to Moscow for military protection against his local enemies as far back as the early 1750s. This was a clear indication that confidence in Iranian abilities to provide consistent protection had clearly faded, while trust in Russian "protection" and influence had grown. Karim Khan did attempt to re-establish authority upon Georgia through diplomacy, but when Heraclius ignored Karim's letter, no further action was taken. What symbolic political links that Georgia had left with Iran completely dissolved after Karim Khan's death. By 1783, Russian's "protection" of Georgia had become official and Heraclius no longer considered his kingdom legally bound to Iran.

This situation did not go unnoticed by the Russians or Ottoman Turks, both of which had long coveted the fertile Caucasus region. From the 1760s, the southeastern Caucasus (encompassing khanates such as Shirvan, Baku, Sheki, etc) had fallen under the sway of Ali Khan Darbandi (also known as Ali Khan Qobbai). Darbandi looked to Russia for military assistance in conflicts against his rivals. In addition, he had a close relationship with the Georgians in Tbilisi. Russia had in fact worked vigorously to cultivate political links with the khanates against Iran in the Caucasus, notably in Karabakh, which under Panah-Ali Khan had become virtually independent of Iran after Nader Shah's death.[19] Mohammad Hassan Khan Qajar had unsuccessfully attempted to capture Karabakh during the 1750s. Panah-Ali Khan not only beat back Mohammad Hassan Khan's assaults but managed to counterattack as far as Ardabil in northwest Iran. Panahabad-Shusha withstood yet another assault by Fathali Khan Afshar who unsuccessfully besieged the city for six months. Panah-Ali's son, Ibrahim-Khalil Khan Javanshir (r. 1763–1806), continued his father's independent policy. By the time Karim Khan Zand had established his authority in Iran, Panahabad-Shusha had became an important fortress and city inhabited by both Muslims and Armenians. Karabakh was of vital strategic importance to Iran as it was the key to controlling the southern Caucasus and projecting northwards towards Ganja and Georgia. Karim Khan made no serious attempt at reaching out to Javanshir or at enforcing Iranian authority in Karabakh or the other khanates of the Trans-Caucasus.

The province of Gilan remained under Iranian rule; however the laxity of the Zands led to a dangerous increase of Russian mercantile influence at Bandar Anzali. Karim Khan appointed Hedayatollah Khan as the province's governor, but Hedayatollah tended to look to Russia rather than Shiraz in times of crisis. Of equal concern was the ability of Russian traders to gain special privileges on Iranian soil. From Karim Khan's perspective Gilan was secure as Hedayatollah Khan paid regular taxes to Shiraz and sent Karim Khan gifts on a regular basis. There were also family ties between the Zands and Hedayatollah Khan as his sister was married to Karim Khan's son. Karim Khan's contentment with the state of Rasht-Shiraz relations may partly explain why Hedayatollah Khan's "tilt" towards the Russians was never seriously scrutinized.

Perhaps one of the most damaging gestures made by the Zands was by Ali Morad Khan Zand. He specifically stated to the Russians that if they afforded him political recognition and offered him military assistance against the Qajars, he would yield Iran's Caucasian khanates to Russia.[20] All Moscow had to do to absorb the Caucasian territories without firing a shot was support Ali Morad Khan. Empress Catherine II of Russia obliged by dispatching an embassy to Ali Morad Khan by spring 1784. While Ali Morad Khan's "offer" may be viewed within the context of his desperate quest for survival against the Qajars, it placed Iran in a very dangerous position. It was only relatively recently, during Nader Shah's time, that the Russians had evacuated their troops from the khanates and the northern provinces. But now, thanks to Iranian political instability, Russia knew it could march its army back into the Caucasus. Ali Morad Khan's action also opened the door to Russian interference into Iran's internal issues of political succession.[21] The Zands evidently failed to evaluate the quality of Russo-Iranian relations; specifically they lacked appreciation, or interest, in gauging Russian military and economic objectives toward Iran. Even less appreciated was the power differential, especially with respect to military might and technology, factors which had strongly shifted in Russia's favor. It was only a matter of time before Russia would translate her growing military ascendancy into territorial conquest at Iranian expense.

PART IV

THE QAJARS

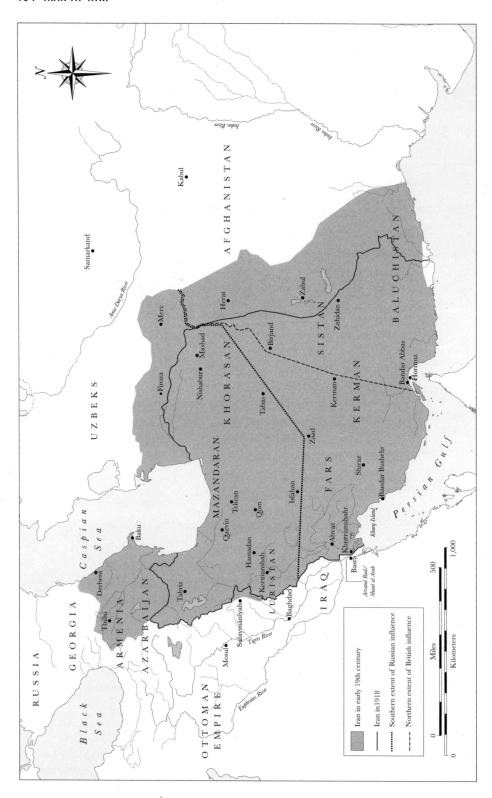

RUSSIA

GEORGIA

Black Sea

Caspian Sea

Derbent

Tbilisi

Baku

ARMENIA

AZARBAIJAN

Tabriz

UZBEKS

Amu-Darya River

Samarkand

AFGHANISTAN

Kabul

Indus River

Indus River

Merv

Firoza

Nishabur

Mashad

KHORASAN

Herat

Birjand

Zabul

Zahidan

SISTAN

BALUCHISTAN

Tabas

Yazd

Kermane

KERMAN

Bandar Abbas

Hormuz

Qazvin

Tehran

Qom

Isfahan

MAZANDARAN

Hamadan

Kermanshah

LURISTAN

Baghdad

Ahwaz

Khorramshahr

Basra

*Arand Rud/
Shatt al-Arab*

FARS

Shiraz

Bandar Bushehr

Khong Island

Persian Gulf

Sulaymaniyah

Mosul

IRAQ

Tigris River

OTTOMAN
EMPIRE

Euphrates River

Iran in early 19th century

Iran in1918

Southern extent of Russian influence

Northern extent of British influence

Miles

0

500

1,000

Kilometers

0

CHAPTER 19

AGHA MOHAMMAD KHAN QAJAR (1785–97)

Origins of the Qajars

The term *Qajar* has been defined as "marching quickly" in Turkish.[1] The Qajars are descendants of Turkic tribes from Central Asia;[2] however, the exact date of their arrival into Iran has been a matter of speculation. Hambly provides the most likely scenario; the Qajars first migrated as far as eastern Anatolia and/or Syria after the break-up of the Il-Khanate in the wake of Abu Said's death in 1335. During the second half of the 15th century, the Qajars established their influence in Iran's Azarbaijan province, Yerevan in Armenia, and the southeast Caucasian khanates of Ganja and Karabakh. The Qajars, according to Hambly, became Twelver Shiites during the Aq-Quyunlu ascendancy, having become the followers of the religious leaders of Ardabil.[3]

The first historical mention of the Qajars is of a certain Qara Pir Beg Qajar, cited as one of the followers of the Safavid sheikh Haydar.[4] Qara Pir Beg Qajar and his warriors are also reported as having been one of the seven major tribes of the Qizilbash Turkic warrior clans who were instrumental in supporting the rise of Shah Ismail to power.[5] By this time, the Qajars had become a powerful influence in the Caucasus as well as in parts of eastern Anatolia. The status of the Qajar tribes was certainly significant by the time of Shah Abbas I, who split them (established at this time mainly in Karabakh and the Araxes region) and sent large numbers of these to eastern Iran.[6]

The Qajars in eastern Iran were settled along Merv and Astarabad to defend against Uzbek and Turcomen raiders. Qajar tribes settling in Astarabad were two distinct groups. Those settled in the upper areas of the Mobarakabad castle (modern-day Agh-Qale situated about 11–12 miles (18–19km) north of Gorgan and on the fringes of the Gorgan River) were mainly the Develu clan, who became known as the Yukhari-bash (Turkic: settlers on the upstream) and those below the castle were generally the Quyunlu who became known as the Ashaqa-bash (Turkic: settlers on the downstream).[7] This may have been done deliberately to keep the two clans (Quyunlu and Develu) separate; by the 18th century, the two clans had developed deep-rooted feuds.[8] Despite their relatively small numbers, the Qajars were well known due to their prowess as warriors. By the time of Nader Shah, the Qajars in the Caucasus and Merv had been absorbed into nearby tribes and peoples, but those located in Astarabad survived.

Agha Mohammad Khan

Agha Mohammad was 38 years old when he escaped from Shiraz after the death of Karim Khan in 1779.[9] Zarrinkoob asserts that the severity of Agha Mohammad Khan's early experiences explains his insatiable lust for power, wealth, and vengeance and his cruelty and deep suspiciousness.[10] "Agha" means eunuch in Persian. Agha Mohammad was captured and castrated by Adil Shah, a nephew of Nader Shah in 1748, when he was just five years old.[11] According to Sykes, this singular experience helps explain the subsequent vindictiveness of the future Qajar shah.[12] He was captured again in 1762 by Karim Khan Zand who forced him to live as a virtual prisoner at the Zand court in Shiraz. While Karim Khan did treat his "guest" with kindness and honor, Agha Mohammad Khan had every intention of inflicting a terrible revenge upon the Zands who had been responsible for the death of his father (Mohammad Hassan Khan) and brother (Hussein Qoli).

Agha Mohammad Khan's vengeance would literally reach into the grave. Karim Khan's remains were exhumed and reburied in the gateway of Agha Mohammad's Tehran palace to ensure that the late vakil would always be under the Qajars' feet.[13] Also exhumed were the remains of Nader Shah, which were then buried at the gateway of his palace.[14] Agha Mohammad had finally satiated his motivation for vengeance against the Afsharids and Zands.

However, as Zarrinkoob and Yekrangian correctly point out, Agha Mohammad Khan was also a brilliant and charismatic military commander deeply trusted and popular among his troops.[15] Agha Mohammad was not arrogant with his men, whom he treated as friends and comrades. Not only was his clothing the same as that of his ordinary troops, he also often dined with them in their quarters.[16] Agha Mohammad Khan also took great care to ensure that his men were well provided for with food, clothing, and pay.[17] These genuine displays of humility may partly explain why Agha Mohammad Khan's men were so steadfastly loyal to him up to the end of his rule and fought so hard on his behalf. The picture that emerges is that of a ruler with contradictory impulses: merciless cruelty against his opponents and fraternal benevolence towards his trusted allies.

The morning following Karim Khan's death, Agha Mohammad Khan was allowed to go hunting outside Shiraz's walls; instead he fled to the north.[18] He immediately arranged a meeting to heal the rift between the Develu and Quyunlu branches of the Qajar tribe; he then rapidly gained ascendancy over Mazandaran in the north.[19] With the settling of his conflicts with his brothers and the allegiance of the Develu branch of the Qajars, Agha Mohammad was able to defeat subsequent Zand attempts at entry into the north. Ali Morad Khan had negotiated with Russia in 1784 over the possibility of allowing it to absorb Iran's northwestern provinces and the entire Caspian Coast.[20] He had calculated that a Russian arrival would crush the Qajars in the north, but his death in 1785 terminated such scenarios.[21] Agha Mohammad Khan made Tehran his capital in 1786 after having secured it in the same year.[22] Tehran has been the Iranian capital ever since.

Armies of Agha Mohammad Khan Qajar

Agha Mohammad Khan was able to draw upon approximately 200,000 troops composed of 140,000 tribal cavalry, 60,000 infantry, and 3,000 artillerymen.[23] The majority of the "artillerymen" were most likely responsible for the operation of the 200 lightweight camel-mounted zanbouraks that were practically useless against contemporary European armies.[24]

A key achievement of Agha Mohammad Khan was his ability to unite local non-Qajar Turkic (e.g. Turkmens and Afshars) and non-Turkic (e.g. Mazandarani and Damghanis) tribes to his banner, a success that greatly expanded the manpower base of his army. The best infantry hailed from

Mazandaran and were known as the *Tofangchian e Mazandaran* ("musketeers of Mazandaran"), whom Agha Mohammad affectionately called the *Pirahan e Jan e Shah* ["the shirt that protects the life of the shah"].[25] These, alongside the Qajar cavalry, played a vital military role in Agha Mohammad Khan's campaigns against the Zands from 1779–94.[26] Agha Mohammad Khan's central corps of 70,000 troops was housed in various camp-type settlements or *Ordus* around old Tehran.[27] These later became the *Padegan e Tehran e Janbaz* ["the Tehran army base of those who risk their lives in battle"].[28]

Sir John Malcolm reported that Agha Mohammad Khan had introduced a high level of organizational efficiency, discipline, and professionalism into his army.[29] Great emphasis was placed on marksmanship and equestrian skill among Agha Mohammad's troops.[30] James Baille Fraser, another contemporary of the early Qajars, concurs by observing that Agha Mohammad had "the talent of forming good and brave troops … kept his army constantly engaged … kept a veteran hardihood and expertness, that rendered them superior to any other Asiatic troops."[31] By this time however European troops were far more advanced than their Iranian counterparts with respect to drill discipline, mass-musket firing infantry, artillery, naval warfare, and coastal defense.[32] The deficiencies of Iranian forces within these domains would become painfully evident in future wars.

The most capable of Iran's forces were the cavalry, whose excellent marksmanship and equestrian skills made them a formidable force.[33] Qajar cavalry tactics were of the traditional Turco-Iranian military tradition: a powerful emphasis on rapid mobility, encirclement and striking at the rear, and surprise lightning strikes.[34] When campaigning inside enemy territory, Agha Mohammad Khan's army secured supplies while simultaneously applying a devastating scorched-earth policy against the enemy.[35]

Interestingly, the cavalry (and combat troops in general) appear to display a quality recorded over a thousand years before amongst the Savaran Sassanian elite cavalry. These were most powerful and formidable in the attack but lacking in endurance as the main impulse of their attack was expended.[36] Almost 1,200 years later, Artemi provides an identical description of Qajar cavalry by asserting that "The Persians indeed attack like lions but they exert their strength in the first blow, and if this fails they return home."[37] Agha Mohammad Khan fully appreciated the daring and prowess of his forces but was aware that these troops lacked endurance when faced with steadfast opposition. In this case, Agha Mohammad was concerned with the highly disciplined ranks and devastating firepower of Russian troops and how these could withstand the determined assaults of Iranian forces. This speaks highly of Agha Mojammad's keen analysis of his army's strengths and weaknesses. Agha Mohammad died just before Russia's wars with Iran began in earnest, with the absence of his martial wisdom becoming a major loss for Iran.

The Qajars initially did not possess the large pool of tribal allies their Zand predecessors had had, especially in western Iran. Agha Mohammad ameliorated this by forming a series of alliances with tribes in western and northern Iran, sometimes by playing off rivals against each other. One example is the Qajar favor shown to the Dumbuli Kurds versus their Shaqqaqi Kurdish rivals in Azarbaijan. Agha Mohammad was adept at attracting many of Iran's tribes (e.g. the Ard-Alan Kurds and the Qaraqozlu of Hamadan) to his cause by offering marital alliances, plunder opportunities, provision of superior pasture grounds, and even opportunities to settle scores with rivals.[38] Conversely, non-compliant tribes could be punished by promoting a rival tribe, confiscation of lands, or forced migration.[39] The most powerful tribal alliance became that between the Ard-Alan Kurds and the Qajars.

Agha Mohammad Khan Qajar secures the north

After his escape, Agha Mohammad keenly observed the internecine Zand battles, especially those between Sadegh Khan and Ali Morad Khan. The feuding Zands similarly watched the steady growth of Agha Mohammad Khan's power in the north.

Russia's first contact with Agha Mohammad Khan occurred in 1781 when Count Voinovich arrived with a flotilla off the Caspian coast of Gorgan province.[40] Voinovich had been sent on behalf of the Russian government to apply for "permission" to build a trading post on Ashraf but Agha Mohammad Khan refused. Thanks to Iran's lack of a Caspian navy, Voinovich was then able to land off the Gorgan coast on the islands of Ashurada. Qaraduvin was also occupied. The Voinovich expedition was part of Empress Catherine II's overall plan to invade and annex northern Iran.[41] Agha Mohammad Khan reacted quickly by arresting and deporting the Russian expedition, an action which Catherine took as a personal insult which explains her subsequent efforts to "punish" the Qajar by invading the Caucasus in 1796.[42]

Just as the operations in Gilan were drawing to a close, more Qajar armies thrust west towards Qazvin. Leading these operations was Jaafar Qoli Khan who first confronted and defeated a Zand force in the Karaj or Rayy area and then entered Qazvin.[43] From there Jaafar Qoli Khan marched towards Zanjan and captured this city as well. Agha Mohammad Khan now arrived with his armies from Gilan and joined Jaafar Qoli Khan to capture Sultaniyeh where upon their arrival they built the large Sultaniyeh military base.[44] Agha Mohammad then imposed a 40-day siege of Tehran but was forced to withdraw after a Zand counterattack.[45]

The constantly feuding Zands had by now realized the danger posed by Agha Mohammad to Zand control of Tehran and the northwest. Ali Morad Khan decided to crush the Qajars in Mazandaran and dispatched an army to the north in 1784 led by his son Sheikh Vais Khan and another army led by Mohammad Zahir Khan.[46] At first all seemed to be going well for the Zands; many of the local khans and leaders submitted to the Zand army with the most important defection being that of Agha Mohammad's brother Morteza Qoli.[47]

The two Zand armies arrived in Sari, where Sheikh Vais Khan proceeded to build a fortress. Mohammad Zahir Khan then peeled off towards Astrabad with 10,000 troops. Agha Mohammad Khan decided to fall back and took positions along an old Safavid defense line with a very large ditch, known as Kolbad, situated near Ashraf (modern Behshahr) and Kordkoy, which had been originally constructed to keep the local Turkmen at bay. Mohammad Zahir Khan however managed to force a successful crossing of the obstacle obliging Agha Mohammad and his army to retreat into the traditional Qajar fortress and safe haven at Astrabad. The city's defenses were quickly fortified and Agha Mohammad ensured that the city would be well stocked with supplies, foodstuffs, and weaponry. Mohammad Zahir Khan soon arrived at Astrabad, but was decisively defeated by Agha Mohammad Khan's Qajar troops and allied Turkmen cavalry.[48]

The Qajars and their allies now made the final push to crush what was left of the Zands in Mazandaran. Sari, the provincial capital, fell to the Qajar army and the remnants of the fleeing Zand army were liquidated. Ali Morad Khan's last gasp was to send Rostam Khan Zand in a desperate bid to stem the Qajar tide in the north but to no avail: these were decisively crushed by Jaafar Qoli Khan.[49] By November 1784, all of Mazandaran had been cleared of Zand troops and there was no longer any dispute as to who was the master of Mazandaran.[50]

The battle of Kashan and the capture of Tehran

After his military disasters in the north Ali Morad Khan returned to Isfahan. Jaafar Khan had already marched against that city in an attempt to capture it while Ali Morad Khan was campaigning in the north.[51] Ali Morad Khan died of natural causes in February 1785. He was succeeded by Jaafar Khan Zand who occupied Isfahan shortly later.[52] Agha Mohammad Khan, now anchored securely in the north, lunged southwards once again towards Tehran. As he approached Tehran, he was visited by a delegation from that city. Their message was straightforward and simple: the city was loyal to the house of Zand. There was however one important proviso: whoever seized the throne would earn the unquestioned allegiance of Tehran.[53] Accepting the message from the Tehran delegation, Agha Mohammad redeployed his army further south towards Isfahan. His army marched first to Qom, reduced its fortress with cannon fire and occupied the city, then proceeded towards Kashan on his way to Isfahan.[54]

Jaafar Khan, having witnessed these alarming developments, sent a counterforce to block Agha Mohammad Khan, but this turned back at Qom without fighting.[55] A more powerful Zand force of several thousand cavalry led by Jaafar Khan and the Zand governor of Yazd, Taqi Khan, advanced to Kashan to force a major showdown. The Qajars arrived near Kashan and proceeded to make their battle preparations. The Qajars emerged victorious after a four-hour battle and put the Zands to flight.[56]

With opposition all but crushed, Agha Mohammad entered Isfahan, the main Zand base for operations in central Iran. Jaafar Khan had escaped to Shiraz. Isfahan was plundered and Jaafar Khan's possessions confiscated. The Bakhtiari Lurs were subdued and another son of the late Azad Khan Afghan, Ahmad Khan, was forced to acknowledge the authority of Agha Mohammad. With these successes, Agha Mohammad marched to Tehran which, as promised, opened its gates without battle in March 1786.

As soon as Agha Mohammad Khan marched north, Jaafar Khan returned and recaptured Isfahan. However, he lost it again to Agha Mohammad.[57] With his second capture of Isfahan concluded, Agha Mohammad marched to Hamadan to formally receive the submission of Khosrow Khan of the Ard-Alan and his allies at Golpayegan. The incorporation of these formidable clans into Agha Mohammad Khan's forces was of major importance as this now tilted the military balance overwhelmingly in favor of the Qajars. The Ard-Alan and the Qajars cemented their alliance with marriages between their respective clans.

New battles in Gilan

Despite the campaigns four years previously, Gilan was still defiant of Qajar authority. Hedayotallah Khan's resumption of his throne was a dangerous development due to his attitude towards Russian interests on Iranian soil. Though Agha Mohammad Khan was not against trade with the Russians per se, he objected to the granting of special privileges to Russian traders and nationals on Iranian soil.

The second Qajar thrust into Gilan in 1786 proved as successful as the first expedition, and was facilitated by the fact that Hedayatollah Khan had already cultivated plenty of enemies already in his own native Gilan province. As the Qajar armies drew closer to Rasht, they gained an important new ally: Mehdi Beg Khalatbari of Tunakabon. The accounts of Hedayatollah Khan's demise vary however what is certain is that upon his arrival to Rasht Agha Mohammad discovered Hedayatollah's treasure trove in his palace. This gave the Qajars ample funds for future campaigns. The second Gilan campaign had also raised new suspicions over Russian motives in Iranian soil as Agha Mohammad Khan had noted how the Russians treacherously armed Qajar troops upon their arrival to Gilan at the expense of Hedayatollah Khan.[58]

Jaafar Khan strikes back

By 1787 Agha Mohammad Khan was ready for another round of battles against Jaafar Khan. The Zands had not been idle as Jaafar Khan had moved with his troops to the Kuhguliye region and taken Behbehan. Another Zand contingent had been dispatched to Khuzistan province to subdue the local Banu Ka'ab Arabs. As soon as he returned to Shiraz by March 1787 Jaafar Khan had to deal with another crisis: the rebellion of his governor (Taqi Khan Zand) in Yazd. Jaafar Khan lost no time in deploying a powerful army to Yazd. Taqi Khan, expecting this response, strengthened his city's defenses and sent appeals to Amir Mohammad Khan, the chief of Tabas for help. Jaafar Khan engaged in a number of unsuccessful assaults to break into Yazd. Amir Mohammad Khan's arrival at Yazd then greatly surprised the Zand army which rapidly lost its cohesion. As the Zands retreated in disorder Amir Mohammad Khan captured vast quantities of supplies and artillery. He now combined forces with a number of Taqi Khan's troops and marched towards Isfahan, gathering more cavalry from allies on his way.

In Isfahan, Jaafar Qoli Khan appreciated the danger that was brewing to his east. He marched out with his army to battle against Amir Mohammad Khan. The battle ended in a decisive Qajar victory with Jaafar Qoli Khan capturing the haul that Amir Mohammad Khan had seized from the Zands. Agha Mohammad Khan had been keenly observing these events in Tehran, and once again plunged southwards in 1787.[59] He arrived in Isfahan and joined forces there with his brother Jaafar Qoli Khan, preparing to subdue the Qashqai tribesmen and strike towards Shiraz. When the Qajar army deployed towards the Qashqai, the latter simply melted into the mountains. The Qajars then proceeded towards Shiraz which was ringed by powerful walls and fortifications. Jaafar Khan felt no need to emerge from the city and the two armies sat and observed each other. Realizing the futility of this "sitzkrieg" Agha Mohammad Khan marched back to Isfahan. He was joined by Fathali Khan who had been sent earlier to forcibly obtain the submission of Taqi Khan, making Yazd a Qajar possession. With the end of these operations Agha Mohammad Khan returned to Tehran.

Jaafar Khan waited for Agha Mohammad Khan to return to Tehran before striking out from Shiraz towards Isfahan. Ali Qoli Khan reacted quickly by sending a force of Qaraquzlu warriors to block their advance. The Zands defeated the Qaraquzlu, Isfahan changed hands once again and Ali Qoli Khan escaped to Kashan. Agha Mohammad Khan reacted by rapidly marching on Isfahan. Jaafar Khan fled for the last time in his career to the safety of Shiraz, while Agha Mohammad Khan returned to Tehran. A stalemate had developed where the Qajars dominated the north but their hold on Isfahan was constantly vulnerable to Jaafar Khan's attacks. The key to knocking out the Zands would be ejecting them from Shiraz.

The last of the Zands

Once again Zand disunity benefitted the Qajar cause when the assassination of Jaafar Khan on January 23, 1789 was followed by internecine fighting until May.[60] From the ashes of the fighting emerged the last ruler of the Zands: 22-year-old Lotfali Khan (r. 1789–94) the son of the late Jaafar Khan Zand.

Agha Mohammad Khan may have underestimated his new opponent's martial abilities possibly due to his youth. Agha Mohammad deployed towards Shiraz just over a month after Lotfali Khan had assumed power. Lotfali Kahn had defeated the Qajar siege of Shiraz by early September.[61] After the Qajar departure, Lotfali Khan arrived with his army at Kerman and made an unsuccessful attack.

In May 1790, Agha Mohammad Khan led another army to Shiraz.[62] Behbehan readily submitted to the Qajars and Lotfali Khan marched out of Shiraz with his army. No clash of arms was to occur at this juncture as Agha Mohammad was obliged to deploy his army to Azarbaijan in the northwest. Agha Mohammad's march into Azarbaijan was preceded by stops at Qazvin and Khamsa whose political matters were settled in Qajar favor. Azarbaijan and the Talysh region in the northwest and the Karabakh khanate in the Caucasus were secured by Agha Mohammad in 1791.[63] Agha Mohammad then entrusted the governorship of Khoy and Tabriz to Hossein Qoli, a Dumbuli Kurdish warlord.

The Zands remained at large in the south but they too were embroiled in battles. Lotfali Khan had departed to Shiraz to attack Fathali Khan just south of Isfahan at Qumishah. While there, Lotfali was informed that his chancellor, Haji Ibrahim Khan Kalantar, was openly plotting against him in Shiraz and Kalantar's brother had encouraged many of the Zand troops to defect.[64] Lotfali abandoned his drive against Fathali and marched back to Shiraz. Denied entrance, Lotfali retreated into the mountain range near Kazerun where he rebuilt his forces.

Kalantar sent a formal message to Agha Mohammad Khan requesting that he become the ruler of Fars province.[65] Having concluded his campaigning in Azarbaijan, Agha Mohammad accepted the "request" and appointed Kalantar as beglarbegi (Turkic: provincial governor) of Fars. Fathali Khan was instructed to position his forces at Abadeh (located between Shiraz and Isfahan). This would allow Qajar troops to deploy southwards to assist Kalantar upon Lotfali Khan's arrival at Shiraz.

Lotfali marched to Shiraz, and prepared to capture it by siege. Kalantar expelled a number of warriors from Shiraz who, though originally opposed to Lotfali Khan, were still loyal enough to the House of Zand that they were not prepared to fight for the Qajars. These warriors joined Lotfali Khan's army outside the city. Though militarily ineffective, they were symbolic of the increasing support that Lotfali was gaining in the environs of Shiraz. To forestall further bloodshed, Lotfali attempted to resolve the standoff by negotiation but this failed. Instead of accommodating Lotfali, Kalantar requested military assistance from Fathali Khan in Abadeh.

Qajar troops moved towards Shiraz and successfully repelled a Zand force dispatched to intercept them. Lotfali Khan then directed the army to confront the incoming Qajar army and defeated it. With the Zand position solidifying around Shiraz, Agha Mohammad dispatched 7,000 cavalry to Shiraz to reinforce the battered Qajar force at Abadeh.[66] Lotfali Khan did not contest the ingress of these forces into Shiraz, apparently concluding that a reinforced garrison would be more willing to step out from Shiraz to engage in open battle. This would finally allow him to destroy Kalantar and his Qajar allies. If this was his actual intent, he was indeed proven correct: the Qajars and Kalantar's troops emerged out of Shiraz to fight in late 1791 or early 1792 and were thoroughly beaten by the Zands. Meanwhile a number of Kalantar's troops had begun to defect to the Zands.

With the situation deteriorating, Agha Mohammad Khan decided to march towards Shiraz himself to crush Lotfali Khan. Despite initial successes, Lotfali Khan was forced to flee from Shiraz.[67]

Agha Mohammad Khan captured Shiraz on July 21, 1792 and remained there until his departure for Tehran on August 29, 1792.[68] Prior to his departure, Agha Mohammad Khan exhumed the body of Karim Khan and took it back to Tehran. He returned to Shiraz a year later to politically consolidate his position there. The Qajars were now clearly dominating the province of Fars while Lotfali's military and political options were steadily decreasing. Since his defeat at Shiraz, Lotfali had been on the run. He first went to Nayriz and from there managed to escape to Tabas via Kerman. He maintained an active stance and soon took Yazd with the help of his allies from Tabas. Abarkouh was next to fall, however Lotfali did leave a garrison to ensure its retention for the Zand cause. Lotfali then deployed towards Darab.

The Qajars were concerned with this resurgence of Zand activities. Despite their occupation of key cities such as Isfahan and Shiraz, the mere fact that Lotfali was at large meant that their hold of central Iran was potentially vulnerable. Qajar forces puched towards Nayriz[69] as Lotfali was located there at the time, but after eleven days of battles, many of the Zand troops deserted. Lotfali pulled back towards Tabas and eventually arrived to Kerman which became his base.[70]

Agha Mohammad Khan made thorough preparations for his final showdown with Lotfali Khan. He assembled a powerful force, and even ordered troops from the Astrabad garrison to deploy to the south. He left Tehran in May 1794 however the Qajars were forced to subdue a number of petty khans who had not yet offered their allegiance to Agha Mohammad. Fathali conducted a thorough expedition across Kerman province by entering locales such as Jiroft, Narmshir, Bam, Larsitan and even territories to the north of Bandar Abbas. These campaigns occurred when the siege of Kerman was underway.[71]

When Qajar forces arrived at Kerman in May, Agha Mohammad was cautious. He travelled around the city on a reconnaissance mission for a number of days to examine the state of its walls, towers and defenses.[72] Elaborate siege works were constructed and bloody fighting ensued in which the Zand defenders fought with special ferocity and gallantry but their cause was ultimately doomed.[73]

Lotfali Khan had gallantly held onto Kerman for four months, but he knew that all was now lost. He desperately looked for some means to escape with his last band of warriors. By now almost all means of egress had been lost as the Qajars were controlling the gates. Lotfali and his men decided to storm the Soltaniyeh gate and after fighting for three hours managed to secure it temporarily by nightfall.[74] Lotfali Khan escaped that evening through the gate and across one of the ditches.[75] Apparently misinformation had also facilitated the escape; there were false rumors that Lotfali had been killed during the assault.

Perhaps one of the most tragic episodes in the history of Iran occurred when Agha Mohammad Khan learnt of Fathali's escape, and displayed his terrible wrath by ordering his troops to tear out the eyes of the civilians and captives. He was shown a display of 20,000 eyes.[76] The women and children of the city were enslaved and the city's possessions were literally stripped bare: Kerman was so devastated that it did not recover until the 20th century.[77]

Lotfali Khan had fled to the fortress of Bam but was soon betrayed and handed over to Agha Mohammad Khan.[78] Agha Mohammad Khan subjected his youthful rival to the harshest possible punishment. After having Lotfali raped in public in front of the Qajar troops, Agha Mohammad personally blinded him.[79] Lotfali Khan was then taken to Tehran to be imprisoned, horribly tortured and finally killed by having a spear driven through his heart.[80] Lotfali had fought with dignity against Qajar military superiority while having to face the disgraceful treachery within his own ranks. He is now buried in Imamzadeh Zaid in Tehran.

The Qajars deploy to the Caucasus (1795-96)

With his hold over western, northern and central Iran secure, Agha Mohammad Khan finally re-asserted Iranian authority in the former Safavid domains of the Caucasus. Agha Mohammad Khan, like the Safavids and Nader Shah, viewed these as Iranian territories no different from provinces such as Fars, Azarbaijan or Yazd.[81] After the demise of Nader Shah, Georgia and the khanates of the Caucasus had become autonomous, and Georgian bonds with Iran continued to weaken during the Zand tenure. The Georgian question became more pronounced in the late Zand era as Russian Empress Catherine II (r. 1762–96) signed the Treaty of Georgievsk with Georgia's King Heraclius II in 1783, acknowledging Georgia as the virtual protectorate of the Russian Empire.[82] The treaty specifically stipulated Georgia's formal renunciation of her former dependence on Iran and even allowed Russian troops to enter Georgian territory.[83] Assured of Russian backing, Heraclius annexed the khanate of Ganja. Despite these actions, Agha Mohammad Khan was willing to accommodate Heraclius. The Qajars offered him control of Caucasian khanates such as Karabakh, Shirvan, Sheki and Yerevan on the condition that he sever his ties with Russia and restore Georgia's tributary status with Iran.[84] Heraclius predictably rejected Agha Mohammad Khan's overtures and made preparations for war.[85]

Agha Mohammad set out to conquer the Caucasus, spanning the Araxes River to the south and bordering Azarbaijan to the Kura River in Georgia further to the north. Mirza Mohammad Khan Dolavi Qajar was appointed as the beglarbegi of Tehran by Agha Mohammad as he marched towards the Caucasus in May 1795. Heraclius again made appeals for Russian military assistance but was again rebuffed by Saint Petersburg. While precise estimates are difficult to ascertain, Qajar forces departing from Tehran most likely numbered between 40,000 and 60,000 men.[86] As the Qajar armies thrust into the Caucasus they ran into stiff resistance at Yerevan and Javanshir's Panahabad fortress at Shusha.[87] The Qajars did defeat Javanshir's army but the latter simply retreated into the powerful fortress at Shusha. Even as many of Javanshir's allies abandoned him and joined the Qajars, the Panahabad fortress held out and Shusha remained outside the Qajars' grasp. Agha Mohammad then besieged Shusha for one month (July 8–August 9, 1795) but failed to capture it.[88]

The key to prying open the powerful defenses of the Panahabad fortress of Shusha and the walls of Yerevan was artillery, weaponry that the Iranians lacked. Javanshir however was under severe pressure and it is unclear how much longer he could have held out against the Qajar blockade. Javanshir finally ceased fighting and agreed to accept Qajar authority, provide hostages, and pay tribute but refused to allow Agha Mohammad's troops to enter Shusha.[89] Nevertheless this compromise allowed Agha Mohammad Khan to resume the march with the main Qajar army towards Tbilisi.[90] Javanshir, though seemingly subdued, would soon reemerge as a threat to Qajar ambitions in the Karabakh khanate.

Agha Mohammad linked up with his right wing after it secured Shirvan and Qobbeh and was then joined by Javad Khan of Ganja.[91] He left portions of the left wing at Yerevan to enforce that city's blockade then amalgamated the rest into his main force.[92] At Ganja, Agha Mohammad Khan sent one final message to Heraclius offering to allow him to stay as governor if he confirmed his obedience immediately, otherwise he would be "treated as the others."[93]

Unbowed, Heraclius reaffirmed his allegiance to Russia and began to mobilize an army. The combined Qajar force that marched towards Tbilisi is estimated at 40,000 cavalry.[94] The first clash occurred on September 10, 1795 when the advance elements of the Qajar army were beaten back by the Georgians who numbered no more than 5,000 men. This brief success was of little solace to the Georgians as Agha Mohammad and the main Qajar army arrived the next day to make battle against a greatly outnumbered Georgian force.[95] The Georgians fought gallantly and ferociously for an entire day during which they forced the Qajar forces back three times.[96] The Georgian forces however had suffered high casualties by the same evening and could hold out no longer. They retreated into Tbilisi's citadel while Heraclius and numbers of the Georgian nobility fled for the mountains.[97] Heraclius died shortly after in 1798, still hopeful of Russian assistance.

Agha Mohammad Khan once again proved his capacity for cruelty. He not only executed those Georgian nobles and commanders who had submitted to him, but also issued orders for his troops to plunder and burn the city and gave them free reign in killing innocent civilians.[98] Churches were deliberately burnt and their priests drowned in the Kura River,[99] a macabre spectacle which Agha Mohammad reputedly took pleasure in witnessing.[100] The final act of brutality was the taking of between 15,000 and 50,000 slaves (including young girls and boys) from Tbilisi to Iran.[101]

News of the massacres at Tbilisi led Yerevan to submit to the Qajars,[102] but Javanshir of Shusha again proved defiant.[103] After nine days in Tbilisi, Agha Mohammad turned south to subdue all remaining opposition. After marching through Sheki, he arrived at Shirvan, defeated its ruler Mostafa Khan and captured the capital Shamakhi.[104] As in Georgia, Agha Mohammad Khan inflicted considerable harm to local civilians. Much of the local agriculture of Karabakh and Shirvan was destroyed, leading to famine and the dislocation of much of the population.[105] Javanshir, however, continued to hold out against the Qajars.

On the surface, Agha Mohammad had restored the lost Caucasian domains, especially the prized Georgian kingdoms. Russian authority had certainly been damaged, but the prestige of Iranian arms would not last long, and Agha Mohammad had harmed the Qajars' cause in Georgia and the Caucasus by alienating much of the Georgian nobility and populace.

The Qajars' conquests in the Caucasus could only be fully consolidated with the total subjugation of Shusha's Panahabad fortress. Agha Mohammad Khan deployed his forces towards this formidable fortress.[106] Agha Mohammad's artillery failed against Panahabad's powerful defenses but he did crush all of Javanshir's assaults.[107] Javanshir and his commanders realized the futility of their resistance, and feared the terrible wrath of Agha Mohammad Khan and the possible massacre of the civilians of Shusha. Emissaries were sent to Agha Mohammad requesting his forgiveness and the withholding of retribution in exchange of Shusha's submission. This was accepted by Agha

Mohammad who also demanded that Javanshir yield one of his sons as a hostage to the Qajar court. Satisfied that their authority had been imposed, the Qajar forces left for Iran. They would, however, be forced to deal with Javanshir yet again in the near future.

Agha Mohammad Khan Qajar becomes shah

Agha Mohammad had refused to accept the title of the shah of Iran as much of Iran's domains had yet to be conquered when he finally defeated the Zands in 1794. With northern, central and western Iran secure and the Caucasus conquered, only Khorasan remained outside of the Qajar orbit. Haji Ibrahim, accompanied by numerous nobles and government officials, arrived at Mughan where Agha Mohammad had encamped and formally requested that he accept the mantle of the shah of Iran before marching into Khorasan.[108] Interestingly, some Iranian historians report Agha Mohammad Khan as having declared his kingship in 1785 or 1786,[109] but this is believed to be incorrect.[110] Agha Mohammad Khan is generally believed to have been crowned as the shah of Iran at Mughan (like Nader Shah six decades before him), in March 1796.[111] Much effort was made to emulate Safavid traditions. The sword of Shah Ismail was hung from the roof of the sacred shrine of Sheikh Safi at Ardabil.[112] Agha Mohammad further legitimized his kingship by wearing that sacred sword followed by the placing of a crown on his head.[113] Once the coronation ceremonies ended, Agha Mohammad Shah departed with his main army to Tehran. Baba Khan also known as Fathali Khan who was Agha Mohammad's nephew was nominated by the latter as the Crown Prince.[114]

The Qajars enter Khorasan (1795-96)

The key eastern province of Khorasan was still ruled by the descendants of Nader Shah. Intending to restore Khorasan to central control, Agha Mohammad Shah once again mobilized his main army, now standing at around 60,000 troops (infantry and cavalry) and left Tehran for the northeast. The new shah arrived at Astarabad and from there successfully subdued a number of rebellious Goklen Turkmen tribes who had been attacking the province.[115] With the conclusion of these campaigns, the Qajar army thrust into Khorasan and headed towards the provincial capital, Mashad.[116] Khorasan was by this time barely governable as much of the province was being run by various tribes (i.e. Turkmen, Kurd) engaged in raids, plundering and the acquisition of slaves. These, however, chose not to fight Agha Mohammad Shah and offered their submission to him and his arriving army.[117] No battle would take place at Mashahd either as Shahrokh, the blind grandson of Nader Shah, and a number of nobles greeted Agha Mohammad Shah honorably at the environs of Mashad.[118] The shah sent 8,000 troops into the city led by Qajar nobles and he himself arrived into the city the next day.

Mashad was spared from violence but Shahrokh himself was doomed. He was captured and tortured so as to confess the whereabouts of the late Nader Shah's hidden jewels.[119] Shahrokh died later as a result, but not before confessing to the location of at least a portion of the hidden treasures.[120] With these, Agha Mohammad was able to finance his next Caucasian campaigns.[121] He also exhumed the remains of Nader Shah and had these reburied in his Tehran palace alongside those of Karim Khan Zand.

Agha Mohammad's Second Caucasian War

Despite the Qajar army's recent successes, the Iranian hold over the Caucasus had yet to consolidate. The French had been especially concerned with Russian ambitions in Georgia. They dispatched two emissaries, G. A. Olivier and J. G. Brugieres, to Tehran. They met Haji Ibrahim who handled affairs of state during the shah's absence, and warned the Iranians to consolidate their hold on Georgia as soon as possible before Russia began to send her armies there.[122] They strongly advised Iran to secure western Georgia, especially the Mingrelia region adjacent to the Black Sea, as this would facilitate Iran's contacts with Europe.

The news from Georgia obliged Empress Catherine II to dispatch a massive Russian army of 80,000 troops supported by 100 cannon led by General Ivan Gudovich and Count Valerian Zhubov towards the Caucasus in 1795–96.[123] Catherine had every intention of eventually toppling Agha Mohammad Khan and replacing him with the more compliant Morteza Qoli Qajar.[124]

When Agha Mohammad Khan returned to Iran after his Caucasian campaign to campaign in Khorasan in 1796, and just as just as Catherine the Great was set to conquer the Caucasus, Javanshir opened negotiations with the Russians. He agreed to support the Russians on the condition that they recognize him as ruler of Karabakh. A number of other khanate leaders also saw an opportunity to take advantage of the Russian invasion to challenge the authority of the Qajars. Heraclius also recaptured Tbilisi and much of Georgia.[125] In what appeared to be a repeat of the conquests of Peter the Great 73 years previously, Russian armies advanced along the eastern marches of the Caucasus capturing Darband, Baku, Salyan, Talysh, Shamakhi and Talysh. The empress, however, passed away in November 1796. Catherine's son and successor, Paul I (r. 1796–1801) opposed his mother's expansionist policies and ordered Russian forces to vacate the Caucasus.[126] Agha Mohammad had arrived from Khorasan to Tehran and began to mobilize his army for a new and prolonged Caucasian campaign. The Qajar army arrived in the Soltaniyeh region in Azarbaijan in June 1797 and prepared for a long and extensive campaign to (once again) re-assert Qajar authority upon the khanates and Georgia. The departure of Russian forces gave the Qajars more flexibility to choose the timing and locale of their assaults.

With Russian forces now out of the Caucasian theater, Georgia was at least nominally an Iranian possession. Agha Mohammad Khan opted to permanently eject Javanshir from Karabakh in 1797. The Qajars first advanced from Mianeh to Ardabil to thrust towards Shusha.[127] At this juncture, just as Agha Mohammad and the main army were at Adinehbazar, the Qajars received a stroke of good luck: a delegation from Shusha arrived to inform the shah that Javanshir and his kin had fled into Daghestan.[128] The delegation also invited the shah to march into city. Agha Mohammad crossed the Araxes accompanied by a ceremonial guard of 10,000 and arrived without incident into the city.[129] Accompanying Agha Mohammad was Sadeq Khan, leader of the Shakak Kurds.[130] Qajar authority had been fully established in the Karabakh khanate. Javanshir had to wait until the Russians decided to resume their advances into the Caucasus. As events were to soon transpire, he did not have long to wait. King Heraclius of Georgia was also fortunate as Agha Mohammad was planning to enter Georgia once more to revive his authority there.[131]

Assassination of Agha Mohammad Khan and the ascension of Fathali Shah

Agha Mohammad Khan spent his last days in Shusha. Angered by an argument between two of his servants, he ordered them executed. The Shakaki Kurdish leader, Sadeq Khan, argued for clemency, but Agha Mohammad only delayed their execution for a day. Incredibly he ordered the doomed servants to wait on him on their last evening. Predictably the servants took advantage of their situation to slay the shah on the night of June 16, 1797[132] with the help of a third servant. They stole the shah's jewels and sought sanctuary with Sadeq Khan who accepted.

Sadeq Khan and the Shakak Kurds left Shusha the same night and marched towards Azarbaijan to the south in Iran.[133] At Shusha the local mullahs buried Agha Mohammad while the local populace raided the shah's camp. Agha Mohammad's guards at Shusha left to join the main force at Adinehbazar that was also in disarray.[134] The main part of this army was taken by Haji Ibrahim towards Tehran[135] but was harassed in Azarbaijan by Sadeq Khan and the Shakak Kurds.[136] When the main army finally arrived at Tehran's gates, they were denied ingress by the city's major, Mirza Mohammad Khan Develu. Other arriving Qajar nobles were also denied entrance to the city. The mayor was loyal to Baba Kahn (also known as Fathali Khan; the late shah's nephew) and awaited his arrival from Shiraz.[137] The situation began to dissolve into a state dangerously akin to the civil war that had characterized the late Agha Mohammad's own quest for power. In the meantime, Javanshir had taken advantage of the departure of Iranian troops to return to Shusha after his brief exile in Daghestan.

Sadeq Khan also appointed his brothers Jaafar Khan and Mohammad Ali Soltan as the governors of Qarajedagh and Tabriz respectively. The brothers were also ordered to attack Khoy. Meanwhile the garrison at Qazvin held out just long enough for a Tehran force to relieve them. Sadeq Khan continued to besiege Qazvin and in the meantime did his best to raise an army from Ardabil, Maragheh, Moghan, Solduz and Tabriz. In the meantime Ali Qoli Khan, the late shah's brother, now arrived from Yerevan and approached the gates of Tehran that remained closed to him. He then left for a fortress at Karaj and declared himself the shah of Iran.[138]

Fathali Khan, who was in Shiraz, proceeded to take charge. He marched towards Tehran and was joined by a number of loyal princes as well as Haji Ibrahim. Fathali Khan also captured his rebellious uncle, Ali Qoli Khan, and blinded him.[139] Tehran opened its gates to Fathali Khan on August 15, 1797.[140] With the capital secured, Fathali Khan quickly marched to the northwest to restore order. The Qajar army marched towards Qazvin to break the siege of the Shakak Kurds there. Fathali Khan and his army were met in battle by Sadeq Khan and his troops approximately 60 miles from Qazvin.[141] After a bitter battle Sadeq Khan was defeated and forced to flee to Sarab. His military power was broken but he still had the late Agha Mohammad's royal jewels. Sadeq Khan was pardoned in return for the return of the jewels. Two of the assassins of the late shah were also caught in Qazvin and soon put to death.[142] The remains of Agha Mohammad were exhumed from Shusha and brought to Tehran and then to the sacred shrine of Imam Ali in Najaf, Ottoman-ruled Iraq where his body was put to rest as that of the Safavid Shah Abbas.

Fathali Khan proved his statesmanship by not partaking in harsh retributions and the granting of generous offices and positions to the chieftains in Azarbaijan, including the Dumbuli and Shakak Kurds. With the situation in the critical northwest secured, Fathali Khan had succeeded in preventing Iran from plunging into another catastrophic civilian war. With his tasks accomplished, Fathali Khan returned to Tehran in late 1797.[143]

With the political situation in Iran partially stabilized, Fathali Khan was crowned as Fathali Shah in March 1798 at Tehran's Golestan Palace. Abbas Mirza, Fathali's fourth son, then just ten years old, was made crown prince and assigned as the governor of Azarbaijan.[144] Stout opposition to Fathali's kingship was still in existence. Fathali's brother (Hussein Qoli Khan) revolted in Fars province but this proved unsuccessful. The main crisis was to once again flare up in Azarbaijan. Sadeq Khan of the Shahak Kurds had attacked Jaafar Kahn Dumbuli (not to be confused with Sadeq Khan's brother of the same name) as the latter marched in to assume governorship of Tabriz and Khoy on behalf of Fathali Shah. Sadeq Khan was defeated and fled to Shirvan. He then gained the trust and alliance of Jaafar Khan Dumbuli and the Afsharid Mohammad Qoli-Khan converging with them at Sarab and then fanning across Azarbaijan.[145] Sadeq Khan, no stranger to perfidy, soon betrayed his newfound allies in favor of the Qajar house. Fathali however had had enough and had the fickle Sadeq Khan imprisoned in the Golestan palace in 1800. With stability having returned to Azarbaijan, Fathali Shah was now secure on his throne.

CHAPTER 20

QAJAR ARMIES 1800–48

The armies of Fathali Shah were initially those inherited from his predecessor, Agha Mohammad Khan, with changes being introduced mainly due to the disastrous wars with Russia. Information of the composition and weaponry of the infantry, cavalry and artillery of Fathali Shah is available from European sources such as Gardane, Joubert, Sir John Malcolm, Stoddard, and Fabvier.[1] While these sources have some discrepencies, together with Iranian sources they generally provide a consistent description of the state of Iran's forces.

The backbone of the army was provided by the provinces, notably Azarbaijan and Ardalan. As noted previously, the forces of Agha Mohammad Khan were reported as 270,000 strong, with 70,000 being the shah's personal corps stationed in Tehran. The total number of Iranian army personnel (shah's bodyguard units and all other units such as tribal contingents, etc) appear to have varied somewhat by the time of Agha Mohammad Khan's successor Fathali Shah. Sir John Malcolm (who wrote shortly after Agha Mohammad's death) reports the total size of the Iranian army of Fathali Shah (infantry, cavalry, artillerymen, etc) as standing at a total of 254,000 men, with Stoddard reporting a total of 100,750 men.[2] Gardane reports the infantry as numbering some 60,000 troops, with Malcolm describing these as being divided into two groups, one being regular troops and the other *Janbaz*-type troops.[3] Stoddard reports the total number of regular troops as standing at 39,000 men and irregular fusiliers at 20,000 men.[4] The commander-in-chief of the army was known as the *Sardar* with the tribal leaders, khans, being designated as sultans during wartime.[5] Interestingly Turkic military terms continued to be used, with some Persian now appearing as well. Examples include *Dah-Bashi* and *Panjah-Bashi* to designate units of ten and fifty men respectively.

The royal guard units were typically stationed in the capital and Tabriz. By 1809, the royal bodyguard stood at 12,000 janbaz (lit. those who toy with their lives), and 3,000 gholam (lit. slave) cavalry.[6] The bulk of Fathali Shah's janbaz were the vaunted tofangchi (lit. fusiliers) of Mazandaran and Astarabad.[7] These were later augmented with more troops trained in the European style.

Mobilization of troops for war would take place as a consequence of the shah's *Farman* (lit. command. edict), which also designated the common place of assembly.[8] As in previous centuries khans would arrive at the head of their various tribes; the same occurred with the nobles who would be leading troops from their particular provinces or towns. The khans and nobles would then become part of the regular high command of Abbas Mirza.[9] After the conclusion of military campaigns, the contingents would return to their respective provinces and regions. The royal corps would not disband during peacetime.

Infantry

Recruitment of the infantry is described as being from Iran's various tribes (i.e. Qashqai, Afshars) and provinces (especially the north in Gilan and Mazandaran) and the peasantry.[10] Fabvier's assessment of the regular musket-armed infantry was generally negative,[11] and their firearms evaluated "very heavy … very badly built."[12] These liabilities were to prove to be a major disadvantage against highly trained European infantry wielding lighter, more reliable and more rapidly firing rifles. Traditional weapons such as daggers, sword and bows continued to appear in early Qajar armies, especially those from tribal units and outlying provinces.[13]

Cavalry

The cavalry of Iran was described in 1805 by Napoleon's emissary to Persia, Colonel Alexandre Romieu as "the best in the entire Orient."[17] The irregular cavalry hailed from western (i.e. Lurs, Bakhtiaris, etc) and eastern Iran (i.e. contingents from Khorasan, Turkmen, Baluch, etc). The total number of cavalry was estimated as ranging between 140,000 and 150,000 with the tribal element of the cavalry numbering 80,000.[18] Their weapons are generally described as being very long guns, lances and shields.[19] Colombari notes that by the time of Mohammad Shah, the army was able to raise 190,000 tribal cavalry.[20] Each tribe was expected to provide a cavalry contingent at times of war with cavalrymen being expected to provide their own mounts, however salaries were provided to these when engaged in government service. In peacetime, cavalry units would be generally available for full-time service for around two months of the year before retiring to their homes in winter.

There were a number of elite cavalry units in service. Fathali Shah had in his personal contingent a "full-time" elite cavalry unit of 3,000–4,000 men, the *Gholaman e Shahi* (gholams of the shah) who were uniformly armed with muskets, daggers and lances.[21] Other Qajar princes had their own elite guards.[22] By the time of Mohammad Shah the regular cavalry arm had risen to 10,000.[23]

The Iranian cavalry force was beset by three weaknesses.[24] The first was inherent to the traditional system of recruitment. There was no consistent system of payment for the mass of the cavalry recruits, obliging them to rely on plunder and booty in compensation for their military services. Secondly, each cavalryman had to pay and provide for their own weapons and horses and neither the government nor the army was responsible for replacing the material losses incurred by their cavalry troops in battle. This seriously hampered the Iranian cavalry force, especially at those times when battles hung in the balance or when the fighting was prolonged and/or intense. The third weakness of the cavalry was a consequence of one of their greatest strengths: fluidity and looseness of organization. According to Gardane, Iranian cavalry would attack en masse without any particular doctrine or strategy and retreat in the face of resistance.[25] Retreating cavalry would often engage in the "Parthian shot." Despite these types of equestrian combat skills, Iranian cavalry had no formal standardized training or doctrine in terms of methodical coordination and focus of strikes in the manner seen with contemporary European armies. Despite these liabilities, the cavalry arm was potentially Iran's most effective military arm.

Artillery

The number of artillery personnel are variously reported at 1,550, 2,500 and even 150 men,[23] with the majority of these being Armenians and Georgians.[24] Estimates of the numbers of reliable standard cannon vary between 20 and 60 pieces[25] described as being of the "Russian type" (Gardane).[26] Fabvier very clearly describes the decrepit state of Iran's artillery at the time of Fathali Shah by observing that "the Iranian army lacks proper artillery … the few cannon that remain from earlier times are completely useless."[27] These reports indicate that the artillery of Iran had seen little improvement since the death of Nader Shah. The reliability of the contemporary western reports need to re-examined after recent studies of Qajar-era artillery.[28] Not only do these reports fail to substantiate the prevailing view of Iranian artillery at the time but also indicate that the Iranian workshops and engineers had designed and fired unguided rockets.[29]

The lighter camel-mounted zanbourak artillery continued to see service as late as the reign of Fathali Shah. Fabvier describes the Qajar zanbouraks as "having very short barrels and small munitions at approximately 250g each. These are mounted on the backs of camels."[30] Militarily these were of dubious value against the modern contemporary armies of the British and Russian empires. The decrepit state of the armaments industry, especially with respect to the mass production of modern guns, artillery and ammunition, was to be another one of Iran's major military weaknesses.

European missions to Iran (1801–48)

The Iranian army experienced attempts at reforms during the reign of Fathali Shah following Iran's disastrous defeats against Russia in the early 19th century. Crown Prince Abbas Mirza was perhaps the most vociferous figure in pushing for reforms in the Iranian army. The impact of most of these military reforms were to be felt in Azarbaijan as this was the front-line province of Iran against Russia, and the seat of Abbas Mirza.[31] Although his reform attempts were ultimately compromised by a variety of factors, a number of important initiatives were introduced which helped to lay the seeds of the modern Iranian army in the twentieth century.

The first Qajar shah to introduce European instructors in an effort to modernize the Iranian army was the late Agha Mohammad Shah who recruited a number of Russian officers to train Iranian troops in Qazvin; these were also later used in a similar capacity by Abbas Mirza.[32] Both Fathali Shah and crown prince Abbas Mirza concluded that the only way to prevail against Russia was by modernizing the Iranian military along European lines as much as possible.[33] The army had fallen into decline after the Afsharid-Zand interlude, while European military technology was in the ascendant. Some knowledge of European methods of warfare had been brought to Iran by Russian adventurers and deserters however the first significant European influences were to come from the English and the French.

The first English mission into Iran in the early Qajar era was led by Sir John Malcolm in 1800.[34] Malcolm and the Iranians signed a commercial and political treaty in January 1801. The relationship broke down a few years later when the British refused to support Iran militarily against Russia.[35]

Europe's military genius Napoleon Bonaparte had had much success in the European mainland. His expedition into Egypt had brought him into contact with the Near East and Iran. After a series of lengthy negotiations, a Franco-Iranian alliance, known as the Treaty of Finkelstein, was finally signed in 1807. By this time Iran was battling Russia in the Caucasus.[36]

Abbas Mirza had managed to train a handful of his men in the European style with the help of the Russian instructors, but the French mission provided him with a full complement of NCOs and professional instructors.[37] The treaty however became null and void just two months later in the same year, when Russia and France signed a treaty of alliance against the British Empire. This forced a halt to the constructive efforts of the French mission in Iran, and the officers were soon expelled by Fathali Shah.

The French arrivals into Iran had alarmed the British, and a second mission resulted in the Treaty of Friendship and Alliance in the spring of 1809.[38] The treaty obliged the Iranians to cut their ties with the French in exchange for a British subsidy to help pay for British military supplies, officers and NCOs for Iran. British and Indian military personnel arrived into Iran from India and Britain in 1810–13.[39] By 1813, fifty officers and men from the British Empire were engaged in continuing the work of the departed French officers.[40] Iran was to also lose the British mission as the Russian and British empires agreed on an alliance against the French in 1812–13. The majority of the British personnel left Iran, with a very small number staying in Iran on condition that they would not partake in any combat operations against Russia. The British departure (like the French one before it) once again bought the modernization of Iran's forces to a dangerous halt.

A number of French officers did arrive to Iran by late 1814, after Napoleon's defeats against Russia (1812) and the sixth coalition (composed of Russia, Prussia, Austro-Hungary, Sweden and Britain) at Leipzig (1814). They arrived too late to make a military impression on Iran's Caucasian front. The French arrivals however did see service with the Iranian army.[41] A trickle of European military officers did manage to find their way into Iran after 1820. These were mainly veterans of Europe's Napoleonic wars. They saw service with Abbas Mirza and the Qajar prince governing Kermanshah, Mohammad Ali Mirza. European observers provide negative reports on the capabilities of these Europeans as military instructors who often quarreled and even fought duels![42]

The final British military mission arrived by ship from India and landed in the port of Bushehr in 1833. This was a team of eight officers, fourteen sergeants and an apothecary, followed shortly later with the shipment of military supplies from Britain and India.[43] The British agreed to supply Iran with 2,000 muskets along with 500,000 flints, and parts of howitzers[44] along with another eight officers to train the Iranian army.[45] The officers arrived in 1836, just one year before the Qajar army besieged Herat. These were the last British efforts aimed at reforming and modernizing the Iranian army. Diplomatic relations between Tehran and London soured and nearly flared into an all-out war over the thorny question of Herat. The treatment of the British officers by their Iranian counterparts caused further tension.[46] By 1839 the British had completely withdrawn their military mission, never to return.

In 1838, Mohammad Shah sent an embassy to King Louis-Philippe (1773–1850) to enlist French military expertise, which after prolonged negotiations, secured the dispatch of five infantry officers, two cavalry officers and three officers and military instructors for artillery. The mission was plagued by interference by Russian and British officials from the outset, finally departing from Iran just four years later.[47]

While these missions were often ephemeral and their immediate effects modest, the long-term consequences of these cumulative efforts were to prove positive for the Iranian military. A growing cadre of Iranian officers absorbed valuable lessons in European modes of warfare and this allowed for the genesis of a modernized cadre of military personnel. Despite numerous obstacles, the seeds of military reforms had been laid, which though slow-paced, proved to gradually institutionalize itself into Iran's first true military academy, the Dar ol Fonoon.

An interesting Iranian viewpoint is provided by Matofi, who argues that one of the reasons for the failure of the military missions was the concern of European governments that successful reforms would lead to the modernization, striking power and martial ardor of the Iranian army.[48] Such a situation would not necessarily be in favor of European geopolitical interests at the time. Russia was certainly not eager to see the Iranians challenge their recently lost possessions in the Caucasus just as the British were not eager to see a powerful and revitalized army on their doorstep in India.

The *Nezam e Jadid*

Abbas Mirza's hard work for reforms resulted in a total of 20,000 troops trained along European lines with 9,000 of these serving as Fathali Shah's personal guards.[49] The remaining 11,000 troops were to form the core of Abbas Mirza's forces in the wars against Russia. All of these new units known as the *Nezam e Jadid*[50] (lit. the new military/order) were issued with consistent uniforms, fought in the methodical and disciplined style of European units and featured distinct rank and status designations.[51] These features however were most typical of the army units in Azarbaijan with many of Iran's other units and tribal levies remaining wedded to antiquated modes of warfare and weaponry. Traditional weapons took some time to disappear and numbers of troops continued to appear with mail, swords, daggers and archery equipment.[52]

With the assistance of French embassy staff in Tehran, Abbas Mirza studied French military manuals pertaining to infantry and artillery warfare as well as the construction of modern barracks and military factories.[53] His son, Bahram Qajar, worked hard at producing writings of military sciences in Persian, especially after studies in Europe. He wrote Iran's first modern military manual, which became known as the *Aeen Nameh e Nasseri* [Protocol Book of Nasser e Din Shah].[54]

Abbas Mirza was keen to modernize Iran's own production centers so they could mass-produce modern weapons. The Austro-Hungarian Empire sent one of their rifles to copy in 1819,[55] but in practice Iran's new rifle production centers became accustomed to making copies of British and French rifles.[56] There were also a number of important artillery and munitions production centers which opened in Azarbaijan and Isfahan. The increase in artillery production also resulted in the greater use of such weapons in sieges. With these developments, the old tactic of "surround and starve" by building structures around besieged cities finally fell into obsolescence.[57] Abbas Mirza also placed much effort towards the creation of an *esprit de corps*, by emphasizing qualities such as military professionalism and military reviews.[58]

Iran's critical military error

The Qajars' quest to modernize their military forces mirrored the efforts of the Ottomans during the 19th century.[59] Abbas Mirza equated the survival of Iran and the Qajar dynasty with the ability to "match European military power by imitating European military organization."[60] Abbas Mirza worked hard at introducing the Nezam e Jadid military units into the Iranian army and in doing so committed a major error: he failed to appreciate the importance of the "traditional" arms of Iran, most especially her cavalry, the marksmanship and equestrian skills of which were highly praised by European observers.[61] The retention of older military methods continued to present advantages for the Iranians, especially when dealing with European armies. Traditional methods could be of military merit, especially in supporting the Nezam e Jadid units of the Iranian army in battles against Russia. The Russians experienced great operational difficulties against the Iranian cavalry in the Caucasus in the early 19th century.[62] Russia was kept at bay for nine years by Iran's tribal cavalry, one major reason being that these often chose not to fight the Russians in formal set-piece battles. European observers at the time were quick to point out Iran's loss of "Asian agility and quickness" as the new military increasingly de-emphasized its formidable cavalry arm.[63]

By the early twentieth century, Iran no longer had the benefit of being able to call upon its masses of tribal cavalry but had no effective standing army capable of resisting foreign invasions. Even if the cavalry had been fully appreciated, the Iranians simply did not have enough time to work out the practical aspects of having the "modernized" and "traditional" branches cooperate effectively on the battlefield before they needed to meet the Russians in battle.

The Iranian Army under Fathali Shah and Mohammad Shah

The Iranian army was beset by a number of profound weaknesses at the time of Fathali Shah. When the showdown came with the Russian and British Empires, the Qajars found their armies hopelessly outclassed. Lambton has argued that the solution to Iran's military problems during the time of Fathali Shah (and by implication much of the Qajar era) required reforms at the top levels of government and administration.[64] Fathali's son and successor, Mohammad Shah (r. 1834–48) was unable to effectively sustain the reforming efforts of his father and Abbas Mirza due to challenges posed by Qajar nobles as well as the disastrous war at Herat (1837–38).[65]

Perhaps one of the most serious problems reported was the lack of a consistent and long-term officer tradition. There were no military schools in the European sense[66] in which veterans trained the next generation of officers. Despite Abbas Mirza's best efforts, officers were often promoted due to political ties rather than military merit, which soon led to corruption and nepotism.[67]

Iran's tribes had traditionally been one of Iran's greatest military strengths. While these certainly provided tough and resilient fighters, their overall efficiency in the Iranian army was often compromised by intertribal politics. Tribal chiefs were often rivals, jealous of each other's political influence, and military successes. This meant that cooperation was not always ensured as tribal chiefs could place their own personal interests ahead those of their own troops and even the Iranian army. There were serious problems with maintaining military secrets in the Iranian army.[68] The failure to maintain military secrecy was to cost the Iranians dearly in their wars against Russia.

Despite the efficiency of Nader Shah's army in the 18th century, there was little appreciation for European developments in military sciences and doctrine, especially with respect to sieges, fortress construction, offensive and defensive modes of warfare.[69]

Even as serious attempts at reform were implemented by Fathali Shah's son, crown prince Abbas Mirza, the "conservative" branch of the army remained obstinate and resistant to change. The "conservatives" were against modernization, partly due to the inevitable disruptions these would casuse to their favorable military/political position in the army and society.[70]

Economics dictated the pace and intensity of Iran's efforts to rebuild her military. The Iranian national budget and economy were simply not up to the task of reforming and re-equipping an entirely new army in a short span of time.[71]

With the exception of Abbas Mirza's units in Azarbaijan, there was no consistent system of training in the Iranian army at the time of Fathali Shah. Training in general would take place when conscripts were being recruited for an impending war.[72] One major consequence of this was that military discipline among regular troops was often low,[73] excepting the elite formations and some European-trained units. Despite Abbas Mirza's best efforts, the sense of professionalism would never permeate across the entire Iranian army. Iranian troops remained tough and resilient, however these factors by themselves could not compensate against contemporary European armies such as those of Russia.

With the exception of royal units, the payment of soldiers and the provision of uniforms and supplies were wholly inconsistent and unreliable.[74] Inefficient systems of payment for government troops in full-time employ of Fathali Shah or the regional governors also led to social discontent, especially in rural areas.[75]

Many volunteers for campaigns and especially tribal levies felt entitled to plunder the townships and locales of defeated foes. This would inevitably lead to the animosity of the local populace against Iranian central authorities, especially in the sensitive Caucasian theater.[76]

The Qajar army had a serious problem with failed logistics. Supplies for campaigns would often be secured from the villages and townships en-route to campaign theaters. Civilians would suffer from the appropriations made by the marching Qajar army, who often didn't pay.[77]

Iran also lacked the reliable roads and railways enjoyed by contemporary armies in Europe meaning that transportation of supplies was undertaken with horses, mules and camels. Iran had yet to develop an effective office to specifically oversee the efficient management of military logistics. Abbas Mirza's reforms saw some improvements such as English-designed horse-drawn wagons for the transport of war supplies.[78] Irrespective of such developments, the gap between Europe and Iran in terms of logistics and transport was clearly to the disadvantage of the latter throughout the 19th century.

The naval arm had been neglected by the Zand and early Qajars with disastrous consequences. The Caspian Sea was to become a Russian lake, thanks in large part to the treaty of Turkmenchai in 1828. Even before the treaty had been signed, Iran had no fleet with which to oppose the Russians in the early nineteenth century. The situation was equally critical in the southern waters of the Persian Gulf. When the British sent a naval squadron to occupy Kharq Island in June 1838 for example, there was no Iranian navy to oppose them.[79] As the 19th century progressed, the Persian Gulf came increasingly under British naval, and political influence.

Iran's technology gap with Europe

It was not until their disastrous wars against Russia in the early 20th century that the Iranians finally realized how much their nation lagged behind the Europeans in European tactics and technology. Military weaknesses resulted in defeats of great magnitude leaving profound political, economic and social consequences that resonate in Iran to this day. Europe had made gigantic strides in the social, economic, and political domains as well in industry and technology. Much of this had occurred when Iran was in overall economic, political and military decline in the late Safavid era. The rule of Nader Shah saw Iran's most serious step towards modernizing her military technology and industry, but the time was too brief to establish long-term benefits for the Iranian army. The rule of the succeeding Zand dynasty did little to improve Iran's armaments industry or technology. By the onset of Qajar rule in the late 19th century, the technology gap between Iran and Europe had continued to widen, with disastrous military consequences for Iran throughout much of the 19th and early 20th centuries.

In Russia, Iran faced a colossus of gigantic proportions. Western historians have often referred to the Tsarist military machine as a "steamroller" which was able to overwhelm its opponents by sheer force of numbers in infantry and artillery. But when facing Iran, Russia's military was so much better that she could prevail even when outnumbered on the battlefield.[80]

CHAPTER 21

IRAN'S DEVASTATING WARS WITH RUSSIA (1804–26)

Imperial Russia had not forgotten the dreams of Peter the Great: the conquest of the Caucasus, domination of Iran and the Persian Gulf with ambitions towards British India. Fathali Shah and Iran would soon be facing the might of imperial Russia, a military challenge for which the armies of the Qajars were wholly unprepared.[1]

Iran was ruled by a series of princes in the major cities and provinces as well as tribes beholden to their leaders. The country would be stable so long as these forces acknowledged the shah's authority, however the large degree of autonomy in the provinces did facilitate rebellion against the government or center. When Iran faced the armies of Russia, a series of rebellions broke out in the northeast (Khorasan) as well as the north (Astarabad and Mazandaran).[2] These types of rebellions often forced the diversion of troops to provincial areas when they could otherwise have been used in critical battles against foreign armies. An example of fickle khans and the threats these posed to Qajar military activities in Khorasan as late as 1832 is provided by Hedayat's *Fihrist ol Tavareekh*.[3] Iran was to eventually lose all of the Caucasus due to a combination of Qajar mismanagement, outdated technology, and opportunistic khans who were willing to side with the Russians in hopes of increasing their personal wealth and status.

Iran and Russia: clash of hegemonies in Georgia and the Caucasus

Agha Mohammad Khan's assassination left his conquests in Georgia unconsolidated, inviting the Russians to forcibly pursue the establishment of their preferred Russo-Iranian border, as far south as the Kura River and even the Araxes River bordering Azarbaijan.[4]

There are indications that Fathali Shah did seek better relations with the Russians, especially in the earlier days of his rule.[5] Tsar Paul was willing to accommodate Fathali Shah's overtures and reciprocated by agreeing that Russian merchants should pay duties on goods they imported to Iran, the export of 18,000 tons of iron into Iran and that Russian warships not enter the port of Anzali arbitrarily.[6] Despite these constructive acts of accommodation, the thorny issue of Georgia remained. No Iranian shah could conceive of ruling just a part of Iran by abandoning its other provinces, a practice which had occurred at the time of Karim Khan and Shahrokh Afshar. Fathali viewed Georgia as a prized province that had to be restored to the Iranian state. Tsar Paul I in turn was determined to treat Georgia as his protectorate, making the prospect of war all but inevitable.

The pattern of events unfolded as they had before. Fathali Shah wrote a highly threatening letter to Giorgi XII (son of Heraclius who had died in 1798), the new king of Karli-Kakheti, in the summer of 1798 ordering him to submit to his authority or face the prospect of "doubly increased

188 IRAN AT WAR

subjection… Georgia will again be annihilated… Georgian people given to our wrath."[7] Giorgi XII sent emissaries to St. Petersburg in September 1800 in order to negotiate a new pact with Tsar Paul I (r. 1796–1801), The pact entitled Paul I to nominate himself as the tsar of Russia and Georgia, thereby considering the latter as a Russian protectorate. Giorgi also demanded that his eldest son David succeed him as king of Georgia.[8]

Confrontation was also hastened by Russian imperialist ambitions. Andreeva has noted that "Territorial aggrandizement … would make the empire rich and … the empire could in return benefit subject peoples by introducing them to civilization and Christianity."[9] Russia was a major European power, thanks to her "absorption of western technology and military skills…"[10] as well as her participation in the Napoleonic wars and European politics. From St. Petersburg, Iran and her Caucasian possessions looked ripe for imperial conquest and economic domination.

Catherine the Great had considered Georgia as the lynchpin of Russian foreign policy to her south. From Georgia Russia could project its military power against both the Iranians and the Ottomans.[11] The Russian navy would also benefit greatly from having access to Georgia's western ports along the Black Sea.[12] With ports already established in southern Russia, access to Georgian seaports would transform the Black Sea into a Russian-dominated lake. As Georgia and the Caucasus stood at the crossroads between Europe and Asia, control of this region would greatly benefit Russian commerce. Control of Georgia as well as the khanates to its east and south would allow the Russians to dominate the maritime trade of both the Black and Caspian seas. Control of the Caspian Sea would allow the Russians to extend their maritime and commercial interests into northern Iran and Central Asia.[13]

The First Iranian-Russian War

The Russians sent a diplomatic note to Iran as early as 1799, stating their intention to "defend" Georgia.[14] The Iranian prime minister, Haji Ibrahim Shirazi, replied stating in no uncertain terms that Iran considered Georgia as her territory and that this claim would be enforced with troops.

Prince Pavel Dimitrievich Tsitsianov was appointed as the commander-in-chief of military operations in the Caucasus in 1802.[15] Tsitsianov and the Russian army entered Tbilisi in 1803,[16] following a smaller Russian force that arrived with Kovalensky in November 1799. As soon as Tsitsianov arrived into Georgia he hoisted himself as governor. By almost all accounts, Tsitsianov held a contemptible view of Iranians and Caucasian Muslims.[17]

The Russians had clearly misjudged the willingness of the Georgians to be simply absorbed into Russia. The late Giorgi's brother, Alexander, his family and members of the Georgian nobility left Tbilisi on March 1803 to seek refuge in Iran.[18] Anti-Russian rebellions soon broke out in Georgia, and were assisted by the Iranians.[19] Dupuy and Dupuy note that "Persian assistance to Georgian factions resisting annexation aroused Russian ire."[20]

Tsitsianov and 8,000 troops fanned out from Tbilisi in early 1804 to occupy the khanates to the south of Georgia.[21] The first target was Ganja which fell to Tsitsianov on January 1804 and was renamed Elizavertpol, which then became a district of Georgia.[22] Tsitsianov not only killed its ruler Javad Khan but also massacred thousands of civilians.[23] The fall of Ganja was a heavy blow against Qajar authority, but also a strategic threat to Azarbaijan and Gilan.[24] Following this success,

Tsitsianov's forces reached Yerevan on May 1, 1804. With Karabakh and Ganja relatively secure for the time being, Tsitsianov quickly forced Yerevan's commander, Mohammad Khan Qajar, to surrender.[25] The Russians had by and large been welcomed by the Armenians who had already aided the Russians in the capture of Ganja.[26] Despite this, Tsitsianov held a low opinion of the Armenians whom he later characterized as "unreliable Armenians with Persian souls."[27] Tsitsianov however could not permanently station Russian troops at Yerevan as he had to engage in more military conquests in Caucasian regions not yet reconciled with Russian rule. It is also likely that Tsitsianov was not overly concerned with the possibility of a serious Iranian counterthrust into Yerevan.

The loss of Tbilisi and the khanates had a deep impact on Iran's populace, military and political leadership. The Russian arrival into khanates considered to be Iranian dependencies set alarm bells off in Tehran.[28] The Iranians now realized that Russian ambitions were not confined to the Georgian kingdom: they were aiming for all other Caucasian territories reaching to the Araxes River, and possibly beyond.

The news from Karabakh in particular allowed the Qajars to easily mobilize a large force in a relatively short time and refugees arriving from the Caucasus swelled the ranks of volunteers to fight. A total of 55,000 cavalry and infantry were raised from the various tribal levies. Crown Prince Abbas Mirza (1789–1833), just 15 years old, was chosen to lead the Iranian army, and departed with his troops from Zanjan in the northwest towards the Araxes River on May 25, 1804.[29]

Abbas Mirza crossed into the Caucasus and rapidly approached Yerevan. He faced no meaningful Russian opposition to this maneuver, a clear indication that the Russians were preoccupied in trying to absorb their recently conquered territories. Abbas Mirza ordered his army to set camp just half a mile (1km) from Yerevan.

Tsitsianov and his army set up camp near the ancient Armenian monastery of Echmiadzin also known as Uch Kelisa, on June 28, 1804.[30] Abbas Mirza, accompanied by Prince Alexander, known as Alexander Mirza to the Iranians, rapidly deployed the Iranian army to face Tsitsianov at Shooreh Gol. Tsitsianov deployed his army in three rows. Three days of inconclusive fighting followed, characterized by the fury of Iranian infantry-cavalry assaults and cannon fire countered by the deadly barrage of modern Russian artillery.[31]

The fourth day of battle proved decisive, with Tsitsianov abandoning his mainly defensive posture. He unexpectedly struck with a furious attack with three raiding parties. At this crucial juncture Abbas Mirza faced treachery from within his own ranks: a good portion of his cavalry were led by Shams e Din-Lu into the ranks of Tsitsianov.[32] This loss forced Abbas Mirza to retreat and seek sanctuary in Yerevan.[33]

In pursuit of the Iranians, Tsitsianov reached Yerevan and rapidly surrounded the city with 3,000 Russian troops and their local Armenian allies by July 2, 1804.[34] Despite the apparent hopelessness of his situation and with supplies running low, Abbas Mirza prevented the Russian force from entering Yerevan. It is not clear how this was done, however it is likely that the Russians were reluctant to engage Abbas troops, in costly hand-to-hand combat. Tsitsianov relied on his excellent artillery and kept his noose tight around Yerevan to starve the Iranians out. Subsequent events demonstrated that Tsitsianov had not completely surrounded Yerevan, a dangerous oversight that was soon to cost the Russians dearly.

The Russians were facing new challenges in Caucasus. Just after the Ganja campaign, Tsitsianov's policies had resulted in the outbreak of anti-Russian revolts in Christian Georgia in May 1804, notably in Mtiuleti and Ossetia.[35] Prince Alexander sent emissaries to these regions promising them that he would be arriving with Iranian armies to expel the Russians from all of the Caucasus.[36] The presence of Russian troops had led to a number of rebellions that had been suppressed with brute force. One example is the tragic revolt that took place in August 1804 at the khanate of Karabakh.[37] The Russians brutally and indiscriminately killed both combatants and civilians.[38] If the intent was to cower the opposition in the Caucasus with an "iron fist" policy, then it failed, as such actions only helped swell the Iranian ranks and prolong the war.

Meanwhile back in Azarbaijan, Fathali Shah was keenly following the military developments in the Caucasus. He now moved into the Caucasus with 5,000 cavalry to support his son in Yerevan. Fathali Shah's cavalry managed to join the Iranian garrison at Yerevan through a gap that the Russians had failed to close off. Just a day later, apparently through the same gap, a vast supply of weapons, ammunition and food from Tabriz succeeded in reaching Abbas Mirza's besieged troops in Yerevan.[39]

The relief forces and supplies changed the tide in Abbas Mirza's favor. The reinforced Iranian garrison led by Abbas Mirza attacked the besieging Russian artillery pits and troops, heavily defeating them in close-quarter combat.[40] The morale and composure of the Russian troops wavered and then collapsed. Tsitsianov's troops retreated northwards in a disorganized fashion towards Tiblisi, pursued by the Iranian cavalry. The Iranians captured abandoned Russian supplies of ammunition, rifles and artillery from the battlefield. Armenia and the khanate of Karabakh had been practically cleared of Russian troops.[41] The Russians remained very much at large in the Caucasus, notably in Georgia. From St. Petersburg's view, these defeats were simply a disappointing setback in their quest to wrest the Caucasus from the Iranians.

Ibrahim Khalil-Khan Javanshir, who had been temporarily forced out of the khanate of Karabakh by Agha Mohammad Khan Qajar in 1797, saw an opportunity in the Russian invasion to regain his position there. General Tsitsianov obliged by signing the Treaty of Kurakchay accord with Javanshir in 1805, acknowledging Karabakh as the protectorate of Russia.[42]

The exact nature of the Kurakchay treaty has been disputed. Mostashari notes that the treaty was a capitulation document imposed upon Javanshir,[43] apparently desperate to maintain his authority against the Qajars. She further adds that Tsitsianov falsely portrayed the accord as Javanshir's willingness to join the empire when in fact these terms had been imposed by force.[44] Tapper notes that "Tsitsianov … wrote the letter of capitulation, addressed to the Tsar and forced the Khans to sign the terms."[45] This may partly explain why Javanshir switched his allegiance to the Qajars after the death of Tsitsianov.[46]

Abbas Mirza mobilized his army in anticipation of combat in Ganja and Karabakh. Meanwhile, Fathali Shah, now in Soltaniyeh, deployed an army towards the Araxes River. Tsitsianov moved swiftly. His first action was to place a number of formations to block the Iranian entrance to Ganja at the Khodafarin Bridge. These troops were expelled and pursued by a cavalry formation of Abbas Mirza, led by the veteran Ismail Beg Damghani.[47]

Tsitsianov's main action was to move towards Shusha and establish his base near the fortress of Panahabad. The aim was to re-install the "pro-Russian" Javanshir (who was accompanying Tsitsianov) as the ruler of Karabakh. It would appear that the Panahabad garrison did not take much convincing to join the Russian force; Tsitsianov soon dispatched troops and 20 cannon to bolster that fortress.[48] With Javanshir now in place as the local ruler in Karabakh, the Russians awaited the Iranian counterstrikes. Abbas Miraz launched a number of attacks and with the arrival of fresh infantry, cavalry, and cannon, defeated the Russians and forced them to retreat.[49]

With the Russians expelled from the arena, Abbas Mirza was able to capture Shusha and the Panahabad castle. Javanshir managed to escape along with his Russian patrons. With Karabakh once again in Iranian hands, Abbas Mirza and his cavalry pursued and captured numbers of Tsitsianov's retreating forces to the south of, then within, Ganja.[50]

Tsitsianov's defeats at Karabakh and Ganja obliged him to adopt a new strategy. He sent Russian warships across the Caspian Sea towards the seaport city of Bandar Anzali in the northern Iranian province of Gilan. The Russian fleet rapidly landed Major-General Zavalishin and 1,345 troops at Bandar Anzali,[51] an action which caught Abbas Mirza completely by surprise. Tsitsianov then threatened Fathali Shah in an insolent letter stating the Iranians should bow to his specific demands. If the Iranians did not comply, then Tsitsianov would make Rasht break away from Iran and become a Russian province.[52] The Russian landing was a complete disaster: Rashti fighters killed 1,000 of Zavalishin's troops and forced the remainder to flee to their ships, which then escaped into the Caspian Sea.[53] Tsitsianov's gambit of opening a second front against the Iranians from Rasht had ended in failure.

With the defeats at Karabakh and Gilan, Tsitsianov decided to retreat to the environs of Baku, which had yet to fall to the Russians. The logical course of action for the Iranian armies was to stay put, observe Russian intentions and strike while they were still trying to reorganize. Instead, Fathali Shah inexplicably departed with his armies for Tehran leaving Yerevan and the Araxes River practically defenseless. Abbas Mirza marched into the Yerevan khanate but he simply did not have the forces to prevent the Russians and Javanshir from marching back into Shusha to recapture the Panahabad castle. Fathali Shah had squandered the recent sacrifices and valor of the Iranian troops at Karabakh and Ganja. The combined strength of Abbas Mirza and Fathali Shah had been just equal to the task of defeating the Russians at Ganja, Karabakh, Yerevan and Gilan, but Abbas Mirza could not hold the entire Caucasus region alone.

Meanwhile, Zavalishin had landed with his ships around the city of Baku. He was soon joined by Tsitsianov and their combined forces advanced to Baku's gates by February 1806.[54] Their efforts to capture Baku failed, with Tsitsianov being killed on February 20, 1806, followed by a devastating Iranian cavalry raid against local Russian forces.[55] Zavalishin and his troops panicked and fled to their ships, sailing back into the Caspian Sea; they landed at Lankaran, in the Talysh region.[56]

Tsitsianov's death, combined with new defeats of Russian arms, prompted Javanshir to switch his allegiance to the Qajars in Karabakh. Javanshir now asked Fathali Shah to eject the Russian garrison out of the Panahabad fortress in Shusha. Qajar forces then advanced close to Shusha and set up their camps. This led Javanshir and some of his entourage to leave the Panahabad castle and join the Qajar host. The alarmed Russians decided to rapidly strike at the Qajar forces on June 2, 1806.[57] Interestingly, the Russian attack was also instigated by Javanshir's grandson, who feared that he would lose his position in the event of an Iranian victory.[58] The Russian assault on the Qajar camp resulted in the death of Javanshir and his wife.[59]

After the death of Tsitsianov, General Ivan Gudovich assumed command of the Russian army in the Caucasus in 1806. Gudovich had achieved recognition for his role against the Ottoman Turks in the Russo–Turkish war of 1787–92. He soon distinguished himself in the Caucasus by launching attacks from the northeast Caucasus along the Caspian Sea. First to fall to his 7,000-strong force in 1807 was Daghestan, followed by Darband (or Derbent). With the capture of Darband, Gudovich proceeded to capture Shirvan, Salyan, Baku, Moghan and Sheki. By this time Russia was also engaged in a bitter war against the Ottoman Turks (1806–12), and Gudovich marched westwards to engage the Ottoman army at the Akhurian River in Armenia in what is known as the battle of Arpachai, fought on June 18, 1807.[60]

Abbas Mirza was defeated by another Russian military commander, General Nebolsin at Nakhchevan in November, 1808.[61] Gudovich, having consolidated the Russian forces stationed at Karabakh and the nearby regions, made preparations to eject the Iranians from the Caucasus. Knowing that many of Abbas Mirza's troops were on leave away from the front, Gudovich launched an all-out attack from Karabakh towards Yerevan in early December 1808. He had timed the offensive very well as there were only 3,000 troops and 11 cannon protecting the city.[62] Gudovich surrounded the city with little difficulty and a great victory seemed all but assured. Unfortunately for Gudovich, high-quality Iranian cavalry arrived at Yerevan to cut the besieging Russian forces to pieces.[63] The Russian survivors now fled back to Ganja.[64] This battle marked Russia's fifth defeat by the armies of Iran. Abbas Mirza was congratulated for this victory by General Gardane.[65] This new blow against Russian military prestige resulted in the appointment of General Alexander Tormasov.[66]

Despite her technical superiority, Russia was unable to comprehensively defeat Iranian forces between 1804 and 1812. The primary reason was that Russia's military was also heavily engaged in the European theater and against the Ottoman Empire, preventing her from fully concentrating on the Caucasus. This allowed the Iranians to field large enough armies to help offset Russian tactical and technological superiority. While estimates vary, Russia may have been variously outnumbered by 5-1 by the Iranians.[67] The Iranians also avoided facing Russia's top generals, who were committed in other theaters. Iranian traditional cavalry forces, highly adept at rapid attacks and harassment often proved their value as shock forces against the Russians, who were vulnerable when caught in close-quarter combat situations against Iranian cavalry and infantry. Nevertheless, they were able to rely on their superior training, weapons and artillery to stave off total defeat.

Russia benefitted greatly from the long-standing Ottoman–Iranian rivalry. Even as Russia simultaneously made war against the Ottomans and the Iranians, the old foes could not even contemplate of coordinating their military efforts against their common enemy. Instead, both the Ottomans and the Iranians often sought opportunities to cooperate with Russia against each other. A perfect example of this was Ottoman Sultan Selim III allowing the Russian military to stage its forces along the southeastern portion of the Black Sea coast during their 1804–13 operations against Iran.

In the spring of 1809, just as the British mission arrived in Iran, Russia resumed her offensives in the Caucasus. The main weight of operations was again focused around Karabakh and Yerevan. This led to the mobilization of 60,000 men.[68] Fathali Shah arrived at the army barracks of Tabriz with 20,000 troops; Abbas Mirza had 20,000 fighters of whom 11,000 were of the Nezam e Jadid composed of Azarbaijani fighters recently trained along European lines; while his brother Mohammad Ali Mirza arrived in the Caucasus with 20,000 cavalry and infantry from Iranian Kurdistan.[69]

The Russians were to be countered with a two-pronged strategy: Abbas Mirza was to attack towards Ganja with Mohammad Ali Mirza thrusting all the way to Tbilisi in Georgia. As in previous campaigns, Fathali's armies were to act as a reserve force close to the Araxes River. Abbas Mirza struck into Nakhchevan and soon received peace overtures from the local khan.[70] His winter 1809 offensive into Ganja failed to secure victory, petering out mainly due to the lack of supplies and the onset of the bitter Caucasian winter.[71] Mohammad Ali Mirza and his Kurdish warriors did manage to achieve penetrations into Georgia in what may be described as a large-scale cavalry raid.[72] This was of little consequence militarily as these cavalrymen focused mainly on raids and plunder without engaging Russian troops in battle.[73] A notable success was a surprise raid by the shahsevan cavalry in the vicinity of Baku which destroyed a Russian force.[74] These operations however failed to alter the military situation in Iran's favor. Following these inconclusive operations, Abbas Mirza and Mohammad Ali merged their forces in the vicinity of Gugchai.

By the spring of 1810 the Russians had counterattacked, retaking Karabakh and forcing the main body of Iranian troops across the Araxes River into Azarbaijan.[75] The Iranians retaliated by sending cavalry to raid the Russian positions at Karabakh while concentrating on the construction of a new and modern castle (known later as Abbasabad Castle) along the Araxes. A number of troops were also trained along European lines with British assistance. The war took on a religious dimension in 1810 when the Shiite clergy declared a jihad against the Russians.

The Russians had designated Pyotr Stepanovich Kotlyarevsky as the commander of Russian troops in the Caucasus. The arrival of the new commander began to slowly turn the tide of war in Russia's favor. Kotlyarevsky decided to strike at the Iranians in Armenia. He captured the Meghri citadel in southern Armenia from the Iranians after a bitter battle in 1810. The Iranians then attempted to besiege Meghri, but the Russians managed to defeat these actions. More skirmishes followed in 1811 but failed to yield any major successes for Iran.[76]

The stage was set for final battles between Kotlyarevsky and Abbas Mirza. With 2,260 Russian troops Kotlyarevsky attacked Abbas Mirza's 30,000 men at Aslanduz near the Araxes River[77] on October 31–November 1, 1812.[78] Kotlyarevsky had timed his attack perfectly, striking just as Abbas Mirza was leaving on a hunting expedition.[79] Kotlyarevsky's attack achieved total surprise and nearly 2,000 Iranians in the camp were killed, taken prisoner or missing in action.[80] The Russians captured Abbas Mirza's camp with its vast stores of supplies, weapons, ammunition and twelve of the cannon that had been commanded by British officers.[81] The Russian losses were very light at just 127 dead and wounded.[82] The year of 1812 was especially significant in Georgia as by then Russian rule was highly resented, leading to a mass revolt which was put down with force.[83]

The crushing defeat at Aslanduz led to yet another disaster nearly two months later in the Talysh khanate. Kotlyarevsky, noting the disorder now spreading among the Iranian forces, chose the Talysh Khanate for his next strike. Despite the bitter winter snows, he deployed 2,000 troops to storm the castle of Lankaran[84] which had had its defenses recently rebuilt by British engineers.[85] Unlike at Aslanduz, Kotlyarevsky did not have the advantage of surprise. Lankaran's 4,000-man Iranian garrison fiercely repelled the Russian assaults for five days.[86] Kotlyarevsky finally broke the deadlock by having his sappers successfully blow a breach in the main wall of the fortress walls, allowing his troops to finally break through. After desperate hand-to-hand fighting, the Russians secured the city's surrender by January 1, 1813. They then put to the sword the survivors of the city's garrison.[87]

The Golestan Treaty

The war was for all practical purposes over and had decisively ended in Russia's favor. While the Shiite clergy urged the troops to fight on, no amount of Iranian national ardor, battlefield valor or religious fervor was able to overcome the Russian advantage in training, tactics and technology. The knockout blows delivered against Abbas Mirza at Meghri, Aslanduz and Lankaran sent shock waves at the House of Qajar, the nobility and the common folk of Tabriz, Tehran and Isfahan. The brutal reality of defeat forced Fathali Shah to dispatch Haji Mirza Abol-Hussan Khan Ilchi to St Petersburg in search of a peace treaty.[88] The British ambassador to Iran, Sir Gore Ouseley, also travelled to St. Petersburg where he acted as chief mediator.[89] The Russians were waiting, ready to negotiate a hard bargain.

The Golestan Treaty was signed on September 24, 1813 in the village of Golestan in the khanate of Nakhchevan.[90] This was one of the most humiliating treaties ever signed by Iran, dwarved only by the treaty of Turkmenchai in 1828. It forced Iran to relinquish all her Caucasian khanates (except Armenia and Nakhchevan) situated between the western shore of the Caspian Sea and Armenia to Russia. These included the khanates of Karabagh (Qarabagh), Ganja, Sheki, Shirvan, Darband, Mughan, Kuba, Baku, and the northern part of Talysh (including the strategic fortress of Lankaran).[91] Iran was also forced to renounce all of her claims to Georgia (as well as the territories of Mingrelia, Imeretia, and Abkhazia) and Daghestan.[92]

The treaty obligated both Iran and Russia to exchange all prisoners three months after the signature of the treaty.[93] Article 7 laid the early foundations of Iran's eventual loss of her economic independence to the European powers. It granted Russian merchants wide-ranging economic freedoms within Iran. This was viewed with much trepidation by Iranians who rightly feared the "India precedent" where overly generous economic concessions granted by an Asiatic empire (i.e. Mughal India) to a powerful European power (the East India Company) would lead to the former losing their political independence.[94] The Russians were certainly doing everything possible to realize (as much as possible) the dream of Peter the Great of turning Iran into a weak protectorate economically and politically subservient to Tsarist imperial ambitions.

Article 5 practically transformed the Caspian into Russia's *Mare Clausum*: the Russians were allowed to station a navy in the Caspian Sea with the Iranians being deprived of all of their rights to navigate in that sea.[95] These restrictions were a bitter blow as the Caspian Sea had been a major sea for Iran since at least Achaemenid times.[96] The consequences of this article left a profound geopolitical legacy in the Caspian Sea basin.

The terms of the Golestan treaty, especially the catastrophic territorial losses in the Caucasus were a heavy blow to Iranian national pride. The issue was not just the diminution of the landmass of the Iranian empire. Iran's ceding of territory also involved the surrender of 3,000,000 citizens (i.e. Persians,[97] Azarbaijanis and Talysh resident in the Caucasus) to Russian rule.[98] This would be a major contributing factor to the growth of a national revanchist sentiment in Iran. From the Iranian perspective, many of their kin had been forcefully torn from the motherland and had to be liberated from the Russians. The sense of injustice felt by the Iranian populace against Golestan was to lead to a new war against Russia just 14 years later. The outcome of that war was to lead to a treaty even more humiliating than that of Golestan.

Prelude to a new war

Hoping to secure Russian concessions through negotiations, Fathali Shah sent the former Iranian ambassador to England, Abu Hassan Khan Shirazi, to St. Petersburg to meet Count Karl von Neselrode, the Russian foreign minster.[99] Shirazi asked that the vague borders be clarified and raised the thorny issue that Russian troops had violated the border. Neselrode made no effort to accommodate Shirazi but the Russians were willing to make some minor concessions. General Aleksei Petrovich Ermelov (a veteran and hero of the battle of Borodino in 1812), the new commander-in-chief of Russian forces in the Caucasus was sent by the Russians to Tehran as ambassador in 1817 to arrive at a compromise with the Iranians.

If the Russians were hoping to send a diplomat to assuage their relations with the Iranians, Ermelov was definitely the wrong man for the job. Ermelov's behavior and attitude towards the natives of the Caucasus had earned him the nickname "Ghenghiz Khan" in relation to methods of governance.[100] Diplomacy was certainly not one of Ermelov's virtues and his attitude was reminiscent of the late Tsitsianov's antipathy towards non-Europeans. His behavior in Tehran did much to fan the flames of war between his country and Iran. From the outset he was not only inflexible, but rude and disrespectful to his hosts, including Fathali Shah.[101]

Even as he had originally crossed the (ill-defined) border from the Caucasus into Iran, Ermelov was provocative to say the least. He immediately began to embark on a military reconnaissance mission in Iranian territory despite the fact that there was no state of war.[102] Rather than assume the position of a diplomatic negotiator upon his arrival to Tehran, Ermelov brazenly made a series of demands. General Ivan Paskevich, who succeeded Ermelov as commander in the Caucasus in 1826 later placed part of the blame for the new Russo-Iranian war on his predecessor's style of diplomacy.[103]

Popular opinion in Iran was increasingly hostile to the state of affairs in the Caucasus. The Caucasian khans and refugees who had been displaced across the border into Azarbaijan across the Araxes River in Iran were restless and hostile to the Russian presence in the Caucasus. In addition the Shiite Ulema, buoyed by stories of Russian atrocities in the region, soon declared a jihad in Azarbaijan against the Russians in June 1826.[104]

Abbas Mirza was supportive of a new war as he was eager to retrieve Iran's lost territories and Qajar prestige. He and his brother Mohammad Ali Mirza Iran scored some military successes against the Ottomans in 1821–23, a factor which helped bolster Iranian morale. It is possible that the Decembrist coup in Moscow following the death of Tsar Alexander in 1825 was viewed as a major distraction to the Russian government in Tehran, which would allow for an opportune Iranian military strike into the Caucasus.[105] A new war with Russia seemed inevitable.

Abbas Mirza's army however was far from ready for a major war with Russia. The financing of his troops and arsenals were inadequate. The British no longer paid the subsidies they had during the previous confrontation[106] and no contributions came from Fathali Shah.[107] The financial burden fell on Azarbaijan province which was incapable of bearing the costs of Abbas Mirza's army.[108] This meant that arsenals, munitions, weapons, etc were often unreliable, training inconsistent and payments to troops often in arrears.[109]

The Second Iranian-Russian War (1826-28)

The year of 1826 witnessed a number of dramatic successes by the Iranian army. Abbas Mirza crossed the Araxes River on July 16, 1826 with 35,000 troops to engage Russian garrisons occupying the Caucasian khanates since 1813.[110] Iranian forces had the advantage of having the support of massive anti-Russian rebellions in the southern Caucasus. The focus of the first rebellions was in Moghan, and Talysh where the local populace assisted Iranian troops in driving out the Russians.[111] The heavily fortified fortress of Lankaran was also cleared of Russian troops with local assistance. Nakhchevan was also captured with the help of local rebels. Like their subjects, the local khans rapidly switched sides and joined Abbas Mirza's forces. The Iranian advance sparked more anti-Russian rebellions in the khanates of Sheki, Shirvan, and Baku.

The Iranian advance and widespread rebellions forced the Russians to retreat north. Abbas Mirza exploited the disorder in the Russian military positions to strike further northwards into the Caucasus. A very large military force composed of 10,000 infantry, 4,000 cavalry and an artillery detachment was placed under the joint command of Amir Khan Sardar and Mohammad Mirza.[112] Poor Russian military leadership soon contributed to further Iranian successes. Ermelov did much to contribute to Russian reverses with his military passivity. Rather than take advantage of Russia's more advanced technology to contain the Iranians until the arrival of reinforcements, Ermelov simply abandoned Ganja to the forces of Amir Khan Sardar and Mohammad Mirza.[113] This vacuum allowed the force of Amir Khan Sardar and Mohammad Mirza to advance to Yerevan further west, with Iranian troops also approaching Tbilisi further north.[114] The Iranians now struck along a broad front from Georgia in the northern Caucasus to Baku along the Caspian Sea.[115] However, the Russian garrisons at Baku and Shusha held out, and this proved to be the limit of the Iranian advance.

For a brief moment it seemed as if Iranian arms had been avenged and Qajar honor restored. Alarmed at these developments, the Russians dismissed Ermelov during the winter lull in the fighting and placed General Ivan Paskovich, a veteran of the Ottoman wars, in command. Paskovich patiently built up a highly efficient and compact fighting force that emphasized mobility and striking power. Russia returned to the formula that had succeeded in 1813; relying on technical military superiority and more advanced training to negate the larger numbers of Iranian troops. Paskovich selected a small force of 1,000 first-rate infantry armed with high-quality rifles and 2,000 Cossacks. Supporting this force was a formation of local anti-Iran (presumably Sunni Muslim) Caucasian troops, numbering (according to Iranian sources) in "the few thousands."[116] The new Russian force soon proved its mettle, utterly defeating the Iranian forces in a series of battles fought at Shamkour.[117]

The battle of Ganja, fought on September 26, 1826, sealed the fate of Iran in the Caucasus. Abbas Mirza fielded about 30,000 troops (10,000 of these cavalry) against Paskovich's 15,000. The Iranians fought well with their infantry, cavalry, and cannon, but the battle swung against them when Paskovich concentrated all of his artillery's firepower into the Iranian center.[118] Abbas Mirza was forced to retreat south into Azarbaijan.

The army that Abbas Mirza led into Azarbaijan in September 1826 was in complete disarray. The troops were already disaffected by delayed payments and short supplies.[119] Fathali Shah, realizing the extent of the disaster, issued a general call for troops. The appeal received an enthusiastic response across Iran, including Iranian-Arabs from Khuzistan, as well as Lurs, Kurds,

Malayeris and Bakhtiaris from western Iran, Turkmen from Khorasan, as well as Mazandaranis and Gilanis from northern Iran.[120] While motivation was high among the new recruits, problems with corruption, logistics, and payment, greatly reduced their overall military effectiveness.

Capitalizing on the Iranian army's difficulties, Paskovich struck with a vengeance all across the Caucasus. The new fort of Abbasabad and the khanate of Nakhchevan fell to Paskovich by June 1827 after Echmiadzin fell in April. Yerevan was unsuccessfully besieged by General Kraskovsky.[121] On July 3, 1827, 4,000 Iranian troops sprang a major ambush against a large Russian supply column of 500 supply wagons bringing supplies from Tbilisi to Yerevan. The convoy had been escorted by 4,000 Russian troops, 1,000 mounted Cossacks and four cannon.[122] The Iranians struck just as the Russians were crossing the Araxes River and quickly achieved surprise. The Russian force was surrounded and destroyed leaving at least 500 men dead and the supplies in Iranian hands.[123] A major battle was fought against Kraskovsky at Echmiadzin, also known as the battle of Astarak or Oushakan (roughly 7 miles (12km) northwest of Yerevan) on August 17, 1827.[124] Western sources generally report this as either inconclusive or a costly Russian victory.[125] There is general agreement however, that at one point during the battle, Russian troops suffered heavy losses to the deadly fire of 22 Iranian cannon.[126] Iranian sources cite this as a major victory for Abbas Mirza, with Hedayat reporting 2,300 Russian troops killed, 1,500 taken prisoner and five siege cannon captured.[127] British sources report 1,150–1,200 Russians killed with the Iranians losing 400–2,000 men.[128]

Whatever the outcome at Echmiadzin, the Iranian cause was clearly doomed. Russian troops and large numbers of Armenian fighters scored a major victory against Abbas Mirza by capturing Sardarabad fortress on September 20 after a four-day siege followed by the capture of Yerevan on October 1.[129] Yerevan's 3,000-man Iranian garrison had put up a valiant defense, repelling numerous attacks before surrendering.[130] The fall of Yerevan was a major blow as it was a major Iranian stronghold, with the Russians capturing all of its artillery and ammunition stores.[131] Even more humiliating was Kraskovsky's appropriation of Hassan Qajar's (Iranian governor of Yerevan) prized sword of Tamerlane, which was then presented to the Romanov court.[132] These disasters severely shattered Iranian morale, leading to the virtual evaporation of their resistance. Russian troops, led by General Aristoff now easily crossed the Araxes River into Azarbaijan to capture Tabriz in mid-October.[133] The Nakhchevan khanate in the Caucasus was also captured by General Paskovich at this time.[134] Abbas Mirza and Fathali Shah had no choice but to negotiate surrender terms as Tehran itself was now open to Russian occupation.

The Treaty of Turkmenchai

General Paskovich, representing Russia, and Haj Mirza Abol-Hassan Khan and Asef o-Dowleh representing Iran arrived at Turkmenchai, between Tabriz and Mianeh, to sign the treaty of Turkmenchai on February 21, 1828. The terms were even harsher than those of Golestan in 1813.

Article four ensured that Iran lost even more territory that she had in the Golestan treaty. In addition to those ceded at Golestan, Iran had to cede the khanates of Nakhchevan, Yerevan (modern Republic of Armenia), Talysh and other regions such as Mughan and Ordubad to the Russian empire.[135] This was disastrous for the Iranian army as many of its fortresses, stores of supplies and weapons were now under Russian jurisdiction.[136] The eighth article maintained Russian maritime and naval supremacy in the Caspian Sea, meaning that Russia could attack Iran's coastal regions with impunity as the Iranians had no right to maintain their own navy.[137]

The Treaty also damaged Iranian sovereignty. Russian nationals committing crimes were now immune from the Iranian legal system. This term was to echo in Iranian politics well into the twentieth century when President Johnson signed a military aid agreement with Iran in the late 1950s. Article 10 allowed Russia to send consular envoys anywhere in Iran and also forced the Iranians to sign economic treaties that mainly accommodated Russian interests. Iran had to also "apologize" to Russia for having broken the terms of the Golestan Treaty and pay reparations of thirty million silver rubles. Russia also imposed military obligations on Iran by stipulating that Iran would not allow its territory to be used as a conduit by any power hostile or at war with Russia.[138] Russia was also very sensitive about the Russian deserters who had joined the Iranian army, and insisted that their formations not be stationed along the common Russo-Iranian border.[139] Iran was in fact to assist Russia whenever the latter was engaged in military conflict. The most "benevolent" term of the treaty was for prisoners to be exchanged within four months (Article 13). Provisions were also made for Armenians in Iran (including prisoners from the earlier Caucasian wars) to settle in Armenia (former Yerevan khanate) proper. The Russians also agreed to support Abbas Mirza's accession to the throne after Fathali Shah's death, but this proved impossible to enforce with the premature death of Abbas Mirza in 1833.

Iran was finished as a military power for the remainder of the 19th century and would not fight a sustained war until well into the late 20th century. Economically Iran would, like the Ottoman Empire, become more and more economically subservient to the Russian and British empires. Industrial, economic, educational, social and political developments were affected as a result. The Turkmenchai treaty however was more than just a military and economic treaty. This was a profound psycho-social blow against the Iranian people who realized the reality of the permanent loss of the prized Caucasian districts.[140] Following Turkmenchai, Russia embarked on a massive anti-Persian cultural campaign in the Caucasus in order to eradicate the region's cultural, linguistic and historical ties with Iran.

CHAPTER 22

FAILURE IN THE EAST AND THE OTTOMAN WAR (1798–1838)

Mohammad Mirza becomes shah

Fathali Shah's successor was supposed to have been his son Abbas Mirza but the latter's death prompted Fathali to choose Abbas' son, Mohammad Mirza Qajar (1808–48), who had been ruling as the crown prince in Tabriz since his father's death. Mohammad Mirza was proclaimed shah on November 8, 1834 with the support of Mirza Abolghassem Farahani and arrived in Tehran accompanied with British and Russian cavalry contingents.[1]

The nomination of Mohammad Mirza as shah by Fathali however was contested by the Qajar royal house. Prior to Mohammad Mirza's arrival to Tehran, one of Fathali's son, Ali Mirza Qajar, effected a coup d'état. When Mohammad Ali arrived at Tehran's outskirts from Azarbaijan, he found the city's gates closed. This state of affairs did not last long, thanks to the intercession of Ali Mirza's war minister Mirza Agha Khan. Ali Mirza opened Tehran's gates, allowing Mohammad Mirza and his escort to peacefully enter the city. In return, Mohammad Mirza pardoned Ali Mirza, who had ruled as shah for just 40 days. Mohammad Shah awarded the chancellorship of Iran to Farahani in return for his support. However, Mohammad Shah had Farahani executed in 1835, mainly due to the court intrigues of Haji Mirza Aghassi, who then received the chancellorship. Aghassi's appointment as chancellor would have profound military consequences as he lacked professional training or schooling in military affairs. Lambton has stated that the Chancellor's incompetence resulted in the continuing "state of decay"[2] of Iran's military, despite some successes such as his establishment of Tehran's munitions factory.[3]

While Tehran was secure, rebellions had broken out in Khorasan, Khuzistan, Azarbaijan, Luristan, the Bakhtiaris and Fars. These were soon extinguished thanks in large part to the assistance of British officers such as Henry Lindsey-Bethune and Henry Rawlinson.[4]

The Herat question

Herat was a major city of the Safavid Empire, with the city and surrounding areas often being a part of both pre and post-Islamic Iranian empires.[5]

Agha Mohammad Khan had had every intention of reincorporating the city of Herat into Iran, but his preoccupation with the Caucasus prevented him from marching east. The Qajar aim was in fact to re-establish former Safavid rule as far northeast as the Oxus River. Herat was the lynchpin upon which a successful reacquisition of Iran's eastern realms would depend.

The conclusion of the first Iranian-Russian war (1804–13) allowed Fathali Shah and his son Abbas Mirza to finally shift their attention northeast. Iranian troops were assembled at Ghorian

Castle on the left bank of the Hari Rud (River), just 50 miles (80km) from Herat (from *c.* 1814).[6] An outright invasion was temporarily halted, thanks to the intercession of the governor of Herat who paid tribute to Fathali. This action displeased the vizier of Afghanistan who had the governor of Herat arrested and exiled.[7] This prompted Fathali to send his forces toward Herat. The Afghans agreed to Fathali's demands and soon blinded the vizier, however the latter's clan then seized power. This led to an Iranian invasion and capture of Herat in 1816, but fierce resistance by local Afghan tribes forced the Iranians to withdraw.[8] Two years later in 1828, Mohammad Vali Mirza (Khorasan's beglarbegi) defeated an Afghan force at Kafar Qaleh.[9] Fathali was nevertheless prevented from resuming his campaign against Herat as the Iranians became increasingly distracted by the Russians to the northwest and the outbreak of the second Russo-Iranian war in 1826.

As Iranian forces struggled against the Russians in the Caucasus, the Qajar governor of Khorasan, Prince Mohammad Vali Mirza (one of Fathali's sons), engaged in bitter conflicts with the local khans. Following the disastrous conclusion of the second Russian war in February 1828, Fathali Shah decided to restore order in Khorasan. He deposed Mohammad Vali Mirza in favor of another son, Hassanali Mirza.[10] At around this time, Fath "Fateeh" Khan and his followers in Afghanistan saw an opportunity to break away from Iran. Shoja ol Saltaneh was then authorized by his father Fathali Shah to bring Fath Khan and the rebel to heel. Shoja ol Saltaneh deployed first to Mashad to assemble an army of 10,000 infantry and cavalry and then proceeded towards Herat.[11]

Fath Khan arrived with a powerful army of 40,000 men near the region of Kusuyeh and prepared for his showdown with Shoja ol Saltaneh, who was at the head of 10,000 troops. After a furious battle characterized by the heavy use of firearms, cannon, and hand-to-hand fighting, the Afghans were defeated and put to flight.[12] Fath Khan was arrested and handed over to Fathali Shah who had him blinded. Abbas Mirza also campaigned against the Afghans after the Treaty of Turkmenchai in 1828, capturing Torbat, Quchan, Amirabad, Sarakhs and Turshiz in preparation for a final blow against Herat.[13] His premature death at Mashad in 1833 spared Herat from an Iranian assault and put a temporary halt to military operations in the Afghan theater.

As Mohammad Mirza fought to quell rebellion in western Iran after his accession, the political situation in Khorasan deteriorated. This was especially the case in the north of the province. A massive Qajar army including 10,000 cavalry (4,000 from Khorasan) successfully fanned out to subdue rebellious tribes which culminated in the defeat of the Oymaq Turkmen cavalry.[14] With Khorasan secured, the Qajars now looked further east.

The governor of Herat, Kamran Mirza, had made a pact with Mohammad Mirza when he was still crown prince in Tabriz, to accept Iran's authority. However as soon as Fathali Shah died, Kamran Mirza reneged and Herat again broke out of the Iranian orbit. Iranian attempts to establish dialogue proved futile, obliging Mohammad Shah to prepare for military action just after the conclusion of the campaigns in Khorasan.[15] As the army assembled for war, great efforts were expended to increase artillery production, but serious problems continued to plague the army's organization and logistics.[16]

Even as the army reached Khorasan, polio broke out in the province, with the army soon gripped by famine and disease.[17] Mohammad Shah had no alternative but to pull back from Khorasan, never even reaching Herat.

Even as Muhammad Shah made the decision to resume the advance, the general populace was skeptical of the prospects of military success at Herat. These doubts were indeed corroborated as logistical chaos once again plagued the 30,000-strong Qajar army as they marched out of Tehran on June 23, 1837.[18]

Mohammad Shah and his senior commanders agreed that the conquest of Ghorian and the confiscation of its supplies would help ameliorate the army's desperate state.[19] The castle surrendered to the besieging Qajar forces on November 15, 1837 after one of its walls was destroyed by a great explosion.[20] The castle's supplies provided some respite from the terrible shortages the Qajar army was facing. With Ghorian subdued, the Qajar thrust to Herat was resumed against increasingly fierce Afghan resistence.[21]

As the Qajar army approached Herat, Kamran Mirza's vizier, Yar Mohammad Khan, ordered the defenders to engage in scorched-earth tactics, destroying wells, farms and any other potential sources of supply. These tactics proved devastatingly effective, especially as the Qajar armies began their siege of Herat on November 24, 1837.[22] With the bitter winter just months away and vital supplies of foodstuffs and war materiel already in jeopardy, the Qajar siege of Herat was vulnerable at the outset.

The Herat dispute had led the British to withdraw their last military advisors from Iran in 1838.[23] The British wished Afghanistan to remain a buffer state between British India and the Russians.[24] They feared that an Iranian Herat could be used as a gateway into India by the Russians.[25] Having failed to persuade the ruler of Kabul, Dost Mohammad Khan, to assist Kamran Mirza,[26] the British sent the very capable Lieutenant Eldrid Pottinger into Herat to organize the city's defenses, especially the artillery.[27] The Qajars also had European military assistance,[28] notably Russian minister Count Simnovich and a regiment of Russian troops, and Isidore Borowsky, a Polish officer in Iranian service killed during the siege.[29] A surviving, very large Qajar map of Herat drafted just prior to the siege shows that the Qajar planning for the siege was incredibly detailed, in stark contrast to their logistics.[30]

The fighting at Herat was especially brutal, desperate and bitter, with close-quarter causing high losses on both sides.[31] A number of towers exchange hands several times during the siege. The Qajars nearly captured a number of gates[32] and at times even broke into the city[33] but all their efforts were beaten back.[34] All the Qajars' efforts continued to be undermined by the haphazard arrival and distribution of supplies.[35] Attempts to secure supplies from the environs proved fruitless, thanks to the scorched-earth tactics of Yar Mohammad Khan. Even the arrival of 2,000 reinforcements and five cannon failed to alter the military balance in the Qajars' favor.

When the British realized that the Qajars had no intention of abandoning the siege, they resorted to diplomatic means. Sir John McNeill, the British representative in Tehran, travelled to Herat to meet Mohammad Shah and the Qajar commanders. The message was simple: end the siege, make peace, and withdraw.[36] Despite the suffering of his troops, Mohammad Shah, whose prestige was on the line, rejected the demands. The Russians, through Count Simnovich, encouraged the shah to continue the siege, which may have bolstered Iranian hopes. However, the reality was that British political networks in Iran were now significant.[37] London had channels of communication open with numbers of the Qajar leadership, giving them important knowledge of the weaknesses of the army and the situation at Herat.[38] This knowledge was to prove crucial in the formation of British military plans against the Qajars. The British did make one further attempt to avoid military conflict, sending Colonel Charles Stoddart, McNeill's military attaché in Tehran, to reiterate London's demands to the shah. Having exhausted their diplomatic initiatives, the British terminated their diplomatic relations with Iran in May 1838.[39] The following month, five naval vessels and 400 troops captured Kharq Island, and remained there until March 1842.[40] Iran was now paying for not having an effective navy in the Persian Gulf. With Kharq secured, the British warned that they would thrust into the center of Iran should the siege of Herat continue.[41]

The shah was further demoralized by rebellions led by Qajar princes, including in Kashan, Isfahan, and Astarabad. The combination of internal unrest, dogged Afghan resistance and British diplomatic and military pressure finally forced Mohammad Shah to withdraw from Herat on September 9, 1838.[42] The Qajars blamed their withdrawal on British machinations, an assertion not wholly contested by the British.[43] The defeat left Mohammad Shah broken and demoralized.

Despite his failing health Mohammad Shah remained preoccupied with Herat and looked for opportunities to avenge his defeat there. Keenly aware of this, the British supported a major rebellion by Agha Khan Mahallati to help divert Iranian attentions towards her center and southeast.[44] Mahallati marched towards Kerman in 1839 with a rented force of 500 high-quality cavalry.[45] By the spring of 1840, Mahallati and his troops, now 4,000 men, were engaged in bitter clashes with government troops from Kerman and Yazd.[46] This finally forced the Shah to dispatch army units from Tehran to bring Mahallati's rebels to heel.[47] The decisive showdown occurred at Kerman. Mahallati was defeated, and fled with his surviving followers to Baluchistan.[48] British India sent Seyyed Khan Baluch with large supplies of cannon, ammunition, to reinforce Mahallati, but he still suffered a string of defeats. Following his final defeat at Shamil, the British arranged for Mahallati to escape to India in December 1841.[49] While the rebellion was finished, it had forced Iranian attentions away from Herat. This state of affairs would not last as Mohammad Shah's successor, Nasser e Din Shah, would make his own bid towards the city in 1856.

The Ottoman-Iranian War

The nature of the Ottoman-Iranian border was a constant source of friction. The demarcation of the border zones had been laid down in the Treaty of Zuhab (1639), which itself was based on a treaty of 1555. The Kurds to the north (often migratory or settled in the mountains) simply ignored the border, making them difficult to administer and control. The same was true of the Arab tribes of the Khuzistan/Arabistan province in Iran's southwest. These were keen to maintain their autonomy outside of Turkish rule and so gave their allegiance to Iran but maintained familial and commercial links on both sides of the Arvand Rud/Shaat al Arab waterway.[50]

A number of issues propelled the two sides toward war; these included border disputes (especially Sulaymānīyah in the north and Muhammara in the south), the Shia-Sunni divide, and even the Russians who attempted to intrigue the Qajars against the Ottomans.[51]

The final descent into war came in October 1820 when the Ottoman rulers of Ottoman-Armenia stationed in Van provoked anti-Iranian rebellions amongst those tribes straddling the border with Iranian Azarbaijan and Kurdistan.[52] Abbas Mirza in turn gave refuge to political dissidents fleeing from the Pasha of Baghdad, Davood Pasha, but then acquiesced to their repatriation.[53] These events further damaged relations between the empires and the Ottoman sultan duly declared war on Iran.[54]

The actual clash of Iranian and Ottoman armies did not immediately materialize as Fathali only formally gave the order for an Iranian military strike in September 1821, almost one year after Istanbul's declaration of war. In Azarbaijan, Abbas Mirza possessed 24,000 troops (mainly Azarbaijani), which could be boosted to 35,000 in times of war.[55] Abbas Mirza could also count on the support of Hussein Khan the *Sardar* (head commander) of the Yerevan khanate, who had 5,000 troops (including 2,000 Kurdish cavalry and 1,000 *Tofangchis* or fusiliers), and the ability to raise a further 5,000 in times of crisis.[56] In Western Iran, Mohammad Ali Mirza, described as the "most able and warlike of all the princes of Persia"[57] had a regular infantry force trained along European lines.[58] He could raise 40,000 troops (two-thirds cavalry, mainly Kurds, Lurs and Bakhtiaris). He was also able to count on the 12,000 warriors of Kurdish leader Suleiman Khan in the event of war. Fraser described Mohammad Ali Mirza's army at Kermanshah as "the most effective military force in Persia."[59]

As for the Ottoman forces, Khosrow Pasha, the Ottoman governor of Erzerum, could field 30,000 provincial troops, mainly foot militia, mounted Kurdish infantry from eastern Anatolia and other tribal cavalry units.[60] He could also call on at least another 75,000 troops from the provinces.[61] In total the Ottomans would then be able to field 105,000 troops against Abbas Mirza and Hussein Khan's 45,000. While this looked impressive on paper, the Iranian troops had been well trained by European instructors, whereas the Ottoman forces in the east had not had the benefit of modernized training, nor could they count on the support of the excellent units in the Ottoman west. Khosrow Pasha's own Janissaries and personal guards were better trained, but these could not compensate for the overall deficiencies of the Ottoman forces. The Ottomans also had problems coordinating such large numbers of troops against the Iranians whose smaller numbers and better training made them more amenable to coordination and maneuver.

Davood Pasha, the governor of Baghdad, was handicapped by having to face rebellions in Ottoman Iraq, and as the Kurds in northern Iraq often looked to Iranian governors in Kermanshah and Luristan for protection. Kurds from Ottoman Iraq could often be seen fighting alongside regular Iranian troops, meaning that the Ottomans could not wholly rely on them in case of a war with Iran.[62] Overall the Ottomans facing western Iran could field a maximum of 35,000 troops (including 10,000–15,000 Arab and Kurd cavalry) with another 10,000 recruited from eastern Anatolia.[63]

In September 1821, Abbas Mirza and his army deployed towards the Ottoman border. The Iranian army advanced from Khoi to Maku and from there aimed towards Bayezid and Erzerum.[64] Abbas Mirza's army moved swiftly, advancing 27–28 miles (44–45km) a day,[65] soon reaching Toprak Qale, a key Ottoman strategic asset sitting astride the Tabriz–Erzerum road. It was here where the first Ottoman-Iranian clash took place with Ottoman forces suffering a decisive defeat. The remnants of Ottoman forces then sought refuge in Toprak Qale, which was quickly surrounded by Hassan Khan Qajar Qazvini. After inflicting 4,000 casualties on the Ottomans, Qazvini forced Toprak Qale to surrender.[66] The rapidity of the advance may have caught the Ottomans off-guard as Agh Sarai Castle also fell to Abbas Mirza, followed by Bayezid. After clearing the Bayezid area of Ottoman troops, appointing sympathetic governors in the conquered areas and quickly erecting military bases, Abbas Mirza attacked the areas close to Malazkert (Manzikert) and inflicted another serious blow against the Ottomans by capturing 16 of their cannon and large stores of ammunition.[67] The road to Erzerum was now open to the Iranian army. By November 1821,

Iranian troops had cleared the Ottomans out of Narein Qale, Hassan Qale, Malazkert Qale, Mosh Qale, Van, Ekhlat, and Bitlis.[68]

The Ottomans were now facing another military crisis further south in Mesopotamia. The Ottomans had invaded western Iran with a powerful army of 50,000 fresh troops under the leadership of Mohammad Pasha in 1821.[69] In response, Mohammad Ali Mirza had clashed with the Ottomans along the border and then counterattacked towards Baghdad in October 1821.[70] The thrust first went through Shahrezur along the Sirvan River, supported by Feili Kurds and Lurs who defeated the Ottoman opposition and forced them to retreat to Kirkuk. Mohammad Ali Mirza conquered Sulaymānīyah and following the capture of Samarra, besieged Baghdad. Davood Pasha of Baghdad dispatched an emissary to negotiate with Mohammad Ali Mirza. However, cholera had broken out among the Iranian troops, and Mohammad Ali Mirza fell victim to it, dying near the ancient Sassanian site of Ctesiphon on November, 22, 1821.[71]

The Ottoman plan of counterattack was straightforward: first they would retake lost territory and then cross into Iran. The main obstacle was the Iranian garrison at Toprak Qale. The Toprak Qale garrison was not able to withstand 40,000–70,000[72] Ottomans indefinitely, but their resistance gave Abbas Mirza time to mobilize and thrust into eastern Anatolia with 20,000 troops by May 1822.[73] Despite their larger numbers, the Ottomans were resoundedly defeated by Abbas Mirza, whose troops proved more efficient in their use of firearms and artillery.[74] Iranian sources reporting on the ferocity of Ottoman resistance note that only 20,000 Ottoman troops manged to escape.[75] The Ottomans had had enough, they were receptive to negotiations with Tehran.

The peace agreement between the Ottomans and Iran, known as the Treaty of Erzerum, was signed by Mirza Taghi Khan Farrahani (representing Iran) and Mohammad Pasha (representing the Ottoman Empire) in 1823. The treaty merely confirmed the territorial status quo and did not resolve any of the major long-standing territorial disputes.[76] It did however stress the importance of both states pledging non-interference in one another's internal affairs. Iranian Shiite pilgrims into Iraq or in transit to Mecca would also not be harassed by Ottoman officials. The movement of tribes along the Ottoman–Iranian borders was to be regulated by the provisions in the treaty and both sides were to avoid granting political asylum to their respective dissidents.[77] The treaty however was to beset by many challenges and was to receive much attention and amendments as a result.

Frictions with the Ottomans and the second treaty of Erzerum

Despite the Erzerum Treaty, a number of major incidents took place between 1833 and 1842 that nearly led to the renewal of war. In 1837, Alireza Pasha of Baghdad decided to take advantage of the Qajar army's preoccupation with Herat by launching a punishing attack into Mohammara (Khorramshahr) and setting the city on fire.[78] Ottoman troops also plundered all of the city's government stores before their departure.[79] Mohammad Shah responded to the Ottoman attack by marching into Ottoman territory and capturing Sulaymānīyah .[80] An all-out war seemed inevitable, but in 1843, Russia and Britain offered to mediate. The offer was accepted but tensions remained high. Alireza Pasha launched an all-out attack against the Shia holy city of Karbala in Ottoman-ruled Iraq, massacring 9,000 civilians.[81] Despite this the overall peace held and the negotiations proceeded.

Negotiations were long and arduous but by 1845 some important compromises had been outlined. The Ottomans agreed that Mohammara, Khizr island (renamed later as Abadan) and other territories on the southwestern areas of Khuzistan would fall under Iranian jurisdiction. In return Iran surrendered the strategic area of Sulaymānīyah. Iran ceded the lowlands of Zuhab to the Ottomans who in turn ceding the highlands of the Zuhab to the Iranians. The Ottomans also promised not to harass Iranian travelers and pilgrims into Iraq.[82]

The efforts of the four-party commission culminated in the second treaty of Erzerum, signed on May 31, 1847. Crucial to the treaty was the Ottoman acknowledgement that the Shaat al Arab waterway delineated the border between Qajar Iran and the Ottoman Empire. The Qajars were still dissatisfied as the confirmation of Iran's sovereignty was affirmed over the eastern bank of the Shaat al-Arab but nowhere upon the waterway itself.[83] British cartographers and Russian topographers then charted the Iranian–Ottoman border corresponding to Iran's modern western borders with Turkey (to the northwest) and Iraq (west) all the way to the egress of the Arvand Rud/Shaat al Arab waterway into the Persian Gulf. These efforts resulted in the production of map at the scale of 1/73050, copies of which were sent to Istanbul and Tehran.[84] The Ottoman and Qajar governments were then asked to specify their land claims on their respective maps.[85]

The commission met in 1849,[86] however proceedings were interrupted by the Crimean War (1854–56) and the Anglo-Iranian War (1856–57). A protocol was finally signed in 1869 but progress continued to be painstakingly slow. The main problem was recurrent border flare-ups between the Ottomans and the Iranians. Nevertheless, the frontier was formally delimited by the Constantinople Protocol of 1913–14, just prior to the Ottoman Empire's entry into The First World War.[87] The convoluted and complex protocol would become the basis of the post-Ottoman Iraqi state's claim to the entire Shaat al Arab waterway; and the Iranian dispute to this claim would lead into one of the causes of the Iran–Iraq War.[88]

The British motivation for mediation may partly be explained by their contemporary "balance of power" policy of keeping the Ottoman Empire as intact as possible. Ottoman wars with Iran would further weaken the already embattled Ottoman state, now dangerously besieged in southeast Europe and by Russia. The British were content to see the Iranians confined to their borders and not expand at Ottoman expense. The Russians simply did not want to witness any Iranian military revival, even if it was against one of Russia's traditional enemies.

The Erzerum treaty failed to put an end to Ottoman and Iranian interference into each other's affairs. The Ottomans attempted to mobilize the Kurds using pan-Sunni Muslim sentiments, while the Iranians attempted to cultivate anti-Ottoman rebellions among the Kurds.[89]

The Russians seize Ashooradeh Island

The Russians remained keen to undermine British influence in Iran. The ultimate aim was that of Peter the Great: reaching the Persian Gulf and India. Just months after having supported the Qajars against Herat, the Russians resumed an aggressive stance against the Iranians. Their immediate ambitions however were to secure their position in Central Asia and the northern Iranian coast.

The first pretext for Russian intervention was that Russian merchants, travelers and citizens had been murdered in Khiva in Central Asia. The Russians complained to Fathali Shah, even though

Khiva was not under Iranian rule.[90] Fathali Shah told the Russians that for him to secure Khiva he had to first gain control over Herat, Bukhara and Balkh.[91] With the Qajar failure at Herat the Russians decided to take Khiva for themselves. If the Russians could secure Khiva they then could thrust south into the Turkmen areas and menace Iran's northeast province of Khorasan and Afghanistan. The Russian attempt to secure the khanate and city of Khiva in December 1838 proved to be a disastrous failure. The commander was killed, and the 5,000-strong army thoroughly routed. Having failed to secure Khiva, the Russians resorted to deploying their navy southwards towards the northeastern coasts of Iran. Thanks to the Treaty of Turkmenchai, the Iranians had no navy of their own to contest the Russians. The pretext for this action was that Turkmen raiders were harassing Russian mercantile shipping in the southern waters of the Caspian Sea. The Qajars, clearly worried about the threats this posed to Iranian territorial waters, asked the Russians to loan them combat vessels to allow them to pacify the waters on behalf of Russian merchant ships. The Russians rejected these demands and continued to sail towards the Iranian coasts. Their vessels arrived just 19 miles (30km) of the northwest coast of modern Gorgan and occupied the island of Ashooradeh in 1842.[92] The Russians built a military base there, which was soon the target of Turkmen raids.[93] Qajar protests for the Russians to leave the island fell on deaf ears, and the occupation of the island only ended in 1941.[94]

CHAPTER 23

THE LONGEST-RULING QAJAR: NASSER E DIN SHAH (1848–96)

Early challenges of Nasser e Din Shah

The death of Mohammad Shah Qajar in 1848 was followed by an interregnum of 40 days before his 17-year-old son, Nasser e Din (1831–96), arrived in Tehran with an escort of 20,000 troops.[1] Nasser e Din was crowned as Shah on September 17, 1848, destined to become the longest reigning Qajar Shah. One of his first actions was to appoint Mirza Taqi Khan Amir Kabir as his chief minister or *Sadr e A'zam*. Nasser e Din Shah himself was a man of varied interests, he was remarkable for his interests and talents in writing, photography, drawing, languages, and for his travels to Europe.[2] During Nasser e Din's five-decade reign, British and Russian economic, political and military supremacy over Iran became paramount.

The rebellion of Hassan Khan Salar in Khorasan during the late shah's reign had caused considerable disruption in security and trade routes, with Nasser e Din Shah determined to stamp out the problem once and for all. Hassan Khan Salar was a powerful warlord with an army of 35,000 troops, who were also armed with heavy cannon. Amir Kabir assigned Sultan Morad Mirza to crush Hassan Khan Salar. By late 1849, Morad Mirza had destroyed Hassan Khan Salar's army at Mashad, capturing vast stores of weapons, cannon, ammunition, and supplies.[3] Salar was executed in early May 1850, despite the pleas for the sentence to be commutated from the British envoy to Tehran, Sir Justin Sheil.[4] With the conclusion of these battles, stability, and order returned once again to Khorasan.[5] In appreciation, Tehran appointed Sultan Morad Mirza as vali of Khorasan, and he was henceforth known as Hessam ol Saltaneh Morad Mirza.[6]

Another early challenge faced by Nasser e Din Shah was the Bahai movement, which left a significant imprint on the military history of Iran.[7] Before 1825, there were no major clashes between this Shiite sect and the government or religious authorities, but this changed with the accession of new leaders and theological doctrines. In 1844, one of the leaders of the sect, Seyyed Ali Mohammad, announced himself as a prophet in 1844 citing himself as the "bab" or "gate" to the hidden (twelfth) imam of the Shiite branch of Islam.[8] This was soon viewed by the Shiite Ulema as a challenge to the Shiite theology and they encouraged the Qajars to suppress Seyyed Ali Mohammad Bab and his followers, the Babis. Seyyed Ali Mohammad Bab was arrested, imprisoned, and put on trial by the religious and political authorities in Tabriz. He was executed in Tabriz, aged 25, on July 9, 1850.[9] Armed clashes occurred between the Babis and government troops, with the most notable showdown occurring at Zanjan (between Tehran and Tabriz).[10] The Babis shut Zanjan's gates, forcing government troops to storm into the town and fight house to house to regain control.[11] Similar clashes occurred at Mazandaran between local Babis and government troops.[12] After an assassination attempt on Nasser e Din Shah in 1852, 3,000 Babi were killed by the government authorities.[13] The military campaign resulted in the defeat of the Babis, but the movement continued primarily under the guise of the Bahais and the Azalis.[14]

Amir Kabir's reforms and the Dar ol Fonoon Academy

Mirza Taqi Khan Amir Kabir (1807–52) was Iran's most capable first minster of the entire nineteenth century and one of the most remarkable Iranian statesmen of recent Iranian history.[15] Despite his brief tenure, Amir Kabir is recalled with great admiration by Iranians due to his reforms of the economy, education and military.[16] He immediately recognized that Iran's ability to retain her independence and territorial integrity depended on her military ability to repel invading foreign armies.[17]

Amir Kabir's most significant reform was the establishment of Iran's first secular school, the Dar ol Fonoon (Place of Leaning) by 1851. This military school, with 50 classrooms and a library, was designed to train a new cadre of military officers in political science, foreign languages, medicine, surgery, pharmacy, military sciences, engineering, mathematics, physics, chemistry, mineralogy, agriculture, and music.[18] The faculty included many European military and civilian instructors, including many from Austro-Hungary.[19]

In his four-year tenure as Iran's first minister, Amir Kabir instituted seven crucial reforms for the Iranian army. Military plants were established in Tehran, Tabriz, Isfahan and Mashad to produce epaulets, cannon, small arms, and ammunition.[20] Great efforts were made towards increasing efficiency of production, and orders for up to 200,000 rifles were placed in Britain and Russia.[21] Amir Kabir also established fifteen civilian factories for the production of samovars, carriages, sugar, metals (lead, iron, copper), textiles, and paper.[22] He made great strides in administrative reform, especially with regard to the correct and punctual payment of troops and government personnel.[23] Reforms were implemented within recruitment processes and organization. The recruitment of troops was now based on a quota system which varied according to villages, tribal regions, and administrative districts.[24] Amir Kabir further developed Abbas Mirza's original *Bunichah* system for conscription in Azarbaijan, making it applicable across the country.[25] He abolished the widespread practice of "legal looting" during military campaigns, which vastly improved relations between regular army troops and civilians.[26] Nezam units were reorganized with the formation of 16 new regiments being ordered. At least one was formed from Iran's Christian population. These included old regiments from Russian army deserters in the Iranian army.[27] Attempts were also made to produce standardized Nezam uniforms in factories.[28] New barracks and fortifications were built across Iran (including a new artillery park in Tehran), and fortresses were built in sensitive provincial regions.[29] At Astarabad a total of 52 new fortresses were built, which were collectively able to accommodate 8,000 troops.[30] Amir Kabir was also keen to modernize the training of Iran's powerful tribal cavalry and worked to raise new units from the provinces and tribal forces along Iran's borders.[31] Had he had longer, Iran's tribal cavalry and the army could have been transformed into a more formidable force.

Perhaps one of the most important legacies of Amir Kabir's Dar ol Fonoon academy was that the Iranians realized that military reform was a more complex process than just adopting European weapons and tactics: Amir Kabir realized that military reform could only work if in tandem with overall reforms in modernization and education.[32]

To help secure the costs of his reforms, Amir Kabir engaged in a highly effective fiscal reform program. Tax collectors were now more closely supervised, fief holders who no longer provided troops paid a new tax, and import duties were increased.[33] In addition, court expenses were reduced and a halt was put to the practice of selling offices and the exchange of "gifts" for government services.[34] These measures might have been the beginning of an economic miracle in Iran, leading to major social and economic progress for the general Iranian populace. But they also gave rise to tremendous resentment among some members of the harem, court and conservative nobles.[35] As noted by Keddie "the values of honesty, integrity, efficiency, and genius were not appreciated by those who most conspicuously lacked them. Amir Kabir's efforts to weed out corruption, restrain fiscal abuse, and overturn traditional interests inevitably made him a host of enemies."[36] The British and Russians were also unhappy with the reforms, particularly the customs on imported goods.[37]

Nasser e Din Shah's mother had always disliked Amir Kabir, and almost from the start of his tenure as Iran's first minster, she conspired with Amir Kabir's rival, Agha Khan Nouri Etemad o Dowleh.[38] They worked to arouse Nasser e Din's suspicions, alleging among other things that Amir Kabir was building up the army in preparation for a coup d'état.[39] The shah was eventually swayed by these intrigues. He dismissed Amir Kabir from his office on November 16, 1851 and imprisoned him in palace near Kashan. On January 10, 1852, the shah sent an executioner to forcefully drag Amir Kabir to the local bathhouse, sever the arteries of his limbs and then leave him to die in a slow and painful death.

In the long term, Amir Kabir's reforms could have eventually awoken Iran from its stupor and acted as a catalyst of modernism. Social, economic, and technical advancement could then translate into military modernity. According to Browne, "had the administration of the Amir-i-Nezam (Mirza Taqi Khan) been prolonged, the King of Persia would have been the master of an army of one hundred thousand men, regularly drilled and accoutred."[40] But the vizier's execution deprived Iran of a fine administrator and planner and put an end to Iran's hopes for adaptive social and political changes concomitant with economic and industrial progress.[41]

Iranian ambitions in the East and Britain's jewel in the crown

Seyyed Mohammad Khan assumed power in Herat around the time that Mohammad Shah Qajar died in 1848. Concerned that he would be ejected by Dost Mohammad at Kabul or Dost Mohammad's step-brothers at Kandahar, Seyyed Mohammad Khan turned to Nasser e Din Shah for protection. In response the shah captured Herat in 1852, formally annexing it as an Iranian province.[42] The British appeared diplomatic at first, but their overall policy on Herat and Afghanistan had not changed: a strong Afghanistan would act as a buffer state between India's northwest and any Russian (or other European) ambitions. The Iranian acquisition of Herat would prevent the formation of a contiguous Afghan state. Fearing another British landing at Kharq Island, the shah reluctantly withdrew his troops and signed an agreement with Sir Justin Sheil that no Iranian troops would arrive at Herat unless it was directly attacked from Kandahar, Kabul or by a foreign power.[43]

The changing winds of continental European politics however began to exert their influence on the east. The Russian army had invaded the Danubian territories of the Ottoman Empire in early July 1853, leading to a declaration of war by the sultan by early October. This was the opening phase of the Crimean War (October 1853–March 1856), which pitted Russia against the Ottomans, French, and British. Nasser e Din Shah briefly contemplated forging an alliance with the Russians against the Ottoman Turks, but was persuaded otherwise by Mirza Agha Khan Nuri.[44] The Russians had offered the Iranians money, portions of captured Ottoman territory, and even arms if the shah joined them, a fact which Mirza Agha Khan was to point out to the British. The British had certainly done their bit to dissuade the shah from entering the war by having their navy engage in massive maneuvers in the Persian Gulf between the months of February and May 1854.[45] This was a reminder to the Iranians that they could again risk British landings in their possessions in the Persian Gulf and lose Kharq Island. The Shah was soon inclined to cooperate with the British, French, and Ottomans against the Russians to help reverse the humiliating terms of the Turkmenchai treaty.[46] A new Iranian ambassador was sent to Istanbul with orders to strengthen Ottoman-Iranian ties. The Shah also tried to forge an alliance with the British to retrieve Iran's lost Caucasian lands from Russia, but was rejected.[47] Realizing that Iran had no chance of retrieving her lost Caucasian lands, Nasser e Din Shah again looked east.

By April 1855 Sir Charles Murray, the new British envoy to Iran had told the Shah in no uncertain terms that the British government was completely opposed to any Qajar moves to extend Iranian authority upon Herat. The shah was far from satisfied with this state of affairs, as no real incentive had been given to Iran for its neutrality. Finally on October 19 Murray was summoned by the shah and told that Iran could not simply remain neutral without receiving any sort of recompense.[48] Murray warned the shah that if he were to forge an alliance with Russia, this would be interpreted as a declaration of war by London. Murray lacked the skillful diplomacy of his predecessor, Sir Justin Sheil.[49] Later in November Murray took down the British flag in Tehran and left with his archives and staff for Baghdad.[50]

The situation in Afghanistan was rapidly deteriorating. Dost Mohammad marched against his step-brothers in Kandahar and captured the city in December 1855.[51] Having conquered Kandahar, Dost Mohammad could now secure Kabul and Herat and mold these territories into his own independent kingdom. The British authorities in India were amenable to his takeover of Herat, while steadfastly opposed to any Iranian moves towards the city.[52] This of course infuriated the shah and the Iranian authorities. In October 1855, political events in Herat took a decisive turn when Shahzadeh Mohammad Yusef, possibly with Tehran's connivance, took over as ruler of the city.[53] Yusef was of the Saduzai clan and had received a pension from the Iranian government in the past.[54] The shah's relations with England had been broken off by November 19, which gave Tehran a freer hand to march into Herat. By December, Dost Mohammad, who had just absorbed Kandahar, was preparing to conquer Herat. Mohammad Yusef appealed to Tehran for help. Nasser e Din Shah responded by dispatching Hessam ol Saltaneh Morad Mirza at the head of an army towards Herat to assist Mohammad Yusef.[55] Morad Mirza reached the environs of the city by February 1856.[56] Relations between Yusef and Iranian authorities broke down, leading to the expulsion of a small Qajar contingent that had been allowed into Herat upon Morad Mirza's arrival.[57] Mohammad Yusef now raised the British flag over Herat, declared himself a vassal of the Queen of England and appealed to Dost Mohammed for help.[58] Appeals were also sent to the British for military assistance.[59]

After watching events unfold, Morad Mirza proceeded to capture Herat. His army of 20,000 included units mobilized from a wide array of Iranian regions, and Arab and Persian warriors from

Bastam.[60] After winning a bitter battle in early March 1857 Morad Mirza reached Herat; after failed diplomacy with Issah Khan (Herat's new ruler) the city was besieged by Morad Mirza's troops.[61] Herat resisted fiercely but was eventually overcome by highly effective Iranian siegeworks and strongly concentrated artillery fire; Issah Khan finally surrendered on October 1856.[62]

The Anglo-Iranian War

After Murray's departure from Tehran, Anglo–Iranian relations were at an all-time low. The Iranians did attempt a reconciliation, and as early as April 10, 1856, the Iranian chargé d'affaires in Istanbul formally requested a meeting with the British ambassador, Lord Stratford de Redcliffe.[63] The Iranians were prepared to settle many of the issues of the Murray affair to British satisfaction but their proposals were met with indifference. After some inconclusive correspondence, the British government met on July 5 to find ways of bringing an Iranian withdrawal from Herat. The British view was that the Heratis were requesting that London come to their aid, knowing (by mid-June) of Dost Mohammad's intentions to march to Herat.[64] On July 11, London transmitted its ultimatum to Mirza Agha Khan: Iranian troops must be pulled back from Herat or face such "[British] measures as a regard for its own honor and its own interests may prescribe."[65] Mirza Agha responded that the Iranians had only gone to Herat at the request of the Heratis themselves, due to their concerns about Dost Mohammad's ambitions. He said that the Iranian army would retire if Dost Mohammad vacated Kandahar and returned to Kabul and finally, that issues could be resolved more quickly if the British mission returned to Tehran. Unimpressed by this reply, London sent orders to its forces on July 22, 1856 in Bombay to prepare an expedition against Iran in the Persian Gulf.

The British finally dispatched their expeditionary force from Bombay, Vingoela, Karachi, and Porbandar towards the Persian Gulf by mid-November 1856,[66] just a month after the fall of Herat. The British force comprised 6,100 troops (2,700 Europeans and 3,400 Indians) aboard a total of 47 vessels.[67] In overall command was Major-General F. Stalker. He captured Kharq Island on December 4, 1856, encountering no resistance as the Iranian garrison had already been evacuated.[68]

The lightning-fast British landing at Kharq Island caused considerable agitation in Tehran and Tabriz. The nobles and military immediately divided into two camps: the "war party," and the "doves." The war party viewed the British military demonstration as "showing off," believing that a firm Iranian stance would force the British to back down.[69] The major flaw with their thinking was their failure to understand the distinction between the British Army and the British Royal Navy. While the army was busy in India, Iran was facing the Royal Navy, which was quite capable of conducting its own operations independently of Britain's land forces.

The doves favored rapprochement with the British and hoped for Russian intercession in their favor.[70] Well aware of Iran's military weaknesses, they pointed to the precedent of Iran's crushing defeats at the hands of their European counterparts during the Russo-Iranian wars. In addition, the "doves" almost certainly realized that irrespective of the attempts at military reform, the Iranian military had yet to transform into a modern force capable of meeting its European counterparts on equal terms.

It quickly became apparent that the British were not simply showing off. On December 6, 1857 a 30-strong flotilla soon broke off from the Kharq force and headed to the port of Bushehr on Iran's southern Persian Gulf coastline.[71] In the meantime the British had been gathering supplies from the Basra region in Ottoman ruled southern Iraq.[72] Bushehr had sent messages for military assistance in anticipation of the British arrival, and the reinforced garrison included an unspecified number of infantry, cavalry and approximately a dozen antiquated cannon, dispersed around the walls.[73] The British fleet landed some distance from Bushehr on December 7, 1857.[74] The landing party brought 30 cannon, including 4-, 5-, 6-, and 9-pounders.[75] The British force included Hindus, Arabs, Baluchis, and Sindhese. The British expeditionary force headed towards the Bahmani castle along the route to Bushehr. It was here where the first battles between the Iranians and the British took place.

Bahmani castle (approximately 4 miles (6–7km) from Bushehr) was defended by a total of 1,500–2,000 troops,[76] including the venerable Bagher Khan, who had arrived with his 400 Tangestani warriors from Fars province with two cannon.[77] As soon as the exchange of fire began, the British flotilla, just off-shore, opened fire with their 66-pounder cannon.[78] These salvos combined with the withering fire from the expedition's 30 cannon inflicted very heavy casualties on the Iranians. The flotilla now directed its fire towards Bahmani castle, inflicting considerable damage, though the garrison still held out. Despite a heroic charge by small force of Tangestani warriors, who engaged the British in hand-to-hand fighting and hauled off three British cannon, the castle was doomed.[79] The Tangestani raid had failed to break the British expeditionary force, and the British flotilla methodically maintained its barrage against Bahmani castle. With the fall of the castle to the British on December 9, 1857, Bagher Khan retreated into the Tangestan gorges.[80] The British expeditionary force now reached Bushehr. The city put up a stout but very brief resistance before surrendering on December 10, 1857.[81]

Meanwhile, in Afghanistan, the British had agreed to pay a subsidy to Dost Mohammad in January 1857. Despite receiving a large number of British muskets Dost Mohammad took no action against the Iranians and proved of little military value to the British for the duration of the war.[82] By early January 1857 a 7,000-strong Iranian force arrived at Borazjan, just above Bushehr.[83]

The British had not been complacent. Reinforcements had arrived from India on January 27, 1857, among them the highly capable Sir James Outram.[84] Trenches and ammunition dumps were dug around the city just as the surrounding water wells were destroyed. A total of 60 cannon were also placed just outside of the city far outgunning the Iranians with their modest artillery complement of eight cannon and one mortar.[85] Outram marched towards Borazjan (almost 47 miles (75km) inland) from Bushehr) on February 3, but found the area already abandoned by Iranian troops who had left behind large stores of supplies and ammunition.[86] Outram finally caught up with the Iranian forces near the village of Khoshab on February 5, 1857.[87] The battle is recorded by Iranian sources as having been desperate and bloody, with acts of exceptional bravery especially among the Tangestanis.[88] Crucial to the British victory were their cavalry charges, which wrought havoc in the Iranian formations.[89] The British attacks resulted in the death of 700 Iranian troops and the capture of 100 prisoners.[90] The remaining Iranians rapidly retreated.[91]

On March 14, General Stalker in Bushehr committed suicide, followed just two days later by Commodore Ethersley, commander of the British naval forces.[92] The reasons for two suicides in three days remain unclear, however the strain and responsibilities of command may have played a role. General James Outram now assumed full command of the British expeditionary force, which sailed towards Mohammara with 4,400 troops (4,000 Indian and British infantry and 400 cavalry)[93] on March 18.[94] Ironically the Treaty of Paris had been signed three weeks earlier (see below), but the news had not yet reached Outram.

The Iranians had reinforced their defenses at Mohammara (up to 13,000 with 7,000 being regular soldiers) and stationed at least 3,000 troops in Shushtar and additional troops further north in Kermanshah in reserve for the Khuzistan theater. The commander of the Mohammara garrison, Khanlar Mirza, had been ordered by the Sadr e Azam to avoid combat outside the city and to keep all his cannon inside of the city to avoid exposing them to the powerful guns of the British ships.[95] Khanlar Mirza, however did exactly the opposite by building earthen defenses on the Arvand Rud/Shaat al Arab, Abadan island, and along the north side of the Karun River. He then placed 30 cannon within the defenses so that these would cover as much of the ingress into the Arvand Rud/Shaat al Arab waterway as possible.[96]

Outram decided to run the gauntlet of the Arvand Rud/Shaat al Arab. Almost immediately after entering the waterway on March 25, 1857, the British ships opened fire with their cannon and rapidly dispatched a raft with four mortars (5.5 and 8 inch) which landed undetected across Iranian batteries to their north. The next day, the four mortars directed further devastating fire against Iranian cannon positions, and seven more British ships sailed up the waterway firing their cannon. Despite the best efforts of the Iranian gunners, the British combination of mortars and cannon virtually wiped out the Iranian defenses, destroying many of the Iranian cannon. The British naval and land artillery had decided the course of the battle and the rest of the war.

British troops disembarked from their vessels and secured their foothold on the coast while artillery fire continued to pound the remaining Iranian positions. Khanlar Mirza, realizing the hopelessness of his position, abandoned Mohammara and fled with the remainder of his troops to Ahwaz. British troops entering Mohammara captured vast stores of ammunition, gunpowder, supplies, and 16 cannon.[97] British casualties had been surprisingly light; they only lost five naval personnel and 21 wounded soldiers in comparison to 85 Iranian dead and 100 wounded.[98]

The war had gone completely in Britain's favor. Immediately after the fall of Mohammara, a reconnaissance in force was made towards Ahwaz (roughly 75 miles (120km) away) prompting the city's governor to offer his surrender on March 27, 1857 despite possessing 9,000 troops and numerous cannon.[99] Outram sent a small force of 300 men in three small vessels upstream along the Karun River to occupy Ahwaz whose governor retreated to Shishtar.[100] By April 5, 1857, news of the Paris peace treaty had reached Outram, putting an end to the fighting.

The Paris Treaty

When Nasser e Din Shah and the leading nobles realized that continuing the war with Britain was no longer an option, Farrokh Khan Amin o Dowleh, the Iranian ambassador to France, was given full powers of negotiation to arrive at peace terms with the British ambassador in Paris.[101] The French, who had good relations with the Iranians and Farrokh Khan in particular, acted as the primary mediators. The Treaty of Paris was signed on March 4, 1857. London's primary aim was to maintain the peace and status quo between Iran and Afghanistan. With Iran's acceptance of London's terms, British forces evacuated the occupied Iranian territories and the two sides exchanged prisoners.[102]

The treaty was viewed as a major humiliation by the Iranians, especially the articles that forced Iran to relinquish her claims to Herat.[103] Iran was to withdraw its forces from Herat and Afghanistan, refrain from making any claims on any territory in Afghanistan, any demands of leaders in the country, or become involved in Afghanistan's internal affairs. Afghanistan was to be considered independent territory, and Iran was not to take any action to jeopardize the independence of Herat or Afghanistan.[104] Just as the Golestan and Turkmenchai treaties had forced the Iranians out of the Caucasus, so too had the Treaty of Paris severed Iran's links with one of the key centers of the Persian literary and cultural revival after the arrival of Islam.

Over twenty years later, the fickle pendulum of international affairs seemed to swing momentarily in Iran's favor. By 1879, the British had gone through two difficult wars in Afghanistan and were now willing to accommodate Iranian claims in Herat. Lord Salisbury offered Nasser e Din Shah the city of Herat and even offered to give Iran a subsidy.[105] In return, Iran was to allow British troops to be stationed in Herat to facilitate the construction of the Herat–Kandahar railway and to allow the British to improve transportation from the Persian Gulf into the Iranian plateau and Afghanistan.[106] The agreement was never ratified due to Russian pressure as well as certain provisions in the treaty which the Iranians could not accept.[107] This was the first and last British offer for the Iranians to have Herat.

Turmoil in Central Asia

Just as Nasser e Din had assumed power in Tehran, Iran was in turmoil in the east. Up to the time of Fathali Shah much of Central Asia had maintained at least a nominal or symbolic allegiance to Iran. This changed as the Iranian army suffered defeats against the Russians and the British, and Tehran's political authority and prestige were diminished in Central Asia. The effects of the Iranian military vacuum were now exploited by three Turkmen clans in Central Asia.[108] These, especially the Tekke, Goklan, and Yamut, became increasingly bold, launching punishing raids into Iranian Khorasan.[109]

These Turkmen raids finally prompted the Iranians to action. The Iranians captured Merv in 1858 and again in 1860; but as they returned to Iran after the 1860 campaign, Iranian troops lost up to 40,000 men to Turkmen attacks.[110]

The Russians had keenly observed the Iranian defeat in Central Asia and sought to take advantage. The Russian army moved forward once again and this time avoided the errors of their previous campaigns in Central Asia. By 1868 Russian troops had occupied Samarkand and Bukhara.[111] Bukhara's khan had requested for Iranian military help, but Tehran was too weak to provide this and knew full well that they could not realistically fight a war against Russia.

The Russian army successfully conquered Khokand, Buokhara, and Khiva[112] by 1868. As the Russians moved south they occupied the Turkmen village of Qizik-Su in what the Qajars considered Iranian territory. In response to Iranian protests the Russian minister in Tehran confirmed that Russia did not recognize any Iranian authority north of the Atrak river, one excuse being that Iran wielded no authority in the Central Asian regions. The Iranians were forced to formalize this new humiliation in a treaty with Russia and in 1869, Nasser e-Din Shah agreed to a new frontier along the Atrak River.[113] This was followed up by yet another treaty known as the Akhal–Khorasan

Boundary Convention in 1881.[114] Russian dominion in Central Asia became cemented with the fall of the castle of Goktappeh in 1881 and Merv in 1884.[115]

In the British and Russian rivalry over supremacy in Central Asia, India, Iran and the Persian Gulf, the Russians had achieved great success and drawn closer to India. From Iran's view, this was yet another display of Russian strength and diminishing Iranian political, economic and military strength. The recent Russian conquests meant that Iran now faced Russian troops to her northeast and northwest.

The Qajar Army 1850-99

By the accession of Nasser e Din Shah, the Qajar army was already in sharp decline.[116] The Iranian army by the 1890s was very impressive on paper, numbering 150,000 regulars and 50,000 reservists.[117] Factoring in men on leave, deficient complements and incorrect reporting, the total number of troops was closer to 80,000, of which many were not fully trained or equipped.[118] While the army was organized hierarchically, each of the distinct branches had become very disorganized and inefficient. The Nezam were the most "European" in appearance, and by the time of Nasser e Din Shah many of these were responsible for protecting the Qajar leadership and the shah.[119] Some contemporary reports on discipline and training in the army note of considerable discipline and efficiency in a number of Nezam units in the 1850s.[120] Iranian troops were also described as being especially rugged, being able to march on average 30 miles daily over a number of days.[121]

The government tended to emphasize recruitment from those areas that had traditionally provided Iran's best warriors, such as Azarbaijan. While many men did enlist, many did so as a result of government pressure on villages, and there was much bribery and corruption. Troops were reported as being rarely fully dressed in regular uniforms.[122] Training had become very limited with even drills being confined to ceremonial occasions (i.e. the shah's birthday).[123] There was hardly any consistent time devoted to small-arms training on firing ranges, and training was almost impossible anyway as troops were allowed just five rounds for training purposes each year because of the overall shortage of ammunition.[124] Weapons were often out of date, with antiquated percussion muskets still in use. The more modern breech-loading Werndl rifle became available as a result of the Austrian mission of 1879–81, but reputedly 10,000 of these were placed in reserve to be used only when necessary in critical situations so many troops continued to use the older weapons.[125]

The best infantry elements were the tribal Kurds and Bakhtiaris as they worked hard to implement their own training and owned their own weapons. Their military quality had much to do with their practices of raiding, local police/patrol duties, and inter-tribal warfare.[126] The least efficient infantry units were the town militias responsible for general security purposes; they were armed with obsolete weapons and their training was rudimentary at best.[127]

Despite reforms made during Amir Kabir's brief tenure, corruption had once again established itself within the armed forces. Soldiers were often not paid for two or three years.[128] It was also not uncommon for troops to bribe officers to be given "permanent leave."[129] There were cases where officers would simply pocket their troops' pay, thereby obliging the soldiers to find other jobs to make ends meet.[130] The selection of officers was often done through favoritism, or through the purchase of positions.[131] The professionally trained officers from the Dar ol Fonoon struggled to find employment due to opposition from officers who had purchased their positions.[132] In this fashion the number of officers with no military merit proliferated.[133]

The state of the Iranian artillery corps by the late 19th century was so pathetic that in the 1880s Russian officers commented that despite having 200 cannon and 8,000 artillerymen, the Iranians simply had no artillery force of consequence due to the poor training of the troops and the quality of the cannon.[134] In practice the Iranian army by the 1890s had one functional artillery regiment (four battalions of two batteries each): one battalion was equipped with machineguns, one with mountain guns, and the other two with second-hand Austrian-made muzzle-loading guns.[135] The latter were only provided with three rounds per gun for training purposes over the course of a year. One of the machinegun batteries had four multi-barrel Nordenfelt models and the other battalion had six rapid-firing Mauser Maxims.[136] As with the gunners, the machinegunners were not well trained and the Qajars provided the Maxims with just 100,000 rounds of ammunition.

Tribal cavalry tended to fight in their own locales and provinces and often formed the first line of defense against foreign invading armies. Numbers of these were often employed by the government on a full-time basis to patrol roads and critical areas. The tribal cavalry remained Iran's most effective arm. Tribal cavalrymen began their training at a young age, and provided their own horses, weapons and equipment.[137]

The rise of the Persian Cossack Brigade

The disastrous outcome of the 1856–57 Herat war convinced Nasser e Din Shah of the need for military reform. The Iranians turned once again to France who were keen to support Iran to counteract the Ottomans and the British, and a mission arrived in October 1858 tasked with raising and training troops and teaching at the Dar ol Fonoon.[138] This mission failed to achieve any notable success and was terminated in 1867. Three years later, the Iranians turned to the British for help but London refused.

In 1875, the shah, under the influence of his prime minister and minister of war, Mirza Hussein Khan Moshir o Dowleh, attempted to institute new reforms.[139] The costly war over Herat had exhausted the already meager Iranian treasury, but despite the fiscal challenges, Mirza Hussein Khan Moshir o Dowleh attempted to imitate the late Amir Kabir's reforms, such as the regulation of the army budget, a high standard of military education, and regularized conscription.[140] The success of these reforms would depend on foreign advisors. During Nasser e Din Shah's second trip to Europe in 1878, he requested that the Austro-Hungarian emperor loan him a number of military instructors.[141] The emperor complied and Austrian military instructors arrived by January 1879, bringing with them a number of Austrian cannon purchased by Iran.[142] The Austrian mission, however, left Iran just four years later in 1881.[143] Some positive developments did take place, such as the establishment of at least two new military academies and a small military hospital by 1895.[144]

Nasser e Din Shah's attempts at reform had had no meaningful results, and the Austro-Hungarian mission had not made a significant impression, so the Qajars again sought foreign help, this time from their nemesis, imperial Russia. During his visit to Russia in 1878, Nasser e Din Shah requested help to form an Iranian version of the Cossack brigade.[145] This became known as the Gazaghan to the Iranians and the Persian Cossack Brigade in the west. The force was first formed in 1879 with the arrival of Colonel Alexei Ivanovich Dumantovich and a Cossack contingent.[146] The Russians trained two brigades of Iranians (400–600 men each). Recruitment was from those Iranians descended from Caucasians who had fled the Caucasus following the imposition of Russian rule from 1813–28. Dumanovich introduced a number of positive practices, including strict discipline, prompt pay, and promotion through military merit rather than family/political connections.[147] The brigade offered many incentives for Iranian volunteer recruits: the regular pay was double that of the Nezam troops, and they would receive the benefits of Russian political immunity.[148]

The Persian Cossack Brigade became the best-trained unit in Iran, becoming Nasser e Din's palace guard, and (by implication) a powerful political instrument responsible for maintaining law and order in Tehran, protecting European nationals and governors in the provinces (and related miscellaneous duties outside of Tehran).[149] However, the brigade was a double-edged sword for Iran. While capable of enforcing the shah's authority they were not strong enough to firmly establish Qajar authority throughout Iran. This is because the Persian Cossack Brigade had been formed to primarily serve Russian interests and not those of Iran, and was commanded by Tsarist officers beholden to Moscow.[150] Soon enough, this police force wielded by Russian imperial interests would demonstrate that its actions were not in the interests of the people or nation of Iran.

Caught in the pincers of the Great Game

The Great Game was a power struggle over the dominance of Central Asia, Iran, and the Persian Gulf fought mainly between Russia and Britain, joined by the Ottoman and German empires, and briefly by the French in Napoleon's time.[151] This was initially born out of British countermeasures to prevent Russia from gaining access to India.[152] British interest in Iran and Central Asia was duly increased after Iran's signature of the treaties of Golestan and Turkmenchai which signaled increased Russian dominance in Iran and Central Asia.[153] Russia, whose northern ports were frozen for the winter and better part of the spring, was eager to expand her shipping into the Caspian Sea, and eventually towards the Persian Gulf.[154] This clashed with British interests, whose imperial navy already dominated the waters there. Within this conflict Iran became a central (and coveted) pawn.[155] Perhaps the greatest irony is that Iran was saved from becoming a colony precisely because the two imperialist powers fighting over it wished to prevent one another from dominating it.[156] Nevertheless, in the great tussle of the Great Game, Iran by the early 1900s had come dangerously close to becoming a virtual protectorate of Russia, especially in the north, with the British having gained considerable influence in the south of Iran and the Persian Gulf.[157]

The late Qajar era therefore saw the rise of British and Russian economic power in Iran, and the development of communications, transportation, industry, and banking in Iran. The 1857 Treaty of Paris enabled the British to expand their business interests in Iran. British economic influence was to steadily increase in the ensuing decades of the 19th century.[158] The British also had considerable difficulty penetrating the northern Iranian markets as the Russians had had significant influence over northern Iran since 1828. The British however had much easier economic access to southern Iran (thanks to their base in India) and the Persian Gulf where their navy was militarily dominant.[159] The British for example, showed a keen interest in southwest Iran, notably the Karun River, where Nasser e Din Shah granted the Lynch brothers the right to operate a steam vessel service[160] between Mohammara (Khorramshahr), Ahwaz and Shushtar from 1888.[161] Iran also made concessions to other European states. While the Russians and British were the main competitors for economic concessions in Iran, the British would score a major success with the D'Arcy oil concession in 1901. Iran's economic state had deteriorated considerably by the early 1900s, due in large part to the country's huge debts derived from British and Russian loans.[162]

Despite the precarious nature of Iranian political and economic independence, Iran did gain a telegraph network linking Iran's major cities by 1872; postage reforms underway by 1879; its first (8km) railway line in 1884, between Tehran and Shabdolazim, followed by a second line established further north between Amol and Mahmoud Abad by 1890; and much-needed reforms in coinage.[163] While the introduction of modernized coinage production and its distribution across the country was a step forward in modernizing the economy, the impact of this was of course tempered by the banking concessions that Iran had given to the British and the Russians.

The Persian Gulf: Nasser e Din Shah reasserts Iranian authority in the south

As the 19th century progressed, the British Empire proceeded to set a series of semi-autonomous protectorates in Iran's south, notably in the southwest region and along the Persian Gulf coast, to offset Russian economic, political, and territorial ambitions in the north of Iran.[164] These protectorates could be used to impose dismemberment upon Iran if this suited the British Empire's geopolitical and economic interests, though in practice this did not happen and London did not militarily prevent Iran from re-imposing its authority along its Persian Gulf coastline.[165] The early Qajars were mainly preoccupied with Iran's other theaters, and it was only during the reign of Nasser e Din Shah that Iran finally reasserted herself along the Persian Gulf coastline from Bushehr to the borders of India.

During Nasser e Din Shah's reign, Arab raids in Bandar Abbas, Bahrain and other Iranian possessions in the region forced the leadership to address Iran's vital naval weaknesses. Britain and Oman were the biggest naval powers in the Persian Gulf. Oman's disputes with Iran regarding the lease of Bandar Abbas had led to threats to blockade the Iranian coastline if Tehran failed to come to terms.[166] Nasser e Din Shah actually had to rely on the British navy to help dissuade the Omanis from taking hostile naval action.[167]

Nasser e Din took steps to revive the Iranian navy. By 1865 orders were placed with British shipyards to build two sloops of war (25 guns each)[168] suited for protecting the Iranian coastline and island possessions in the Persian Gulf.[169] The British refused to accommodate the order as they feared that the Iranians would then use these against their Arab clients in Bahrain and upset British–Arab relations in the area.[170] Nasser e Din Shah then approached Germany in 1883 for assistance and after prolonged negotiations Iran took delivery of two steamship combat vessels, the *Persepolis* (600 tons and 4 75mm cannon) in January 1885 and the smaller *Shoush* (Susa) (250 tons) which was delivered in kit-form to Mohammara and assembled there.[171] These ships made very little impression in the Persian Gulf, which may explain why the Iranian government lost interest in building up a navy.[172] Bushehr had been cleared of the Al-Mazkur Arabs by 1850 and Bandar Abbas (which had fallen under Omani domination) had been restored to Iran by 1868.[173]

Since the fall of Nader Shah, the Omanis had gained dominance in Chahbahar and Gwatar in Iranian Baluchistan, which bordered British India. The region was propelled into prominence by British interest in establishing a telegraph line from England to India following the Indian Mutiny of 1857. By 1864 the Iranians were asserting their sovereignty over Gwadar and Chahbahar, launching raids up to outskirts of Gwadar. Oman contemplated the dispatch of a powerful fleet to bolster both Chahbahar and Gwadar against Iran but were persuaded not to do so by the British.[174] The Iranians, the British and representatives from the Kalat Kingdom (in British India), met in 1870, and in 1871 Iran was awarded those lands in Baluchistan up to the town of Gwatar. Though Chahbahar was clearly on the Iranian side of the boundary, it was held by Oman until 1872 when the Omanis were expelled by an Iranian army.[175]

Kangan on the Iranian coastline was captured from Sheikh Mazkur in 1880.[176] Further east across the Iranian coastline to the Gulf of Oman was Jask, where Iranian authority was reasserted by 1886 through the appointment of a government official and the stationing of Iranian troops.[177]

Bandar Lengeh had also been restored to Iran, especially after the clearing of the Qawasim Arabs by 1857.[178] The capture of Bandar Lengeh also led to the arrival of Iranian troops to Sirri Island (which had also been administered by the Qawasim Arabs).

Iran also claimed the Tumbs and Abu Musa in 1887 as these had been administered from Bandar Lengeh.[179] As protectors of the Arab sheikhdoms of the southern portion of the Persian Gulf, the British rejected the Iranian position.[180] The British specifically supported the Qawasim Sheikh of Ras al Khaimah's claims to the Tumbs and Sharjah's claims to Abu Musa.[181] There was little acknowledgement of Iran's authority in the islands by the British as they occupied them in 1903 and advised Sharjah, then a British protectorate to hoist its flags there.[182] The Iranians protested that these actions were illegal as the Tumbs and Abu Musa were administered from the Lengeh district of the province of Fars.[183] The repercussions of these issues resonated in the 20th century and continue to do so to the present day.

The Iranians had been driven out of Bahrain in 1783 during the Zand era but had not ceased their claims to that island.[184] By 1855 the Iranians had even worked at securing American naval assistance for asserting Tehran's authority upon Bahrain and other Iranian possessions in the Persian Gulf.[185] This project never materialized and just six years later in 1861, the British recognized the Sheikh of Bahrain as independent from Iran and by 1880 had even taken over the foreign policy of the island.[186] This was very much a function of military force as the British enjoyed uncontested naval dominance in the Persian Gulf. Iran's lack of a navy and her overall military weaknesses meant that she had no choice but to acquiesce with this state of affairs, but they were to claim Bahrain as Iranian territory well into the 20th century.

The Kurdish Question

One of the greatest internal challenges to arise in Iran during the reign of Nasser e Din Shah was the Kurdish rebellion in northwest Iran. Political borders have often meant little to the Kurdish tribes straddling across the borders of the Qajar Iran and the Ottoman Empire and Kurdish warlords within one empire often made political and military alliances of convenience with the bordering empire just to strengthen their position. Even if the warlords remained "loyal" to their state, there was always the possibility that they could switch alleigance. By the 19th century however the Kurds no longer viewed the Iranians or the Ottomans as the supreme powers in the region, instead viewing the Russians and the British as the stronger parties. Kurdish nationalists from 1880–1930 openly envisaged an independent state that would be a client of the British or the Russians.[187] The Ottomans proved especially adept at directing Kurdish nationalist aspirations towards Iran. This was done by mainly appealing to the pan-Islamic (anti-Shiite and anti-Christian) tendencies of the Kurds, while de-emphasizing their historical, and cultural affinity with Iran and the common Pahlavi language roots of Persian and Kurdish.[188]

While many of Iran's Kurds did identify with the Iranian state, there were also those who did not, notably the Shikak. Interestingly many of these endeavored to carve a state inside Iran, rather than Ottoman Turkey where a much larger proportion of Kurds predominated (and continue to do so). Ali Khan Shikak of the Shikak Kurdish tribe erupted into revolt against the Iranian state almost as soon as Nasser e Din Shah came to power. Tehran and Tabriz swiftly dispatched contingents to face down Ali Khan resulting in a number of bruising battles.[189] Ali Khan was defeated and fled into Ottoman territory. The Ottomans then handed him back to the Qajars, who imprisoned him until his death. Ali Khan's brother, Jaafar Khan, continued to engage in battles against government troops resulting in his defeat and death.[190] This was by no means the end of the Shikak challenge to Iran.

The first serious attempt to carve out an independent Kurdish state inside Iranian territory was made in 1880 by Sheikh Obeidollah.[191] The latter's major base of support and residence was not in Iran but in the southeast area of Lake Van in the Ottoman Empire. The Ottoman Sultan Abdulhamid II (1842–1918) openly supported the idea of using Ottoman Kurds to create a Kurdish homeland at Iranian expense.[192] Obeidollah recruited a large army inside Ottoman Turkey and invaded Iranian Azarbaijan, an action which encouraged a number of Iran's local Kurds in the region to join his banner.[193] The Ottoman sultan may also have been hoping to use the proxy Kurdish state to suppress Armenian nationalists, thereby killing two birds with one Kurdish stone.[194]

Obeidollah however soon became bogged down in Iranian Azarbaijan. Not only was he facing government troops and local Azarbaijanis, but also numbers of Iranian Kurds who opposed Obeidollah. Judging Istanbul's support as insufficient he then made contact with the British authorities in his quest to solicit their support.[195] After a slow mobilization of three months resulting in the raising of twenty thousand troops,[196] the Iranians managed to defeat and eject Obeidollah's forces back into Ottoman territory, where the sultan offered him sanctuary, but also promised Iranian authorities to prevent him from returning to Iran.[197] Despite the defeat in 1880, the notion of creating a Kurdish-Sunni state inside Iran had by now entered the consciousness of numbers of Kurds who were well aware of Iran's growing weaknesses. Tsarist, and later Communist, Russia would work at cultivating and permeating pan-Kurdism against the Iranian state by the early 1900s.

Russian cultivation of anti-Persianism in the Caucasus and Kurdistan

Before the Tsarist Russian conquests of the early 19th century, Persian and wider Iranian civilization had a deep-rooted historical, linguistic, and cultural influence in the Caucasus as well as Central Asia."[198] Even after the treaty of Turkmenchai, Persian remained the main language of administration in these provinces.[199] The Shiite clergy who held considerable influence over the local courts and schools helped maintain the influence of Iranian culture in the Caucasus. Tsarist authorities realized that the persistence of Persian language, traditions and literature was a potential threat against Russian rule as it perpetuated a common cultural bond with Iran to the south across the Araxes River. Russia successfully promoted the local Turkish vernaculars to eventually replace Persian as the dominant language in the region. By the early 1860s, local sentiments against Russification had been successfully channeled away from an Iranian cultural-literary expression into a distinctly Turkic-Tatar form. By 1910, only one of Baku's 41 primary schools taught in Persian.[200] The Russian authorities also invested in the propagation of anti-Iranian literature in the eight Caucasian khanates, such as the *Akinci* (*Cultivator*) newspaper (1875–77) which mainly targeted the local Turkish speaking peasants of Albania and was hostile towards Persian-speakers and the Shiite religion, also targeting Persian culture and civilization.[201] Written in the Azarbaijani vernacular of Turkish, the paper made a deliberate effort towards avoiding the use of Persian and Arabic words, even to the extent of inventing new vocabulary. The Tsarist Russians continued to sponsor Persophobic literature into the early twentieth century, one notable journal of this genre being the cartoons of the *Mulla Nasrredin*.[202] The cultural warfare against the Persian language and culture in the Caucasus met with almost total success, though some pockets of Iranian language remained, such as the Talysh.[203]

Russia's anti-Persian activities soon extended to the Ottoman Kurds, and then against Iran's Kurds. The aim was to weaken the Kurdish cultural and historical ties with the Iranian realm. The Russians sponsored and supported Abdulrazzag Bedir Khan of the Bedirkhanid clan who had left his kinsmen in Istanbul for exile in Russia in 1906 due his falling out with Sultan Abdul Hamid. In 1912, Abdulrazzaq arrived in the west of Iranian Azarbaijan to vigorously promote separatist Kurdish sentiments. This task was easy to accomplish as Russian troops were occupying much of northern Iran and Iranian Azarbaijan, therefore Abdulrazzaq was guaranteed that his efforts would not be molested by any authorities.[204]

The efforts at de-Persianization especially among the Kurds were simultaneously joined by efforts at arming Iranian tribes to the detriment of the political integrity of the Iranian state. By 1901 Russia was sending weapons to a number of tribes (especially the Kurds) in efforts to further expand its influence.[205] Particular emphasis was placed on recruiting tribal levies to the Persian Cossack brigade extend Russian influence into Iran's provinces, notably in the Azarbaijani, Kurdish, and Bakhtiari areas.[206] Russia's approach was unique in that it sought to further its geopolitical objectives by combining "educational" methods with the age-old practice of forging political-military links along Iran's peripheral provinces. Perhaps more interesting are Russian "conferences" that were set up in (Russian) occupied Iranian Kurdistan in 1917 which aimed to unify Kurds from Iran and the Ottoman Empire towards a pro-Russian policy.[207] The Russian chargés d'affaires in Tehran at the time (Minorsky) went so far as to advocate "national rights" for the Kurds within Iranian territory.[208]

CHAPTER 24

THE CONSTITUTIONAL REVOLUTION

Nasser e Din Shah did not live to see the 20th century. As he was preparing to celebrate the fifty-year anniversary of his reign, he was assassinated in 1896 in the holy shrine of Imam Reza in Mashhad by Mirza Mohammad Reza Kermani. The Shah's assassin had been a close follower of Jamal e Din Assadabadi "Afghani," one of the forerunners of the pan-Islamic movement.[1] Nasser e Din Shah was succeeded by Mozzafar e Din Shah (r. 1896–1907). The shah very much owed his ascension to the Peacock throne to the Persian Cossack Brigade which had immediately deployed throughout Tehran to maintain law and order and prevent two rival Qajar princes from contesting the new shah's right to rule.[2] Mozzafar e Din's eleven-year reign saw the rise of western Asia's first popular democracy movement: the Iranian Constitutional Revolution.

One of the most fascinating developments during the latter part of the 19th century was the rise of the Iranian secret societies. By the early 20th century these had given way to the Anjomanhaye Melli (the Nationalist Societies), which helped spawn the Melliyan (Nationalists).[3] The Melliyun expressed great concerns with respect to the military and political ascendancy of other powers (especially Russia and Britain) over Iran, the despotic and corrupt system of government, and the threat to the very social fabric of Iran itself.[4]

A year after he assumed the throne, Mozzafar e Din Shah dismissed the unpopular minister Amino ol Sultan and appointed the reformist-minded Amino ol Dowleh in his place in 1897 (his tenure lasting only one year into 1898).[5] Mozzafar e Din Shah continued his predecessor's policy of maintaining a close relationship with Russia, which partly explains why the growing democracy or constitutionalist movement of the Melliyun looked increasingly to London for support.[6]

The Anjomans disseminated a number of declarations and articles relating to their proposed reforms to the political and social structures of Iran.[7] In May 1905, the Anjomans made a declaration addressed to the Prime Minister Ayn o Dowleh, which specifically demanded an overhaul and reform of the armed forces.[8] Iran's lack of a strong military allowed the Russians, British, and Ottomans to virtually enter Iran at will and there was rising discontent over the Qajar state's unwillingness or inability to effect reforms to the army. Meanwhile, the defeat of the Russians by the Japanese in the Russo-Japanese War (1904–5) shattered the myth of Russian invincibility and Iranian constitutionalist nationalist thinkers may have concluded that Russia's defeat at Japanese hands and the internal upheavals in Russia had rendered the Tsar too weak to support the shah.[9]

The constitutional movement essentially began as a protest movement in December 1905 in which a coalition of reformers, Ulema and *Bazaaris* (merchants/entrepreneurs) put pressure on the government to accede to their demands for a Constitutional government.[10] Matters came to a head in July 1906 when a large group of people engaged in a *Bast* (lit. seeking refuge, sanctuary) at the British embassy.[11] The Constitutional Movement had looked to the British for support who were willing to oblige at first as Britain was (unlike Imperial Russia) a parliamentary democracy.[12]

Perhaps most significant in the protests were the shouts of "Long live the nation of Iran" by the crowds, an indication of unity across a broad spectrum of secular and religious society.[13]

Mozzafar e Din Shah finally caved into the protestors' demands and signed a decree in August 5, 1906 allowing for a constitutional assembly to convene.[14] The Majlis (parliament) had four other general objectives other than limiting the powers of the Shah: defending themselves against internal and domestic enemies; halting the process of political and economic disintegration that threatened the unity and territorial integrity of the Iranian state; engaging in state building and; constructing a modern national army capable of defending the state.[15] This was of special concern to the constitutional movement as they were strong advocates of an indigenous (Iranian) military organization that would be capable of defending Iran's political and economic independence, frontiers and national security.[16]

Mozaffar e Din Shah's son and successor, Mohammad Ali Shah (1872–1924, r. 1907–09) approved the Supplementary Fundamental Laws, but was soon to challenge the Majlis with a vengeance.[17] He arrived in Tehran from Tabriz on December 17, just weeks before his father's death, and was crowned Shah on January 19, 1907. Mohammad Ali Shah was well-known for his strong pro-Russian stance, in effect being a tool of their imperialism in Iran.[18] His main source of strength in Iran was the Russian-officered Persian Cossack Brigade.[19]

It was this stage, just as the constitutional movement was struggling to maintain itself, that Britain and Russia agreed to settle their differences over Iran and to divide it into their respective "spheres of influence." The Anglo-Russian accord was signed in St. Petersburg on August 31, 1907. Russia and the British had arrived at an overall settlement over their differences in Iran, Afghanistan and Tibet.[20] Fears over the rise of Imperial Germany was also a major factor in motivating the Russians and the British towards a closer relationship.[21] The treaty's clause with respect to Iran stated that the north and central areas (including Tehran and Isfahan) would be part of the Russian "sphere of influence," the southwest, especially Iranian Baluchistan bordering and a major part of Iran's coastline on the Gulf of Oman roughly up to middle part of Laristan (around the straights of Hormuz), would be part of Britain's sphere of influence; and there was to be middle "neutral" zone that also included Khuzistan in the southwest.[22] The treaty was a major blow for the Iranians as they had neither been consulted nor informed of its points while the treaty was being negotiated. This also dashed any hopes that the Constitutionalists may have entertained regarding British support against Russian intervention against them. The Iranians were alone against the Russian colossus, who no longer had to fear London's reaction when they decided to march straight to Tehran. The Iranians had realized the harsh fact that their democratic movement had few friends in the democratically governed west.[23] Nevertheless, British public opinion was appalled by Foreign Minister Edward Grey's betrayal of Iran. The London Persia Committee headed by Professor Edward G. Browne (1862–1926) for example spoke out vociferously against the Anglo-Russian treaty.[24]

On August 31, 1907, the very same day the Anglo-Russian Accord was being signed in St. Petersburg, Mohammad Ali Shah's prime minister (Amin ol Sultan, known as the *Atabak e Azam*) was assassinated.[25] The shah apparently hoped to use this incident as an excuse to stifle the Constitutionalists, however the latter simply became more strident in their demands. By early December 1907 Mohammad Ali Shah had made up his mind to crush the Majlis by mobilizing the 1,200–1,800 man Persian Cossack Brigade and a band of ruffians.[26] The Iranian army by this time was no longer a military factor domestically or internationally. By mid-December Mohammad Ali Shah unleashed his attempted coup d'état by having his ruffians agitate against the Majlis. These actions were foiled by the quick reaction of the Anjomans resulting in armed citizen volunteers guarding the Majlis.[27] In Tehran alone there were 140 Anjoman societies with an estimated membership of 30,000.[28] Telegrams of support arrived from all across Iran expressing support for the Majlis. Mohammad Ali Shah backed down and even agreed to consider bringing the Cossack brigade and other Royal troops under the jurisdiction of the Majlis.[29] Tensions died down by December 20 when the Majlis and the shah appeared to be arriving at conciliation.

The first Russian military invasion of Iran in the 20th century occurred on April 29, 1908.[30] But this was not the only foreign military power to invade Iranian territory in the early 20th century. Almost a year earlier, in 1907, an Ottoman force of 6,000 men had marched into Iranian Azarbaijan, occupied its western Kurdish inhabited regions and threatened the city of Urumiah.[31] The Ottomans struggled to maintain control of their occupied territories and were ejected by Russian forces in 1911.[32]

The Russian army led by Colonel Vladimir Platonovitch Liakhov escorted Mohammad Shah and his entourage to the Bagh e Shah district in Tehran on June 4, 1908.[33] It was at this juncture when the Persian Cossack Brigade (by now a force ranging between 1,500 to 2,000 men) openly displayed themselves as a tool of foreign interests.[34] The efficacy of the unit had actually declined by 1904 mainly due to decreasing funds and by 1905 many of the Russian officers were distracted by events back home in Russia.[35] The major consequence of this was decreased overall morale among the Iranian troops of the brigade.[36] On June 23, Liakhov attacked the Tehran Majlis with four cannon and 1,000 troops of the Persian Cossack Brigade.[37] The brigade's primary weapon was the US-designed and Russian-produced Berdan single-shot bolt-action rifle that was markedly superior to anything in the Iranian arsenals at the time.[38] Just prior to the bombardment 400 Iranian troops left the Cossack Brigade to avoid partaking in Liakhov's actions.[39] This is of interest as Liakhov had already expunged the brigade from all those Iranians who harbored "nationalist" sentiments.[40] Opposing Liakhov were just 100 members of the local Anjomans along with their comrades from Azarbaijan.[41] Despite impossible odds, these men fought against the Cossacks with incredible courage, knocking out three of their cannon and resisting for eight hours before being overwhelmed.[42]

After the "conquest" of the Majlis, Liakhov executed many prominent members of the Constitutional movement[43] and then run amuck for days in Tehran looting and bombing the homes of all those disliked by the shah.[44] In appreciation to his Russian mentors for having re-installed him as shah, Mohammad Ali Shah appointed Liakhov as the governor of Tehran with full powers over the police and military.[45] This was the first time in history an Iranian Shah had appointed the military leader of an invading army to govern his capital.

With the Majlis now forcibly closed and royalist control re-asserting itself throughout the country it seemed that the Iranian experiment with democracy had been crushed. But thanks to Azarbaijan, the Constitutional movement was about to gain a new lease of life. Tabriz had a well-organized and -armed militia which refused to bow to Mohammad Shah.[46] It was here where one of the modern heroes of Iran, a Tabrizi by the name of Sattar Khan (1868–1914) defied the royalist authorities by tearing down the white flags that had set up as a sign of submission to the royalists.[47] The center of political authority in Tabriz was the Anjoman e Melli (the National Council).[48]

The battle of Chaldiran, 1514, between Ottoman and Safavid forces, from the 1597 manuscript *A History of the Kurds*. (The Art Archive / Bodleian Library Oxford, MS Elliott 332 folio 207–8)

Shah Abbas in battle as depicted in the Chehel Sotun Palace in Isfahan. (The Art Archive / Palace of Chehel Sotun Isfahan / Gianni Dagli Orti)

The reception for the Ambassador of the Grand Mughal at the court of Shah Tahmasp, 1573–76. (Chehel Sotun Palace, Isfahan, Iran / Giraudon / The Bridgeman Art Library)

Nader Shah's artillery repelling the attacks of Ashraf the Afghan, as seen in the *Jahangoshay-e Naderi*. The infantry stand behind the cannon, ready to deploy when given the order. There is a space after the first two cannon where Nader's cavalry stand ready for the counterattack. (Khorasani, Maouchehr, Mosthagh (2009), *Classic Arms and Militaria*, p.26)

The battle of Karnal (February 22, 1739) as depicted in the Chehel Sotun. Nader Shah is shown riding a horse on the left, with the Mughal Mohammad Shah riding a white elephant. The battle ended in an overwhelming victory for Nader Shah. (Courtesy of Youngrobv / Flickr.com)

The *Arg-e Karim Khan* (Citadel of Karim Khan) in Shiraz. (© Arthur Thévenart / Corbis)

Agha Muhammad Khan Qajar, *c.* 1820. (Private Collection / Photo © Christie's Images / The Bridgeman Art Library)

Top: Despite limited resources, an antiquated military, and the increasing lethargy and corruption of the Qajar court, Prince Abbas Mirza made a valiant, but ultimately futile effort against one of Europe's most powerful empires, Imperial Tsarist Russia. (Georgian State Picture Gallery, Tbilisi, Georgia / The Bridgeman Art Library)

Bottom left: Abbas Mirza defeating Russian troops, helped by a company of zanbouraks. Illustrations from *Shahinshahnama*. (The Art Archive / Bodleian Library Oxford, Elliott 327 folio 428r)

Bottom right: A gun with a British percussion cap mechanism with a barrel from the Zand era. (Khorasani, Maouchehr, Mosthagh (2009), *Classic Arms and Militaria*, p.22)

Constitutionalist *Melliyun* (nationalists) of Iranian Azarbaijan fighting against anti-Constitutionalists in 1908. Note the tricolor Persian flag. (*Illustrated London News* / Mary Evans)

A parade of Iranian troops from the new Iranian army for the coronation of Shah Reza in 1926. Iran finally had a national army that was unified and beholden exclusively to the interests of the Iranian state. (© Bettmann / Corbis)

Iranian cavalry during the Second World War. Despite procurements of armored vehicles and their integration into the Iranian army, cavalry remained Iran's prime asset for rapid strikes and shock and maneuver tactics on the battlefield. (National Library of Australia)

Iranian soldiers in training during the Allied occupation of Iran. When Russia withdrew her military umbrella from her satellite states in northern Iran, Pishevari and Ghazi Mohammad were ultimately doomed. (National Library of Australia)

Revolutionaries in control of a tank in Tehran in February 1979. (© Michel Setboun / Corbis)

Iranian army troops fraternizing with clergy holding posters of Khomeini atop an armored vehicle in Tehran, January 15, 1979. (© Patrick Chauvel / Sygma / Corbis)

An Iraqi soldier posing in front of a bullet-ridden portrait of Khomeini after Operation *Ramadan Al Mubarak* which recaptured Fao on April 17–18, 1988. (© Shepard Sherbell / Corbis)

Jubilant citizen volunteers celebrate after one of the numerous operations which expelled Iraqi troops from Khuzestan, 1982. Up to 22,000 Iraqi troops surrendered at Khorramshahr and the mass surrender imposed major challenges to the Iranian transportation system as numerous trucks had to be diverted from the main war effort to transport the prisoners to detention camps. (© Françoise Demulder / Corbis)

Iranian F-4 Phantoms with Maverick air-to-ground missiles in action during the Iran–Iraq War. Phantoms such as these proved vital in supporting the Iranian offensives which expelled Iraqi troops from Khuzestan in 1982. (Farzad Bishop and Tom Cooper)

Sattar Khan and his co-commander Baqer Khan now led a powerful defense of Tabriz against a determined siege by royalist troops lasting well into the winter.[49] The resistance effort at Tabriz was supported by the Iranian community of the Caucasus as well as sympathetic Georgians and Armenians.[50] The success of the Azari resistance served as an inspiration for the Gilanis in northern Iran and other provinces in Iran.[51] The resistance of Sattar Khan and Baqer Khan was so effective that it forced Mohammad Ali Shah to divert the bulk of his forces to Tabriz, leading to the slackening of Royalist authority in Iran's provinces. It is estimated that 10,000 constitutionalist defenders at Tabriz held a besieging royalist force of up to 30,000 troops at bay.[52]

The obstinacy of Tabriz resulted in the outbreak of pro-Constitutionalist protests in Mashad, Gilan and Isfahan.[53] Sattar Khan and his men vowed to fight until the constitutional government was reinstated in Tehran.[54]

Following a food shortage in Tabriz, 4,000 Russian troops (four squadrons of Russian Cossacks, three battalions of infantry, two artillery batteries and company of sappers),[55] led by General Sharski entered Tabriz[56] on the pretext of protecting Europeans on April 29/30, 1909. Their real motive was to break the back of the Tabriz constitutionalists in favor of Mohammad Ali Shah.[57] The Russian invasion however only resulted in nationalist fighters leaving Tabriz to join the like-minded Rashti forces of Gilan now led by Sepahdar e Azam and pro-constitutionalist Armenian fighters led by Yeprem Khan.[58] Together the Azari-Gilani-Armenian forces marched towards Tehran on March 1909.[59] These forces first thrust to Qazvin in May 1909, approximately 110 miles (180km) from Tehran, where they decisively defeated the local royalist garrison.[60] This resulted in 400 Cossacks deploying from Tehran to Karaj in its northwest (today a suburb of Tehran) to build a line against the constitutionalists coming from the north.[61] The German ambassador to Constantinople, Baron Wangenheim, openly expressed concerns that the actions of Russian troops were part of an overall and longer-term plan by Russia to annex Azarbaijan as well as Kurdistan in Iran.[62]

As pro-constitutionalist forces were arriving towards Tehran, Bakhtiaris from the southwest in Isfahan were also on the move towards the capital. These had successfully overcome a royalist force (1,200 infantry, 300 cavalry and six field guns) and threatened to outflank the Cossacks at Karaj obliging them to retreat to Shahabad (around 37 miles (60km) from Tehran).[63] The Azari-Gilani-Armenian forces and the Bakhtiaris linked up in Karaj on July 8, 1909, creating a true national army.[64] The Russians threatened that they would send more troops into Iran if the nationalist-constitutionalist forces continued to advance towards Tehran. They made good on this threat by dispatching another 2,000 troops from Baku on July 8.[65] Russian actions may partly explain why the Bakhtiaris sent another 600 cavalry to support the nationalists fighting their way into Tehran.[66]

Qajar forces, a few thousand troops with three Maxim machineguns, deployed to defend the city with 1,000 formidable Cossacks policing the town itself.[67] The royalist forces put up an effective resistance for a number of days, blocking the ingress of the 4,000 nationalists, and their one field gun.[68] The nationalists broke to the city by July 13, 1909.[69] Meanwhile the Russian force from Baku had reached Qazvin two days earlier on July 11, 1909.[70] In Tehran fighting continued for a few more days until Mohammad Ali Shah fled to the Russian embassy and took sanctuary there on July 16, 1909.[71] Two days later Mohammad Ali Shah was dethroned and his young son Ahmad was made Shah.[72] Mohammad Ali left for Odessa, Russia on September 9, 1909.[73] Sattar Khan and Baqer Khan arrived in Tehran on April 17, 1910 and were greeted as national heroes by the populace.[74]

Liakhov had surrendered to the nationalist troops (with the mediation of the Russian embassy) in early September. The nationalist-constitutionalists agreed for Liakhov's arms to be returned in exchange for acknowledgment of the authority of the Majlis.[75] When Liakhov was succeeded by Colonel Prince Vadbolsky in November 1909, he was apparently cooperative with the Majlis at first but soon refused to comply with their directives.[76] The Iranians would soon pay a hefty price for allowing the Russian officers to remain in control of the Persian Cossack Brigade.

As he sat in exile in Russia, Mohammad Ali had every intention of restoring himself on the throne. A new plot was hatched to launch a three-pronged assault on Tehran (two from the north and one from the west) to overthrow the Iranian experiment with democracy once and for all. The first attack materialized in the north, originating from Gumish Tappeh where Mohammad Ali landed from a Russian ship (carrying a massive stockpile of ammunition in crates[77]) from the Caspian Sea by July 19, 1911.[78] He immediately recruited local Turkmen, disaffected Qajar troops and shahsevan cavalrymen to his banner. In practice it would be the forces of Arshad ol Dowleh (Mohammad Ali's close confidant in Russia and main military commander) who would fight the nationalists from the north towards Tehran. The western thrust was launched by Salar ol Dowleh (Mohammad Ali's brother) from the west with a force of 3,000–4,000 troops[79] (800 of these being Kurdish and Luri cavalry from Kermanshah). Hamadan in the northwest easily fell to the Kurd-Lur cavalry force of Salar.[80]

The nationalists devised their defense on three fronts. A force of Bakhtiari cavalry went west to harass Salar and slow his advance towards Tehran while a second force organized from the nationalists of Gilan went north, heading through Mazandaran to confront royalist forces assembling in the northeast region along the Caspian Sea. In Tehran, organization of the defense was entrusted to the Armenian Yeprem Khan (head of Tehran's police and gendarmerie).[81] He had at his disposal a total of 2,500 troops (1,800 gendarmes and police from Tehran and 600 gendarmes from Qazvin, 200 Armenians and 1,200 police). The Persian Cossack Brigade refused the government's request for assistance. More troops were organized by Tehran's politicians and even Morgan Shuster, the American fiscal reformer, organized nationalist volunteers and a few hundred students. These were soon joined by Bakhtiari cavalry who had been scattered between Isfahan and Tehran. Yeprem needed the gendarmes or police to maintain order and security inside Tehran. He turned to Bakhtiaris and 600 of these formed the backbone of the nationalists' defense of the capital. As the royalist forces began to arrive near Tehran, in mid-August, Yeprem stationed bodies of troops to guard the strategic mountain passes leading to Tehran.

In early August another anti-nationalist force led by Arshad ol Dowleh had coalesced with a force of Turkmen warriors in the northeast, close to Semnan. Arshad won a victory against the nationalists at Damghan capturing two cannon, munitions and even recruiting some defectors. By late August Arshad had won another victory at Ayvanekey, approximately 70 miles (112km) from the capital. Yeprem send a force of 400 Bakhtiari cavalry to harass Salar's Turkmen troops, and succeeded in slowing down their advance. This bought valuable time for Yeprem who had been careful not to disperse his modest forces too widely and conserve these for the inevitable showdown with the royalists. Adopting a cool and collected approach, Yeprem's aim was to first observe where the enemy's axis of attack would fall before committing the nationalists to a set-piece battle. His overall strategy was to hold the mountain passes and then to strike the royalists from the rear. He then went to support the Bakhtiaris with an elite force of just 350 men and a small but highly effective force of Maxim machineguns and three fast-firing Shneider-Cruezot 75mm cannon under a German artillery instructor. More nationalists joined the banner and all of these forces formed a line of defense around 50 miles (80km) from Tehran at the outskirts of Varamin.

By September 5, 1911 Arshad had arrived with 2,000 Turkmen warriors (1,600 cavalry and 400 infantry), outnumbering Yeprem's Gendarmes, Bakhtiaris and Armenians. While less numerous, Yeprem's 1,200 nationalists were highly motivated and well-led. Yeprem had carefully placed his 75-mm cannon and Maxim machineguns in strategic positions to defend Varamin. This proved decisive. The battle opened with Arshad sending a force of 300 Turkmen cavalry to attack Varamin to create a diversion. Instead the Turkmen were cut to pieces by the 75-mm cannon and Maxim machinegun fire.[82] The survivors fled back in haste through their lines causing a general panic in Arshad's ranks. The rest of the Turkmen now fled back to the northeast. Arshad was captured, and shot by firing squad. Mohammad Ali, who had chosen to remain north, attempted once more to recruit anti-nationalists for his quest to become shah once again. This proved to be failure and he and his troops were crushed by a nationalist force. Mohammad Ali fled back to Gumish Teppe and boarded his Russian ship on the Caspian Sea to flee Iran for good.[83]

Tehran still had to face the forces of Salar who was on move from Hamadan by the middle of September, now hoping to become shah himself.[84] Numbering now at around 6,000 fighters, these confronted Yeprem and his 2,000 Bakhtiaris on the outskirts of Qom.[85] Once again it was the adept use of artillery and Maxim machineguns that probably won the battle for the nationalists: they reputedly suffered only eight casualties with Salar's forces enduring 500 dead and wounded (and another 200 taken prisoner) and having lost six cannon and much ammunition.[86] Salar escaped westwards into the Ottoman Empire engaging in looting and plunder on his way.[87] The Russian gambit at using Mohammad Ali to overthrow the Majlis in Iran had failed.

The Iranian parliament (Majlis) sought the services of Morgan Shuster to help implement badly needed reforms to Iran's financial system.[88] Iran's financial difficulties were making it increasingly difficult to maintain central authority over the provinces, which were now being raided and plundered by tribal warriors with little interest in paying taxes.[89] Arriving in Iran in May 1911, Shuster encouraged the development of Iran's Gendarmerie to act as the national government's arm in restoring law and order and the collection of taxes from across the country.[90]

The Melliyun had long argued for military reform towards a truly national army geared towards the protection of Iran's interests. The Majlis had wanted to replace the Russian officers of the Persian Cossack Brigade with Iranian ones in 1911, but this was firmly opposed by the Russians and the British who also rejected almost every Iranian effort towards military reform.[91]

Shuster persuaded British military attaché Major C. B. Stokes to lead the Gendarmerie but the Russians applied pressure on London to prevent Stokes' appointment from being realized.[92] The Iranian parliament had voted as early as 1910 to hire officers from neutral countries and Sweden was soon chosen for the task. The Swedish mission led by Colonel H. O. Hjalmarsen arrived in Iran by May 1911 and work proceeded quickly to build up an indigenous Iranian gendarmerie. The British were supportive of the Gendarmerie at this time as they were eager to find a way towards counterbalancing the Persian Cossack Brigade. They offered both political and financial support towards the Gendarmerie hoping that this force would help protect London's interests in the south.[93]

However, Russia was fiercely opposed to Shuster's tax-collecting Gendarmerie. As soon as Shuster's tax reform measures were put into practice, Russia issued a terse ultimatum (with British approval) to Iran on November 2, 1911 through the Russian consul in Iran to the Iranian Foreign Ministry.[94] The demand was that the Iranians remove their tax-gendarmes from the residence of Shua ol and issue a formal "apology" to Russia[95] regarding an alleged "insult" to Russian consul officials.[96] On November 18, Russia severed her diplomatic relations with Iran and declared that she would send additional troops into Iran.[97] Fears of a full-fledged Russian invasion led the Iranian foreign minister to officially comply with Russia's demands on November 23, 1911.[98] The Russian minister handed the Iranians a second ultimatum on November 29, 1911 demanding that Shuster be immediately dismissed, that the gendarmes be dismissed and wholly replaced by Cossacks and that no foreigners were to be appointed to Iranian government positions without the prior approval of Russia and Britain.[99]

The rapacity of these demands infuriated Iranian public opinion across the provinces and social strata. The most dramatic demonstration of these sentiments was expressed by 300 Iranian women who entered the parliament with handguns, threatening to shoot any parliament members who contemplated accommodation with the Russian ultimatum.[100] The Majlis predictably rejected the ultimatum on December 1, 1911.[101] Meanwhile more Russian soldiers, Cossacks and artillery landed by ship at Bandar Anzali while others arrived by land from Tbilisi, Baku and Julfa, raising the total number of occupying Russian troops in northern Iran to approximately 12,000 men by mid-December.[102] On December 15, 1911 Russia informed the Iranians that if they did not capitulate to their demands in six days, their 4,000 troops stationed in Qazvin would begin to march towards Tehran.[103] In practice Russian troops had advanced towards Tabriz by December 1 and were well underway towards Tehran by December 3.[104] The Iranians were now practically at war and alone against Russia.

By December 20, a force of 2,000 Turkmen warriors, taking advantage of the Russian advance from Qazvin, thrust from the north towards Tehran, reaching as far as Damghan.[105] This was particularly dangerous as Tehran could barely spare the 600 men which Yeprem Khan dispatched to block the Turkmen advance. In the meantime the political parties collectively agreed to resist the Russian advance against Tabriz and Tehran. The total number of troops that could be used to counter against the 15,000 Russians was a maximum of 6,400 men (2,000 Bakhtiaris, 3,000 nationalist volunteers, 1,100 Gendarmes and 300 Armenian fighters).[106] Tabriz put up a desperate fight for six days against virtually impossible odds before being occupied by Russian troops. Tehran was the next target.

Despite the decision to resist, there was also great concern in Tehran as to the consequences of resisting the Russians. The Russians had stationed an additional 50,000 troops along the border,[107] ready to support their armies in Iran in case the resistance at Tehran proved too obstinate. Anglo-Russian pressure was a major factor in the shut down of the Majlis on December 24, 1911 and in the expulsion of the Shuster from Iran by January 11, 1912.[108] The British and Russians appointed Belgian national Mornard as the director-general of Iran's finances alongside his post as director general of Iranian customs).[109] A major consequence of Shuster's dismissal was the further strengthening of the British and Russian domination of Iran.[110] In fact, Iran in 1911 also witnessed the arrival of British troops into the south.[111]

One of the major reasons the nationalists had capitulated was the desire to spare the civilian population from harm. The very same day that the Iranian cabinet had complied with all Russian demands, Russian troops stationed at Tabriz began to massacre the citizens apparently over a dispute with local sentries over a telephone wire.[112] Over several days the Russians "indulged in terrible brutality, killing women and children in the streets and hundreds of other non-combatants … unrestricted shootings, hangings, tortures, blowing of men from cannon … the cynical butchery of women and children … and even worse things."[113] Russian troops also executed any Iranian nationalists they found, hanging their bodies in pieces in the local bazaar.[114] Russian troops also shot and killed Iranians and police without provocation in Rasht and Bandar Anzali.[115]

CHAPTER 25

THE FIRST WORLD WAR: IRAN ON THE EDGE

The country that Ahmad Shah (1898–1930) inherited in mid-July 1909 was in dire economic and political disarray, and wholly unprepared to meet the challenges of the First World War. Iran declared her neutrality in a royal farman (edict) on November 1, 1914, but this failed to spare her from invasions by Russian, Ottoman, and Anglo-Indian troops in the north and south. Foreign operations in the north were mainly focused in Iranian Azarbaijan and Gilan with the south mainly confined to the Persian Gulf coastal areas, Shiraz and Isfahan. The Russians treated northern Iran like a protectorate, facing fierce resistance in Gilan. Fierce fighting also broke out in the south between the British and Iranian nationalists allied with the Gendarmerie. The Germans sought to exploit anti-Russian and anti-British sentiments while the Ottomans sought to expand into Iranian Azarbaijan and the Caucasus. The scope of foreign military operations and high-handed political meddling brought Iran perilously close to the edge of partition and destruction. Much of Iran's predicament was due to the fact that it had no real operational army capable of maintaining law and order in the country and defending its borders. This left the brunt of Iran's defense on the Melliyun nationalists, their Democrat allies and the Gendarmerie.

The Qajar regular army at the eve of the First World War

The Iranian military of the early 1900s was in a desperate state and quite unable to defend the country against invasion. Tribal levies were nominally obligated to support the government but in practice became increasingly beholden to the security issues of their respective provinces.[1] While these could effectively fight against foreign invaders, recruiting these troops for the state became increasingly difficult, thanks in large part to the weaknesses of central Qajar authority.

While Iran had on paper a total of 150,000 troops at Mozzafar e Din Shah's time, barely a fraction of this number could be raised when the Great War began in 1914. The few available troops were hardly effective as a fighting force. Farjollah Hosseini, the chief consul of Iran to England in the early 1900s summarized: "the military office is nominally 70,000 men but is officially nil as numbers of our formations have never seen service … it would take six months to get our army to move if we were to mobilize available formations. We have no weapons, no ammunition reserves, no military schools … no military regulations, no factories and no battleships."[2] While Hosseini's observations regarding military factories and schools were somewhat exaggerated, much of what he stated was accurate. Many officers lacked knowledge of modern military doctrines, and most troops were characterized by poor training, discipline, and morale. Military equipment (especially guns and cannon) were mostly outdated and of low quality with arsenals poorly managed. The last military acquisitions were Austrian artillery pieces delivered in 1898 with negotiations for further purchases made in 1901.[3] Antiquated percussion and matchlocks continued to appear alongside more modern Snider and Martini (single-shot breech-loading) rifles.

Despite the dire state of the army, resistance against military reform remained strong, and corruption undermined any attempts. Prime Minister Ain ol Dowleh's attempt at reform was opposed by the war minister who feared that these would disrupt his enrichment schemes.[4] Recruitment was wholly inconsistent and arbitrary with troops sometimes having to serve for an entire lifetime! Regular troops, levies, and conscripts continued to suffer from arrears in pay. Troops were not provided with housing or meals, and had to take extra jobs to make ends meet while their officers pocketed their pay.[5] This inevitably led to much anger, resentment, and protests among ordinary troops. The issue of payment arrears became so acute that reservists called up to fight rebels in Rasht in 1903 refused to serve unless their concerns were addressed.[6]

All military reforms and foreign missions instituted since the early 19th century had ended in failure by the early 1900s. The formation of the Gendarmerie was Iran's first true success in creating an indigenous military force beholden to the country's interests. Created during the Russian invasions in 1911, the Gendarmerie project set the basis for a modern Iranian military force capable of tax collection, maintaining order, and protecting roads for travel and trade.[7]

The Gendarmerie was a truly indigenous Iranian force which succeeded in recruiting high-quality, well-educated and nationalistic recruits. The force gained rapid popularity among Iranians who appreciated its dedication to Iran's independence and territorial integrity. These sentiments were expressed by civilian spectators in the presence of Ahmad Shah during a march-past of the Gendarmes. The spectators proclaimed in unison "Long live the government's Gendarmerie, long live the soldiers of the nation."[8]

Financial and political support for the force in its early years came from the British, but British support would be withdrawn during the First World War when the Gendarmerie turned against them. By the eve of the First World War, six distinct units of the Gendarmerie had been formed in the Bagh e Shah, Yusef Abad, Shiraz, Kerman, Ghazvin, and Isfahan districts.[9] Bagh e Shah had a military academy which trained new recruits for six months.[10] The gendarmes were not provided with sufficient amounts of heavy equipment (notably artillery and machineguns) and the largest contingent (at Shiraz) numbered around 3,500 men.[11] By early 1915, the Gendarmerie stood at 10,000 men, armed with several machineguns and a few field guns.[12]

Though markedly superior to the Persian Cossack Brigade in terms of morale, training, weapons and their officers, the gendarmes were in no position to challenge the invasions of powerful foreign states.[13] As the primary loyalty of the Gendarmerie was to the Iranian state, the Cossacks often did not support them in internal security operations. One example was the refusal of the Cossacks to assist the Gendarmerie's operations against the Lurs in western Iran in 1913.[14] The Persian Cossacks' subservience to Russian imperialism became even more pronounced in 1914. The brigade and occupying Russian troops took control of Iran's wheat and transport caravans, resulting in serious bread famines. The Cossacks (Russian and Persian) openly intimidated landowners in northern Iran, forcing them to yield their properties to Russian nationals and "protected persons."[15] Many members of the Persian Cossack Brigade in Tabriz and Tehran were simply absorbed into the Russian army.[16] The Persian Cossack Brigade had dramatically declined in effectiveness and importance by 1915, especially as the Russians became increasingly preoccupied with their battles against the Central powers in Europe. The force would be greatly expanded after the Sepahsalar agreement of late 1915.

By 1900 Iran did have six major centers of armament production: Tehran, Tabriz, Shiraz, Isfahan, Khansar, Golpayegan, Mashad, and northern Iran (Shahsavar and Rasht).[17] Non-ballistic items such as swords, spears, body armor and martial musical instruments continued to be built in a number of workshops across Iran, especially Tehran, Tabriz, Isfahan and Mashad. At least one modern cartridge production facility had been purchased from France during the latter years of Nasser e Din Shah's reign.[18] While these facilities were wholly inadequate at meeting Iran's contemporary military needs, the basis for a future Iranian arms industry had been built. Mozzaffar e Din Shah attempted to improve Iran's military output by instituting European methods of production and purchasing modern industrial machinery.[19] A number of innovations and military inventions did take place in Iran, such as an automatic light-cannon capable of firing and reloading seven rounds per minute, but these could not be mass produced due to Iran's inadequate industrial base.[20]

The First World War introduced the country to military aviation for the first time. The first aircraft to fly over Tehran was a French Berliot in late February–early March 1914.[21] The sound of the aircraft's engines apparently caused a stir among the Tehranis who rushed from their homes into the streets to witness the strange flying object. Iran's first combat pilots were *two* Iranian pilots, known as "Hussein Khan and Ahmad Khan" by the Turks, who flew missions for the Ottoman air force, mainly against British troops in Syria.[22] Iran's most notable pilot and first air combat ace was the enigmatic Colonel Taghi Khan Pesyan (1892–1921) who lived in exile in Imperial Germany from 1916 and trained as a fighter pilot for the German Air Force. He distinguished himself by shooting down 25 allied aircraft in aerial dogfights along the western front. Pesyan then returned to Iran where he fought on behalf of the Gendarmerie and the Melliyun.[23] Pesyan became a potent national Iranian symbol. The British were especially concerned with Pesyan's martial capabilities, declaring openly that he should be killed to undermine the military leadership of the Melliyun.[24]

The Iranian navy was still practically non-existent at the outbreak of the First World War. This meant that Iran's southern coastline and other Persian Gulf possessions were dangerously exposed to military incursions and raids. Mozzaffar e Din Shah did order one small combat vessel from British shipyards which later became known as "Kashteeye Mozzafari" (Mozzafar's ship).[25] Another effort at reinforcing the navy was made by Ahmad Shah (1898–1930) with his acquisition of four 75-ton vessels[26] from Britain. Iran's "fleet" was certainly no match against the more modern and powerful western flotillas (especially the Royal Navy). At best it was a coastal guard force intended to confront smuggling and piracy along Iran's Persian Gulf coastline.

Battles in northern and western Iran

The Ottomans had held sections of territory adjacent to the Irano-Ottoman border within Iranian Azarbaijan since 1907, and as the war began, Enver Pasha resumed the Ottoman invasion of Iran.[27] The Ottomans had territorial ambitions in Iran's north, notably in Iranian Azarbaijan, and across the Araxes in the Caucasus. They also aimed to assist indigenous anti-British and anti-Russian forces and battle against British and Russian forces. Enver Pasha was anxious to have the Ottoman army arrive into Iran as liberators, assisting the Iranians in ejecting Russian and British troops from the country. A number of Iranian constitutionalist fighters from Tabriz (in exile in Istanbul since 1909) had arrived into Iranian Azarbaijan in November 1914 to attack the Russians.[28] The Ottomans attacked Kars in December and thrust into the Russian-held Caucasus. Many Russian troops in Iran were redeployed to the Caucasus in December 1914 to fight invading Ottoman troops.[29] The Ottomans took advantage of the weakened Russian presence in Iran to thrust into Iran's Azarbaijan province in January 1915.[30] Tabriz fell to the Ottomans in early January followed by Khoi and Urumiah. The Ottomans had received the help of Iranian Kurds from the western area of Azarbaijan during these operations.[31] Enver Pasha's objective was to achieve a pan-Turkic state by incorporating Iran's Turkic-speaking Iranian Azarbaijan province and the Caucasus' Turkic-speaking regions into the Ottoman Empire. But by the end of January the Russians, led by General Chernozoubov, had not only forced the Ottoman Turks out of the Caucasus but also expelled them from Tabriz. The Ottoman army had been mostly cleared out of Iranian Azarbaijan by late April 1915. The Ottoman retreat was also due to their military difficulties in Iraq. An Ottoman force led by Rauf Bey did attempt to enter western Iran towards Kermanshah in early June 1915 but was forced back by numbers of Melliyun assisted by local Kurdish fighters.

Russian troops landed in Anzali in northern Iran in mid-May 1915 and from there marched towards Qazvin to openly threaten the Iranian government and Ahmad Shah. A number of Melliyun, realizing that they could not hold Tehran against a Russian invasion, decided to deploy further south to Isfahan and form their own government. Their plan was to build a nationalist army around the Gendarmerie and stiffen these with tribal forces and local volunteers from the Isfahan area. The Germans were counted on to provide logistical-organizational support.

Tehran had in the meantime become increasingly unstable, mainly due to British and Russian pressure on the Qajar government. Ahmad Shah and the prime minster had been forced to reshuffle a number of cabinet positions. The eventual outcome of the reshuffles was not favorable to the British and Russians. There was now a new (Democrat nationalist) prime minster who leaned more towards the Central Powers. Through secret talks, he obtained a German guarantee of Iran's territorial integrity on condition that the Iranians join the Central powers. Meanwhile the Germans at Borujerd had managed to persuade the governor of Luristan and Khuzistan (Nezam ol Saltaneh) to become the head of Iran's new nationalist army. Nezam ol Saltaneh recruited Lur and Bakhtiari warriors to the nationalist cause. The nationalists were assisted by northern Iran's Mirza Kuchik Khan and other nationalists in Semnan.

Mirza Kuchik Khan (1880–1921) was an enigmatic leader who had done much to further the cause of the Constitutional Revolution.[32] An ardent nationalist, he took the lead in organizing the Jangali (Persian: of the forest/jungle) movement in Gilan (in northern Iran). The origins of Gilan's Jangali rebellion are largely rooted in foreign intervention in Iran, especially Russia's 1915 invasion of northern and northwestern Iran. They published a newspaper, the *Jangal*, and soon gained a strong following across Iran.[33]

The Jangali movement began fighting Russian forces that had entered Iran in 1914–15. Russian brutality in Gilan did much to contribute to the resistance movement against them, as did their forcefully enforcing the authority of the unpopular feudal elites.[34] Mirza Kuchik Khan and his Gilani fighters were soon joined by a number of gendarmes and Kurds.[35] While precise numbers of Gilani fighters in that period cannot be ascertained, Iranian historians estimate them as having stood at 4,000–6,000 fighters in 1917, rising to 10,000 men by 1918.[36]

Kuchik Khan proved to be an effective military leader. His forces launched a series of successful partisan attacks against the Russians and their feudal allies. This forced the Russians to assign a special task force of 1,000 crack troops to finally rout the Gilanis in 1916.[37] The latter remained intact as a fighting force and retreated into the dense forests of northern Iran. The Jangalis then engaged in guerrilla warfare against the Russians. The Jangali movement was to be also directed against the British and the Qajar authorities of Tehran.[38]

Despite fighting against highly effective nationalist forces in the north, Russian forces were sufficiently large to spare troops to march on Tehran on November 7, 1915.[39] The Majlis had been shut down by late December, allowing the British and Russians to apply their political machinations with greater ease. The Russians secured the Sepahsalar Agreement in late 1915. This allowed the Russians to revitalize the Persian Cossack Brigade into a complete division of 10,000 men. In practice, the force's total number of troops, including all dispersed units, reached a total of just 6,000–7,000 men by early 1920.[40]

The British were also allowed to organize the South Persia Rifles (SPR) for the protection of their assets in the south against attack and sabotage.[41] The SPR was formed by the fall of 1916, initially recruiting around 8,000 Iranians and Indians into its force with units being stationed in Fars, Kerman and Bandar Abbas.[42] The force was to have a maximum size of 11,000 troops.[43] Iranian politicians opposed the SPR as they viewed this as the British version of the Persian Cossack Brigade. London first assured them that the force would be relinquished to Tehran's control after the conclusion of the First World War. The SPR proved crucial in suppressing anti-British revolts in the south during the war and was then disbanded in October 1921.

The Melliyun vacated Tehran when Russian troops arrived in the capital on November 7, 1915. The Russians, who wanted to crush Iranian Democrats and the Melliyun, had been urged to do so by the British who had also warned the shah and Iranian government to not align themselves with the Axis powers. The Melliyun fell back to Qom and formed a provisional government known as the National Defense Committee of Iran (NDCI). The NDCI hoped that Ahmad Shah would join them and finally declare war on the British and Russians, but this never happened. The combination of a dithering Ahmad Shah and Russian troops ensured that he and the majority of his ministers would remain in Tehran. Under these circumstances, the shah issued no war declaration against the Anglo-Russian allies. By December, Tehran's government had been reshuffled to include a strong dose of ministers amenable to British and Russian interests. This new cabinet signed a treaty ensuring Iran's neutrality, which was farcical as Iran was now an Anglo-Russian pawn with an ineffectual figurehead.

Having secured Tehran, the Russians proceeded to destroy the Melliyun. Having assembled 20,000 troops in Qazvin, General Baratov attacked towards Hamadan in November 1915.[44] The city had been under the control of Melliyun fighters and Gendarmerie units since the early part of the year. Colonel Taghi Khan Pesyan, acting in concert with Azizollah Zarghami, valiantly fought against Baratov but lacked sufficient quantities of heavy guns and machineguns; Hamadan fell to the Russians by mid-December.[45]

Another Russian force of 15,000 troops was sent to Qom to confront the NDCI there. The NDCI could at most muster 6,500 men: 5,000 gendarmes and 1,500 mounted troops led by

German officers.[46] The defense was organized around two key strategic points to block the Russian advance: the Sultan Bolaq Pass on the road between Qazvin and Hamadan and Avab just north of Qom. The Germans had been providing funds, uniforms and other supplies for the NDCI, but this did little to offset the Russian edge in heavy weaponry. What the Iranians desperately needed was heavy weaponry, especially heavy artillery and machineguns.

As Baratov pressed towards Qom, he was met with fierce Iranian resistance well into the bitter winter cold of December. Baratov, relying on his superiority in numbers and heavy equipment, pounded the Iranians with constant assaults and heavy artillery barrages. Avab and the Sultan Bolaq Pass were finally taken by Russian troops by mid-December, which led to the fall of Qom.[47] By early 1916, Kashan and Isfahan had also been captured.[48]

The battered Gendarmerie, who had fought at Sultan Bolaq Pass retreated to the southwest of Russian-held Hamadan, covering their withdrawal with a rearguard force. The Melliyun and the NDCI retreated westwards to Kermanshah. Despite their ejection from Qom and Hamadan, the Melliyun were able to hold much of southwest Iran (albeit briefly) with the exception of Khuzistan and the Persian Gulf which was in the British "sphere of influence."

Nizam ol Saltaneh had worked hard to re-establish the provisional government in Kermanshah, a rival or "alternative" government to that seated in Tehran. Kermanshah was a wise choice as the area was populated with tough Kurdish warriors who shared the Melliyun's goal of ejecting foreign troops from Iran. The Kurds were especially supportive of the Melliyun, notably the Kurdish feudal leaders of Kermanshah and the (Kurdish) Shikak and Sanjabi tribes.[49] Nizam ol Saltaneh had worked feverishly with German support since at least early 1915 to rebuild the Melliyun army with around 3,000 gendarmes already in Kermanshah. The call for volunteers met with success, attracting Iranians from across the country as well as 4,000–5,000 Kurdish warriors.[50] The Melliyun army and its allies struck out of Kermanshah by May 1915 to take control of Qasr e Shirin, just as Russian troops were menacing Tehran. The Melliyun then linked up with Gendarmerie units in (predominantly Luri) Borujerd. The Germans favored these operations, as these would help block Russian thrusts from northwest Iran into Iraq. If the Russians entered Iraq they could then link up with British forces moving up from the south. It was at this juncture that a large Ottoman force of 14,000 troops, including 10,000 Kurdish levies, arrived to the west of Kermanshah to support Nizam ol Saltaneh.[51]

A major liability was the lack of trust between the Iranian Melliyun and their Ottoman and German advisors.[52] The primary German advisor, Field Marshall Colman von der Goltz had (as in German efforts at Qom) failed to deliver the vitally needed supplies and weapons to the Iranians.[53] The Iranians were also handicapped by the lack of a clear and organized chain of command. Most of the Ottomans' Kurdish levies also deserted upon the Russian arrivals; this greatly diminished the strength of the Ottoman forces.[54] Despite these shortcomings, the Iranians and their allies put up stiff resistance against Baratov who arrived near Kermanshah by early February 1916. As before, the Russians outgunned the Iranians which resulted in another defeat for the Melliyun; Kermanshah fell to Baratov on February 26, 1916.[55] The Russian victory at Kermanshah sealed all Melliyun prospects of seizing control of Iran and linking it to the Central Powers.[56]

With Kermanshah secured, Baratov's advance towards Qasr-e-Shirin on the Ottoman–Iranian border seemed secure. Nevertheless, Iranian resistance at Kermanshah bought precious time for the Melliyun to retreat to Qasr-e-Shirin along with numbers of allied Ottoman troops. By late March a strong defensive perimeter was set up around the town along with approximately 12 pieces of artillery. The resistance at Kermanshah had also benefitted the Ottoman Turks fighting the British in Iraq.

Baratov's supply lines were now dangerously stretched. The Russians were also paying for their failure to subdue Gilan in northern Iran. Mirza Kuchik Khan's Gilani warriors had conducted a successful partisan campaign against local occupying Russian troops and often interdicted their supply lines meandering from Bandar Anzali to Qazvin. Baratov's troops had also suffered heavy casualties throughout the campaign, especially during the recent battles at Kermanshah.

Meanwhile, the British had run into serious difficulties in Iraq, where the forces of General Townsend had been defeated by the Ottoman Turks at Ctesiphon (approx 25 miles (40km) from Baghdad) on November 22–23, 1915.[57] Townsend retreated to Kut, where he was besieged by the Turks from December 7, 1915.[58] The British then asked their Russian allies to attack the Turks to help relieve the pressure on Kut. Baratov gathered his remaining forces, now numbering 7,500 troops and approximately twenty heavy guns, to storm the Melliyun's defenses at Karand on April 10, 1916.[59] Karand was defended by 1,000 gendarmes and 1,000 Kurdish warriors. They were backed by up to 6,000 Ottoman troops who were apparently acting as a reserve force.[60] The gendarmes resisted bitterly, suffering a casualty rate of up to 50%.[61] The Russians became bogged down in a slugging match, suffering heavy casualties all the way to Qasr e Shirin, which they finally reached in May. The remnants of Iranian resistance retreated across the western border into Ottoman Iraq and entered Baghdad. But Baratov's belated success at Qasr e Shirin provided little solace to the British as Townsend had been forced to surrender unconditionally at Kut on April 29, 1916.[62] Despite the British defeat, Baratov tried to enter Iraq, with disastrous results. He was heavily defeated by the Ottoman XIII Corps in the battle of Khanaqin on June 3, 1916.[63] With half of his forces destroyed, Baratov beat a hasty retreat to the Sultan Bolaq Pass.

Flushed with their recent successes against the British and the Russians, the Ottomans prepared their counterattack. Ottoman General Ali Ehsan, supported by German artillery, machinegun units, aircraft and other detachments, thrust into Iran to eject the Russians from Kermanshah (July 1, 1916), and Hamadan (middle of August) soon threatening Russian forces as far away as Qazvin.[64]

General Ehsan's thrust into Iran was supported by the remnants of Iranian nationalists who had recently fled into Ottoman Iraq. Meanwhile, Nizam ol Saltaneh and the Melliyun were working hard to rebuild their forces with German assistance. This major effort led to the build-up of at least 10,000 Gendarmerie and allied tribal cavalry. The main purpose of these troops was to garrison liberated regions, incite anti-British and anti-Russian tribes, notably the Bakhtiaris, to revolt. The Iranians protected the Ottoman flanks as they advanced against the Russians. Interestingly, the Germans at this time referred to Iranian nationalist forces as the *Unverstandliche Gruppe* (German: incomprehensible group)![65]

The Ottoman success was not destined to last. General Ali Ehsan failed to destroy Baratov's forces at the Sultan Bolaq Pass. This allowed the Russians to resupply Baratov with men and supplies just in time. Conversely, the Ottomans now lacked the military strength and necessary supplies to enter Tehran. This resulted in a relative stalemate for a number of months, with events in Iraq once again having an impact on the military situation in Iran. The British had recovered from their defeat at Kut to vigorously resume their advance against the Ottoman Turks from December 1916. Ottoman units in Iran were now recalled to Iraq to deal with the increasingly dangerous British threat. By January many Ottoman units had been withdrawn from Iran, weakening the Melliyun's supply and logistics base. The Russians counterattacked that same month and reoccupied Kermanshah and Hamadan.

Turkish fortunes reached a new low when Baghdad was lost to the British in March 1917.[66] At the time, Ottoman troops were also fighting the Russians inside Iraq along the Diyala River northwest of Baghdad.[67] This was the last armed resistance of the battered Melliyun, with their comrades in the south defeated in 1916. By the end of 1917, many of the surviving Melliyun had escaped to Turkey, where they soon lost their cohesion. In the north Iranian nationalists led by Mirza Kuchik Khan maintained their resistance against the Russians and the British.

Russia had been increasingly wracked by political upheavals since early 1917 with the tsar overthrown in early March. The provisional government of Alexander Kerensky had planned to send up to 70,000 Russian troops into Iran but these came to naught with the Bolshevik takeover in St. Petersburg (or Petrograd) on November 6–7.[68] This had a major impact in Iran where many of Baratov's officers and men deserted by late October 1917. By November (when the Bolsheviks began negotiating peace terms with the Central Powers), Baratov could barely raise one regiment. As Russia descended into civil war, the Bolsheviks demanded that all remaining Russian officers in Iran return to Russia. Large numbers of the Persian Cossack Brigade's Russian officers did return to Russia, with many of these joining the White Russians against the Bolsheviks. Britain soon assumed the costs of running the outfit by December 1917 and took complete control by the autumn of 1920.[69] The British then took over the main Russian operational headquarters in Qazvin.[70] The chaos in Russia allowed the British to finally gain full supremacy in Iran. British forces proceeded to occupy those areas that had been earlier been under Russian control. By March 1918 Mashad was under British control followed by Qazvin, Hamadan and Kermanshah in April.[71]

The termination of Tsarist operations in Iran prompted the Qajar government to order the appropriation of as many abandoned Russian military stores as possible. This proved difficult to implement due to the weakness of Qajar authority. In practice many Russian weapons ended up in either Armenian, Assyrian or Kurdish hands in northwest Iran. Many weapons stores were sold off by Russian deserters to whoever would purchase them, including the anti-Russian Mirza Kuchik Khan fighters and Iran's tribal warriors.[72]

Berlin was very impressed with the Jangalis' stance against the British and soon demanded that German forces in Russia do their part in assisting Kuchik Khan. This resulted in the arrival of the largest and most significant body of German troops into Gilan by March 1918. The size of these forces are generally cited as having been "a few hundred" and led by Wilhelm Grutzmacher, Walter Strich, and Christian Schneider.[73] Strich demanded that Berlin deliver 10,000 rifles, four million cartridges, 10 machineguns, six mountain cannon, 30 heavy trucks, 10 tanks, and five aircraft.[74] Had these supplies arrived Kuchik Khan's partisan army would have transformed into a formidable striking force. Fortunately for the British, the Germans never delivered the supplies to Kuchik Khan.

Further to the north in the Caucasus, the Germans had already established themselves in Georgia and had managed to renew their communication with Kuchik Khan by May 1918.[75] Around this time two German officers[76] arrived to Gilan from Georgia and agreed to train 5,000–6,000 of Kuchik Khan's fighters. This was followed by more German arrivals, mainly ex-POWs. These also began to train the Jangalis. Overall, the Germans failed to make the necessary military commitment in the Iranian theater, despite the dramatic exploits of the Wassmuss mission in southern Iran.

General Dunsterville had initially arrived at the head of a British motor column into Gilan but had been forced back to Hamadan. He told his superiors that the only way to enter Gilan was by combat or accommodation with Kuchik Khan. The British Norperforce (North Persia Force) then stationed its base in Qazvin by late May–early June 1918.[77] They were then reinforced with two aircraft and two armored cars.[78] By this time, nearly all of the Germans had left Gilan.

The British attempted to deploy the Persian Cossacks against Kuchik Khan with unsatisfactory results, and in March 1918, Kuchik Khan's fighters had forced the surrender of Rasht's contingent of Persian Cossacks.[79] By June 1918 the British had delivered a number of ultimatums to Kuchik Khan asking him to grant passage for Norperforce. Dunsterville was hoping to avoid fighting by using diplomacy but Kuchik Khan and the Gilanis were deeply anti-British.[80] Kuchik Khan rejected Dunsterville's requests and prepared for battle at Manjil, around 93 miles (150km) from Qazvin. He formed a trench manned by up to 3,000 Gilani fighters armed (along with a number of Austrians).[81] These troops were mainly armed with rifles and machineguns but were deficient in heavy guns and antiaircraft artillery.[82] Another liability was the hastily prepared trenches, which proved wholly inadequate against determined British assaults.[83]

Norperforce opened its attack with a powerful artillery barrage supported by bombing aircraft. The British then attacked Mirza Kuchik Khan on the left and right flanks: the strike on the left flank was led by British armored cars and on the right by Russian Cossack cavalry acting in concert with the British.[84] Virtually helpless against Norperforce's artillery, armored cars and aircraft, the Gilanis had no choice but to retreat.[85] Kuchik Khan had inexplicably placed his forces in front of a bridge spanning a deep gorge and now had to flee in haste to the other side of it. The bridge was left intact with the Gilanis melting into the forests for cover. With its victory at Manjil, Norperforce streamed over the bridge and reached Bandar Anzali and then captured Rasht by June 1918.[86]

Kuchik Khan responded by assembling around 1,200 men in July 1918 to counterattack Rasht. A number of telegraph stations, the local British consulate and banks were hit but the British beat back the Gilani assault against Norperforce's main headquarters. During the fierce battle at Rasht, the Gilani fighters felled large trees onto the city's main streets to block the movements of British armored cars.[87] Trenches had also been dug in the city for close-quarter combat against British troops. Norperforce responded by using its aircraft to bomb Kuchik Khan's positions along Rasht's environs with British artillery targeting Gilani fighters in the city. Dunsterville's firepower and airpower had prevailed once again, forcing Kuchik Khan to abandon his offensive at Rasht.[88]

Gilan provided Dunsterville with the launch pad he needed to advance into the Caucasus towards Baku and its oil fields, these being of great interest to London.[89] After his defeats at Manjil and Rasht, Kuchik Khan had been obliged to sign a non-aggression pact with the British in August 1918. He did share one major concern with the British: the recent Ottoman capture of Baku.[90] The Germans too were increasingly wary of their Ottoman ally's (pan-Turkist) ambitions in both the Caucasus and Gilan. They may have interpreted Kuchik Khan's "alliance" with the British as a temporary geopolitical necessity. The Germans did feel a sense of gratitude to Kuchik Khan and the Gilanis in general for having provided their escaped prisoners with safe haven in Gilan.[91] They probably felt that despite his recent accord with Dunsterville, Kuchik Khan remained anti-British. What is certain is that the Germans attempted once more to send supplies to Mirza Kuchik Khan. By the summer of 1919 they had dispatched 12 machineguns, 4,000 rifles, ammunition, a wireless set and money to Kuchik Khan.[92]

Mirza Kuchik Khan's rapprochement with Dunsterville did not prevent him from engaging in actions against British interests. His fighters once again expelled the British-sponsored Persian Cossack Brigade from Rasht in early June 1920.[93] The latter success had been partly indebted to recent Soviet landings at Bandar Anzali.[94] The initial intention of the Soviet landings had been to root out White Russian forces hiding in the region.[95] The Bolsheviks had become firmly ensconced in Gilan by the summer of 1920. They were regularly landing armed troops by ship into northern Iran; typically Russian and Caucasian Bolsheviks. Bolshevik landings included political commissars who most likely intended to export Communist ideology into Iran. The British responded to the Bolshevik arrivals by deploying the Persian Cossacks for gathering intelligence and dispersing Soviet agents at large in northern Iran.

Ottoman Ambitions in Northern Iran and the Caucasus

The elimination of Russia from the First World War in 1917 allowed Ottoman forces to once again thrust into Iranian Azarbaijan. Istanbul still aimed to incorporate Iranian Azarbaijan and the eastern Transcaucasus (modern Republic of Azerbaijan) into the Ottoman Empire. It is also possible that they harbored territorial designs on northern Iran (Gilan, Mazandaran, Semnan, etc) as this would allow them to link towards Central Asia through the southeast area of the Caspian Sea. The first primary objective of the Ottomans in the Caucasus was Baku. The Ottomans knew well that any successful thrust into Baku required them to be on good terms with Kuchik Khan's fighters in Gilan. At first the Ottomans attempted to win over the Gilanis (and Iranians in general) by appealing to pan-Islamic tendencies. To that end Turkish agents had been active in Iran since 1911 in their attempt to inculcate pan-Islamic sentiments against the Russians, the British, and the French.[96] While Islam was certainly an important facet of Iran, pan-Islamism per se had failed to replace indigenous national sentiments. The Ottomans also had a serious "image" problem as the memories of past wars against the Ottoman Empire were alive in Iran, especially in Azarbaijan and northern Iran. Despite this, relations with the Ottomans were initially cordial.

Even as the Ottoman situation in Mesopotamia against British troops remained critical, their prospects in the Caucasus and northern Iran were gradually shifting in their favor. As the Ottoman "Army of Islam" prepared for its invasion of the Caucasus, Kuchik Khan was contacted by Ottoman military leaders. The first was General Khalil Pasha who sent a letter dated September 23, 1917 to Kuchik Khan stating that he intended to link up with Jangali fighters in Gilan via Lankaran after they captured Baku.[97] As a gesture of friendship to Kuchik Khan, Khalil Pasha dispatched a German officer to bring arms and ammunition to Gilan.[98] Kuchik Khan's cooperation would greatly facilitate the Ottoman attack into Baku (and the Caucasus in general) and perhaps even pose a threat against Russian positions facing Erzerum in eastern Anatolia.

The next Ottoman contact with Kuchik Khan was made by Enver Pasha in March 1918 who sent gifts. He also sent a letter to Kuchik Khan requesting his assistance in organizing the Ottoman "Army of Islam" for its upcoming campaign in the Caucasus.[99] Enver Pasha also promised to follow up with arms and ammunition for the Jangalis. The reasons for the Ottoman courtship of Kuchik Khan were practical. The Gilanis had been supplying Baku with foodstuffs thereby protecting her inhabitants against starvation.[100] This was done even as Iran was suffering from a terrible famine.[101]

Nuri Pasha's "Army of Islam" entered Tabriz on May 6, 1918 with all of Iranian Azarbaijan falling into their hands by June.[102] Ottoman actions had been supported by a number of Iranian Kurdish tribes in the area.[103] Before their capture of Tabriz, the Turks had tried to make contact with Kuchik Khan since at least March 1918. Ubeydollah Effendi, who had been assigned as the Turkish ambassador to Afghanistan, sent messages to Kuchik Khan asking him to first disarm ex-Tsarist Russian troops still inside Iran and then to march southwest towards Hamadan to cooperate with Ottoman troops.[104] Kuchik Khan was skeptical. First, he lacked enough guns, heavy artillery and ammunition to neutralize the Russians by himself. Second, a march onto Tehran was dangerous and fraught with political and military risks. In any case, Kuchik Khan's immediate focus was the north of Iran and the Caucasus. The third and perhaps most serious problem was that the "Army of Islam" was primarily pan-Turkist with ideological borrowings from pan-Islamism. Kuchik Khan knew after the fall of Tabriz to the Turks in May, that Istanbul had territorial ambitions towards Iran. Despite their capture of Tabriz, the Ottomans did their utmost to continue their efforts towards cultivating friendly relations with Kuchik Khan and the Jangalis. When the Ottoman "Army of Islam" arrived to join forces with Kuchik Khan in May, he forced them to leave Gilan and offered them no military assistance. Kuchik Khan also refused to support an Ottoman-inspired coup in Tehran spearheaded by Bakhtiari tribal warriors in late July 1918, an effort that was quickly defeated by the British.

Enver Pasha's Army of Islam captured Baku on September 14, 1918.[105] The Ottomans fortified their military gains by establishing air bases in Tabriz, the Kermanshah locales, and Baku.[106] These actions aroused much suspicion, especially in Iran's north. Kuchik Khan's relations with the Ottomans soon deteriorated due to Ottoman territorial intentions in Azarbaijan province and the Caucasus.[107]

After the Ottomans took Baku in mid-September, they dispatched a force into Zanjan, possibly meaning to outflank Gilan province. Gilan was also threatened by a possible thrust by Ottoman forces in Baku. In August 1918, Kuchik Khan found common ground with General Dunsterville against Ottoman territorial ambitions. As noted by Dailami "Kuchik Khan had made peace with the British because of the unbelievable Turkish actions in Azarbaijan and to prevent a Turkish march into Gilan."[108] Just two days prior to the armistice of November 11, 1918, General Thompson, commander of British forces in Baku, expressed British gratitude in a letter sent to Kuchik Khan stating "I wish to take the opportunity … to thank you … in regard to your repeated refusals to join the Turkish forces or to admit them to the area under your control."[109]

The Ottomans and their messages of pan-Turkism completely failed to win over Iranian Azarbaijanis.[110] Their failure to "win over" Iranian (Turkophone) Azarbaijanis into pan-Turkism may explain why the Ottomans engaged in a number of atrocities against civilians in that province.[111] The Ottoman jailed prominent Iranian Azarbaijanis such as Sheikh Mohammad Khiyabani. The Iranian famine became especially pronounced in Iranian Azarbaijan, thanks to the Ottoman occupation. Ottoman forces finally vacated Iranian Azarbaijan after the armistice of November 11, 1918.

British interests in the South: Khuzistan province and petroleum

British interests in Iran had changed dramatically by the First World War. Before the discovery of petroleum, Iran had simply been a major pawn in the Great Game between Russia and Britain in their contest for supremacy in Central and Western Asia. But with the advent of the petroleum era, Britain now viewed Iran as a geopolitical economic asset. William Knox D'Arcy had won exclusive oil rights in Iran in 1901, for a term of 60 years with just 16 percent of profits to be given to the Iranian state.[112] D'Arcy approached the Anglo Persian Oil Company (APOC), which discovered oil in commercial quantities in Khuzistan province in 1908, the first such discovery in the Middle East.[113] By 1912, the British Navy was converting the fuel systems of its ships from coal to oil.[114] While oil-powered ships were faster and more efficient, oil had to be secured from overseas.[115] By spring 1913, the British Navy and APOC were engaged in business deals.[116] The British government became involved and soon Iran became the world's first and most important oil producer for the British Empire. The Iranian government had not even been consulted: they had originally provided their concession to one individual but were now notified that APOC was under the control of the British government.[117] Iran, the major financial loser in this arrangement, had few options. Cancelling the concession would mean a direct confrontation with the British. Tehran had to meekly accept the new arrangements. The APOC arrangement had major repercussions in the southwestern province of Khuzistan.

The British had significantly increased their influence in southwest Iran, especially since 1888 when Iran granted a steam-ship concession to the Lynch brothers.[118] British political influence throughout Iran grew significantly in the early twentieth century and by 1918 England had forged ties with many of Iran's southern tribes, notably the Bakhtiari and Sheikh Khazal, the leader of Khuzistan's Arab-speaking population.[119] The Bakhtiari leader, Sardar Zafar, received a monthly stipend of £500 provided that he "conformed to our [British] wishes in every way."[120]

Khuzistan had been semi-autonomous but subject to the Iranian crown for several centuries. The Qajar shahs would appoint a governor-general to manage the affairs of the province. Leadership of the Bani Kaab and the city of Mohammara was assumed by Maz'al Khan in 1881. The Qajars confirmed his position as governor-general by a royal edict. Maz'al Khan however was killed in 1897 by his brother Khazal, who became the sheikh of Mohammara. The Qajars approved Khazal's position as governor-general of Khuzistan and gave him the *Neshan e Aqdas* medallion in 1920. Qajar authority was now in name only as Khazal achieved complete dominance of the province by 1921. The British signed a treaty with Khazal in 1909–10 assuring him of their support against any attack against his rule.[121] Khazal in turn undertook to protect British oil assets and ensure stability in the region.[122] This was clearly indicative of London's lack of confidence in the Qajars.[123] Khazal's refusal to pay taxes to Tehran and the British annual payments soon gave him a strong financial base with which to recruit levies from Bakhtiaris and Lurs. Sheikh Khazal did not support the Constitutional Revolution and was known for promoting a separate Arab state by dismembering Khuzistan from Iran.[124]

British battles in Khuzistan, Fars, and the South

At the beginning of the First World War, the British had a powerful presence in southern Iran, with at least one cavalry detachment in Shiraz, a naval presence along Iran's Persian Gulf coast and regular troops stationed in Khuzistan.[125] The latter protected British petroleum interests in that province and nearby Kuwait. British interests became increasingly endangered by rising anti-British sentiments in the south; German agents working to instigate anti-British rebellions among tribal elements such as the Bakhtiaris and the defeat of British forces at Kut in Iraq in 1916 which led to the arrival of Ottoman troops in Iran.[126]

The first military action in the south was by Ottoman forces in Iraq, which advanced as far as Ahwaz, the provincial capital of Khuzistan, in the early part of 1915.[127] This was a direct threat to British petroleum interests in the south. The British responded by capturing the Fao peninsula in Iraq in November followed by Basra. The Ottomans retaliated by striking again at the soft underbelly of the British: oil-rich Khuzistan. The British turned to Sheikh Khazal for help against the Ottomans, but were quickly disappointed by their protégé. Khazal argued that his followers were not willing to fight fellow Muslims on behalf of the (non-Muslim) British.

The British prevailed in Khuzistan as they scored military successes against the Ottomans in southern Iraq. This allowed British troops in Iraq to enter Khuzistan and fan out to secure London's petroleum facilities and the city of Ahwaz. With Khuzistan and its petroleum assets secured, the British moved to consolidate their hold over the rest of southern Iran and Fars province.

Relations between Iranian Gendarmerie officers and the British had been steadily deteriorating in central and southern Iran during 1915. Two factors led the gendarmes to turn against the British. The first issue was rooted in fiscal mismanagement. The Swedish commander of the third Fars regiment of the Gendarmerie (Major Pravtiz) had written a terse letter to Mr. Heynssen (director general of Iranian customs) complaining of his "aggressive behavior" and his withholding of funds for the Gendarmerie.[128] Pravtiz also threatened to expose this information to his men and local populace. Heynssen's actions succeeded in aggravating the gendarmes' hostility against the British. Another factor leading to resentment was the Mokhber ol Saltaneh affair. Mokhber ol Saltanah was the German-educated anti-British governor of Fars province, whose support of the German agent Wassmuss led the British to force Tehran to remove him from his post in September 1915.[129] He yielded his position to Habibollah Ghavam ol Molk e Shirazi and left for Tehran. By this time the financial situation of the Gendarmerie had become critical.

The Germans scored a number of successes in the south and west of Iran thanks in large part to the efforts of Wilhelm Wassmuss (1880–1931), who spoke fluent Persian.[130] He had been a German diplomat based in Bushehr, where he remained as a consul official until early 1915. Wassmuss met with German officials in Istanbul at the outbreak of war and successfully proposed plans for organizing an anti-British Iranian revolt and guerrilla campaign. Funded by the German Foreign Office, the German plan was to eject Russia and England from Iran, and threaten British India.[131] In the south they aimed to disrupt Anglo-Indian telegraph lines; to encourage forcible removal of pro-Russian and pro-British politicians; to incite Iranian tribes to fight the British and the Russians; and to sabotage Britain's petroleum assets.[132] The British were aware of German intentions. They landed 20,000 troops at Bushehr and to build the Bushehr–Kazeroun road.[133] The British also surrounded the German consulate at Bushehr on March 9, 1915, capturing its chief consul (Listermann) and his family. Listermann had been plotting to incite local tribes against the British prior to his arrest.[134] He had also been advised of the imminent arrival of Wassmuss. Wassmuss and a small number of officers had come from Baghdad to southern Iraq and then entered Iranian territory.[135] He arrived in Shiraz to assume the post of German consul there.[136] The British then demanded that local Gendarmerie and other Iranian authorities expel Wassmuss from Shiraz or face British military intervention.[137] Wassmuss moved quickly by inciting the Qashqai, Tangsir and Bakhtiari tribes into rebellion against the British.[138] The rebels inflicted great damage against oil pipelines in the southwest.[139]

Wassmuss arrived near Bushehr by May 1915 and incited local Tangestani tribes against British forces.[140] Bitter fighting soon spread from Tangestan to Dashti and Dashtestan in that same month.[141] These operations occurred just as Russian troops were menacing Tehran and the Melliyun there were contemplating setting up their capital in Isfahan. The British had apparently anticipated trouble in the south and relocated a number of units from the Ottoman-Iraqi theater into Iran.[142] The British succeeded in crushing the tribal rebels but their harsh methods further alienated the population of cities such as Shiraz and Isfahan as well as the Gendarmerie.[143]

Tensions against the British finally came into the open on November 10, 1915 when the Shiraz Gendarmerie surrounded the city's British Consulate and sent their members to Bushehr.[144] By this time a "nationalist committee" had been formed in Shiraz just as strong nationalist sentiment was spreading across the south and Fars province. The nationalists fiercely opposed the governor of Fars, Habibollah Ghavam ol Molk e Shirazi, who was regarded as a British asset.

Bitter battles ripped through Fars province for three weeks. The Gendarmerie rejected its British patronage, superseded its Swedish officers, and with the Melliyun, ejected all British and Russian citizens from Shiraz, Isfahan, Kerman, Kermanshah, Soltanabad, and Yazd.[145] British banks and companies in many of these towns were raided for bank notes, allowing the Melliyun to raise funds for their cause. The Melliyun and gendarmes (1,500 men in all) were supported by Iranian-Arab sharpshooters, Basseris and other local warriors.[146] Iranian tribal warriors, gendarmes, and Melliyun also gave assistance to a German mission to cross over into Afghanistan from southeast Iran in late 1915.[147]

The fighting resulted in a victory for the Melliyun, and Ghavam ol Molk fled to India. The British responded by landing large amounts of weapons and ammunition in Bandar Abbas by March 1916.[148] Sykes recruited local Iranians for the SPR in order to secure the south. The British planned a two-pronged assault for expelling the Melliyun and Gendarmerie from Shiraz.[149] A major thrust was led by Ghavam ol Molk, who on his return to Iran had been furnished with weapons and supplies.[150] He struck towards Shiraz from Bandar Lengeh with as many as 10,000 Khamseh warriors. A second thrust towards Shiraz from Bushehr was led by General Douglas. The two columns converged and crushed the Melliyun, who numbered no more than 2,500.[151] Shiraz fell to Ghavam ol Molk in April 1916.[152] He took brutal reprisals against the Melliyun, including hangings, poisonings, and placing captives in front of cannons for execution.[153]

Kerman was captured by Burmese and Indian infantry and SPR units without resistance by June 1916 followed by Yazd (August) and Isfahan (mid-September). Despite these successes, the fighting was far from over. Local anti-British tribes in the south conducted a number of successful attacks against SPR outposts, but Sykes managed to retain Shiraz well into the spring of 1917. He used the time to train his SPR units and then defeated his tribal opponents. The methods of the SPR were harsh which may partly explain why many southern tribes continued fighting until the very end of the war.

The First World War left Iran battered.[154] A disastrous famine followed, killing two million Iranian citizens, one-fifth of the population. Influenza killed countless more. The arming of warriors from Iran's peripheral regions by foreign powers would result in the rise of autonomist movements. These movements had a severe impact on the economy as communications and trade links were thrust into disarray. Finally, despite some American support at the Paris Peace conference in 1919, London ensured that Iran did not receive its demands for the abrogation of the 1907 Anglo-Russian partition treaty; the cancellation of past capitulation treaties; restoration of former Iranian territories; or war reparations.

PART V
THE PAHLAVIS

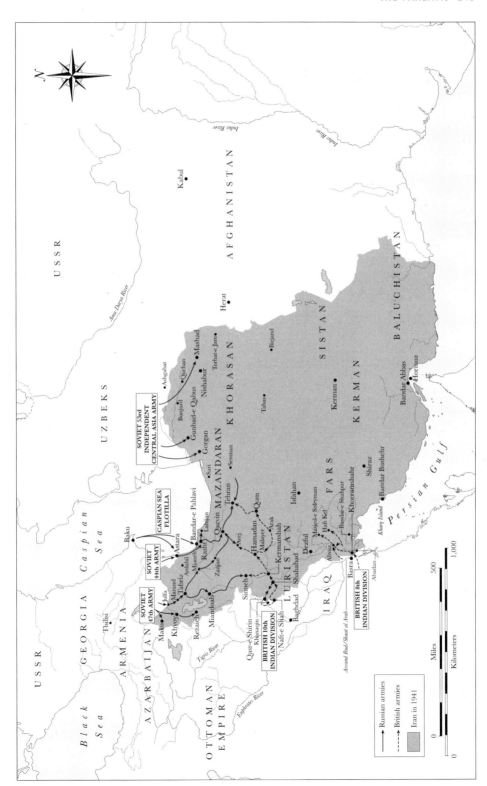

CHAPTER 26

POSTWAR REVOLTS AND THE RISE OF REZA SHAH (1919–25)

The Anglo-Iranian Agreement: proposals for a new Iranian Army

Iran had no real army capable of defending its borders at the end of the First World War. Instead, there were two distinct forces, the Persian Cossack brigade and the South Persia Rifles (SPR) commanded by British officers. Nationalists now demanded that both forces be replaced with an "Iranian" force.[1] The Constitutionalists had strongly advocated for the formation of a modern, indigenous and unified army led by Iranian officers. The Gendarmerie, born during the Constitutional Revolution, had performed well during the pre-war to post-war years despite its relatively small size and modest inventory. Despite this promising start, the Gendarmerie had yet to become the basis of a new indigenous Iranian army.

The Anglo-Iranian agreement led to the formation of a joint (Anglo-Iranian) commission. Their task was to oversee the comprehensive overhaul, re-organization and unification of all armed forces in Iran into a single force. The commission formed in January 1919 and by April that year submitted a full report to Tehran. This proposed the formation of a unified Iranian army (with the SPR as the core model) led by British officers.[2]

The proposal was bitterly opposed by nationalists vehemently opposed to any Iranian forces led by foreign officers. The Iranian officers of the Gendarmerie and the Persian Cossacks also protested in the strongest terms.[3] From the Iranian view, this "new" army was no different from the Persian Cossack Brigade or the SPR whose foreign officers acted in the interests of their respect governments. Iranian nationalists also saw the overall terms of the treaty (i.e. British economic advisors for financial affairs etc) as London's veiled attempt to transform Iran into a British protectorate.[4] Iran's strong nationalist climate prevented the ratification of the Anglo-Iranian Agreement in the Majlis. The British in turn remained steadfast, demanding that their officers assume the leadership role of the new Iranian army.

The revolt of Sheikh Mohammad Khiyabani in Azarbaijan

By 1915, Azarbaijan, Iran's key center for protest against foreign domination and political change, had seen the rise of a number of anti-government rebels.[5] The 1919 Anglo-Iranian agreement caused a negative backlash across the entirety of Iran, and in Azarbaijan in particular.[6] Sheikh Mohammad Khiyabani (1880–1920), the leader of the Democratic Party in Azarbaijan, vociferously protested against the 1919 agreement, setting the stage for his rebellion. Like Mirza Kuchik Khan in Gilan, Khiyabani was both a dedicated nationalist and a staunch anti-colonialist advocating a strong government to safeguard Iran's interests.[7] Like Mirza Kuchik Khan, Khiyabani had been an active supporter of the Constitutional Revolution. In 1911, Khiyabani had ardently defended Morgan Shuster as a symbol of Iran's independence in the Majlis.[8]

Prior to the revolt, Tabriz's citizens had been angered by the government's appointment of the generally unpopular Ayn o Dowleh as provincial governor of Azarbaijan.[9] This and a host of other grievances led rebellion breaking out on April 5, 1920 when Khiyabani, his followers, and the local barracks commander, stormed a local prison to free a political prisoner.[10] By the next day, numbers of veterans from the constitutional movement, democrats, and students had joined Khiyabani. Khiyabani was soon joined by disaffected soldiers and local security forces. Khiyabani published an official proclamation on April 7 in Persian and French against the government and demanding the establishment of a constitutional government.[11] Unlike Ismail Agha Simko, the leader of the Kurdish Shikak rebellion in western Azarbaijan, Khiyabani was not a separatist. British Foreign Office archives at the time clearly stated that Khiyabani and his movement wanted to promote the Iranian constitution and the welfare of Iran as a unified state.[12] Khiyabani's relations with local British representatives were cool at best, while those with the Bolshevik authorities of Russia being outright contradictory. He would at times appear conciliatory towards them and then bitterly criticize them in public.[13] The Tehran press was alive with debates showing a clear divide between the supporters and opponents of Khiyabani.[14]

Khiyabani strongly opposed pan-Turkism and the Ottoman armies that had invaded Iranian Azarbaijan during the First World War.[15] He also strongly opposed the policies of the newly established Republic of Azarbaijan. The Turkish Democratic Musavat Party (TDMP) of Baku had convened on May 27, 1918 in Tbilisi to select the name "Azarbaijan," rather than the historical appellations of Albania or Arran, as the title of their new "Independent Republic of Azarbaijan" (IRA) in the Transcaucasus.[16] The Musavat regime soon proposed to annex the historical Iranian Azarbaijan into their newborn republic.[17] Iranians in general, and Azarbaijani activists in particular, opposed the new name for the Republic.[18] Khiyabani even proposed that the Iranian Azarbaijan change its name to "Azadistan" (Land of Freedom) to distinguish it from the recently created Republic of Azarbaijan.[19] The term Azadistan also referred to the "heroic" role of Azarbaijan in Iranian history, especially during the constitutional movement.[20] Mirza Kuchik Khan also protested against the Musavats' use of "Azarbaijan" for their Republic.[21]

The only force capable of confronting Khiyabani was the Persian Cossacks, 85% of whose Iranian contingent were of Azarbaijani and Kurdish origin.[22] On June 22, 1920, Khiyabani officially declared that the Cossacks were no longer entitled to roam Tabriz's streets to terrorize its population and that they could leave their barracks by leaving their arms behind.[23] This made a major showdown between the Cossacks and Khiyabani all but inevitable. Two days later, Khiyabani and his followers appropriated a Qajar palace in Tabriz for their headquarters.[24]

The central government sent Haji Mokhber ol Saltaneh to Azarbaijan by late August 1920 to suppress Khiyabani.[25] Mokhber ol Saltaneh induced the Shahsavan tribe, Ismail Agha Simko, and the Shikak Kurds (in western Azarbaijan) to attack Khiyabani.[26] The task of destroying Khiyabani and his followers was finally accomplished by the Cossacks who stormed out of their barracks on September 13, raided the city and attacked the palace, clearing it of Khiyabani's followers.[27] Khiyabani refused to surrender. He continued to fight from the basement of his friend's home but was killed by Cossack gunfire.[28] Despite the suppression of Khiyabani, Qajar authority in Azarbaijan remained tenuous.

Towards the end of the First World War, the German consulate in Tabriz had stocked large amounts of war supplies and explosives intended for Ottoman forces operating in northwest Iran. With the end of the war and the Bolshevik arrival in Russia, the consulate became a center for pro-Bolshevik, anti-Constitutionalist, and anti-British activities.[29] Kurt Wustnow, the German consul in Tabriz, died on June 1, 1920, putting an end to the threat of Bolshevist activities in Tabriz.[30] These events were then followed by the Soviet invasion of Iran's Azarbaijan province in 1921. The Soviet government had in the fall of 1920, alleged that Shahsavan tribes from Iranian Azarbaijan had launched attacks into the Caucasus. Following this announcement, the Soviet forces invaded the province through Astara in January 1921 but were literally wiped out by local Azarbaijani fighters.[31] Another Soviet attempt to enter Azarbaijan through Mughan in the spring was also crushed.[32] Soviet efforts were then to be mainly confined to northern Iran's Caspian Sea coastline.

Reza Khan's Coup

Reza Khan (1878–1944) hailed from northern Iran's Savad-Kooh region of Mazandaran.[33] He was energetic, ambitious, and an ardent nationalist. Known originally as Reza Savad-Koohi, he joined the Russian-trained Persian Cossack Brigade in 1894 at the age of 16. He also served with the Iranian army during the Qajar era when he attained the rank of gunnery sergeant and the coveted Qajar *Neshan e Aqdas* (Medallion of Aqdas).[34] Though illiterate, he taught himself to read and write in adulthood.

As a result of negotiations between General Edmond Ironside (in command of Norperforce), the Iranian government, and a somewhat reluctant Ahmad Shah in October 1920, the Persian Cossack Brigade's Russian commander, officers, and NCOs had been removed and replaced by the British.[35] Ahmad Shah lamented the departure of the Russian officers and Ironside promised him that the Persian Cossacks would "in future have only Iranian officers."[36] Ahmad Shah placed Sardar e Homayoun in overall command of the Cossacks, but the latter proved incapable of asserting his authority over the primary force in Qazvin.[37] The British appointed Reza Savad-Koohi in Qazvin as deputy of the force. Ironside then sent Homayoun on leave making Reza Savad-Koohi the *de facto* commander of the force, especially at Qazvin.[38] A highly capable soldier, Reza Savad-Koohi attained the rank of brigadier and then brigadier general in the Persian Cossacks. He earned the title "Reza Khan," as he also was the only Iranian to have ever commanded the Persian Cossacks.

The Cossack Brigade's shake-up in late 1920 set the stage for Reza Khan's bid for power. Acting in concert with Seyyed Zia e Din Tabatabai, Reza Khan staged a successful coup d'état on February 21, 1921.[39] Traversing a distance of almost 93 miles (150km) from Qazvin, Reza Khan and 2,500 Persian Cossacks, equipped with eight cannon and 18 heavy machineguns, seized Tehran with virtually no violence.[40] Reza Khan's troops methodically took over Tehran's government buildings, extinguishing the last vestiges of Qajar power in Iran.[41] Despite this, Reza Khan professed his loyalty to Ahmad Shah. Interestingly, General Edmond Ironside had noted, as early as December 1920, to London that he supported the takeover of the Persian Cossacks by a strong Iranian officer.[42]

The general argued that this was a constructive and face-saving way for the British to depart from Iran, and allow the Iranians to finally put their house in order.[43]

Reza Khan initially became the head of all of Iran's armed forces. By April 1921 he had merged his office with that of the minister of war, entitling him to the designation, "Reza Khan Sardar e Sepah" (Reza Khan commander of the army). Tabatabai became prime minister. Despite the coup's success, much work remained to be done. Iran's disparate military units had to be amalgamated in a short time into a national Iranian army. This new force then had to campaign to reassert authority in a country that had lacked an effective government for decades.

London was supportive of Reza Khan's coup. The British were anxious to see a strong and united Iran capable of standing up to the new Communist regime in Russia. London feared that a Russian takeover of Iran would threaten British interests in southern Iran, the Persian Gulf, and British India. Cronin notes that British support for the coup derived from hopes of working with a new government willing to accept the 1919 Anglo-Iranian agreement.[44] The British, according to Cronin, placed their hopes on their protégé Tabatabai, who was sympathetic to London's proposals in the 1919 agreement.[45] London was soon to be disappointed as just months after the takeover, a serious rift developed between Reza Khan and Tabatabai. Reza Khan adamantly opposed Tabatabai's demand that British officers from the Cossack brigade be placed in operational command of the new Iranian army. Tabatabai was overruled and exiled. Reza Khan then dismissed the British officers of the Persian Cossacks and the SPR, as well as the remaining Swedes of the Gendarmerie.[46]

Nevertheless, no Iranian political leader, even Reza Khan, could have acted in a vacuum given Iran's serious political and military disarray and her precarious geopolitical situation at the time. Reza Khan was realistic and knew that he needed to gain the approval and support of the British before he engaged in his endeavors. British and American archives indicate that London initially supported Reza Khan through General Ironside. A number of contemporary historians have suggested that the British provided funds, supplies and ammunition as well as political support for Reza Khan, but the extent of British military support in terms of war materiel has been recently questioned by the detailed analyses of the Iranian military by Babaie.[47]

The Soviet-Iranian Border Treaty: pretext for future invasions?

Iranian authorities in Moscow were negotiating terms for the withdrawal of Bolshevik troops from northern Iran. The end result of these negotiations was the signing of the Soviet-Iranian Friendship Treaty on February 26, 1921, just five days after Reza Khan's coup in Tehran.[48] A number of the treaty's articles were constructive for Iran. Article 11 reversed one of the humiliating terms of the Turkmenchai treaty, allowing Iran to have armed vessels with the Iranian flag on the Caspian Sea.[49] Article 3 returned Ashooradeh Island to Iran, under Russian occupation since 1842.[50] Russian highways, ports and railways in the port city of Bandar Anzali in Gilan, and barges in Lake Urumiah in Azerbaijan were handed over to Iran.[51] Article 1 in particular was a major success for Iran: the new Communist government of Russia renounced all former Tsarist-gained concessions in Iran.[52] The Russians also renounced all former Tsarist banking assets in Iran.[53] The treaty also affirmed the permanence of the Russo-Iranian borders.[54] This meant that Iran would not to be handed back any of its Caucasian territories lost to Russia in the early 19th century. Interestingly, Iran had laid territorial claims (i.e. Baku, Nakhchevan, etc) against Russia during the post-war peace conferences at Versailles.[55]

Article 6 provided the Russians with the legal justification to march their army into Iran should they feel threatened by any "third powers" situated upon Iranian soil.[56] The article stipulated that Russia would have the right to send its troops into Iran for "self-defense" if any "third powers" introduced their forces into Iran (by armed intervention or otherwise), or used Iranian territory to menace or invade the Soviet Union in any way should the Iranian government prove unable to deter the incursion.[57] The Soviet interpretation of Article 6 was to prove rather elastic when it suited their purposes.

Outbreak of provincial revolts 1900–22

Iran was on the brink of disintegration. The combination of an economy in disarray, widespread famine, mismanagement by an ineffectual central government, unchecked banditry, rampant lawlessness, and the presence of foreign troops, had facilitated the rise of a number of regional rebellions by 1918. The rebellions could be roughly classified as those with earlier links to the constitutional movement (i.e. Mirza Kuchik and the Jangalis of Gilan) or rebellions unrelated to the constitutional movement. The latter were typical of 20th-century Iranian history: whenever the central government grew weak, demands for local autonomy increased.[58] Ismail Agha Simko's separatist Kurdish rebellion in northwest Iran proved to be one of the greatest threats to Iran's political and territorial integrity in the early 20th century. Before his movement was finally crushed by Tehran's reorganized army under Reza Shah, Simko had captured large tracts of northwest Iran, especially in Azarbaijan and adjoining Kurdish-speaking areas.

Battles in the northwest: rise and fall of Kurdish warlord Simko

Prior to 1914, occupying Russian troops had kept Iran's Kurds in the northwest from exploding into the heart of Azarbaijan province. Iran's Kurds in the northwest and west had suffered great economic deprivations and injustice mainly due to government corruption and mismanagement and many were receptive to rebellion. With the outbreak of the First World War the Kurds got their chance to raid the interior of Azarbaijan province. Iran's military weaknesses had been clearly demonstrated even before the war when Azarbaijan had been invaded by Russia and the Ottoman Empire. It was these very chaotic circumstances that gave rise to the Kurdish warlord Ismail Aqa Simko (Simitqho in Persian) of the Shikak tribe. Simko wanted to carve out his own independent Kurdish kingdom in Iran's northwest, which would act as a magnet for a larger pan-Kurdish empire encompassing all Kurdish populated regions in Iran, Turkey, and Iraq.[59] He was supported by Seyyed Taha Ibn Abdolqader, the grandson of Sheikh Obeidollah[60] who had invaded Iran in 1880 to carve out his own independent Kurdish state.

Simko's rebellion suffered from three major weaknesses. First, he lacked the organized bureaucracy needed to run a government.[61] Second, despite his pan-Kurdish credentials, Simko excluded the Kurds of Mahabad from his grand council of Kurdish chiefs.[62] He also failed to unite with the Kurds of Kermanshah[63] who were to lead their own rebellion against the central authorities. The third and perhaps greatest liability proved to be many of Simko's future followers. Many of these joined his cause to mainly engage in plunder and raids. These did much to alienate fellow Kurds and solidify resistance against Simko.

Soon after the First World War, Simko was joined by a few hundred well-trained and battle-hardened ex-Ottoman officers and soldiers. These had deserted (along with their machineguns and artillery) from the main Ottoman force withdrawing from Azarbaijan at the end of the war.[64] Numbers of these were Kurds who had been won over by Simko's pan-Kurdism while other ex-Ottoman (Turkish) troops acted as mercenaries. These deserters were paid handsomely by Simko who even gave them wives.[65] Simko also benefited from the withdrawal of Russian General Baratov after 1917. He quickly expanded his arsenal by appropriating abandoned Russian arms, ammunition and at least three mountain guns, which he entrusted to his ex-Ottoman artillerymen.[66] By 1918 Simko had also built a powerful castle on the heights of Chehreeqh (near the Ottoman border). This was soon strengthened with more powerful fortifications and additional towers. Chehreeqh, which became Simko's main base, soon threatened all of Iranian Azarbaijan.

Simko was well known by the major European powers, who also bestowed honorary titles on him.[67] Simko proved especially adept at using the Ottoman Turks and the Russians against the Iranians. Simko viewed the British as essential to his cause by stating that "only a fool could not see the need for British support for Kurdish national aspirations."[68] He certainly was careful not to alienate the British; despite receiving Ottoman assistance, Simko refused to help them against the English during the Great War.[69]

Simko also developed strong links with Russia, which had invaded northern Iran during the Constitutional Revolution. By 1911 Russia had even stationed some troops in predominantly Kurdish Sawoj-Bolaq (now Mahabad) in Iran's northwest.[70] The Tsarist sponsored Ottoman-Kurdish Abdulrazzaq Bedir Khan was brought in from Russia in 1912 to Rezaieh (now Urumiah) in Iranian Azarbaijan. Abdulrazzaq's role was to cultivate anti-Persian sentiments among Iranian Kurds, and to cultivate links between the region's Christians and Kurds.[71]

Simko had been initially captured by (Tsarist) Russians in 1916 but released that same year. The Russians then placed Simko on a regular subsidy and made him governor in parts of Iranian Kurdistan.[72] It is also possible that the post-Ottoman Turkish government at least partly supported Simko at first, but then distanced itself from him, especially when Reza Shah came to power.[73] Perhaps the Turks realized that Simko's pan-Kurdism posed an equal threat to both Turkey and Iran. Simko's scheme for a Kurdish state was consistent with overall allied policies, at least at first. The allied Treaty of Sevres with the defeated Ottoman Empire had already guaranteed independence to the Turkish-Kurds in Article 64 (August 10, 1920).[74] In practice the British and the West preferred to carve out both a Kurdish and an Armenian state out of eastern Anatolia.[75] Simko's bid to create his own (pan-) Kurdish state was indeed a case of being at the right place at the right time.

The authorities in Tehran and Tabriz had long taken issue with Simko's lack of cooperation with the central government. Ahmad Shah had tried to win his allegiance by giving him the governorship of Kotur, but this had little impact.[76] This was because the government's actions had done much to cultivate Simko's intransigence. Simko's clan had been the victim of government treachery as far back as 1904. The Qajar official, Nizam ol Saltaneh, had invited Jaafar Agha (Simko's older brother) to Tabriz, swearing on the Koran that he would not be harmed. Instead, Jaafar Agha had been killed as soon as he had arrived in Tabriz, on Ali Mirza's orders. Local Kurds were outraged as were Iranian exiles in Istanbul who protested against this assassination.

Simko is known for his massacres of Christians in Iran in 1918. One of these was the murder of Mar Sharmon, the Assyrian Christian patriarch, and 150 of his retinue just as they arrived to engage in negotiations.[77] It is possible that Simko had been encouraged to do this by Tabriz's governor.[78] The Hakkari Christians took revenge by massacring Salmas' Muslims, with Simko killing Khoi's Christians in turn. This was followed by the massacre of at least 1,000 Christians in Salmas, with Simko playing a major role.[79] When Ottoman armies entered the area against the Christians, Simko cooperated with them and again massacred many of the fleeing Christians.[80]

Two critical incidents following the First World War clearly demonstrated the political ineptitude of Qajar authorities. The governor of Rezaieh (now Urumiah) had obtained an audience with Simko in February 1919 and appealed to him to stop raiding his city.[81] Simko viewed this appeal as a sign of government weakness, which further emboldened his dream of an independent Kurdish state.[82] Three months later, Qajar authorities sent Simko a "present": a bomb.[83] The package exploded when opened on April 14, 1919, killing Simko's brother Ali Agha.[84] Simko and his young son survived with slight injuries.[85] This clumsy assassination attempt further alienated Simko, who mobilized his forces for an open rebellion against the government.[86] Simko and the Shikak Kurds then launched a furious attack against Rezaieh which was repelled by the town's populace and militia. More raids followed against towns such as Salmas, Khoi and other northwestern Iranian towns in April–May 1919.[87] Simko then succeeded in capturing Rezaieh (along with a number of Iranian soldiers) and had it completely looted.[88] Simko only withdrew to Chehreeqh when the British consul (escorted by a British-Indian force) arrived in Rezaieh by January 1919.[89] This did not prevent Simko from continuing his raids well into the fall and early winter, launching a major attack with 4,000 men (including the Ottoman deserters) against Shapur (in the Salmas region).[90] Shapur's citizens raised 7,700 men to resist Simko but could only supply 340 of them with firearms.[91] The battle was joined on December 19, 1919 with Shapur's defenders bitterly resisting for two days before Simko broke through their defenses.[92] Showing little mercy, Simko had many of the fleeing citizens pursued and killed as they attempted to escape to Tabriz and Sharafkhaneh.[93]

Qajar authorities first assigned Commander Kopal to suppress Simko but his efforts proved futile.[94] The one notable success was achieved by Russian officer General Filipov of the Persian Cossack Brigade. He arrived from Tehran to Tabriz where he organized a mixed force of Cossacks and gendarmes.[95] Filipov then forced a major showdown with Simko near Salmas on February 25, 1920.[96] The battle decisively crushed Simko, who witnessed many of his Kurdish warriors deserting him.[97] Simko and the remnants of his battered forces then hastily retreated to Chehreeqh.[98]

Entessar, one of the local Iranian commanders, wrote a letter in Ottoman-Turkish and sent this to Simko's Turkish mercenary soldiers and artillerymen. They were promised immunity from persecution and safe passage to Turkey if they surrendered and came to Tabriz. Entessar's appeal proved persuasive. A number of Turkish soldiers left Simko's camp and were repatriated to Turkey without incident.[99] It was here where Filipov committed a major mistake. Instead of pursuing and destroying the battered remnants of Simko's forces, Filipov chose to negotiate with him. Simko and his Chehreeqh fortress were spared on condition that no further attacks were made in northwest Iran.[100] Simko's promises were just a cunning ploy to buy time. Just months after Filipov's departure in early 1921, Simko organized new forces, this time mainly from the Herki Kurds. He then resumed his attacks around Rezaieh and went as far as Khoi. A government force from Tabriz was easily crushed at Shakar Yazi. Simko was now completely transparent: he was fighting to carve out a Kurdish state inside Iranian territory.

The morale of government troops had suffered greatly due to repeated defeats by Simko's forces. Disorganization in Tehran and the lack of a unified national army resulted in the dispatch of piecemeal forces which were easily crushed by Simko. After Reza Khan seized power in Tehran he worked feverishly to build a national army, but it required time and in the meantime, the small government forces available in the region would continue to suffer more defeats against Simko.[101] Much of the failure of government forces stemmed from problems in coordination, command, and control. With each government defeat Simko became militarily stronger as he captured more guns, cannon, and ammunition.[102] Continuous victories boosted Simko's prestige, leading more warriors to join his banner. Simko's forces, described by Western sources as marching under "a Turkish flag," more than tripled, from 1,500 to 4,000 men, between March and summer 1921.[103]

By the end of August, Simko's forces had become even better equipped, thanks to the additional capture of government military supplies.[104] By autumn, his forces had expanded to 7,000 men.[105] By September 1921, Simko had marched against Mahabad (south of Rezaieh Lake).[106] The town's garrison of 800 troops (mainly gendarmes) and many of its Kurdish inhabitants put up fierce resistance.[107] Simko overcame the town's defenses and defeated the local garrison.[108] Captured officers, soldiers, and local (Kurdish) townspeople who had fought against Simko were mown down execution-style by machinegun fire.[109] Only a few officers and Kurds managed to escape. These actions contradicted Simko's pan-Kurd cause and may partly explain why he failed to rally more Kurds under his banner. Nevertheless, Simko's Mahabad victory increased his control over a wider chunk of territory in the northwest, and attracted additional warriors to his cause.

Realizing the gravity of the danger at last, garrisons from Hamadan and Qazvin, infantry and cavalry units from Ahmadi, and a mountain combat unit from Tehran were ordered to deploy against Simko. Another 700-man force led by Gilan's Khalo Ghorban also joined the government forces.[110] Despite this vigorous response, problems with coordination, command, and control, and petty rivalries between local military commanders severely diminished the effectiveness of the government forces.

Simko's allies inflicted a major defeat on Khalo Ghorban's forces in the vicinity of Mahabad on April 3, 1922, capturing up to four cannon and perhaps 20 machineguns.[111] Khalo Ghorban's forces, though highly effective as guerrilla fighters in northern Iran's dense forests, lacked the military training of regular troops to repel Kurdish attacks from the nearby hills.[112] Iranian sources also report the Kurds capturing two European military advisors and prominent Qajar officers (i.e. Pooladeen).[113] Morale among government forces, anti-Simko Kurds, and in Azarbaijan province now sank to a new low. Simko's sway reached its zenith by July 1922 when he ruled as far east and south as Sain Qaleh (Shahin Dezh) and Saqqez.[114] Simko was also in communication with other Kurdish tribes such as the Hawroman (Avroman) and Mariwan and even Luristan.[115]

In the summer of 1922, Reza Khan was finally able to send an 8,000-man force from Tehran to Tabriz to join local forces already there.[116] In overall command was army chief of staff, General Amanollah Mirza Jahanbani, who would later engage in battles against rebels in Baluchistan. Before confronting Simko and storming Chehreeqh, Jahanbani first secured the northern portion of Lake Urumiah in Iranian Azerbaijan. After assembling from the port of Sharafkhaneh, his forces struck towards the foothills of Ghizil Dagh and from there crushed and cleared Simko's forces from Deilamghan (Shapur), Salmas, Khoi, and Mahabad.[117] Jahanbani successes opened a direct route towards Chehreeqh which was to be attacked by five forces.[118] The first force (the "Guard") deployed from Meshev Dagh and Qizil Dagh towards Chehreeqh. The second force (the "Azarbaijan") deployed from Shekar Yazi.[119] The third deployed from Khoi and was essentially an all-cavalry force, supported by gendarmerie and anti-Simko partisans. The fourth force included armed civilian militias led by Armenian officers from the north of Lake Urumiah. The fifth was elements of the "Sang e Kazem" barracks, which were to combine with the forces of Sharafkhaneh in the march towards Chehreeqh.

Jahanbani's forces struck on August 9, 1922.[120] Simko's men showed special daring and resoluteness as their Turkish artillerymen fired their heavy guns with great effectiveness.[121] Simko's men beat back the assault of the Guard and succeeded in prying open a gap between the former and the Azarbaijan forces. He now tried to isolate both forces and destroy them piecemeal. Simko's efforts were frustrated by Zafar o Dowla, the commander of the Azarbaijan force. Zafar o Dowla used his cavalry to swiftly close the gaps between his forces and the Guard. He then ordered his cavalry to attack Simko's flanks. Simko's men, who were well-armed with machineguns, cannon, and rifles, did everything possible to maintain the gaps between the Guard and Azarbaijan but they stood no chance against Zafar o Dowla's brilliant use of his Azarbaijani cavalry and the grim determination of both the Guard and Azarbaijan troops; the gap was closed.[122] The deadly Azarbaijani cavalry now delivered a decisive blow and forced Simko's flanks to collapse. With Simko's forces in disarray, the entire Iranian force counterattacked and captured three field guns and all of the Turkish artillerymen.[123] Simko also suffered the indignity of witnessing the desertion of 9,000 of his 10,000 Kurdish warriors.[124] The Kurds quickly sued for pardon by declaring that Simko had deceived them into rebellion.

It is probable that so many of Simko's followers deserted him because their primary motivation was profits and plunder.[125] When these prospects disappeared (as at Chehreeqh), so too did Simko's base of support. Van Bruinessen suggests that "for the majority of the followers nationalism was as best an additional motive."[126] With his dreams of an independent Kurdish kingdom shattered, Simko and his remaining forces fled into Chehreeqh castle.

The myth of Simko's invincibility had been broken, leading to a sharp increase in the army's morale. Chehreeqh fell to the army on August 12, 1922. Simko, who was still at large, urged his men to recapture Chehreeqh. Simko lost many of his remaining men and heavy equipment in ill-conceived and futile assaults against the army. Simko's days of easy victories over disorganized and demoralized troops were clearly over. Many of the survivors fled to Turkey where they were attacked by Turkish troops. The last vestiges of Simko's "empire" in Iranian Azerbaijan disappeared as government troops cleared out the last pockets of Simko's men from the city of Rezaieh on August 14, 1922. Simko's defeat was met with rapturous celebrations in Iranian Azerbaijan among

Azaris, Armenians and anti-Simko Kurds. They were elated to witness the end of decades of chaos, invasion, carnage, and banditry.

Simko refused to give up. On August 23, 1922, government troops discovered him trying to assemble the remainder of his followers in the Golreesh region. A cavalry regiment entering the area was heavily attacked and forced to retreat, but quickly returned with additional government troops to crush what remained of Simko's forces. Simko had no option but to escape to Turkey. Tehran, however, was intent on reconciliation; Simko was officially pardoned in early October 1922 by Abdollah Amir Tahmasebim, the army commander in northwest Iran. Simko was allowed to return to Iran on condition that he refrain from rebellious activities. He did not keep his word. Simko unsuccessfully tried to organize another rebellion, then asked and received a further pardon from Tehran. Once again, Simko broke his word and tried to organize yet another rebellion in June 1930. Tehran's patience had run out; Simko met death at the hands of government troops.

Battles in northern Iran: Mazandaran, Gilan, and Lahijan

Soviet authorities had been landing armed Communist activists along the northern Iranian coastline during the 1920s and possibly earlier. These and local Communist sympathizers occupied Babolsar and nearby locales. The Communists were then defeated by a mixed force of Persian Cossacks, gendarmes, and local anti-Communist militias at Bandar Goz in early July 1920. The Communists fled by ship to Baku with their Iranian allies retreating into the local forests.

It was around this time that Ismail Khan Amir Bavand Savadkoohi, a powerful feudal lord in Mazandaran, challenged Tehran. Savadkoohi refused to pay taxes, created his own fiefdom, allied himself with Gilani anti-government forces and declared his intention to conquer Tehran. An army unit marched in on July 7, 1921 and demanded Savadkoohi's disarmament. While Savadkoohi won the first round of fighting, he was completely routed on July 27. He retreated into the forest, then returned to be defeated in a 12-hour battle before retreating to Alasht. The city fell to government troops on September 9, with Savadkoohi losing much of his military equipment. Realizing the inevitable, Savadkoohi signaled his submission via telegraph to Reza Khan in Tehran. The rebellion in Mazandaran was over but it would take another nine or ten months of fighting to clear out Soviet fighters who had landed there by ship.

Soviet Bolsheviks had also landed in the Lahijan region. A force of 1,000 Soviet fighters and local Communist sympathizers had moved from Lahijan to Tankabon on May 1921, with the ultimate aim of marching to Tehran. Iranian forces, which had anticipated this move, attacked and defeated the Communists in a series of battles lasting until May 31. By October 1921, all Soviet forces had been ejected from Lahijan, Tankabon and Mazandaran.

It was in Gilan that the Soviets became most influential, especially with the Gilan Soviet Socialist Republic (or Persian Soviet Socialist Republic), which was proclaimed on May 1920. These developments were not approved by Mirza Kuchik Khan, an ardent Iranian nationalist who had fought to preserve Iran's independence against foreign domination. As noted by Zirinsky, "Kuchik Khan … and most of his followers were motivated by Iranian patriotism and Shia Islamic values."[127] Kuchik Khan left the city of Rasht in protest on June 9, 1921. The Iranian Communist Party (the Edalat),[128] which seized power in Gilan was unmistakably pro-Soviet.[129] A number of the "Gilan

Soviet" such as Mirjaafar Pishevari, was to be later used by Moscow in an unsuccessful attempt to attach Iranian Azarbaijan to the Soviet Union in the 1940s.

By early 1921, the "Soviet army of Gilan," accompanied by Soviet Red Army "volunteers," was ready to march south towards Tehran with "a guerrilla force of 1,500 Jangalis, Kurds, Armenians, and Azarbaijanis."[130] From the Iranian perspective, this was simply another manifestation of Russian imperialism trying to absorb Iran. Kuchik Khan, apparently suspicious of Bolshevik-Russian motives in northern Iran, expressed his readiness to cooperate with Reza Khan in Tehran. Kuchik Khan then inexplicably attacked Massooleh. Reza Khan ordered a massive counterattack which destroyed Kuchik Khan's forces. These made their last stand at Roodkhan Castle on December 1, 1921 with Kuchik Khan dying of exposure on January 31, 1921. The Iran-Soviet Treaty of February 1921 also doomed the Gilan Republic: the Soviets vacated their forces from northern Iran and ended their support for the republic. Reza Khan was then able to assert Tehran's authority over Gilan province with the "Republic" ceasing to exist by September 1921.

Battles in the west: Iranian Kurdistan and Luristan

The prelude to the revolts of Iranian Kurdistan and Luristan can be traced to 1912 when Salar ol Dowleh, brother of deposed Mohammad Ali Shah, recruited Kurdish and Lur warriors to help him seize the Qajar throne in Tehran. Salar ol Dowleh failed as his force was defeated by Yeprem Khan in Hamadan in May 1912. The battle however, encouraged a number of Kurds and Lurs to revolt against the central government. Soon a certain "Skeikh Mahmood e Kurd" began to organize sympathetic Kurdish tribes towards independence, much like Simko in western Azarbaijan. Nevertheless, the most dangerous rebellion in this region was that of Rasheed Khan who led 6,000 Kurdish cavalry in the vicinity of Nowsood and Hawraman. A number of other tribes (i.e. the Ghobadi) also revolted, each pursuing their own separatist agenda. The weak government presence in Iranian Kurdistan was further exacerbated by the departure of government military units to the northwest to resist the incursions of Simko.

Qajar authority in Luristan had been weak ever since the reign of Nasser e Din Shah. The mountainous nature of the region made it difficult to access. The Lurs had little loyalty to the Qajar house as it had overthrown the Zands who originated in Luristan. The Gendarmerie mounted a general offensive in May 1912, managing to capture Khorramabad against fierce opposition. They then were forced to withdraw from the city by April 1913. The end of the First World War witnessed a renewed push into Luristan by a force of Persian Cossacks but these quickly became bogged down near Boroujerd.

By early March 1922, Tehran was ready to reassert its authority in Iranian Kurdistan. The army launched its first offensive towards Baneh and Saqqez. Its main opponent was Rasheed Khan whose plans to dismember Iranian Kurdistan were opposed by many of Iran's Kurds. These Kurds supported the army units in their final attack against Rasheed Khan at Ravansar in late March 1923. Rasheed Khan's 6,000-strong cavalry force was crushed and he fled to Turkey. He was soon issued a pardon and allowed to return to Iran by Reza Khan. Rasheed Khan however, attempted to raise another army and resumed his attacks against the government by June 1923. He was again defeated by government troops and anti-Rasheed Khan Kurds on April 1924. Sporadic revolts however, continued until 1931. By 1935 Tehran had expanded the local Kurdistan Brigade into a full division.

Brigandage, raiding, lawlessness and rebellion continued in Luristan. The army deployed into the province in April 1921 to restore Tehran's authority. The government had plans to connect Luristan and Khuzistan by new road and rail networks. The army finally entered Boroujerd on October 27, 1923 and by late November Khorramabad had also been secured. The establishment of law and order did much to terminate the disorders in the province. Some isolated rebel pockets continued to resist as late as 1930, but these too were subdued. By June 1928, the highway between Luristan and Khuzistan had been officially opened.

Khuzistan: Fall of Sheikh Khazal (1924)

Khuzistan's Sheikh Khazal remained outside of Tehran's orbit as late as 1923.[131] Price notes that his rise had been made possible by three factors: "an uneducated and isolated population, a weak central government, and British support."[132] By 1919, the British had provided Khazal with 3,000 rifles, ammunition and a steamer for the specific purpose of protecting British oil assets.[133] Cottam has noted that the Iranians "regarded the British treaty with the Sheikh as a national humiliation."[134] Sheikh Khazal collected taxes, but paid only a tiny fraction of this to Tehran.[135] By 1922 Khazal was acting in almost complete independence from Tehran. Khazal also contributed funds to prevent the restoration of peace in Luristan in an effort to bog down the Iranian army there.[136] The British were also on good terms with Reza Shah who was establishing a strong central government in Tehran.

On October 23, 1923, Tehran demanded that Khazal yield much of his possessions to the government. Khazal rejected this and forged an alliance with some Bakhtiari chiefs over the next nine months. A number of Bakhtiaris who guarded the oilfields in Khuzistan on behalf of the British had an economic stake in keeping Reza Shah out of the province. Khazal was also joined by Reza Gholi Khan Arghavan, the local chief of the Iranian gendarmerie in Khuzistan. He also got help from the Qajar dynasty, as Salar ol Dowleh brought him tons of arms and ammunition in fall 1924. Interestingly, Khazal offered Ahmad Shah help in restoring his authority in Iran if he joined him in Khuzistan; the offer was rejected.[137]

Tehran was now determined to crush Khazal for good. The Iranian army arrived in the city of Behbahan in Khuzistan in late August 1924. A force also arrived from the west to concentrate on Dezful, with another deployed towards Khuzistan from Janeki. Crack infantry, cavalry and artillery units were were also ordered to deploy south from Azarbaijan. The army was ready to deploy into the province by early November, just as Sir Percy Lorraine arrived at Mohammara (Khorramshahr). Meanwhile, British authorities in Bushehr, Shiraz, and Isfahan did their best to discourage Iranian forces from attacking Khazal.[138] Ignoring the British, the army deployed into Khuzistan to quickly defeat Khazal's Bakhtiari, Arab and Bahmani tribal warriors. Casualties on both sides were light.[139] Bakhtiari tribesmen did manage to surround an Iranian army barracks near Shushtar, but Khazal was already doomed as his friends had begun to desert him.

The army prevailed with the Iranian prime minister entering Ahvaz, the provincial capital, on December 4, 1924. That same day, Khazal sent his son to the army commanders to declare his allegiance to Tehran. He also promised to pay his expected share of the national taxes.

The government issued a general amnesty in the province and peace was restored. Political lobbies in Tehran's Majlis opposed to central government reforms in Khuzistan soon collapsed as their chief source of revenue, Sheikh Khazal, was no longer able to support them.[140] Britain also bowed to the inevitable and withdrew support for Khazal.[141] Khazal continued to dream of re-establishing his rule in Khuzistan, leading Iranian authorities to arrest him. He was sent to Tehran where he died in 1936.

End of the Qajar dynasty and the coronation of Reza Shah

Reza Khan's success in ending the rebellions within Iran greatly elevated his popularity among the populace.[142] Unity and political order had finally been restored and lawlessness and banditry had finally come to an end.

Reza Khan had allowed Ahmad Shah to retain his throne after the February 1921 coup. But, after being forced to elevate Reza Khan to prime minister on October 28, 1923, Ahmad Shah was exiled to Europe.[143] Two years later, the Majlis formally deposed Ahmad Shah as king of Iran on October 31, 1925.[144] Ahmad Shah's lackluster interest in politics combined with the Iranian public's overall lack of confidence in Qajar rule certainly facilitated the abolition of the dynasty.[145]

Reza Khan had originally been sympathetic to the idea of an Iranian Republic, and elements of the Iranian press had been promoting the notion of a republic with Reza Khan as president.[146] The Iranian army was unable to legally back the notion of a republic in the Majlis as it lacked a political wing.[147] The feudal lords and especially the conservative clergy were opposed to the notion of a republic.[148] The clergy also offered a concession: the monarchy would stay but the dynasty could be changed.[149] Reza Khan accepted this compromise and made an official declaration to that effect on April 1, 1925.[150] He was finally proclaimed as shah of Iran by the Majlis, on December 12, 1925,[151] becoming the first shah of the new Pahlavi dynasty. The surname Pahlavi was a deliberate link to Partho-Sassanian Iran. It is ironic that the Pahlavi dynasty's demise in 1979 would be realized by the very same clergy who had defended it so passionately just five decades previously.

Khorasan: battles in the northeast

Reza Shah's authority was significantly enhanced, having defeated rebels in the north, northwest, west, and southwest. More battles had yet to be fought as rebels in Khorasan, Fars and Baluchistan continued to defy the government.

Colonel Mohammad Taghi Khan Pesyan was one of the Gendarmerie's most respected officers. By late September 1921, Pesyan had been appointed governor of Khorasan and the commander of Khorasan's independent 9th Regiment.[152] Pesyan led the 9th Regiment in an effective campaign against armed brigands who had been terrorizing roads and looting towns. He soon gained an excellent reputation as a military commander with an impeccable sense of integrity. Meanwhile Prime Minister Tabatabai had decided to remove select members of the nobility. In early April, Pesyan was ordered to arrest Ghavam ol Saltaneh, the vali of Khorasan, and send him to Tehran.[153] The actual reasons for Ghavam's arrest remain a matter of heated conjecture, as the label of "corruption" was hard to substantiate: he was a positive force during the Constitutional Revolution and played a statesmanly role during the Soviet Union-Azarbaijan crisis in 1946.

Ghavam ol Saltaneh was arrested and imprisoned in Tehran but Iran's fickle and chaotic political climate then led to a surprising and unexpected twist: Ghavam ol Saltaneh was not only released but made prime minister by early June! Intent on revenge, Ghavam issued a decree, abolishing Pesyan's post as Khorasan's governor. Samsam ol Saltaneh Bakhtiari was then sent from Tehran to assume that office. Pesyan refused to bow to Ghavam and cut off his relations with Tehran. Pesyan's loyal men prepared to defend him in the inevitable confrontation. A delegation failed to successfully negotiate with Peysan and in late August, Ghavam sent a telegram to Khorasan's various tribal leaders and military commanders, ordering them to combine forces against Pesyan.[154]

The first battle occurred between one of Pesyan's major commanders, Major Alireza Khan Shamshirvaziri, and the riflemen of the Hazara tribe in Khorasan. After a battle in Fariman, Shamshirvaziri defeated the Hazara. Other armed tribal units successfully attacked Ghoochan in the north and defeated a detachment of Pesyan's men. Pesyan deployed with his horsemen towards Ghoochan. They reached Jafarabad on October 1, 1921, 4 miles (6km) from Ghoochan. Pesyan planned to occupy the hills around Jafarabad but the rebels struck first, surrounding Pesyan and his men. After a long and bitter firefight, Pesyan's ammunition was exhausted. The rebels closed in and engage in close-quarter fighting to destroy Pesyan's force. Pesyan himself went down fighting and was decapitated.[155] Despite his tragic demise, Pesyan remained immensely popular and was given an honorable military burial at the Naderi graveyard.[156] But Ghavam's sense of retribution reached literally into the grave: he ordered Pesyan's body exhumed from Naderi to be reburied in a less prestigious locale.[157] From a purely apolitical standpoint, Pesyan's death was a loss for Iran: this was a highly capable officer who could have contributed much to Iran's newly forming army. His experience as a fighter ace during the First World War could have been of immense value to the nascent Iranian air force.

The steady erosion of Qajar authority had resulted in the rise of lawlessness along the Caspian Sea's southeast regions. By the early 20th century, many of the Kuklan and Yamut Turkmen were conducting deep raids into northeast Iran and even as far as Damghan and Varameen. To their west, the Turkmen raided deep into Khorasan. Iranian army units stationed in Khorasan were incapable of subduing the rebels themselves. Turkmen would often retreat into Soviet territory only to return to mount fresh raids into Iran.[158] Tehran was finally able to dispatch a number of powerful regiments and cannon in March 1925 to support Khorasan's army contingents.[159] They were soon joined by tribal partisans and riflemen. The army carefully drafted battle plans and built supply dumps over four months. The strike against the Kuklan was finally launched in the Jooyeen, Vamand, Samalghan and Jarghalan regions on July 6, 1925. The assault broke the Kuklan, forcing them to scatter. Tehran paused again for three and a half months to carefully prepare its plans and logistics against the Yamut. Northern Iranian units supported the army by launching probing attacks and reconnaissance sorties.[160] The army's main strike finally fell on October 10, 1925 when infantry and cavalry units attacked the Yamut at Khajeh Nafas. Once again the tribal warriors were broken and scattered. This was followed by the army's capture of Takhmagh and Altun by October 26, 1925. The remaining Yamut and Kuklan warriors retreated to Gonbad Ghaboos, hoping perhaps to lure the army into a costly siege. Such hopes were quickly dashed when Gonbad Ghaboos fell to government troops on November 3, 1925. The fall of Gonbad Ghaboos led to the final disarming of all remaining Turkmen raiders by late February 1926. The end of these military operations was followed by Tehran's accommodation with the defeated chieftains, with the government building schools and public works in their locales. This tempered approach may partly explain why no further dissensions or armed clashes occurred in Iran's Turkmen regions until the aftermath of the 1979 revolution.

Battles in Fars and Boyer Ahmad

Fars province had, like all of Iran's provinces, suffered during the First World War and rebellions broke out among the Qashqais and the Boyer Ahmadis in the south by 1929. Reza Shah dispatched forces from Tehran, led by Brigadier-General Mohammad-Hussein Firouz, to Shiraz on February 1929. These were to reinforce Brigadier-General Shahbakhti (the commander of the Independent Brigade of Fars).[161] Also dispatched were Ahmad Nakhchevan (commander of the air force at the time) and Brigadier-General Fazlollah Zahedi. These reinforcements made virtually no impression against the tribal rebels. By late March 1929 a frustrated Shahbakhti telegraphed Tehran to report that "the few Brigadier-Generals sent here waste their time with amusements and play tennis" and take no action against raiding tribes at Shiraz.[162] The telegram also noted plummeting troop morale and the need for a new and more capable senior officer to take charge and subdue the tribal rebels.

An angry Reza Shah relieved and demoted Firouz, Zahedi, and Nakhchevan. Habibollah Sheibani was appointed to assume command of all armed forces in Shiraz on May 1929. Sheibani's tenure was fraught with risk from the outset. As he left Isfahan for Shiraz with an armed escort he was attacked by up to 800 Qashqai horsemen. The situation became so desperate that the officers, including Sheibani, were forced into close-quarter gun battles against the attackers. After heavy losses, Sheibani reached Shiraz in early June 1929. The very next day, the Qashqais, led by Mehdi Sorkhi, launched a deadly raid against Shiraz airport.[163]

Sheibani immediately led the armed forces out of Shiraz to force a final showdown with the Qashqais. After three battles, the two major leaders of the Qashqais, Solar ol Dowleh and Ismail Khan Qashqai, surrendered after having suffered heavy losses. Sheibani proved magnanimous and took no reprisals. In return Solar ol Dowleh and Ismail Khan Qashqai joined the Iranian army. Together these forces campaigned to restore government authority among other rebellious tribes in the area. Iranian army units then mopped up remaining Qashqai resistance during July and August. Shahbakhti and his forces had in the meantime moved out of Shiraz to pacify the Mamasani tribes. By the early September the Rezapour regiment supported by artillery had obtained the submission of Molla Qobad Sisakhti and disarmed his men at Sisakht near Kohgiluyeh. The Rezapour regiment ran into some trouble in Dashtestan (near Bushehr) in early October but prevailed with the arrival of reinforcements and disarmed the local tribes. By December 1929, the Pahlavi regiment had successfully disarmed the tribes at Lar. The Rezapour regiment simultaneously swung to the south of Fars province to disarm other tribes in Bushehr province along the Persian Gulf. By early June 1930, all remaining pockets of resistance in Fars province and the south had been cleared.

With Fars and Bushehr secured, Sheibani now had to face the formidable Boyer Ahmad region in the southwest. The region is especially strategic as it is situated between Khuzistan and Fars. Its geography is also unique in the area as it is mostly mountainous and connected to the Zagros mountain range. The area was completely out of central government control and Tehran wanted its tribal warriors disarmed. The leaders of the Boyers, Imam Gholi Khan, Mir Gholam, Shokrollah Khan, and Gholamali Khan placed Sarteep Khan in overall command against the army. They recalled their exploits against Nader Shah and Nasser e Din Shah, whose armies had been blocked from entering Boyer territory, thanks to its difficult and narrow passes. The Boyers had nicknamed the Tang e Namoradi (Namoradi narrow pass) ingress into their territory the "Tang e Sarbazkosh" (lit. soldier-slaying narrow pass).

Sheibani assembled four regiments (Rezapour, Pahlavi, Naderi, and Fateh cavalry), units from the Fars Division, and 500 Qashqai tribal cavalry.[164] The force was supported by two armored vehicles and mountain artillery. Sheibani deployed his forces forward towards the Boyer heartland on July 5, 1930. Sheibani's troops were ambushed on the night of July 17, with a number of senior officers killed and injured. This failed to deter Sheibani's advance, who weathered constant hit-and-run attacks by the Boyers. Fighting intensified as Sheibani's forces reached Cheshme Chenar and Kakan, finally reaching Tall e Khosravi on July 30. Sheibani then bogged down in heavy fighting against the Boyers but succeeded in reaching Dashte Rum on August 1. Fighting continued to escalate as Sheibani advanced closer to Tang e Namoradi. The Boyers launched another furious assault at Dashte Rum, resulting in a 24-hour battle. Sheibani dispersed the attackers and reached Tang e Namoradi on August 4 after fighting off yet more hit-and-run attacks. Sheibani now had to force his way through the Tang e Namoradi pass.

The attack to force the pass quickly ran into trouble. Elements of the Pahlavi regiment were so badly mauled that they were unable to retreat. A rescue was attempted by elements of the Rezapour brigade but these were beaten back by the Boyers. The Pahlavi troops soon ran critically low on supplies and water. Bitter fighting then continued for another four days, resulting in at least 300 Pahlavi casualties. The Boyers succeeded in capturing stores and supplies from their opponents. Sheibani's forces were reaching the end of their tether, as available forces in Isfahan could not arrive on time to rescue them. It seemed that the deadly Tang e Namoradi would defy Sheibani as it had Nader Shah and Nasser e Din Shah generations before. Tehran turned to the nearby Bakhtiari tribes for help. These obliged by furnishing 400 of their excellent cavalry which immediately proceeded towards Tang e Namoradi. In the meantime, the Naderi regiment had managed to pry open a route, eventually reaching Mamasani. By the end of August, the Rezapour regiment had finally stormed through the Tang e Namoradi and disarmed the Boyer Ahmadi warriors. The fighting in the south had come to an end.

Baluchistan: battles in the southeast

Baluchistan had been one of Iran's most severely neglected regions, and by the 1920s the region was clearly ripe for revolt. The government's writ in Baluchistan was tenuous at best: banditry, smuggling and raids were commonplace. By 1923, Baluchi raiders had reached as far as the cities of Bam and Kerman, causing alarm in Tehran. Reza Khan responded by sending forces from Fahraj (in Kerman province) towards Bampour to confront the Baluch rebels led by Dost Mohammad Khan Ismailzai. A number of forts were established in Zahedan and Iranshahr, but these proved inconsequential. Policing the vast 530-mile (850-km) frontier with British India was virtually impossible. For seven years (1923–30), Ismailzai successfully obtained weapons from British Indian territories adjacent to Iranian Baluchistan.

In 1930, Reza Shah appointed Brigadier-General Amanollah Jahanbani to defeat Ismailzai and disarm his Baluchi tribesmen. By late November, Jahanbani's forces were ready to move against Ismailzai and assembled in Zahedan, the capital of Baluchistan province.[165] These deployed into the interior of the province in three columns on December 8. Two aircraft also supported Jahanbani by acting as observation scouts and dropping leaflets on rebellious tribes, urging them to disarm and surrender. By late December, serious clashes were taking place between Jahanbani's forces and Ismailzai's men. Baluchi warriors engaged in hit-and-run attacks but Jahanbani forced them to retreat. Ismailzai and his men then fled into the vicinity of Koohak and took refuge inside a fortress. Jahanbani soon caught up and surrounded the fortress. Seeing this, Ismailzai and his followers requested surrender and immunity from prosecution. Jahanbani sent Colonel Bagher Davarpanah and a small cavalry escort towards the fortress for negotiations, but just as they approached the fortress gate, they were all killed at close range by gunfire. Jahanbani responded to Ismailzai's treachery by ordering his artillery to fire into the fortress. After a few hours of continuous bombardment, Ismailzai's men surrendered. Jahanbani set firm conditions for accepting the surrender. All fighters and local inhabitants of the fortress were to evacuate the area and all weapons were to be unconditionally surrendered. Jahanbani's demands were met, leading to an end of all hostilities. The fortress was renamed as Qale Davarpanah (Davarpanah fortress).

Ismailzai and fellow rebel chiefs were pardoned and brought to Tehran, where they were given homes and government salaries. After a short stay, Ismailzai and his followers left Tehran to restart their rebellion in Baluchistan. They were intercepted by the army at Semnan, returned to Tehran, and executed. This action, along with the brutality of a number of army personnel in Baluchistan, ignited a new rebellion by 1935. Brigadier-General Abbas Alborz was appointed to bring the rebels to heel and operations unfolded much as they had before: the rebels engaged in hit-and-run attacks, the army chased them back into a fortress and then forced them to surrender. Despite Alborz's assurances, 40 of the rebels were executed. This action greatly angered Tehran; Alborz was demoted and sent to prison for 15 years. Tehran worked to make amends by ordering its new commanders in Baluchistan to engage in construction works and housing projects for the local populace. The fighting in Baluchistan had come to an end. Iran now witnessed peace after decades of turmoil.

CHAPTER 27

THE IRANIAN ARMY (1921–41)

The origins of Iranian nationalism are often attributed to the Reza Shah era, but in fact can be traced to the writings of Tarnscaycasian Fathali Akhundzadeh (1812–78), at least fifty years before Reza Shah.[1] Akhundzadeh first made reference to the glory of pre-Islamic Persia and lamented its downfall at the hands of Arabs.[2] Akhundzadeh's writings exerted a profound influence on subsequent Persian-language writers who became vociferous advocates for reforms in Iran.[3]

Iranians had become sensitive on the issue of territorial integrity. They had witnessed the Anglo-Russian agreement of 1907 dividing their country into "spheres of influence," occupation before, during and after the First World War, the separatist rebellion of Simko, and demands for secession by the Caucasian Azerbaijan Republic and Istanbul pan-Turkists for Iranian Azerbaijan.[4] These developments alarmed Iranian intellectuals, a handful of which reacted by writing chauvinistic anti-Turkish poems.[5] This was soon followed by the *Ayandeh* (*Future*) magazine's first issue penned by its editor, Mahmoud Afshar, entitled "*Gozashteh-Emrooz-Farda*" (*Past-Today-Future*) which expressed concerns for the future of Iran's unity, namely its long-term political independence and territorial integrity.[6] The Soviet Union expended considerable efforts towards undermining Iranian national identity and by the 1930s accused the Iranian establishment of "Persian chauvinism."

Four years before the Second World War, Iran, Turkey, Afghanistan and Iraq signed a major treaty of cooperation and friendship on July 8, 1937 in Reza Shah's palace at Se-adat-abad. The three overall objectives were that the states would respect each other's territorial boundaries; support each other against attacks by outside powers; and refrain from interfering in each others' internal affairs.[7] One of the provisions of the treaty pertaining to Iran, Iraq, and Turkey, was their pledge to stop inciting Kurds in adjacent states against their respective governments.[8] The treaty became meaningless when the British and the Russians invaded Iran in 1941.

Modernization comes to Iran

Iran's first drive towards modernization can be traced to the aims of the Constitutional Revolution of 1905–09.[9] These were finally put into motion during Reza Shah's 16-year reign. Iran's achievements were miraculous, especially for an economically bankrupt nation that was on the verge of political and territorial disintegration by the end of the First World War.[10]

Reza Shah built over 14,000 miles of highways and roads and the number of cars rose exponentially from just 600 in 1925 to 25,000 in 1942.[11] Perhaps his greatest achievement was the 850-mile Trans-National railroad, which finally linked southern and northern Iran.[12] The development of Iran's road and railway system dramatically reduced the cost and time involved in transporting goods.[13] The cost of transport by 1933 had been cut to a third of what it had been in 1920 and the time involved had been reduced to one-tenth.[14]

By August 1941, over 6,000 miles of telephone cables had been laid across the country.[15] The 1926 Civil Service Act introduced reforms to Iran's civil service and educational systems. By 1934 Iran's first European-style university had been inaugurated.[16] Women were encouraged to obtain secondary and post-secondary education, and to enter public life and the professions.[17] The wearing of the veil for women also became illegal by law, an action later criticized by the clergy and by members of the Iranian Left.[18]

Reza Shah pushed for industrial self-sufficiency by ordering components for a steel-mill factory, but plans were thwarted by the Anglo-Soviet invasion in 1941.[19] Nevertheless the number of industrial plants increased 17-fold during Reza Shah's tenure with over 64 state-owned industrial plants established.[20] The industrial workforce increased seven times in comparison to 1900.[21] By the late 1930s, all of Iran's major cities had electric power.[22]

Taxation was regulated and national banking was finally brought under Iranian control through the offices of a national bank. New commercial treaties were negotiated with Western states. Higher tariffs were now imposed on foreign goods, finally protecting Iranian domestic industries, especially the traditional sector. Iran had come a long way since its humiliating economic concessions with Russia and the British. The elimination of rebellion, banditry and raids in the provinces finally allowed for a stable legal system in Iran, and civil courts on the French model were established. The cumulative impact of these reforms was a ten-fold increase in the country's revenues, a statistic also a function of Iran's petroleum revenues.[23]

However, despite massive efforts towards industrialization, the Iranian industrial sector by 1947 was only around 5% of the total Iranian economy. The agricultural sector had also been neglected resulting in the decrease of agricultural workers' living standards. Iranian industrial goods were generally inadequate for export. Government efforts at subsidizing local industries contributed to inflation. The cultural programs of "Europeanization" by enforcing uniform dress and urbanization upon Iran's disparate nomadic tribal regions also elicited resentment which helped contribute to the revolts in the south and the west.

The clergy were wary of the rapid pace of changes and the social impact these would have on society's traditional (Islamic) values, while Reza Shah was increasingly contemptuous of the religious establishment.[24] Reza Shah showed a very firm hand against the clergy, attacking the Goharshad Mosque in Mashad in August 1935 with artillery, machineguns and small arms.[25] Reza Shah also disbanded the Sharia court systems further undermining the clergy's influence.[26] Former representatives of the constitutional movement were also disappointed to witness Reza Shah's increasingly autocratic system of rule.[27] Saikal offers another view by observing that "He had been severely criticized for his absolutism, and his reforms have often been overlooked."[28] In practice many of the deeply-rooted and long-term problems of Qajar Iran persisted well into Reza Shah's time. Despite the massive strides in the economic, education and legal domains, Iran still had a long way to go.

The Iranian army (1921–41)

With the rebellions in Iran's provinces finally quashed, the country could focus on building a single Iranian military machine. When Reza Shah conducted his coup in early 1921, the total number of "official" forces (excluding the SPR) stood at a total of 22,800 men, organized within the Persian Cossack Brigade (7,000 men), the Gendarmerie (12,000), former Qajar-era brigades in Tehran (1,800) and units beholden to the former (Qajar) ministry of war (2,000 men).[29] On December 6, 1921, Reza Shah ordered the unification of the Gendarmerie and Persian Cossacks into a single force.[30] The SPR were disbanded by October 1921, with some of its Iranian officers and troops entering the new Iranian army.[31] The army was finally a united force led by Iranian officers, one of the original aims of the Iranian Constitutional Revolution.

Reza Shah placed a high priority towards the modernization and expansion of Iran's armed forces, now known as the Imperial Iranian Armed Services (IIAS). By January 5, 1922 Reza Shah had ordered the formation of five *Lashgars* (divisions) composed of 10,000 men each.[32] These were the First (Central) Division based in Tehran, the Second (Northwest) Division based in Tabriz, the Third (Western) Division based in Hamadan, the Fourth (Southern) Division based in Isfahan, and the Fifth (Khorasan) Division based in Mashad.[33] The defense of Iran was rationalized by dividing the country into five military regions composed of the north (Gilan, Mazandaran, Semnan, Tehran), northwest (Azarbaijan), west (Kurdistan, Kermanshah, Luristan), south-southwest (Fars, Khuzistan, Persian Gulf coast, Seistan-Baluchistan) and northeast (mainly Khorasan and environs to its south and west).[34]

By 1930, up to 50% of Iran's gross national product had been assigned to the military sector to help in the creation and expansion of a Ministry of War, the purchase of aircraft, combat vehicles and ships, the building of armaments factories, formation of security forces, and the provision of scholarships for cadets to study in European military academies.[35] Iran's inventory of rifles, machineguns, and artillery stood at 37,325; 66; and 86 respectively in 1922. By 1941 Iran possessed 507,587 rifles, 8,158 machineguns, and 874 cannon.[36] While Iran ordered much of its equipment from abroad, the buildup of these items was also assisted by the Iranian armaments industries. By the Second World War most units were equipped with modern rifles and machineguns.[37] During that period Iran ordered approximately 300,000 rifles, 350 cannon (mainly light and medium calibers – some motorized) and 6,000 heavy and light machineguns.[38] The artillery force continued to use antiquated equipment such as the Bofors 75-mm mountain guns and the Shneider-Cruezot 75-mm cannon. Nevertheless, in just 19 years, Iran's inventory of rifles and cannon had increased ten-fold and its machinegun inventory had grown 120-fold.

Iran also built up its armored combat vehicles and tanks during the interwar years. The first tanks arriving into Iran in 1925 were the French FT-17 light tanks armed with a 7.92-mm machinegun followed by the US-made Marmon Herrington also armed with machineguns.[39] By the onset of the Second World War, Iran had around 200 tanks, with the most modern of these being the Czech-built AH–IV and TNH light tanks armed with the 37-mm gun.[40] The TNH was very popular in both military and civilian circles. Up to 300 more were ordered but never delivered due to the Anglo-Soviet invasion. Iran also possessed 120 armored vehicles on the eve of the Second World War. These included the British Rolls Royce India (1921) Pattern armored cars with Vickers machineguns, along with more potent types such as the American-made LaFrance TK-6 armored car armed with a 37cm main gun and two machineguns. Despite the rise of the armored corps, cavalry remained Iran's primary weapon for rapid attack and maneuver. This was because Iran's armored forces had yet to assume the primary role in such operations. For this to evolve, the Iranian army needed a professional cadre of officers knowledgeable in the latest methods of European armored warfare. Iran did have numbers of such officers trained in European schools, but these could not advance to higher ranks due to overall problems in the upper echelons of command.

Cconscription continued to be based upon the antiquated Qajar-era Bunichah system where each district was called upon for recruits, with numbers based on calculations of that region's amount of cultivated land.[41] This helps explain why each of the army's five divisions remained below its target strength of 10,000 men and by 1926, the army only had a total of 40,000 troops.[42] Mass conscription finally allowed for a dramatic expansion of Iranian army personnel.[43] By 1930 the army stood at 85,000 men (supported by a newly established 12,000-man Gendarmerie service, the Amnieh), expanding to 105,000 by 1937, and reaching a maximum of 126,000 men in 16 divisions by the onset of the Second World War.[44]

Iran had a number of military training academies in 1921, but these were geared to serve the separate organizations of the Persian Cossack Brigade, the Gendarmerie, and the Tehran contingents of the former Qajar military. While a number of good education programs were already in place, especially at the Gendarmerie, Iran's military education program was disorganized as each service had its own distinct curriculum. Efforts at military education reform were considered in 1921. All of the academies and their curricula were finally brought under a single management through a new organization named "Madares e Kol e Ghoshoon" (all of/entire schools of the army). This new organization had by 1936 created an entirely new military education system. Institutions were established at the elementary (*Dabestan e Nezam* or military school), secondary (*Dabirestan e Nezam* or military high school), and post-secondary levels, notably the *Daneshkadeye Afsari* (officers' college), *Dansehkadeye Fanni* (technical military college) and the *Daneshgahe Jang* (war university).[45]

The rising armaments industry

Efforts were made from 1921 to reform existing Qajar-era factories, which already had machinery of Austrian, French, and British manufacture. German expertise was brought in to organize and manage the plants with new machinery also delivered.[46]

When Reza Shah began to organize a unified army, he was faced with the problem of multiple types of armaments as the different services all had their own unique weapons; the Qajar army had used the old British four-pounder cannon while the Gendarmes used the French Shneider-Cruezot 75-mm cannon.[47] The variety of weapons increased as the army captured the weapons of recently subdued tribal rebels. Despite these challenges, the high command succeeded in standardizing much of its equipment and aummunition by the late 1930s.

Iran's armament industries began to show signs of high efficiency by 1941. The implementation of administrative reforms in military factories resulted in better management and organization. This resulted in increased production and quality control. Newly built plants included Saltanatabad's rifle factory, the Doshan Tappeh machinegun factory, and the Parchin military research facility.[48]

The Iranian air force

On June 1, 1924, Reza Khan issued a directive separating the Air Office of the IIAS into a distinct branch of the armed services independent of the army. Two years later the air service was officially recognized as the Iranian Air Force. By August 1924, Iranian air cadets were training in France and Russia. The Junkers Company had begun operating a civilian air service shuttling between Tehran, Mashad, Shiraz, Bushehr, Anzali, Baku, western India, and Turkey. Junkers aircraft and personnel were utilized to provide military air reconnaissance and possibly transportation for the IIAS in 1924. In that year, Iran took delivery of 10 combat aircraft from France, Germany, and Russia; by 1926 this number had doubled to 20 machines and increased to 30 with the arrival of 10 Russian Polyakareyev R-5 aircraft by June 1933. Iran's air force grew to 122 Hawker series combat aircraft (Audax, Hind, and Fury) by 1941 with only 40 of these outdated machines fit for combat when the Anglo-Soviets invaded in August 1941.[49] Iran also had around another 160 aircraft (i.e. trainers, transport, etc).[50] In practice, only the ten P-38 Curtiss combat aircraft at Ahvaz were capable of challenging British and Russian aircraft, but only one of these had been assembled from its kit.[51] Iran's obsolescent aircraft were distributed to four major airbases in Tehran, Ahvaz, Tabriz, and Mashad.[52] The latter three were decommissioned after the Anglo-Soviet invasion of Iran in August 1941. The Iranian air force had a total of 1,000 trained personnel at the eve of the Anglo-Soviet invasion.[53]

The Iranians worked hard to develop indigenous aircraft maintenance and production facilities. By August 1932 technical schools for the repair of aircraft and pilot training had been established. Three years later, production machinery for aircraft manufacturing had arrived from England, France, and the United States.[54] The Shahbaz Aircraft manufacturing plant was then formally inaugurated at Doshan Tappeh on September 12, 1936. The plant produced ten Hawker Audex combat aircraft that same year under license.[55] Plans were underway to produce more combat aircraft but the onset of the Second World War put a halt to these projects.

The Iranian navy

The Nasser e Din Shah-era *Persepolis* and *Shoush* were finally decommissioned in 1921. This left just the four vessels acquired by Ahmad Shah to form the nucleus of a new Iranian navy. After the fall of Sheikh Khazal, three of his ships were appropriated. One of these, renamed as the *Homa*, was capable of carrying 1,000 troops and could operate as far as the Indian Ocean. The other two were contracted to American naval engineers for repairs.

Iran took delivery of its first German-built minesweeper (141 tons) in April 1925. Despite this, the navy remained incapable of disrupting piracy and smuggling along the Persian Gulf coastline. The seriousness of the situation prompted the Majlis to legislate the buildup of the Iranian Navy on March 20, 1928.[56] Italian naval experts were used to purchase ships suitable for Iran's needs. The first cadre of European-trained Iranian naval officers arrived from Italy in 1933. The Navy then took delivery of nine Italian-built ships (two ships of 950 tons each, four ships at 330 tons, and three smaller craft at 75 tons).[57]

The Caspian Sea had a diminutive "navy" of one ship. A few gunboats and tugs were later added, and by 1936 Iran had formed a coastguard for its Caspian Sea coastline.[58] The northern (Caspian Sea) coastguard and the small southern (Persian Gulf) fleet were each supported by naval repair facilities at newly built docks, mobile repair ships, fire-fighting ships, hospital ships, and floating barges.[59]

CHAPTER 28

THE SECOND WORLD WAR AND THE ANGLO-SOVIET INVASION OF IRAN

Shortly after his seizure of power in 1921, Reza Shah had sought foreign expertise to help Iran's drive towards modernization. While relations with Russia and England were cordial and constructive, the Iranian populace and intelligentsia retained vivid memories of recent British and Russian domination. The Iranians first turned to the United States for help in their industrialization drive, but their overtures were ignored. This led them to seek assistance from Germany, another country which had no history of imperialism in Iran. Iranian fears of Communism and Russian imperial ambitions helped propel the Iranians towards cooperation with Germany.[1]

The German Junkers Airline Company were contracted to develop Iran's postal services, railway system, and the Bank Melli of Iran in 1927–30.[2] As Iranian dependence on German technical expertise grew so too did pro-German sentiments.[3] By the onset of the Second World War, Germany was Iran's major trading partner.[4] Iran declared her neutrality on September 4, 1939, but the pro-German wing in Iran was soon equating German victories with Britain's ultimate defeat.[5] Britain was also concerned with the real possibility of a Soviet collapse which would allow the Germans to advance through the Caucasus into Iran.[6] Even before Britain invaded Iran in August 1941, she was already making aggressive moves at sea to diminish the growing German–Iranian relationship. A vivid example of this was the British confiscation of a German ship bringing parts for a steel mill factory in Iran.[7]

Germany invaded Russia on June 22, 1941, leading to a new alliance between London and Moscow. Iran declared her neutrality in this Russo-German conflict just four days later.[8] This again failed to assuage British and Soviet concerns about the German presence in Iran.[9] However, the situation was nowhere near that simple. Irano-British relations were actually improving as late as May 1941, when the British offered to ease the war's pressure on Iranian merchants suffering losses to their businesses.[10] The British retained enormous influence in Iran, especially in the vital petroleum sector and the Anglo-Iranian Oil Company's tanker fleet was contributing to the British war effort.[11] British influence was also highly significant in Iran's military sector. Reza Shah had signed an arms deal with London in 1939, but the British soon backtracked from this stating that they needed all their available military supplies.[12] British influence in Iranian military aviation was already significant with many of Iran's aircraft being of British design.[13] Conversely, there are now believed to have been only 600 Germans within Iran rather than the 3,000 estimated by the British.[14] The Turks had been skeptical of British claims from the outset and in August 1941, Shukri Saracoglu, the Turkish foreign minister, told the British ambassador to Turkey that they rejected the British estimate, as Turkish observers reported just 580.[15] Saracoglu did not consider there to be much of a German threat in Iran, especially as the Germans were employed in education, commerce, domestic industries and the construction of an armaments plant.[16]

Reza Shah was also increasingly suspicious of German plots to eject him from power in favor of a pro-German government.[17] Berlin wanted to distract the Soviets towards Iran and calculated that a pro-German coup would encourage a Soviet invasion, resulting in a clash with the British.[18] All German efforts at intrigue were mainly blocked by Iranian surveillance services, and British intelligence officials were aware of this.[19]

These reports failed to allay British fears of a pro-German coup in Tehran. This had a lot to do with events in Iraq where Rashid Ali al-Gilani's nationalist and pro-Axis revolt in April–June 1941 had received not only supplies from the Germans, but Germany had even flown a number of combat aircraft into Iraq to bomb and strafe British forces.[20] Interestingly, German demands for Tehran to supply fuel lubricants for Iraqi fighters were refused due to fears of British military retaliation.[21] After his defeat, Rashid Ali and his followers fled to Tehran and then to Ankara.[22] His departure from Iran did little to assuage London's concerns. British planners remained worried about the possibility of German action in Iran and the defeated Iraqi revolt was to have profound long-term consequences for Iran as well.

Finally, while Nazi propaganda sought to make much of the "Aryan" connection between Iran and Germany, the Iranians had very little affinity with the anti-Semitic policies of Nazi Germany. This is aptly seen in the works of Mr. Abdol Hussein Sardari (1895–1981), the "Schindler of Iran."[23] Sardari was the head of the Iranian consular mission in Nazi-ccupied Paris in 1941. He saved Iranian Jews there from certain death by insisting they be treated as full Iranian citizens, and then issued up to 1,500 Iranian passports to European Jews to shield them from the Nazis.[24] Sardari's actions were fully supported and celebrated by the Iranian government.[25] This helps puts the nature of the so-called "pro-German" Iranian sentiments in perspective. Iranians were more anti-British and anti-Russian than "pro-German," due to their experiences with British and Russian imperialism in the 19th and early 20th centuries.[26]

Cronin provides four reasons for London's decision to invade Iran: to secure the Iranian railway to provide supplies for the Soviet war effort against Nazi Germany; to expel German and Axis nationals in Iran; to prevent a pro-Axis revolt and; to eject Reza Shah from power.[27] To this list may be added the securing of Iranian oilfields for the Allied war effort.[28] Abadan refinery was able to produce around 8,000,000 barrels of oil per year by 1940. This was of vital importance to the Allied war effort, and the British were determined to retain this at all costs. The securing of the Iranian land-route was especially vital as German U-boat attacks made the shipping of supplies to Arkhangelsk in Russia dangerous and costly. Reza Shah, who had already declared Iran's neutrality, had yet to take serious steps to expel German nationals from Iran. He was not inclined to allow open Anglo-Soviet access to the Iranian railway, nor was he prepared to renounce Germany altogether.[29]

The Soviets hardly needed any persuasion to join the British in an invasion of Iran. Soviet intentions for invading Iran however were far more long-term than the British. Moscow wanted to annex Iranian territory. The Soviets had already engaged in the forcible annexation of territory before the German invasion of Russia in places such as Estonia, Latvia, and Lithuania. As the war drew to a close in 1945, Soviet territorial appetites in Iran would become rapaciously transparent.

The British soon realized that they could not count on unqualified American support for their intended invasion of Iran. The American position was initially not all that different from the Turks. The British had yet to convince the Americans and the Turks that there was a need for military action against Iran. Turkish newspapers openly disparaged the Anglo-Soviet position on Iran on August 15, 1941.[30] The same Turkish papers praised Iran's position of neutrality.[31]

The British proved much more successful in swaying the Americans. Winston Churchill, realizing that American support for his Iranian adventure was not guaranteed, personally discussed the issue with President Roosevelt on August 11, 1945. It is generally believed that Churchill discussed with Roosevelt the virtues of expelling the Germans in Iran and securing the Iranian railway to facilitate the transport of supplies for the Soviet Union. Churchill now had his "green light" to invade Iran in concert with his Soviet ally, Joseph Stalin.

Reza Shah was highly surprised when the Allies struck on August 25, 1941. He summoned Sir Reader Bullard and Andrey Andreyevich Smirnov, the British and Soviet ambassadors to Iran. He then asked them "I need to know why your forces have invaded my country? You haven't declared war on us."[32] The ambassadors' response was that the invasion had been triggered by the presence of German nationals in Iran. Reza Shah then replied "I will expel all the Germans. What then?"[33] The ambassadors could give no clear answer. Reza Shah then sent a telegram to Roosevelt asking him to mediate between himself and the Anglo-Soviets. Roosevelt, already aware of Anglo-Soviet intentions, proved evasive. He did not offer to mediate but stated in general terms that Iranian territorial integrity and political independence would be respected.[34]

The Iranian military on the eve of the Anglo-Soviet invasion

Iranian armed forces were rapidly defeated by the Anglo-Soviet invasion in late August 1941. Anglo-Soviet military forces certainly outmatched their Iranian counterparts, but there were also a number of profound liabilities in the Iranian military that had not been addressed by the Iranian high command.

There was little expertise at the highest echelons in fighting against modern armies equipped with tanks and combat aircraft. This was partly because the upper echelons of command were composed of Reza Shah's comrades from the former Persian Cossack Brigade.[35] These were mainly sycophantic "yes men" with more interest in their wealth and social position than in new military theories.[36] Their combat experience was limited to fighting tribal and regional forces during the early days of the rise of Reza Shah. In contrast, the promising young cadre of European-trained officers. was barred from making any meaningful contribution due to the entrenched conservatism of the senior commanders.[37] Similarly, Reza Shah had failed to delegate many of the military's more mundane duties. He retained the command of almost every trivial detail in the military. This led to the development of a rigid top-down system of command, grossly impeding initiative and decision-making among the officer corps.[38]

While the Iranian military was a large force in 1941, it was mainly geared towards internal security operations rather than fighting well-led and equipped Western and Soviet armies, and the army lacked a coherent battle doctrine in the event of a major war.[39] There was no effective land–air doctrine for armored forces supported by air power.[40] The regional system of defense also proved to be a disastrous failure because the regions failed to coordinate their actions against the invasion.

The above problems were related to another serious weakness: an over-estimation of the army's efficiency. Reza Shah had witnessed a number of maneuvers in which the army gave a very "modern appearance": but these maneuvers may well have been carefully orchestrated, leading to unwarranted conclusions about the army's combat capabilities.[41] Even after the rapid collapse of the army in August 1941, many top army commanders failed to admit the fundamental causes of their failure. They tended to selectively attribute their defeat to inferior equipment and lack of mechanization.[42] Financial mismanagement continued within the army, meaning that soldiers were not always paid. When war broke out, supply and logistics systems failed to supply troops with the necessary equipment, some troops received the wrong ammunition or equipment, and most were given far less ammunition than required.[43]

Almost all the army's armored vehicles and mechanized regiments were concentrated in the capital, while divisions in critical border regions were inexplicably neglected.[44] This meant that Iranian units along the border regions had no adequate means of confronting mechanized enemy forces. The state of affairs was even worse against aircraft: the northern divisions had a combined total of just eight antiaircraft guns against the Soviet air force![45]

While conscription had certainly increased the army's size, it also led to a concomitant decrease in the force's overall fighting effectiveness.[46] Improving the military quality of the conscripts would require a new officer corps able to motivate the recruits and introduce better treatment and physical accommodation for them.

No plans had been made to make modern and rapid transportation a priority, and mobility was highly problematic as army units outside Tehran had a combined total of just 300 trucks, 66 motorcycles and 100 other vehicles. With the exception of Tehran (where the bulk of motorized transport was located) transportation and logistics was mainly reliant on horses and pack animals.

Excepting a few units, most of the army's divisions were deficient in modern wireless communications equipment. This obliged them to rely on civilian telephone lines, telegraph and even the postal services. Inexplicably the army did not incur the costs of communications services for its units. This meant that each unit had to pay from its own budget for communications, resulting in communications being kept to a minimum to save costs.[47] No serious efforts were made to arrive at a comprehensive, efficient and rapid communication system that would allow all units to coordinate their actions against enemy invasions. The air force also lacked wireless capabilities.[48] As events soon demonstrated, communications between the military's higher and lower echelons were wholly inadequate to confront the needs of modern mechanized warfare. It is no exaggeration to state that when the Anglo-Soviet invasion struck in August 1941, the Iranian military's left hand did not know what the right hand was doing.

Russians invade the north

The Soviet buildup was conducted in the utmost secrecy at a considerable distance from the Irano-Soviet border.[49] Moscow planned to invade Iran through the north and northwest. The forces entrusted for this invasion were Lieutenant-General Dmitri T. Kozlov's Transcaucasus Front, which consisted of the 44th and 47th armies.[50]

The 47th Army struck into Iranian Azarbaijan on the morning of August 25 at Pol Dasht.[51] The 47th Army was led by Major-General Vasilly V. Novikov. Novikov spearhead his assault with an overwhelming force of tanks into Tabriz and from there he intended to swing to Qazvin, the traditional invasion route used by Tsarist armies earlier in the century.[52] His second objective was to capture Rezaieh and then drive into Iranian Kurdistan. Novikov also thrust towards Maku to cut Iran off from the Turkish frontier.

The Soviet force of 40,000 troops, supported by 1,000 tanks, was double that of the 20,000 Iranian cavalry and infantry in Azarbaijan.[53] Even more crushing was the Soviet advantage in the air. The Transcaucasus Front was able to call upon 409 combat aircraft, including heavy bombers.[54] Against this vast air fleet stood Colonel Sheibani's 14 outdated Audax and Hind biplanes of the Second Iranian Air Regiment in Tabriz.[55] The rest of Iran's vintage fighter fleet was stationed in Tehran, Ahvaz, and Mashad.

The Iranians were badly underequipped and especially low on vital supplies and ammunition. The situation against Soviet armor was virtually hopeless. Iran could field a maximum of 200 tanks against a Soviet tank force five times their size. Soviet tanks were perhaps among the world's best at the time with machines such as the medium T-34 and the heavier KV-1 and KV-2 tanks which were far more powerful in terms of weaponry and armor than any vehicle found in Iran's modest inventory.

In practice most Soviet tanks invading Iran in August 1941 were of the T-26 light tank type (weight 9–10 tons). Iran's most modern tanks were the Czech-built CKD TNH (8.2 ton) series which though somewhat outgunned by the Soviet T-26 (37mm vs. 45mm main gun of the CKD TNH), were otherwise evenly matched in terms of armor (8–15mm vs. 6–15mm of the CKD TNH) and were slightly more mobile than its Soviet counterpart (38km/hr vs. 31km/hr of the CKD TNH). Even if Iran could have assembled all 50 of its CKD TNH tanks in northern Iran in time, these would have been too few to make any impression against the Soviet armored colossus. Despite their military superiority, the Soviets were apparently cautious at first as they quickly ran into resistance against a local Amnieh Gendarmerie border post armed with light weapons. These fought against vastly superior numbers of Soviet troops and tanks for a number of hours before being overwhelmed.[56]

The mainstay of Azarbaijan's defense rested on the 3rd Division of Tabriz and the 15th Division of Ardabil.[57] The 47th Army's 63rd Georgian Mountain Infantry Division charged forward to Maku from Pol e Dasht with T-26 light tanks.[58] Soviet bombers bombed Maku, but this failed to stop its troops from marching towards defensive positions commanding the ingress towards the local river and gulley.[59] They put up stout resistance against the Russian infantry and armor, but heavy losses forced them to retreat to Rezaieh.[60] Soviet forces and the Georgian 63rd then pushed towards Khoi and Rezaieh. Panic set in at Khoi as its 1,800-man cavalry force simply mounted their horses and fled towards the Turkish border.[61] At Rezaieh the 4th Infantry Division barracks had been bombed by Soviet aircraft, having been inadvertently guided by the firing of Iranian antiaircraft guns.[62] The 4th Infantry Division wanted to resist but its commander Major-General Moini was unable to organize a coherent defense, realizing that his stocks of ammunition and weapons were alarmingly low. He sent appeals to Tehran to send him ammunition and supplies while issuing a general call-out for his reservists to report for duty.[63]

Further to the northwest the Soviets easily crossed the Araxes to seize the town of Julfa. The left wing of the 47th Army, comprising one cavalry and one infantry division, led by tanks, thrust south into Azarbaijan aiming for Tabriz. Soviet bombers targeted the 3rd Division army base in

Tabriz, and antiaircraft gunners shot down one of them. The intensity of Tabriz's antiaircraft fire forced the other bombers to flee and jettison their bombs around Tabriz's city limits. Those bombs that did fall on the Tabriz base failed to inflict any significant damage. The garrison then quickly reorganized and prepared to fight the Russian invasion, but local arsenals could provide just five rounds of ammunition for each soldier![64] A convoy of 14 trucks laden with ammunition bound for the city was intercepted by Soviet troops.[65]

The army also had no food rations or medical supplies for wound care.[66] Major-General Matbooi had telegraphed Tehran for instructions and received orders to hold Tabriz, but this was clearly impossible. Matbooi considered marching towards Maragheh to make contact with the 4th Division at Rezaieh.[67] Soviet bombers soon returned to bomb Tabriz several times with incendiary bombs, igniting fires across the city.[68] Sheibani's aircrews undertook reconnaissance flights, which revealed a massive Soviet armored column of several hundred tanks south of Julfa rapidly pushing deeper into Iran towards Marand.[69] It would have been possible to block their advance at Shibli but the site remained unmanned as Matbooi failed to take advantage of his motorized capabilities to rapidly reach Shibli.[70]

The 44th Soviet Army crossed over into Ardabil and launched bombers against that city which caused minimal damage. The local garrison, 15th Division supported by two regiments, made preparations to march further south to confront the Russian troops. Two regiments were marching towards Nir to make their stand against the arriving Soviet troops when Brigadier-General Qaderi, after promising to bring supplies, weapons, and rations, drove off in his car leaving his men to their fate. The column had been transporting vital supplies of ammunition, artillery for the 15th Division but Qaderi had ordered that these be removed from the vehicles to make way for his personal belongings.[71] The 44th Army however was not interested in Nir but in pushing further south into Iran's Gilan province.

By the next day, August 26, Iranian forces in the northwest had fallen into disarray due to persistent problems with supplies, communications and organization. The 3rf Division from Tabriz was marching west but this was soon forced to halt and disperse due to lack of food, water, ammunition, and medical supplies. By now, many top commanders had simply taken to their heels and abandoned their men to the Russians. The troops managed to maintain order but were soon forced to abandon their heavy equipment, especially cannon. Perhaps one of Matbooi's greatest failures was failing to quickly destroy vital roads and bridges despite having access to large supplies of explosives for demolition purposes.[72]

The 15th Ardabil Division, east of Tabriz, was marching to Sain Gaduki but their efforts were also in vain due to lack of supplies, food, and ammunition. This led to widespread demoralization and desertion. The desperate situation prompted Sheibani and all local pilots in Tabriz to try and prevent the capture of their biplanes. The pilots were given the option to flee by car, but they all volunteered to fly with Sheibani.[73] They flew west to Zanjan, where they refueled, and then resumed their flight towards Tehran.[74] The remnants of the 3rf Division and Matobooi reached Malayer and remained there until Reza Shah's departure from Iran.[75] Isolated pockets of machinegunners and snipers gallantly fought against the Soviets, who extinguished them in short order. The occupation of Azarbaijan had begun.

The first Soviet action against Gilan was by Rear-Admiral Sedelnikov's Caspian Sea Flotilla. Thia sailed from Baku towards the northern Iranian coastline, escorting freighters and tankers laden with troops and equipment. Sedelnikov's force was composed of a small naval force of six gunboats, four auxiliary escort patrol boats, as well as torpedo boats, submarine chasers, small patrol craft, and an unspecified type of aircraft carrier.[76] Three floating antiaircraft platforms were also deployed in case of Iranian air attacks.[77] Sedelnikov split his fleet in two on August 25: one headed for Astara and the other to Bandar Pahlavi (now Anzali). The Iranian Caspian navy had no more than three 30-ton gunboats and two other vessels to confront the Soviet armada.[78]

The Soviet land invasion into Gilan was led by General A. A. Khadeev's 44th Army. Khadeev proceeded along the Caspian coastline into Gilan and northern Iran. Landing Soviet troops at the port city of Astara, very close to the Soviet border, were soon joined by Khadeev's tanks and motorized infantry advancing from the north. In contrast to Astara, initial Soviet efforts to take Bandar Pahlavi ran into unexpected resistance. General Iranpour, the local regimental commander, deployed his forces in the dense forests facing the beach where Russian troops were hoping to land by sea. Captain Daftari sank a platform in front of the beach barring the entry of Soviet ships into the harbor. As the area lacked coastal guns, Iranpour placed a battery of four 75-mm guns for defense.[79] The second Soviet flotilla from Baku arrived at Bandar Pahlavi to be greeted by two volleys of Iranpour's cannon. The Soviets responded with three salvos but then withdrew.[80] In the meantime Soviet bombers had attacked Bandar Pahlavi, Rasht and the Gilan army barracks. The Soviet fleet returned to bomb Bandar Pahlavi but Iranpour's guns and the blocked harbor prevented Soviet troops from landing. Iranian gunners were careful not to fire their guns at Soviet ships when Soviet aircraft flew overhead. This prevented Soviet planes from pinpointing the guns' location. Soviet planes were also kept at bay by the machineguns and 47-mm guns of the three Iranian gunboats.[81]

Soviet aerial assaults were more successful the following day when large numbers of bombers were dispatched in groups of four all over Gilan. Their most successful strike was against a machinegun position at Qazian (near Rasht).[82] Soviet bombers returned to bomb Gilan's naval stations, military barracks and a rehabilitation center. Resistance was finally crushed by Soviet troops advancing to Bandar Pahlavi and Rasht by land. An Iranian motorboat with a white flag approached Soviet vessels on August 28 to declare that Iranian forces had been ordered to cease fire.[83] Russian forces then disembarked at Bandar Pahlavi, to be later joined by a motorized battalion from Soviet Azarbaijan.[84] Soviet Azarbaijanis interrogated Captain Daftari at Bandar Pahlavi demanding that he yield the location of non-existent Iranian submarines![85]

The Soviet arrival into Bandar Pahlavi was not the end of resistance in Gilan. A Soviet aircraft flying over Rasht dropping leaflets came under fire from the antiaircraft guns of the Iranian 11th Division. Soviet bombers killed 100 soldiers in the barracks but the bulk of the division's troops remained defiant.[86] Before Soviet troops entered Rasht, troops of the 11th took what weapons and supplies they could and dispersed into the northern Iranian forests to continue their resistance.[87] Others retreated further into Ramsar, the westernmost district of neighboring Mazandaran.

Russians invade the northeast

Two days after the Anglo-Soviets struck, Colonel Motazedi and Major-General Mohtashemi, the commanders of the 10th Division at Gorgan and 9th Division at Mashad respectively, had received no instructions on how to counter a Soviet invasion from Central Asia. Anticipating an invasion, Mohtashemi, who had four regiments in Mashad, organized his forces into two mobile strike groups comprised of one infantry and cavalry regiment each supported by 75-mm and 105-mm artillery.[88] There were another two cavalry regiments stationed outside of the city.[89] The 10th Division's forces at Gorgan were spread dangerously thin and less prepared to face a Soviet invasion.

Lieutenant Sergei G. Trofimenko, based in Central Asia, attacked with his 53rd Independent Central Asia Army into the Iranian northeast on August 27. This crossed the Atrak River along the exposed Iranian border from Afghanistan to the eastern shores of the Caspian Sea. Trofimenko's primary target was Mashad. The outnumbered Iranian border guards were quickly overcome and resistance by scattered elements of the 10th Division quickly crushed. Mohtashemi sent one of his task forces from Mashad to the northwest to confront the Soviet invaders and another to the Mazduran pass to defend the western approaches to Mashad.

Soviet air attacks against Mashad airport in the early dawn were met with fierce Iranian antiaircraft fire. Their resistance drastically reduced the effects of Soviet bombing against the main hangar and other aerodrome assets. The Soviets bombers returned against heavy Iranian antiaircraft fire, but succeeded in destroying six of 22 Iranian aircraft on the ground, demolishing a hangar and killing a number of crews.[90] Soviet aircraft, facing no Iranian fighters, proceeded to attack Mohtashemi's strike force at Mazduran. These now had no choice but to retreat to Mashad. Mohtashemi's other strike force in the northwest had also been forced to reatreat to Mashad after having been pummeled by Soviet artillery at Qhoochan. By now, many officers and men from the 9th and 10th Divisions had simply deserted. Mohtashemi did his best to salvage the situation by leading the remnants of the 9th Division towards Tehran for the anticipated last stand.[91] Other surviving regiments from Gorgan also began retreating south. Retreat orders were unpopular with many of the ordinary troops; many wept for not being allowed to stand and fight the Soviets.[92]

After the war, Mohtashemi noted his liabilities against the Soviets were his "lack of antitank/antiarmored vehicle weapons, ammunition, transport vehicles, supplies, and credibility."[93] Mohtashemi's candidness and brutal honesty is commendable especially in his usage of the term credibility. But the undermining of his credibility among his troops derived from factors beyond his control, namely the high command's problems with logistics and communications.

British invasion from the south

British forces invading from Iraq were under the overall command of Lieutenant-General Sir Edward Pellew Quinan. These forces were first known as the IraqForce, soon renamed PaiForce (Persia and Iraq Force). PaiForce was mostly composed of Indian troops who fought alongside the 4th British Cavalry brigade. Quinan's orders were to assemble military forces in the Persian Gulf to attack and seize Bandar Shapur, its port facilities and shipping assets; occupy Abadan, its refinery and oilfields; and attack the Qasr-e Shirin area to seize the Naft-e Shah oilfields.[94]

Bandar Shapur was of key strategic importance to the Anglo-Soviets. It was the southern terminal of the Trans-National railroad. British forces opened their attack with a naval bombardment of Bandar Shapur at precisely 4:00am on August 25. This was almost exactly the time that Prime Minister Ali Mansour received the ultimatums of the British and Russian ambassadors in Tehran.[95]

The British-Australian naval group attacking Bandar Shapur consisted of 16 combat vessels led by Rear-Admiral Adams aboard the armored merchant-cruiser, HMAS *Kanimbla*.[96] The British captured up to eight German and Italian ships, though it is disputed how many were scuttled by their crews.[97] *Kanimbla* fired its six-inch guns at a train hurriedly departing Bandar Shapur's railway station which Adams suspected was transporting fleeing Axis sailors.[98] The train escaped unscathed but British operations soon netted 100 Axis prisoners.[99] Adams also captured two Iranian vessels; the *Kafkaz* and the *Shahbaz*.[100] Their crews offered some resistance but the ships could not operate their heavy weapons thanks to the lack of ammunition.[101] Bandar Shapur was soon captured by the *Kanimbla* which landed Baluchi troops from British India.[102] The Iranian commander of the port, Captain Abdollah Zeile, surrendered his sword, but the Iranian 18th Infantry Regiment refused to surrender.[103] With the 18th overcome, the fighting at Bandar Shapur came to a cordial end. That same evening, the British entertained the Iranian commander of the two gunboats as an honored guest aboard one of Adams' ships.[104] The captured high-ranking German and Italian officers were not invited.

The Iranian vessel *Palang* (commanded by Hassan Milanian) protected Abadan and its refinery.[105] The day before the outbreak of hostilities, the British sloop HMS *Shoreham* sailed into the Abadan area and took its position alongside the *Palang*. Yekranigian reports Milanian welcoming the British ship and extending an invitation for his British counterpart to visit.[106] Instead of a visit, the *Palang* received the firing of the *Shoreham*'s four-inch guns at 4:00am on August 25, causing massive explosions.[107] Milanian attempted to return fire but the damage was too great. One version of events states that Milanian and all hands were lost with another claiming that he led much of his crew safely ashore.[108] The *Shoreham* ceased firing, evidently fearing that more explosions from the *Palang* could spread to Abadan's refinery.[109]

Alerted by the explosions, Iranian troops in Abadan's refinery rushed to man their positions. The troops in Abadan city could not open their armory to distribute weapons.[110] Two British transport craft fired their three-inch guns against Iranian machinegun nests and landed their troops followed by more landing craft. Iranian machinegunners and riflemen fired furiously from the roof of the pumping station and jetty. Their resistance pinned down the British who suffered the loss of a few officers. British sources report that the Iranian troops "resisted with the highest bravery and … fought with tenacious gallantry."[111]

Shoreham now entered the fray by firing its machineguns to silence the Iranian machinegunners and riflemen. There was more fighting in the palm groves where a company of 60–70 Iranians withdrew after suffering 25 dead.[112] Further resistance was encountered in the European bungalow area where the Iranians trained an antiaircraft gun and machinegun against the invaders.[113] During this melee Sikh troops gunned down three employees of the AIOC, who they had mistaken for Iranian troops. The Sikhs also gunned down three Iranian ambulance men trying to evacuate the AIOC men.[114]

Abadan and its streets had to be cleared against fierce Iranian resistance which "fought to the last man."[115] The Iranians were finally overcome by the guns of the *Shoreham* and some landing craft. Colonel Ahmad Nackchevan arrived in the early morning, and discovered to his horror that Abadan's armory doors were still locked! These were finally forced open but it was too late as the remaining unarmed Iranian troops had been forced to take cover along the Bahmanshir River.[116]

Realizing that Abadan was lost, Nackchevan ordered all remaining personnel and weapons transported by trucks towards Khuzistan's provincial capital, Ahvaz. Nackchevan's plans were foiled by British aircraft which quickly destroyed many of the trucks at the ferry terminal.[117] British air superiority was demonstrated by their unimpeded bombing of Iranian air bases, communication hubs, and supply lines. Nackchevan, Rear-Admiral Bayandor and Major-General Shahbakhti were all handicapped by inadequate communications and coordination.[118] By the next day, August 26, Iranian resistance had virtually ceased as British forces conducted vigorous patrols in Abadan city, the refinery and its environs.

Just minutes after the attack on the *Palang* at Abadan, the HMAS *Yarra* prepared its deadly assault against the *Babr* moored at Khorramshahr approximately 11 miles (16km) upstream from Abadan along the Arvand Rud/Shaat al Arab. The *Yarra* slammed ten salvos of four-and three-inch shells into its victim.[119] The *Babr* erupted into a series of explosions killing any of her crew.[120] Iranian naval marines at Khorramshahr's local barracks and navy staff building began returning fire with rifles and machineguns, but a single deadly shot by the *Yarra* into the barracks put an end to their resistance.[121]

The British attack had achieved perfect timing: the two Iranian gunboats (*Shahrokh* and *Simorgh*) that could have opposed them were not battle ready. The *Shahrokh* was undergoing a refit and had almost no ammunition to fight, while the *Simorgh's* crew were on shore leave![122] The only naval opposition was by a small naval training ship, the *Ivy*. This bravely but vainly fired at the *Yarra* which responded by tearing its wooden hull to pieces with its heavy machineguns.[123] The British then trained their machineguns on the decks of the *Simorgh* and *Shahrokh* to prevent their crew from manning their loaded Maxim machineguns. One machinegun crew reached the Maxim on the *Simorgh* but was cut down by the alert British machinegunners.[124] Both vessels were then captured. An armed tug and its barge also offered resistance and were boarded by force. The *Yarra* now landed its British-led Baluchi troops into Khorramshahr; the troops immediately ran into resistance from the Iranians at the waterfront, barracks, and various buildings. These were all cleared by bitter fighting, resulting in the capture of 30 Iranian prisoners, 400 rifles, 30 vehicles, and four machineguns.[125]

Rear-Admiral Bayandor, in command of the south Khuzistan-Persian Gulf area's 4,000 naval and ground forces had left Khorramshahr by car heading for the Pol-e-Now Bridge. He ordered the local forces to split into two. One force would defend the route to Khorramshar while the other would defend a munitions depot. Bayandor, accompanied by Captain Mokri-Nejad, commander of 6th Division's artillery, then continued on towards a wireless station to attempt communications with Tehran.[126] But time was running out as British (and Indian) forces were already advancing towards the wireless station. The British were halted by a group of Iranian troops with machineguns and rifles. The Iranians had also constructed a 2m-wide antitank ditch which held back a number of the British attacks. The British quickly changed tactics by bringing forward armored cars supported by heavy guns and mortar fire. As the armored cars fired their machineguns, British troops finally reached the ditch and after bitter close-quarter fighting cleared out the Iranian troops. This was followed by the British capture of the wireless station. Just as the station fell, a staff car carrying Bayandor and Mokri-Nejad sped out of the station's compound. The British fired a warning shot but the car continued. British forces gave chase and fired at the car, forcing it to stop. The driver,

Bayandor and Mokri-Nejad jumped out of the vehicle and were machinegunned. Mokri-Nejad was killed immediately and Bayandor was fatally wounded, dying soon after. The following day the British conducted a military ceremony in Khorramshahr honoring Bayandor.[127] Bayandor is still commemorated as a hero among Iranian army personnel.

There had also been resistance to the north of Khorramshahr, notably at the Qasr e Sheikh fortress.[128] This was held by Tehran's 1st Pahlavi Regiment supported by a battery of 75-mm howitzers. An attack by British armored cars and Sikh troops was stalled by Iranian artillery and machineguns but much of their firing was inaccurate and failed to inflict much damage. The nearby trenches were cleared of Iranian troops and the fort was finally encircled by the armored cars which fired machineguns. The fortress finally surrendered, but what highlighted the occasion was the exemplary behavior of Major Colin McVean who went out of his way to care for the Iranian prisoners and wounded; he also did much to restrain the excesses of the Sikh troops under his command.[129]

Brief but fierce resistance was offered by an artillery battery at Pol-e-Now, pinning down British forces and hitting a pipeline leading into Basra, causing a terrible blaze. The artillery commander then surrendered. Just as British forces were consolidating their gains at Pol-e-Now, they were attacked by a large number of Iranian-Arabs, who were defeated by the Gurkha Rifles.[130] British forces then mopped up remaining snipers and troops who refused to surrender in the Abadan and Khorramshahr area. The Iranians' last hope in Khuzistan rested on their defense at Ahvaz further northeast.

The RAF had bombed Ahvaz airbase just two hours after the attacks on the *Babr* and *Palang*. Two waves destroyed eight aircraft, damaged two more and destroyed two hangars.[131] To the west of Ahvaz six British *Valentia* transport aircraft, under escort by Hurricane fighters, landed at an abandoned landing strip at Haft Khel, using markers on the ground placed by local AIOC personnel.[132] The task force then proceeded to secure Haft Khel. Masjid Suleiman was secured by British paratroopers who had landed over 150 miles (240km) behind Iranian lines.[133] By August 26, Shahbakhti had placed artillery to protect Ahvaz's approaches.[134] He also set up vigorous tank and armored car patrols supported by infantry on trucks around Ahvaz.[135]

British forces steadily advanced towards Ahvaz supported by Rolls Royce armored cars. They were on the alert for Iranian tanks but Shahbakhti had pulled most of them back for the defense of Ahvaz. The RAF continued to rule the skies and also launched punishing attacks against Iranian positions at Ahvaz.[136] Some Iranian officers muttered about withdrawing across the Karun River but Shahbakhti stood firm. He ordered his demolition crews to prepare the blowing up of the Karun Bridge but Tehran countermanded these orders. In fact there were general orders that no bridges, roads or railways were to be demolished.[137]

The situation deteriorated severely by the end of August 26. Bandar Shapur, Khorramshahr and Abadan were now lost with Ahvaz under threat. Russian forces in the north were overrunning much of Azarbaijan and Gilan with Tehran also threatened. Nevertheless Shahbakhti's tanks did succeed in repelling a British reconnaissance force that had come near Ahvaz's city limits.[138] Shahbakhti had prepared his defenses well, covering Ahvaz's west and the east bank of the Karun River with infantry regiments supported by artillery. Shahbakhti's mobile strike group of tanks and cavalry along Ahvaz's northwest stood ready to strike into the flank of the British advance.

Nevertheless the same problems plaguing the other divisions caught up with Shahbakhti by August 27. By the morning of August 28, an Iranian envoy arrived to the British lines to announce Reza Shah's order for the cessation of all hostilities. Major-General Harvey, in command of British troops in the theater, was greeted by an honor guard of Iranian troops at Ahvaz and was warmly received by General Shahbakhti.[139] The British conquest of southern Iran and the Persian Gulf was thus concluded.

British invasion from the west

Just as British forces were occupying the south, a major military push erupted along Iran's western frontier in Iranian Kurdistan. There were three general thrusts. The first was from Khaneqin in Iraqi Kurdistan towards Kermanshah. This thrust was led by Major-General William Slim in command of the Indian 10th Division. The second thrust deployed towards Qasr e Shirin. Another force attacked Naft-e Shah (31 miles (50km) south of Qasr-e Shirin) from the Iraqi border town of Naft e Khaneh. Naft-e Shah and the local oil fields were quickly seized as Gurkhas caught the small Iranian force there by surprise and forced them to surrender.[140]

Qasr-e Shirin, the object of the second thrust, was a strategic location as it links up to the road leading to Kermanshah, a key junction for roads leading to Iran's northwest, north, east and south. British forces advanced with two columns towards Qasr-e Shirin. The first quickly captured the border post of Khosrovi and cut off its telephone lines running into Qasr-e Shirin. A second column of light tanks ran into Iranian troops with small arms. While their firing had no impact against the tanks, the Iranians did succeed in damaging a number of British trucks. Another British column arriving towards Qasr-e Shirin from the south captured a number of hills against heavy Iranian opposition. A major tank thrust then forced the Iranian garrison to evacuate the town and withdraw east. British forces entered Qasr-e Shirin and then joined the offensive towards the Paitak pass leading to Kermanshah. The column that occupied Qasr-e Shirin also managed to capture Sar e Pol e Zohab by that same afternoon.[141]

Major-General Hassan Moghaddam at Kermanshah reacted quickly. He realized that the British were aiming towards the Paitak pass but would also try and outflank this by driving through the village of Gilan further south. General Puria's 12th Division was already defending Paitak pass, but Gilan had to be reinforced. Moghaddam rushed an infantry regiment supported by artillery and antitank guns into the valleys and ridges around Gilan. He then joined them with his staff and took command of the defense of Gilan pass.[142]

The British pushed towards Gilan village through "European" landscape, with rising ridges and trees. They passed through the village without difficulty, but as British tanks and Bren carriers pushed beyond the village, they ran into well-concealed Iranian artillery, antitank guns, machineguns, and riflemen, which began a withering volley of fire.[143] Unpanicked, the British deployed 18-pounder artillery as their tanks charged forward, knocking out one Iranian antitank gun. The British attack however was decisively beaten back by intense fire. Two further British attacks were repelled.[144] By the next day, August 26, the successful Iranian defense was beginning to fall apart. Once again low supplies of food, water, and ammunition undermined the morale of Iranian troops. In contrast, the British were getting stronger with the arrival of reinforcements and supplies. Moghaddam could count on no such blessings from Tehran. He evacuated his troops and cannon from the Gilan pass and fell back to Kermanshah to organize a new line of defense. Moghaddam also issued explicit orders for the Gilan–Shahabad road to be demolished at as many points as possible to slow the British advance.

Paitak pass was also well defended, and presented a rude surprise to General Slim and Brigadier Aizelwood.[145] As the two men drove towards the Pass to survey the area, their car ran into accurate artillery fire. Fortunately for the British officers, their driver reversed their car just in time to avoid a shell that landed exactly where they had been a moment before. An Iranian cavalry patrol surprised elements of a British advance guard, forcing them back and taking a number of prisoners.[146] British Gurkha troops quickly resumed the advance toward Paitak against heavy Iranian artillery fire. The British responded by firing their own artillery but the Iranian positions held, albeit temporarily. The next day 12 Blenheim bombers finally blasted the Iranians from their positions.[147]

As Iranian positions collapsed, British forces pushed closer to Kermanshah. They ran into more resistance at the village of Zabiri, along the Shahabad road to Kermanshah. Zabiri was fortified with Iranian troops with well-concealed artillery and supported by cavalry.[148] On August 27, just as the British were preparing to attack Zabiri, an Iranian staff car bearing Major Abdollah Massoud arrived to discuss ceasefire terms with Slim. After intense negotiations it was agreed that the British would enter Kermanshah. In the meantime four Iranian cavalrymen galloped towards an Iranian cavalry unit to prevent it from attacking the British. Moghaddam's forces retreated from Kermanshah while being monitored by British aircraft and ground observers.[149] Further south in Khuzistan, Quinan had reached Ahvaz by August 28. By August 30–31, British forces had linked up with their Russian counterparts in Senna and Qazvin. Iran had lost approximately 800 army, naval and air personnel while the British and Indians had suffered only 22 fatalities.

Ceasefire

When the Anglo-Soviets attacked on August 25, Reza Shah immediately ordered military chief of staff Major-General Azizollah Zarghami to deploy Tehran's garrisons to defend all approaches leading to the capital. By August 28, with the situation clearly hopeless, Reza Shah ordered Iranian army units to cease hostilities and withdraw to Tehran. This was followed by Iran's acceptance of the Allies' surrender terms on August 31, 1941. Just weeks later, Reza Shah abdicated in favour of his 21-year-old son Mohammad Reza Pahlavi on September 16, 1941.[150] British and Soviet forces entered Tehran the very next day.[151]

The ceasefire orders resulted in many troops and officers simply melting into the civilian population. Zarghami's staff then ordered the army to release all conscripts from military duty. This caused a chain reaction as Tehran's police units also deserted their posts by early September. This posed grave dangers for civil and political stability in Iran. Reza Shah, who had not approved of the General Staff's release of the conscripts, ordered them to return to active duty at once. A few did return but the disordered state of the barracks compelled them to return to their civilian lives. The situation in the western provinces dissolved almost immediately. Many army warehouses in Iranian Kurdistan were looted, leading to cases of armed rebellion which were suppressed by Major-General Slim.[152]

Hassan Arfa, a key Iranian military figure at the time, argued that Tehran's orders to spare roads, bridges, etc from demolition only facilitated the Anglo-Soviet advance. He later speculated that Reza Shah's aim had been to offer token resistance to avoid destruction and to convince Berlin that he had done all he could to resist the Anglo-Soviet advance.[153] In August 1941 the Germans had swept the British out of Western Europe and seemed likely to defeat Russia, so a German arrival into Iran through the Caucasus was not altogether unlikely in the Iranian imagination.[154] Judging from their dire military situation against the Germans in August 1941, the Soviets were very fortunate that Iranian resistance had been brief. Had the Iranian army managed to maintain resistance, it would have put the Soviets and the British in a difficult situation. In such a scenario, Arfa proposed that Iran destroy all its key bridges and deploy Tehran's powerful garrisons into the Iranian mountains.[155] This could have possibly prolonged Iranian resistance for months.

Not all Iranian military personnel were content with the ceasefire. Even as Soviet troops entered Anzali, Rasht, Astara and Azarbaijan, continuing incidents of sniping, ambush and resistance by isolated pockets of Iranian troops persisted for weeks after the ceasefire.[156] Defiance was especially prominent in the air force. A number of air force personnel refused to comply with August 30 orders to not resist the Soviet paratroops if they landed at Tehran's Qaleh Morqhi 1st Air Regiment airbase.[157] The mutineers then arrested the chief of the air force, Brigadier-General Khosrovani. News of these events prompted the Iranian high command to crush the rebels. Brigadier-General Bozorjemehri ordered all antiaircraft units to fire at all planes taking off from Qaleh Morghi base. He also ordered armored units to advance into the base. Two Hawker Fury aircraft managed to take off, strafe the armored columns approaching the airbase, then escape unscathed.[158] The aircraft must have landed in safety somewhere in northern Iran because they intercepted five Soviet Polikarpov I-16 fighters on September 17, 1941 over the Caspian Sea.[159] One was shot down by the Soviets and the other ran out of fuel and crashed in forest.[160]

The Russians and the British divided Iran into northern and southern zones of occupation, not unlike the Anglo-Russian Accord of 1907.[161] Iran's newly constructed railway system, road networks and bridges were used to funnel military equipment to the Russians. The Iranian railway transported over 4 million tons of war materiel to Russia with Iranian roadways and bridges conveying another million tons.[162] US estimates are higher at 7.9 million tons of Lend-Lease Aid. Much of this was due to the arrival of American troops in Iran by December 1942 whoe reorganized and expanded the Iranian rail networks and port facilities. Many Iranian drivers were trained to assist the Allied war effort. By the war's end American troops and Iranian personnel had delivered a staggering total of 3,500 planes, 1,400 bombers, and 150,000 vehicles to Russia.[163] Few would argue that these gargantuan supplies helped contribute to Soviet victories. None was more appreciative of Iran's role than Winston Churchill, who said in no uncertain terms in the Tehran Conference on December 1, 1943 that Iran was the Allied "bridge to victory."[164] The abundant supply of Iranian oil was also a critical asset in the Allied war effort.[165]

The Allied occupation of Iran caused hyper-inflation, which ran as high as 450%, food shortages, and famine.[166] The latter were partly due to the disruption of food distribution networks as a result of British and Russian control of Iran's rail and road networks. The Russians in the north had already caused food shortages by forcibly shipping food stuffs to Russia. The massive influx of foreign troops awash with foreign currency put severe pressure on Iran's already strained food supplies, causing yet more shortages for the Iranian population.[167] These problems caused great resentment among the populace and the majority of the Majlis, already embittered by how rapidly their country had capitulated to the Anglo-Soviet invasion.[168]

The Anglo-Soviet occupation caused considerable bitterness among numbers of nationalists, government officials, journalists, ordinary citizens, tribal elements and army officers. The nucleus of a pro-German resistance cell composed of some army officers and Majlis members had been formed by mid-1942. This was led by General Fazlollah Zahedi. The Germans obliged by successfully parachuting six of their agents into Iran on January 1943 to join the German secret agent Franz Mayer. A handful of other Germans entered Fars province in March to join another German agent, Berthold Schulze-Holthus. Schulze-Holthus made significant efforts towards inciting Qashqai tribal warriors against the British. Had this succeeded, the rebellion could have seriously distracted the Allied effort to supply Russia. Fortunately for the Allies, Iranian central authorities proved highly diligent and British intelligence also came to the rescue. They captured a key German operative in August 1943, and Iranian authorities then arrested over 200 pro-German Iranian activists, including General Zahedi, and forty Iranian officers.[169] The discovery of the conspiracy led the Iranian government to declare war on Nazi Germany in September 1943.

On December 1, 1943, Joseph Stalin, Winston Churchill and Franklin D. Roosevelt met in Tehran. The most critical aspect of conference for Iran was the declaration guaranteeing Iranian political independence and territorial integrity.[170] But Stalin would break his pledge and soon tried to partition Iran.

CHAPTER 29

COLD WAR SALVO: SOVIET UNION ATTEMPTS TO PARTITION IRAN

The Soviets refuse to evacuate Iranian territory

The German army formally surrendered in May 1945, meaning that there was no longer any reason for the Allies to stay in Iran. American and British forces departed from Iran by December 31, 1945, and March 1946 respectively.[1] But in contrast to the punctual departure of the Western Allies, the Russians reneged on their pledge to evacuate occupied Iranian territory. Soviet troops were still inside Iran at the end of 1945. There were around 100,000 troops in Iran's north, and as noted by Roosevelt, "the Soviets were considering … the attachment of northwest Iran to the Soviet Union."[2] Soviet Russia's intentions in Iran were essentially a continuation of those of the Tsars: annexing northern Iran and dominating the entire country as far as (and including) the Persian Gulf. As early as 1940, V. M. Molotov, chairman of the USSR Council of People's Commissars, had told Hitler that the Soviet Union aspired to dominate the "area south of Batum and Baku in the general direction of the Persian Gulf."[3]

With the Red Army occupying northern Iran, the Soviet Academy of Sciences cooperated in oil exploration expeditions with the engineering corps of the Central Asian District and the Trans-Caucasian Front in 1942–43.[4] The studies found potential oil deposits in northern Iran. The Soviets "pointed out that serious exploratory work would require large amounts of investments and the annexation of a part of Iranian territory."[5] It was in this context that the Soviets helped to organize and arm separatists and communists in northwest Iran into what both Roosevelt and Sicker have characterized as "puppet governments."[6] With their armies in northern Iran, the Soviet Union encouraged and supported Azari and Kurdish insurrections in northwest Iran "with the aim of detaching Azarbaijan from Iran and annexing it to the Soviet Union."[7]

The Tudeh Party and support of Soviet aims in Iran

The Soviet build-up in Iran in 1944 was accompanied by the arrival of very large numbers of Soviet agents and political officers into northwest Iran, with the majority of these hailing from Soviet Azarbaijan.[8] The Soviet International Propaganda Organization set up a number of "Iranian-Soviet Cultural Relations Societies" in Iran with chapters in Azarbaijan advocating ethno-nationalist separatist ideology among Iran's Azaris and Kurds.[9] Iranian communists were also incited to promote Moscow's aims. Instructions were also given by Moscow to promote separatism in Iran's northern provinces.[10]

The political party supporting Soviet aims in Iran was the Tudeh (the Masses). The Tudeh was formed in late September 1941.[11] The movement was mainly composed of Iranian communists and left-wing intellectuals, and was soon drawn into Moscow's orbit. According to the British Foreign Office, the Tudeh became an increasingly "one-sided pro-Russian party" after the battle of Stalingard in 1943.[12] The Tudeh was to become, over the decades, a very effective tool for implementing Soviet aims in Iran.

The Soviet appetite for Iranian fossil fuels was transparent. A Soviet oil delegation led by Sergei Kavtaradze on September 15, 1944 noted of the link between Soviet policy in Iran and northern Iranian oil. At first the Soviets put pressure on the Iranian government to comply with their demands but when this failed, they turned to the Tudeh for help. The Tudeh obliged by first distancing itself from its original antipathy against oil concessions with foreign states.[13] This stance severely damaged the Tudeh's standing among the Iranian populace and intelligentsia. The Tudeh's kiss of death occurred when they demonstrated, under Soviet military escort, in Tehran's streets demanding that Iran surrender concessions to Moscow.[14] The reputation of the Tudeh as a pro-Russian organization would continue to haunt it for decades.

An even greater blow to the prestige of the Tudeh was their acquiescence to Russian territorial ambitions. The Azarbaijan branch of the Tudeh was ordered by Moscow to disassociate itself from the mainstream Iranian Tudeh to form a separatist party.[15] Thanks to declassified Soviet-era archives, it is now all but certain that the idea originated with Stalin himself.[16] Some members protested, but in vain.[17] The Tudeh party in Azarbaijan relabelled itself as the "Ferqeh e Democrat e Azarbaijan" or the "Azarbaijan Democratic Party" (referred to henceforth as "Democrats"). The leader of the Democrats was Mirjaafar Pishevari (1892–1947), a veteran Iranian communist from Iranian Azarbaijan. This was the first time in history that a political party inside Iran had been organized by a foreign state with the specific purpose of promoting ethno-linguistic separatism. From the outset the Democrats tried to utilize the language issue (i.e. Azari-Turkic) as way of distancing Iranian Azarbaijanis from the rest of Iran and her people. This was mainly done at the behest of the Soviet-Azarbaijani leadership, namely Mirjaafar Baghirov (1896–1956) the communist leader of Soviet Azarbaijan,[18] and Soviet writer Mirza Ibrahimov.

The exploitation of a country's ethno-nationalist or minority issues to serve the geopolitical interests of another state is known as the fissionist technique.[19] Iran is highly vulnerable to the fissionist technique as it is a nation of many linguistic and ethnic communities. The Soviets used this technique to create separatist movements in Iran's northwest. Iranian Kurds and Azaris were vulnerable to Soviet manipulation because they share cultural and linguistic ties with analogous ethnic groups across Iran's borders. The Soviets portrayed Iranian culture and the Persian language as "oppressive," "bourgeois," and "imperialistic." Soviet efforts at promoting ethnic disunity in Iran had three additional objectives: to divide Iran's ethnic groups into warring and antagonistic parties; to discredit the government to undermine the "establishment"; and to portray the Soviets as "champions" of social justice and as the only party capable of improving the conditions and rights of "the oppressed."

The Soviets had put considerable effort towards expunging the Iranian cultural legacy from the Caucasus and Central Asia between 1920 and 1941. These processes lasted until the collapse of the Soviet Union. These have led to long-standing geopolitical and military challenges against Iran's territorial integrity. One of these is the notion of a Greater Azarbaijan which aimed for the union of Soviet and Iranian Azarbaijan.

Like their Tsarist predecessors, the Soviets were "… eager to deny the existence of close cultural ties between [Soviet] Azarbaijan and Persia."[20] Stalin's role in falsifying history books to suit political and military purposes has been characterized by Leon Trotsky (1879–1940) as "Stalin's School of Falsification."[21] Applying the Musavat and pan-Turkist term "Azarbaijan" for Caucasus' ancient khanates allowed Soviet Russia to lay territorial claims to the historical Azarbaijan in northwest Iran.[22] Stalinist historiography generated a mindset in Soviet Azarbaijan which viewed Iranian Azaris as "oppressed" and requiring "liberation" by the Soviets. The Soviet attempt to import this thinking into Iranian Azarbaijan in the 1940s failed.

The Soviets attempted to seize on any potential social, economic, regional or political issue that could divide Iranian society in favor of Moscow.[23] Reza Shah's centralizing policies had resulted in economic imbalances and mismanagement between Tehran and the provinces. A powerful term invented by the Soviets (notably Baghirov) was "Persian Chauvinism," used to characterize the centralizing and "Persianizing" policies of the Reza Shah administration. One of Reza Shah's policies had been to recreate the Iranian state as a nation with one official language. Most of the advocates for this policy were Turkic-speaking Azarbaijanis who feared foreign states abusing Iran's multi-ethnic nature to promote secession. Another ban was against the wearing of traditional dress. This caused a great deal of resentment among many Kurds who otherwise acknowledged their kinship with Iranian peoples.[24] Despite their championing of "democracy," the truth of Soviet motives became quickly transparent. Soviet troops began seizing farmlands in northern Iran and Azarbaijan and forcibly took foodstuffs away from the Iranian people in favor of the Soviet war effort. These actions resulted in severe economic hardships and food shortages in those areas under occupation.[25]

The autonomous republic of Azarbaijan

Pishevari and the "Democrats" announced the formation of the Autonomous Republic of Azarbaijan on September 3, 1945, followed shortly after by similar developments in western (predominantly Kurdish) Azarbaijan.[26] There was very little Tehran could do as the Democrats were backed by Soviet troops and tanks. In Azarbaijan province alone, the Soviet occupying force stood at 60,000 troops and rose to 75,000 in October 1944 to beef up support for Pishevari.[27] The Soviets had been content to confine local Iranian army garrisons to their barracks, and took no military action against them.

The Soviet consul-general in Tabriz soon organized a "rebellion" by using his office to distribute weapons to the Democrats on November 15, 1945.[28] The next day witnessed a "revolution" in which local government offices, Gendarmerie stations and army barracks in Azarbaijan were systematically attacked.[29] Iranian army units outside Azarbaijan attempting to support their colleagues in the province were forced to halt by the Soviets at Qazvin on November 20, 1945.[30] The Soviet commander in the theater had bluntly told his Iranian counterpart that he would open fire if the Iranian columns proceeded further.[31] Just a day after the Qazvin incident, the Democrats had succeeded in taking control of most of eastern Azarbaijan.[32] By December the Tabriz garrison had been forced to surrender. Soviet military power had been indispensible in helping the Democrats sever eastern Azarbaijan from Iran. What occurred next in Iran was similar to the Soviet takeover of Eastern Europe after the Second World War. The Democrats took power in elections (closely watched by the Soviets) to form a nationalist assembly, backed again by Soviet troops and pro-Soviet militias. The Democrats selected Mirjaafar Pishevari as their leader who declared his government on December 13, 1945 in Tabriz.[33]

Many of the Democrats who had engaged in the "revolution" were foreigners: imported by the Soviets into Iran from Soviet Azarbaijan or from the greater Caucasus area.[34] With Pishevari in place, the Soviets proceeded to create a "national" army for their protégés. This was composed of new local recruits known as the Qizilbash, acting as "volunteers," whose role resembled that of the *Fadaian,* acting as the local Gendarmerie, and the *Mohajerin* (lit. immigrants).[35] The Qizilbash and the Fadaian were militarily unreliable to the Soviets, as "many had no desire to fight their fellow [Iranian] countrymen for the sake of Pishevari and the Russians."[36] This left the Mohajerin as the most loyal element to Pishevari's cause. These were Soviet citizens of Iranian origin who had been "deported" to Iran in the 1930s. Having grown up under Tsarist and Communist rule, these immigrants were alienated from mainstream Iran, speaking Russian and Azari-Turkic but no Persian. These provided invaluable political and military assistance to the Soviets in their attempt to separate Azarbaijan province from Iran.[37] Soviet forces had been bussing in additional Mohajerin just days before the "revolution."

Pishevari aimed to raise 10,000 troops with Moscow providing Soviet uniforms and equipment.[38] In case of an emergency, Pishevari could theoretically raise another 70,000–100,000 men.[39] The Soviets also turned over to Pishevari much of the Iranian army equipment they had captured in 1941.[40] The Democrats also established military schools at primary, secondary and college levels, a police college and a separate "political study" program.[41] As in the Red Army, political officers, mostly from the Soviet Union, provided the link between Pishevari's army and his Democrat party.[42] All movements, appointments and activities of Pishevari's government were closely supervised by Baghirov in Baku who provided daily updates to Stalin.[43] This helps explain why the Pishevari regime "quickly became an unpopular police state dependent on the Soviet Union for its survival."[44] Just months after the declaration of the Pishevari regime, an underground Azari army had emerged to fight it, a fact confirmed by the *New York Times* in early January 1946.[45] As events soon demonstrated, the real military muscle backing Pishevari was the Red Army.

The republic of Mahabad

Pan-Kurdish nationalism did not immediately surface upon the Soviet arrival into northwest Iran in August 1941. The predominantly Kurdish western regions of Iranian Azarbaijan had witnessed a number of revolts in recent years, the most spectacular being that of Simko. The Soviets now wanted to weaken Tehran's authority in the region in favour of Moscow. They first prevented Iranian army units from entering the area. This was the prelude to the Kurdish "Mahabad Republic," which like the Democratic Party of Azarbaijan, was also to be engineered by the Soviets.[46] Moscow aimed to incorporate this region, along the rest of Azarbaijan, into the Soviet Union after the Second World War.[47]

The Soviets were initially circumspect as to how to promote Kurdish separatism. The Komala-e-Zhiyan-e Kurd (Committee of Kurdish Youth) had been formed by mid-August 1943, a pan-Kurd movement which soon sprouted chapters in the Kurdish areas of Turkey and Iraq.

The operations run by Soviet agents in the last years of the war in western Azarbaijan involved Kurds from the Soviet Union who were mainly directed by the Soviet consulate at Rezaieh.[48] One of these, "Abdullaov," established contact with the Komala and by April 1945, contacts were made with Qazi Mohammad (1893–1947), a religious leader and hereditary judge of Mahabad. Qazi Mohammad became the head of the Komala, approved by the Soviets.[49] Qazi Mohammad fully acknowledged the Kurdish kinship to the Iranians while also entertaining pan-Kurdish aspirations.[50]

Under Qazi Mohammad, the Komala became a one-man autocratic party. The Soviets however, remained dissatisfied as the Komala did not politically fit into Pishevari's Turkic (or pan-Azari Turkic) nationalism. Qazi Mohammad and members of his entourage were taken to Baku to meet Baghirov. The latter made clear that he had little regard for the Komala whom he considered to be a creation of British intelligence.[51] Baghirov also made a point of attacking the policies of Reza Shah and encouraged Qazi Mohammad to create a new "Democratic Party."[52] Baghirov promised financial and military support for Qazi Mohammad's quest for independence from Iran and a Greater Kurdistan (comprising all Kurds in Iran, Iraq, Turkey and Syria).[53] Qazi Mohammad returned to Mahabad and announced the formation of the "Kurdish Democratic Party" (KDP). The Komala was dissolved and its members absorbed into the KDP.

Qazi Mohammad's position in western Azarbaijan and the Mahabad region was far from secure. Despite Soviet pressure to acquiesce, local Kurdish tribes were wary of Qazi Mohammad's close ties with Baghirov and the Communists. Help for the KDP soon arrived from Iran's northwestern border with Iraq. Barzani tribal chief Mulla Mustafa, along with 1,000–3,000 of his warriors and their families arrived from Iraq into Iran on October 11, 1945, to support Qazi Mohammad and the KDP.[54] The Barzanis were seasoned fighters and included numbers of deserters (of Kurdish descent) from the Iraqi army, including 12 officers. Many of these had held high posts in the Iraqi high command and received military training in England.[55] The Barzanis were armed with British-made rifles, machineguns, and an artillery piece captured from the Iraqi army.[56] Soviet military authorities instructed Mulla Mustafa Barzani to place his forces under Qazi Mohammad's command. These Iraqi Barzani Kurds formed the backbone of Qazi Mohammad's KDP party until their collapse in December 1946.[57] The Soviets encouraged local Kurdish tribes to support the KDP in its bid to separate western Azarbaijan and Mahabad from Tehran. These efforts were not completely successful as three major Kurdish tribes, the Dehbokri, Mamesh, and Mangur, refused to cooperate with the KDP and the Soviets.[58]

On December 15, 1945 Qazi Mohammad declared his separation from Iran by announcing the establishment of the "Kurdish People's Republic," just three days after Pishevari's announcement in Tabriz.[59] The ceremony was attended by members of the KDP, various tribal chiefs, Mulla Mustafa Barzani, and three Soviet officers.[60] This appears consistent with reports that the KDP included many Kurds from the Soviet Union.[61] Qazi Mohammad's overtly pro-Soviet stance soon alienated those Kurds who were opposed to Moscow's agenda.[62]

Moscow provided Qazi Mohammad's regular 1200-man militia with Soviet uniforms, and captured Iranian army equipment.[63] Barzani's Iraqi officers and Soviet military advisors began training Qazi Mohammad's forces. The villages were policed by local Kurds dressed in traditional Kurdish costume, supervised by officers from Mahabad. Qazi Mohammad could draw upon another 2,000–3,000 Kurdish warriors but these were fickle and subject to the wishes of their tribal chiefs. The Soviets pledged Qazi Mohammad much military aid, but this was never delivered.

The Kurds and Azaris had a number of disputes, mainly over territory, with the flashpoint being Rezaieh, which had been captured by the Democrats. Much of the Rezaieh area in the vicinity of Lake Urumiah is populated by Azaris with Kurds occupying the hills surrounding the plains around the town. There are also areas with mixed Kurd-Azeri populations. Battles soon broke out between the Kurds and the Azaris. The Soviets were unhappy, as the fighting between their two satellite states was a major political embarrassment. Qazi Mohammad was brought to Tabriz to resolve the dispute, and a treaty was signed on April 23, 1946.[64] This caused alarm in Tehran as Pishevari and Qazi Mohammad were clearly behaving like heads of independent states. Indeed, the Iranian government had not even been consulted in the signing of the treaty. Pishevari then went to Tehran to negotiate his own separate treaty there, which was nothing less than forcing the Iranian government to legally recognize the Democrats. Qazi Mohammad now demanded a greater share of Azarbaijani territory from Tehran. The Iranian government seemingly agreed with Qazi Mohammad, but skillfully left the final decision to the Pishevari regime which predictably rejected the request. This ensured that tensions between Moscow's clients would remain.

The Soviets overplay their hand

Just as the Soviets hoisted their client regimes in Mahabad and Tabriz in December 1945, they also made an all-out effort to occupy Tehran and overthrow its government. The major offensive was to be conducted by the Soviet Army supported by Soviet-armed Tudeh allies and Pishevari's fighters.[65]

The similarities with the early 1900s when Russian forces would enter Tehran to bomb the Iranian Majlis into submission were unmistakable, but this time the Iranians were more prepared, they had an organized and unified army, supported by an effective Gendarmerie. Iranian commanders organized their army and gendarmer units to protect Tehran. They also supplied weapons, communications gear and ammunition to Iranian tribes along the communist routes of advance. By January 1946, the Iranian army, gendarmerie and Iranian tribal fighters had succeeded in halting the advance of thousands of Soviet troops and their allies. Tehran also had the support of Washington. The Americans wanted an intact Iranian army to maintain Tehran's authority throughout the country. To this end they sent the Ridley and Schwartzkopf missions into Iran to implement highly effective reforms for the army and gendarmerie. These greatly assisted the Iranians in eliminating a number of problems, especially in logistics and communications.

Stalin's gambit to seize Tehran and install puppet figures as he had in Tabriz and Mahabad was more than just a military failure. He had also lost face in the court of international opinion. The Iranians, with the support of the British and Americans, now took their complaint to the United Nations Security Council (UNSC).

Ahmad Qavam ol Saltaneh became prime minister of Iran in January 27, 1946, right in the midst of the failed Soviet offensive and the involvement of the UNSC. Despite the support of the British and Americans and the UNSC, Qavam adopted a very compromising attitude to the Soviets. He dismissed General Hassan Arfa who had played an important role in halting Moscow's march to Tehran. In Arfa's stead Qavam appointed General Ali Razmara, an open Russophile with strong ties to the Communists.

Stalin responded by pouring more troops into Soviet-occupied territories in northern Iran[66] and again pushed towards Tehran with tanks, reaching as far as Karaj (approximately 28 miles (45km) from Tehran) by mid-March.[67] Washington and London were clearly displeased with Moscow and insisted that Iran's independence and territorial integrity be respected. Washington's military chiefs warned the Russians that if they continued their offensive into Iran, they risked igniting a Third World War. America's readiness to fight the Soviets over Iran was expressed by President Harry S. Truman (1884–1972), who told Stalin that unless he ceased his actions in Iran, the US would send military forces to eject Soviet troops from the country.[68] Had Moscow really wanted to fight the Americans in a conventional war in Iran, Truman would have had difficulty assembling enough military forces and warships for such a showdown.[69] The Russians realised that Truman meant business. He certainly had not hesitated to deploy nuclear weapons against Japan to secure her unconditional surrender.[70] Stalin got Truman's message and decided not to press the British and Americans much further.

Qavam managed to secure an agreement with the Soviets by April 5, 1946. The Soviets would evacuate Iranian territory in exchange for petroleum concessions in the north. The agreement stipulated the establishment of a joint Irano-Soviet oil company in which the Soviets would hold 51 shares and the Iranians 49.[71] Qavam also agreed to withdraw Iran's complaint against the Soviet Union in the United Nations, open negotiations with the Pishevari government, and even allot three seats to the Tudeh party in the Majlis.[72] The British were displeased and stated in a diplomatic dispatch that "Qavam had sold his country to the Russians."[73] British misgivings would soon be assuaged as Qavam's agreement had yet to be ratified by the Iranian Majlis, and Qavam had outfoxed Stalin. The 14th Iranian Majlis had ensured that elections for the 15th Majlis would be postponed until all Iranian territory had been evacuated by foreign troops. The Russians were now willing to withdraw, believing that the Majlis would endorse Qavam's oil concession treaty. Moscow may have also hoped that the treaty's ratification would ensure Azarbaijan's "autonomous" status; facilitate the spread of Communism across Iran; and enforce Soviet control over all of Iran's political and economic domains.[74]

Meanwhile Pishevari was negotiating the treaty with Qavam that acknowledged that Azarbaijan was (at least nominally) Iranian territory, but in practice not much had changed. Pishevari continued to wield an independent army with the Democrats in full control of Azarbaijan. Iranian army and government officials were still banned from the province. Pishevari's agreement added further insult to injury by forcing the Iranian government to "appoint" them to posts they already held inside Azarbaijan!

Soviet forces completed their pullout from Iranian territories by May 9, 1946.[75] Pishevari was bitter about the Soviet withdrawal and concerned with the imminent arrival of the Iranian army.[76] Pishevari then received a letter from Stalin on May 8, 1946 stating "you [Pishevari] say that that we first raised you to the skies and then let you down into the precipice and disgraced you. If this is true it surprises us."[77] Stalin's letter also made clear that he had used the Azarbaijani movement to force oil concessions from Tehran, and to hoist Russophile politicians into the Majlis at the expense of Iranian Anglophiles.[78] Stalin also noted that he withdrew his forces from Iran to remove the British and American pretext for stationing troops in Europe, Asia, the Middle East, etc.[79] Pishevari and Qazi Mohammad must have finally realized that they had been sacrificial pawns in Moscow's game of geopolitical chess against the British and Americans.

Pishevari and Qazi Mohammad now had to fend for themselves. The army generals and the young Shah remained concerned with Iran's political-military situation and were unhappy with Qavam's compromises with the Soviets. The Iranian army also refused to recognize the legitimacy of Pishevari's army. Pishevari however remained steadfast in his demand to keep his army and sent two officials to negotiate with Tehran on August 20, 1946. Despite the intervention of the Soviet ambassador, Ivan C. Sadchikov, they were unsuccessful.[80]

The pro-Soviet regimes in the northwest soon created new geopolitical dangers for Iran. London was deeply concerned with Russian political penetration in Iran as this could compromise the security of British assets in the south (i.e. petroleum) and it was proposed that London encourage an autonomy movement in southern Persia.[81] The British encouraged tribal rebellions in Fars province and Khuzistan as a counter-response to Soviet influence in the north.[82] By July 1946, London had sent two battleships to Abadan and reinforced her troops in Basra. Anti-Tehran rebellions finally erupted among the Qashqais and other tribes by October 1946. The rebels even managed to temporarily occupy government buildings in Kazerun and Bushehr.[83] There were even a number of British officials who wanted to accommodate Stalin. Recent studies paint a different picture of British foreign policy, one that diverged with the UN and the US at the time. These documents suggest that not all in London were sympathetic to Iran's territorial integrity. There were in fact British officials who seriously contemplated "sharing" Iranian oil with the Russians, similar to the intervention of Britain and Russian in Iran in the early 20th century.[84]

The rising chorus of domestic political criticism, British and American concerns, and the potential for more revolts in the south finally forced Qavam to reverse his support for the pro-Russian lobby.[85] While some historians have interpreted Qavam's actions as "opportunistic" it is possible to interpret his action in a more "Iranocentrist" light. Qavam's diplomacy had facilitated the withdrawal of Soviet troops without the need to resort to combat. With the Soviet army out of Iran, the Iranian army could finally focus on removing the pro-Moscow governments and militias ensconced in the northwest. Time was now running out for Pishevari and Qazi Mohammad.

Fall of the Democrats: Iranian army deploys into Azarbaijan

Qavam declared that in order for free elections to take place, Iranian security forces had to be in control of all Iranian provinces, including Azarbaijan. Only then could the elections for the 15th Majlis take place.[86] The Iranian army general staff and the shah engaged in careful preparations before they proceeded to eject the pro-Soviet regimes in the northwest. By November 1946 the army had sent arms and ammunition to local anti-Pishevari and anti-KDP fighters in east and west Azarbaijan. Equally important was the intelligence operation which obtained valuable information on the state and morale of the separatist militias. These operations went well due to the support of local anti-separatist and anti-communist citizens in all of Azarbaijan. The Iranian army also infiltrated the province with Iranian soldiers of Azarbaijani and Kurdish background. These quickly blended in and gathered yet more valuable intelligence for the army. These also succeeded in arranging for the defection of (non-Barzani) Kurdish and Azarbaijani recruits from the separatist militias. As events soon demonstrated, morale among the separatists was very low.[87]

Prior to their departure from Iran the Soviets had left Pishevari a large amount of ammunition and automatic weapons. Also, despite the "official" pullout, at least 6,000 Soviet personnel or agents had remained behind.[88] There are also reports from Iranian-Azari ex-Tudeh members that the Soviets had brought in hard-core communists from the Balkans to battle the Iranian army on their behalf.[89] This may partly explain why Qavam was worried about the possibility of renewed Soviet military action.[90] The Americans unequivocally declared that Iran had the right to maintain her territorial integrity.[91]

Iranian army units stationed in Qazvin were absorbed into the 3rd Division[92] led by General Mir Hossein Hashemi, an Azarbaijani with great popular support in Tabriz. The 3rd Division marched into Zanjan on November 22–23, 1946, where the Democrats surrendered without a fight.[93] This may be because the local populace had already risen against the Democrats as soon as the Iranian army arrived at the city's outskirts.[94] The Democrats now held a line to the south of Zanjan of 1,500 men armed with numerous machineguns.[95]

With Zanjan secured, the 3rd Division and Saqqez's 4th Division were soon heavily reinforced with tanks, troops, artillery, and additional soldiers, resulting in a combined force of 17,000 troops.[96] This force was supported by at least 3,000 irregular Azari and Kurdish troops. The army's drive into Azarbaijan brought it into an area between Mianeh and Zanjan.[97] The army lunged towards Democrat positions on the Qaflankuh Pass just south of Mianeh on December 10, 1946.[98] Witnessing the rapid evaporation of Democrat military resistance, Pishevari demanded that the Azarbaijanis "fight to the death."[99] The Azarbaijanis did fight, but Iranian Azaris, many of them armed by Tehran or having captured their own weapons, directed their efforts against Pishevari. Pishevari's army disabled an important bridge on the road to Tabriz on December 10, but the Iranian army rapidly crossed the river against minimal resistance. Another Iranian army column easily dispersed remaining separatist resistance on December 11, forcing the surviving Democrats and Tudeh fighters to flee to Tabriz.[100]

Realizing the futility of resistance and their unpopularity among the Azarbaijani populace, the Democrats and their allies opted to flee towards the Soviet border. Numbers of those trying to escape Azarbaijan's cities were caught and killed by locals.[101] Hundreds of surviving separatists fleeing through the mountains were intercepted by the Azarbaijani Shahsavan tribe but Pishevari and his entourage reached the safety of their Soviet patrons across the border. The Iranian army met virtually no resistance in Azarbaijan, and were greeted as liberators as they entered Tabriz.[102] With the Soviet army out of the country and its clients in Iran swept away, the Soviet oil concession was doomed. When the Majlis convened in October 1947, Mohammad Mossadegh of the Iranian National Front ensured the complete defeat of that concession.[103]

The reasons for Pishevari's collapse are often attributed to the departure of the Red Army, but Pishevari was also handicapped by three factors which severely weakened his ability to resist the Iranian army in December 1946, namely the local economy, domestic politics and cultural/historical factors. The decrepit state of the Iranian economy, especially after the food shortages following the Anglo-Soviet invasion in 1941 was a major source of discontent in Azarbaijan. At first, Pishevari did well in addressing local complaints, but the impact of his reforms proved ephemeral.[104]

Despite the adoption of the term "Democrat" Pishevari's government quickly came to resemble a Soviet-style dictatorship.[105] By December 1946, his regime had become so dictatorial that listening to radio broadcasts from London or even Ankara risked the death penalty in Tabriz.[106] Finally, while the Democrats and Soviet authorities put considerable effort into erasing Azarbaijan's historical associations with Iran, encouraging hostility towards the Persian language and encouraging Iranian Azarbaijanis to join the Soviet Republic of Azarbaijan,[107] Azarbaijanis became increasingly apprehensive about being severed from Iran and attached to the Soviet Union due to their shared history and culture.[108]

Despite Pishevari's safe arrival in Soviet Azarbaijan, it soon became clear that Pishevari and Baghirov cared little for each other. Tensions came to a head in a stormy exchange about why the Democrats fell during a reception in Baku.[109] Shortly after the meeting, Pishevari died. The official Soviet explanation was that Pishevari died in a car accident.[110]

The fall of Qazi Mohammad at Mahabad

As the departure of the Soviets in May 1946 approached, General Homayuni's 4th Division from Saqqez became more aggressive in its operations against Qazi Mohammad. Previously, army operations had been characterized by sniping exchanges and skirmishes. Homayuni's first major action by mid-April 1946 was to pry open the roads to rush badly needed supplies to Iranian army garrisons in Saqqez, Sardshat and Baneh. After a number of small, intense battles the army's drive to Saqqez was beaten back by a motley force of Kurdish tribal warriors. The army's losses were relatively modest with 20 killed, 30 taken prisoner and two machineguns captured. Emboldened, the Kurds soon attempted to cut the Sanandaj Road. Their larger goal was to break out of western Azarbaijan into the Kurdish areas of western Iran.[111] The KDP were not only beaten back but also lost their positions in the hills of Saqqez. Homayuni then rapidly built towers on the hills, manning each with 30–40 troops.

Many of the Iranian Kurdish tribes had refused Soviet demands that they fight against the Iranian army.[112] A number of Kurdish tribes such as the Tilekuhis were now supporting the Iranian army against the KDP.[113] At this juncture, the KDP and Homayuni negotiated a truce in which the former held the upper hand. The KDP continued to block supplies from being delivered to Iranian army garrisons in Baneh and Sardasht. This state of affairs was unsustainable as local Kurdish support for Qazi Mohammad's cause had progressively weakened. The Mamesh, Dehbokri and Mangur had never been on good terms with Qazi Mohammad, but now even the Shikak Kurds in the Rezaieh area further north were distancing themselves from the KDP. The Barzanis were also restive as they were no longer receiving free local provisions. This meant that Qazi Mohammad had no real military muscle in late 1946. The only credible support for his cause by that time came from tribal forces, barely numbering over 1,000 fighters. Despite Moscow's best efforts and Qazi Mohammad's impassioned pleas for assistance, "the [Kurdish] tribes almost all sided with the Iranian army."[114]

By mid-December Qazi Mohammad had seen the writing on the wall. He dispatched his brother Sadr Qazi (who was a deputy in the Iranian Majlis) to inform General Homayuni on December 13, 1946 that the KDP would not resist the arrival of the Iranian army. Homayuni asked that the

Barzanis depart prior to his arrival.[115] Then the General sent Lieutenant-Colonel Ghaffari forward to lead Dehbokri, Mamesh and Mangur tribal warriors to enter Mahabad. Qazi Mohammad requested that the Kurdish tribes be stopped from entering Mahabad, and so the Iranian army peacefully entered the city on December 15, 1946, to be warmly received by Qazi Mohammad.[116] Qazi Mohammad was arrested just two days after the arrival of the Iranian army and sent to the gallows the following year. Ironically, the military tribunal had relied on the testimonies of the local Kurds to arrive at their decision. His death made him a martyr, which largely helped diminish his associations with the Soviets. Perhaps sparing his life would have been brought better closure to what can be seen in many ways as the consequences of Soviet imperialism.

Farther to the north of Mahabad the Shikak, led by Amr Khan, had abstained from partaking in any operations against the Iranian army. Earlier Soviet appeals for them to attack the Iranian army had fallen on deaf ears and the Shikak were even contemplating military action against the Democrats before their downfall. The one exception was Zero Beg, once one of Simko's supporters, who had been courted by the Soviets since 1941.[117] In practice he was willing to negotiate, and met General Homayuni near Rezaieh, but his tribesmen inexplicably attacked the Iranian troops in the vicinity. Zero and his allies fled to Oshnuyeh, where he linked up with Barzani who had been ordered by the Iranian army to disarm or return to Iraq. Rejecting Tehran's request, Mulla Mustafa Barzani then fought until June when he finally reached the Soviet border.

Several factors explain Qazi Mohammad's failure. During his rule, the Kurds of Mahabad suffered severe economic hardships because the important export of tobacco to the rest of Iran was stopped.[118] Food resources were also becoming scare by late 1946, and having to share meager supplies with the Barzanis led to a decrease in the latter's popularity. Memories of past Russian atrocities by Tsarist troops in northwest Iran, most recently during the First World War, were very much alive among local Kurds. Despite the Soviets trying to keep a low profile in the Mahabad Republic, Qazi Mohammad's greatest political liability was his close association with the Soviets. Many Kurds realized that theirs was not a truly independent Kurdish state but a Soviet puppet state. The Soviets also failed to appropriate pan-Kurdish nationalism. The Soviets hoped to merge all Kurds into Soviet Azarbaijan, but the Kurds felt that if they should join a larger state, they had far more affinity with Iran.[119] When the Iranian army arrived in December 1946, the vast majority of Kurds (like the Azaris) showed little desire to die on behalf of Moscow.[120]

CHAPTER 30

POSTWAR DEVELOPMENTS TO THE FALL OF MOSSADEGH (1946–53)

The state of the army

The Iranian military was still the most organized government apparatus in Iran despite its reduction in size following the 1941 Anglo-Soviet invasion. The main question during the Allied occupation of Iran was who was in control of the Iranian army. The shah wanted the Iranian army to focus on internal security to facilitate the safe transfer of military materiel across Iranian territory to the Soviet Union. The Majlis wanted to steer the army out of the political arena. The shah's position towards the Majlis was partly conciliatory as he transferred much of the wealth accumulated by his late father, Reza Shah, back into state hands and even yielded more powers to the prime minster's office.[1]

However, coming from an extensive military education background, the shah wanted to maintain as much involvement with the military as possible.[2] He attended graduation ceremonies and even organized army maneuvers. Like his father before him, the shah considered the army to be his chief source of support. As a result, commanders who had deserted their posts during the Anglo-Soviet invasion were protected by the shah against investigations and scrutiny. This meant that the old system of commands directed from the royal palace to commanders and from them to subordinates was maintained. The War Ministry was also primarily staffed with the shah's close allies. These successfully blocked the prime minister's office from dismissing them in 1942. The occupying forces certainly recognized the shah as the primary head of the army, which they viewed as critical in maintaining law and order. The Allies had little desire to divert their troops towards security duties in Iranian cities.

The shah had sought closer relations with the United States from the early days of his rule. Such an alliance would allow Iran to be linked to the West without having to rely on Britain to counterbalance the Soviet Union. Iran had been declared eligible for US Lend-Lease assistance but this had been very modest and specifically geared to serve the overall war effort against the Nazis. The US wanted to improve the Iranian army's capabilities with respect to internal security. Of key importance was the protection of Allied supply routes from the Persian Gulf northwards towards Russia. This led to the arrival of two missions into Iran to help improve the performance of the Iranian armed forces. The work of these American missions was often challenged by the meddling of the Soviets and the British.[3] The Americans also had to face the vicissitudes of the Iranian political scene. In just six years (1941–46) Tehran had witnessed the rise and fall of 11 administrations. Despite these challenges the American missions greatly benefited the Iranian gendarmerie and regular army.

The Gendarmerie was a prime force in implementing law, order and security, especially in Iran's outlying regions and provinces. The US dispatched Colonel H. Norman Schwartzkopf to Iran in August 1942. Schwartzkopf carefully examined the Gendarmerie, then called for its complete reorganization and overhaul. Schwartzkopf's suggestion was met by opposition, even within the Gendarmerie, but support by other Iranian officials prevailed and the plans were implemented. By November 1943 the Gendarmerie had been jointly placed under the Ministry of the Interior and with Schwartzkopf's mission known as GENMISH. The shah was reputedly unhappy with Schwartzkopf's expanded authority over the Gendarmerie. Efforts to reassert direct military control over the Gendarmerie by the shah's top commanders proved unsuccessful.[4] By the end of 1944 Schwartzkopf had established an effective communications system for the Gendarmerie, which allowed dispersed units to greatly increase their coordination and rapidity of response.[5] Schwartzkopf also established effective training facilities for the Gendarmerie. These trained an array of truck drivers, motorcyclists and sergeants which led to a sharp rise in the Gendarmerie's efficiency. Schwartzkopf managed to procure vital military supplies and trucks for the Gendarmerie, even as these had been primarily intended for the Soviets. Schwartzkopf's successes allowed the Gendarmerie to successfully reinstate Tehran's authority across Iran, excepting the Soviet-occupied northwest. But perhaps most important was the cultivation of a new sense of professionalism in the force. Operations became characterized by transparency, efficiency, discipline and reliability.[6] Schwartzkopf also recommended reforms against corruption and bureaucracy, advocated a better pension system, and suggested the allocation of a separate budget for the Gendarmerie.

The US dispatched General Clarence Ridley to Tehran on October 1942 to begin work on reorganizing the Iranian military. An earlier mission led by General John Greely in July 1942 had been recalled due to Greely's ambitions to rebuild the Iranian army as quickly as possible to fight the Nazis, as the US simply wanted an Iranian army capable of maintaining internal security.

Ridley was given full and unrestricted access to all military records. He was also authorized to promote, dismiss or assign Iranian army officers. Ridley's overall objective was to create a force of 88,000 men led by the most militarily capable officers. Ridley focused on those domains requiring critical attention: supply (equipment and salaries), logistics (along with motorization and transport reforms), training, equipment shortfalls, and recruitment procedures.

Iran's key Achilles heel during the Anglo-Soviet invasion had been in supply and logistics. Special attention was accorded to upgrading military education with respect to finance, management, supply and logistics. These same schools also taught courses in engineering and medicine. Ridley also subjected the offices of the Chief of Finance and the Ministry of the Quartermaster General to close scrutiny. These were then given rigorous reforms in management procedures. These reforms had a positive impact on the distribution of equipment and payments. Prior to Ridley's arrival, the distribution of basic equipment and uniforms had been centralized in Tehran with local commands responsible for all other items. This resulted in uneven efficiency and corruption. To stop the abuse of payments for troops outside of Tehran, Ridley set up a system of local depot offices, ensuring that payments for soldiers were regulated by Tehran's central authorities. Provisions were made to equitably adjust payments in accordance to inflation. Accounting procedures were also put in place to keep track of all stocks. These measures did much to eliminate waste and corruption, which led to a sharp increase in consistency and accountability. Tehran was also empowered to procure all supplies and distribute these in a balanced fashion to depots all across the country.

Ridley recognized that a major liability reducing the Iranian army's efficiency was motorized transport. There simply weren't enough trucks, jeeps, and motorcycles available. This dangerously compromised the army's ability to deploy quickly. Ridley succeeded in having 600 trucks delivered to the Iranian army. He completely reorganized the Iranian army's transport department and set up special schools for mechanics and truck drivers. Tehran, Kermanshah and Isfahan were provided with maintenance and repair facilities, along with depot stations.

The one area where Ridley failed to achieve major success was in recruitment. There were serious issues with recruitment as eligible recruits from higher social classes were often able to buy their way out of military service, leaving unfit men of lower status to fill the ranks. Recuits even faked their medical exams to receive exemption from service.[7]

Dr. Arthur Millspaugh and a financial mission arrived in Iran for a second time in early 1943 to overhaul the country's financial system.[8] His mission was a failure, succeeding only in uniting both royalists and nationalists against his plans to drastically cut the army in size to release funds for education, health care, and agriculture. The British also objected to his plans, instead endorsing Ridley's plan of creating an 88,000-strong army. While Millspaugh did have some Iranian advocates for his plans, he was dismissed from Iran for the second and final time after failing to find a compromise. The Majlis then voted to increase the army's budget. The legal size of the army was approved at 90,000 men by mid-1945, followed by another resolution to have that force increased by another 12,000 men.[9]

The Truman Doctrine

The conclusion of the Second World War was soon followed by the Cold War between the West, led by the United States, and the Communist bloc, led by the Soviet Union. Truman, who had already stood up to Soviet attempts to dismember Iran, was eager to further integrate Iran into the Western anti-Communist alliance. By March 1947, Iran was being offered American military and economic assistance within the context of the Truman Doctrine, which offered help to states threatened by the Soviet Union.

Tehran and Washington ratified an agreement on June 9, 1947 allowing for the sale of US military materials to Iran.[10] The first batch was delivered by March 1948 with another shipment arriving in Bandar Shapur on February 9, 1949. In total, the Americans only sold the Iranians a modest 10.7 million dollars' worth of equipment, supplies and ammunition as Washington had refused the 175 million dollar purchase limit originally requested by the shah and General Ali Razmara, the Army chief of staff.

By 1950, the army had more than doubled its forces from 80,000 to 200,000 men.[11] The steady growth of the armed forces, increasingly equipped with American hardware, necessitated the recruitment of US expertise to increase the military's efficiency. This resulted in the US and Iran signing a military agreement on October 16 1947. The agreement legalized the arrival of a US military mission to help upgrade the Iranian army's overall efficiency.[12] The agreement was to last for two years, with the Iranians then having the option of requesting another two years. The US had the option of unilaterally terminating its mission at any time. The terms of the treaty would be renewed twice. The treaty stipulated that US personnel were allowed to inspect any Iranian military installations at any time; that Iranian military personnel were to grant their US counterparts access to all documents; that Iran was not allowed to hire any other foreign military advisors during the US mission; and that any US personnel accused of crimes were to be immediately deported to the US.[13]

On a visit to the US in November 1949, the shah was warned by US Secretary of State Dean Acheson that the US's proposed $650 million aid offer could be jeopardized if the shah intended to shift the majority of this to the military.[14] Acheson was especially critical of Iran's ambitions to develop a military potential capable of withstanding Soviet military aggression.[15] In March 1950, the shah appointed Al Mansur as Iran's prime minster on March 23, 1950. Mansur was generally considered as an Anglophile, and the Americans applied various strategies to undermine him, including scaling back US military and economic assistance to Iran.[16] The shah replaced Mansur with General Ali Razmara on June 26, 1950.

The rise and fall of Mohammad Mossadegh

The Iranian military was also drawn into Tehran's tumultuous politics in 1949–53. The three power blocs at that time were the rising Iranian nationalists, the clergy and the conservative bloc. The latter were mostly landowners and aristocrats closely aligned with the shah, who was supported by much of the army.[17] There was also the Tudeh Party, which despite its association with the Soviet Union, had done very well in reorganizing itself to enter the political mainstream.[18]

Following an attempted assassination by Nasser Fakhrai, whose papers linked him with the Tudeh and religious extremists, the shah declared martial law and outlawed the Tudeh party.[19] The latter were also charged with treason for having inflamed the 1944–46 riots in Abadan, organizing strikes in Khuzistan, arming workers in northern Iran's Mazandaran province and promoting separatist movements in Azarbaijan and Kurdistan.[20] The Shah also introduced changes to the constitution allowing him to dissolve the legislature of the Majlis[21]. He also attempted to influence the 1949 elections of the Majlis and sought greater control over the media.[22]

The shah's greatest challenge was the highly educated Mohammad Mossadegh (1882–1967), an older veteran of Iranian politics, who had served in the first Majlis. Mossadegh had been one of the firm opponents of the 1919 Anglo-Iranian treaty. He had been again nominated to the Majlis in 1923. Mossadegh, a nephew of Mozzafar e Din Shah Qajar, had been initially supportive of Reza Khan as a strong constitutional prime minister but opposed his ascension as shah of Iran in 1925.[23] He was briefly arrested in 1930 and later imprisoned in 1940 for his criticism of Reza Shah's policies. He was then released as part of general amnesty issued by Reza Shah Pahlavi's son.[24]

Mossadegh had taken the lead in organizing the *Jebbhe Melli e Iran* (National Front of Iran) and became the party's leader in 1949. From its inception, the anti-imperialist National Front aimed to ensure that Iran's natural resources were the property of the Iranian state and eliminate all concessions to foreign powers. Mossadegh had certainly been instrumental in defeating the Soviet oil concessions in the Majlis on October, 1947.[25] Also of note was the ratification of a bill in the Majlis which forbid the granting of oil concessions to foreign countries. This stipulated that the Iranian government was henceforth responsible for the exploitation of Iranian petroleum.[26] This was the main stepping stone towards the nationalization of all petroleum assets in Iran by 1951. This set the stage for the showdown with the AIOC (Anglo-Iranian Oil Company). In principle, the Shah was in agreement with the National Front's overall objectives of reducing foreign influence in Iran, but was concerned over possible British reactions, political instability and Iran's national security.[27]

Iran's economy was performing poorly in 1949, with its most vital asset, petroleum, being largely under British control.[28] There had been growing resentment over AIOC's role in extracting and exporting Iranian petroleum to Britain. It is generally agreed that a major source of friction was the AIOC's refusal to share its profits more equitably with its host country, Iran. The issue of ownership of Iranian oil was now a unifying point across a broad spectrum of Iranian society.[29] There was also much popular resentment against the AIOC's blatant discrimination against its Iranian employees, who received substandard housing and low wages in contrast to their British counterparts.[30] Another problem was the "imperialist" and even racist attitude of a number of British statesmen against Iranians during the AIOC affair.[31] These attitudes did much to contribute to the rise of nationalism among the AIOC's Iranian employees and the Iranian populace.

In the late 1940s, the British were especially sensitive towards their assets in Iran because their economy had been battered in the aftermath of the Second World War, and India achieved independence from the British Empire in August 1947, just as Iranian nationalists were demanding control of Iranian oil.[32] The demands of the Iranian nationalists clearly clashed with London's economic interests.[33]

The Iranians extracted a supplemental agreement from AIOC in September 1949 with better terms than those negotiated by Reza Shah in 1932.[34] Nevertheless, this was turned down by a commission led by Mossadegh on November 25, 1950.[35] Razmara became prime minister in June 1950. His appointment meant that he would soon be identified with the unpopular stance of compromising with the AIOC. The Americans were initially pleased with the shah's new prime minister, and hoped that Razmara would work towards stamping out corruption but soon realized that this was not to be the case. Their dislike of Razmara was influenced by Razmara's closeness to the British and the AIOC. The British placed high hopes in Razmara finding a favorable settlement for them in the AIOC dispute.[36] Razmara also accommodated British and Soviet desires to restrict the activities of US diplomatic and military personnel in Iran.[37] Razmara was in fact well known for his pro-Soviet and Tudeh sympathies.[38] He even refused to continue negotiating with the Americans regarding the transfer of loans to Iran.[39] Razmara was also unpopular in Washington due to his refusal to send Iranian troops to fight in Korea. Given these factors, it is not altogether surprising that Iranian–American relations sank to their lowest level since the Second World War.

Some British statesmen at this time agreed that the Iranians should be more fairly compensated, to the chagrin of London's "imperialists."[40] Realizing the strength of the rising nationalist movement in Iran, the AIOC came forward in early 1951 with the same 50–50 profit-split which the Saudi Arabian government had reached with the American-owned ARAMCO (Arabian American Oil Company).[41] The caveat for the Iranians was that they had to approve the supplemental agreement first.[42] The offer was rejected by the Iranian nationalists who now aimed at completely eliminating all British influence from Iran.

On March 3, 1951, Razmara appeared before the Majlis to dissuade them from full nationalization and to encourage them to ratify the supplemental agreement.[43] His main concerns were over Iran's lack of knowledge and technology. Razmara's days however were numbered. Just four days after his speech at the Majlis, he was assassinated.[44]

With a majority of votes the Majlis named Mossadegh for premiership of Iran on April 28, 1951. The shah accepted, and appointed Mossadegh as the prime minister on May 1.[45] The Majlis voted to nationalize the AIOC and just days after becoming prime minister, Mossadegh cancelled the Iranian oil concession, officially taking over all of the assets of AIOC. This was a significant move as the concession would not be up for another 42 years, in 1993. On the other hand, this was nothing irregular in the international arena as Britain itself had nationalized a number of assets as had Mexico.[46]

London, which viewed the AIOC as a British corporation and asset, was infuriarated. The British became further incensed by the arrival of Majlis representatives into Khuzistan, to implement Mossadegh's action.[47] Basil Jackson (a representative of AIOC) again re-extended the British 50-50 offer to Mossadegh in June 1951, but Iranian nationalists were determined to nationalize Iran's petroleum.[48] As noted by Katouzian, the primary objective of oil nationalization was to achieve complete oil independence as a prerequisite towards an enduring democratic Iranian government.[49] Mossadegh and his colleagues argued that Iran stood little chance of establishing true sovereignty and lasting democratic government as long as the British owned and operated the petroleum industry in Khuzistan.[50]

After first discounting military action to take Abadan and its AIOC facilities, by July 20 the British government was reconsidering its options. Emmanuel Shinwell, the British minister of defence, wanted to demonstrate British resolve to those Arabs of the Middle East who thought that they could nationalize economic assets such as the Suez Canal.[51] An ardent imperialist, Shinwell wanted to show Tehran that the AIOC could never be evicted from Iran.[52] He seriously believed that the crushing of Iran would elevate London's prestige in Arab eyes.[53]

The British drafted operations *Midget* and *Buccaneer*.[54] Operation *Midget* was the evacuation of all British citizens in Abadan and the AIOC facilities. This would be followed by Operation *Buccaneer*, the military seizure of Abadan/AIOC. The next phase was to hold Abadan/AIOC against Iranian counterattacks. Despite Foreign Secretary Herbert Morrisson's enthusiasm, British military planners remained skeptical. London had few troops capable of coping with Khuzistan's hot summer climate and harsh terrain.[55] Bringing acclimatized British troops from Egypt was possible, but risky, as thinning the British presence there could risk Egyptian nationalists seizing the Suez Canal. There were serious supply and transportation shortages. British generals were also highly appreciative of fierce Iranian resistance. There were vivid memories of Iranian troops fighting to the last man in Abadan in 1941. This time the Iranians would be better prepared and expecting a British attack. These challenges forced the British to scale down their military objectives to just seizing Abadan Island. However, unfolding political events in the domestic Iranian and international arenas provided the British with other means to realize their objectives.

The AIOC withdrew its technical staff from Abadan by August 1951. The lack of indigenous technical expertise meant that the Iranians were unable to produce the oil in quantities required for export. London also lodged its complaint against Iran at the United Nations.[56] The British also arranged for a major boycott of Iranian oil and reinforced their warships in the Persian Gulf. The measures forced Iranian petroleum production to drop to virtually nil, just as the shah and the late Razmara had feared. This denuded Mossadegh of the funds he required for his planned reforms.

Mossadegh's main base of support rested in the major cities.[57] Despite Mossadegh's efforts at curtailing his royalist and conservative opponents, the shah with the support of the army did secure many royalists into the Majlis during the 1951 elections.[58] The tug of war between the shah and Mossadegh now came into the open. Mossadegh demanded that the shah appoint him as minister of war in July 1952. The shah refused, leading Mossadegh to resign. Veteran politician Ahmad Qavam was appointed as prime minister. On the day of his appointment he announced a reversal of Mossagegh's policy. This led to the breakout of riots in Tehran and other major cities.

The shah turned to the army to maintain order but the army was reluctant to fight civilian protestors, and Ayatollah Kashani issued a fatwa demanding army troops join the protestors against the government.[59] This was dangerous for the Shah as a number of younger officers began to consider mutiny. The shah backed down and yielded control of the ministry of war to Mossadegh. Having gained the upper hand, Mossadegh now began to undermine a key part of the shah's support: the army. Mossadegh cut the army's budget by 15%, transferred 15,000 from the army to the Gendarmerie, purged a number of senior ranking officers, and considered severing Iran from US military aid.[60] Mossadegh also set up commissions to investigate corruption, nepotism, military promotions and acquisitions in the army.[61] While Mossadegh had won over the loyalty of many factions in the military and police, the overall loyalty of the 200,000-man Iranian army and 50,000 police to Mossadegh remained far from certain.[62] Many in the army were suspicious of Mossadegh's seemingly lax attitude towards the pro-Soviet Tudeh party as its patron, the Soviet Union, looked favorably on any weakening of Iran's military potential; of the threat posed by Mossadegh's budget cuts; and royalist elements within the armed forces were at odds with Mossadegh's stance towards the shah.[63]

In the meantime British intelligence operatives in Tehran had been active since the early 1950s, spreading funds to undermine Mossadegh.[64] Morrisson turned to Iran experts such as Ann K. S. Lambton, who suggested that the British not compromise with Mossadegh and to use "effective lines of propaganda" to mobilize Iranian public opinion against him.[65] Lambton also suggested rejecting US attempts at finding a compromise, as in her opinion "The Americans do not have the experience or psychological insight to understand Persia."[66] British intelligence soon established links with discontented army officers to plan for an anti-Mossadegh takeover. The British strongly favored General Fazlollah Zahedi, due to his extensive links with many key army officers. Zahedi had actually been arrested by the British in 1943 for his pro-German sympathies, but the British viewed this as an asset, as Zahedi could not be easily tainted as pro-British.[67] The British also forged ties with a number of key gendarmerie officers, the air force, the imperial guards and even the Iranian secret police.[68]

The Truman administration was not altogether sympathetic to the British but they did attempt to mediate between them and the Iranians.[69] American public opinion was in fact sympathetic with Mossadegh. This was exemplified by the 1952 *TIME* magazine's choice of Mossadegh as "Man of the Year," describing him as "The Iranian George Washington."[70] US sympathies for Mossadegh quickly changed with the 1953 presidential election which ushered in the administration of Dwight D. Eisenhower.

British-Iranian relations took a turn for the worse when Mossadegh severed Iran's diplomatic ties with London in October 1952.[71] British intelligence operatives lost no time in proposing to the Americans that they cooperate in the overthrow of Mossadegh. The British convinced their

American counterparts that Mossadegh was becoming increasingly pro-communist and pro-Soviet.[72] This rang alarm bells in Washington, and British intelligence and CIA (Central Intelligence Agency) worked together towards the dislodgement of Mossadegh. The British and American press now began printing articles critical of Mossadegh. In March 1953, John Foster Dulles, US Secretary of State, ordered his younger brother, Allen Dulles, the head of the CIA, to implement plans for ejecting Mossadegh from power. Four months later, on June 25, 1953, Kermit "Kim" Roosevelt, a grandson of Theodore Roosevelt, met John Foster Dulles and gained his approval for Operation *Ajax* to remove Mossadegh.[73] The British nickname for the project was Operation *Boot*.[74] Eisenhower gave the final order for Operation *Ajax* to commence after Mossadegh opened trade negotiations with the Soviet Union on August 8, 1953.[75]

A *New York Times* report of October 1, 1951 opined that Russia's advocacy of the AIOC issue was self-serving and geared for the promotion of communism in Iran.[76] The interpretation was clear: Russia's sense of helpfulness in this case was self-serving rather than a genuine concern for the Iranian people. The American decision to support the British in removing Mossadegh was primarily animated by the fear of a communist takeover of Iran rather than a concern for British petroleum interests.[77] How dangerous was the Tudeh party? Did they have the capacity to force a pro-Moscow communist coup? How powerful were the Tudeh in Mossadegh's governing apparatus? The strength of the Tudeh was not so much in their numbers but in their Soviet-style organization and discipline. CIA estimates placed the overall strength of the Tudeh in October 1952 at around 25,000 members, with 8,000 of these in Tehran.[78] They had certainly played a major role in organizing protests in support of Mossadegh, from the summer of 1951 to late 1952. Their role was even acknowledged by Ayatollah Kashani who wrote a (public) letter to pro-Tudeh organizations thanking them for their efforts.[79] While the issue of whether the Tudeh and the Soviet Union could have taken over Iran can be debated, there are few doubts as to their ultimate objective. An interesting observation is made by Louis in reference to a discovery in the Tudeh offices of Tehran, "a packing case of postage stamps overprinted with the words 'Republic of Iran' … a reminder of what might have happened had the Soviet Union intervened."[80] Mossadegh himself had opened trade negotiations with the Soviet Union on August 8, 1953, an action which prompted President Eisenhower to give his final sanction for the commencement of Operation *Ajax*.[81]

Operation *Ajax*

The British-led boycott of Iranian oil was now sharply undermining the Iranian economy. This led to a weakening of the Mossadegh administration's support base, as the strict measures used to manage anti and pro-Mossadegh demonstrators.

The British and American plan to remove Mossadegh hinged on the Shah's decision to issue a Farman to have Mossadegh removed from office. This would give legal sanction through the constitution for Mossadegh's removal as prime minster; issuing such a Farman was within the legal and constitutional powers invested in the shah. Kermit Roosevelt spoke to the shah, but the monarch stated that he was reluctant to confront Mossadegh.[82] Roosevelt is then reputed to have told the shah that his failure to act could lead to a communist takeover of Iran or even another Korea.[83] The shah finally issued his Farman a few days later, but his inability to act quickly would cost the conspirators.

Nematollah Nassiri, the head of the imperial guards, failed to capture the army chief of staff, General Taqhi Riahi, and the latter, who had learned of the plot, began directing Mossadegh loyalists to counter Operation *Ajax*. Not realizing that Riahi was aware of his intentions, Nassiri went to Mossadegh's private residence, intending to personally deliver the shah's Farman to Mossadegh and arrest him. Instead Nassiri was arrested by pro-Mossadegh army troops on August 15, 1953.[84] With Nassiri captive, *Ajax* fell apart. Numbers of royalist army officers, including General Zahedi, went into hiding, while many others were arrested. The shah, realizing that the plan had collapsed, boarded an airplane for Baghdad. Once there, he declared on Baghdad radio that he had issued two decrees: one for dismissing Mossadegh as prime minister and another appointing General Zahedi to that post.

Despite his thwarting of Operation *Ajax*, Mossadegh had failed to hold his alliance with Ayatollah Kashani. This was a crucial failure as Kashani was a leading member of the clergy and commanded the respect and admiration of Iran's conservative religious elements. The relationship had deteriorated as early as January 1953 when Kashani had rebuffed Mossadegh's demands that he be given more powers in the Majlis. Kashani had also shielded Zahedi from arrest by providing him with sanctuary in the Majlis in April 1953.[85] By this time Kashani was no longer an ally of Mossadegh, mainly due to the latter's advocacy of secular reforms.[86] Like the royalists, the conservatives soon forged their own ties with the British and Americans.[87] Mossadegh came to increasingly rely on the left and the Tudeh for support as he lost the support of influential figures like Kashani.[88]

The failure of Operation *Ajax* simply prompted Kermit Roosevelt to revise his tactics. This time the key emphasis would be placed on disaffected units in the army. Roosevelt ordered the surviving anti-Mossadegh leaders to begin a massive propaganda campaign against Mossadegh. First, it was declared that recent events were in effect a coup by Mossadegh. Second, army troops were encouraged to collectively side with Zahedi and the shah. This message proved only partially successful. Finally, the shah's Farman dismissing Mossadegh as prime minister, was vigorously promoted.

At this juncture the American military mission led by General Robert McClure directly intervened in support of Operation *Ajax*. McClure ensured the delivery of vital military supplies to Zahedi and his supporters. Roosevelt pressured McClure to go further by recruiting as many Iranian army leaders as possible. This was a tough sell as many army commanders such as Riahi could not be bought off by promises of money or future advancements. Persistence and financial inducements finally led to the winning over of one tank battalion and two infantry battalions in Tehran. The big prize was Colonel Teymour Bakhtiar's powerful Kermanshah garrison, armed with tanks and armored vehicles.

The CIA also played on genuine Iranian fears of a communist takeover by staging crowds posing as Tudeh demonstrators, who then ran amuck in the streets.[89] Mossadegh, acting on the advice of the US ambassador, sent in security forces to subdue the alleged Tudeh demonstrators, while asking the National Front to stay off the streets. This failed to stabilize the situation as by August 16, 6,000 armed pro-shah demonstrators reportedly funded by the CIA, began spilling into the streets.[90] There is evidence that the CIA attacked the homes of prominent clergy members, using written threats and intimidating graffiti to attribute these actions to Mossadegh's followers.[91] The riots got progressively worse by August 18. This was the beginning of the end as large numbers of soldiers simply melted into the pro-shah crowds. The majority of the soldiers were simply supporters of the shah who were unhappy with Mossadegh's policies towards the army. The CIA's plan worked as these not only made common cause with the crowds but even began to organize these and provided support with their tanks and artillery.[92] This swung the balance against pro-Mossadegh army troops who were forced to yield many streets to anti-Mossadegh forces. The latter proceed to sack all pro-Mossadegh government stations and media outlets. The situation further deteriorated when Nassiri, now freed from captivity, rapidly proceeded to mobilize imperial guard units to support Zahedi's factions. It was now General Riahi's turn to be arrested. Police and army units loyal to Zahedi and Nassiri fanned out across the capital to crush all remaining pro-Mossadegh units.

As the streets were being cleared of pro-Mossadegh forces, Zahedi finally emerged from hiding to climb aboard a Sherman tank to declare a new government.[93] He had driven with a military escort to Tehran's radio station to officially proclaim the shah's Farman that he was now replacing Mossadegh as prime minister. But Mossadegh's supporters would not give up so easily. Army troops loyal to Mossadegh fell back to make their last stand at Mossadegh's residence. Standing firm with a few Sherman tanks and a handful of machineguns, these troops beat back attack after attack of pro-Shah army tank units in a bloody nine-hour battle.[94] The pro-Mossadegh army troops finally ran low on ammunition but fought on to allow Mossadegh to escape. By now Bakhtiar's tanks and armored cars had rolled into Tehran from Kermanshah. With the National Front crushed, the shah returned to Iran from his brief exile in Rome on August 23, 1953.

Mossadegh chose to surrender to the authorities on August 21. He was put on trial for high treason, sentenced to solitary confinement for three years in a military prison and then allowed to return to his home in Tehran's environs, where he stayed under house arrest until his death in 1967.

In the strict military sense, Mossadegh's fundamental error was in forcing the "royalist" elements in the army to choose between himself and the shah.[95] Mossadegh's association with the Tudeh certainly did not help his cause among those army officers who were undecided until the eleventh hour. Perhaps it may be speculated that had Mossadegh attempted to reach out more to the military's undecided elements, he may have had more support from them in his hour of need. Mossadegh did indeed have an extraordinary talent in reaching out to factions outside of his political *weltanschauung*, such as the clergy, and the Tudeh. In the case of the military Mossadegh remained content with those troops and police whom he had already won over. In the end it was these loyal troops who stood by him to the bitter end.

Mossadegh remains a national hero among a wide spectrum of Iranians to this day. He was an Iranian nationalist propelled by a determined anti-imperialist zeal to wrest Iran's petroleum out of AIOC hands. There is little disagreement among mainstream historiographers that Mossadegh was the victim of imperialist forces bent on preserving their petroleum interests.[96] The irony of this tragic chapter of Iranian history and Iranian–Western relations is that Mossadegh continued to hold a high regard for the Americans and blamed the orchestration of his removal on the British, whom he profoundly disliked.[97] Though successful, Operation *Ajax* had come at great cost: it had damaged the image of the US amongst many Iranians over the long term. Mackey notes that it was in the wake of *Ajax* when the term "nest of spies" came to be applied to the US embassy, with the Iranian acronym for the CIA, "*Siya,*" transforming into a defamatory term across the political spectrum.[98] These sentiments would fester until their explosion in the 1979 revolution.

CHAPTER 31

THE IRANIAN MILITARY: DEVELOPMENT, DEPLOYMENT, AND CHALLENGES (1946–78)

The Iranian Army 1946–79

The occupation of northern Iran by the Soviet Union and its attempt to absorb Azarbaijan was a major basis for Iran's alliance with the West during the Cold War. The major expansion of the armed forces took place from the early 1960s. The total size of the armed forces rose from 218,500 in 1963 to 413,000 in 1977.[1] By that time Iran had a total of three armored divisions, three infantry divisions, four independent brigades (with Special Forces and commandos) and an imperial guard.[2] Iran could also draw upon a reserve force of 300,000 men, along with 60,000 gendarmes in case of a major war.

The flow of arms and economic support from the US steadily increased after 1953.[3] US military and economic aid delivered between 1949 and 1952 totaled 32 million USD, while aid between 1955 and 1957 totalled 500 million dollars.[4] Of the latter sum, 125 million USD was for the military sector.[5] Much of this was due to the looming Soviet threat and the Cold War, though the devaluation of the dollar also had an effect. Iran also began to face the serious threat of Arab nationalism allied to the Soviet Union. By the 1970s, Iraq was being heavily armed by the Soviet Union, obliging Iran to increase its military expenditures.

Iran's total number of towed artillery pieces by 1979 was 1,072 alongside 482 US-made self-propelled M-107/M-109 artillery.[6] Iran had a total of 825 armored personnel carriers that included US- and Soviet-made vehicles.[7] Iran in fact concluded an overall economic agreement with the Soviet Union in 1967 which committed the latter to furnish Iran with 110 million dollars' worth of weaponry.[8] For air defense, Iran had a total of 1,800 antiaircraft guns (including the radar-guided Swiss-designed Oerlikon systems) and the highly effective US-made I-HAWK (Improved Homing All the Way Killer) medium- to high-level surface-to-air missiles. The HAWK was to give a very good account of itself in the defense of Iranian ground forces Kharq Island, and cities throughout the Iran–Iraq War. For low-level air defense, the Iranians relied on British-made Rapier missiles.

Iran had a total of 400 Huey, CH-47 Chinook (heavy transport), and various other transport helicopters before the Iran–Iraq War. These were crucial for the rapid troop transport, medical evacuations, reconnaissance, as well as command and control. Orders for another 186 Chinooks were not delivered due to the Revolution. The Iranian army would have become possibly one of the most air-mobile in western Asia had these joined the 22 Chinooks already in Iranian service in

1971. This capability would have allowed the Iranians to rapidly deploy large numbers of commandos in the path of invading forces or behind enemy lines.

The arrival of at least 220 AH-1 Cobras armed with a multibarrel mini-gun and antitank TOW missiles made it a great combat asset against enemy armor. Iranian Cobra pilots were trained to use geographical features to camouflage their approach, then "pop up" unexpectedly to attack enemy armor. The Cobras played a crucial role in compensating against larger numbers of Iraqi tanks during the Iran–Iraq War. Another 890 helicopters (transport and combat) had been ordered but never delivered due to the Revolution.[9]

There was a major emphasis on acquiring heavy firepower from the 1960s, especially with regards to self-propelled guns and tanks. There was also an impressive array of antitank missiles, notably the TOW. Despite the impressive increase in personnel and expenditure, the land army had yet to develop its full potential as many tanks, self-propelled guns, and armored personnel carriers were never delivered as a result of the Revolution. This meant that despite its rising military strength, Iran's tank forces were smaller than those of Iraq. Iran's total inventory of tanks just prior to the outbreak of the Iran–Iraq War stood at just 1,735 machines (400 M-47/-48, 460 M-60, 875 Chieftain) along with 250 light tanks unsuitable for tank-to-tank duels. Iraq's tank force in 1979 totalled 2,650.[10] In addition, nearly half of Iran's tanks were the older US-made M-47/48/60 tanks which were upgraded with gun stabilizers and laser-range finders. Iran had ordered 3,000 tanks and 9,000 antitank missiles in a bid to overcome Iraq's edge in armor, but these never arrived due to the Revolution.[11]

Iran's fleet of early-production Chieftain tanks proved to be a disappointment during the Pahlavi era and the subsequent Iran–Iraq War. Numerous Iranian officers were legitimately concerned that the early-production Chieftain's weak engine would dangerously compromise its mobility against Iraq's rapid-moving Soviet armor in Khuzistan's flat terrain.[12] There were also problems with the early Chieftain series' computer data feed device for the fire-control system.[13] These problems led to negotiations with London to ship a number of the tanks back to England for engine refits and computer overhauls. These plans never materialized due to the Revolution. This may partly explain Iran's large losses of the Chieftain to Iraqi forces during the early phases of the Iran–Iraq War.

The expanding armaments industry

Iran had made large strides in the development of its indigenous arms industries by 1977. The shah's decision to reduce Iran's dependence on the West for weapons systems appears to have been made right after the 2,500-year celebrations in 1971. Until that time Iranian arms industries were mainly capable of producing light weapons, heavy machineguns, artillery and ammunition. Iran's industrialization drive had received a major boost with the establishment of a machine tool manufacturing plant and a steel plant in Isfahan.[14] This reaped major benefits for the Iranian arms industries. Despite the Soviet origins of the steel mill and machine tool plants in Isfahan, Iran mainly relied on Western technology and knowledge to develop its industrial and defense industries. By 1978, vast strides had been made with respect to armored vehicles, aeronautics, missiles, and electronics technology. Despite major disruptions as a result of the Revolution, these developments were resumed during the Iran–Iraq War and have continued to this day.

Facilities were established for the repair and overhaul of tanks and armored vehicles. The most ambitious plan was the design of the *Shir Iran* (Lion of Iran) tank with British expertise. On a par with cutting-edge western designs such as the US M-1, the Shir Iran featured Chobham armor and a 120-mm main gun. The tank underwent a series of trials and evaluations in England in 1977 and plans were underway to produce it in Shiraz and Isfahan.[15] The Revolution put a halt to the project, with the initial UK-produced batch of undelivered tanks later sold to Jordan as the Khaled. The design of the Shir Iran weapons platform provided the basis for the British Challenger.[16]

The shah had expressed an early interest in developing Iranian capabilities for the construction of jet fighters. One notable proposal in the 1960s was for a joint Iranian-Pakistani venture to produce the French-designed Mirage fighter in Iran. The Mirage proposal never materialized as the Iranian military brass preferred US-aeronautics technology. By 1978, Iranian contracts with US companies (i.e. Northrop, Bell, Lockheed) had resulted in the establishment of a vast infrastructure for the overhaul, manufacture, research and design of aircraft and helicopters. These factories came with state of the art manufacturing technology, accompanied with management systems training for supervisors, along with specialized programs for engineers, technicians and workers.[17] This was to be the basis of a powerful, high-tech, indigenous military aeronautics industry that would collaborate in weapons production for the army and navy. By 1977 two major plants had been established in Tehran and Isfahan. Many of these projects had become operational before the Revolution, notably factories for the final assembly of Huey helicopters from imported kits.

The Parchin facility had become a major research and development centre for missiles, warheads and explosives by 1977–78. It is possible that the shah was also pursuing a nuclear development project at Parchin. A massive production facility for the venerable Maverick missile was being constructed in Shiraz, complete with a "clean room" for the assembly of sensitive equipment such as electronics gear and specialized optics.[18] The Maverick remains highly popular with Iranian pilots given its excellent track record as a "tank buster" during the Iran–Iraq War. There were also assembly plants for rocket-propelled grenade launchers, artillery rockets, and other types of missiles. Plans were underway for the establishment of repair workshops and production facilities for the entire US-designed HAWK missile system, as well as extensive training programs for managers, technicians and engineers.[19] The Iranians also made strides towards the development of their electronics capabilities.[20]

Expansion of the Iranian Air Force: 1946–79

The Anglo-Soviet invasion of 1941 had been a powerful setback to the progress and development of the small Iranian Air Force. The conclusion of the Second World War allowed for the reinvigoration of Iranian air power. By late 1949 Iran had obtained more modern aircraft for its inventory, notably the P-47 Thunderbolt fighter-bomber and C-47 Dakota transporters. The Iranian air force slowly rebuilt until the late 1950s when the service began to dramatically augment its equipment and capabilities.

The name of the Iranian air force was officially changed to the "Neero Havaye-e Shahanshahi-e Iran" [The Imperial/Monarchial Iranian Air Force or IIAF] on June 30, 1956. The IIAF entered the jet age on receipt of T-33 trainers in 1956, the F-84G Thunderjet fighter in 1957, and the more modern F-86 Sabre in 1960. Just before the arrival of the F-84Gs, the Iranian government had sent 15 pilots to the USAF's Fursten Feldbrook base to engage in jet pilot training. Among the Iranians were Mohammad Khatami and Nader Jahanbani, who played crucial roles in leading Iran's air force into the jet age. Ten of these pilots (including Khatami) returned to Iran after a round of intense training with another five (including Jahanbani) remaining in Fursten Feldbrook to continue more advanced jet flight training. Jahanbani and the rest of the Iranian team returned to Iran after completing their courses in Germany. They then quickly began to work with their colleagues in Iran to develop the Iranian air force.

Jahanbani worked very hard to develop Iran's first acrobatic jet team, after becoming familiar with the USAF's Sky Blazers aerial acrobatic team in Fursten Feldbrook. He eventually succeeded in inaugurating Iran's first jet acrobatic team of four F-84Gs. Known as the "Taj e Tallaee" [The Golden Crown], these made their first public performance on October 30 1958. The Golden Crown team was soon equipped with more modern aircraft by 1971 the team had upgraded to the F-5 Tiger. The Taj e Tallaee was much more than just aerial entertainment. The team became one of the venues for developing sophisticated aerial flying skills for Iran's new generation of top-gun pilots. Khatami and other high-level air force brass realized that Iranian pilots would one day be called upon to bomb and strafe Soviet-type armored formations. Nevertheless, the US refusal to sell Iran avionic anti-radar electronic equipment in the 1970s obliged Iranian pilots to train in flying at very low levels. Most significant was the fact that the Iranians received the best US training, often from combat-seasoned Vietnam-era pilots. The Iranian government's heavy investment in air-combat training resulted in the rise of a world-class cadre of pilots.

Air transport capabilities were significantly improved with the arrival of the robust C-130 Hercules transport planes, which numbered 54 by 1979. These finally gave the Iranian military the means to rapidly deploy troops and equipment across Iran's diverse and often difficult terrain. Orders had been placed for an additional 57, but the Revolution prevented the deliveries from taking place. Iran's fleet of Boeing jets was also intended to rapidly transport arms into Iran in case of a major war.

A substantial budget was earmarked for the development of the air force by the Shah, who appointed Air Marshall Mohammad Khatami to oversee this process. Iran received the F-5 Tiger from February 1, 1965 giving it a significant boost in fighter-bomber capabilities. The air force in 1965 was equipped with a modest total of 75 combat aircraft and 7,000 personnel. Just three years later, the service had expanded its compliment to 15,000 personnel and 200 combat aircraft.[21] The delivery of the more powerful F-4 Phantom from September 18, 1968 transformed the IIAF into a world-class air force. By 1979 Iran possessed 190 F-4s alongside 160–166 F-5s.[22] The F-5/F-4 combination granted Iran a clear edge against the Iraqi air force. The Iranians also armed their aircraft with the latest air-to-air missiles (i.e. Sparrow) and guided bombs (especially the deadly Maverick). They also worked to establish an extensive ground crew support and maintenance system.

The arrival of 77 F-14A Tomcat fighters by 1977 ensured that Iran became the most modern air force in the Middle East, second only to Israel. A marvel of aeronautical engineering, the Tomcat allowed Iran to challenge the latest Soviet aircraft, and drones within its airspace.[23] The Tomcat was capable of tracking multiple targets simultaneously with its deadly AWG-9 radar system and posed a mortal threat against enemy aircraft with its potent and accurate Phoenix missiles. Iran had ordered a total of 714 Phoenix missiles from the US, but only 284 of these were delivered before the Revolution.[24] Another advantage of the Tomcat was its ability to quickly take off from short runway spaces.[25] Quick air interceptions were crucial given northern and western Iran's proximity to Soviet and Iraqi air bases respectively. The Tomcat was to prove its worth in spades throughout the Iran–Iraq War.

Iran also "multiplied" its air fleet of 400-plus combat aircraft with its acquisition of 24 KC-707 and KC-747 "Jumbo Jet" airborne tankers by 1977; orders had also been placed for an additional 24, but these were never delivered. The air tankers significantly increased the combat times and radii of Iran's combat aircraft, greatly enhancing their ground strike and aerial interception capabilities. But these developments were just the beginning. Plans were underway to further expand and modernize Iran's already formidable air fleet. Iran had placed orders for an additional 250 F-4 fighter-bombers and 78 F-14A fighters by 1977. There were also orders for 140 state-of-the-art F-16s and 250 F-18s with keen interest being expressed for at least 53 F-15 all-weather air superiority fighters.[26] The F-16s were to replace the F-5 fleet by the early 1980s;[27] the F-5s would then be relegated to training. The F-18s were to replace the F-4s over a longer period of time. With the exception of some spare parts for the F-16s, no F-16 aircraft ever arrived in Iran, nor the additional F-14s, newer F-18s, or F-15s.[28] The Revolution also resulted in a number of trials, purges, and executions, misleading Iraqi war planners (and many Western analysts) to the erroneous conclusion that the IIAF could no longer pose a threat against an Iraqi invasion. Iran had also ordered seven airborne aerial radar platforms (AWACS), with the ability to monitor a radius of 200 miles, but these were not delivered. The AWACS airborne radar platform could have possibly elevated the striking accuracy and capabilities of Iranian aircraft to Western or NATO levels of effectiveness.

The Iranian navy: 1946–79

The Iranian navy proceeded to rebuild its modest fleet after the Second World War. Its first move was to negotiate with British India for the repatriation of four ships (*Shahrokh*, captured by British forces in August 1941. These were returned to Iran in December 1946. Britain also donated two combat vessels to Iran in compensation for the two Iranian ships she sank in August 1941; these were christened the *Babr* and *Palang*.

The build-up of the Iranian navy was slow at first, with modern naval equipment first being delivered in 1955 after Iran joined the Baghdad Pact.[29] The navy's personnel then increased six-fold in 1965 from 1,000 to 6,000 men, reaching a total of 30,000 men before the Revolution.[30] By this time Iran had acquired a small but effective fleet of mainly US- and British-built vessels organized into five divisions (a major fleet, light fleet, minesweeping, coastguard, and auxiliary-support services) in the Persian Gulf. Iran also operated a single base at Bandar Pahlavi (Bandar Anzali) in the Caspian Sea.

The major Persian Gulf fleet consisted of three destroyers (three armed with surface-to-surface missiles (SSMs), two also armed with surface-to-air missiles (SAMs), four frigates (all armed with Seakiller SSMs and Seacat SAMs),[31] and four corvettes. The light fleet was organized around seven large patrol craft, three patrol gunboats, and five formidable French-built Combattante II Fast patrol boats armed with missiles. The minesweeping group consisted of three coastal and two inshore minesweepers. There was an extensive coastguard of 62 coastal patrol vessels, 40 harbor patrol vessels, and another two vessels specialized for customs operations. The auxiliary, transport and services division consisted of four landing/logistical support ships, six landing craft (for tanks), two ships for logistical support, three water tanker ships, five survey and research craft, one ship for repair operations, one supply ship, two floating docks, one yacht, and 14 tugs.[32]

The Royal Navy departed from the Persian Gulf in 1971, and by 1977 the Iranian navy had grown to virtually dominate the waters of the Persian Gulf. Iranian naval bases were located at Bandar Abbas, Kharq Island, Bushehr, Bandar Shapur, and Hengam Island. Iranian planners were also looking towards the Indian Ocean. A major naval and air base was being built at Chahbahar to enable Iran to project its military assets into the Indian Ocean. Plans were also underway to significantly expand the Iranian navy with a new inventory of ships, aircraft, and helicopters before the revolution. Among the items ordered were four Spruance-class destroyers (8,000 tons each), 12 Frigates (3,000 tons each) armed with Harpoon ship-to-ship missiles, 12 Combattante II Class missile boats, 12 submarines (three US-made and nine German-made), 14 hovercraft, 50 Sikorsky (transport) and Sea Cobra (combat) helicopters, tankers, landing craft, and transport ships.[33]

Iran's navy was not comparable to Western, American or Soviet navies, but it was more than a match against any potential adversaries in the Persian Gulf.[34] By the mid-1970s Iran had established the world's largest hovercraft base at Kharq Island, and Iran's fleet of hovercraft enabled commandos to be rapidly deployed into the islands and coasts of the Persian Gulf. The landing craft could easily follow up any operation.

Considerable attention had been accorded to reducing the vulnerability of the Iranian navy and petroleum assets to Soviet and/or Iraqi military action. Both Abadan and Khorramshahr are very close to southern Iraqi border, making them highly vulnerable to Iraqi artillery strikes and infantry-tank thrusts. As a result of these concerns, Kharq Island had replaced Abadan as Iran's main oil export outlet, with the main headquarters of the Iranian navy transferred from Khorramshahr to Bandar Abbas.

CENTO, the Soviet threat and the Arab frontiers

The US was eager to prevent the spread of communism in the Middle East and looked to Iran, Iraq, Turkey and Pakistan to create a regional pro-Western and anti-Soviet alliance. This was the brainchild of John Foster Dulles which materialized as the Baghdad Pact, first signed between Iraq and Turkey in Baghdad on February 24, 1955.[35] The Baghdad Pact was soon joined by Britain, Pakistan, and Iran.[36] It would not be long before the Baghdad Pact lost its Iraqi member. A brutal revolt erupted in Iraq on July 14, 1958 in which King Faisal II was overthrown and slain by General Abdolkarim Ghassem. Ghassem, an ardent Iraqi nationalist, began distancing himself from the Baghdad Pact by refusing to partake in any of its conferences. The center of the alliance then shifted from Baghdad to Ankara and was soon renamed as CENTO (Central Treaty Organization) in August 1959. By that time Iraq had produced a written declaration that she was no longer a member of the alliance and finalized this by February 24, 1960.

The US did not formally join CENTO but provided it with military and political support. The Eisenhower doctrine committed the Americans to support regional allies threatened by communism, and in the case of Iran and Turkey, threatened by Soviet invasion.[37] Iran for example, received its first jet fighters from the US to help strengthen it against the Soviet Union.[38] By 1959, Iran and the US had signed a bilateral military agreement. There were hopes that Afghanistan would also join CENTO but its border disputes with Iran dissuaded her from doing so.[39] Moscow was antagonized by CENTO and feared that the US would use Iran as a military base against the Soviet Union.[40]

Iran's military brass perceived the main threats to Iran's security as emanating from the Soviet Union to the north and the Arab world (mainly) to the west/southwest. The Soviet Union had already tried to absorb Iranian territory in the 1940s and continued to pose a special threat along Iran's northern borders. Iran, as a military and political ally of the West, was especially important to CENTO. Her Zagros Mountain chain was viewed as a strategic asset by Washington against a potential Soviet invasion.[41] Iran's petroleum assets and her strategic role in the Persian Gulf were critical to the West, as today. These factors ensured that the West and the US would militarily respond against Soviet forces attempting to invade Iran. US war planners recommended that Iran's defensive line against a Soviet invasion begin along the Zagros Mountain chain.[42] This was unacceptable to the Iranians as northern Iran would then have to be ceded to the Soviets, a factor that would severely undermine Iranian military morale.[43] The Iranians preferred a system of forward defense.

The role of Iran's regional CENTO partners in response to a Soviet advance into the Iranian plateau and the Persian Gulf would be crucial. The Turks, situated along Iran's northwest border, would be ideally positioned to laterally slice into Soviet forces invading Iran's Azarbaijan province. The Pakistani military would have the option of sending its units through Baluchistan to bolster their Iranian allies in the south or further north as military circumstances dictated.[44] The British could at best field a token land force against the Soviets in Iran, but their naval and air assets, in conjunction with US fleets and aircraft carriers, could prove deadly to the Soviets in southern Iran and the Persian Gulf.

Neither the shah nor the Iranian military had any illusions regarding Soviet military might, conventional or nuclear. Nevertheless, serious planning for a forward system of defense against a Soviet invasion were prepared.[45] Ground defense emphasized highly trained professional troops specialized in anti-armor and commando operations. The Shir Iran II tank was part of a long-term plan to create highly mobile armored and mechanized forces supported by antitank helicopter gunships and combat aircraft. These would presumably be held in reserve, perhaps to act as "fire brigades" by selectively counterattacking at the most threatened sectors. In reality, the best that the Iranians could do was to delay the Soviet armored juggernaut just long enough (optimistically 2–4 weeks) for US and Western help to materialize. The IIAF would have been central to Iran's defense, notably its F-14A fleet. Had the build-up of the Iranian air fleet been completed, invading Soviet aircraft and armor would have faced serious challenges. Iranian pilots had already been effectively trained to destroy Soviet armor, a capability which they demonstrated in July 1974.

By 1978, CENTO had become increasingly a ceremonial organization for the simple reason that its member states often failed to support each other in times of crisis. This was dramatically demonstrated in Pakistan's wars against India in 1965 and 1971. The exception was some military assistance by the Shah to Pakistan in its 1965 war with India.,[6] but the US blocked Iran from sending her US-made weaponry to aid Pakistan's war effort.[47] Iran also offered indirect support for Pakistan during the Indo-Pakistani war of 1971.[48] The US offered some military support for Pakistan in its

1971 war with India but not under CENTO auspices. With the breakaway of Bangladesh from Pakistan in the aftermath of the 1971 war, Iran officially declared that she was opposed to any further weakening of Pakistan.[49] Turkey's invasion of Cyprus in 1974 also weakened CENTO.

The Soviet Union had easily circumvented CENTO by establishing close alliances with the Arab world, notably Iraq, Egypt, Libya, Yemen, Somalia and Syria. Tehran had genuine concerns that Arab states, notably Syria and Iraq, would combine their forces against Iran. Iraq in particular had been militarily built up by the Soviets against Iran, especially after 1971. Iranian forces facing Arab armies to the south-southwest would be operating in "Middle Eastern" climates with warm temperatures and desert-like geography. Iran's Khuzistan province is especially vulnerable as its flat terrain is ideally suited for a blitzkrieg-style tank invasion. Arab armies (esp. Iraq and Syria) posed a serious threat against Iran with their large quantities of Soviet-built tanks.

In case of an invasion, the Iranian army envisaged a rapid armored build-up along its western frontier in the Mehran and Qasr-e Shirin area (to the north of Khuzistan). The Chieftain and US-made M-47/48/60 series tanks would be spearheaded by the Shir Iran II tanks. The tank force, supported by combat aircraft and helicopters, would advance towards Baghdad. Another armored force would counterattack from Khuzistan, supported by combat aircraft and helicopters, into southern Iraq to capture Basra. The Iranian army had in a series of intense exercises and maneuvers, worked extensively to hone its skills in maneuver and massive tank thrusts, in coordination with the helicopter fleet and air force. The buildup of the armored forces remained incomplete as a result of the Revolution as the Shir Iran II project remained in the prototype stage, much of Iran's tank orders remained undelivered, and a significant number of earlier Chieftains were in serious need of overhauls. The aftermath of the Revolution also reduced the efficiency and striking power of Iran's armored forces.

The combat doctrine of the IIAF in a possible war with Iraq was straightforward and based on that of the USAF. The IIAF was to initiate an overwhelming air offensive against Baghdad to achieve complete air superiority. The F-14 would be entrusted with high-altitude, long-range interception duties, with F-16s tasked with low-altitude, short-range interception against Iraqi fighters. Powerful strike packages of F-4s (to be eventually replaced by the F-18) would enter enemy airspace escorted by F-14s and F-16s.[50] The F-4s (to be later replaced by F-18s) supported by F-5s (to be completely replaced by F-16s) would strike to destroy enemy air defense sites, airfields and runways. Having secured complete air superiority, the IIAF would then shift its focus to supporting Iranian ground and naval services. Had the ordered combat aircraft arrived, Iran would have fielded a formidable air fleet of nearly 1,000 state-of-the art combat aircraft. The shah's ultimate aim was to have a core air superiority wing composed of 150 F-14s and 300 F-16s.[51]

The Persian Gulf: the Tunb and Abu Moussa islands

The Shah had been increasingly attentive to Iran's long and exposed Persian Gulf coastline. He was especially concerned with radical, leftist or revolutionary movements aiming to overthrow friendly governments in the Persian Gulf region. The shah was in fact to soon support the Sultan of Oman against a rebellion in that country's Dhofar region. The US and the West in general shared many of the shah's concerns in the 1970s and were keen to maintain the stability of the Persian Gulf.

The British Empire had engaged in a system of "indirect rule" in a number of Persian Gulf sheikhdoms. In practice, the sheikhdoms were London's colonies under her military protection.[52] By the early 1970s London had treaties in place to militarily defend Bahrain, Qatar, and the seven Trucial states or sheikhdoms (Abu Dhabi, Dubai, Um al-Quwain, Fujairah, Ajman, Ras al-Khaima and Sharjah). The main objective of these treaties was to protect the sheikhdoms against Iranian and Iraqi military actions.[53] The British also worked to keep the peace between the Arab states in the Persian Gulf.

In January 1968 Prime Minister Harold Wilson announced that Britain would completely withdraw her military assets and defense obligations "east of Suez" by December 1971.[54] This immediately placed British policy in a dilemma. Britain was an ally of Iran, especially through CENTO; she sold arms to Tehran and conducted joint naval exercises with the Iranian navy. The shah had also reluctantly consented to the UN-sponsored plebiscite report that stated Bahrain as being independent from Iran,[55] and the founding of the United Arab Emirates (UAE) from the seven Trucial states. He also militarily assisted British forces in Oman.

Positive Tehran–London relations hardly assuaged Iran's long-standing claims to the three islands (Greater Tunb, Lesser Tunb and Abu Moussa) strategically located on the western ingress of the Straits of Hormuz. The shah made it clear that he viewed the three islands as Iranian territory. In an interview with the Indian magazine *Blitz* on June 24, 1971 the shah asserted that the islands had been usurped from Iran in the 1890s, when Iran "had no central government."[56] Three days later Iranian Prime Minster Amir Abbas Hoveida reiterated the shah's position and emphasized the importance of these islands to Iran's economic and territorial security.[57]

Sharjah administered Abu Moussa, the largest of the three islands with the Greater and Lesser Tunbs being administered by Ras al-Khaima. The British took the side of their Arab clients (emirates of Ras al-Khaima and Sharjah) by supporting their claims to the islands.[58] But time was running out for London as the Royal Navy was to be fully withdrawn by December 1971. The Iranian government continued to pursue negotiations with the British and the Arabs right into late November.[59] Tehran concluded a "Memorandum of Understanding" with Sharjah on November 29, 1971 allowing Iranian forces to be stationed at Abu Moussa and that both governments would jointly administer the island.[60] Iranian troops then landed on the three islands the following day. This was just one day before the termination of the British treaty with Ras al-Khaima, which disputed the Iranian arrival to the Tunbs.[61] This led to a very brief and limited clash on the Greater Tunb.[62] Ras al-Khaima (which soon joined the UAE) was also offered a compromise by allowing her to exercise authority over the small Arab population of the Lesser Tunb[63] as the larger Tunb was largely uninhabited at the time.[64] To this day the issue of the three islands remains a source of friction between Iran and the UAE.

As strident pan-Arab nationalists, the Baath government of Iraq took great issue with the shah's arrival to the three Persian Gulf islands. Baghdad severed its diplomatic relations with Tehran and London over the issue. This was followed by a warming of relations between Iraq and the Soviet Union resulting in a 15-year Treaty of Friendship and Cooperation in April 1972.[65] The treaty led to a massive Soviet military aid program for Baghdad, which would soon receive advanced combat aircraft such as the supersonic Tu-22 bomber and the MiG-23 fighter-bomber, and top-of-the-line Soviet tanks (i.e. T-72). After their break with Tehran in late 1971, the Baath expelled "tens of thousands of persons of Persian descent" from Iraq into Iran during the 1970s.[66] Large numbers of Iraqi citizens of non-Iranian descent, suspected of disloyalty, were also deported during the summer of 1980, including 15,000 Shiite Kurds and 35,000 Arab middle-class Shiites.[67] The total number of citizens forcibly deported into Iran may have been as high as 200,000.[68] The Baath also sponsored Arab separatists in Iran's Khuzistan province.[69]

Iraq, the Kurdish question and the Algiers Accord

Iraq had emerged as one of the Arab successor states of the former Ottoman Empire following the First World War. Almost immediately, new Iraqi state's border demarcations with Iran became a major issue. Reza Shah was also focused on Iranian territorial issues regarding the Arvand Rud/Shaat al Arab waterway. He argued that the 1913 Protocol regarding the waterway had been unfavorable to Iran, and Iran had been forced to sign it. Broadly speaking, the origins of the waterway dispute can be traced right back to the Treaty of Zohab. By 1928, the Iranians preferred the boundary to be on the Thalweg principle: a median line along the waterway 'constructed from the main navigable channel."[70]

Iraq's foreign minister Nuri al-Said (1888–1958) took the matter to the League of Nations pointing out the strategic importance of the waterway for Iraq; that Iraq's maritime access was confined through the Arvand Rud/Shaat al Arab while Iran had a long coastline, numerous ports and a deep-sea harbor; and that Basra, Iraq's major port on the waterway, was vulnerable to Iran's ability to command its maritime traffic.[71] The British, who owned over 90% of local commercial shipping, were generally unsupportive of the Thalweg principle.[72] This was one of the reasons why the ensuing 1937 Treaty essentially affirmed Iraqi sovereignty over the waterway. The boundary was set at the low-water mark at the Iranian or eastern side of the waterway. This obliged ships entering it to host Iraqi pilots, fly the Iraqi flag and pay tolls to the Iraqi government.[73] Exceptions to the rule were areas near Khorramshahr and Abadan (where the Thalweg principle applied).[74] The Iranians were dissatisfied with the 1937 treaty.

Abdolkarim Ghassem, who overthrew Iraq's King Faisal II in 1958, exhibited anti-Western tendencies from the beginning of his time as prime minister.[75] He withdrew Iraq from the Baghdad Pact, and brought Iraq closer to the Soviet Union and Iraqi Communists. The last British forces departed from Iraq's Habbaniya airbase in 1959.

Ghassem also engaged in vigorous anti-Iranian rhetoric.[76] Just 18 months after his coup, Ghassem declared on December 18, 1959 that Iran's Khuzistan province was Iraqi land ceded to Iran by the Ottomans during the 19th century.[77] Ghassem began to sponsor separatist movements in Khuzistan. Ghassem's land claims against Iran met a cool reception at the Arab League. This was in large part due to his advocacy of indigenous Iraqi nationalism versus the pan-Arabist discourse of Egypt's Gamal Abdul Nasser.[78] Ghassem vacillated over joining the pan-Arab League of Syria and Egypt, a policy that angered the pan-Arabist officers of Iraq's military. Nevertheless, Ghassem had succeeded in laying the ideological foundations for the future Iraqi invasion of Iran. Even when Ghassem was overthrown, his irredentist ideology of "liberating" the Iranian Arabs would endure into the 1980s.

The Kurds of northern Iraq, who had aided Ghassem in his quest for power, began to demand greater autonomy.[79] Mullah Mustafa Barzani, the leader of the Iraqi Kurds, engaged in negotiations with Baghdad until 1961, after which fighting broke out between the Iraqi army and the Kurdish Democratic Party (KDP) at Ramiyah. Barzani's struggle aimed at achieving full Kurdish autonomy if not outright independence. By the 1960s, Iran began to provide support to the Kurds, as Iran felt increasingly threatened by her western neighbor's territorial ambitions.

Ghassem was finally overthrown by a coalition of pan-Arabists, army officers and Baathists led by Abdul Salem Aref and supported by the CIA and British intelligence in February 1963.[80] The Baathist leader, Hassan al-Bakr, became prime minster and vice president.[81] The US also supplied arms to the Baathists.[82] By 1966 he Soviets were reputedly attempting to send arms to the Iraqi Kurdish rebels through Iranian territory. It is not clear why such an attempt would be made. Iranian garrisons, gendarmerie and police stations, stationed across 190miles (300km) from the Soviet border to Iraq, could easily intercept the Soviet efforts.[83] Infighting within the Baathist party allowed Aref to strike with his own coup and ejected the Baath from political power.[84] Aref's death in 1966, led to the ascension of his brother, Abdur Rahman Aref.[85] He in turn was the victim of another CIA-supported coup in July 1968.[86] The coup was led by the Baathist leader Hassan Al-Bakr and his right-hand man Saddam Hussein.[87] Just one year after their return to power, Baathist government officials and radio stations began to reiterate Ghassem's propaganda against Khuzistan, encouraging Iranian Arabs to secede from Iran to join Iraq. Similar messages were also broadcast to the Baluchis of southeast Iran near Pakistan. This led the Shah to increase his support for the Iraqi Kurds who were increasingly armed and trained by Iranian "advisors."

On April 15, 1969 Iraqi officials declared that all Iranian ships entering the Arvand Rud/Shaat al Arab waterway had to lower their flags and that all Iranian nationals on those ships would have to disembark.[88] The shah put the Iraqi demand to the test by dispatching a merchant ship under escort by an Iranian gunboat into the waterway on April 24, 1969.[89] Iraqi forces did not open fire but Baghdad's frosty relations with Tehran rapidly took a turn for the worse. Five days after the arrival of the Iranian vessels, Amir Khosrow Afshar, the Iranian foreign minister, officially declared that Iran had unilaterally abrogated the 1937 treaty.[90] Iraq protested that the shah's action was in violation of international law. Both states mobilized their troops along their common border. Iranian artillery was quickly positioned on the eastern bank of the Arvand Rud/Shaat al Arab waterway with Iranian vessels in that waterway provided with air cover.[91] The Shah's Western-equipped and -trained military was more than a match for Iraq at the time, and Iraq opted out of a direct conflict with Iran.

By the 1970s Iran was concerned with Iraq's rising economic and military strength characterized by close ties with Iran's long-time nemesis, Russia. Baghdad signed a Friendship and Cooperation Treaty with Moscow in 1972, further raising concerns in Tehran and Washington. Baathist pan-Arabist discourse continued Ghassem's policies of encouraging secession among Iran's Khuzistan Arabs. Iran in turn sought ways to undermine the Iraqi state. The Americans had suggested that the shah support Mullah Mustafa Barzani of the KDP in northern Iraq. The Shah was reluctant to do this at first, as he suspected Barzani of being a communist.[92]

Baghdad, which was anxious to resolve its Kurdish problem, had come to an understanding with the Iraqi Kurds by 1974, and granted them considerable autonomy. The KDP remained dissatisfied as Baghdad retained control over Iraqi Kurdistan's oil-rich regions. Fighting was resumed as Barzani mobilized 45,000 fighters to quickly tie down 80,000 Iraqi troops in Iraqi Kurdistan.[93] Baghdad was also forced to divert 695 tanks, half of its entire tank force, against the KDP.[94]

Tehran, in concert with its American and Israeli allies, took advantage of Baghdad's Kurdish woes. The KDP began receiving US and Israeli weapons through Iranian territory. Iran began deploying its own Kurds to ferry supplies, ammunition and weapons to the Iraqi Kurds. The shah went further; he ordered Iranian antiaircraft guns and artillery to be positioned inside Iraqi territory. Key to these was Operation *Ararat* which entailed the dispatch of artillery elements from Rezaieh into Iraqi Kurdistan through the Tamarchin Pass.[95] This was a great boost to the KDP whose antiaircraft guns were from the First World War, incapable of shooting down modern Iraqi jets. Iran's actions were clearly provocative but there was little Baghdad could do. Four-fifths of Iraq's troops were now locked in battle against the KDP. Saddam Hussein retaliated by providing succor and assistance to the shah's political opponents. He also established up to five anti-shah radio stations in Iraq, and even tried to incite the Baluchis of southeast Iran against Tehran.[96]

Iraqi troops were deadlocked in their fight against the KDP, who engaged in guerrilla tactics. To break the stalemate, Baghdad launched a strong offensive in April 1974, relying on massive aerial bombardment, which also targeted Kurdish towns and villages. Tanks however, proved ineffective against the Kurds fighting from formidable mountain strongholds. The Iraqi army remained bogged down but aerial bombings continued well into June, with further (ineffectual) bombings in late September.

Saddam Hussein launched a new offensive in August 1974 towards the east of Mosul. The offensive went well at first with a formidable Iraqi armored force of 300 tanks managing to seize Ramiya, Qaleh Dizeh and Rawanduz.[97] The *Peshmerga* (Kurdish-Persian: those close to death/those who risk their lives) guerrillas of the KDP remained undefeated in the mountains. As Iraqi tanks again bogged down, Iranian artillery fire just across the border supported the Peshmerga. Despite having suffered heavy casualties in August, Baghdad refused to cave in. The Iraqi army launched yet another massive attack in November 1974, this time supported by swarms of fighter-bombers and bombers.[98] The Kurds succeeded in shooting down their first Iraqi aircraft in mid-November, apparently using more modern Iranian-supplied antiaircraft guns. By December, Iranian military personnel were fully engaged in supporting the KDP, with many of these (especially Iranian special forces elements) operating up to 31 miles (50km) inside Iraqi territory.[99] Tehran even placed Rapier and Hawk antiaircraft missiles inside Iraqi Kurdistan which shot down up to 18 Iraqi aircraft.[100]

By January/February 1975, two Iranian army regiments had moved into Iraqi Kurdistan.[101] A very serious confrontation took place on "Bloody Sunday," February 10, 1974, when both sides deployed heavy weaponry.[102] Baghdad was at a disadvantage as it had already lost much of its heavy equipment and up to 40,000 troops against the KDP.[103] Iran also succeeded in shooting down two more Iraqi jets. Iranian Phantoms were also active in southern Iraq, destroying an Iraqi army pontoon bridge over the Arvand Rud/Shaat al Arab waterway. Iraqi air defenses and aircraft had been virtually silent during these operations. The KDP was dominating a large chunk of northern Iraq.

The situation was now escalating out of control with both sides seeking a way to resolve their disputes. The UN Security Council called on both Iran and Iraq to de-escalate the situation in favor of negotiations.[104] Baghdad and Tehran urged the Turks and then the Algerians to engage in mediation. Representatives of Iran and Iraq began meeting to work towards a comprehensive settlement covering border disputes, the Arvand Rud/Shaat al Arab waterway, the Kurdish issue, etc. This resulted in the Algiers Treaty, signed on March 6, 1975. The treaty was in essence a *quid pro quo* arrangement. Baghdad yielded to Tehran's demand that the Thalweg principle be applied across the entirety of the Arvand Rud/Shaat al Arab waterway.[105] Iraq would also refrain from sponsoring separatist movements among Iranian Arabs and Baluchis.[106] In exchange, Iran agreed to cede small pockets of its territory to Iraq and to cease support of the KDP.[107] Iran withdrew its forces the day the treaty was signed, leaving the Kurds without artillery support.[108] More ominously, the withdrawal of the Iranian missile umbrella allowed Iraqi aircraft to finally press home their attacks against the KDP. Denuded of supplies and Iranian support, Kurdish resistance was doomed. Barzani, now an exhausted and shattered man, sought refuge along with hundreds of thousands of his followers in Iran, which granted them asylum and shelter.[109]

An Iranian delegation arrived in Baghdad in April 1975 to work out the details of their border demarcation treaty with the Iraqis. This resulted in the signing of the Iran–Iraq Treaty on International Borders and Good Neighborly Relations on June 13, 1975.[110] This stipulated the re-affirmation of the Algiers treaty; the demarcation of the fluvial boundary in accordance with the Thalweg principle; a pledge by both sides to halt any activities of "a subversive nature" upon each other's territory and; a re-emphasis on the indivisible nature of the treaty (meaning that the political and territorial concessions by both sides were crucial to the integrity of the treaty).[111] Just days after the signing of the treaty, Saddam Hussein ordered the Iraqi military to cross the border into Khuzistan.[112] Saddam, like much of the Iraqi leadership, may have been hoping to overturn the terms of the treaty to Iraq's advantage, or he may been testing the mettle of the Iranian armed forces.

Whatever Saddam's aims may have been, they certainly backfired. Iraqi military units crossed the Arvand Rud/Shaat al Arab waterway into Iran and rapidly built a pontoon bridge near Abadan on June 16, 1975. With near-lightning speed, Iraqi T-55 tanks, protected by the deadly self-propelled radar-guided ZSU-23-4 antiaircraft guns, rolled onto Iranian soil. For a brief moment Saddam Hussein may have concluded that he had gained a quick victory as the only opposition was a screen of lightly equipped border guards who were easily overcome. But, as events soon demonstrated, the Iranian military had prepared contingency plans for possible Iraqi tank thrusts into Khuzistan.

On the very same day when Iraqi tanks rolled into Iran (June 16), the IIAF dispatched four F-4E Phantoms armed with the new air-to-ground Maverick (AGM-65A) missiles. Another four F-4Es acted as fighter escorts against Iraqi jets trying to interfere with the "Maverick" Phantoms. The fighter escorts proved unnecessary as no Iraqi fighters scrambled to challenge the IIAF. Baghdad's recent experiences against Iranian HAWK and Rapier missiles in Iraqi Kurdistan may have dissuaded Iraqi jets from entering the combat zone.

The Phantoms closed onto the leading tanks of the Iraqi spearhead and in less than 20 minutes fired 12 Maverick missiles, destroying 12 Iraqi tanks.[113] The Iraqi bridgehead was now in complete disarray and at the mercy of Iranian forces. These quickly moved in the following day to wipe out the last surviving Iraqi forces on Iranian soil. The cost of ejecting the Iraqi advance was surprisingly light: three Iranians had been killed in exchange for 88 Iraqi personnel.[114] The relative ease with which the IIAF crushed the Iraqi armored advance came as a profound shock to the Iraqi military. Especially suprising was the absence of Iraqi SAMs and the inefficacy of their mobile antiaircraft guns. This may explain why just weeks later, Iraq ordered vast numbers of SAMs from the Soviet Union.[115] This battle was significant as it clearly demonstrated to Saddam and the Baath leadership that Iran's military power was superior to theirs. These humiliations were never forgotten by the Iraqi leadership, who patiently waited for a future opportunity to avenge their defeats.

Eastern Arabian Peninsula: operations in Oman

Oman had become embroiled in a serious struggle against tribal rebels in its Dhofar province by the early 1970s. The Dhofari rebels (generally known as the Dhofar Liberation Front) had separatist ambitions and were Communist in orientation.[116] They were based along the South Yemen border and received support by the South Yemeni state. They also had the support of a wide array of mainly anti-Western powers such as China,[117] the Soviet Union, Palestinian organizations and Iraq.[118] There was also a noticeable presence of Cuban and Libyan (Cuban-trained) "advisors" among the rebels.[119] Less known was the presence of Iranian anti-shah Leftist guerrillas known as the *Cherikhaye Fadayian e Khlaq e Iran* (Organization of Iranian People's Fadayian Guerrillas) (see following chapter) who fought alongside Dhofari rebels against Iranian forces.[120]

The Dhofari rebellion began in earnest in 1963, largely with support provided by Iraq and Egypt. In less than ten years the rebellion had become a dangerous movement threatening the authority of the Omani sultan. Thanks in part to foreign support (i.e. Soviets, Cuba, Iraq, etc) the rebellion succeeded in taking over much of Oman's western territory in Dhofar province. By 1969 the strategic coastal town of Rakhyut and the nearby Shirshitti cave complexes had fallen into rebel hands. This critical state of affairs prompted the (British-supported) overthrow of Oman's Sultan Said Ibn Teymour by his son Qaboos Ibn Said Al-Said.[121]

Qaboos took the initiative in reconstituting Omani resistance against the rebels. British officers and Pakistani-Baluch troops soon assumed key positions in the Omani army. The revitalized Omani army successfully blocked further rebel expansion, but was unable to eject the rebels from their previously captured territories. The rebels remained especially dangerous as proven by their dramatic June 1972 attack against the British Royal Air Force barracks. Qaboos was now looking north to Iran for military assistance against the rebels.

The shah was acutely concerned with the growth of Soviet and Soviet-allied influence along his southern (Persian Gulf) periphery.[122] He accepted Qaboos' appeal for military assistance, which led to the arrival of Iranian personnel and equipment in Oman. An elite battalion of 1,500 special forces troops[123] landed in Oman in spring 1973 to assist British and Omani forces in establishing the (approximately) 54-mile (70-km) Hornbeam defense line.[124] The line, which was completed by August 1974, featured minefields, barbed wire, and blockhouses. Prior to the arrival of Iranian troops, the shah had given five AB205 helicopters to Omani forces, which proved invaluable against the rebels. The Iranians also stationed 6-10 F-4 Phantoms[125] and up to 35 helicopters[126] in Oman.

The establishment of the Hornbeam defense line was followed by the arrival, in December 1974, of another elite group of 1,200 troops known as the Imperial Iranian Battle Group. The Iranian army now launched a major offensive known as Operation *Thimble*. *Thimble's* primary objective was to secure Midway Road, which was a major communications and supply link between the capital (Muscat) and Dhofar. Constant rebel attacks against Omani-British convoys at Midway Road had effectively undermined Omani authority in Dhofar province.

The Iranians concentrated their forces in Thumarit, transforming its local air base into a major military centre. Iranian troops then proceeded to capture a number of strategic positions in the mountains. This allowed them to launch attacks (with infantry patrols and mortar attacks) against rebels operating along Midway Road. The support of heavy artillery, combat helicopters and aircraft allowed the Iranians to secure the entire road. After this success, the Iranians handed Midway Road over to Omani authorities in October 1974. Dhofari rebels vowed on the radio to retake the road (which they dubbed as the "Red Line") but never managed to carry out their threat.[127] The British were also instrumental in helping the sultan win the "hearts and minds" of Dhofar populace. They did this by assisting Omani authorities in the construction of important facilities such as schools, clinics, wells, and other essential services.

The Iranians concentrated 3,000–4,000 troops along the north and south axes of the port town of Rakhyut in early December 1974.[128] This force (now based in Manston) included veterans from the earlier Thumarit operations.[129] The capture of Rakhyut was essential as this had become the "capital" of the rebels and symbolized the sultan's inability to exercise his authority in the region.

The Iranian force was composed of naval assets, Huey combat/transport helicopters, Chinook heavy transport helicopters, two infantry battalions, and a gun battery unit.[130] The offensive quickly ran into heavy rebel resistance and slowed down. Another problem was the Iranian army's excessive caution and lack of experience in such operations.[131] The rebels held out against the Iranian assaults, but their time was running out. The Iranians regrouped and revised their strategies with the assistance of British Major-General Timothy Creasy. This was followed by the resumption of the Iranian offensive to the south from positions already established in the mountains.[132] Despite bitter fighting, the operations proved successful and finally led to the capture of Rakhyut in January 5, 1975.[133]

With Midway Road and Rakhyut secured, operations shifted towards the South Yemen border which was the major supply conduit for the rebels. The Iranians now built the Damavand Line to cut off the ingress of incoming rebel troops and supplies from their bases in South Yemen. The Damavand Line also deployed special sensor devices to rapidly pinpoint attempted rebel crossings. The Omanis had in the meantime launched a series of operations to clear remaining rebels adjacent to South Yemen. The Iranians supported the Omani operations by launching their own attacks against the rebels. This tied down many rebel fighters, allowing Omani troops to establish their authority along the South Yemen border. South Yemeni aircraft were prevented from supporting the rebels due to the presence of deadly Iranian antiaircraft systems.

The rebels had fired scores of Soviet-supplied shoulder-fired SA-7 antiaircraft missiles. These destroyed three Omani and two Iranian helicopters as well as one British combat aircraft in 1975.[134] These minor losses could do little to turn the tide in the rebels' favor. British Hunter aircraft flew devastating combat missions alongside Iranian Phantoms to bomb rebel positions.[135] The landing of Iranian commando units (supported by two Iranian navy destroyers) in South Yemen proved decisive. The commandos broke the back of the resistance by destroying two key rebel bases in South Yemen in October 1975. The vast majority of the rebels had been finally ejected out of Dhofar prompting Sultan Qaboos to declare in mid-December 1975 that the rebellion was over.[136] By March 1976 all military operations had ceased and Iranian forces left Oman the following year.[137]

Pakistani Baluchistan

Pakistan fought a difficult campaign against a Baluchi insurgency with up to 80,000 troops in 1973–77. Tehran was especially concerned as Iraq had been attempting to foment a Baluch separatist movement in Iran's Sistan-Baluchistan province for years. Baghdad, which had been host to the Baluch Liberation Front in 1973, spread its activities into Pakistan's Baluchistan region adjacent to Iran.[138] Direct evidence for Baghdad's complicity was found by Pakistani authorities who after raiding the Iraqi embassy in 1973, found 300 machine-guns and 60,000 rounds of ammunition destined for Pakistan's Baluchi rebels.[139]

The shah was concerned that the Pakistani-Baluchis might encourage a separatist rebellion in Iran's Sistan-Baluchistan province.[140] He lent his support to the Pakistani military by loaning them Iranian army helicopters and their pilots.[141] There are two versions as to the types of Iranian helicopters involved and their overall impact on the campaign. The first version reported by Harrison asserts that Tehran sent thirty AH-1 Cobra combat helicopters to support the Pakistani army and air force in its operations against the rebels.[142] The Cobras, according to Harrison, played a crucial role in defeating the rebels, notably during the decisive six-day battle of Chamalang fought in early September 1974 against 15,000 Baluchi rebels.[143]

Harrison's version of events has been disputed. Wirsing asserts that the Iranians only loaned CH-47 Chinook (non-combat) heavy transport helicopters which played no decisive role in the fighting, with these being withdrawn before the battle of Chamalang.[144] One factual liability with Wirsing's report is that Iran may have loaned the Pakistanis up to 30 Chinooks, which is clearly impossible as Iran only had a total of 22 before the Revolution.[145]

Other combat operations of note by the Iranian army on the Pakistani border involved battles against drug traffickers. One notable success was the capture of two Pakistani drug kingpins (Mirza Rasefi and Sharif Ali Khan) who had imported thousands of tons of drugs and narcotics into Iran and from Iran to Western countries. To this day, Iranian security forces continue to clash with drug traffickers arriving from Pakistan's Baluch region.

Cold War spy missions against the Soviet Union

By 1978, Iran was host to five stations set up for monitoring military and missile activity in the Soviet Union. Three were jointly operated by the CIA and the IIAF with the other two run entirely by the CIA. These would relay information on Soviet missile locations and activities to US forces.[146] These five bases coordinated their activities with data provided by four specially modified C-130 planes known as the Khofash (Bat in Persian). Khofash aircraft continuously flew along the Soviet border, keeping a close watch on Soviet military intentions to the north of Iran.

Before satellite spying technology came of age from the mid-1970s, US spying aircraft often flew from bases in Pakistan into Iran in the 1960s before proceeding into Soviet airspace. A key refueling station for the U-2 spy planes en-route to the USSR was the Zahedan airbase in Iran's southeast. Iranian pilots and aircraft also engaged in reconnaissance, sometimes with US personnel. One dramatic case occurred on November 28, 1973 in which an Iranian RF-4E reconnaissance aircraft flown by Major Shokouhnia and Captain Saunders was rammed by a MiG-21 which exploded upon impact. The Iranian and American pilots ejected safely but were captured by the Soviets.

They were then handed back to Iranian authorities. On June 21, 1978, a Soviet MiG-23 shot down two of four Iranian CH-47 Chinook heavy helicopters flying in Soviet airspace.[147] The unfortunate Iranian Chinooks were probably engaged in a reconnaissance or spying mission.

Soviet attempts to dominate Iranian skies during the Cold War are little known. The formidably fast and high-flying MiG-25 Foxbats began to violate Iranian air space to engage in reconnaissance. But the Soviets soon learned that IIAF pilots were a force to be reckoned with. Many F-4s scrambled to intercept but the MiG-25s were easily able to evade their Iranian pursuers. The Soviets' luck finally ran out when an F-4 finally managed to surprise a MiG-25 in 1977, successfully firing an AIM-7 Sparrow missile at the Foxbat which then crashed inside the Soviet Union.[148] The Soviets continued to launch more Foxbats into Iranian air space, and eventually the shah permitted the F-14 Tomcats to combat the Foxbats. In tests in August 1977, four of five Phoenix missiles fired by F-14s hit their target drones, the fifth malfunctioned.[149] The next Foxbat into Iranian airspace was greeted by an F-14. Despite flying at 65,000 feet at Mach 2+, the Foxbat was locked on by the AWG-9 radar of the Iranian Tomcat.[150] The Soviets got the shah's message and backed down, all Soviet flights into Iranian airspace ceased.

Iranian military: strengths and weaknesses

While the IIAF was still maturing as an air arm, most Western assessments agreed that Iranian airmen had approached near Western and Israeli levels of performance by the late 1970s. Not all Western observers agreed, as shown by a scathing 1974 report from the Pentagon which concluded that Iranian pilots were substandard in performance in comparison to their counterparts operating US-made aircraft in Western and non-Western countries.[151] Another 1974 report made by the USAF Aeronautical Systems Division in partnership with the Hughes Aircraft Company specifically highlighted the rising skills of the Iranian airmen.[152] As noted by Farhad Nassirkhani, a major in the IIAF Test/Instructor Pilot, "in less than 20 years by their hard work and dedication made the impossible possible ... created 10 air force bases, 15 radar sites, operated the most modern machines and equipment at their best performance." [153]

The Iranian military had yet to be tested in battle like its counterparts in Egypt, Jordan, Syria, Pakistan, Israel or India. The battles against Dhofari rebels for example, were certainly too small and limited in scope to provide the military with any comprehensive battle experience. The border battles with Iraq in 1974–75 certainly suggested that the Iranian military was ascendant over Iraq. However, the Iranians may have failed to appreciate that their opponents' performance was as much due to flaws in their leadership as combat doctrine and equipment. Perhaps most dangerous were those in the leadership who glossed over Iranian weakness, especially with respect to armored warfare. Iranian forces had yet to be tested in massive ground battles involving large bodies of mobile armored vehicles.

Prodigious efforts had been made in raising a skilled tank force and many highly qualified tank crews and officers began to staff the armored corps. Nevertheless, some army commanders raised concerns with respect to logistics and armored maneuvers. Colonel Hedayat Behzadi noted in a 1976 report that Iranian army capabilities for the rapid transport of troops, supplies and tanks to threatened sectors were inadequate citing an Iranian army maneuver from Tehran to Khuzistan taking 10 days whereas the Iraqi army would travel similar distances in less than 48 hours.[154] Behzadi's observations stand in stark contrast to favorable British assessments made during the Oman operations.[155] British observers were also positive about Iran's field medical support and especially their naval operations at Rakhyut.[156] Nevertheless Iranian forces in Oman had not engaged in massed armored operations. The British were critical of the Iranians' use of massive firepower to compensate for their lack of tactical initiative on the battlefield, which they blamed on American training.[157] Many of the Iranian army's liabilities were being addressed by the late 1970s but these came to an abrupt halt with the Revolution.

Plans were underway to expand Iran's radar stations and early detection systems, but these remained incomplete, the AWACS systems never arrived, and existing radar systems were only partly operational following the Revolution. Any potential adversary wishing to launch a massive military attack could now take advantage of the weaknesses in Iran's early warning system.

Iran had shortages of skilled personnel to service its rising inventory of modern weaponry.[158] There was a need for more instructors in all services. Iran's educational system was not yet able to train enough students with the necessary professional skills.[159] As in Reza Shah's time, many young Iranian cadets and civilians in search of higher education were sent overseas, especially to the United States, to acquire military expertise and training. Ironically, numbers of these students turned to anti-shah political platforms during their educational sojourn in the West.[160]

The total number of foreign military specialists and technical personnel in Iran stood at 24,000 in 1975–76 and was expected to rise to 50,000–60,000 by 1978.[161] But Western technicians often barred Iranian engineers and technical personnel from obtaining access to "sensitive" equipment.[162] Iranian personnel were often prevented from replacing even the most rudimentary parts, which were instead shipped back to the country of manufacture for repairs, imposing great financial burdens on Iran.[163] This led to serious concerns that Iran would not unable to operate its increasingly sophisticated equipment without Western assistance in the event of a major war.[164] This may partly explain why there was such a determined drive from the early 1970s to create an indigenous industrial base led by Iranian managers, technicians, and engineers.

The Iranians often complained that they paid too much for the equipment they purchased from the West. Western estimates suggest the Iranians often paid two to three times more than America's partners in NATO for identical US-made equipment.[165] The shah noted that standard Russian fighters cost on average 600–700 thousand dollars apiece, in comparison to three million dollars Iran had to pay for each F-4 Phantom fighter-bomber.[166] There were also reports of widespread corruption in Iranian arms deals, with middlemen, civilian and military often milking exorbitant personal profits.[167]

The Iranian military had made large strides by the 1970s, with a number of top-notch personnel in place. However, the shah, who encouraged military professionalism and excellence, was also intolerant of officers displaying too much independence and initiative.[168] The latter were often cashiered or shunted into "less threatening" positions such as diplomatic posts, probably to stop them forming an independent power base.[169] While the shah encouraged excellence in political and military elites, he was insecure in his position, excluding these elites from critical decision-making processes.[170] There are also reports of a number of forced retirements of highly qualified military leaders due to their independent-minded approach. There were also reports of lower-level colonels being cashiered for being too candid.[171] The Iranian military brass was certainly far more effective than it was during Reza Shah's time, however the system of promotion by loyalty also meant that the Iranian military continued to be denuded of a number of high-caliber commanders.

The shah in turn became deeply absorbed in micromanaging the entire military's daily operations, trying to run the entire establishment himself.[172] Despite the fact that there was a Supreme Defense Council (SDC), there was little in the way of true team-like staff meetings as the shah preferred to meet his various chiefs of offices individually. The shah frequently rotated commanders from their posts, probably to prevent the formation of strong bonds. Commanders selected by the shah were often at odds with one another. This ensured that they would not form alliances against the shah. The end result was that nearly all decisions had to pass by the shah first. In the meantime, the system of espionage and informants ensured that commanders would withhold information from each other and only share these with the shah. This system of checks and balances ensured that the Shah was in full control and the primary source of all critical decision-making. This same process worked against the formation of a truly integrated and unified high-level command. This meant that Iran lacked a military body capable of quickly, decisively and independently reacting against internal or external crises. When the Revolution exploded in 1978, the shah was left alone to manage the greatest challenge to his throne.

An ambivalent relationship? The West and the shah

Despite his official status as a Western ally, and British and American support in the ousting of Mossadegh in 1953, the shah's relationship with the West was complex by the 1970s. Western media and political outlets often criticized the shah's domestic and international policies, and unflattering remarks about the shah were made on record.[173] There were also grave concerns in the West over Iran's rising military strength and its potential to become a "mini-superpower" with regional ambitions.[174] The shah's nuclear program raised questions, as nuclear reactors had been ordered from West Germany, the United States, and France for the civilian sector, and it was not clear whether there might be future military applications for this technology.[175] The shah even told *Newsweek Magazine* in 1973 that the Americans should not expect to enjoy world hegemony indefinitely.[176]

US support for the shah became increasingly ambivalent during the administration of President Jimmy Carter (1977–81). Prominent members of the Carter administration were unfavorable towards the shah. George Ball (former diplomat and high-ranking advisor) urged Carter to either sever America's ties with the shah or find ways of curtailing him.[177] Carter openly demanded that the shah institute human rights reforms and loosen his rule in favour of more liberal political processes and press.[178] More bad press for the shah was provided by Amnesty International's scathing reports on the state of human rights in Iran's courts and prisons.[179]

Even before the election of Carter as president, the shah had been levelling criticism against his Western allies throughout the 1970s.[180] Petroleum in particular became a sore point between the shah and his Western allies. When President Gerald Ford and Secretary of State Henry Kissinger cautioned oil producing states against raising oil prices to "dangerously high levels," the shah thundered back that "if this is a serious policy of the US Government then on this subject we are going to have a very serious clash."[181] There was a clash, but not in the international arena. This was the Iranian revolution, an event that shook not only Iran but the entire Middle East and international arena.

CHAPTER 32

THE ISLAMIC REVOLUTION (1978–79): RISE OF THE PASDARAN AND MILITARY IMPLICATIONS

The Islamic Revolution of Iran and its implications continue to generate much discussion among Iranians, and the international community. The main focus of our discussion in this chapter pertains to the role of the military during the Revolution and the implications of the arrival of a new governing establishment.

Prelude to the Iranian Revolution

The Iranian army had been involved in operations against a number of small-scale revolts mainly among the Qashqai in Fars province in the early 1960s, and sporadically against the Kurds in Western Iran during the 1960s and 1970s.[1] These were neither long-lasting nor widespread, and easily contained. Far more problematic were the shah's problems with an increasingly militant conservative religious movement as well as leftist guerrillas opposed to his rule. It was in this domain where Iran's internal security apparatus known as SAVAK took the lead.

Following the shah's return to Iran after Operation *Ajax*, a US Army officer working for the CIA arrived in Tehran to cooperate with Teymour Bakhtiar, Tehran's military governor, to lay the basis of Iran's first true intelligence organization. Success came less than a year later when the fledgling organization penetrated a large communist cell, known as the Tudeh, inside the Iranian military. Thanks to the discovery of critical documents pertaining to the Tudeh's organization, Iranian security forces arrested up to 430 military personnel.[2] The success of this operation led to the inauguration of "Sazman e Ettleat va Amniate Keshvar" (The Organization for Information/ Intelligence and Security of the Country), also known as SAVAK, in 1957.[3]

By 1964, SAVAK was closely cooperating with Israel's Mossad in intelligence affairs.[4] The Iranians were soon trained by the Americans and Israelis in surveillance, networking, interrogation methods and the penetration of opposition networks. SAVAK was ultimately composed of an internal wing (responsible for ensuring internal security) and an external wing (intelligence gathering and operations against foreign threats). SAVAK's American advisors had modelled the "internal" on the FBI and the "external" on the CIA respectively.[5] The organization aimed to gather information vital to state security; identify and neutralize foreign agents working against Iran's independence and territorial integrity; and block the activities of anti-government organizations and political parties.[6] By 1972 SAVAK had up to 5,000 full-time members with thousands of associates.[7] "SAVAK" became a dreaded term, increasingly perceived as a tool of government coercion.[8] Citizens in social and work places often dreaded the prospect of being reported to the authorities by a SAVAKI (a SAVAK associate or agent). In a sense, SAVAK became the "eyes and ears of the king."

By 1962 a new nucleus of anti-government opposition had been formed. These were Shiite theologians and members of the left comprised of Ezatollah Sahabi, Mehdi Bazargan, and Ayatollah Taleghani.[9] The flashpoint for the 1963 riots was the shah's reforms in land distribution, education and family laws as a consequence of his White Revolution, announced in January 1963.[10] A prominent cleric and theologian in Qom, Ruhollah Khomeini, denounced the shah's White Revolution in the strongest terms by January 22.[11] The shah arrived in Qom with army troops followed by armored vehicles just two days later. He delivered a speech denouncing the Ulema who were opposing his plans. The situation escalated by March 22, when government security forces stormed into Qom's Faiziyeh Mosque to clash with religious students, killing two.[12] Events escalated further and in June, Khomeini was arrested and placed in a military prison in Tehran.[13] Riots erupted in Qom, Tehran, Mashad, Shiraz, and Isfahan. The Tehran riots were the most serious with protestors emerging from southern Tehran's slums towards the capital's center. Pictures of Khomeini appeared on a number of Tehran's walls, and rioters destroyed shops, parts of the bazaar and attempted to storm Tehran's radio station and government centers. Army troops opened fire into the crowds. When the crowds refused to disperse, tanks were brought in. It took 7,000 troops three days of fighting to subdue the rioters. Estimates of casualties range from 85 to 6,000 demonstrators killed.[14]

Khomeini was released from jail on August 3, 1963, and placed under house arrest in Tehran.[15] The shah's attempt to persuade him to stay out of politics proved futile.[16] With the coming of elections on September 17, Khomeini asked the public to refrain from voting, leading authorities to arrest him; he was again released in April 1964.[17] Two months later the granting of diplomatic immunity to US servicemen and citizens working for the Iranian military (part of a deal made with President Johnson to provide Iran with 200 million dollars in credits to buy US weapon systems), caused great resentment among the general public.[18] Majlis members were bitterly divided over the agreement, which barely passed the test of ratification in the Majlis.[19] Khomeini strongly protested against the agreement in a speech on October 26, leading once again to his arrest.[20] A few days later Khomeini was exiled, going to first Turkey, then Iraq.[21] SAVAK continued to monitor the religious opposition and soon arrested pro-Khomeini activists such as Hashem Rafsanjani, Ali Khamenei, and Hussein Ali Montazeri; these become the future leaders of the 1979 Revolution.[22] SAVAK agents were sent into mosques to prevent the rise of political opposition. Religious student associations in universities were closed down.[23] Conservative opposition had been stifled, but the Pahlavi establishment would again be challenged by them 15 years later.

The Soviets and their KGB spy network were highly active in Iran, especially from the early 1960s and throughout the 1970s. The pro-Soviet Tudeh had been battered after Mossadegh's removal in August 1953 but they had not been destroyed. A number of Tudeh members remained at large with others breaking off to join or form other leftist cells. Ilya Dzhirkvelov, a key Soviet spy in Iran, describes how the KGB trained operatives to lead Iranian leftist guerrillas in sabotage operations.[24] The Soviets also provided additional training to many Iranian leftists to support the Soviet army should it wish to invade Iran.[25] The Soviets had made extensive preparations in

1967–73 for a possible invasion of Iran. With the help of their leftist allies, the Soviets were able to tabulate and select key bases, depots, and landing sites in Iran's northwest (Azarbaijan), west (Kurdistan) and south (Khuzistan).[26] One of the key foci for Soviet operations in Iran was the TASS news service in Tehran which was almost entirely staffed by KGB operatives.[27] Preparations for subterfuge in Iran were among the most extensive made by Moscow.

There were intermittent revolts among the Kurds (1960s and 1970s) and the Qashqai (1960s).[28] The Qashqai of Fars skirmished with Iranian security forces from 1963, with their revolt losing its impetus over the next few years and being finally defeated by 1967. In that same year another rebellion broke out in Iranian Kurdistan. Led by Mullah Avareh, Abdollah Moini and Sharifzadeh, this rebellion was defeated by 1969. Far more challenging was the resurgence of an increasingly militant left who had formed resistance cells by the 1960s. By the early 1970s these had begun to engage in armed clashes against the establishment. Of particular note was the rise of the "Sazmane Enghelbiye Hezbe Tudeye Iran" (The Revolutionary Organization of the Tudeh party of Iran or ROTPI), a Stalinist and Maoist Communist movement which broke from the old Tudeh due to its alignment with Khrushchev's de-Stalinization policies.[29] These sought to support the aforementioned tribal rebellions in Fars and Iranian Kurdistan.[30] It was in February 1971 that 16 leftists armed with machineguns, grenades, and rifles attacked the Gendarmerie station in Siyahkal village in Gilan.[31] Despite its small military scale, the impact of this attack led to the establishment of the Cherikhaye Fadayian e Khlaq e Iran (Organization of Iranian People's Fedaiyan Guerrillas); it reinvigorated Iran's Communist movement, soon becoming known as the Jonbeshe Novine Komonisthaye Iran (The New Communist Movement of Iran) and other Marxist groups; and also inspired armed resistance by the politicized religious opposition.[32]

Leftist organizations proved exceptionally difficult to penetrate, diffuse and pin down. This was because these operated according to the communist doctrine of guerrilla warfare in which the guerrillas were organized in compartments and decentralized.[33] If members were captured, not much critical information could be obtained, and if a cell was crushed, others would continue operating, and new ones formed. The Fedaiyan were especially strident against the shah and even sent their fighters to Oman to aid Dhofari rebels against Iranian forces. They were supported by the Palestine Liberation Organization (PLO) and possibly Libya.[34] They often financed their operations through bank robbery.[35] The Fedaiyan tended to target foreign interests in Iran, members of the state apparatus, and ruling caste.[36]

By 1978–79 a whole host of small Marxist[37] and Islamic organizations were operational in Iran.[38] The most notable of these to combat the Shah's government was the Mujaheddin e Khlaq e Iran (The People's Mujaheddin of Iran, also known as the MEK or MKO), founded in 1965 by six students.[39] The Mujaheddin combined Marxism with Islamic concepts.[40] A major split developed, with one branch completely declaring itself Marxist and the other remaining Marxist-Islamist.[41] Both branches remained committed to violent opposition against the Pahlavi establishment. The PLO provided Mujaheddin recruits with much of their military training.[42] The Mujaheddin made their military debut in August 1971, launching a series of guerrilla actions to disrupt the shah's 2,500-year celebrations of Iranian history and monarchy.[43]

The government mobilized SAVAK to track down the opposition, especially the leftist guerrillas. SAVAK set up a joint anti-terrorist committee in 1972 which cooperated with the police, gendarmerie and army in hunting down the guerrillas.[44] By 1976 SAVAK had arrested numbers of leftist guerrillas, who then divulged under torture the whereabouts of dozens of their comrades. Abrahamian reports a total of 341 guerrillas from all political groups having lost their lives in battles against the government, 172 Fedaiyan and 103 Mujaheddin.[45] The Mujaheddin continued their struggle against government forces and engaged in terrorist actions against US military, diplomatic and civilian personnel inside Iran including assassinations and kidnapping.[46] SAVAK forced the leftists to curtail their activities by 1976, but the leftist movement had not been destroyed; they had simply pulled back to recoup their losses and bide their time.[47]

A heavy price had been paid for SAVAK's partial success. They had used heavy-handed tactics to root out the leftitsts, including intense spying operations.[48] The impact of the counter-guerrilla operations was especially felt by those university students, professors and other intellectuals who were suspected of support or sympathy for the left. Western media and human rights outlets became especially vocal and critical of SAVAK, citing reports of torture and brutality.[49] When in exile after the Revolution, the shah later told reporter David Frost that all physical torture had been stopped in Iran since 1976.[50] Perhaps the shah had never been informed about the minute details of SAVAK's interrogation techniques.[51] If so, it raises the possibility that the system of information communication, from subordinates to the shah, was flawed before the Revolution.

Some factors behind the Revolution

A thorough analysis of the causes of the 1979 Revolution lies far beyond the scope of this text.[52] The discussion here aims to provide only an overall sketch.

The Shah's base of support had been dangerously limited as land-owners remained unhappy with his 1963 reforms. His overall ties with the crucial bazaar business class and the clergy had also been unfavourable from at least the early 1960s. Freedom of political expression became highly restricted with the shah reducing the two-party system to a single party by 1975 which became known as Hezb-c-Rastakhiz-e-Iran (Party of Resurgence of Iran).[53] Many students (especially foreign educated ones) were agitating for more political freedom by the mid-1970s. The shah, encouraged by US President Jimmy Carter, agreed to loosen the political restrictions. Prime Minster Jamshid Amouzegar was replaced by Jaafar Sharif-Imami. This proved to be a double-edged sword for the shah. While allowing greater political freedoms was constructive and the Majlis witnessed lively debates, the loosening of the political climate allowed the shah's opponents to come out into the open with their descriptions of oppression and torture.[54] The first to become noticeable were the religious right (and Khomeini in his Iraqi exile), followed by leftists, university students, intelligentsia and the mass of the people.

The presence of Western personnel had a profound social impact in Iran, being possibly one of the myriad factors leading to the Revolution. By the mid-1970s there were a total of 50,000 Americans in Iran. Outside Tehran, the majority of these were in Isfahan and Shiraz working in Iran's growing military helicopter sector. The vast majority conducted themselves well, but a troublesome few created a negative overall impression of Americans among the Iranian citizenry. Reports of rowdiness, public drunkenness, pugnacious and culturally insensitive behavior began to surface in the mainstream press, greatly angering the public.[55] The fact that the Americans were immune from Iranian laws and courts, thanks to the Status of US Forces Agreement, further fanned popular resentment against American residents and eventually, against the shah.[56] Leftist groups made much of the fact that many of the Americans were former Vietnam War veterans, hence their characterization of the "Vietnamization" of the Iranian army.[57] Many Iranians also felt that Americans occupied positions in place of qualified Iranian personnel.[58]

The Revolution explodes

A major Iranian paper published an editorial in January 7, 1977 linking Khomeini to British intelligence, and describing opposition to the shah as being confined to the religious right and leftists.[59] Riots broke out the very next day among Qom's religious students. In what appeared to be a repeat of 1963, security forces responded swiftly and harshly. Estimates of those killed vary from just five, to over a dozen killed and hundreds wounded.[60] Stern action failed to cow the protestors. Instead riots began to spread to the Tabriz in Azarbaijan. The Tabriz riots became especially fierce, forcing the government to bring in tanks to re-impose order.[61] The application of force was again unsuccessful. By April, riots had spread to a number of provincial cites such as Kermanshah and Yazd. The government were still unable to contain the rioters in Qom.

In May when the government committed a major blunder by firing into protestors supporting Ayatollah Shariatmadari. The main part of the pro-Shariatmadari protestors demanded the full implementation of the 1906 Constitution in which a popularly elected Majlis held power of governance with the monarchy enstrusted with a more symbolic role.[62] Shariatmadari had been among those clergy, who had been critical of the shah's reforms and policies in the early 1960s. He had encouraged his followers to engage in peaceful demonstrations by avoiding violence, but the events of May changed that.[63] Shariatmadari and his followers merged with the more strident rioters. By July, anti-shah demonstrations had broken out in other key cities such as Arak, Mashad and Isfahan. The situation further escalated when government workers from Iran's industrial plants began joining the protestors. It would not be long before the chant *Marg bar Shah* (Death to the shah) would be echoing throughout Iran's streets.

The dynamic providing continual impetus for the riots was the *Arbain* mourning ceremony, undertaken 40 days after a person's death.[64] This created the deadly Arbain cycle: demonstrators would mourn for the dead 40 days after they were killed, resulting in clashes in which more people would be killed leading to a fresh round of Arbain ceremonies. The government never found a constructive solution to assuage this dynamic in its favor.

On August 19, 1978, over 400 moviegoers died when Abadan's Cinema Rex was set alight, and all the exits blocked.[65] The shah's government placed the blame on religious fanatics, while the shah's opponents pointed the finger at SAVAK.[66] The events transformed the riots into a massive march of hundreds of thousands in Tehran by late August. Significant was the presence of students and middle-class citizens in that march. The shah formed a government of conciliation following the resignation of the established government, but to little avail. The revolution was now a widespread movement.

By early September more widespread marches and protests erupted across Tehran and Iran's major cities. Protestors demanded the release of political prisoners, the inauguration of free elections and the complete implementation of the Constitution of 1906. The latter demand may have allowed a way for the Iranian monarchy to survive in some sort of ceremonial fashion, but time for even such a compromise was running out. By September 6, approximately half a million people were marching in Tehran's streets, doubling to one million the next day.[67] The scope and potential of these protests finally swayed the shah to declare martial law in September 8, placing Major-General Gholamali Oveissi as Tehran's governor.[68] But Oveissi and the Iranian military had been caught completely off-guard with the massive scale of the riots. They were not equipped with enough tear gas and riot gear, nor did the troops have adequate training in crowd management. This meant that the military had no real means to contain the demonstrations. The shah turned to his US ally for help in procuring riot gear equipment in November, but ran into stiff opposition from the Carter administration's Human Rights office.[69] When the equipment finally arrived, it was already too late.

Following the shah's orders for martial law, army troops were quickly deployed onto Tehran's streets. On Friday September 8, 5,000–20,000 protesters gathered in Jaleh Square (central Tehran).[70] Each of the four streets into Jaleh square were blocked by a single tank, then what are described as "elite royal guards" surrounded the square, sealing off all exits. The demonstrators were then ordered to disperse, and when they refused to do so the troops opened fire.[71] It is possible that many of the demonstrators were unaware that martial law had been declared at the time.[72] The crowded nature of the area and the sealing of all exits prevented non-demonstrators from escaping.[73] Estimates of casualties again diverge widely, ranging from 58 to thousands killed.[74] The government claimed 122 were killed and thousands wounded.[75] Black Friday was another tragedy the government could ill-afford. The shah ordered his troops to avoid further bloodshed but it was too late.[76] Black Friday swayed more Iranians against the shah and weakened Western support for his administration. Protests increased in size and intensity over the next four months. The name of Ayatollah Khomeini also began to appear in the press. He was, at the shah's request, under house arrest in Najaf, Iraq.[77] As the protests gained momentum, the ayatollah gained greater and greater prominence, becoming the indisputable leader of the Revolution.

As the Revolution gathered momentum, the leftists, especially the Fedaiyan, moved to lend their support to the protestors. They soon managed to smuggle weapons into Iran through the Persian Gulf in the south and Afghanistan in the east.[78] This allowed them to resume their armed struggle against the government by attacking the Tabriz police station in September and assassinating Mashad's police chief in October.[79] More significantly, these joined demonstrators in the streets, adding their military muscle against the shah. By October the country was facing a mounting series of strikes, especially in the petroleum industry, a major factor which helped cripple the shah.[80]

The shah continually tried to find ways to accommodate the demonstrators, after bouts of violence.[81] None of his conciliatory gestures helped, especially after the Black Friday tragedies.[82] He attempted to mollify the escalating crisis by recalling General Nematollah Nassiri from Pakistan, and placing him and a number of other SAVAK chiefs under arrest. Other unpopular officials were arrested or fired and some political prisoners were freed. Troops were ordered to fire into the air and shoot only in self-defense.[83] These measures were interpreted as hesitation and weakness by the shah's opponents. The shah and the army were also hesitant to use brute force to crush the

Revolution.[84] They were evidently wary of further inflaming the Iranian population against them. By late 1978 the shah's options were all but exhausted. In contrast, Khomeini's position was characterized by initiative, unwavering determination and resolve. He had little fear of head-on confrontation with the shah's security forces even if this could result in heavy casualties.[85] The shah was also reluctant to appoint a strong military leader capable of making decisive decisions. General Azhari, who was appointed to lead the military government from November 1978, reputedly told the US ambassador, William Sullivan, that "this country is lost because the king cannot make up his mind."[86]

The shah's deteriorating health, due to cancer, must have had an impact on his decision-making processes. Partial corroboration of the shah's battered state is provided by William Sullivan who noted that the Shah had become a "totally ravaged man who had lost all of his self-confidence."[87]

The Iranian military and the Revolution

The Iranian army collapsed in February 1979. Zabih inquired, "Was the disintegration of the armed forces brought about by internal socio-economic conditions or by the breakdown of their leadership? To what extent did the departure of the shah create a vacuum and thus cause the collapse of the military?"[88] There are a number of possible domestic and international factors specifically pertaining to the military's collapse.

The shah's micromanagement of the army had resulted in the promotion of leaders who were militarily professional but dependent on the shah for overall leadership. These generals lacked the requisite abilities to work as a team to respond quickly and flexibly to fluctuating circumstances. The Shah's methods of ensuring the loyalty of the officer corps since 1953 had resulted in an upper military clique increasingly out of touch with the ordinary people.[89] When the Revolution took place, many of these had few links with mainstream society, preventing them from understanding the protestors.

The Iranian military had, since 1963, become increasingly preoccupied with external threats, paying little attention to preparing for internal insurgencies.[90] The army had dealt with revolts in Kurdistan and among the Qashqai during the 1960s, but these were neither large-scale nor sustained. Prior to 1978, the leftists and conservative religious groups had generally been dealt with by SAVAK.

Leftist guerrillas and religious activists mounted an effective campaign of attacking checkpoints and army patrols. More subtle means involved the successful infiltration of armed forces units. This soon led to incidents of sabotage, with fighting breaking out within some units.[91] The revolutionaries would converse with soldiers and commanders on the street, and many conscripts, hailing from modest and religiously conservative backgrounds, proved receptive to their religious messages. Religious activists also proved especially successful in weakening the internal bonds of the military.[92] This was all part of Khomeini's increasingly successful appeal to the "hearts" of the troops in the streets.[93]

Other leftists and numbers of religiously conservative demonstrators mixed with demonstrators in the streets, intending to provoke the troops. As the revolution gained momentum, more and more troops refused to follow orders. Demoralization also affected the non-political officers, frustrated by the confusion permeating the upper echelons of command. Meanwhile, the combination of the revolutionaries' tactics combined with inconsistencies in the high command resulted in confusion among regular troops. Many became unsure when they should or should not fire into demonstrating crowds. The number of deserters increased as morale plummeted. In early 1978 desertions ran at an average of 100–200 per day, increasing to at least 1,000 per day by the end of the year.[94] Whole units and even divisions had already melted away by the time of Khomeini's arrival.[95]

Khomeini arrives in France

Iraq expelled Khomeini in October 1978, and Khomeini arrived in Paris on October 5. Khomeini's arrival to France solidified his position as the uncontested leader of the Revolution. His sojourn in France also gave him sympathetic international media exposure for his cause.[96] The scope of Western attention is indicated by the 120 interviews provided by Khomeini during his four-month stay in Paris.[97] Western media coverage was soon followed by expressions of support for Khomeini by a select number of US officials.[98] The ayatollah soon made clear his ultimate goal, which was the overthrow of not only the shah but the Iranian monarchical tradition, in favor of an Islamic republic. Communications media also played a major role in directing anti-shah demonstrations. Iran's mosques already provided an instant network for conveying information and directives throughout the country. Cassettes of Khomeini's speeches were copied and distributed throughout Iran. The BBC Persian service in particular, became a major medium for conveying Khomeini's messages to the Iranian populace.[99] Their coverage of Iranian events and the transmission of Khomeini's messages was so extensive that it elicited protests from the Iranian government, especially as the service "acquired a progressively pro-revolution tone."[100] The BBC retorted that it was an independent organization dedicated to the impartial reporting of major international events.[101]

The military government

The anniversary of Khomeini's exile from Iran in 1963 led to major riots and the burning of many buildings on November 4–5, 1978. These led the shah to officially announce the formation of a military government on November 6.[102] The shah placed General Gholam-Reza Azhari as prime minister and promised on television to hold free elections once order was restored. While certainly loyal to the monarchy, Azhari had great difficulty coping with the extreme stress of his critical post.[103]

The Azhari military government was "military" in name only and was beset with major weaknesses from the outset. It was not given any new powers required to implement martial law, so little was to change in the streets. The Azhari administration was not a full "military" government, as civilian personnel continued in their posts in all key ministries. Azhari had problems ensuring the cooperation of key military leaders. This resulted in more military inefficiency and confusion. Azhari preferred a low-key approach by arresting high-profile former government officials, including former prime minister, Amir Abbas Hoveida.[104] These tactics not only failed to assuage the opposition but helped undermine the morale and loyalty of the establishment's civilian and military officials.

Protests and riots during the month of Muharram would prove critical.[105] Azhari insisted at first that the curfew would be strictly enforced and that no permits for any type of religious protests would be granted.[106] Clashes took place with up to 700 protestors being killed, prompting the oil workers to go on strike.[107] Realizing the rising power of the opposition, Azhari backed down; he had no military solution. The ban against marches was lifted with curfew hours relaxed and troops placed away from the protestors' path of marches.[108] In early December up to two million protestors congregated in Azadi Square (former Shahyad Square) to demand the removal of the shah and the return of Khomeini to Iran.[109] Kurzman has estimated that by December 10–11, up to 10% of the entire Iranian population were marching, making it possibly the largest mass protest in history.[110] Clashes did take place, one notable confrontation occurring in Isfahan, resulting in protestors attacking banks, a movie theater, and various government buildings.[111]

The Bakhtiar interlude

With the failure of the military government, the Shah decided to terminate martial law.[112] The shah approached Shapur Bakhtiar of the newly revived National Front in early January.[113] He requested that Bakhtiar become the prime minster of a new civilian government. Bakhtiar assumed this office on January 4, on condition that he was allowed to appoint a regency council. He also wanted the army's support, but this proved challenging given Bakhtiar's background of opposition against the shah.[114] Bakhtiar also wanted to name his own minister of war and fire commanders such as Oveissi, Khosrowdad and Rabii but they could not be replaced.[115]

It is unclear why the shah chose Bakhtiar as he had no links to the religious establishment, the left or the military. This meant that Bakhtiar had little hope of reaching out to the opposition or counting on the army's unqualified support. The political and military situation continued to deteriorate as Bakhtiar proceeded with the near-impossible task of building a viable civilian government.

The Bakhtiar interlude is widely believed to have hastened the demise of the Iranian army in the face of the Revolution.[116] Other key players in the unfolding drama were the US military. While President Carter had been supportive of the shah in the early days of the crisis, the Carter administration was split between those who wanted the shah to show a firm hand, those who wanted him to accommodate the Revolution, and those who profoundly disliked the shah.[117] This resulted in what Foran characterized as the US' "nonaction" to the Iranian crisis.[118] Following the Ball report into the situation, numbers of US officials began considering the possibility of accommodating the opposition by mid-December.[119] By late December US embassy officials in Tehran were in contact with key members of the revolution.[120] Following the Ball report, General Robert E. Huyser of the USAF and Major-General Philip Gast were dispatched to Tehran to consult with the Iranian military.[121] They arrived unannounced in Tehran on January 4, 1979, just as Bakhtiar had become Prime Minister.[122] The two immediately set to work with their Iranian counterparts. The latter were organized into a five-man *Heyat* (board) composed of generals Qarabaghi (chairman of the joint chiefs), Badrei (ground forces commander), Rabii (air force commander), Toufanian (head of Iranian military industries and chief of foreign military purchase program), and Admiral Habibollah (navy commander), occasionally joined by Moghaddam (the new head of SAVAK). The board met daily with the US generals, then meeting with Gast after Huyser's departure from Tehran on February 3, 1979.

The actual nature of Huyser's mission remains unclear. Some American sources report that Huyser's mission was to ensure that the Iranian military held together and that plans for a coup d'état were to be drafted as a "last resort."[123] Huyser's major liability was the damaging political image he projected upon the government and the shah. Zabih notes that "the shah had told them [the Iranian commanders] to trust, listen to, and obey the US General [Huyser]."[124] Qarabaghi was to later deny in exile that the shah had ordered Iranian commanders to "obey" Huyser.[125] Religious conservatives and leftists predictably portrayed Huyser's presence in Tehran as further evidence of how the shah and the army were puppets of the United States. But the shah soon came to believe that Huyser's mission was to arrange for an accommodation between the military and the revolutionaries at the monarchy's expense.[126] General Qarabaghi later wrote that Huyser had ulterior motives by conducting a secret mission against Iran's interests.[127] The revolutionaries believed that Huyser was in Tehran to arrange for a coup against them.[128] Huyser's memoirs characterize his mission to Tehran as "one that started with desperation and disunity and ended in disaster."[129]

It appears that Huyser told Iranian commanders that the US and the West no longer supported the shah and that the restoration of law and order was conditional on his departure from Iran.[130] Later during his exile, the shah accused Huyser as having thrown him "out of the country like a dead mouse."[131] The shah also noted other Westerners insisting on his departure from Iran, including US ambassador William Sullivan, Lord George Brown of England and the French.[132] The shah's departure had also been one of Bakhtiar's key demands for accepting the premiership.[133]

The shah left Iran from Tehran on January 16, 1979.[134] Qarabaqhi literally begged the shah to stay, fearing (correctly as it turned out) that his departure would lead to the army's collapse.[135] Even as he was boarding his jet to leave, the shah failed to provide his commanders with thorough instructions for dealing with the crisis.

Qarabaghi had to quell rumors of a coup after the shah's departure. He declared in no uncertain terms that any coup attempt would be sternly dealt with. The military kept up a brave front by issuing press releases, pouring more troops into the streets, and conducting over flights over Tehran. But the military's morale had been badly shaken, forcing them into the dilemma of either accommodating the opposition or the unpalatable option of cracking down. With the shah gone and loyalty to Bakhtiar tenuous at best, more and more members of the high command began to consider their options.

By late January, Huyser had adopted Sullivan's view that the old order was close to collapse. Arojmand notes that Huyser and Sullivan put forward a proposal to Washington on January 23, 1979 to build a coalition between the revolutionaries and the army.[136] Washington rejected this, instructing Huyser to support Bakhtiar and to draft contingency plans for a military coup in case Bakhtiar collapsed.[137] Meanwhile, Mehdi Bazagran stated in late January that Sullivan had proposed a referendum to replace the monarchy with a republic.[138] Huyser appears to have succeeded in having a five-man board draft plans for terminating the crushing strikes crippling the economy as well as seizing oil production-distribution facilities and customs services.[139] These plans never materialized but Huyser reputedly believed that a triumvirate of Rabii, Badrei and Toufanian could take charge if Bakhtiar gave the order.[140] It is doubtful that a coup would have succeeded at this late stage.

Morale had drastically plummeted among many of the army's conscripts, professional troops and officers, with top commanders being far from united. Huyser was particularly critical of Qarabaqhi, deriding his courage to take charge just as Bakhtiar's administration tottered on collapse.[141]

The arrival of Khomeini: fall of Bakhtiar and the monarchy

In late January, the BBC reported that US officials were working to prevent Khomeini's return to Iran.[142] All Iran's airports were closed on January 27–28 to prevent Khomeini from flying into Iran.[143] This resulted in serious riots, in which at least 28 people died in a single day.[144] This had major repercussions within the air force. A considerable number of air force technicians, officers, and NCOs across Iran engaged in a hunger strike to protest against Mehrabad airport's seizure.[145] Around 800 *Homafaran* (air force cadets) seized the strategic airbases of Hamadan and Dezful.[146] The military retaliated by having 160 of the air force technicians arrested, but such measures were stopgaps at best.[147] Bakhtiar finally acquiesced to Khomeini's arrival.

Even as Khomeini's Air France jet was taking off from Paris towards Tehran, many members of the Iranian military were contemplating how to compromise with Khomeini and the revolutionaries. Qarabaghi even met with some of the revolutionary activists in hopes of finding a solution through the impasse. Predictably, these efforts came to naught. Demands by the revolutionaries to have the army join them were summarily rejected by Qarabaghi, but as events soon demonstrated, it was Khomeini who held the initiative.[148] Qarabaghi had threatened to resign but Huyser persuaded him to retain his command.

Khomeini's arrival to Tehran on February 1, 1979 had major repercussions for the Iranian military. As the jet entered into Iranian airspace, Iranian jet fighters provided an escort to Tehran. Iranian TV provided live coverage of the aircraft's arrival at Tehran's Mehrabad airport. Among those present to greet the ayatollah and his entourage were pro-Revolution air force personnel. Security arrangements for Khomeini's arrival had been entrusted to revolutionary activists. The army staged a powerful presence in Tehran's streets, but this did little to bolster Bakhtiar's position; the cheering crowds simply fraternized with the troops. The revolutionaries escorted Khomeini through Tehran's rapturous crowds towards the Behesht-e Zahra cemetery. Upon his arrival there he delivered a speech declaring the Pahlavi monarchy, the Bakhtiar administration and the Majlis as illegal. He also invited the army to join the revolutionaries. Khomeini soon made his challenge clear by appointing Mehdi Bazargan as the head of the provisional government on February 4.

Khomeini's appeal for the military to join the rRevolution proved increasingly effective. Increasing numbers of troops and officers began to desert to the revolutionaries. Just days before Khomeini's arrival, workers from a machinegun factory and other military plants in Tehran organized a major pro-Revolution march on January 29.[149] This was followed shortly later on February 8, 1979, by another pro-Revolution march by numbers of Homafaran and air force officers.[150] Iranian newspapers showed pictures of these events, including air force officers saluting Khomeini, delivering yet another mortal blow to the military's morale. The Homafar split was clearly indicative of the ideological chasm that had developed within the armed forces. Fights and gun battles now broke out between pro- and anti-revolutionary factions across Iran's military bases. It was the beginning of the end.

Just one day after their official declaration of solidarity with Khomeini, the Homafaran became engaged in major firefights against pro-government air force officers, elements of the regular army, and the imperial guard at Dushan Tape on February 9, 1979.[151] The opening up of the arsenals by the Homafaran proved decisive: weapons and ammunition were handed out to revolutionary fighters and leftist guerrillas. Bakhtiar realized that the fighting at Dushan Tape could explode across Tehran's military bases and into the streets. He ordered a major curfew the next day to clear the streets. The aim was to facilitate the arrival of reinforcements in support of the beleaguered imperial guards at Dushan Tape.[152] But it was too late. The fighting at Dushan Tape spread across Tehran's bases, with their arsenals being opened to pro-revolutionary fighters. Tehran now thundered with rifle and machinegun fire as armed revolutionaries and leftist fighters fanned out onto Tehran's streets.

The main target after Dushan Tape was the military industrial complex. The capture of the machinegun factory was especially crucial as this had thousands of assembled weapons and large supplies of ammunition. This was followed by the storming of police stations, military bases, government buildings as well as radio and TV stations. One by one, Tehran's police stations and army bases fell.[153] There are reports that Bakhtiar ordered the air force to precision-bomb the machinegun factory, but Rabii objected.[154] In any event, the presence of so many unarmed civilians within the ranks of the revolutionaries and their Homafaran allies made any sort of "precision" bombing impossible. At this stage, any heavy-handed military action would have resulted in Khomeini issuing an official call for Jihad against the military. By this time whole units had either completely deserted or joined the revolution. With Dushan Tape in the revolutionaries' hands, Rabii had no choice but to capitulate.

The old order was now breathing its last gasp. General Mehdi Rahimi (martial law commander) announced that he was unable to resist the revolutionaries.[155] At 10:30am on February 11, 1979, the military high command of 27 top commanders and support staff officially declared the neutrality of the armed forces. This signaled the fall of the Bakhtiar government and the monarchy.[156] Despite this, the imperial guards' barracks had to be subdued by fighting the following day with all hostilities ending by February 13.[157] Western reports cited 500 killed and 2,000 wounded[158] with local Iranian newspapers reporting 650 killed and 2,500 wounded.[159] Bakhtiar escaped to France.[160] A number of high-ranking generals (including Rabii, Rahimi, and Nassiri) were captured and executed shortly thereafter. These, along with hundreds of other officers and former government officials, were rapidly tried and executed over the ensuing months. The overthrow of the Pahlavi establishment and its replacement by the Islamic Republic bore immediate geopolitical consequences. The CENTO alliance had now become null and void.

Rise of the Pasdaran

The "Sepah e Pasdaran Enghelab e Eslami" (Army of the Guardians of the Revolution), commonly known as "Sepah e Pasdaran" was officially formed in the consolidation of the revolutionary Islamic Republic of Iran in May 1979. Before May, the disparate Islamic fighters formed around 20,000 men (along with numbers of Palestinian and Lebanese Shiite allies), along with another 20,000 armed revolutionaries (not members of MEK, Fedaiayn and Tudeh) in Tehran.[161] The Islamic fighters rapidly organized into *Komiteh* (committee) units to maintain law and order, as well as introducing Sharia law. Their immediate task was to purge the armed forces of suspected pro-Shah officers, generals, and pilots. A number of these, including a number of personnel from the SAVAK secret services, were executed.

The Pasdaran soon developed into a military force parallel to the professional armed forces. This kept the army in check with respect to potential possible coup attempts, but also resulted in the rise of "two armies." Mohsen Rafiqdoust, commander of the Pasdaran, noted the force's three main responsibilities by 1985: provision of internal security against political opponents and separatists; participation in combat alongside the regular army against foreign invasion; and organization of powerful and ideologically loyal popular militias, notably the *Basij e Moztazafan* (lit. mobilized forces of the oppressed.)[162] By 1982 the Pasdaran stood at 100,000 men and were playing a major role in the Iran–Iraq War.[163] The Basij acted as the Pasdaran's strategic reserve and suffered very heavy casualties during the Iran–Iraq War.

Battles with the KDPI

The KDPI (Kurdish Democratic Party of Iran) rapidly fell out with Khomeini and the emerging government in Tehran. Abdolrahman Ghassemlu, the leader of the KDPI, arrived in Qom to discuss the issue of Kurdish autonomy with Khomeini. When no meaningful accord was reached, revolts began breaking out in western Iran's Kurdish regions in mid-March.[164] Protestors in Sanadaj fought against with local army forces and then stormed a number of government buildings, military installations and police stations. There were also conflicts between Shia and Sunni Kurds, as well as fighting between Kurds and Azaris in northwest Iran. The army and then the Pasdaran became locked in battles well into the summer of 1979. The KDPI were soon joined by members of the Fedaiyan.[165] The rebellion became serious in August when the Peshmerga succeeded in defeating a major Pasdaran offensive at Paveh. Tehran responded by sending a combined force of gendarmes, regular army and Pasdaran forces backed by Phantom fighter-bombers and combat helicopters. Success was finally achieved as government forces entered Saqqez and Paveh. Mahabad, now the KDPI's main base, became the scene of major clashes as Tehran's forces fought to secure the city's TV and radio stations.[166] Entrance into the city was bitterly contested with the Peshmerga repelling two tank thrusts before giving way in early September.[167]

The KDPI retreated into the mountains to resume their attacks against government forces. The KDPI and their allies were already well-armed; they had captured stocks of 105-mm cannon, antiaircraft guns and even a few tanks from Iranian army arsenals during the latter days of the Iranian Revolution.[168] The KDPI also got military assistance from Iraqi army helicopters which transported weapons for them in Iran.[169] Baghdad was clearly taking advantage of its neighbor's chaotic post-revolutionary state.

By the mid-November the KDPI returned to attack Mahabad. By the end of that month, attacks were being made against almost every significant Kurdish city. Mahabad once again became the KDPI's headquarters. Ghassemlou soon declared that he could muster up to 7,000 Peshmerga. Despite this boast, the KDPI was vulnerable. Numbers of Iranian Kurds opposed the KDPI and began joining Tehran's forces. The KDPI remained intact and held its ground during the fighting in January–August 1980.[170] By this time Iraqi air and land intrusions into Iranian territory, especially the Kurdish-populated regions, were becoming increasingly frequent.

Iraqi incursions materialized into the full-scale invasion of Iran on September 22, 1980. By December 1980, the Iraqi army had launched major thrusts into western Iran in coordination with KDPI.[171] This proved counterproductive for both Iraq and the KDPI. First, numbers of Iranian Kurds, already opposed to Iraq's invasion of Iran, stopped supporting the KDPI. Iraq's attempt to use the "Kurdish card" backfired as Iran soon made common cause against Baghdad with Iraq's own Kurds. Tehran managed to defeat the KDPI, thanks to the help provided by Iranian Kurds and neighboring Iraqi Kurds who cut off much of the KDPI's supply lines from Iraq. By 1983 the KDPI was increasingly bottled up in its mountain strongholds, capable of sporadic resistance at best.

The Left and the MEK

As the Islamic Republic worked to consolidate its political power, it faced opposition from various Islamic groups notably the Forqhan. These launched a number of attacks against clerical and government officials in 1979, their most dramatic action being the assassination of Ayatollah Motahari, a close ally of Ayatollah Khomeini.[172] These were soon crushed. Various secular and nationalist groups were also shunted out of mainstream politics by the Islamic Republic Party (IRP). This task was easily accomplished as neither the secularists nor nationalists were armed.

Bazargan and his more liberal group with the Islamic government managed to survive politically but were quickly eclipsed by the IRP. The remaining factions in the contest for power were the leftists, namely the Fedaiayn e Khalq, Tudeh and the MEK (Mujaheddin e Khalq). These posed the greatest military threat as they were well-armed and highly experienced in guerrilla warfare. As the theocratic-based system of government established itself in Tehran, leftist fighters began joining the various provincial rebellions that broke out in Iran.

The Fedaiyan soon became politically divided. Significant numbers considered joining the new Islamic establishment and withdrew their support for the KDPI.[173] The Tudeh, which had had around 7,000 armed fighters in Tehran at the time of Bakhtiar's overthrow, used more indirect tactics to spread its influence.[174] They resorted to traditional communist tactics of subtle infiltration of government, military and educational posts, with hopes of increasing their influence over the years. They also helped the conservative elements within the clerical establishment to reduce the power of Bazargan and other liberal-secular politicians within the Iranian parliament.[175] The Tudeh remained operational until July 1982 when it was outlawed, followed by the arrest of leader Noureddin Kianouri and many Tudeh members and sympathizers in February 1983.[176] Notable was the arrest of Admiral Bahram Afzali, commander of the Iranian navy, evidence of the Tudeh's efficacy in infiltration.[177] The destruction of the Tudeh, which was cooperating with Soviet officials, was one of the factors that shifted Moscow towards Saddam Hussein against Iran during the Iran–Iraq War.[178]

The MEK and the Fedaiyan had around 15,000–20,000 armed fighters after the Revolution.[179] Relations between the MEK leader Massoud Rajavi and the new establishment had rapidly deteriorated by the summer of 1979. By the following year, increasingly serious clashes were taking place between the MEK and the Pasdaran. MEK operatives escalated their attacks by setting off a huge explosion in the Iranian parliament on June 29, 1981 killing over 70 government officials including Ayatollah Mohammad Beheshti. Rajavi and President Bani-Sadr fled Iran and sought asylum in France.[180] This did little to stop the violence. Another bomb blast in late August 1981 killed Mohammad Rajai and Mohammad Bahonar, the president and prime minster respectively. By October 1982 Rajavi was claiming that the MEK had slain over 2,000 pro-government religious and political activists in Iran.[181]

The MEK's actions elicited a brutally rigorous military response just as Iran was locked in a major war with Iraq. By 1983, MEK logistics, manpower and communications in Iran had been severely damaged by the Pasdaran and Iranian security forces. According to MEK reports, 5,000 of their members had been killed with another 25,000 imprisoned.[182] Though militarily the MEK in Iran was badly mauled, their overall organization was far from finished. Rajavi left France for Iraq in 1986 to join MEK exiles already there. It was here that he and the MEK committed a most serious blunder: they struck an alliance with Saddam Hussein. Rajavi's MEK organization began receiving Saddam's support in military training and weaponry. The MEK's military alliance with Saddam Hussein's army proved to be immensely unpopular with Iranians across a wide political spectrum.

Provincial revolts

Turkmen at Gonbad Kavoos had a number of land grievances and were boycotting the Constitutional referndum. This led to brief fighting with the Pasdaran in late March–early April.[183] The Pasdaran were supported by air force personnel, while the Turkmen were bolstered by leftist fighters. The cease-fire on April 3, 1979 was quickly followed by negotiations and the granting of greater local autonomy.[184] The brief clashes had resulted in just over 100 men killed on both sides.

In late April a number of local Iranian Arabs began demonstrating in a number of locales, mainly Khorramshahr. This soon led to clashes with the Pasdaran. Baghdad's support for separatist movements in Khuzistan had steadily increased as the Iranians had become preoccupied with the Revolution in 1978–79. Arab historian Al-Azhary notes that by 1979, "Baghdad armed and trained guerrillas who waged a sabotage campaign against Iranian oil installations."[185] These Iraqi actions were not unlike their involvement with the KDPI. Saddam Hussein also activated cells of the Baath party in Khuzistan, sending them arms and ammunition through the Iraqi consulate in Khorramshahr.[186] This was part of Saddam's attempt to ensure that Iranian Arabs would be "won over" to the Baathist cause before Iraqi tanks began rolling into Iran. Baghdad's involvement may partly explain why 115 Iranian Arabs and Pasdaran were killed in clashes in April–May 1979.[187] Tehran's dispatch of Admiral Madani to Khuzistan seems to have played an effective role in helping curtail Baghdad's activities in the province.

The majority-Sunni Baluchis were unhappy with the constitutional referendum. Fighting soon broke out between them and the majority-Shiite Seistanis by early December. Baluch fighters also attacked parolling Pasdaran and army armored vehicles which prolonged clashes until December 25.[188] Baghdad had previously supported separatist movements among the Baluchis in Iran, but it is not clear how much foreign involvement was implicated in the December 1979 incidents.

Unlike most of those who rebelled following the Revolution, the Azaris, like the majority of Iranians, are Shiite. Azaris are not confined to Azarbaijan province but tightly integrated throughout Iran. This meant that what happened in Azarbaijan had serious repercussions throughout Iran. The Azarbaijanis had been among the first Iranians to lead the anti-shah demonstrations in 1978.

The Azari protests had much to do with the philosophical underpinnings of the new government now forming in Tehran. The implementation of the *Velayat e Faqhih* (lit. Guardianship of the Jurist) and the notion of a supreme leader (i.e. Khomeini) or *Rahbar-e Enqhelab* (leader of the revolution) into the new government and constitution was not agreed by all leading clerics, notably Ayatollah Mohammad Kazem Shariatmadari.[189] Shariatmadari's objections did not lead him to boycott the referendum and he voted for the Islamic Republic, but the Muslim People's Republican Party with support in Azarbaijan and among Iran's educated and middle-classes, remained unreconciled.[190] Clashes erupted in Qom between the followers of Khomeini and Shariatmadari on December 5, resulting in the death of a guard outside Shariatmadari's home. This set off serious riots in Tabriz where locals took control of the governor's office, and broadcasting stations by December 9–10.[191] More serious was the capture of the Tabriz airbase and local army and police units joining the protestors.[192] The new government was keen to negotiate but numbers of Pasdaran continued to battle local rebels in Tabriz.[193] The government finally got the upper hand when elements of the 64th Infanry Division rolled into Tabriz, forcing an end an the fghting by late January. Shariatmadari was placed under house arrest but the government also worked to accommodate the Azaris by promsing them greater autonomy. Shariatmadari also appealed to his followers to desist from protests as he had no wish to provoke further violence.

Military impact of the purges

The post-revolutionary purges, mandatory retirement and executions led to a sharp decline in the professional military leadership of the armored corps, combat helicopters, and fighter aircraft. Overall, 4,500 professional personnel from the air and ground services were "purged."[194] Much of the military's top echelon was simply executed. There was even talk of selling off much of Iran's advanced equipment including the Chieftain tanks and F-14 Tomcats. Had this occurred before Saddam Hussein's invasion in 1980, Iran would have been at even more of a disadvantage. The army was reduced from a total of 200,000 to 100,000 men, the air force from 100,000 to 20,000–25,000 men and the navy from 25,000 to 10,000 men. There were numbers of commentators in the new establishment who expressed alarm at the purges and anti-military measures. They were aware that these dangerously imperiled the country's security against foreign invasion.

The new government consolidated its political authority upon the armed services, including the air force. Executions and trials of former air force commanders and regular army officers alienated numbers of air force and army personnel.[195] These, along with SAVAK members and imperial guards, conspired to overthrow the new Islamic Republic.[196] The conspirators were apparently linked to the former prime minister, Shapur Bakhtiar, and Ali Akbar Tabatabaie in Washington, DC.[197]

Planning for the coup was done in some haste, with inadequate provisions being made for protection against infiltration. The top tier of conspirators were higher level officers who planned the coup, while the second tier would implement the plans. Coup members were selected on their ability to access critical domains such as combat aircraft (mainly F-4s), aviation fuel, barracks, arsenals, and ammunition dumps. It is unclear as to whom or what organizations funded the coup attempt.

The final plan was comprised of three phases and hinged on the Nojeh airbase close to Hamadan. Nojeh was within easy striking distance of Tehran and was equipped with F-4 Phantom fighter-bombers, which were to be the main instruments of the upcoming coup. The first stage entailed the launching of 30–50 Phantoms equipped with anti-personnel cluster bombs, Maverick air-to-ground missiles, and 20mm cannon. These would blitz Tehran on the evening of July 10–11, 1980. The strike package would attack Tehran's Mehrabad airport, the nerve centers of the new government, radio and television stations and Khomeini's home at Jamaran.[198] Jamaran was to be continuously attacked after the bombing by Phantoms firing 20mm guns. Military targets had also been selected, including regular army barracks, the newly established Pasdaran headquarters and ammunition dumps. Military and political targets in five other cities (including Qom and Mashad) were also selected. The conclusion of the aerial assaults (lasting half a day) was to be followed by the deployment of up to nine regular army divisions. These would seize government buildings, Pasdaran headquarters, the Tehran bazaar, and radio and television stations. The third phase entailed the recruitment of up to 50,000 Kurdish, Azeri and Baluchi paramilitary fighters to support the coup.[199] It is unclear as to how so many of these could be so quickly recruited. In addition, not all of these spoke Persian and many were unfamiliar with Tehran's important locations. There were also questions as to how effective the regular armed forces would have been. Even if the aerial assaults had been carried out, many regular army troops had been severely demoralized by the events of the Revolution. In contrast the supporters of the new government were imbued with revolutionary ardor.

The coup was doomed just hours before it was due to unfold. The revolutionary authorities were alerted to the plan and made arrests on July 10.[200] Following the exposure of the coup, the revolutionary authorities arrested up to 300 suspects, most of them military officers, along with 30 pilots.[201] Many of the latter and numbers of army personnel were executed, followed by a large wave of purges, forced retirements, imprisonments, and exiles. The vacuum left in the top echelons of the military was filled by younger colonels and officers.

The hostage crisis

If there is one event that Westerners and indeed Americans vividly recall from Iran's recent history, it is the seizure of the US embassy in Tehran by Islamic student militants (known as "Daneshjooyan e Mosalman-e Peyroye Khat-e Imam" or Muslim Student Followers of the Line of Imam Khomeini) on November 4, 1979. It is believed that planning for this action had been made by Ibrahim Asgharzadeh who had consulted the Muslim Student Followers of the Line of Imam Khomeini associations from Tehran's various universities. Sixty of these "students," along with at least 300 confederates, scaled the US embassy walls capturing its personnel and a small group of marines.[202] The "students" then demanded that President Carter return the shah to Iran to face trial. This was categorically rejected by the US, beginning an international crisis lasting 444 days. The shah had entered the US for cancer treatment in late October. He left the US on December 15, staying briefly in Panama and then settling in Egypt where he died on July 27, 1980.

Khomeini had not instigated the takeover of the US embassy[203] but decided to support the action, which now had massive support from radical anti-American and conservative Islamic activists.[204] It is also not clear whether the students actually wanted to occupy the embassy for a prolonged period.[205] As the Pasdaran took no action to expel the students from the US embassy compound, the takeover became a long-term affair.[206] The Pasdaran then replaced the students guarding the hostages at the embassy.[207] Prior to the embassy seizure, numbers of Iranian officials were open to the idea of a rapprochement with the US.[208] Efforts towards an Iranian–US reconciliation were ultimately doomed mainly due to the hostility of the left and hard-line clerics.

Washington dispatched naval units towards the Persian Gulf, raising the prospect of American military action. Awareness of this fact may explain why the new establishment ordered numbers of regular troops be restored to pre-Revolution levels.[209] Washington had no intention of engaging in massive bombing or invasion; her sole interest was to extract the hostages. This objective led to Operation *Eagle Claw*, which would land commando-type troops in Iran to free the hostages.

On April 24, 1980, eight US Navy Sea Stallion helicopters left USS *Nimitz* and headed for the desert of Tabas (approximately 250 miles (400km) from Tehran). Also en route to Tabas were six C-130 transport aircraft carrying fuel for the helicopters, various equipment and approximately 90 Delta Force commandos, accompanied by support personnel. Entering Iranian airspace was not much of a problem, as revolutionary chaos had disrupted much of Iran's early warning and radar net. Despite this, the operation was complicated and fraught with risk. The plan was for the helicopters and C-130s to arrive at Tabas. The helicopters would be refueled, then transport the commandos to Garmsar near eastern Tehran. From Garmsar the commandos would board trucks stationed there by CIA operatives. The commandos would then drive into the US embassy compound. Achieving surprise, the commandos would quickly overpower the Pasdaran and free the hostages. Helicopters would then transport the commandos and freed hostages to C-141 transport aircraft, protected by US jet fighters.

From the outset, Operation *Eagle Claw* went terribly wrong. As soon as the helicopters entered Iranian airspace, three suffered mechanical problems. *Eagle Claw* was still-born: a minimum of six helicopters were needed to proceed with the operation. The mission was cancelled. The extrication proved disastrous. A C-130 collided with one of the helicopters as it was ascending to leave Tabas, causing a massive explosion. Scores of Americans were injured and eight were killed. The other helicopters were grounded. Their crew, along with remaining US troops and personnel, boarded the remaining C-130s to depart from Iran without incident by the morning of April 25. Just one day after the failed rescue mission, tensions between Iranian and American forces were heightened in the Persian Gulf.[210] The Pasdaran quickly dispersed the hostages in Tehran to various locations.[211] The hostages would finally be released on January 20, 1981, twenty minutes after Ronald Reagan had been sworn in as the president of the United States.

The hostage crisis and the doomed Operation *Eagle Claw* strengthened Iran's radical anti-US/Western factions. Anti-American rhetoric and demonstrations became commonplace, with images of these beamed to Western audiences. Logically, the major consequence of the crisis was the political estrangement of Iran and the Western hemisphere. The capture of the American diplomats sent profound shock waves of disbelief and anger throughout America. Daily American television coverage of the crisis did little to endear Iranians to the American administration or public. Some Western analysts believe that this factor may have been partly responsible for the profound anti-Iranian stance taken by the American administrations during the 1980s.[212] Few would argue that the hostage crisis eroded international support for Iran during the Iran–Iraq War of 1980–88. The US in particular became a determined and most dangerous enemy.

Saddam Hussein was the major beneficiary of the rupture in US–Iranian relations, especially in the military domain. Iran had paid billions of dollars to the US and Britain for military equipment yet to be delivered. The US now placed a strict military embargo for spare parts, which had an immediate impact on Iran's ability to operate its fleet of US-made aircraft and tanks.[213] From Baghdad's perspective, a golden opportunity was opening.[214] The US provided assistance to the Iraqi war effort, especially after Saddam Hussein's forces were expelled from Iran in 1982.

American antipathy against Iran as a result of the hostage crisis may explain why US media reports during the Iran–Iraq War often portrayed Saddam Hussein favorably. Western (especially US) media also glossed over Saddam's use of chemical weapons against Iranian troops, civilians and Iraqi Kurds.[215] The pro-Saddam stance of the US media and political establishment was such that even when an Iraqi jet attacked the USS *Stark* in 1987 killing 37 US servicemen, Washington refused to condemn Iraq, attempting to shift the blame for that incident to Iran.[216]

PART VI

THE IRAN–IRAQ WAR

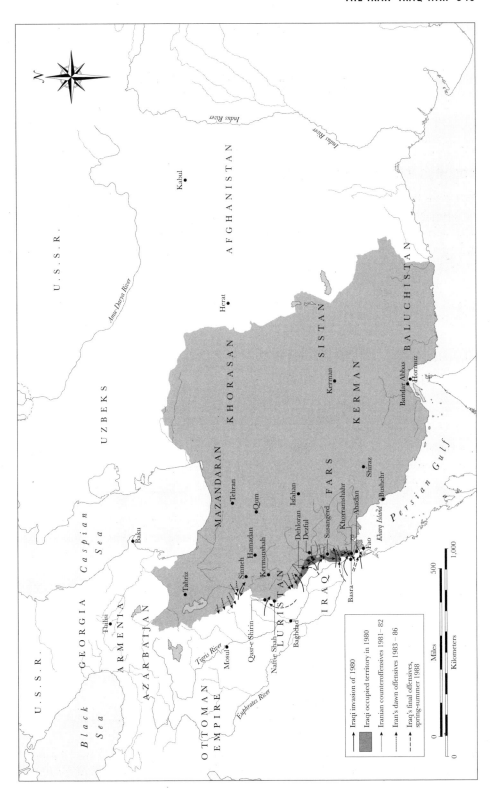

U.S.S.R.

Black Sea

GEORGIA

Tbilisi

ARMENIA

AZARBAIJAN

OTTOMAN EMPIRE

Euphrates River

Tigris River

Mosul

Baghdad

Nahe Shah

Qasr-e-Shirin

IRAQ

Basra

LURISTAN

Simeh

Kermanshah

Hamadan

Tabriz

Caspian Sea

Baku

U.S.S.R.

UZBEKS

Amu-Darya River

MAZANDARAN

Tehran

Qom

Isfahan

Dehloran

Dezful

Susangerd

Khorramshahr

Abadan

Fao

Kharg Island

Bushehr

Shiraz

FARS

KHORASAN

Herat

AFGHANISTAN

Kabul

Indus River

Indus River

SISTAN

KERMAN

Kerman

BALUCHISTAN

Bandar Abbas

Hormuz

Persian Gulf

Iraqi invasion of 1980

Iraqi occupied territory in 1980

Iranian counteroffensives 1981–82

Iran's dawn offensives 1983–86

Iraq's final offensives, spring–summer 1988

0   500   1,000
Miles

0   500   1,000
Kilometers

CHAPTER 33

IRAQ INVADES IRAN

Baghdad exploits Iran's military disarray

Even as the Iranian Revolution was fully underway, the Iranian military brass was concerned about the possibility of foreign powers taking advantage of Iran's internal disarray. The shah ordered one detachment of F-4 Phantoms from Tehran to fly into Chahbahar (southeast Iran) and an F-5 Tiger detachment from Tabriz to augment the air wing at Dezful.[1] Orders were also issued for the entire radar and early warning net to operate at maximum alertness.[2] Tehran's anxieties would soon be proved justified.

Saddam Hussein and the Iraqi military had keenly noted the collapse of the Pahlavi order. Iran's military was now cut off from its main weapons suppliers and the Western economic embargo and political isolation also worked to Baghdad's advantage. Saddam had neither forgotten his disastrous tank thrust into Iran in June 1975 nor the punishment Iraqi forces had received as a result of Iranian support for the Iraqi–Kurdish rebellion in the 1970s. The Iraqi leadership also viewed the 1975 Algiers Treaty as a humiliation, signed under pressure from a militarily superior Iran. They had patiently waiting for the right time to "correct" the terms of that treaty.[3]

Saddam Hussein and the Baath party saw many opportunities in attacking what was perceived as a militarily weakened Iran. Baathist irredentist propaganda made it clear that the greater Arab nation consisted not only of the territories of the members of the Arab League but also those "outside" of the Arab world, namely Alexandretta (Iskenderun) in Turkey and Khuzistan in Iran. The time to "liberate" Khuzistan seemed ripe. Annexing Khuzistan would greatly expand Iraq's coastline and maritime access to the Persian Gulf and the Indian Ocean. Iraq's already booming economy would become an international powerhouse with the appropriation of Iran's port facilities and petroleum assets in Khuzistan. The politically prestige of dismembering non-Arab Iran would also transform Saddam Hussein into the new leader of the Arab world.

Just months after the overthrown of the Bakhtiar administration, the Iraqi military proceeded to "test" Iran's defensive capabilities. The first intrusion was an Iraqi helicopter which flew at low level over Mehran in Iranian Kurdistan in early April 1979. This was followed by severe air and helicopter strikes in Iranian Kurdistan in May–June. The situation deteriorated by early October when Iranian aerial reconnaissance photos revealed heavy concentrations of Iraqi troops and tanks massing along the Iranian border. There was little doubt as to the seriousness of the Iraqi threat, but there was little the Iranians could do about it.

Saddam Hussein's first political action was to send a formal letter to the UN in April 1980 demanding that the Iranians vacate the islands of Greater Tunb, Lesser Tunb and Abu Moussa in the Persian Gulf.[4] Saddam's next action was to dispatch Iraqi troops to "liberate" 130km² of territory on May 10, 1980, claimed by Baghdad under the 1975 treaty.[5] Tensions rose further with the outbreak of bitter border clashes in the Mehran region of Iranian Kurdistan in August. More clashes followed in early September 1980, with Iraqi forces capturing pockets of territory around Zain ol Qaws in Iranian Kurdistan, again claimed by Baghdad under the 1975 treaty.[6] Iraqi land forces were now repeatedly crossing into Iran to seize a number of Iranian border posts. Tehran's only meaningful military response was the artillery shelling of Mandali, Khaneqin and Zarbatiyah on September 4.[7] This did little to alter the situation on the ground. Baghdad confidently stated by September 10 that all claimed territories had been "liberated" by its armed forces.

With conclusion of his "liberating" operations, Saddam Hussein delivered a speech to the Iraqi national assembly on September 17, 1980, abrogating the Algiers treaty. In that same speech he declared that "We in no way intend to launch war against Iran."[8] One day later, Saddam's forces proceeded to attack more Iranian border posts in the south to prepare for the large tank thrusts into Iran's Khuzistan province. The Iraqi 4th Infantry Division attacked border posts leading to Bostan with the Iraqi 7th Mechanized Division doing the same along border posts leading to Fakkeh.[9] Despite the post-revolutionary purges, the Iranian air force, now known as the Islamic Republic of Iran Air Force (IRIAF) had managed to support the army, Pasdaran, and Gendarmerie against the Iraqis. Despite Iran's edge in the air, the reality was that Iran's land forces were in no condition to repel a major Iraqi invasion. Baghdad was confident that it now had the military edge over Iran and would score a quick and easy victory. It was in this spirit that Iraqi tanks rolled into Iran on September 22, 1980.

Volumes of ink have been spilt to explain the "causes" of the Iran–Iraq War. Previous chapters have outlined the historical territorial disputes (especially over the Arvand Rud/Shaat al Arab waterway) between Iran and Iraq which were a cause, alongside other, non-territorial, factors.

Arab, Iranian and Western historians have offered a variety of "historical" reasons for the conflict. One of the least convincing "causes" are the supposed "Aryan versus Semitic" rivalries that have allegedly existed since the arrival of Indo-Europeans onto the Iranian plateau thousands of years ago.[10] While this interpretation was often conveyed by Saddam Hussein and the Baath party as a root cause of the war, the notion that "pure" racial differences exist between Iranians and Iraqis are oxymoronic, simply because the Iranian plateau, fertile crescent, Anatolia, Caucasus, and Central Asia have witnessed multitudes of ethnic groups and languages ebbing and flowing across these territories for millennia.[11] Iran and Iraq have experienced centuries of admixture and synthesis, especially in the cultural domain.[12]

The notion of religious differences, namely the Shia-Sunni rivalry, may appear superficially more convincing, especially given the centuries-long wars between the Ottoman Empire and Iran. But the "religious" explanation as a "trigger" for war has been questioned.[13] In practice, Baghdad's administration was driven by a racialist-secularist ideology with Tehran's leadership being imbued with the fervour of pan-Islamism.

Pan-Islamic rhetoric was in essence the antithesis of Baathist ideology. Baathism viewed Islam as "a revolutionary Arab movement whose meaning was the renewal of Arabism."[14] Tehran's pan-Islamism challenged this view by emphasizing that Islam went beyond Arabism to appeal to the entire Islamic world (Arab and non-Arab countries). Pan-Islamism distinctly disdains national identity in favor of a trans-national pan-Islamic one. The new Iranian administration combined religion and state while the Baathists were strictly secular. This meant that the political systems of

Baghdad and Tehran were diametrically opposed. The Baathist vision was that of all Arab states (including Iraq) were provinces of a single (secular) pan-Arab super-state. In contrast, pan-Islamism views Arab and non-Arab Muslim states as borderless provinces within a larger pan-Islamic state.[15] Staudenmaier argues that one of the causes of the war was due to the Iranian clergy's demands that the Iraqi people overthrow the Baathist party.[16] Some Arab historians conclude that the psychological circumstances created by the Iranian Revolution led the Baathists to the conclusion that resolute action was necessary before it was too late.[17] Nevertheless, Iraqi Shiite sectarian violence already had roots in internal Iraqi politics, and was not a simple "product" of the Iranian Revolution. Iraq's Sunni elements were generally more affluent and influential than the country's more numerous Shiites, which helps explain in part one of the reasons of the rise of the Shiite Al-Dawaah party. What is certain is that a number of terrorist bombing incidents did take place in Iraq. Tariq Aziz, Iraq's deputy minister was also the target of a failed assassination attempt in April 1980 while visiting Iraq's Al-Mustansiriya University. Cockburn now questions the veracity of that event by reporting that an Iraqi "ex-minister believed that the assassination attempt on Tariq Aziz was faked by Iraqi security."[18] If this is the case, then it was certainly a macabre affair as 11 innocent Iraqi students were tragically gunned down in that attack. More research is required to verify Cockburn's controversial report that the Baath party may have staged the assassination for propaganda purposes.

As relations steadily deteriorated and border clashes increased, bellicose rhetoric began escalating on both sides. Iraq's highly capable and efficient security services were more than capable of quickly crushing any challenges against Baathist rule. Baghdad was also politically secure with a robust and prosperous economy. It is true that disaffection against the Baath did exist amongst Iraq's Shiite and Kurdish communities. But the notion that Tehran somehow had the organizational and logistical capacity to mobilize these into a massive pan-Islamic style revolution is difficult to substantiate. Baghdad had in fact already suppressed Shiite political organizations such as the Al-Daawah before Saddam's invasion of Iran.[19] What is almost certain is that Tehran's fiery post-revolutionary rhetoric calling for the overthrow of the Baath posed little military threat to Iraq. Iran's armed forces, caught in the midst of post-revolutionary purges and trials, were wholly incapable of posting any serious challenge against Baghdad.

The Baathist propaganda machine openly promoted racialism during the war by often portraying Iranian people as animals.[20] By the 1980s, Nazi-style race laws had been instituted against Iraqis of Iranian descent.[21] Racist and anti-Semitic literature was widely distributed to Iraqi government institutions, education centers and front-line troops.[22] The Baathists even resorted to "archeological warfare," deploying artillery, missiles and aerial bombardment against ancient Iranian historical sites.[23]

Iraqi military capabilities and plans

Iraq committed seven of its 12 army divisions for the invasion of Iran. Iraqi supply lines had been prepared well in advance of the invasion.[24] Saddam Hussein had in fact been planning for war since at least the spring of 1980 or earlier.[25] His armies faced just two under-strength Iranian divisions across the border. This meant that Iraq not only had the advantage of surprise but numerical superiority. The Iraqis carefully struck at those points where the Iranians were at their weakest, often outnumbering the defenders by a margin of at least 2-1.[26]

Iraq's invasion plans aimed to sever Khuzistan's refineries, oilfields, and communications from the rest of Iran.[27] The capture of Iranian Khuzistan was to be achieved by a massive tank thrust, the focal point of the invasion. The Iraqi offensive was based on an invasion plan provided by British military instructors at the Baghdad War College in 1941.[28] These "called for Iraqi forces to occupy Khuzistan province and then negotiate an armistice with the Iranian government that would include the relinquishment of the province to Iraq."[29] The plan recommended that Iraqi forces thrust into Iran on a broad front along five major axes (Panjvin, Qasr-e Shirin, Mehran, Susangerd–Dezful–Ahvaz, Khorramshar–Abadan). Iraqi invasion forces in fact entered Iran (north to south) along a wide front of approximately 1000km. The first three axes (Panjvin, Qasr-e Shirin, Mehran) were mainly blocking actions to prevent Iranian counterthrusts into Iraqi Kurdistan and towards Baghdad, while the fourth (Susangerd–Ahvaz–Dezful) and fifth (Khorramshar–Abadan) axes were completely offensive aiming at seizing as much of Iranian Khuzistan.

Khuzistan's flat desert-like terrain is ideal "tank country" and was ideally suited for Iraq's Soviet-style mechanized army. Nevertheless, Iraq's military doctrine was beset by three serious weaknesses. First, despite their proficiency in deploying their armor en masse, the Iraqis had tended to overemphasize massive defense systems (earth works, bunkers, etc). This became the mainstay of their war effort, especially after their ejection from Iran in 1982. The second weakness derived from the Iraqi army's experiences against Iraqi Kurdish rebels. In those battles, the Iraqis had often heavily relied upon massive artillery preparations to suppress enemy infantry. Iranian infantry would be far more lethal as they would be heavily supported by artillery, armor, combat helicopters, and aircraft. The third weakness (one shared by Iran), was a serious lack of proficiency in Western-style combined arms operations. The Iraqis often made rapid tank thrusts without effective air cover, helicopter escorts or infantry support.

The efficiency of the Iraqi military was strongly compromised by a rigid "top-down" command model. Saddam Hussein, who had no professional military training, was supreme commander-in-chief. Iraq also partly suffered from militarily and morally unfit officers. These officers were often promoted based on their ideological reliability rather than military merit. Like Jordan, Syria and Egypt, Iraq also possessed significant numbers of well-trained, daring, and innovative officers. The problem rested again on the person of Saddam Hussein and his leadership. He often insisted on "micromanaging" the activities of the armed forces. These shackles in command loosened somewhat during the war, but were re-imposed after the 1988 ceasefire.

A number of Western analysts writing at the end of the Iran—Iraq War provided a selective view of the power differential between the combatants. Pelletiere for example noted that "The Iranians vastly outnumbered the Iraqis" during the entire war,[30] a statement that is strictly true if one considers the demographic difference between Iraq (16–17 million in 1980) and Iran (around 45 million in 1980). Iran certainly could and did draw upon its larger population base to sustain its war effort, but this could not overcome a number of key military advantages held by Iraq throughout the war. At the outset of the invasion, Iraq held a numerical edge in tanks, fielding 3,000 operational Soviet-built tanks versus Iran's less than 2,000 Western-built tanks.[31] Iran was also unable to field its full complement of tanks: many tanks were in need of repair or refit; many of Iran's top tank officers had either been retired or purged from the army after the Revolution;[32] and many of Iran's operational tanks were stationed close to the Soviet and Afghan borders to the north and northeast. These had to be transported over very long distances, and many suffered breakdowns and required overhaul and repair.[33] There are also indications that the sights and detection systems of numbers of Iranian tanks were out of order or in need of repairs.[34] These problems ensured that many arriving Iranian tanks were unfit for battle against the Iraqi advance in September 1980.[35] These factors may partly explain Iraqi successes against Iranian armor during the early stages of the war. By the end of 1980 the Iraqis had captured an impressive array of Western-built Iranian tanks, including 31 Chieftains, 25 M-60s, and 43 other armored fighting vehicles.[36]

There were other military discrepancies between Iran and Iraq in 1980. Examples include Iraq's 2,500 armored fighting vehicles and armored personnel carriers against Iran's 1,075.[37] The one area where Iran held a slight advantage on land was artillery, which at 1,000 pieces was more than Iraq's 800, but much of Iran's heavy artillery was in desperate need of repair and service, and the serviceable artillery was dispersed across the country.[38]

The Iraqi Air Force (IrAF) was beset by a number of disadvantages. Ever since the assumption of power by Saddam Hussein, the overall command of the IrAF had come increasingly under the domination of the Baath party. The leadership's fear of coups resulted in Iraqi pilots receiving insufficient air-combat training. Iraqi airmen were often outclassed in air-to-air combat, although this was also due to the far superior US-based training of Iranian pilots and their more sophisticated combat aircraft. The IrAF's air-to-ground support and bombing skills also failed to achieve conclusive results at the outbreak of hostilities. Iraqi aircraft were also hampered by mediocre Soviet avionics equipment.[39] The weaknesses of the IrAF had been demonstrated several months before the war when numbers of Iraqi aircraft and helicopters had been badly mauled in a series of engagements.[40] More ominous for Baghdad was the ability of Iranian aircraft to destroy large bodies of Iraqi armor. One example was the destruction of up to 30 to 40 Iraqi tanks by Iranian fighters in Qasr-e Shirin (September 8, 10 and 17).[41] Another example right before the war was the retreat of the Iraqi 7th Mechanized Division in Khuzistan after Iranian aircraft destroyed three of their tanks.[42] Despite these engagements, the Iraqi high command failed to appreciate the lethality of the IRIAF. Perhaps they viewed the IRIAF as a temporary nuisance against their impending invasion.

Whether or not Saddam Hussein received a "green light" from the West (notably the US) to invade Iran remains a matter of heated debate.[43] Some Iranian sources claim that the US encouraged Saddam Hussein to invade Iran and annex Khuzistan.[44] Both President Carter and Zbigniew Brzezinski, US national security advisor in 1980, deny all allegations of connections to Saddam Hussein and his invasion of Iran.[45] The general consensus among contemporary Western analysts is that the US played an encouraging role towards Saddam Hussein's ambitions to invade Iran.[46] As the war progressed, Western and US military assistance to Iraq (not to mention Arab and Soviet aid) proved highly significant.

Saddam Hussein met the leaders of Saudi Arabia and Kuwait in August 1980 and informed them of his plans to invade Iran.[47] The Kuwaitis and the Saudis in turn are believed to have encouraged Saddam's jingoism against Iran.[48] There were fears of Iran's Revolution among the monarchy-ruled states of the Persian Gulf and Jordan. Not all Arab states supported Saddam, Oman for example refused to assist Iraq's plan to attack Iranian islands in the Persian Gulf, and the UAE did not allow Iraqi jets to use its airbases.[49] Syria and Libya were the only Arab states to openly side with Iran during the conflict.

The Iranian opposition at this juncture was fundamentally composed of members of Iran's previous political and military establishment. These are indications that small numbers of these were in contact with Saddam Hussein prior to his invasion of Iran. Six months before Iraqi armored units entered Iran, Former Prime Minister Shapur Bakhtiar, along with a number of exiled Iranian political and military leaders, met Saddam Hussein in Baghdad and provided four reasons why an invasion of Iran could quickly succeed: the air force would allegedly defect with its aircraft in the event of war (as presumably would the navy with its vessels); Iranian military forces, especially those in Khuzistan, were in such disarray that they could mount no defense against an Iraqi invasion; the Iranian army resented the newly formed Pasdaran; and middle-class opposition to the clerics and other political turbulences in the country virtually assured an Iraqi victory.[50] Iran's state of post-revolutionary political flux was buoyed by consistent reports of friction between President Bani Sadr and the conservative clerics.

The Iranian military was in tatters. Many top officers had been purged, exiled, executed or retired. Many pilots were also languishing in jail, especially after the Nojeh coup. Military discipline had dangerously slackened with much equipment in desperate need of rehabilitation and repairs. Politically, a dangerous rift had developed between President Bani-Sadr and Rajai, head of the cabinet and overall commander of the Pasdaran. This meant that coordination between the regular army and the Pasdaran could be dangerously undermined in the event of war.

To Baghdad's war planners and Western analysts this was Iraq's golden opportunity. All the Iraqis had to do was to thrust their tanks and troops into Iran as quickly as possible and annex Khuzistan within a week.[51] To outside observers the Iranians would at best offer meek, disorganized and token resistance. The war would be over in a matter of weeks with the new Iranian administration overthrown, Khuzistan severed with the rest of Iran probably dismembered as a result.[52] At the very least, an Iraqi success would give Baghdad full control of the Arvand Rud/Shaat al Arab waterway, chunks of Khuzistan and other lands along the common border. Iranian exiles in Baghdad, aiming to topple the new revolutionary government, had failed to realize that their Baathist hosts were using them as pawns in their plans to annex Khuzistan.

Iraqi military planners made the fatal mistake of trivializing Iranian nationalism, especially among Iran's non-Persian speaking population. Saddam Hussein (and pan-Arabist Baath ideology in general) sincerely believed that Iranian Arabs would make common cause with Iraq's invading army. Instead, many Iranian Arabs fought bitterly against the invaders.[53] There was also a tendency to deride Iranian martial abilities; documents seized from Iraqi POWs indicated that the Iraqi high command expected to win a complete victory within 10–14 days.[54] This may partly explain why the Iraqis chose to believe the Iranian opposition's assurances that a quick air strike on Iran's airfields followed by a massive armored drive would shatter Iran's military and lead to the overthrow of the government.[55] The tendency to underestimate Iranian military potential would cost the Iraqis dearly. Instead of achieving quick victory, Saddam thrust his nation into one of the most bloody, futile, drawn-out, catastrophic and inconclusive wars of modern history.

Iraq invades

The Iranians finally realized that an Iraqi invasion was imminent at least one week before it actually struck. Regular army units in Kurdistan province were ordered to deploy towards the Iraqi border on September 14. Two days later orders were issued for all available army units to head towards Iran's western provinces. Naval units in Abadan and Khorramshahr were placed on alert on September 19, with reservists summoned to duty by the next day.[56] It was too little, and too late. When the Iraqi military machine rolled into Iran on September 22, 1980, it faced 25,000 regular army troops spread along (or in close proximity to) the entire length of the border supported by few tanks or heavy equipment.[57] In contrast the initial Iraqi thrust into Iran had 70,000 troops and 2,000-plus tanks, augmented with another 35,000 men.[58] The border posts were poorly manned and their guards were ill-equipped to face a full-scale invasion.[59] The disorganized nature of the Iranian defense in the first few days of the invasion greatly assisted the Iraqi invaders. It was during those first few days that the Iraqis achieved their greatest advances into Iran. Despite these initial advantages, the Iraqis quickly ran into unexpected resistance against elements of the Gendarmerie, regular army, tribal warriors (Kurds, Lurs, Khuzistan Arabs), Pasdaran, and armed civilians.

The Iraqi high command had been greatly impressed with Israel's 1967 air blitz which annihilated the combined air forces of Egypt, Syria and Jordan on the ground. They mimicked Israeli methods by opening their invasion with an air blitz against the IRIAF's airbases on September 22. These attacks failed completely due to a combination of inaccurate intelligence, inadequate pilot training, substandard Soviet equipment, and the use of high-altitude bombing instead of more effective low-level attacks. The IRIAF had also dispersed most of its aircraft in hardened and underground shelters, highly indicative that they had suspected an Iraqi air attack. The score for Iraq's air raid was a very modest two Iranian jets destroyed, and a number of airstrips temporarily damaged. Iraq was to pay very dearly for its failure to knock out the IRIAF. Iraq's attack only served to galvanize the IRIAF and led to the release of many jailed air force personnel, who quickly rejoined their air bases. The initial shock of the attack had rapidly transformed into martial prowess against Saddam's invasion.

Iranian aircrews worked feverishly during the night of September 22 to ready their F-4 Phantoms, F-5 Tigers and F-14 Tomcats for action.[60] The planned attack was relatively simple, aiming to wrest complete air superiority and support ground operations. A total of 120 F-4 Phantom IIs and 20 F-5 Tiger IIs were tasked for a massive air strike against Iraq. This was a formidable task as Iranian aircraft lacked the capability to defend against radar-guided SAM systems. The Iranians compensated for their lack of anti-SAM defenses by training their pilots to fly very low (sometimes at rooftop level). This tactic allowed Iranian fighters to utilize the terrain to mask their approach against enemy targets.

The Iranians also could not refuel all of their jets during their mission over Iraq as they only had 18 flying tanker aircraft.[61] Thanks to US-based training and planning regimens implemented during the Shah's era during the 1970s, this was not a major liability. The 18 tankers selectively provided fuel to those aircraft engaged in the deepest strikes inside Iraq. The other pilots knew that dogfights had to be concluded quickly and decisively as they did not have enough fuel for lengthy air-to-air engagements, and bombers would also have to deliver their ordinance accurately after a single pass to conserve fuel for the flight home.

The first Iranian air strike on September 23 was a complete success. Massive numbers of aircraft arrived over Iraq to achieve complete surprise. With the partial exception of Baghdad, Iraqi air defenses failed to blunt the Iranian attacks. A large number of key Iraqi air bases and two army barracks were bombed.[62] The Vassileyah oil complexes were severely damaged. The air strike cost the Iranians just four aircraft; three to enemy ground fire and one which crashed on take-off. There are no reports of Iraqi jets intercepting Iranian fighters that day.

The dramatic success of the air strikes bolstered the morale of the Iranian airmen who quickly follow up with another strike the next day. Iranian fighters pounded Iraqi air bases around Mosul, Baghdad, Kirkuk, and Basra, and severely damaged the Zubair petrochemical facilities; further south, Fao was also struck. Iraqi radar and SAM sites again proved ineffectual. One Phantom was finally damaged in air-to-air combat when a formation of four MiG-21s unsuccessfully tried to stop a massive air raid against Iraq's Tahmouz and Al-Taghadom air bases. In that raid at least one Iraqi AN-24 transport aircraft, and nine or 10 combat aircraft were destroyed on the ground with serious damage inflicted on the airbases' runways and aircraft shelters.[63] Also notable was the attack on the aviation fuel facility near Al-Hurriya in which the strike leader, Captain Dowran dove low, using his 20-mm cannon to destroy fuel trucks near hardened aircraft shelters in the vicinity. This set a precedent for other Phantoms to do the same against Iraqi vehicles, especially in Khuzistan.

The scale and precision of the IRIAF's response came as an unpleasant surprise to the Iraqi military. Iraq had not only failed to eliminate the IRIAF, but had now lost control of the air. Saddam Hussein relocated many Iraqi aircraft to Iraq's western bases and sent others to countries such as Jordan and Yemen. Advancing Iraqi land forces and supply lines were now at the mercy of Iranian fighters. The IRIAF's success in wresting control of the air proved invaluable in blunting the Iraqi blitzkrieg. Iranian jet fighters also bought valuable time for Iranian defenders to organize their defenses, especially in Khuzistan.

The five axes of invasion

Panjvin was the northernmost tip of the Iraqi invasion, situated to the north of Qasr-e Shirin, The Iraqis wanted to secure the Panjvin area to prevent an Iranian thrust into Iraq's Kurdish-populated Sulaymānīyah province.[64] They invaded the Panjvin area and blocked all roads from Sanandaj which Iranian forces would need if they wanted to invade Sulaymānīyah and its Kirkuk oilfields.[65] As Iraq went increasingly onto the defensive after 1982, Iranian forces gradually moved into Sulaymānīyah, making their greatest gains towards the end of the war in 1988.

On September 22, 300 Iraqi tanks crossed the border near Qasr e Shirin and seized the town.[66] Iraq's second axis targeted Qasr-e Shirin, a major stop along the vital Tehran–Baghdad highway, due to fears of a major Iranian tank thrust towards Baghdad. The IRIAF had the necessary air superiority to support an attack of this kind, but the state of Iran's tank forces meant they were unable to contemplate it.[67] The drive beyond Qasr-e Shirin to Sar e Pol e Zahab, Gilan Gharb, and Sumar took 6–10 days, as resistance had already begun to solidify. The Iraqis often fired large numbers of their Soviet-made "Sagger" antitank missiles into roadblocks and other Iranian strong points.

Iraqi tactics in this theater resembled those used against Iraqi Kurdish insurgents during the 1970s. Artillery was often used to keep Iranian fighters away from advancing Iraqi infantry. The Iranians soon began responding with numbers of their own artillery, which slowed the Iraqi advance. Another unexpected surprise was the Iranian Kurds who instead of supporting the invasion as expected, began fighting against the Iraqis.[68] These fought a guerrilla-style campaign against

Iraqi troops, buying the Iranian army precious time to organize their defenses.[69] The Iraqis were soon contained with their 10,000-man force blocked from reaching Kermanshah.[70]

The third Iraqi axis targeted Mehran, which was critical for the Iraqis as Iranian forces could thrust from there to the Iraqi town of Al-Kut, around 80km. The fall of Al-Kut would entail the loss of a major road and communications hub allowing Iranian forces to threaten central, northern and southern Iraq. Mehran was weakly defended by just one Iranian infantry battalion, supported by a small number of tanks and artillery.[71] These were quickly overrun by 3,000 Iraqis in the early hours of September 22.[72] The Iraqis then pushed towards Dehloran which fell just 10 days after Mehran. The loss of Dehloran was a heavy blow as the city was host to a vital missile and radar site. The Iraqi advance was then halted, partly due to Iranian Cobra helicopter gunships, which utilized the terrain to conceal themselves and then "popped up" to surprise and destroy Iraqi soft-skinned and armored vehicles.

While the Iraqi advances towards Panjvin, Qasr-e Shirin and Mehran aimed at shielding central and northern Iraq from Iranian counterthrusts, the main Iraqi offensive was towards the south, into Iran's Khuzistan province. The fourth axis, Susangerd–Ahvaz–Dezful, was the most vital for a complete Iraqi victory. Even if the Iraqis could be prevented from entering Khorramshahr and Abadan, Iranian efforts at the "three cities" (Susangerd, Ahvaz, Dezful) were critical to holding Khuzistan. The Iraqis rapidly propelled three armored and one mechanized division towards Susangerd.[73] If this was captured, they could then drive into Khuzistan's provincial capital, Ahvaz. The Iraqis also planned to cross the Karun River to capture Dezful, which is a major communications hub and host to a major hydroelectric station and oil pumping centre. Dezful is also host to the strategic Vahdatiye airbase featuring underground facilities, a major operations center, powerful concrete shelters, and extended runways.

The Iraqis had split their armored strike force into three spearheads, and had stripped down much of their divisions' infantry formations to facilitate a more rapid "tank charge" into Khuzistan. So as Iraqi tanks, self-propelled and towed artillery pushed towards Ahvaz and Dezful, they were accompanied by just 5,000 infantry.[74] This plan could have worked if the Iranians had not resisted, but contrary to Saddam's expectations, Iranian resistance solidified after just a few days of fighting. Iraq brought in more infantry, but it was already too late. The Iraqi planners also failed to appreciate the lethal threat of the IRIAF and Iran's helicopter gunships against Iraqi land forces.

The "northern" portion of the Iraqi armored division deployed from Iraq's Amara area and quickly thrust into Iran seizing Fakkeh (on the border), then Bostan (near Susangerd) and Musian (near Dehloran). The column then pushed northeast towards Shoush as this was pivotal for entering Dezful. The central spearhead of the Iraqi armored thrust was aimed at Susangerd, but seeing as they had little infantry to fight into, occupy and garrison the town, the Iraqi column simply drove past the city towards the Ahvaz–Dezful highway. This was a gross departure from Iraqi plans and a major strategic blunder, as it allowed the Iranians to build up their defensive positions in and around the city. Later, when the Iraqis realized their mistake and attempted to storm the city, their efforts were defeated. This meant that a dangerous salient would soon be projecting into the Iraqi lines.

The "southern" portion of the Iraqi armored thrust aimed towards Ahvaz, Khuzistan's provincial capital. This was a city of approximately 300,000 residents and served as a major economic communications grid, as well as an oil management center. When Iraq struck, the city was home to an Iranian armored division, although numbers of their tanks were unprepared for combat. The "southern" column deployed out of Qornah and placed itself on the Khorramshar–Ahvaz highway, quickly occupying the small border town of Ahu. The Iraqis advanced northeastwards towards Hamid en route to Ahvaz, located just east of the Karun River.

In the first few days Iraqi tank columns moved very rapidly into Khuzistan, but this soon changed. By the third or fourth day the advance had slowed considerably, resulting in Iraqi forces being halted just 10–12 miles (15–20km) from the cities of Ahvaz and Dezful.[75] The Iraqis resorted to using long-range artillery against these cities but to no avail. Though somewhat disorganized, the Iranian regular army managed to rush just enough men and equipment to help stabilize the front lines. The Iraqis however did not give up on their drive to simultaneously capture Khorramshahr, Abadan and Dezful.

By early October the IRIAF had not only demonstrated its ability to dominate the Iraqis in the air, but were also proving very effective in damaging Iraqi armored thrusts. Between October 2 and 4, Iranian Tomcats covered formations of Cobra helicopters and F-4 and F-5 fighter-bombers flying attack runs against Iraqi tank thrusts in the Dezful, Susangerd and Ahvaz areas. Up to 60 Iraqi jets had been lost to Iranian fighters who also supported helicopter strikes against Iraqi armor knocking out 65 tanks on October 2 and 3 around Dezful and Khorramshahr.[76] Iranian fighters completely dominated air combat in Khuzistan, allowing the air strikes to continue against Iraqi armor, supply lines and rear areas as far as Basra. The Iraqis brought forward ZSU-57-2 and ZSU-34-4 mobile antiaircraft guns, which shot down numbers of Cobra helicopters, but this did little to break the power of the Iranian fighters and the Cobras, who continued to wreak havoc on Iraqi aircraft and armor. The Iraqis were paying dearly for having underestimated their opponent's abilities in the air.

Saddam was frustrated that his air force was unable to support his tank thrusts towards Ahvaz, Susangerd, and especially Dezful. Iranian airmen and Cobra helicopters played a very significant role in defeating Saddam's tank thrusts into Dezful, Susangerd and Ahvaz, buying precious time for the front lines to organize and solidify. Meanwhile Iraqi aircraft sought other ways of damaging Iran, and they soon resorted to sending supersonic Tu-22 Blinder bombers against residential districts in Tehran, Dezful and Khorramabad. Iranian Hawk missiles only managed to shoot down two of the Blinders. A very damaging Iraqi air raid was then launched by Tu-16 bombers against the housing section of the airbase of Tabriz, killing 42 air force personnel and many civilians. These actions only further motivated the Iranian population and military to eject Saddam's forces from Iran.

The Pasdaran entered the fighting from the outset and in conjunction with local armed civilians and army personnel formed an impenetrable barrier against Saddam's invasion. Significantly, the Iranians managed to rapidly equip their troops with antitank missiles, rocket launchers and even made numbers of their artillery operational. This may partly explain why Iraqi armored thrusts towards Dezful and Ahvaz failed to break through the Iranian lines. By this time much of the local populace had already taken arms to resist Saddam's invasion, including Iran's indigenous Arabs.

The Iraqi assumption that Iranian Arabs would welcome the invasion may explain why the Iraqis felt confident in dispersing their armored thrust into three segments in Khuzistan, accompanied by small numbers of infantry. But the Khuzistani Arabs took up arms against the Iraqi invaders.[77] In the early days of the war, Ahvaz residents witnessed large numbers of Iranian

Arabs in jeeps arriving in the town center, dance the traditional Arab war dance, declare in Arabic and Persian their allegiance to Iran, before departing to the front lines to support Iranian troops defending Ahvaz.[78] Many Khuzistani Arabs rose to prominent military and political positions during and after the war. One such person was Ali Shamkhani who fought against the Iraqi forces and lost a number of his brothers in that war. Shamkhani later became Iran's minister of defense.

Khorramshar and Abadan sit astride the vital egress of the Arvand Rud/Shaat al Arab into the Persian Gulf. The Iraqis believed that the seizure of Abadan would deliver a devastating blow against Iran's economy. The shelling of both cities began from September 22. Iraq rapidly transported much of its heavy artillery into the theater during the first week of fighting to support the fifth axis, the drive into Khorramshar and Abadan.[79]

Just two days into the Iraqi advance towards Abadan, two F-4 Phantoms destroyed several Iraqi vehicles with 20-mm cannon fire against no IrAF opposition.[80] The Phantoms attacked and destroyed some of the lead elements of an Iraqi armored division that had deployed from Basra to take both Khorramshahr and Abadan. These had erected large pontoon bridges across the Arvand Rud/Shaat al Arab waterway. Three Phantoms targeted and destroyed a primary supply bridge near Basra by using Maverick air-to-ground missiles on September 26. The Phantoms then fired their remaining Mavericks destroying two tanks and a major merchant ship just as it was unloading military supplies.[81] This resulted in a massive series of explosions which gutted the ship and sent shock waves across both sides of the Arvand Rud/Shaat al Arab waterway. The Iraqis did their best to counter the IRIAF but lost up to nine aircraft in dogfights against them over Khorramshahr and Abadan on October 2–4.[82]

The Iraqi assault against Khorramshahr finally began in earnest on September 28, with approximately 100 tanks and armored vehicles.[83] The first attacks ran into fierce resistance with the loss of at least 16 armored vehicles.[84] The Iraqis tried to pound the city into submission by subjecting it to massive artillery fire. The artillery transformed Khorramshahr's buildings into heaps of rubble, which provided ideal cover for determined fighters. The 3,000-man Iranian garrison was mainly composed of Pasdaran, regular army troops and local citizens, including Khuzistani Arabs.[85]

The fighting in Khorramshahr was prolonged and bitter. Local citizens guided Iranian troops to the best ambush and defensible positions. Iranian snipers in particular were very successful. Iraqi Special Forces troops and Republican Guard troops soon arrived to bolster the attacks in Khorramshahr but had no maps of the city.[86] Fighting raged on house to house and street by street until November 10, when the Iraqis finally declared that Khorramshahr had succumbed. The Iraqi high command was alarmed that despite their numerical advantage and firepower, they had lost around 2,000 dead, three times as many wounded and approximately 200 tanks and armored vehicles.[87] There were also some alarming incidents of Iraqi Shia troops having turned their guns against their own forces.[88]

Incessant pounding by Iraqi artillery transformed Abadan's giant oil facilities into a raging inferno. Abadan is surrounded by a number of natural obstacles to its west (Arvand Rud/Shaat al Arab waterway), north (Karun River) and east (Bahmanshir River), with the southeast characterized by heavy marshlands. The Iraqis flanked Abadan from the north by ferrying their forces to the eastern side of the Karun River on October 12, 1980.[89] They were now poised to storm Abadan, but the task would not prove easy, and the Iranians were able to use the Abadan–Khosrowabad road to supply their garrison in Abadan as all Iraqi attempts to sever the road failed.

Iraqi armored forces operating in the Abadan area's marshy terrain soon ran into difficulties. In one case 200 Iraqi tanks and armored personnel carriers (APCs) became stuck in the marshes, and at least 80 were destroyed by the Iranians.[90] Iraqi helicopter gunships did destroy a number of Iranian artillery pieces around October 24, but IRIAF aircraft quickly counterattacked, destroying a number of Iraqi self-propelled guns. Saddam's failure to capture Abadan meant that Iraqi ships trying to access the Arvand Rud/Shaat al Arab waterway were subjected to Iranian artillery fire. The situation became a stalemate. Abadan's garrison tried to link up with regular army columns advancing from the east in November 1980–January 1981, but were stymied by heavy Iraqi resistance. The Iraqis in turn failed to storm Abadan.

Iraq reaches its limit

By mid-November 1980, Iraq was in occupation of 10,000 square miles of Iranian territory. Despite having penetrated as deep as 30 miles (50km) into Khuzistan in the south, Iraq had not won the war. The vital rail links between Ahvaz, Dezful and Tehran remained operational. Khorramshahr had fallen, but this bore no major military advantages for Iraq. Even if Abadan were captured, Iran still had plenty of other outlets for exporting its oil. Iran's real jugular was at Kharq Island but this was well defended by low- and high-altitude missiles and (mainland-based) Tomcat fighters. Another serious problem for Iraq was the IRIAF and especially the Vahdati air base at Dezful. Iran's land forces of Iran, notably the army and Pasdaran, were intact with their defensive lines solidified. Saddam's invasion had become a stalemate.

Just as Khorramshahr fell, Saddam Hussein delivered a major press conference in Baghdad on November 10 outlining his conditions for a ceasefire. His demands escalated to include Iran's shipping routes in the Persian Gulf and the Straits of Hormuz. Saddam also nominated himself as the champion of Iran's various linguistic groups by declaring that "if the Arabistanis [i.e. Khuzistani Arabs], the Baluchis or the Azarbaijanis want their stand to be different [with respect to staying in Iran], then this will be another matter."[91] Saddam's conference failed to impress the Iranians, in fact the speech was followed by a sharp increase in the number of Iranians volunteering to fight.

The IRIAF had continued to pummel Iraqi military personnel and heavy equipment at Susangerd.[92] The Iraqis responded by firing FROG-7 missiles against the airbase. All of these missed to land in Dezful's residential areas. The Iraqis then launched powerful assaults towards Susangerd between November 14 and 17. Their most successful engagement occurred on November 17 when a 12-ship helicopter raid attacked Iranian lines and knocked out numbers of Iranian Chieftains.[93] But every one of Iraq's armor-led attacks was beaten back. The Iraqi invasion of Iran had reached its limit.

Operations *Kafka, Ashkan,* and *Morvarid*

The Iranian military was steadily regaining its confidence. With the exception of Khorramshahr, they had blocked Saddam's war machine from every significant military objective. The Iranian high command now committed its combat aircraft and helicopters to cooperate with the Islamic Republic of Iran Navy (IRIN).[94] This resulted in operations which virtually eliminated the Iraqi navy for the duration of the war.

356 IRAN AT WAR

The small Iraqi navy, acting with Iraqi air forces, could pose a dangerous threat to Iranian coastal installations and shipping routes. Iraqi missile boats were already using the Khor Al-Omayah and Mina Al-Bakr oil platforms to launch lightning raids against Iranian ships.[95] The Iraqis had also placed early warning radar equipment to monitor Iranian air and naval operations in this region of the Persian Gulf. Similar devices had been positioned on Al-Omayah. The IRIN proceeded to knock out the platforms and destroy Iraq's coastal installations and combat vessels. Abadan and Bandar Khomeini (previously Bandar Shapur), became the main base of IRIN's operations. Three Kaman-class fast missile craft, the *Joshan, Gordouneh,* and *Paykan*, were assigned to attack Al-Omayah and Al-Bakr. The IRIAF was tasked with air support for the operation.

Operation *Kafka* commenced on October 28. *Joshan* opened fire on Al-Omayah, and *Gordouneh* attacked Al-Bakr. The *Paykan*, armed with light SA-7 antiaircraft missiles, supported both vessels against air attacks. Iraqi Osa I and II boats fired several SS-N-2 missiles, but these were all decoyed by the *Paykan*'s chaff. Iraqi combat aircraft attacked the 3 IRIN ships, but escaped after losing one of their aircraft to the *Paykan* and the other two to Iranian interceptors. The Iraqi air raid had not been a total failure as their bombs (and antiship missiles) had caused injuries on board the *Joshan*. By this time all guns aboard the Iranian ships had overheated and jammed. The detection of another wave of Iraqi jets obliged the IRIN strike force to depart the theater. The Iranians returned days later, on October 31, under Operation *Ashkan*, escorted by two fighter jets and one helicopter.[96] Once again Al-Omayah and Al-Bakr were heavily shelled, but Al-Bakr continued to resist. Iraqi air responses proved ineffectual with the *Paykan* shooting down another Iraqi jet.[97] Alert to the dangers of the IRIN at last, Baghdad launched an air strike against Iranian warships at Bushehr on November 12, during which the Iraqis lost five of their aircraft to Iranian fighters, four to Phantoms, one to a Tomcat.

Despite the successes of operations *Kafka* and *Ashkan*, Iraqi early warning facilities remained operational. New plans were drafted to destroy these as well as Iraqi oil facilities situated along the lower reaches of the Arvand Rud/Shaat al Arab waterway. Once again the experienced crew of *Paykan* and *Joshan* were selected for the new operation (codenamed *Morvarid*). The Iranian vessels had been able to damage the oil platforms in previous operations, but they lacked the necessary firepower to destroy them completely. Operation *Morvarid* would deploy commandos to secure and destroy the rigs. Greater and more aggressive use would be made of Iranian air power.

Paykan and *Joshan* returned to Al-Bakr and Al-Amayah and resumed their attacks against them, supported by two helicopters. The Iraqis dispatched two OSA-II fast attack boats. These fired SS-N-2 missiles against the *Paykan*, which decoyed these with chaff. The OSA-IIs retreated when *Paykan* fired back with two Harpoon missiles. Another OSA-II attack an hour later was again neutralized by a Harpoon from the *Paykan*. The Al-Bakr and Al-Amayah platforms were now completely cut off from Iraqi support.

Operation *Morvarid* formally commenced on November 29. Meeting no opposition, Iranian CH-47 heavy helicopters landed commandos on Al-Bakr and Al-Amayah. The surprised Iraqis on the platforms were gunned down and the survivors taken prisoner. The Iranian commandos then placed explosive charges. As the commandos and their Iraqi prisoners departed, the rigs and their radar facilities exploded in flames. Sea Cobra and Bel-214 helicopters had covered the arrival and departure of the commandos, while Iranian jet fighters had attacked those Iraqi air bases closest to the operation.

This ensured that very few Iraqi aircraft could harass the operation. The few Iraqi aircraft that did reach Al-Bakr were roughly handled – Iranian commandos shot down two Iraqi jets.[98]

As the *Paykan* and *Joshan* disengaged to return to their bases, the Iraqis sent their P-6 combat boats and OSA II and IIIs to engage the *Paykan*. This time one of the Iraqi SS-N-2 missiles exploded close to the *Paykan*. This caused some damage and injured numbers of the crew. Frantic calls for air support were sent to Bushehr air base which dispatched two Phantoms. These immediately sank one of the Iraqi vessels, prompting the others to flee. The Phantoms were prevented from finishing off the retreating Iraqi vessels due to the arrival of Iraqi MiG-23s. In the subsequent air-to-air combat no jets were downed, but the Iraqis were chased away.[99] The interlude allowed the Iraqi vessels to again fire SS-N-2 missiles against the *Paykan*, which evaded them. Iraqi aircraft also returned to join the attack. *Paykan* shot down one of the attacking aircraft and fired its last Harpoon missile to sink an Iraqi vessel. Running low on fuel and ammunition, the *Paykan* now faced a new wave of MiG-23s. Once again the *Paykan* shot down one of them with a single SA-7 missile. *Paykan* then suffered casualties from missiles fired from two Iraqi helicopters. One of the helicopters was shot down in turn by gunfire from the *Paykan*. Iranian Phantoms returned to shoot down two MiG-23s. Iraqi vessels again approached the *Paykan* and fired four SS-N-2 missiles, scoring two direct hits. The gallant *Paykan*, which had fought against overwhelming odds, finally exploded and sank. Two Phantoms again arrived from Bushehr and destroyed eight Iraqi vessels. Iraq found some solace in having its aircraft intercept and shoot down the Phantoms, at the cost of one MiG-23. The *Joshan* shot down two of four attacking MiG-23s with its missiles; another was destroyed by an F-14. The remaining MiG fled back to Iraq. In the meantime, the IRIAF had been attacking the Fao refinery station and its protecting SAM sites in southern Iraq.

The *Kafka*, *Ashkan*, and *Morvarid* operations were a big blow against Iraqi oil production, which plummeted overnight from a pre-war total of 3.25 million barrels a day to 550,000 barrels per day.[100] The operations also sealed off of the Fao peninsula and its important port from the Persian Gulf, preventing Iraq from using the Arvand Rud/Shaat al Arab waterway to export its oil or import military supplies by ship. The destruction of Iraqi early warning radar sites coordinating Iraqi air attacks over the Persian Gulf handicapped Iraqi air operations for a whole year in this sector. Following the confrontations, the Iraqi navy was eliminated as a threat to Iran, having lost access to the Al-Amayah and Al-Bakr oil rigs. Numerically speaking, Iraq had lost 80% of its navy in exchange for three Iranian Phantoms, one small combat boat, and the *Paykan*. The *Paykan*'s sacrifice had not been in vain, as Iran now held the military initiative in the Persian Gulf. The operations also demonstrated the effectiveness of Iranian commandos and the benefits of their training regimen in the 1970s.

Iranian tank disaster at Susangerd

Thus far, the Iranians had done well in defense but Iraq still held the initiative by occupying a large swathe of Iranian territory. Iranian Kurdish rebels' efforts to link up with Iraqi forces in December 1980 had been defeated by the Iranian army. Clerical factions now demanded that Bani Sadr launch an offensive against the Iraqis as quickly as possible.

The Iranians launched their first major counterattack with 400 tanks to the south of Susangerd on January 11, 1981.[101] As the Iranian armored force constructed bridges to cross the waterway, the

Iraqis calmly observed where the main weight of the Iranian attack was to fall. This led them to give approximately a mile (2km) of ground to the Iranian forces. As the Iranians drove west towards the Iraqi positions, the IrAF bombed the Iranian bridges. The Iraqis then rapidly crossed the river, sealing the Iranian tank force to its front and rear. The Iranian tanks realized that that they had fallen into an Iraqi trap and attempted to retreat back to Susangerd. It was already too late: the Iraqis destroyed at least 100 Iranian tanks and captured another 100.[102] It is not clear whether the Iranians had successfully addressed their Chieftains' engine problems before the advance.[103] The Chieftain's weak engine is consistent with Iranian reports of having to deploy the tank as static artillery pieces.[104] This may partly explain why the Iraqis captured 200–300 Iranian Chieftains during the war.[105]

The surviving 200 Iranian tanks escaped back across the river thanks to Iranian combat engineers who rapidly rebuilt the damaged bridges. The Iraqis lost a total of 50 tanks, along with scores of other armored vehicles, raising their total to 200.[106] Despite the momentum of their victory, the Iraqis failed to launch a powerful new offensive. Instead of rapidly following up with a massive armored thrust, the Iraqis continued their constant shelling, inconclusive air raids and fruitless probing attacks against Susangerd, Dezful, Ahwaz, and Abadan.

Iraq: what to do next?

Although Iraq still held the initiative, there was great confusion in Baghdad as to what to do next. Despite Saddam's claims of "victory," the Iranians were far from conquered. Despite their recent defeat at Susangerd, the Iranians were more than capable of resisting further Iraqi advances. An Iraqi withdrawal was out of the question but staying in Iran without "finishing the job" of destroying the Iranian army was also fraught with risk.

Much to Baghdad's chagrin, Tehran rejected the March 1, 1981 peace plan proposed by a nine-member delegation. Seeing Iran's determination to continue the war, Baghdad then stated that they refused to withdraw "from a single inch of Iranian territory until Tehran recognizes Iraqi rights."[107] As previously, it was not exactly clear what rights Iraq was demanding. Weeks after the failed peace initiative the Iraqi government made official its support for Iran's break-up.[108] In mid-April 1981, Deputy Prime Minister Tareq Aziz openly declared that "Now we don't care if Iran is dismembered."[109] Saddam's support for Iran's dismemberment became more pronounced as he offered to assist separatism among Iran's Baluchis, Kurds, Azarbaijanis and Khuzistani Arabs.[110] In reality, Iraq's "separatist card" against Iran had all but failed. Ironically it was Iraq's Kurds who were to gradually side with Iran as the war progressed.

Following their refusal to withdraw, the Iraqi army made another determined drive against Susangerd on March 19–20. Once again, prodigious Iraqi use of artillery, tanks, helicopters and aircraft proved futile and the Iranians decisively beat back each of the Iraqi assaults. So confident had the Iraqi military been at winning the war quickly that they had failed to draft a contingency plan in case Iran was not overcome; all the Iraqis could do was to sit tight and hope that the Iranians would launch further ill-conceived offensives like that of January 11.

Waiting was not an option for Baghdad. Iranian organization and logistics were improving and lessons had been learnt from the failed January offensive. They continued to launch missile strikes against Iranian civilian centers. FROG-7 surface-to-surface rockets were fired into Ahvaz and Dezful

THE IRAN–IRAQ WAR: Iraq invades Iran 359

on March 12 and 22, ostensibly against Iranian troop concentrations. These succeeded only in inflicting severe civilian casualties. This was significant as it signaled Baghdad's lack of concern over injuring Iranian Arabs resident in Khuzistan's towns.

Iraq's Pearl Harbor: Phantom blitz at H-3

Iranian intelligence had learned of a dangerous development underway at the gigantic H-3 airbase in western Iraq near the Jordanian border.[111] H-3 was staffed by Iraqis and significant numbers of foreign personnel. The Jordanians were building up H-3's infrastructure and transforming it into a conduit for war supplies arriving from Jordan. The Egyptians were working at overhauling and refurbishing Iraq's Soviet-made aircraft (MiGs, Tupolov bombers, etc). As Egypt was itself adopting Western military equipment, it was transferring much of its spares for Soviet-made equipment to Iraq. French technicians were also probably at H-3 as the Mirage F-1 fighters were stationed at the base.

The Iranians realized that they had to strike quickly before H-3 could rehabilitate and strengthen the IrAF. Eight Phantoms took off from Iran on April 4, 1981 to head towards H-3 in western Iraq. A number of Tigers and Tomcats patroled the border along Iran's northwest in anticipation of the Phantoms' return. The Iranians manned a single C-130 Khofash along Iran's northwest frontier to coordinate their strike force.

After refueling, the Phantoms crossed into Iraq, flying at very low altitude, near Turkey. The team's main challenge was fuel, obliging the Iranians to devise an ingenious plan. Two 707 tankers took off from Istanbul International airport on seemed like a routine flight to Iran. The aircraft were secretly diverted to a rendezvous over the western Iraqi desert to fuel up the Phantoms. The refueled jets then peeled off towards H-3. The tankers retired towards the Syrian border and flew in a circular fashion until the mission's conclusion. They fueled up the Phantoms four times during the mission.

As the Phantoms arrived at H-3, they rearranged themselves into three (two 3-ship and one 2-ship) formations. As the Phantoms swooped in to attack, they found scores of Iraqi aircraft neatly lined up at the base. One of the formations headed for H-3's Walid "main" site to successfully draw the attention of Iraqi SAMs and antiaircraft artillery (AAA) fire away from the other two formations. Despite many Iraqi SAMs being fired and the expenditure of much AAA ammunition, the Phantoms methodically bombed H-3's runways, ensuring that no surviving jets could take off. Precise hits by Snake-Eye bombs destroyed scores of hangers and hardened shelters. Cluster bombs made short work of more vulnerable targets such as regular hangers, large aircraft, and radar facilities. Scores of other parked aircraft were also blown to bits by the Phantoms. The aircraft still had plenty of fuel after the exhaustion of their bomb loads, allowing them to engage in one more deadly pass. This time they pounded surviving Iraqi aircraft and helicopters with 20-mm cannon fire. With the mission now concluded, the Phantoms climbed up to make good their escape, and returned to Iran unchallenged.

The Iranians claimed to have destroyed 48 aircraft of various types, including freshly delivered Mirage F-1 fighters. US intelligence estimates put the losses at 26, with eleven other aircraft damaged, some beyond repair.[112] Whatever the exact number, the damage to Iraq's air program and morale were considerable.[113] The debacle at H-3 infuriated Saddam Hussein who executed Colonel Fakhri Hussein Jaber (commander of western Iraq's air defense net) and imprisoned numbers of Iraqi pilots and personnel.

CHAPTER 34

IRAN LIBERATES KHUZISTAN (1981–82)

Iraq's last effort to capture Abadan

The Iraqi failure to achieve a quick victory gave the Iranians time to rebuild their forces. Tehran realized that revolutionary ardor was not militarily sufficient to liberate occupied territory. Such a task required professional military planning and leadership. The operations that led to the liberation of the Dezful-Shoush regions, the breaking of the Abadan siege and the liberation of Khorramshahr were very much under the leadership of the professional army, in coordination with the Pasdaran.[1]

The IRIAF had been severely bombing Iraqi positions at Darkhovein (near Ahvaz). These air attacks had been launched to distract the Iraqis from an Iranian ground offensive further south. On June 11, 1981, Iranian troops and armor attacked Iraqi positions near Abadan. AH-1J cobras soon joined the fight and destroyed numbers of Iraqi heavy vehicles and tanks. Iraqi jet fighters appeared but were intercepted by the IRIAF.[2] When the fighting ended, Iraq had lost a number of key positions.

Through these attacks the Iranians gained invaluable information about Iraqi defenses. They concluded that Iraqi forces could be overcome by well-coordinated air-ground attacks. The Iranians had certainly learnt from their mistakes at Susangerd in early 1981, but Saddam Hussein and Iraq's top command failed to appreciate the alarming rise in Iranian military efficiency. The offensive also helped morale among the Iranian troops, who were gaining confidence just as morale was sagging among Iraqi front-line troops, especially the poorly trained People's Army.

Saddam Hussein and the Iraqi command had been frustrated in their attempts to capture Abadan. Conquering Abadan would boost Iraqi morale and help open up the bottom of the Arvand Rud/Shaat al Arab waterway, increasing Iraq's coastline and reducing Iraq's dependence on neighbors, such as Jordan, for sea ports. Despite these enticements, the Iraqi high command was cautious. Khorramshahr had been taken at great cost against a small Iranian garrison. At Abadan the Iraqis would be facing 10,000–15,000 Iranians: regular army troops, Pasdaran, and Khuzistani Arabs. The regular troops belonged to a naval marine battalion, a mechanized battalion, and an armored brigade of the 92nd Armored Division fielding 50–60 Chieftain tanks.[3] The Iraqis launched a massive assault with 60,000 troops, backed by massive firepower and tanks, in June 1981. Despite being outnumbered 6-1, the Iranian force defeated the Iraqi assaults, and the Chieftain proved decisive in defeating Iraqi armored assaults. The only Iraqi successes were the shooting down of a number of Iranian helicopters.

Bani Sadr flees into exile

The Iranians were not yet able to mount an all-out assault on the Iraqis. This was mainly due to the continuing lack of coordination between the regular army and the Pasdaran (and the Basij).

This posed a serious military problem for Iran. Accused of incompetent leadership, Bani Sadr was impeached by the parliament on June 20 and escaped from Iran nine days later on board a KC-707 tanker aircraft.[4] Bani Sadr's departure led to a significant if not immediate improvement of Iranian military performance.[5] The radical fundamentalists and their new president Mohammad-Ali Rajai were now in control of the legislative, judicial and executive bodies. This now allowed them to exercise full powers to implement cooperation between the army and the Pasdaran-Basij. The "radicals" were now in full control, but they were willing to accept the professional skills and training of the regular army. Baghdad and its allies in the Arab world, the Eastern bloc and the West had failed to appreciate the profound military consequences of the recent government reshuffle in Tehran.

The Karun River and breaking the siege of Abadan

Despite having had the upper hand in the air, many Iranian aircraft had been lost and damaged since the invasion. Some had been lost in air-to-air engagements but the greatest number of losses had occurred in ground-attack missions against Iraqi SAMs, and ground fire. Improved Iraqi antiaircraft defenses necessitated the Iranians improving their suppression of Iraqi SAMs and ground-based antiaircraft systems. As Iraqi air-to-air combat skills had improved, the Iranians had been obliged to revise their tactics to keep their edge in the air.[6] These measures soon showed results as Iraqi air raids over the cities of Ahvaz, Dezful, Tehran, Isfahan, Kermanshah, and the Kharq-Bushehr area were practically stopped. Maintaining air dominance over the front was crucial while Iranians prepared their major ground offensives. Meanwhile, the The IrAF was in the middle of a major reorganization and training program, upgrading their fleet with highly modern French Mirage F-1EQs and Russian MiG-25 fighters.

The Iranians realized that they had to secure the Karun River and lift the siege of Abadan before liberating Khorramshahr and the rest of Khuzistan. The drive to break the encirclement of Abadan began on September 22, 1981, exactly one year after Iraq had invaded Iran. The Iranians first launched a devastating series of bombing runs against besieging Iraqi units stationed around Abadan. The IrAF tried to intervene but was quickly chased out of the theater. Two days later, the Iranians rushed two infantry divisions into Abadan across the Bahmanshir River. The operation was done at night to deny Iraqi tanks the opportunity to maneuver.[7] Besieging Iraqi troops were subjected to a series of intense attacks by commandos, regular army troops, and Pasdaran-Basij troops. These pinned down the Iraqis in their strongest positions, while simultaneously tearing through their weakest defenses.

The Iraqis showed little innovation and failed to use their skills in mechanized maneuver. Instead they simply stuck to their positions, becoming cut off and surrounded. The turning point came when an Iranian armored battalion sliced into a weak spot in the Iraqi lines surrounding the city. Now it was the Iraqi troops' turn to be besieged. Iranian tanks supported by TOW-firing Cobra helicopters fired into Iraqi tanks and APCs. Just as the Iraqi positions were crumbling, the IRIAF bombed the four Iraqi pontoon bridges across the Karun River on September 25 to prevent surviving Iraqi troops from escaping.[8] In response to the evolving disaster, the IrAF responded by sending six aircraft to bomb Abadan with cluster bombs. This proved largely ineffective as the attackers refused to fly low to accurately deliver their ordinance, instead mistakenly bombing a number of their own troops.[9]

Despite having lost their grip on Abadan, the Iraqis kept fighting and refused to be ejected across the Karun River. The Iranians then unleashed the 92nd Armored Division on September 27, which struck to its north and severely damaged two Iraqi divisions. By September 29, all remaining Iraqi troops had been cleared from the eastern banks of the Karun River. Veterans report that Iranian forces suffered their heaviest casualties during this phase of the operation.[10]

Iranian morale had certainly been boosted by the success at Abadan, however in military terms their victory had been relatively modest. The Iranians netted 2,500 Iraqi prisoners and destroyed or captured a few hundred tanks and armored vehicles. Iranian casualties stood at 3,000[11] with Iraqi casualties around half that number.[12] The Iraqis had taken a taken a very heavy toll of Iranian helicopters, downing nine Cobras, two Chinook heavy, and three Bell 214 light transport helicopters. Western sources also report that the Iranians lost 150 M-48A tanks on September 29, 1981, during the Abadan operations.[13] These had in fact been abandoned to the Iraqis, who failed to integrate these into their armored corps. Ironically, the Iranians bought the tanks back from the Iraqis in 1987 through middlemen in the UAE![14] The Iranian high command quickly absorbed the military lessons of these losses: and successfully implemented them in the upcoming offensives at Dezful-Shoush and Khorramshahr.

The Nowruz Offensive: Dezful and Shoush

The commander of the regular army, Colonel Ali Sayad Shirazi, was keen to prepare a meticulous plan to liberate Khuzistan. He was reluctant to commit to a major series of offensives without the benefit of accurate and up-to-date intelligence. Captain Davood Delfani's unarmed RF-4E reconnaissance aircraft flew over Iraqi units in Dezful, Shoush, Khorramshahr, and other occupied regions to obtain critical intelligence. Despite being subjected to heavy antiaircraft fire and the firing of several SAMs, Delfani survived his hazardous mission and delivered valuable aerial reconnaissance photos of Iraqi troop concentrations, land defenses, SAM and AAA nets, communication networks, tank parks, and bridges. It is perhaps no exaggeration to state that the subsequent success in expelling the Iraqis from Iran was partly indebted to Captain Delfani.

The Iranian high command had massively reorganized and re-equipped its forces in January and February 1982. The new Iranian force was roughly the equivalent of seven divisions, including two armored divisions of the regular army (88th and 92nd).[15] The others were two regular army divisions (the 21st and 77th "Khorasan")[16] plus two or three of the less well-trained, but highly motivated, Pasdaran IRGC divisions and accompanying Basij militias. There were also specialized units such as Tehran's 59th Airborne "Zolfaqhar" Brigade and an unspecified number of commando and special forces units. The Pasdaran, the 59th and the special forces/commandos would soon wreak havoc within the Iraqi lines.

Iraqi commanders in Khuzistan were aware that the Iranians intended to launch a major blow against them and on March 19, they launched Operation *Al-Fowz al-Azim*. This was a massive attack with tanks, aircraft and helicopters aimed against the Iranian build-up around the Roghabiyeh pass. Saddam Hussein and the Iraqi leadership interpreted the offensive as a success. This explains why the Iraqi government ruled out an Iranian assault just prior to the Iranian New

Year (Nowruz) on March 21.[17] In reality, operation *Al-Fowz al-Azim* had been a complete failure and Iranian troop concentrations were very much intact.[18]

The Iranians struck back with Operation *Fatah ol Mobin* on March 22, catching the Iraqis completely by surprise. Key to the operation was the rapid landing of commandos and special forces by CH-47C helicopters behind Iraqi lines. F-4 and F-5 fighters from Vahdati air base had provided escortes for the landing. The commandos silenced Iraqi artillery positions that had been firing into Vahdati since the start of the war. In just 40 minutes, Iranian commandos destroyed 30 130-mm guns, captured six officers, destroyed two HQs and killed 80 Iraqi troops in hand-to-hand combat.[19] This created panic and confusion behind Iraqi lines, distracting them from Shirazi's next blow. Just as the commando attacks were taking place, the Iranians launched a two-pronged armored attack. The Iraqi lines initially held, but they were then confronted by wave after wave of Pasdaran-Basij revolutionary guards, armed with rocket-launchers. Each wave of 1,000 fighters advanced in intervals of 200–500 yards.[20] Despite terrible losses, the Pasdaran-Basij broke into Iraqi lines and decimated their demoralized foes in close-quarter combat. Regular army forces followed the Pasdaran, consolidating their gains and driving towards Iraqi command centers and supply depots. The 9th and 10th Iraqi Armored and 1st Mechanized divisions were now surrounded, with another Iraqi armored brigade having suffered heavy losses.

Western and Arab press reports, including Iraqi commanders, at the time tended to exaggerate the military impact of the Pasdaran-Basij's "human wave" assaults. Such tactics were certainly effective against the poorly trained Iraqi People's Army, but could not singularly defeat Iraqi armor, troop concentrations or heavy equipment. The successes of the Iranian infantry (regular army and Pasdaran-Basij) was very much due to the decisive support of tanks, TOW-firing Cobra attack helicopters and APCs. The Iraqis had a preference for sheltering their armored units within heavily fortified "Maginot-style" positions. When the Iraqis did try to maneuver, their actions proved clumsy and confused. Iranian armor knocked out 320–400 Iraqi tanks and armored vehicles in combat, although a number of Iraqi tanks were disabled because they had crashed into each other on the battlefield.[21] Many Iraqi tanks had been knocked out by Cobra helicopter strikes, obliging the crews of the remaining tanks to flee. Iraqi regular troops also abandoned their weapons and yielded their positions to the Iranians. The Iranians suffered the loss of 196 tanks on March 22, indicating that the Iraqis were still determined to retain as much conquered territory as possible.[22]

Iraqi commanders asked Baghdad to send aircraft to save them from total disaster. They were hoping to keep the Roghabiyeh pass open long enough to allow surviving Iraq troops and armor to retreat. The IrAF did well in these operations, as their bombing and strafing runs prevented the Pasdaran's 25th Karbala Brigade from reaching the international border, which helped save what was left of Iraqi troops and armor.[23] This was Saddam's sole positive gloss on what was otherwise a crushing Iraqi defeat. The IrAF battlefield interdiction had not been altogether successful either, as the IRIAF, freely roaming over the battlefield throughout the operation, had shot down five Iraqi aircraft for no losses of their own.[24]

The Iraqi high command however was not prepared to concede the strategic Dezful-Shoush pocket. Saddam ordered the Iraqi 12th Armored Division to assemble at Fakkeh to relieve what remained of the Iraqi 4th Army Corps. The Iraqis launched their tanks to relieve their beleaguered comrades on March 23, but the IRIAF was waiting for them. In less than an hour, 95 F-4s and

F-5s reduced the armored vehicles of the 12th Armored Division into burning hulks. Saddam's attempt to rescue his 4th Army Corps had only compounded the disaster.

The Iraqis refused to give up, prolonging combat for at least another week. This resulted in the Iranian capture of the Dehloran heights on March 27. This was an important victory as the Dehloran heights had been used to strike the Vahdati air base with artillery strikes. Free from artillery and missile harassment, Vahdati would now become even more dangerous to Iraqi forces both inside Iran and in Iraq. Dehloran's radar net had also been recaptured from Iraqi troops and soon used against their former owners. Recent studies reveal that Dehloran's radar emplacements and SAM sites were quickly reactivated and significantly improved by the Iranians. Iranian SAM nests and antiaircraft artillery were now coordinated much more effectively with the IRIAF. The synthesized efforts of these services contributed much to the subsequent downing of at least 27 Iraqi aircraft in the Dehloran theater between late March and early June 1982.[25]

With the land battle practically lost, Saddam Hussein hoped to salvage the situation with his air force. Despite having lost 150 aircraft, the IrAF still possessed 175 machines, including the recently delivered French F-1EQs.[26] Saddam ordered the IrAF to launch strikes against Iranian troop concentrations, armor, airfields and communication nets on April 1, 1982. By this time Iranian ground troops were being supported by ZSU-23-4 antiaircraft artillery and shoulder-held antiaircraft missiles (especially SA-7s). These shot down 20 attacking Iraqi helicopters and aircraft. The bombing efforts of the IrAF proved largely ineffective, but resulted in much collateral civilian damage.[27]

The battle for the Dezful-Shush pocket was over. The Iraqi 4th Army Corps had been decimated, with 10,000 Iraqi troops killed and another 15,000 injured.[28] Surviving Iraqi forces had been pushed 10–12 miles (20km) back towards the international border. By the end of Operation *Fatah ol Mobin*, Iran had liberated 940 square miles of territory and captured 15,000 Iraqi troops.[29] The Iranians had also captured 350 Iraqi tanks and APCs.[30] These same tanks were soon pressed into service against their former Iraqi owners. With the conclusion of *Fatah ol Mobin*, the Iranians sent more antiaircraft artillery and missiles to the front to support their troops for the next round of operations.

Saddam Hussein himself had almost been captured during the operation when his convoy was ambushed during a visit to the front lines.[31] However, despite his own harrowing experience and the defeats of his forces, Saddam Hussein downplayed the dangers of Iran's reviving military machine. In his speech to the Iraqi 4th Army Corps he said "I hope you will not be bitter about the land you are leaving voluntarily, as dictated by the requirements of defensive positions to the rear … we never told you to keep this land as part of Iraqi land."[32] Saddam's speech appeared to be a tacit admission that the Baathist dream of annexing Khuzistan into a greater pan-Arab state had failed. On the other hand, Saddam's statement that his troops had retreated voluntarily was patently unconvincing. The continuing public derision of Iranian martial abilities by Saddam Hussein and the Baath party was probably meant to boost sagging Iraqi troop morale and Iraq's increasingly wary home front. In private, Saddam and the Baath party were under no illusions, acknowledging their military's tactical and strategic errors and even realizing that their troops could be pushed all the way back inside Iraq.[33] Nevertheless for reasons that remain unclear, the Iraqi army simply remained in place, suffering from an apparent lack of initiative that was due to Saddam's rigid top-down control regimen.

Iran liberates Khorramshahr

With Abadan secured, Dehloran liberated, and the Dezful-Shoush pocket cleared of Iraqi troops, Iran was ready to implement the final and most devastating stage of its offensives: Operation *Beit ol Moghaddas* (*Jerusalem*), which led to the liberation of Khorramshahr. The loss of this city and its tenacious defense had left a profound mark across the Iranian populace. The forces that soon converged towards the city had volunteers from across Iran, including Lurs, Azaris, Kurds, and Khuzistani Arabs. Saddam responded by making a dramatic televised visit to his troops in Khorramshahr, swearing to never relinquish the city. But fiery rhetoric could do little to salvage Baghdad's sinking fortunes.

The Iraqi high command ordered its Mirage F-1 and MiG-23 assets to be deployed to Iraqi air bases facing Iran, in an endeavor to counter Iranian air superiority as well as their ability to conduct reconnaissance.[34] The Iraqis had also taken delivery of powerful long-range radars and attempted to use these to direct their Mirage F-1EQs against Iranian F-14s, F-4s and F-5s.[35] The IRIAF had anticipated these moves and launched a massive air strike on April 4, targeting Iraqi air bases equipped with the recently delivered Mirage F-1 and MiG-23 fighters. The Iraqis were caught by surprise as Iranian jets appeared over Baghdad, Basra, Kut, and Nasseriyah. Iraq's major Al-Rasheed air base was hit exceptionally hard: Iranian F-4s bombed 16 Iraqi jets on the ground and destroyed two Mirage F-1EQs in air-to-air combat. The swift dispatch of the Mirage F-1s proved especially demoralizing as the aircrafts' much-vaunted Matra air-to-air missiles had failed to defeat the Iranian jets. The IRIAF bombed another 31 Iraqi aircraft in their airfields close to the front and shot down a number of others in air-to-air combat.[36] Iranian jets continued to strike military targets in Baghdad into late April. Thanks in large part to the constant pounding of Iraqi airfields, Iranian RF-4E reconnaissance jets continued gathering valuable intelligence on Iraqi troop movements and strength levels. Iranian ground forces had also been assured of complete air superiority as they converged towards Khorramshahr.

Iranian forces had deployed to the south of the recently liberated Dezful-Shoush region, threatening to cut remaining Iraqi forces in two. The Iranians made good on their threat by launching a major attack on the night of April 29–30, 1982. Regular army personnel, commandos, and Pasdaran-Basij militia struck along three axes: Bostan–Susangerd, the west banks of the Karun River, and southwest of Ahvaz. The Iranian offensive was supported by 200 tanks and 26 AH-1 Cobra gunships.[37] It is not clear how many of these tanks were Western equipment, as the Iranians were now also using captured Soviet-built Iraqi equipment. Heliborne transport of troops in the theater was provided by Bell 214 and CH-47C helicopters. An effective air defense net was effected by two HAWK and one Rapier batteries. There were also large numbers of SA-7 shoulder-fired SAMs. Bombing operations by F-4s and F-5s were underway against Iraqi troop concentrations, armor and supply lines. Transportation and evacuation of wounded troops was entrusted to C-130 aircraft operating out of Ahvaz airport and air bases at Vahdati and Omidiyeh. Crucial to Iranian operations was the role of the air bridge between Iran's major cities and air bases at the front. The IRIAF set the world record for air transport on May 9, 1982 when their Boeing 747s transported over 6,000 fully armed troops of Khorasan's 77th Division from Mashad to Khuzistan in a single night.[38]

The tactics of Operation *Beit ol Moghaddas* were two-fold. First, infantry assaults backed by tanks were launched against Iraqi forces at night. These were followed by tanks and APCs the next day, closely supported by Cobra gunships which destroyed large numbers of Iraqi tanks, APCs, and soft-skinned vehicles. Iraqi armor in particular received special attention with the Pasdaran focusing their attacks on the already battered Iraqi 12th Armored Division. Iraqi resistance was uneven: the regular Iraqi units generally tried to resist while the Popular People's militias, lacking morale and training, often crumbled when the Iranians struck.

The results of the initial attacks were devastating. By May 3, Iraq had lost another 100 tanks, 10,000 troops, two combat helicopters and 300 square miles to the Iranians.[39] In desperation, the Iraqis launched their battered air force in a bid to wrest control of the air but lost 44–50 combat aircraft to F-4/F-14 fighters and the Iranian SAM net.[40] The IrAF only succeeded in shooting down four Iranian F-4s and three helicopters by May 5–6. The Iraqis then scaled back their efforts to conserve what was left of their air fleet.

Realizing the danger at last, the Iraqis deployed their remaining tanks to launch a powerful counterattack on May 3–4, which actually retook some lost ground. With the failure of their air force the Iraqis were forced to rely on their antitank Gazelle and Mi-25 helicopters for air support.[41] Unfortunately for Baghdad, Shirazi had anticipated the Iraqi counterattack. He ordered a major thrust towards the border town of Fakeh, which was quickly captured. Iranian helicopters (covered by F-4 and F-5 fighters) also landed the 55th Parachute Brigade in the Iraqi border town of Shalamcha in Basra province. Cobra gunships participated by destroying Iraqi armor, bridges, and combat vehicles at Shalamcha. The fall of this town placed Iranian forces just 16–17 miles (26–27km) from Basra. This meant that supply lines between Iraq's remaining occupying forces and southern Iraq had now been virtually cut off.

The only way Iraq could rescue its position was to push the Iranians out of Fakeh and Shalamcha, but their increasing military disarray prevented this from happening. Just six days after the failed May 3 Iraqi counterattack, the Pasdaran tore a wide gap in Iraqi lines. This allowed the 92nd Iranian Armored Division to drive its tanks into the Iraqi rear and destroy two Iraqi army divisions, including the 6th Armored Division.[42] The 92nd then wheeled towards Shalamcha to link up with the 55th Paras. By mid-May the Iraqis had lost more tanks, troops and an additional 116 square miles of territory just north of Khorramshahr. The loss of all land routes to Khorramshahr tightened the noose around the city's occupying Iraqi troops.

To defend Khorramshahr against Iranian frontal attacks, the 35,000-man Iraqi garrison had built three fortified tiers of minefields and earthworks, which they christened "The Wall of the Persians."[43] Fears of Iranian commando landings by air prompted the Iraqi garrison to erect a large number of metal spikes in those areas deemed most vulnerable to helicopter or parachute landings. Bizarrely, hundreds of derelict cars were placed on end to bolster these "anti-commando" defenses!

By May 21, the Iranians had placed 70,000 troops around Khorramshahr.[44] Saddam, finally acknowledging his precarious position in Iran, called on the Arab League's Joint Defense agreement on May 23. He wanted to secure military aid from fellow Arab states against Iran, but nothing came of it. The Arabs clearly wanted to distance themselves from Saddam's failed adventure.

The Iraqi garrison had only one means of access for its supplies: the Arvand Rud/Shaat al Arab waterway. This was also vulnerable as the IRIAF was destroying all bridges across the waterway and sinking any vessels daring to bring supplies into Khorramshahr. To make matters worse, Iranian artillery began pounding the Iraqi garrison and targeted its supply lines along the waterway.

The attack came sooner than Saddam had expected; the Iranians struck on the night of May 23. Spearheading the Iranian assault was the 77th Khorasan Division, the 59th Zolfaqhar Brigade, and the Pasdaran. The Iranian arrival was heralded by massive artillery preparation and devastating air strikes.[45] Saddam's "Wall" failed to halt the Iranian advance: 4,000 Iraqi troops immediately surrendered to Iranian troops as soon as they attacked.[46] Constant defeats over several months had taken a terrible toll on Iraqi morale. The Iraqi garrison at Khorramshahr had little motivation to fight to the bitter end. Approximately 22,000 men, two-thirds of the Iraqi garrison, rapidly surrendered.[47] This meant that in the course of Operation *Beit ol Moghaddas* alone, Iraq had lost 33,000–35,000 combatants as prisoners.

It is not clear how many of the surviving 13,000 Iraqi troops managed to escape in the chaotic Iraqi withdrawal across the Arvand Rud/Shaat al Arab waterway to Iraq. One Iraqi staff helicopter, attempting to take off as Iranian troops were entering the city, was forced down by small arms fire, leading to the capture of its occupants, which included Iraqi officers.[48] Those who did make it to the waterway found almost every bridge already destroyed. The city of Khorramshahr had been avenged 575 days after its fall to Saddam Hussein, and Iran had liberated 5,400km² of its territory from the Iraqis.

Saddam's failure and Iran's military situation

The Baathist regime and Saddam had already lost the war in terms of their primary objectives: securing both sides of the Arvand Rud/Shaat al Arab waterway, annexing Khuzistan province and balkanizing Iran along ethnic lines. Iraq had also paid very dearly for its military failures: two of Iraq's four armored divisions had been cut down to brigade size; many of Iraq's leading generals had been killed or captured; professional troop levels had fallen from 210,000 to 150,000; and the Iraqi air force now had barely 100 combat aircraft operational.[49] The Iraqi armored corps had proven itself to be inefficient at carrying out complex armored operations.[50] Saddam Hussein did his utmost to minimize the scope and importance of Iraq's defeats, which were largely the result of his own leadership. The Iraqi military now had two choices. The Iraqis rejected the option to fight to remain in Iranian territory and instead pulled back to the international borders, conserving what was left of their battered army.

In purely technical terms, Iran had won the war. The Iraqis had been ejected from nearly all occupied Iranian territories.[51] Saddam was more than willing to accept a ceasefire, but his claim of having withdrawn from all Iranian territory on June 29, 1981, was disingenuous; Iraqi forces still held pockets of Iranian territory. Arab states were also eager to promote an end to the conflict. The Iranian military and political leadership were divided. The Pasdaran in general opted for an all-out drive on Basra without much consideration for a methodical military build-up, hoping that Iraq's Shiites would make common cause with their coreligionists. The regular army was more circumspect and lacked the Pasdaran's enthusiasm for an all-out drive into Iraq.

The Iranian military were exhausted after several months of offensives. General Zaher-Nejad argued that the mass of Iran's raw recruits needed to be properly trained before any offensive could be launched across the border.[52] Despite their tanks' recent successes in Khuzistan, the Iranians needed time to replace their heavy armored losses and train more crews. Despite having captured large numbers of Iraqi tanks, the Iranian military was struggling to maintain its fleet of tanks and armored vehicles. Iranian industries simply could not field enough serviceable tanks to counter Iraq's increasing superiority in armor. Procuring quantities of spares was very difficult as Western governments "officially" refused to sell Iran their latest tanks. This forced Iran to procure spares from underground markets at great cost and in insufficient quantities. Iran soon turned to suppliers such as China for Soviet-type tanks, these suppliers also provided similar machines to Iraq.

Despite their terrible losses as a result of Shirazi's recent offensives and during Iran's later attacks into Iraq, Iraq fielded over three times as many tanks as Iran. Iran's shortage of tanks obliged the military to increasingly rely on combat helicopters and antitank teams for defense against Iraqi armor. Iraq's financial support from other oil-rich Arab states allowed Iraq to expand its numerical advantage in tanks as the war progressed. The Iraqis also enjoyed substantial Soviet support. During September–October 1982, the USSR exported an unspecified number of T-72 tanks as well as SA-8 antiaircraft missiles.[53] While Iran was still able to match the T-72 qualitatively, the Iranian armored corps remained handicapped by its numerical inferiority.[54] The Iraqi armored corps, unlike Iran, was also receiving the best of Soviet tanker training.[55]

The professional military also realized that time was needed to replace Iran's losses in APCs, artillery, and helicopters. The air fleet also badly needed to replace its heavy losses in aircraft and pilots. While Iraq had certainly suffered disastrous blows in recent months, it had many foreign benefactors. Thanks to deliveries from Egypt, China, and the Soviet Union, Iraq's heavy losses had been practically replaced. Foremost among Saddam Hussein's Western supporters at this time were the French, who sent over 40% of their military exports to Iraq.[56] By the end of 1983, Iraq had almost completely restored its prewar total of aircraft to 332 machines. By contrast, Iran's operational air fleet was down to just one-quarter of its prewar 440 combat aircraft. This was partly due to combat losses, but many of Iran's aircraft were grounded due to lack of spare parts. The IRIAF did get a new lease of life by January 1983 by breaking the computer codes necessary to access the large storage centers for combat aircraft. By this time some sections of aircraft were being manufactured in Iran. Along with clandestine purchases this allowed the IRIAF to confront Iraqi bombing efforts, but the reality was that no nation with advanced aircraft manufacturing abilities was willing to sell combat aircraft to Iran. Iran had to preserve its dwindling stock of aircraft for defensive purposes in what had become a prolonged war of attrition.

While Iranian aircraft performed very well the Iraqis were definitely gaining advantages because they had enough aircraft to attack many economic, military and civilian targets at once. Iran's available aircraft simply could not compensate for Iraq's growing numerical edge. This situation became increasingly pronounced as the war progressed.

Despite efforts to harmonize if not unify the army with the Pasdaran-Basij, a clear division of command still existed between the two, which seriously compromised Iran's overall military effectiveness. What Iran desperately needed in military terms was the development of a unified and integrated force. At the very least, this would have minimized the very high casualties, especially among the Basij militias.

The Pasdaran-Basij in particular suffered from serious military shortcomings. First, they had yet to appreciate the importance of supply and logistics in battle. They often captured enemy positions after an initial attack, but had no coherent logistics system to support their advance. They also lacked a reliable system of command and control to maintain cohesion and focus in the battlefield. Training and battle doctrine did improve through the war, but the Basij continued to suffer horrendous casualties throughout the war. This was because they often relied on ideological and religious fervor during battle.

Because of the state of the Iranian military, the army argued for short thrusts over modest areas close to the Iranian border. The most maverick proposal for a quick and victorious advance into Iraq was that of air force hero, Lieutenant Colonel Abbas Dowran. Dowran's proposal was to focus on Baghdad rather than Basra. His plan was highly reminiscent of tactics envisaged by the Iranian military during the shah's era. This was an all-out "blitzkrieg" by land forces towards Baghdad, closely supported by a revitalized Iranian air force.[57] Iranian pilots and aircraft had clearly demonstrated their capabilities in air-to-air and air-to-ground combat, but whether Dowran's plan would have worked is difficult to ascertain.

CHAPTER 35

STALEMATE:
THE WAR SHIFTS INTO IRAQ (1982–85)

Iran's Failed Drive to Basra

Iran finally launched Operation *Ramadan ol Mobarak* on the night of July 13–14, 1982, to capture Basra. Iraq's second largest city boasted one million citizens, many of them Shiites. The Iranians were probably also trying to cut the Baghdad–Basra highway. Another objective was to silence Iraqi artillery situated to the east of Basra, which was shelling Khorramshahr.

The defense of Basra was entrusted to the Iraqi 3rd Army Corps, consisting of seven divisions plus special forces and independent brigades. The Iranian force poised for the attack was actually smaller, standing at just five divisions, one of them armored.[1] These succeeded in penetrating up to 9 miles (15km) into Iraq, with Iranian troops soon just 12 miles (20km) from Basra. The Iraqis had constructed a formidable network of earthworks, minefields, trenches, barbed wire lines, machinegun nests and heavy artillery pits to defend Basra and to channel Iranian attacks into "kill zones."[2] The Basij literally ran over the minefields; followed by Pasdaran's direct-infantry "human wave" assaults. At one point it seemed that Basra would fall until four Iraqi divisions counterattacked the Iranian spearhead. At this point 130,000 troops from both sides became locked in close-quarter combat, making it the largest infantry engagement since the Second World War.[3] The Iraqis fought very well and inflicted very heavy losses on Iranian troops and armor. By the end of the week-long battle (July 20), the Iranians had been pushed back. The Iranians attacked again on July 22 and then on July 27 but the results were the same: the Iranians would advance into Iraq only to be beaten back by fierce Iraqi resistance. The last offensive was characterized by the heavy deployment of the ill-trained Basij in fruitless front-line attacks, resulting in heavy casualties.

When the fighting finally subsided, the Iranians retained a pocket of 50 square miles of Iraqi territory after a maximal penetration of 95 square miles.[4] The only advantage this afforded to the Iranians was a better platform from which to shell Basra. The number of Iraqi prisoners was modest at just 1,110 men.[5] Iranian sources reported 7,000 Iraqi troops killed with the Iranians themselves having casualties of 9,000 during their offensives.[6] The Iraqis also captured 200 Iranian tanks, as well as armored vehicles and artillery.[7] The Iranians did capture 101 Iraqi tanks, including 12 new T-72s, which Iran acquired for the first time.[8]

The operation failed because the Iranians had too few tanks, artillery, combat helicopters and combat aircraft to properly support their offensives.[9] Despite their terrible losses in tanks the previous year, Iraq still fielded 3,000 tanks against Iran's barely 900 operational machines.[10] The Iranian logistics system also proved unable to cope with stretched lines of supply and communications. Tehran's hopes of a general Shiite uprising against Baghdad turned out to have been an illusion.

The Iranians now realized that the battle into Iraq would be prolonged and bitter. Nevertheless Tehran's costly failure resulted in one important political silver lining. The Non-Aligned Movement's 97-member conference scheduled at Baghdad in September 1982 (with Saddam as chair of the conference) was now relocated to Delhi, India. Iraq's hopes for gain diplomatic leverage against Iran through this conference had dissolved, thanks to the ongoing fighting. During the offensives Lieutenant Colonel Abbas Dowran was shot down by a Roland missile near Baghdad.[11] The Baathist media made much of the loss of "Iranian bandit Dowran" with Iraqi General Maher Abdul Rasheed expressing his satisfaction in public.[12] Dowran's death as a result of the French-supplied Roland missile was also a vivid demonstration of increasing Western support for Iraq's war effort. The IRIAF now had to adapt its ground attack tactics as Iraqi antiaircraft weapons systems became increasingly formidable, thanks to Western and Soviet-bloc support.

Targeting Iraqi forces remaining in Iran

Despite the ejection of the Iraqi army from much of Khuzistan, small pockets of Iranian territory still remained in Iraqi hands. Baghdad may have viewed these last pockets as strategic assets or "speed bumps" before the Iranians could fully focus their attentions on Iraq. The reduction of these last pockets of occupied territory by Iranian forces bought Iraq just enough time to build up its defenses inside Iraq.

Iraqi forces still retained a number of strategic heights inside Iran overlooking the Iraqi town of Mandali, situated 65 miles northeast from Baghdad. The Iranian army launched Operation *Moslem ibn Aqhel* on October 1, 1982, deploying 50,000–70,000 troops supported by an airborne detachment and an armored brigade.[13] The lack of armor and combat aircraft forced the Iranians to resort to human-wave attacks, resulting in heavy casualties.[14] Mandali remained in Iraqi hands but the Iranians succeeded in capturing the strategic heights in Iran overlooking the town. The Iranians made another determined push towards Mandali but were again repelled. Iran's haul of booty was very modest at approximately 12 tanks, light weapons and just 110 prisoners.[15] This indicates that the Iraqis had retreated to Iraq in relatively good order. Despite their heavy losses and failure to capture Mandali, the Iranians had liberated 65 square miles of their own territory and entered within 25 square miles of Iraqi territory.[16] A few days after the fighting, the UN Security Council called on Iran and Iraq to stop fighting and respectfully return each other's captured territories. Iraq accepted the resolution but Iran dismissed it.

Iraq attempted to strike back by launching a Scud-B missile at Dezful in late October, killing 21 civilians and injuring a further 100.[17] Another rocket attack was launched against Dezful on December 18, killing 64 civilians and injuring over 300. These actions only served to strengthen the position of Tehran's hard-liners who argued that the only way of ending such attacks was to occupy Iraq itself. More importantly, these attacks served to raise more volunteers for the front. The Iraqis also sent their MiG and Mirage-F1 fighters to bomb Kharq Island, its pumping station and its oil tankers. The island however was too well defended by high- and low-level SAMs.

Operation *Moharram ol Harram* launched on November 1 endeavored to liberate the last pockets of Iranian territory in Khuzistan (situated to the northeast of the Iraqi town of Al-Amarah) still under Iraqi occupation. The Iranian high command assembled at least four regular divisions supported by M-60 and Chieftain tanks, along with numbers of Pasdaran-Basij units.[18] The initial strikes close to the Fakkeh area ruptured the Iraqi lines and led to a temporary breakthrough. The Iraqis struck back with much of their newly arrived equipment, including brand-new Soviet T-72 tanks.[19] Iraq also fielded large numbers of helicopters and aircraft but Iranian antiaircraft missiles shot numbers of these down. Baghdad reacted quickly by sending in its Republican Guard, equipped with T-72 tanks. These cleared the Iranians from the town of Zubeidat. After this success, the Iraqis contained the Iranians but failed to conclusively push them back. The Iranians had penetrated approximately 6 miles into Iraq and had secured a total of 360 square miles; 190 square miles of this was Iraqi territory. One factor which prevented Iraq from pushing the Iranians back to the border was the appearance of Cobra helicopters on November 10–12. These fired their cannon and TOW missiles into Iraqi armored columns, destroying at least 107 Iraqi tanks and APCs.[20] The Iranians also captured 40 pieces of 106mm artillery, 139 tanks and APCs as well as 3,500 prisoners.[21] Saddam Hussein's invasion of Iran had now transformed into the invasion of Iraq.

Operation *Moharram ol Harram* worried the Iraqi high command. The conduct of Iranian armed forces during this operation had resembled the devastating 1982 summer offensives that had crushed the Iraqi army from Khuzistan. Baghdad's concerns led to the dispatch of generals Abdul Jabbar Mohsen and Maher Abdul Rasheed of the Fourth and Third Army Corps respectively on a fact-minding mission.[22]

The generals boarded a Mi-8 helicopter on November 20, 1982 to fly towards Iraq's front lines, escorted by two Mi-8s and eight fighter aircraft. What occurred next proved to be one of the most dramatic incidents of the entire Iran–Iraq War. Just 5 miles (8km) away, an Iranian Boeing KC-707 air tanker was standing by to fuel incoming F-4 Phantoms. The Boeing was escorted by two F-14A Tomcats who had been ordered to stay with the aircraft under all circumstances. Despite these orders, one of the Tomcats broke off and began firing Phoenix and Sidewinder missiles into the eight Iraqi aircraft. Two MiG-23s and one MiG-21 plunged downwards in flames in midst of the three helicopters. The debris narrowly missed the helicopter of Rasheed and Mohsen.[23] This and the remaining aircraft rapidly fled. Fortunately for the Iraqi generals, the Tomcat's radar had not picked up the slow-moving helicopters. The Iraqi generals' near-fatal experience had once again proven the deadly effectiveness of the Tomcat. Shortly after this incident another formation of Iraqi aircraft attempted to enter Iran for a bombing mission but this was intercepted by the F-4s that had just been refueled by the Boeing aircraft.

The conclusion of operations *Ramadan ol Mobarak*, *Moslem ibn Aqhel*, and *Moharram ol Harram* were reported as Iranian defeats by Arab and Western media outlets at the time. While Iran had failed to capture Basra or make deep inroads into Iraq, enough pieces of Iraqi territory or "launch pads" had been captured (albeit at great cost) to give the Iranians the option of future strikes against Basra, Baghdad and the Baghdad–Basra highway.

The *Val Fajr I–IV* offensives

The Iraqis were acutely aware of Iran's intention to launch more offensives into Iraq. From early January 1983, the IrAF was deployed in a massive bombing campaign into Khuzistan and against

Iranian oil and maritime assets in the Persian Gulf. The intention was to forestall future Iranian offensives and cripple the Iranian economy. As soon as they commenced their operations, Iraqi air strikes ran into the IRIAF which had just been rejuvenated by the arrival of supplies from both domestic and foreign sources.

The Iraqis had hoped to use their superior numbers of aircraft to "swamp" Iran's interceptors by dispatching very large strike packages of up to 40 aircraft. The Iraqi strikes were quickly defeated because the Iranian pilots had been well trained by US instructors in combating superior numbers of hostile aircraft attacking from different directions; the Tomcat and its Phoenix missile remained far superior to any aircraft in Iraq's inventory; and Iran had managed to close the gaps in its radar blind spots. From now on, arriving Iraqi aircraft would be detected much sooner. The IRIAF had proven its resiliency once again, but their dwindling numbers of combat aircraft prevented them from assisting Iranian ground forces.

Iran launched the first of its many *Val Fajr* offensives on February 7, 1983. Up to 100,000 men were to deploy from Khuzistan's Fakeh region to sever the Baghdad–Basra highway and possibly capture the Iraqi town of Amara. Iraqi Major-General Hisham S. Fakhri, commander of the 4th Army Corps, had prepared for this onslaught. As soon as Iranian troops advanced into Iraq, masses of Iraqi artillery erupted with a withering barrage. Had Iranian aircraft initially supported the advance, the course of the battle may have been different. Some Iranian fighters did appear two days after the offensive and worked in concert with a Hawk missile battery to shoot down 8–10 aircraft, but this had little impact on the ground offensive, allowing Fakhri to hurl his aircraft using cluster bombs against the advancing Iranian troops. These acted in concert with helicopter gunships (especially the deadly Mi-25) and artillery to inflict heavy losses against Iranian troops. Iranian tank units were also battered. These performed well, but in a repeat of the January 1981 Susangerd disaster, one armored unit was cut off by its Iraqi counterparts and decimated. Tehran's only consolation was the expulsion of Iraq's troops from 100 square miles of Iranian territory.[24] Despite their failure to sever the Baghdad–Basra highway, the Iranians had, according to British military reports, captured 1,460 Iraqi Soviet-built tanks and APCs by February 1983.[25] The acquisition of Soviet tank engines allowed the Iranians to replace the damaged engines of captured Soviet-built Iraqi tanks; these then entered Iranian service. It is not clear how many of these were battle ready for the next series of *Val Fajr* offensives.

Fakhri's success was a great boost for Iraqi morale. This led the Iraqi high command to launch a major offensive in the central front in March. The elation proved premature as Iraqi armored attacks from the Miqdadiya region were soundly defeated by Iranian Cobra helicopters and troops armed with antitank weapons.

Following Iraq's failure in March, the Iranians prepared for a fresh offensive. This operation, launched on April 10, 1983, witnessed Iranian armed forces thrusting to the north of Fakeh. The primary target was (again) the Baghdad–Basra highway. The secondary target was a series of strategic heights strewn for over 40km. The outcome of the battle was a virtual repeat of the original *Val Fajr* offensive. The Iranians attacked, with the Iraqis fighting back with superior numbers of tanks, artillery, combat aircraft and helicopters. The Iranians were then forced back with heavy casualties. The end result was the liberation of a modest 60 square miles of Iranian territory and the netting of just 390 Iraqi prisoners.[26] Baghdad still continued to occupy 330 square miles of Iranian territory.

Iran's third attack of the *Val Fajr* offensives came on July 21, 1983. This attack was towards the north. Iranian forces deployed from the Iranian-Kurdish towns of Piranshahr and Sardasht into Iraqi Kurdistan. This operation was supported by the regular army, helicopters and fighter aircraft. Helicopters were essential in this operation with Cobras providing combat support and transport helicopters ferrying commandos. Iranian forces initial thrust into Haj Omran with the ultimate objective being the Kirkuk oilfields. Local anti-Saddam Peshmerga of the Kurdish Democratic Party (KDP) and Iraqi Shiites (The Al-Mujahedin) supported the Iranian troops.

The operations went well, with the abandoned Haj Omran barracks falling into Iranian hands. The fall of Haj Omran was a military disaster for the Iraqis as this was near the Kurdish towns of Rawanduz and Qaleh-Dizeh. From this region Iran could threaten Iraq's Sulaymānīyah province and Kirkuk. The Iranian advance towards Kirkuk did not go well due to effective Iraqi resistance in front of Chuman Mostafa. The Iraqis then counterattacked, but the highly elevated, rugged and mountainous terrain prevented them from pressing home their superiority in armor and artillery. These factors helped the Iranians to prevail and defeat the Iraqi counteroffensive.

Iranian combat helicopters took a heavy toll of attacking Iraqi troops with transport helicopters ferrying supplies to the troops. Iraqi aircraft and helicopters failed to alter the military situation due to the presence of Iranian jets. On July 27 six Iraqi helicopters laden with Iraqi commandos were shot down by Iranian jets. Iranian ground forces then attempted to resume their drive to Chuman Mostafa on August 5 but were again repelled. When the fighting subsided, the Iranians had managed to capture 190 square miles and mountain ranges at an elevation of 9,000ft.[27]

If Iran had hoped to divert the bulk of Iraq's forces away from the southern regions, then the strategy had clearly failed. Iraq's generals realized that the Iranians were trying to keep them offbalance. Baghdad kept just enough troops to try and contain the Iranians in the north. This strategy was also risky as anti-Iraq Kurdish Peshmerga were now supporting the Iranian drives into the region. The Iranians were of course wary of the local Kurds' secular and nationalistic tendencies and made a point of asking Iraqi dissidents, both Kurds and the Supreme Council of Islamic Revolution in Iraq (SCIRI) to set up offices in the Iranian-occupied regions.[28] The problem was that many local Peshmerga would often take over the regions once Iranian troops had thinned out or departed, making the region defacto autonomous. To solve this problem, Iran struck a formal alliance with the Peshmerga against Baghdad.

After attacking northern Iraq, the Iranian military focused on the Iranian town of Mehran, to the north of Khuzistan. The Iraqis were located on heights near Mehran which overlooked the roads connecting the city to Elam and Dehloran. *Val Fajr III* was devised to eject the Iraqis from these strategic locations. The operation was actually two large offensives which were launched on July 30, and August 5. These were covered by Iranian Cobras and support helicopters but air support was lacking at first, which led to low-level attacks by Iraqi jets. Iraqi air attacks were then terminated with the arrival of Iranian interceptors into the theater. The Iraqis were finally cleared off the mountains surrounding Mehran and forced to cede approximately 32 square miles on the Iraqi side of the border. During these operations, Iranian armored forces had assisted in the defeat of three Iraqi counterattacks. Their tanks maneuvered well, capturing 70 Iraqi tanks and armored vehicles.[29] Also captured were 294 Iraqi artillery pieces, 13,000 light weapons and 600 prisoners.[30] The vast cache of captured light weapons were useful in helping arm the large pool of raw Basij recruits now pouring into the front lines. The cost for the Iranians' success at Mehran was indeed horrendous; 15,000–25,000 troops had been killed with 80% being the ill-trained Basij.

The Iranians resumed their attacks into Iraqi Kurdistan with *Val Fajr IV*, hoping to reinforce their recent gains there. They struck on October 20 along a broad front between the Iranian Kurdish towns of Sardasht and Marivan. The main aim was to finally sever the connection between the Iraqi army and the KDPI. The region boasted two mountain passes allowing Saddam Hussein to supply the KDPI. The first phase of the fighting succeeded in ejecting occupying Iraqi troops situated between Baneh and Marivan. Iranian forces had been supported by commando–helicopter operations and Iraqi Kurdish fighters. The Iraqi army responded by counterattacking with combat aircraft and the tanks of the Republican Guard.[31] These blocked the Iranian advance towards Panjvin, but Tehran did succeed in severing Iraq's connection with the KDPI. Despite Baghdad's claim of having destroyed two Iranian armored divisions, the Iraqis had paid dearly in this round of fighting. The Iranians had captured 400 Iraqi tanks and APCs, 20 pieces of 100mm artillery (and large stores of their ammunition), 33,000 mine detectors, 1,800 prisoners, and 20 batteries of SAM launchers.[32] The latter was indicative of the Iraqi command's concern with Iranian helicopters and aircraft. The capture of so much heavy equipment was also suggestive of fragile Iraqi morale in this region. Iran also gained a very modest Iraqi territorial swathe of 65 square miles.

During *Val Fajr IV*, the Iraqi army deployed mustard gas against Iranian troops in October 1983.[33] There is plenty of evidence of a lax attitude towards the use of such weapons by the Iraqi military leadership.[34] Human rights and peace groups in the West condemned these actions as violations of the Geneva protocols banning the use of chemical weapons. On the other hand, Western policymakers remained generally muted. The West's official silence was probably interpreted by the Baathist leadership that it was "ok" to use chemical weapons against Iranian troops. Iraq came to develop a series of chemical weapons munitions for its artillery, aircraft and helicopter strikes against Iranian infantry. Iraqi forces also mistakenly landed chemical weapons on their own troops on a number of occasions, resulting in heavy casualties.[35] This prompted the Iraqi military to increase the accuracy of its chemical weapons.

The military balance in 1984–85

The military stalemate persisted into 1984. Despite its highly motivated infantry force, Iran had failed to achieve a breakthrough mainly due to its shortage of aircraft and heavy equipment. Conversely, Iraq had been able to contain the Iranian thrusts, but had failed to prevail despite its numerical edge in aircraft, tanks and artillery. Baghdad's strategy was to use its heavy equipment, aircraft, and helicopters to preserve its manpower and prevent the Iranians from making deep penetrations into Iraq. Iraqi use of chemical weapons became more pronounced on the battlefield, especially after these helped blunt Iranian attacks.

By February 1984 Iraq was still able to field 3,000 tanks, three times more than the barely 1,000 machines possessed by Iran.[36] The imbalance continued into 1985 with Iran's armored force reportedly having just 950 tanks along with 200 tanks that had been captured from Iraq, with Iraq continuing to outnumber the Iranians with 2,800–3,000 machines.[37] Iraq had also surpassed Iran in artillery. By 1984, Iraqi artillery pieces outnumbered Iran's by three to one (1,800 compared to 600).[38]

More ominous for Iran was the numerical decline of its Cobra antitank helicopter fleet. The shortage of spare parts and heavy combat losses had reduced Iran's operational Cobras to around 50 by early 1984. The state of IRIAF was also becoming desperate. By 1984 Iran's operational Tigers and Phantoms stood at 70–80 and 80–90 respectively.[39] The situation worsened in 1985 with Iran being capable of only operating 50 F-4s and 30 F-14As. The rest of the fleet was grounded due to the shortage of spares. Despite these serious military handicaps, Iran launched its new three-phase offensives into Iraq. When Iraq retaliated by bombing Iranian cities in 1984 and 1985, Iran's dwindling air fleet was unable to prevent these strikes.

The numerical decline of Iranian aircraft gave Baghdad a virtual carte blanche to launch its second round of bombardments of Iranian metropolitan centers known as the "War of the Cities." Iraq's air fleet and pool of qualified pilots had grown steadily by 1984. The French delivered their most advanced technology and looked for ways to eliminate Iran's dangerous Tomcat interceptors. The Soviets delivered supersonic bombers (Tu-22) and other advanced fighters such as the MiG-23. They also began to deliver lethal Fuel air explosive (FAE) bombs which could wipe out infantry in a 200m radius. The qualitative and quantitative rise of the Iraqi air force was soon matched by the Iraqi helicopter corps.

"War of the Cities" begins

Iraqi jets were active against Iranian cities in 1983 with bombing runs on Pol e Dokhtar and Dezful. There were also ballistic missile attacks (FROG-7 and Scud-B) on Andimeshk in May 1983 followed by more such attacks in August 1983 again against Andimeshk and the cities of Nahavand, Marivan, and Dezful. The Iraqis fired additional Scuds and launched more air raids against Iranian cities such as Dezful and Abadan, between December 1983 and February 1984. Iran retaliated with bombing raids of its own against Iraqi cities including Baghdad, ringed at the time by one of the most effective air defense systems in the world. This cycle of bombings, cited by some as the first round of "The War of the Cities," was finally put to an end by an UN-mediated ceasefire on February 5, 1984. Western sources reported that Iraqi air and missile attacks had killed 4,700 and wounded 22,000 Iranian civilians by February 1984.[40]

Saddam's strategy was simple: he wanted to demoralize the Iranian population to force the leadership into accept peace talks. The strategy not only failed in its purpose but served to elevate the anger of Iran's civilian population against the Baathist regime. Undeterred by his failure to cow the Iranian populace, Saddam launched a new war of the cities in March 1985. The Iraqis had so many aircraft that they were able to launch multiple and simultaneous raids over Tehran, Tabriz, Isfahan, Kermanshah, Ahvaz, Dezful, Hamadan, Shiraz, and Bushehr. Iraqi bombing was heavy, with Tehran enduring over 40 air raids. By the end of March, UN efforts led to a temporary suspension of Iraqi air raids, but they resumed in May. Iraq also launched numbers of Scud missiles against Iranian cites.

The Iranians started to launch their own Scud missiles on March 12. In one case, Iranian Scuds struck Baghdad at least 12 times. A small number of air raids were also carried out by Iranian F-4s against Iraqi cities, but the numbers of these paled in comparison to what Iraq was able to deliver. By May, relocated Hawk batteries and Iranian interceptors had managed to shoot down a number of Iraqi fighters and bombers, but this hardly altered the strategic situation in the air. Nevertheless, Saddam Hussein realized that his bombing strikes had only stiffened the Iranian will to resist. The Iraqi air raids and missile strikes were finally called off on June 14, 1985. While estimates vary, Iran lost around 1,450 civilians with another 4,000 injured in the second "War of the Cities."[41] *The Guardian* later reported that Iranian civilian losses since the beginning of the war stood at 7,000 dead and 30,000 injured.[42] Saddam Hussein knew that attacking Iranian civilian and economic targets was his cost-effective way of retaliating against Iranian land offensives.

The Majnoon Islands

By 1984, Iranian infantry were departing from the "human-wave" battering ram tactics. The Pasdaran in particular now appreciated the importance of refining infantry assault techniques. This helped facilitate cooperation with the regular army, although smooth coordination between the two services had yet to materialize. Very heavy combat losses and the inability to procure heavy equipment abroad forced Iran to downsize its armored corps into a single armored division. Iran reorganized its other vehicles into three mechanized divisions in 1984.[43] The Iraqis in 1984 fielded around four times more tanks and three times more artillery, meaning that at this stage of the war, the Iranian armored corps was incapable of spearheading an armored drive into Iraq. Iraq also outnumbered Iran's aircraft by a margin of at least five to one. This placed attacking Iranian armored forces at a severe disadvantage as the IRIAF simply had no way of providing them with sufficient air cover.

The primary Iranian effort, Operation *Kheybar*, aimed to set the stage for capturing Basra by surprising Iraqi forces situated between that city and Amara.[44] Iran assembled close to 300,000 men for its ultimate aim of capturing Basra or at the very least cutting it off from the Basra–Baghdad highway. Cutting the highway would isolate Iraq's oil-rich south, with its predominantly Shiite population, from the country's Sunni-dominated center. Before launching its main offensive, Iran launched a number of diversionary attacks. The first of these was Operation *Val-Fajr V* in which Iranian forces deployed from Changuleh (between Dehloran and Mehran) into Iraqi territory on February 16, 1984. The aim was to sever the Baghdad–Basra highway between Amara and Kut, but the Iraqi 4th Army Corps counterattacked and forced the Iranians back towards Dehloran.[45] Another attack, Operation *Val Fajr VI*, was launched into Iraq's Amara province but this too failed after 7–10 days of fighting. These attacks were meant to divert the Iraqis from the Iranians' true intentions towards the Majnoon and marshland areas. Tehran was also at a major disadvantage as the US was now providing Baghdad with up-to-date satellite photographs and intelligence of Iranian military positions.

Iraq's Haur ol Howeizeh marshland stretched westwards across the Tigris River and extended to the lower sections of the Euphrates River, just before the start of the confluence of the two rivers (at the start of the Arvand Rud/Shaat al Arab). An important area of this region was the artificial series of islands known as the "Majnoon" (lit. insane) buried deep within the marshes. The area had been subject to a major oil extraction project as the region had a potential of approximately 7 billion barrels of crude. When war broke out in 1980, Baghdad sealed off the Majnoon islands' 50 oil wells.[46] Iraqi military planners also made the mistake of considering this area as a natural barrier against Iranian attacks. Here the Iranians delivered their primary blow for Operation *Kheybar*.

Just six days after the offensive from Changuleh, a number of predominantly Pasdaran divisions deployed for another offensive on February 22 in the Haur ol Howeizeh theater. The Iranians surprised the Iraqi army by launching a rapid assault using speedboats and helicopters. This time the Iraqis could not unleash their swarms of tanks as the marshes were unsuitable for armored warfare. Iraq's edge in artillery was also somewhat diminished as the marshy terrain absorbed at least some of the force of the exploding shells. Still, Iraq's artillery posed a mortal threat. It remains unclear how the Iranians coped with the Iraqi artillery. In one of the operations, Iraqi artillery pits were rapidly assaulted by special forces commandos dropped by Huey helicopters. Many of the artillerymen were then quickly killed by the Iranian commandos with hand-to-hand weapons and light automatic weapons. After the conclusion of their raid, the commandos were flown out in Huey helicopters. It is reputed that these landed just prior to the launch of the primary assault.[47] It is also possible that Cobra helicopters proceeded ahead to knock out some of the artillery pits.

Fighting raged bitterly but one Pasdaran division actually broke through the Iraqi lines by February 23. The primary aim of this offensive was to reach the town of Qorna, astride the Basra–Baghdad highway.[48] As Pasdaran advanced towards Qorna on February 25, they began to stage assaults on the western and northern islands of the Majnoons. The Iranian army supported these assaults with transport helicopters to rapidly and successfully land troops and commandos behind Iraqi lines. The Iraqis tried to respond in kind but eight of their own transport helicopters were shot down while carrying Iraqi commandos. Cobra helicopters then crossed into Iraqi territory to destroy a number of Iraqi tanks and armored vehicles that were gathering for a major counterattack. This was only a partial success as the Iraqis managed to shoot down some Cobras; losses which the Iranians could ill-afford.

Some Iranian troops managed to reach the Basra–Amarah road but these were quickly thrown back. Iranian F-4s, F-5s and even a few Tomcats were thrown into the fighting. In one operation Iranian jets and Cobra helicopters scored a major success by knocking out 34 tanks and armored vehicles. Some of the Iranian jets also wreaked havoc on Iraqi supply lines coming from Basra. Though impressive, these operations had little overall impact on the overall course of the fighting. Iran simply did not have enough aircraft and Cobras available to do the job. The main burden of the offensive remained on the shoulders of Iran's infantry.

The Pasdaran performed well using guerrilla tactics. They proved proficient at dispersing and "blending" into the terrain. This made it difficult for Iraqi aircraft to pinpoint and destroy them. However Iraqi helicopters, especially the heavily armored Hind (Mi-25) helicopters proved deadly, inflicting heavy losses on the Pasdaran. Despite these losses, the Iranians did capture the Majnoon islands by February 27 after bitter close-quarter fighting. This proved to be a bittersweet victory. On the very day that Majnoon fell, the Iranians suffered catastrophic helicopter losses to Iraqi air power. On that day, a massive array of Iranian helicopters transporting Pasdaran troops were intercepted by Iraqi combat aircraft (Mirage F-1s, MiGs and Sukhois). In what was essentially an aerial slaughter, Iraqis jets shot down 49 of 50 Iranian helicopters. Despite this, the Iranians advanced to Qorna's city limits by February 29. At last, the evasive Baghdad–Basra highway seemed to be within reach. But the nature of the fighting had changed, the Iranians were now out of the marshes and dangerously exposed in open terrain against Iraqi armor, artillery, combat aircraft and helicopters.

Time was now running out for the Iranians. The Iraqi high command had recovered from its initial shock and quickly laid its plans to counterattack. Baghdad quickly reorganized its forces in the East Tigris region and pressed the Popular Army to fight alongside their regular troops. Together, these stood their ground against the Iranian infantry assaults. The Iraqi edge in aircraft, helicopters, artillery and tanks again proved decisive. These attacks did little to deter the Iranians from pushing towards Qorna. They rushed two Pasdaran divisions forward on March 1 and supported these with tanks and heavy engineering equipment. Once again, this attacking force was handicapped by a lack of adequate air cover, an adequate logistics system and the inability to implement a combined arms system of battle.[49] Iraq's heavy artillery barrages were coordinated with helicopter and aircraft attacks, using both conventional and chemical bombs and rockets.[50] The Iraqis deployed mustard gas on February 25–26, March 2–3, 7 and 9, killing 1,200 Iranian soldiers and permanently injuring 5,000.[51] Punishing losses finally forced the Pasdaran to fall back into the marshes.

Qorna had remained in Iraqi hands, but Iraqi efforts to reenter the marshes towards Majnoon proved to be exceedingly difficult. The Iranians were now adeptly using their helicopters and motorcycles to rapidly move troops in the marshes to blunt the Iraqi counterattacks. These proved effective as the Iraqis could not push their tanks into this theater and their artillery proved ineffectual. Iraqi efforts to eject the Iranians from the Majnoon islands proved largely unsuccessful, but they did capture the southern portion of the westernmost island of the Majnoons. This at least allowed the Iraqis to block future Iranian thrusts towards Qorna. The rest of the Majnoon area was now in Iranian hands.

The Iranians had not given up on Qorna. In desperation, they gambled by throwing in their only armored division for the remainder of March. The dangerous lack of air cover ensured that Iranian armored forces became quickly bogged down. This new failure did little to deter Tehran from Qorna. They assembled a total of 300,000 troops by mid-April, many of them raw volunteers who lacked proper military training. These troops never managed to attack as Iraqi military engineers flooded the southern and western areas of the marshes. This effectively barred the Iranians from resuming their drive towards Qorna.

The cost for Iran's modest gains had been exorbitant. The Iranians had lost 27,000 killed versus 7,000 Iraqis. At the peak of the fighting, half a million troops (200,000 of these Iraqis)[52] had been locked in combat. Four years into the war, the human cost to Iran had been 170,000 combat fatalities and 340,000 wounded.[53] Iraqi combat fatalities were estimated at 80,000 with 150,000 wounded.[54]

Operation *Badr*

The Iraqi high command was determined to retake the Majnoon island complex. General Rasheed assembled four divisions for this task. The assault was launched on January 28, 1985, preceded by an artillery barrage. Rasheed launched his tanks towards the western bank of the islands along two dry roads.[55] Iraqi forces struck frontally at the Iranians at the westernmost point of the islands. As the Iranians became engaged against the main Iraqi thrust, Rasheed's infantry poured in from the flanks, resulting in an Iraqi success. The Iranians were cleared out of the western Majnoon islets in a single day but the remaining islets remained in Iranian hands. Rasheed's assault was followed by another limited Iraqi attack towards Qasr-e Shirin (in the central front) on January 31. There are few reliable reports of this operation but it is clear that no Iraqi breakthrough was achieved. The Iranians do not seem to have made any major military impression in that theater either.

Rasheed's attacks in January 1985 had not altered the balance of the war. The Iranians still held the initiative, but their problem was where and how to strike next. This created a major debate in Iran's military between the mainly "maximalist" Pasdaran versus the predominantly "minimalist" regular army. The maximalists wanted an all-out offensive to end the war while minimalists favored limited objectives across a dispersed front. Despite the very costly nature of operation *Kheybar* at Majnoon the previous year, prominent members of the Iranian leadership (favoring the Pasdaran) remained convinced that an "encore" of *Kheybar* would break through Iraqi lines and lead to the fall of the Baathist regime.[56] Regular army commanders were more circumspect and warned against the use of massive "human-wave" assaults, as these would face an Iraqi army increasingly equipped with more heavy weapons, aircraft and helicopters. They suggested limited attacks against the weakest Iraqi points. The regular army was overruled: Iran would "re-launch" a new (but diminished) version of the previous year's *Kheybar* offensive. Regular army commanders objected by pointing out that repeating last year's operations would clearly be anticipated by the Iraqis, who would know where to counterattack and inflict very heavy casualties.

Operation *Badr* again aimed to cut off the Basra–Baghdad highway and to march to Basra. *Badr* was to unfold in three stages.[57] In the first stage, Iranian forces, supported by artillery, would attack westwards through the Howeizeh marshes. The aim was to break through to dry land on the western edge of the marshes. Attacking through Howeizeh was meant to afford the greatest natural cover possible against Iraqi tanks, artillery and aircraft. The Pasdaran, who were taking the initiative for *Badr*, had absorbed the bitter lessons of the previous year's fighting. They were now lavishly equipped with automatic rifles and RPG-7 rocket launchers.[58] Both regular and Pasdaran troops were given chemical warfare suits, antropine needles for nerve agents, and respirators for poison gas, in anticipation of Iraq's use of chemical weapons. The Iranians were also equipped with Chinese-made 105mm antitank and US-made 106mm recoilless (RCL) weapons to counter Iraqi armor.[59] Despite these preparations, the *Badr* offensive was handicapped from the outset. As the regular army had pointed out, Iran lacked sufficient numbers of heavy artillery, tanks and combat aircraft to sustain such an ambitious offensive.

The second stage (again to be supported by artillery) was to have the Iranians build up their bridgeheads by ferrying in supplies and troops using helicopters and motorboats. By this time the Iranians would have tied sturdy rubber boats together and placed planks upon them to build pontoon bridges. This action was to help unfurl stage three: lunging towards the Baghdad–Basra highway between Qorna and Uzair. Once this was done, Iranian forces were to fan towards the north of the highway (towards Baghdad) and to the south of that highway (towards Basra). The southern (towards Basra) deployment was crucial as this was to link up with another Iranian force that was to be launched from Majnoon to cut off Basra from Baghdad.

Badr was launched on the evening of March 11, 1985, simultaneous with an IRIAF raid on Baghdad.[60] Iraqi and Iranian forces had already been trading artillery barrages and air raids (mainly against economic infrastructures) since March 3.[61] The Iranian attack towards Qorna and Uzair was a three-pronged operation along a narrow 7-mile (12-km) front. This struck the southern end of the Iraqi 4th Army Corps containing 10 divisions.[62] The sheer ferocity of the Iranian attacks crashed through the initial Iraqi defense lines, forcing them to yield ground. Two days into the offensive, Iranian forces had penetrated up to 10 miles (16km) into Iraq. On March 14, a group of Pasdaran supported by some tanks and artillery broke through to the north of Qorna, reaching the Tigris River. Three pontoon bridges were now rapidly constructed across the Tigris; one of which was capable of sustaining heavy armored vehicles.[63] By the nightfall of March 14, 3,000 Pasdaran actually reached the Baghdad–Basra highway.[64] To the "maximalists" in Tehran it seemed as if their arguments had been proven correct, with the Iranian press celebrating the breakthrough to the Tigris. Tehran's euphoria would be short-lived. The Iranians had dangerously overextended themselves without having adequate protection from tanks, aircraft or artillery.

As warned by the regular army's strategists, the Iraqis had thoroughly prepared themselves for the Iranian offensive. In overall command was General Sultan Hashem, working closely with General Jawal Zanoun. In anticipation of the Iranian advance, the Iraqis had constructed numerous earthworks and bunkers, erected vast amounts of barbed wire and laid massive fields of mines. The Iraqi defense grid was meant to channel the Iranian attackers into deadly "kill zones." The Iraqi high command also had a contingency plan in place.

The Hashem-Zanoun strategy consisted of three phases: pin down the Iranians with air power and artillery at the edge of the marshes; counterattack with armor and highly trained mobile troops; and attack the retreating Iranian troops with artillery and helicopter gunships.[65] As a last resort, Iraqi engineers had also constructed pipes that could divert water from the Tigris to flood the area, should the Iranians actually achieve a complete breakthrough. The Iraqis also had the benefit of access to US satellite photos and intelligence. Saddam Hussein also knew that his use of chemical weapons would elicit no Western opposition. For the implementation of the second phase of the Iraqi plan, Zanoun placed major forces to the north and south of the anticipated Iranian thrusts. These "pincers" would hold off from attacking until the main Iranian thrust(s) had manifested itself. The "pincers," along with the highly mobile Republican Guard troops, would then be unleashed. The northern Iraqi pincer was placed under the command of a highly skilled commander who had helped blunt Iran's *Kheybar* operation the previous year: General Hisham Sabah al-Fakhri, assistant chief of army staff of the Iranian army. The southern pincer was commanded by General Saadi Tooma Abbas, an assistant chief of army staff in charge of training.

Zanoun initiated the second phase of his plan by having Iraqi forces strike with their mobile forces, Republican guard and artillery on the night of March 15. The Pasdaran, now at the Tigris and Basra–Baghdad highway, were badly mauled, and the survivors retreated. The Iraqis also pumped water to flood the Iranians out of their trenches. Retreating Pasdaran fighters soon witnessed Iraqi helicopter gunships destroying the Iranian pontoon bridges. Western sources reported the Iraqis losing a number of helicopters, tanks, and armored vehicles to Iranian antitank and antiaircraft defenses but these losses did little to stop the Iraqi counterattacks.[66] All remaining Iranian forces had been forced back into the Howeizeh marshes by March 16. With this success, Iraqi commanders unfurled the third phase of their plan. Using artillery, helicopter gunships, and mobile troops, the Iraqis harassed the Iranian retreat on March 17. By the next day, the Iraqis had recovered all of their territories. The planned Iranian offensive from Majnoon had failed to materialize. Had this attacked simultaneously with the overall *Badr* operation, the Iranians may have had more success. The Majnoon force struck too late on March 19 and 21 with both efforts repelled by the Iraqi 3rd Army Corps.

Interviews with two Iranian veterans of *Badr* detail the Achilles heel of Iranian forces: the serious shortage of heavy equipment. M. T. noted that "The Iraqis had so much artillery that they would pin us in place – then they would unleash wave upon wave of tanks followed by Republican Guard troops who were very well trained, highly motivated and willing to fight us face to face. We lacked the equipment to stop the Guards' tanks who forced us back." K. I. reported that "once we had broken through we simply had no way of advancing further once we were on open ground … our own heavy guns were too few to stop them and we simply did not have enough tanks, while Iraqi tanks attacked en masse – we had antitank weapons and knocked out some of their tanks but could not stop their advance."[67]

Operation *Badr* had proven to be a costly failure. Western analysts reported approximately 10,000 Iranians killed in exchange for just 2,000 Iraqis, with the Iranian press reporting 12,000 Iraqis killed and 3,000 taken prisoner.[68] Despite their heavy infantry losses, the Iranians had not lost much heavy equipment.[69] President Hosni Mobarak of Egypt and King Hussein of Jordan flew to Baghdad to personally congratulate Saddam Hussein on his recent success.

During Operation *Badr*, Iranian commandos managed to capture a number of Soviet-made Scud missiles.[70] Some of these Scuds may have been among those fired against Iraq during the "War of the Cities" on March 12, 1985. The Iranians were also working to reverse-engineer the Scud, eventually producing copies in Iran. Iran would receive at least 130 Soviet-made Scud missiles through Syria and North Korea.[71]

Battles over Kharq Island and the Persian Gulf

The Iraqis were not yet able to attack Iranian shipping and facilities along Iran's long Persian Gulf coastline. Iraq had been using French-built Super Frelon helicopters equipped with Exocet missiles to attack Iranian shipping in the Persian Gulf but these were of limited usefulness due to their short ranges and vulnerability to Iranian fighters and naval vessels. Aircraft such as the MiG-23 had attacked Kharq Island's shipping as early as May 1982, but Iraq still lacked the munitions, pilot training, and tactics necessary to conduct such raids. When Iraq attacked Kharq Island and other Iranian ports in the Persian Gulf in November–December 1982, Iranian Tomcat fighters shot down a Super Frelon and two MiG-25s. Despite these setbacks, Iraq launched more raids against Kharq between January and May 1983.[72] Super Frelons attacked more ships in December 1983, leading some analysts to cite this as the beginning of the "tanker war." Iraq would strike Iranian tankers, with Iran retaliating by attacking ships bound for non-Iranian ports in the Persian Gulf.

In October 1983, five Super Etendard fighter aircraft equipped with Exocet missiles leased from France arrived in Iraq.[73] These were a vast improvement over the Super Frelons but their small numbers did little to affect Iranian shipping. The Super Etendards also lacked the range to reach all of Iran's maritime and oil-loading facilities in the Persian Gulf.[74] These aircraft often attacked Iranian tankers en route to Kharq Island as well as Kharq Island itself, but made little military impression against Iranian exports as the large commercial ships were capable of surviving heavy damage.[75] Iran claimed that a Tomcat damaged one of the Super Etendards with missiles in a dogfight over Kharq on July 26 1984. Another Super Etendard was claimed as shot down on August 7, but neither claim has been verified by the French.[76] The remaining aircraft were returned by Iraq to France in 1985.[77]

Exocet-firing Mirage F-1 aircraft began their attacks against Kharq Island in August 1983, followed by more attacks in February–July 1984 and throughout 1985. The Iranians would also send their F-4s armed with air-to-surface Maverick missiles against shipping, with these operations vociferously condemned in the West. In one incident, one Iranian F-4 was shot down with another badly damaged by Saudi Arabian F-15s on June 5, 1984. The Saudi planes had been vectored in by US AWACS aircraft to intercept the Iranians operating close to the Saudi coast. Both sides then scrambled their jets and at one point 60 jets were in the vicinity, but both sides stood down and no other Saudi–Iranian clashes took place during the war.

Iranian interceptors did engage and shoot down a number of Iraqi aircraft, but their ability to attack shipping declined sharply due to a lack of spare parts. In the latter half of 1985, Iran launched only four air strikes against ships in the Persian Gulf. Irrespective of Iranian aircrafts successes in air-to-air combat and Kharq's highly effective antiaircraft defenses, Iraqi attacks against Iran's tanker traffic and Kharq inflicted serious damage to the Iranian economy.[78] Kharq's infrastructure and other oil and export facilities suffered serious blows with a total of 130 tankers mortally hit in 1984 alone. The end result by 1985 was a 55% reduction in Iranian oil exports. This was a severe blow against Iran's economy, imposing further hardships upon the Iranian populace.

Iran's post-revolutionary state combined with the ongoing war had battered the economy. Factories suffered from a shortage of skilled workers, raw materials and spare parts. Inflation went over the 50% mark by 1987.[79] Iraqi bombardment of Iranian economic facilities, especially oil tankers, ports, and loading facilities, took a very heavy toll on the economy. Oil revenues dropped from 19 billion dollars in 1983 to 12–13 billion dollars in 1984–85, then to 6.6 billion dollars in 1986, resulting in 50% unemployment by 1987.[80] Iraq also faced difficulties in its economy, but the support it received from foreign countries prevented its economy from collapsing and allowed Baghdad to transform Iraq's military into one of the world's largest by 1988.

Iran was actually spending much less on its military than Iraq at this time due to a number of factors. No major arms-producing state was willing to supply Iran with military hardware, and Iran was redeveloping its indigenous military industries. Iran was not yet able to mass-produce heavy equipment, but its ability to repair and manufacture parts was increasing. The military was also aiming for self-sufficiency in the production of ammunition, rockets, and small arms. Iran's military expenditure was also being reduced by the vast quantities of Iraqi military equipment that Iran continued to capture and utilize.

CHAPTER 36

THE CAPTURE OF FAO AND IRAN'S LAST DRIVE TO BASRA

Iran's military shortcomings in 1986-87

Iran's offensives in 1984–85 had been very costly in terms of manpower, tanks, helicopters and aircraft. Iran had also lost many experienced regular army personnel in 1983–85, who had to be replaced soon if Iran was to continue its war into Iraq. The provision of better training for personnel showed results by 1986–87 but Iran was still plagued by the inability to replace its hardware losses. The Iranians still retained around 1,000 tanks (M-47/48/60, Chieftains, and captured Iraqi Soviet-made tanks) by 1986–87. Iran had captured hundreds more Iraqi tanks and APCs but these could not be immediately pressed into service as many required new engines and spares. Iranian war industries were refurbishing existing stocks of tank engines, and producing parts and ammunition for tanks, but these could not compensate for Iraq's growing numerical edge in armor. Iran did succeed in obtaining spares for tanks, the hovercraft fleet, artillery ammunition, and SAMs through the black market in 1986. While these such deliveries did help refit some of Iran's naval and army units, these procurements could not upgrade Iran's armed forces to full strength nor could these match Iraq's massive weapons imports. Despite Iran's best efforts, only half of the army and just two-thirds of the Pasdaran were combat ready before the Fao offensives of early 1986.[1]

By 1986–87, Baghdad was able to field 4,500 tanks.[2] Iraqi tanks continued to be a mix of T-54/55/62 and the more modern T-72. Attempts were made to upgrade these tanks including air-conditioning which allowed Iraqi tank crews to fight over longer periods of time in the very hot temperatures of southern Iraq. This proved crucial as the Iraqis often used their tanks as mobile artillery platforms to counter Iranian infantry assaults. Other improvements included the installation of French fire suppression systems, and electro-optical dazzlers designed to misdirect incoming antitank missiles.[3] By 1986 the expansion of the armored wing of the Republican Guard was fully underway and these were increasingly entrusted with leading armored counterattacks against Iranian offensives.[4] Iraq's increasing edge over Iran in heavy weaponry also extended to artillery, APCs, etc. This was matched by Iraq's ever-increasing array of missiles and antiaircraft weapons. Iraqi road networks had been greatly expanded by European firms, allowing for an unprecedented increase in the efficiency and speed of military communications and transport. Other examples of European assistance include the Yugoslav-built hardened air shelters with standards superior even to NATO.

The IRIAF was having difficulties maintaining its fleet of F-4, F-5, and F-14A fighters.[5] The Tomcat F-14As were the most difficult to maintain, as many of their sensitive parts could not be manufactured in Iran. Again, clandestine contacts and black market procurements did manage to import numbers of bombs, missiles, spare parts and engines for aircraft, allowing Iran keep up to 30–35 of the first-line Tomcats operational.[6] The greatly diminished force of F-4s and F-5s were easier to maintain as Iranian aircraft industries were able to produce more and more parts indigenously. Iran then suffered a major blow when a US sting operation halted a clandestine shipment of 18 F-4s, 46 A-4s, and 13 F-5s, along with bombs, antitank missiles and advanced radars in November 1985. Had these shipments not been intercepted by US officials, Iran's subsequent breakthrough at Fao may have been even more disastrous for Iraq in 1986. The US had been clamping down against arms dealers attempting to do business with Iran; by 1984–85 Tehran was having great challenges securing spares for its US-made weapons. Despite these challenges, the IRIAF was able to maintain combat patrols over vital sectors such as Kharq Island till the last days of the war. In contrast, Iraq's air force witnessed a steady rise in its inventory of aircraft.

Val Fajr VIII: the capture of Fao

Iran launched Operation *Val Fajr VIII* on February 9, 1986. This was a three-pronged assault towards Qorna, Basra and the primary objective, Fao, which was furthest to the south. The Iranians has been assembling a vast array of pontoon bridging equipment and amphibious assault craft for this operation since December 1985.[7] The aim was to cross the Arvand Rud/Shaat al Arab waterway, capture Fao and Um al-Qasr and punch from there towards the Kuwaiti border. This would extend full Iranian control to the lower reaches of the waterway and knock out Iraqi antiship missiles and naval facilities. Capturing this territory would allow the Iranians to form a salient against Basra from the south.

The operation opened a diversionary move towards Qorna. This was well-planned as the Iraqis were expecting a new attack towards the Basra-Baghdad highway. This time the Iranians committed the 92nd Armored Division supported by the 12th Infantry Division against the Iraqi 1st and 5th Mechanized Divisions.[8] This resulted in major tank duels, which were risky given the Iranians' low numbers of tanks. This may partly explain why the Iranian offensive in this sector petered out by February 11. Nevertheless, the operation had succeeded in its primary purpose. The Iraqis were kept guessing as to whether the Iranians wanted to thrust towards the Basra–Baghdad highway or were using the Qorna region as a diversion for a major thrust towards Basra.

The Iranians staged another diversionary assault towards Basra. The real objective of this attack was the Basra–Fao highway, which Iranian troops quickly reached. Essential to this assault was a surprise attack by frogmen who supported the major assault led by the Pasdaran followed by the Basij. With this success, more Pasdaran troops punched toward Um al-Rassas with the 21st and 77th Infantry Divisions of the regular army moving towards Sibeh, resulting in further cuts to the Basra–Fao highway. With these successes, the regular army quickly rushed troops and supplies across the Arvand Rud/Shaat al Arab. In contrast to the Iranians, Iraqi responses were sluggish and labored. The Iraqi 11th Motorized and 15th Mechanized Divisions proved incapable of stopping the Iranian advance. Inexplicably, the Iraqis failed to deploy their crushing edge in tanks. Iraqi air attacks were also ineffective as Iranian forces had learned to quickly disperse and camouflage into the local terrain.

The lynchpin of the assault against Fao was launched by naval and army commandos against Um al-Qasr, and the Al-Bakr, and Al-Amayah rigs. This was in preparation for the follow-up assaults of the 55th Parachute Brigade. The Iraqis reacted swiftly and repelled the commandos, forcing the 55th Paras to alter their plans. As the Iraqis were pushing back the commandos, the Pasdaran attacked simultaneously across a number of points, successfully landing in a number of locations on the western side of the Arvand Rud/Shaat al Arab waterway. These attacks caught the Iraqis by surprise and appear to have contributed to the subsequent panic that spread among local Iraqi forces. Iraqi sentry positions were quickly eliminated followed by the rapid construction of four pontoon bridges across the Arvand Rud/Shaat al Arab waterway.[9] For one of these crossings, the components of the pontoon bridge were brought forward the night before the assault, then welded together underwater. Large canisters were then pumped with oxygen, bringing the bridge steadily to the surface virtually undetected by Iraqi forces and US intelligence satellites. The building of the pontoon bridges allowed for the arrival of more regular army troops, Pasdaran and commandos. By February 10, the Iranians had broken out of their bridgeheads towards Fao. The Iraqis, still believing that the Iranians were preparing for a major Basra offensive, stationed just two mechanized divisions in the Fao theater. The Iranians then struck a major blow when their 21st Infantry Division sliced through Iraqi units, capturing prisoners and a large amount of weapons and ammunition.

Bad weather aided Iran's initial assaults as heavy rains prevented the Iraqi air force from being brought fully to bear. One strike by Iraqi Mirage F-1s did manage to temporarily knock out the radar system of a HAWK missile battery at Abadan, but this was quickly repaired. Iraqi jets dropped chemical munitions against Iranian troops but the harmful effects of the chemical weapons were diminished by the terrain and winds. The Iraqi counteroffensive was stopped by the afternoon of February 10 by Iranian antitank teams supported by TOW-firing Cobra helicopters.

The failure of Iraq's counterattacks led to the Iranian capture of Fao on February 11. Iraqi positions had already started to unravel as the local Iraqi 15th Mechanized Division and a naval brigade had been virtually wiped out. By this stage a very large quantity of advanced French-built radar systems and missiles along with scores of Soviet-built missiles, and Chinese-built shore-to-ship Silkworm missiles, had fallen into Iranian hands. Iraq's southern air defense net and antiship capabilities had now been seriously damaged. The Iraqis had successfully bombed the single Resalat fixed bridge that spanned the Arvand Rud/Shaat al Arab waterway. Iraqi chemical weapons ensured that Iranian engineers were delayed in effecting repairs. Iranian forces were now stranded on the Iraqi side of the waterway, and low on supplies. The IRIAF came to the rescue, as did the Hawk antiaircraft missile battery at Abadan. These shot down close to 20 Iraqi aircraft by February 11, enabling Iranian hovercraft and transport helicopters to land additional supplies, regular troops, and Pasdaran antitank teams. Iranian artillery was also brought across the waterway to shell Iraqi defenses.

Counterattacking Iraqi tanks, forced to operate in cluttered and marshy terrain, suffered heavy losses against Iranian antitank teams. Iranian Cobra helicopters and jets also took a heavy toll of attacking Iraqi tanks, APCs and supply columns. Iraqi artillery fire proved ineffective as the soft terrain absorbed most of the lethal effects of Iraqi conventional and chemical munitions.

The Iraqis had been slow to react as they were still unsure where the Iranians intended to strike. They finally realized that Fao was the main target and ordered their Republican Guard to attack. The Guards, heavily backed by armor, deployed from Nasseriyah to launch their counterattack on the morning of February 12. The Iranians had by now fully dug in and prepared their antitank defenses around the Fao perimeter with their Cobra helicopters still at large. The Iranians had gained another edge by having detected the position and deployment of the Guards. Just as the Republican Guard assembled to move towards Fao, multiple Iranian BM-21 launchers on the Iranian side of the waterway, opened fire. This barrage was quickly followed by ground attacks against the Guards whose tanks become bogged down in the marshy terrain.[10] The ferocity of these assaults destroyed nearly one-third of the Guards in this theater.[11] Fearing the complete loss of the Guards, the Iraqi army did its best to extricate them, relying on air strikes using chemical weapons. These proved ineffective as the close proximity of the combatants resulted in chemical munitions being accidentally dropped on Iraqi troops. The Guards then resorted to using their tanks as mobile artillery platforms; wearing out at least 200 tank-gun barrels due to constant firing.[12] The remnants of the Guards then retreated to the north.

The Iranians suffered a setback at Um al-Rassas on the afternoon of February 12 as their advance parties were thrown out by a successful Iraqi counterattack. At Um al-Rassas Iraq debuted the brand-new Brazilian Astros Multiple Launch Rocket Systems (MLRS). The Iranian defeat at Um al-Rassas actually helped the overall objective at Fao as it confused and dispersed Iraqi efforts at concentrating all their might towards Fao. By February 13 Iranian units were threatening Um al-Qasr. Iraqi army units did their best to stop them. Iraqi gunships and aircraft intervened on the battlefield and against the Abadan area, especially against its bridges. The latter was damaged, but quickly repaired by Iranian engineers. These attacks again cost the Iraqis dearly as Abadan's Hawk missile batteries continued to shoot down attacking Iraqi jets. To make matters worse for the Iraqis, the IRIAF was achieving local air superiority.

Baghdad was not prepared to concede defeat. On February 14, a large formation of Iraqi jets led by Egyptian Air Force Mirage 5SDEs struck a key Iranian airbase in the southern front close to Fao.[13] Their first pass was very successful and caused heavy damage, but the follow-up raid ran into heavy air defenses, forcing the formation to abort and return to Iraq. At the same time F-14A Tomcats appeared and scattered a number of Iraqi helicopters close to Fao. Despite Egyptian assistance, Iraq had failed to win aerial superiority.

The Iraqi army also launched a new three-column counterattack on February 14. Helicopters and observation aircraft were extensively used to help pinpoint Iraqi artillery strikes. The eastern Iraqi column advancing just south of Um al-Rassas was mainly defeated by a combination of Iranian air and artillery strikes, The central column, which had the heaviest concentration of armor, was badly mauled by the TOW missiles of Iranian antitank teams. The third (western) column, an Iraqi armored brigade, was trapped and annihilated between Khowr Abdullah and Mamlaha by Iranian troops. The Iranians had also been deploying many of the Iraqi tanks, APCs and artillery they had already captured from Iraqi forces.

More fighting raged on February 15, when an armored brigade of the Iraqi VII Corps assembled to launch a major counterattack at Fao. They were attacked by TOW-firing Cobra helicopters which destroyed large numbers of Iraqi tanks and personnel carriers. Another Iraqi armored offensive on February 17 fared no better; this too was crushed by a combination of Iranian artillery, infantry antitank teams and Cobras. Iraqi artillery and air strikes remained ineffective as the marshy terrain continued to negate much of the lethal effects of chemical munitions.

The IRIAF launched a series of well-planned strikes against Iraqi airfields in the Basra and Fao regions. These air raids were intended to goad the IrAF into attacking Iranian forces in the Fao theater. The plan succeeded: Iraqi jets flew into repositioned Iranian Hawk missile batteries and the deadly F-14 Tomcats.[14] Despite the IrAF's numerical superiority and foreign expertise, Baghdad admitted to losing up to 45–47 fighter aircraft and 10 helicopters against Iranian fighters and air defenses by February 20.[15]

The success of Iranian jets and the antiaircraft missile net had four major consequences. The first was the damage it inflicted upon the morale of Iraq's air fleet, which had lost some of its best pilots. Concerns about Iranian jets and Hawk missiles greatly impeded subsequent Iraqi attacks, which were often forced to prematurely drop their ordinance to avoid being shot down. The second consequence of Iranian air dominance at Fao was the shift of Iraqi air strikes towards civilian centers, Kharq Island and Iranian shipping in the Persian Gulf. The third consequence was that Iranian transport helicopters and naval transport vessels could rapidly bring in vital supplies and evacuate wounded troops. Iraqi jets scored one notable success against Iranian armor in the southern theater in February 1986. In this engagement an Iranian armored column of M-60 tanks, M-113 APCs and BM-21s was surprised by a flight of attacking Iraqi MiGs.[16] It is not clear how much damage was inflicted in this operation.

The Iraqi VII Corps and two mechanized brigades of the Republican Guard were now led by the battle-tested General Maher Abdul Rasheed. Rasheed began his massive attack on February 23 by first unleashing a massive artillery barrage. The effectiveness of these strikes was seriously compromised as Iranian missiles and aircraft shot down and dispersed Iraqi observation aircraft and helicopters intending to direct Rasheed's artillery. The Iraqi three-pronged offensive fared no better. IRIAF interceptors cleared the skies of Iraqi aircraft and helicopters. The Iranians took advantage of the marshy terrain by flooding as much of the area as possible, leaving Iraqi tanks with little room for maneuver, prime targets for the Iranian antitank teams. The Republican Guard fought ferociously, but without proper tank support they had little hope of success. Stubborn Iranian resistance forced the Guards and the remaining Iraqi army units to retreat. In frustration, the Iraqis fired back with their artillery, again using chemical weapons alongside conventional ammunition.

The Iraqis suffered another deadly blow at Fao on March 4. Two Iranian F-5s attacked the headquarters of Iraq's 5th Mechanized Division, killing the general and his entire staff. No Iraqi aircraft had scrambled to prevent this attack and no attempts were made to shoot down the aircraft once their mission had been completed.[17] The Iraqis realized that the key to recapturing Fao was to achieve complete mastery of the air. They were unable to dominate the IRIAF in dogfights or to knock out the deadly Iranian HAWK missile sites. To break this deadlock, Egyptian Mirage 5SDEs were again deployed to support Iraqi air strikes. These led to a powerful Iraqi air strike escorted on March 7, bombing Iranian positions in the Fao theater. Egyptian electronic countermeasures and chaff prevented Iranian missiles and antiaircraft guns from shooting down any Iraqi aircraft. While the bombing run was effective, it is not clear how much damage was inflicted on the Iranian missile sites.[18]

The Egyptian-Iraqi air strike was meant to "soften up" the Iranians in Fao for Iraq's new offensive. On March 9, they struck again with armor from three directions. A combination of helicopter and amphibious landings of commandos, massive artillery strikes and combat aircraft supported armored thrusts. They finally managed to isolate and destroy numbers of Pasdaran from the main Iranian garrison at Fao, but ultimately the Iraqi offensive was a failure. The Iranians once again dispersed and camouflaged their forces, with their TOW antitank missiles again taking a terrible toll of Iraqi tanks. While the Iranians had suffered heavy losses, Iraqi infantry had also sustained high levels of casualties. Iraqi forces had suffered their greatest defeat since 1982, and would not recapture Fao for another two years. Iraq's generals may have failed to realize that the Iranian troops and antitank teams they now faced were far better trained, led and equipped than those they had fought in 1983–85. The Iraqis also failed to counter the IRIAF's local air superiority and Iran's HAWK's antiaircraft batteries.

Theoretically the Iranians could have followed up their success at Fao with an assault on Basra. One of the veterans of the operation reported "we were full of confidence and were waiting for orders to march to Basra. Instead, to our great disappointment, we were told to stay put."[19] Iran's shortage of tanks, artillery and strike aircraft conclusively militated against a major offensive towards Basra from Fao.

In 1987, Iraq's Prime Minister Taha Yassin Ramadan accused the US of having "doctored" the satellite intelligence in 1986, leading to the Iranian occupation of Fao.[20] The Iranians were aware that US intelligence and satellite information was being passed to Saddam Hussein and had devised techniques to mislead US intelligence. The Iranians sent numerous trucks, heavy equipment, and troops to the Basra front and Howeizeh marshes. These gave off a distinct "heat signature" as the trucks and heavy equipment were constantly moving to and fro as if they were gearing up for a massive push towards Basra or the Basra–Baghdad highway. The resulting intelligence distracted the Iraqi command from the Fao theater. It was clear that the Iranians had not only improved their ability to mount multiple offensives, but were also factoring the role of US satellite intelligence into their military planning.

Following their capture of Fao, the Iranians launched operations at the mouth of the Persian Gulf waterway to secure their recent gains in southern Iraq. Operation *Karbala 3*, launched on September 3, 1986, aimed to attack Al-Amayah and the Al-Bakr platforms. This would put considerable pressure on Kuwait's Al-Bubiyan island which had been hosting Iraqi troops. The operation went smoothly at first, Iranian naval commandos and Pasdaran armed with antiaircraft weapons and shoulder-fired antiaircraft missiles, arrived on Al-Amayah in speedboats and eliminated its Iraqi troops. Almost simultaneously, Iranian artillery began pounding the Al-Bakr platform, which was then gutted by continuous explosions. The Iraqis launched a massive air attack, forcing Iranian commandos and Pasdaran to evacuate the Al-Amayah platform.[21] Despite losing their grip on Al-Amayah, the Iranians did succeed in destroying much of the platform's radar and early warning systems. Ironically, the "blinding" of Iraq's radar capabilities at Al-Amayah prompted the Americans to extend their AWACS coverage for Baghdad.

Saddam's dynamic defense strategy

After Iraq's defeat at Fao, Saddam announced the implementation of "*Al-Defa al Mutahharakka*" (Arabic: dynamic defense). The Iraqi military would abandon its system of static defense in favor of ejecting the Iranians from Iraqi territory and capturing Iranian territory.[22] Mehran was selected as the first target. A number of Iraqi officers had expressed their reservations against an attack on Mehran as it was too difficult to hold against the inevitable Iranian counterattacks.

Iraq's II Corps, supported by the IrAF, attacked across the border towards Mehran on May 15, 1986. Iraqi aircraft also launched a damaging airstrike against a railway station north of Dezful. Mehran fell three days later on May 19, after bitter battles against regular Iranian army troops. Saddam then announced that he would vacate Mehran if the Iranians gave up Fao. Tehran rejected Saddam's "exchange offer." Saddam ordered his troops to fan out and strike deeper into Iranian territory. This proved to be a serious mistake. All Iraqi attacks were defeated by TOW-firing Cobra helicopters, which knocked out an unspecified number of Iraqi tanks and armored vehicles. Iraqi troops in Mehran were also in a precarious position as Iranian troops were still located around the city's surrounding heights. Iran quietly built up its counterattacking forces and struck on June 30–July 1.[23] Mehran had been completely cleared of Iraqi troops by July 3.[24] Saddam dispatched the Republican Guard supported by Iraqi jets and helicopters to counterattack and regain Mehran the following day. The Guards were thoroughly defeated with their air and helicopter support scattered. Iraqi losses were now so severe that Iranian troops managed to cross the border into Iraq. This forced Baghdad to divert troops from the critical southern theater to help bolster the dangerous ruptures further north. Saddam's disaster at Mehran was a major blow against his prestige, and only raised Iran's stature on the battlefield.

Iraq was forced into the strategic defensive for another two years. Saddam's failure did make the West, especially the US, more determined than ever to prevent the Iranians from winning the war.

Following the defeats at Fao and Mehran the Baath regime recognized that Iraq's static defensive strategy was failing in the face of new Iranian tactics; that Iraq would not be able to sustain blows such as those suffered at Fao indefinitely; and the war of attrition was not working in Iraq's favor. The Baath party held an extraordinary congress in July 1986 and decided to expand and improve the Iraqi military, the tank and artillery arms, and the air force; to expand the road and communications networks; and develop Iraq's defense industry, aiming for total self-sufficiency. To fund these ambitious schemes, Iraq relied on its wealthy Arab brethren, especially Kuwait and Saudi Arabia, and also the US. Iraq also received valuable technical assistance from France, Britain, the Soviet Union, the US, Brazil, Venezuela, Pakistan, India, Belgium, New Zealand, South Africa, Australia, and Germany.[25] Iraq addressed its manpower problem by recruiting "volunteers" from other Arab countries such as Jordan and Egypt. Another effective policy was to allow all Iraqi Sunnis (not just those from Tikrit) to enter the prestigious Republican Guard. University students were also encouraged to apply. The end result was the introduction of a fresh batch of highly intelligent, educated and physically fit men into the Republican Guard.[26] These went a long way towards replacing the Guard's heavy losses since 1982.

American support for Iraq reached very high levels by 1986, especially after the fall of Fao. A CIA team in Baghdad prepared detailed reports of Iranian military and industrial targets most vulnerable to air strikes.[27] This resulted in crushing air raids on factories, and economic and military sites at Arak, Isfahan, Shiraz, Iran's ports, and Khuzistan and Kermanshah provinces between August 1 and November 1986. The most devastating strike came on October 15, 1986, when the Iraqi air force bombed Shiraz international airport, destroying vital 747 air-to-air tankers and C-130 transport aircraft on the ground. Punishing Iraqi air raids continued well into 1987.

The Iran-Contra affair

Despite the state of Washington–Tehran relations, a number of US officials were concerned as to what would happen in post-Khomeini Iran. There were genuine fears that the country could break into a civil war, allowing the Soviets to extend their influence onto the Iranian plateau. The Cold War was still a reality in mid-1980s and the US was apprehensive of Soviet goals not only in Iran, but the wider region, especially the Persian Gulf. US worries were compounded as Soviet influence in Iran increased. As access to US-built spares and weapons systems became increasingly limited, the Iranians turned to Soviet-built antiaircraft and surface-to-surface missiles. Iran purchased these through third-party contacts but the transactions had Soviet approval.

The Israeli position was basically in favor of having the Iran–Iraq War continue.[28] From the Israeli and the American perspective, neither an Iranian nor an Iraqi victory was palatable. An Iranian victory would lead to the fall of Iraq, and at the very least encourage anti-Western and anti-Israeli Islamist movements across the Middle East. Tehran would also be able to link up with Syria through conquered Iraq. Western oil interests and tanker traffic would also be sitting astride a strengthened Iran. An outright Iraqi victory would also be harmful to Israeli and Western interests as Saddam Hussein could lay claim to the leadership of the Arab world. This would create a dangerous unified Arabian front against Israel and challenge Western petro-economic interests in the Persian Gulf. A victorious and/or militarily mighty Iraq could also opt to annex small but oil-wealthy neighboring Arab states, as later happened with Kuwait.

Spearheading the drive for a Tehran–Washington rapprochement was Robert McFarlane, US National Security Advisor. By May 1984 five US citizens had been kidnapped by pro-Iranian Lebanese Shiite militias. McFarlane hoped to secure the release of the hostages and revive Washington's ties with Tehran at Soviet expense. By 1985 a number of secret meetings had taken place between Iranian and American officials, despite US media describing Iran as an anti-American terrorist state.[29] A pro-Syrian Lebanese newspaper, the *Shiraa*, exposed the US–Iranian contacts on November 4, 1986 by reporting on McFarlane's visit to Tehran.[30] The stage had been set for the Iran-Contra scandal.

Iran obtained large numbers of missiles between August 1985 and November 1986. A total of at least 2,008 TOW antitank missiles, 238 Hawk antiaircraft missiles and spare parts arrived in Iranian ports.[31] Numbers of the HAWK antiaircraft missiles were from Israeli stocks that were past their shelf-life and were of dubious reliability. Iran's domestic military industries had to restore these to battlefield readiness.[32]

While much media coverage was given to the arms sales to Tehran, little attention was shed upon Western support for Saddam Hussein's military machine. International military, financial and political backing for Baghdad far surpassed that afforded to Iran, dwarfing the arms shipments to Iran as a result of Iran-Contra.[33] The Iran-Contra scandal increased Tehran's diplomatic isolation, and pushed the US and the West closer towards Saddam Hussein. Western public opinion remained unfavorable to Iran, due to memories of the hostage crisis and Iran's links with Lebanese Shiite militias responsible for taking Western hostages, hijackings, etc.[34] Iran's "image problem" in the West was further compounded by the clerical leadership's constant anti-Western rhetoric. The monarchies of Jordan, Saudi Arabia, Kuwait, and the Persian Gulf were especially wary of Tehran's anti-monarchial messages. There were also fears of a pan-Islamic takeover of Iraq and the

Persian Gulf region, leading many Arab states (except Syria and Libya) to support Iraq. Even long-time foes Pakistan and India found common ground against Iran. All of these factors, in combination with the Iran-Contra scandal, benefitted Saddam Hussein as his regime enjoyed unconditional financial, moral, economic and military support from the West, the Eastern bloc and the majority of the Arab world; the international community ignored the Baathist regime's abysmal human rights record; and looked askance whenever Iraq deployed chemical weapons in direct contravention of the Geneva Convention. The expanding Arab-Western-Soviet alliance in support of Saddam greatly alarmed Iran's military leaders and the more pragmatic members of the leadership (notably Rafsanjani). Iraq's military strength was now expanding at an astonishing rate, and the US was promoting a strict arms embargo against Iran.[35] Time was now running out for Tehran.

Karbala 4: Iran's failed attack at Um al-Rassas

After their success in Fao, the Iranian high command conducted a number of studies in May–August 1986 to find ways of breaking through Basra's defenses. A serious wedge again developed between the military's "maximalists" and "minimalists." The "maximalists," led by Mohsen Rezai, commander of the Pasdaran, and the conservative clerics wanted an all-out frontal assault against Basra. They believed that such an offensive would capture the city and end the war in Iran's favor. The "minimalists" represented by a number of Pasdaran commanders and the majority of regular army commanders, including army chief of staff Shirzai, disagreed. They argued that any direct offensive against Basra was extremely risky, given the city's formidable defenses and overwhelming strength in armor, airpower and artillery. The "minimalists" argued that Iran's best option given Iraq's edge in heavy weaponry and air power was to continue a slow war of attrition. These disagreements led to a bitter falling out between Shirazi and Rezai, resulting in the former's removal from command.[36] The "maximalists" again prevailed.

The finalized plan was to drive into the 3rd and 7th Iraqi Army corps with at least 200,000 troops. To counter Iraq's air raids against Iranian positions and supply lines, a number of antiaircraft guns and missile batteries were brought forward to the Basra front. Air sorties were planned by the IRIAF with reconnaissance provided by Iranian-built camera-equipped drones.

Thanks to the sheer size of the Iranian preparations and US intelligence, the Iraqis were aware of the coming Iranian offensive. Baghdad launched a massive pre-emptive strike in mid-October, unleashing a series of very effective air strikes targeting Iranian bridges, supply lines, and military centers in the Khorramshahr–Abadan area. Probably the most successful Iraqi air-to-ground operation of the war thus far, it reduced Iranian military engineering and road construction capabilities by 75–85%.[37] These bombing runs severely diminished Iran's ability to conduct its upcoming offensive.

Undeterred, the Iranians launched their offensive on December 24. Things went very wrong from the start. As the Pasdaran lunged towards Um al-Rassas Island near Basra, the Iraqis shot them to pieces in their boats. A handful landed on parts of the island only to be crushed the following day in a withering Iraqi counterattack. Iraqi aircraft had harassed Iranian preparations from the night of December 23, severely disorganizing their intended assaults. Iraqi aircraft continued their devastating bombing runs on the eastern (Iranian) side of the Arvand Rud/Shaat al Arab waterway, preventing the Iranians from sending in reinforcements for their stranded forces at Um al-Rassas.

This victory finally brought the morale booster the Iraqis needed after their defeats at Fao and Mehran the previous year. Tehran did its best to put a gloss on this defeat by attempting to downplay its original scope and objectives. Saddam and the Iraqi military now made the mistake of underestimating the Iranian military's capacity for launching yet another strike. The Iraqis also failed to appreciate that the Iranians had been holding back much of their best weaponry and aircraft for their most powerful assault yet against Basra.

Iran's final push to Basra: *Karbala 5*

Tehran was now determined to deliver the "knockout" blow against Basra. The Iranian strategy had been to either storm Basra directly or to sever it from Baghdad by cutting the connecting highway. These strategies had failed due to fierce Iraqi resistance. Now the Iranians would have to confront Basra's formidable defense works. These had been under construction since at least 1981, and consisted of powerful bunkers, artificial water barriers, earthworks and barbed wire.

The Iraqis had also taken advantage of the segment of the Arvand Rud/Shaat al Arab waterway to the southeast of Basra. As early as 1981, the Iraqis had constructed a huge trench three yards deep, nineteen miles long and three-quarters of a mile wide.[38] Using the waterway, the Iraqis pumped water into four canals, the largest which was named Jasim. By 1983, these works had been extended into a large water reservoir known as "Fish Lake," which was then extended into channels towards Khorramshahr and the north.[39] By 1987, Fish Lake had extensive underwater barbed wires, sensors and electrodes, making it an even more formidable barrier.[40]

Any direct Iranian drive to Basra would be forced to cross two artificial waterways. Behind each were radar-guided artillery systems, large numbers of ground-attack aircraft, and combat helicopters. A number of earth barriers were also constructed to prevent the Iranians from draining the water defenses. The Iraqis also constructed very formidable land defenses ahead of their artificial lakes in addition to those to their rear. Continued improvements to the defense works ensured that any Iranian assault on Basra would be an extremely formidable task.

Fish Lake was the boundary between the Iraqi 3rd and 7th Army corps, and it was here that the Iranians chose to launch Operation *Karbala 5*. Despite their formidable defenses and overall military edge, the Iraqis were caught by surprise. An initial strike force of 35,000 Pasdaran successfully crossed Fish Lake just after midnight on January 8, 1987. The southern end of Fish Lake was attacked by four Iranian divisions on the night of January 9, capturing the town of Duaji. Surprise was complete when the Iranians used Duaji as a springboard to capture Shalamcha. Iranian tanks also broke through two of four defense lines at the northern extension of Fish Lake. This action aimed to prevent the Iraqis from lunging at the flank of their first assault axis a little further to the south of Fish Lake. The Iranians then reinforced their troops at Shalamcha with up to 65,000 troops. These concentrated on clearing Iraqi troops from the territory between the Arvand Rud/Shaat al Arab waterway and Fish Lake.

The Iraqis counterattacked with large numbers of infantry as early as January 9. Aircraft and artillery bombed the Iranians furiously, again using chemical munitions. Iraqi air strikes, using the newer Su-25 and MiG-29 aircraft, also threatened to disrupt Iran's fragile supply lines to the west of Fish Lake. By January 10, the Iraqis were throwing all available infantry, tanks, artillery, helicopter gunships and aircraft in a bid to eject the Iranians. The situation threatened to become another Um al-Rassas type disaster for the Iranians, but this time the Iranians were prepared. Iraqi tanks and armored vehicles rushing forward were badly mauled by deadly TOW antitank missiles fired by Iranian antitank teams and Cobra helicopters. Iraqi artillery was more difficult to silence, but the impact of their shells was diminished by the marshy terrain.[41] Iraqi aircraft and helicopters were countered by HAWK missile batteries, Chinese-built HQ2s and Iran's new Swedish-designed shoulder-fired short-range RBS-70.[42] The cost of *Karbala 5* to the Iraqi air force and helicopter fleet was very heavy; the Iraqis later admitted to US authorities that they had lost 10% of their aircraft (50–60 jets).[43] These losses forced Baghdad to curtail its air strikes against advancing Iranian troops.

Much like at Fao in 1986, superior Iraqi firepower in the air and on the ground had failed to eject the Iranians from their positions. This can be attributed to several factors. The training and leadership of the Pasdaran had further improved and they now attacked with specific military objectives, coordinating their assaults with efficient logistical support. Iranian troops as a whole were now much better armed, especially with antitank and antiaircraft missiles. The TOW-firing Cobra helicopters proved effective, taking a heavy toll of Iraqi tanks and armored vehicles north of Fish Lake and preventing the Iraqis from pushing the Iranians out of the western end of the lake. The Cobras also destroyed a large number of Soviet- and Swiss-built antiaircraft batteries. The Iranians utilized their antiaircraft missiles as effectively as they had at Fao the previous year, and made maximum use of their aircraft. Despite being outnumbered 10–1 in the air, Iranian F-4 and F-5 aircraft did manage to stage a number of effective bombing runs against the Iraqi positions.[44] The threat posed by Iran's very limited number of operational aircraft explains why Iraq ordered 18,000 SAM missiles from France and fielded around sixty SAM sites in the Basra theater alone.[45] Iran's limited stock of Tomcats was kept back in the "fire brigade" role, intervening only in situations of absolute necessity.

Iraq's formidable land and water barriers came to its rescue, slowing down the Iranian advance and buying Baghdad just enough time to stabilize the situation. The Iranians cleared the Iraqis out of most of the secondary defensive positions, but the primary Iraqi defensive positions were too well-defended. No amount of daring, tenacity or innovation in infantry tactics could compensate for the Iranians' lack of heavy military equipment and strike aircraft. Every Iraqi bunker in the primary defense lines was like a mini-fortress and supplied with massive stocks of ammunition, supplies, and weapons. A week into the offensive Iran had only gained a mere 26 square miles between the Arvand Rud/Shaat al Arab waterway and Fish Lake.

Iraqi aircraft reappeared over the battlefield on January 12–14. Iranian aircraft once again dominated in dogfights and effectively bombed Iraqi troop concentrations and armored assets. Instead of sending more aircraft to overwhelm the Iranians in the air, the Iraqi high command decided to divert its assets towards the bombing of Iranian cities, Kharq Island and Iranian shipping. While these were "softer" targets, this denied Iraqi land forces the shielding they needed against Iranian air strikes. The Iraqis soon realized their mistake and returned their aircraft to Basra. These air strikes, combined with massive artillery barrages and chemical weapons, halted the Iranian advance. Iraq continued to lose numerous aircraft.

Iran responded by unleashing the second phase of its drive to Basra. Pasdaran troops attacked on January 12, breaching the fourth of Basra's five major defense lines. This success allowed Iranian military engineers to construct a route across Fish Lake, finally ensuring the regular arrival of reinforcements and supplies. The Iraqis counterattacked against the Pasdaran at Buwariyan Island in the Shalamcha area. The Pasdaran held their ground but were barred from further advances towards Basra. Iraqi artillery fire, aerial bombardment, and chemical weapons continued to pound the Iranians and slow their advance. But despite their heavy firepower, the Iraqis faced great difficulties. Iranian TOW missiles often punched through the thick walls of Iraqi bunkers with deadly results. TOW-firing Cobra helicopters continued to take a heavy toll of Iraqi tanks and armored vehicles. By January 15, the Iranians were just 9–12 miles (14–20km) from the city. Iranian TV even showed footage of Basra's outskirts, but the Iranians could go no further. The momentum of the advance was lost by January 27, bringing Operation *Karbala 5* to an end.

The Iranians struck again towards Basra from Fish Lake and Shalamcha in Operation *Karbala 8* on April 7. The Pasdaran had attempted more probing attacks during February, but their efforts continued to be stymied. The one solace was that the Iraqi air force had scaled back its operations due to Iran's few jet fighters and ground missiles. This helped them make new preparations from late February until early April. From the outset of the offensive, the mainly infantry force suffered very heavy losses against dense and powerful Iraqi defenses. Just four days into the attack, the Republican Guard, supported by tanks, chemical weapons, and the Iraqi air force, counterattacked and forced the Pasdaran back to their original positions. Iraqi air force activity resumed successfully, pounding Iranian targets, bridges, and supply lines in the Abadan-Khorramshahr areas and Shalamcha. The Iranian offensive in the south had finally died out by April 12. This marked the end of Iran's last major offensive against Basra.

Many Iranian regular army contingents were being concentrated towards the north, facing the Soviet Union, which was concentrating its military forces along its borders with Iran.[46] Iraq now accused the US of "making exaggerated assessments of the Soviet military build-ups on the Iranian borders."[47] The forced absence of these units from the Iraqi theater was of great assistance to Baghdad. The mere presence of a Soviet military threat was enough to produce jitters in Tehran, which was closer to the Soviet border than it was to Baghdad. Memories of past wars with Tsarist Russia were very much alive in the Iranian army.

Attacking the central and northern sectors: battles in Iraqi Kurdistan

Iran, supported by local Kurdish dissidents, launched a successful operation into Iraqi Kurdistan on February 24, 1986. Codenamed Operation *Valfajr 9*, the Iranians and their Iraqi-Kurdish allies thrust into the Sulaymānīyah area. The new territorial gains meant that the Iranians could now threaten Darbandikhan dam, Baghdad's chief source of electricity, and the area provided a staging post for future operations into the region.

Iran's objectives in Iraqi Kurdistan soon focused on the Haj Omran valley. The Iraqis had staged massive helicopter raids from this area into Iran just as they were attacking Mehran in May 1986. Iran wanted to capture Haj Omran as this would open a direct route towards Irbil. These objectives materialized in Operation *Karbala 2*, launched on September 1, 1986. The operation failed as Iraqi aircraft repelled Iranian troops using chemical bombs. Iran's setback at Haj Omran was compensated by its effective use of commando forces on October 11, 1986. The Pasdaran's special forces landed inside Iraqi Kurdistan as far as Kirkuk. They attacked Kirkuk's oil facilities, local airbase, and SAM sites. Attacking in concert with local Kurdish allies, they destroyed some aircraft at the airbase, inflicted damage to the oil infrastructure, and SAM sites. Mortars fired by the commandos prevented the Iraqis from scrambling their aircraft. While certainly spectacular, such raids could do little to win the war for Iran.

To help divert the Iraqi high command from reinforcing Basra to the south, the regular army staged a powerful assault towards Qasr-e Shirin on January 13, 1987. Codenamed *Karbala 6*, this operation claimed to have ejected Iraqi troops from 100 square miles of Iranian territory. A similar attack had been launched a day before towards the border town of Naft-e Shahr. These attacks succeeded in drawing away some Iraqi units in the south, providing some relief to the Pasdaran fighting in the Basra theater.

Iran renewed its attempts to enter Haj Omran in 1987. Operation *Karbala 7* was launched on March 4, 1987, by the Pasdaran supported by the regular army. This time their combined efforts succeeded in capturing Haj Omran's snowy and mountainous peaks. The Iraqis launched a number of desperate but futile counterattacks, losing unspecified numbers of tanks.[48] These operations were followed by *Karbala 10* in late April 1987, when the Pasdaran thrust into northeast Iraq's Mavoot area.[49] Baghdad claimed to have defeated the Pasdaran but Tehran denied this.[50]

War of the Cities ... again

Iraq was able to use its numerical advantage in aircraft to apply pressure on Iranian civilian and population centers, often in response to major Iranian offensives. The bombing of Iranian cities intensified with Saddam Hussein's defeats at Fao in 1986 and the powerful Iranian offensive at Basra in 1987. Iraqi air raids were very damaging in October 1987, especially to refining facilities in Ahvaz, Kermanshah and Shiraz.

Iran's air defense net was unable to detect all possible Iraqi ingress routes. These "blind spots" were used by the Iraqi air force to penetrate Iran's airspace. Limited numbers of antiaircraft missiles and artillery made it impossible for Iran to protect all of its cities. Iraqi jets arrived at speed, released their ordinance and accelerated back to Iraq. This tactic was highly effective as metropolitan centers did not require precise targeting, and the rapid escape minimized the risk from Iran's limited stock of interceptors. To counter the danger of Iranian interceptors, the Iraqis often launched "baits" such as the high-flying and rapid MiG-25s.[51] These attempted to draw Iranian fighters away from Iraqi bombers. Iranian air defenses in cities such as Arak, Ahvaz and Tehran did manage shoot down numbers of Iraqi aircraft.[52] Iranian interceptors maximized their low numbers by engaging in longer air patrols, allowing them to destroy a number of Iraqi aircraft during the renewed "War of the Cities."

Iran's Fao offensive in February 1986 resulted in massive air strikes against Iranian cities. The first of these occurred on February 15, just as Iraqi forces were launching their counterattack at Fao. Other raids against civilian targets occurred, notably against Arak on July 27, 1986, and the bombing of the Dez hydroelectric plant on October 15. The pressure of Iran's *Karbala 5* offensive prompted Saddam Hussein to launch a fresh round of the "War of the Cities." On January 12, 1987, over 100

Iraqi aircraft crossed into Iranian airspace to bomb over 60 Iranian industrial, communications and civilian centers. This round of bombings lasted for 42 days. In response, the Iranians staged a highly successful bombing run with just four F-4 fighter-bombers on February 15 against Iraq's H-2 pumping station situated on the oil pipeline to Jordan. The efficacy of this attack combined with pressure from Baghdad's Soviet allies obliged Saddam to put an end to the air raids.

Kharq Island and Persian Gulf battles

Baghdad's defeat at Fao resulted in the loss of a major base coordinating Iraqi air strikes against Kharq Island and Persian Gulf shipping. This failed to dissuade the Iraqis from attacking a number of Kharq-bound ships with Mirage F-1 aircraft in March 1986. The Iranians retaliated with F-4 fighter-bombers and helicopters against Iraqi shipping towards Saudi Arabian and Bahraini ports. The Iraqis struck at Kharq Island in late April 1986, damaging portions of its infrastructure, causing a serious (albeit temporary) disruption in Iranian oil exports.

Iraqi attacks against Kharq in 1986 reached a climax in July, but their efforts to knock out the facility again proved unsuccessful. Tehran decided to find other (safer) routes for its tanker traffic. Construction began almost immediately at Larak at the Straits of Hormuz, Jask, Bandar Lengeh and Qeshm Island with Sirri's existing facilities being expanded. The Iraqis adapted quickly, attacking Iranian shipping between Kharq and Larak on August 7, 1986. A more dramatic raid by Mirage F-1 aircraft occurred against Sirri just five days later on August 12. The bombing raid took the Iranians completely by surprise and left one of their tankers disabled. The raid compelled the Iranians to transfer more of their loading assets to other ports, notably Larak. Western media reports noted that the Sirri raid had been made possible by heavily laden Iraqi aircraft refueling in mid-air, to fly over 1,300km. What the Western press failed to report was that nearly all of the pilots who partook in the Sirri raid were of non-Iraqi nationality. The "Iraqi jets" then attacked Farsi Island's loading terminals and radar station on August 28, 1986. After Sirri, the Iranians hit back by targeting Iraq-bound shipping with F-4s.

The Iraqis returned to Kharq again on October 6 and disabled one of the island's Hawk missile batteries, but other Iranian missiles shot down one of the Iraqi Mirages. The main terror for the "Iraqi jets" proved to be the venerable F-14 Tomcats. These quickly scrambled from Bushehr to shoot down two more Mirages. Another raid was launched against Kharq the next day, and this time the Mirages put the island's loading berths temporarily out of action. When the Mirages returned on October 8, two Tomcats were waiting. Only one Mirage reached Kharq, as the Tomcats shot down three Mirages and scattered the rest. The Iraqis tried attacking Kharq again with Mirages on October 14, but were again forced back after one of their aircraft was destroyed by patrolling Tomcats. An even more dramatic long-range engagement took place on November 25 in which "Iraqi jets" engaged in air-to-air refueling to bomb Larak near the Straits of Hormuz. Despite the Tomcats' successes, Iraqi strikes became so frequent that they often caused damages to Kharq's facilities as well as Iranian tanker traffic. These strikes along with the decline in world oil prices put a considerable strain on the Iranian economy in 1986.

By 1987, all the damaged facilities at Kharq Island were repaired, and the island boasted a deadly network of radar-guided missiles capable of defending against low- and medium-level air strikes.

Hardened shelters were also built to help protect the island's facilities against air attacks. More difficult to verify are Iranian claims of having developed electronic jamming devices (or beacons) at Kharq, capable of deflecting Exocet missiles. The IRIAF's limited stock of Tomcats was available to defend against Iraqi air strikes.

The Iraqis began their 1987 operations on a high note by launching yet another attack against Larak on January 25, 1987. A series of intense raids occurred between March 21 and 23 but these failed to cut off tanker traffic to Kharq Island. Kharq's defenses combined with the ability of Iranian interceptors to scramble quickly finally forced the Iraqis to scale down their raids against the island.

Iraq launched a very powerful series of strikes with its Mirages against Iranian tanker traffic, Larak, and Sirri on August 29–31, 1987. Contrary to Western reports, not all of these missions were successful. Many Iranian tankers were damaged by Exocet missiles, but a number of Iraqi attacks were dispersed by patrolling F-14A Tomcats and ground-based missiles, which shot down three or four Mirages. The Iraqis struck and severely damaged a number of tankers again on September 21–27 and October 16, as well as numerous other strikes in November and December 1987 but these failed to cut off Iranian oil exports.

The West moves into the Persian Gulf

Iraqi air strikes against shipping had been very successful in the greater geopolitical sphere. While Iranian fighters raided Iraqi oil facilities around Kirkuk and Basra, these failed to affect Iraq's growing ability to export its oil. By 1987 overland routes for the export of Iraqi oil had been established through Turkey and Saudi Arabia. Kuwait was marketing up to 300,000 barrels of oil on a daily basis on Baghdad's behalf.[53] While Iran's relations with Turkey were cordial, Arab states were openly pro-Saddam and had little desire to facilitate Iranian oil exports.

Saddam Hussein's attacks against Persian Gulf shipping were calculated to internationalize the conflict against Iran. Iraqi attacks provoked Iranian responses against international shipping, especially Kuwaiti and Saudi tankers, which rallied Arab and Western powers against Iran. By mid-October 1986, Iranian war vessels were attempting to inspect all ships for possible Iraqi bound military cargo. These actions, in concert with Iranian attacks on a number of ships bound for the Arab littoral states, encouraged the latter to look for foreign powers to intervene in the Persian Gulf.

American policy makers had been concerned with the fighting in the Persian Gulf, fearing disruption of tanker traffic in the Straits of Hormuz. This had resulted in the dispatch of a carrier group to the Gulf of Oman as early as summer 1983. The Royal Navy also prepared a number of its Mediterranean ships for deployment into the Persian Gulf. By early 1987 both the US Navy (USN) and the Royal Navy had increased the numbers of their warships in the Persian Gulf, with the French dispatching an aircraft carrier group to the region. US commando and SEAL personnel were also brought closer to the southern Iranian coastline.

Iraqi–US cooperation with respect to battlefield intelligence had now extended into the Persian Gulf. The Iranians, clearly concerned, began to lay mines around the Straits of Hormuz and the approaches to Kuwaiti ports. Chinese-built Silkworm missiles were installed between Fao and Bandar Abbas. Tensions were inevitably rising between Iran and the West, much to Saddam's delight. The Iranians had no desire to be drawn into any military conflict against the far more powerful Western navies. Such an unequal military contest would divert Iran's limited military resources away from Iraq, exactly as Saddam wished.

On May 15, 1987, an Iraqi Mirage fired Exocet missiles into a USN warship, USS *Stark*, killing 37 crewmembers and injuring 11. Iraq later explained that its pilot had mistaken the USS *Stark* for an Iranian frigate. The reactions of the US political and media outlets were surprisingly restrained, instead lashing out at Iran as the main culprit for rising tensions. The USS *Stark* incident had clearly demonstrated how politically isolated the Iranians had become in the international arena.

The IRIN won a small-scale engagement against Iraqi patrol boats near the Al-Amayah platforms in late July 1987, but this could not alter Iran's deteriorating strategic situation. Concerns with Iranian activities against Kuwait prompted the USN to escort Kuwaiti tankers by July 1987 (Operation *Earnest Will*). Tensions rose higher when a US tanker was hit by a mine around Farsi Island on July 24, followed by the damaging of two more commercial vessels on August 11 and 15 in the Gulf of Oman. These incidents prompted the USN and Royal Navy to dispatch more minesweepers into the Persian Gulf to join US aircraft carriers and battleships already in the area. USN battleship missiles could now target almost any location inside of Iran.

Iran in the meantime had continued its inspection of ships ferrying possible military supplies for Iraq. The IRIN also deployed helicopters and aircraft to direct strikes against shipping. Iraqi aircraft were now forewarned by USN forces whenever Iranian interceptors were detected. This helped spare many Iraqi jets from destruction. The US was also confronting Iranian jets in the Persian Gulf. On August 8, two USN Tomcats fired at two Iranian F-4s approaching a USN task force. The Iranian F-4s evaded the missiles, but Iranian-US tensions continued to escalate.

Tensions took a turn for the worse when Iran fired a Silkworm missile against Kuwait on September 4, 1987, followed by two further Silkworm launches. These strikes failed to damage any Kuwaiti oil installations. On September 24, 1987, an Iranian supply ship, the *Iran Ajr*, was intercepted by USN ships just as it was laying mines near Bahrain. The vessel was tracked by US forces for some time, then seized by USN SEAL commandos. This was a major public relations coup against Tehran, as the US presented the *Iran Ajr* case as evidence of Iranian aggression.

The Pasdaran had been using speedboats to attack ships in the Persian Gulf. The USN was on guard for these and on October 8, their helicopters destroyed four Pasdaran speedboats. This clash did little to dissuade the Pasdaran who continued their attacks against tanker traffic. Silkworms were fired against Kuwaiti-bound tankers on October 15 and 16 causing extensive damage to two ships. The USN retaliated on October 19 by sending in four warships to destroy the Reshadat and Resalat oil rigs, which had been used by the Pasdaran to stage their speedboat raids against tankers. Three days later, the Iranians successfully fired a Silkworm into Kuwait, inflicting serious damage against one of its major tanker terminals.

Encouraged by Iran's increased preoccupation with the USN in the Persian Gulf, Iraq made its most determined bid to destroy all IRIAF air bases in Khuzistan during November and December 1987. The main targets were Omidiyeh, Masjed-Soleiman, Ahvaz, and especially Vahdati. Excepting some damage inflicted upon Vahdati, the Iraqi bombing effort was a resounding failure. Iranian fighters, antiaircraft missiles and antiaircraft artillery destroyed up to 30 attacking Iraqi aircraft. Iraq's failure ensured that Iran's limited numbers of aircraft would remain operational in Khuzistan until the end of the war.

CHAPTER 37

THE END OF THE WAR

The expansion of Saddam Hussein's war machine

By 1988 Baghdad's massive military expansion program had resulted in the creation of a gigantic army composed of 50 divisions in nine corps. Despite having a population one-third the size of Iran's, Iraq had surpassed Iran in numbers of troops. The Iraqi military now fielded 955,000 troops versus Iran's 655,000.[1] This was due to Baghdad's extension of conscription, efficient recruitment from across Iraqi's private, agricultural, industrial and university sectors. Large numbers of foreign laborers were brought in prevent the Iraqi economy from collapsing. This massive expansion was accompanied by parallel developments in Iraq's non-conventional weapons sectors, especially in chemical-biological weapons, ballistic missiles and even a "supergun," a super long-range artillery system which reached design stage just before the ceasefire.[2]

Diplomatically, Iraq was enjoying excellent relations with the US, the West and the Soviet/Eastern bloc. A key diplomatic shift in Iraq's favor occurred when Mikhail Gorbachev became the USSR's last head of state. When elected general secretary of the Communist Party in 1985, Gorbachev had significantly increased Soviet military aid to Iraq. The Soviets had established an air bridge between Moscow and Baghdad, from January 1, 1987, allowing Saddam to safely receive the best Soviet weaponry. These significantly enhanced Iraq's military advantages over Iran. By 1988 Iraq's 5,500 tanks outnumbered Iran's machines by more than five to one.[3] Although estimates vary, Iraq's 800–900 fighter aircraft outnumbered Iran's by a margin of around ten to one by 1988.[4] The Americans, notably Richard Murphy, seemed pleased with Gorbachev's efforts as these supported Iraqi (military) actions, especially during the "Scud Duel" between Tehran and Baghdad in April 1988.[5] Iran viewed Gorbachev's increasingly pro-Iraq position as part of his overall effort to woo the West towards the Soviet Union.[6] The Gorbachev administration even softened its stance against the proposed US-sponsored arms embargo against Iran.[7]

Eastern Europe was closely involved with Iraq's military build-up. Czechoslovakia, Poland, and East Germany provided training, technical expertise and specialized engineers.[8] Yugoslavia afforded extensive support by provided pilot training, technicians, engineers, refurbishing Iraqi aircraft in Yugoslavia, and built a large number of improved runways, underground facilities, and hardened shelters.[9] Western countries, including Belgium, Switzerland, Britain, and Italy, joined the Yugoslavs in building Iraqi "superbases" at a cost of over 4.3 billion dollars. Most of these became operational by late 1987.

Britain and the US were exporting their most advanced super computers and electronic equipment to Iraq.[10] By 1988, 18 US corporations were providing military hardware to Saddam.[11] Perhaps the most significant US support was in the transfer of military technology, including equipment for the production of chemical weapons.[12] The US was also ready to militarily intervene on behalf of Iraq, with contingency plans drawn up for if the Iranians broke through Iraqi lines.[13] British aid became very significant by January 1987[14] with the dispatch of items such as aircraft and helicopter engines, ejection seats, air defense simulators, spares for armored vehicles, naval assault craft (and spares), depleted uranium and plutonium, radar systems, communications gear (and spares), light weapons, body armor, and night vision equipment.[15] Britain also supplied unspecified numbers of hovercraft, Saboteur APCs and the latest Sea King helicopters.[16] Britain also trained up to 4,000 Iraqi military personnel during the war.[17] Britain also worked at refurbishing captured Iranian Chieftains for Iraqi service.[18] Other Western powers including Austria, South Africa, West Germany, Italy, France, and Chile provided Saddam with a plethora of weapons systems.[19] Western laser technology was also adapted to blind or damage the vision of at least 2,000 Iranian troops during the war.[20]

One of the least reported facets of the Iran–Iraq War was the crucial role played by foreign mercenary pilots. Examples include the Sirri raid of August 12, 1986, which was conducted by 23 mercenary pilots, including Belgians, Pakistanis, West Germans, Australians, South Africans, and New Zealanders.[21] The Larak raid of November 25, 1986 was led by the Belgian veteran Max von Rosen.[22] East German and Russian pilots flew MiG-25s in deep raids inside Iran, with several highly experienced Russian pilots being shot down by Iranian F-14As.[23] Iraq deployed mercenaries because they had lost many experienced pilots, who could not be replaced quickly. After Iran's Operation *Karbala 5* the Iraqi air force was left with just 100 qualified pilots, with only half of these fit for dangerous missions.[24] Despite the large numbers and increasing sophistication of the Iraqi air fleet, Iranian antiaircraft defenses and Iranian fighters, flown by excellent Iranian pilots, remained very dangerous.

Arab "volunteers," particularly Jordanians, Egyptians, Lebanese, Syrians, Tunisians, Algerians, and Palestinians, were now fully integrated into the Iraqi army. Jordan played a key role in acting as a conduit for British arms destined for Iraq.[25] Saudi Arabia aided the Iraqi war effort by allowing Iraqi aircraft to land at its airbases for refueling and repairs.[26] Egypt became the third largest supplier of weapons to Iraq after the former Soviet Union and France.[27] Egypt also supplied stocks of chemical weapons. Egyptian officers, commandos and professional troops also took part in combat operations against Iran. The scale of Egyptian commitment is evidenced by the fact that nearly 3,000 Egyptians were held in Iranian POW camps by 1988, though many of these may have been non-military Egyptian guest workers forcibly pressed into Iraqi military service.

Vigorous attempts were made to make Iraq as self-sufficient as possible in weapons production. Iraq was already self-sufficient in light weapons and produced copies of Soviet and Yugoslav automatic rifles, light and heavy machineguns. Iraq began producing its own artillery, including copies of the Yugoslav version of the Soviet 122mm howitzer known as the *Saddam*. Gun barrels for the 155mm howitzer were also being produced with plans to re-barrel existing Soviet-built 130mm and 152mm guns. The *Al-Jaleel* mortar series, which included the 60mm, 82mm, 120mm and 160mm Yugoslav-based models, were all produced in Iraq. Iraq produced a variety of other weapons systems including rocket launchers and guided bombs.[28] The RPG-7 rocket launcher was produced in Iraq as the *Al-Nassira*.[29] Iraq's military industrialization program was assisted by a variety of international technical staff from countries such as India, France and Egypt. Iraq also made a number of strides in the production of armored vehicles, with tangible results appearing after the war.[30]

US, British and German assistance proved indispensable to the advancement of Iraq's non-conventional armaments industry.[31] Western technology helped develop Iraq's "wunderwaffe" systems, such as long-range ballistic missiles and other non-conventional weapons. German (and other Western engineers), Egyptians and Argentineans were active in Iraq's ballistic-missile sector by enhancing the range and warhead effectiveness of Iraq's existing missiles. Their efforts helped Iraq obtain enhanced versions of the Soviet-designed Scud-B long-range missile (nicknamed the *Al-Hussein*) by April 1988. These "super-Scuds" enabled Baghdad to strike Tehran at a range of 700km.[32] Egypt cooperated with Argentina to develop the Condor-2000/Badr 2000 ballistic missile, which would have had a range of 1,000km.[33]

Chemical weapons became fully integrated into the Iraqi order of battle, yielding excellent results for Saddam in the summer of 1988.[34] This was partly due to Baghdad's success in indigenously manufacturing large numbers of chemical munitions for Iraq's 4,000 pieces of artillery.[35] The Baath leadership had also tested chemical munitions on lab animals and Iranian prisoners to help calibrate and improve their effectiveness.[36] Iraqi artillery forces were now able to quickly deliver massive amounts of chemical munitions against Iranian positions, as would be shown in upcoming Iraqi offensives. In practice, Iraqi artillery barrages mixed conventional and chemical shells in order to maximize disarray in Iranian lines. The Iranians lacked the ability to proportionately respond against Iraq's use of chemical weapons. The Iraqis used rapid-dispersal and slow-dispersal chemical agents. Rapid-dispersal agents were directed at Iranian front-lines, forcing Iranian resistance to rapidly disintegrate, and allowing advancing Iraqi troops to swiftly advance into Iranian positions. Slow-dispersal agents, mainly mustard gas, and were directed towards rear Iranian positions. These created a "chemical wall" to prevent Iranian forces from rapidly counterattacking in the combat theater, allowing Iraqi forces to conclude their operations unmolested.[37]

The Iranian military in early 1988

Iran's armaments industries had significantly expanded by 1987. Iranian war industries and research facilities had produced indigenous prototypes for an unmanned reconnaissance aircraft, a fighter plane, and combat helicopters. Prototypes for a main battle tank were also being designed. By 1987 Iran was producing a local version of the Swiss turbo-prop PC-7, 122mm cannon, and a variety of rockets and missiles, the TOW antitank missile, and the antiship Silkworm missile. By the war's end, 115 of Iran's 200 universities were engaged in military research and development with 12,000 workshops being integrated into Iran's arms industries.[38]

By late 1987 the Iranian air force was in a desperate situation. The Vahdati air base, had fewer than 20 F-4s and 20 F-5s in flying condition. Only 15 of Iran's 70 F-14As were fully operational. The Iranians were able to fly another 30 to 35 Tomcats, but these could only fire sidewinders and use their aerial guns. The situation became so desperate that Iran had to import Chinese copies of the MiG-21 (the F-7), a machine derided by Iranian pilots as a "toy." But Iran now made significant advances in the repair and overhaul of airframes and even achieved the ability to completely rebuild jet engines.[39] Much of this was due to the organizational efforts of Colonel Hamid-Reza Ardestani.[40] Iran began producing spare parts for its combat aircraft, with Iranian engineers and technicians restoring severely damaged F-4 Phantoms to service.[41] Iran also graduated its first batch of indigenously trained fighter pilots for its air force.[42] These factors, along with a fresh arrival of spares for F-4 and F-14A fighters by early 1988 allowed the IRIAF to keep fighting. The Iranians also developed guided bombs, and sophisticated electronic and TV equipment for spying aircraft. A crash program was also underway to reverse-engineer sophisticated missiles such as the Phoenix air-to-air missile.

Iranian awareness of the vital role of US intelligence in helping direct Iraqi air strikes was confirmed by the information given by an captured Iraqi pilot in 1987, who told his interrogators that Iraqi forces knew the exact location of Iranian guns, tanks, missiles, troop concentrations, and aircraft.[43] Despite this alarming news, the Iranian leadership failed to consider the possibility that Iraq could effectively launch large offensives, mainly due to complacency and overconfidence. Some members of the press and leadership tended to deride Iraqi technical and martial abilities, partly due to the fact that Iran had held the strategic initiative since 1982. Many in the Iranian leadership retained the misconception that "one more push" would completely defeat Iraq. But if Iraq's huge military were to be unleashed, the Iranian military would be in danger of being overwhelmed. The Iranians may have known of Iraq's military improvements, but they could do little to stop them. The Iranians also had no solution to the comprehensive integration of chemical weapons into the Iraqi armed forces. Despite knowing how far the military balance had tilted against them, the Iranians still had no inkling of what blows were about to descend upon them.

There were continuing problems at the military leadership level. Achieving synthesis between the Pasdaran and the regular army had proven very difficult.[44] This meant that coordinating military actions on land, sea and air was often plagued by problems inherent in competing systems of command and control. These problems continued to seriously diminish Iran's military performance.

The final War of the Cities

Iraqi jets bombed Tehran, Dezful and Hamadan on February 27, 1988. Iran retaliated by firing Scud-B missiles into Baghdad. This was the moment Saddam had been waiting for. Iraq's propaganda ministry announced that they would fire four modified Scuds (the Al-Hussein) for every Iranian Scud fired into Baghdad. Iraq fired its first 16 Al-Hussein missiles into Tehran on February 29. Iraqi aircraft then bombed Tehran, Qorveh, Hamadan, Zanjan, Shiraz, Qom and Rasht on March 1–3 with Iranian F-4s raiding Baghdad and Basra. Fifteen Al-Husseins were shot into Tehran during this time with Iran firing just two Scuds back at Baghdad. Iraq continued to launch air raids and scores of Scuds until April 20. Baghdad's missile strikes were so intense that Tehran was hit 17 times by modified Scud-Bs in just 24 hours. Tehran's populace reacted in anger, protesting in front of the Soviet embassy.[45] Moscow acknowledged having supplied the missiles to Baghdad but claimed that it had done so on the assurance that these would not be deployed against civilian centers.[46] Iranian media, expressing popular frustration, viewed Soviet explanations as disingenuous.[47]

The "Scud Duel" was a heavy blow to both civilian and military establishments of Iran. Up until early 1988, Iran had been able to counterbalance Iraqi air raids with missile strikes into Baghdad. In this "Scud Duel," Iran fired 77 Scuds while Iraq fired at 189 Al-Husseins into Tehran (135), Qom (23), Isfahan (22), Tabriz (4), Shiraz (3), and Karaj (2).[48] Baghdad had demonstrated that its military superiority now extended to ballistic missiles. Iraq also publicized its threat of mounting chemical warheads on its ballistic missiles.[49] Given Saddam Hussein's willingness to deploy chemical weapons against Iraqi-Kurdish civilians, the possibility of him firing chemical weapons into Iranian cities was not far-fetched.

Iran strikes into Sulaymānīyah province: The horror at Halabja

Iraq's defenses in Basra were now even more formidable than in 1987, ruling out any major Iranian offensive there. Iraq's northern front was more practical as Iran had many Kurdish allies in that sector and the terrain was mountainous and partly forested negating Iraq's advantages in heavy armor and aircraft. These factors led to a major Iranian offensive into Iraq's Sulaymānīyah province. The aim was to capture or destroy the Darbandikhan Lake and its associated power-grid.[50] The attack began with a number of diversionary strikes, including Operation *Beit-ol-Moghaddas 3*, directed to the north of Sulaymānīyah .[51] They proved successful, diverting the Iraqis from the main strike.

The main thrust into Sulaymānīyah province, Operation *Val-Fajr 10*, occurred on March 16. Iraqi troops were taken completely by surprise as helicopters landed Iranian commandos behind their lines, supported by TOW-firing Cobra helicopters wreaking havoc on Iraqi armor. The IRIAF was also active, shooting down a number of Iraqi jets. Most notable was the F-5 raid at Kirkuk where Iran first fired its indigenously designed air-to-ground Shahin rockets with success. Iranian troops poured into Iraqi Kurdistan, supported by their Kurdish allies.

One of the ugliest incidents of the war occurred on March 16–17, just as Iranian forces were fanning into Sulaymānīyah province. Iranian forces and their Kurdish allies had ejected Iraqi troops from the town of Halabja by March 16. Saddam retaliated by bombing the city with chemical weapons which killed some 5,000 Kurdish civilians.[52] Saddam Hussein continued to use chemical weapons against the Iraqi Kurds after Halabja. The *Anfal* campaign, which was nothing less than genocide against the Kurds of northern Iraq, reached its height in August 1988, and continued after the ceasefire.[53]

While Iraqi use of chemical weapons against the Kurds was nothing new, willingness to deploy them against cities was.[54] Western responses remained muted. US efforts to diminish (or exonerate) Saddam's role at Halabja proved unconvincing given the testimony of surviving Kurdish victims. Attempts were then made to place the blame on both Saddam and the Iranians. UN Resolution 612 (issued May 9) drafted in response to Halabja simply stated "We condemn without reservation illegal use of chemical weapons by both sides in the Gulf conflict."[55] As noted by Hilterman, the UN resolution "was a bone tossed to the Iraqis … both the administration and the Iraqi regime knew who had committed the offense … by causing diplomatic confusion, the Iran accusation, first aired by the state department's spokesperson on March 23, won Iraq a two-month reprieve. Unencumbered by unanimous condemnation of its warfare methods, it could now trigger the war's endgame."[56]

Operation *Ramadan Al Mubarak*: Iraqis recapture Fao

Intense Soviet training by advisors acting in concert with Indian, Pakistani, Egyptian and French officers had helped alter the Iraqi chain of command and battle doctrine. Live fire exercises under their instructors helped hone the offensive capabilities of Iraq's armored and mechanized divisions, especially those of the Republican Guard. With over 8,000 APCs, Iraqi troops became one of the most mobile forces in the world.[57] Iraqi land and air forces were trained to improve inter-service cooperation in combined arms operations. This intense level of planning and training lasted for approximately one year, resulting in highly methodical and systematic Iraqi offensives beginning in mid-April 1988, at Fao.

One of the reasons for Iraq's upcoming success at Fao was Iraqi success in distracting the Iranians from Baghdad's true military intentions. Saddam staged a number of highly publicized visits to the northern frontier, which may have diverted the Iranians from the south. Just days before the Iraqis struck, the Iranian army again thrust into the Sulaymānīyah province (codenamed *Beit ol Moghaddas 5*) on April 11, 1988. This was Iran's last major offensive into Iraqi Kurdistan. The Iraqi air force also ceased its bombing of Iranian civilian centers on April 10, one week before the eruption of Baghdad's devastating offensives.

Baghdad had been trying to recapture Fao since 1986. The Iranians had downgraded their Fao garrison to 5,000 men.[58] Perhaps the Iranians recognized they would be unable to hold Fao against a massive Iraqi onslaught. The Iranians were finally alerted to the danger, and warned their Fao garrison a week before the Iraqi attack. The revolutionary Basij militias holding Fao lacked professional military training or discipline and failed to act on Tehran's warnings.

The meticulously planned Iraqi recapture of Fao was launched in the early hours of April 17, 1988. Lieutenant-General Ayad al-Rawaii of the Republican Guard, who had undergone US military training, led the assault.[59] Rawaii assigned his helicopters to direct Iraqi aircraft and artillery strikes. Instead of massive Soviet-style artillery bombardments, Rawaii's shelling of northern Iranian positions (facing Basra) lasted barely an hour.[60] Iraqi munitions were mixed in with chemical agents.[61] The Iraqi air force attacked almost simultaneously by bombing and strafing Iranian positions. Despite being forewarned, the Basij had made no preparations against chemical warfare attacks and soon paid the price. The Iranian front lines became engulfed in chemical agents, allowing Rawaii's ground offensive to begin.

Rawaii unleashed a rapid two-pronged offensive with 40,000 troops.[62] The Iraqi 7th Corps struck through palm groves along the Arvand Rud/Shaat al Arab waterway with the Republican Guard deploying across the Khowr Abdulla channel. The Iranians attempted to move part of their garrison forward to block the Iraqi thrusts and even tried to bring more support from Um al Qasr. Rawaii knew that Iranian defenses were facing the north and northwest, with their southern flank very weakly defended. Iraqi helicopters landed commandos right behind the Iranian lines on the southern flank. The helicopters were equipped with spray cans to spread deadly chemical agents on the Iranian troops.[63] Iraqi naval commandos also landed amphibiously behind the Iranian lines sealing off the Iranian garrison.[64]

Despite being subjected to chemical warfare in the van and rear and outnumbered 8 to 1, Iranian resistance was fierce, albeit brief, especially at the command bunker. Iranian TOW missiles managed to repel a number of Iraqi tank thrusts, but failed to block the main impetus of the Iraqi advance, which continued into the night. On the morning of April 18, Iranian jets finally tried to halt the Iraqi progress, but their efforts proved futile. The Iraqis had made such heavy use of chemical weapons that across the waterway Abadan soon became contaminated.[65]

Iranian resistance finally collapsed, forcing the garrison to retreat. This was made difficult by precise Iraqi air strikes that had destroyed all but one pontoon bridge, which itself was very badly damaged.[66] Many Iranians drowned while trying to reach the Iranian side of the waterway. The F-4s of Bushehr airbase finally scrambled and mounted effective bombing runs every 10 minutes to cover the withdrawal of the survivors.[67] The Iraqis captured a large amount of heavy equipment at Fao, but no SAMs or Silkworm antiship missiles, as these had already been evacuated to Iran.[68] One surprising feature of the Fao operation was the relatively light casualties on both sides. This was most likely due to the lightning and unexpected nature of Rawaii's strike as well as the rapid Iranian retreat. Iraq had demonstrated that it was capable of quickly focusing vastly superior numbers of troops and heavy equipment to areas they intended to strike. This may explain why the Iraqis managed to complete their capture of Fao in just 36 hours, when they had originally estimated a five-day battle. The recapture of Fao gave Iraq a major morale boost: massive celebrations erupted in Baghdad.[69] The battle's consequences were both strategic and psychological. Iraqi troops had broken out of their "Maginot line" mindset and were now poised to launch more deadly offensives. The Iranians were shocked to see how quickly Iraq had regained the Fao peninsula. The Iraqi military had transformed itself from battered defender to battlefield giant.

Iran claimed that eight American helicopter gunships had assisted the Iraqi blitz at Fao, with Kuwait allowing them transit over its territory.[70] While direct American involvement during the operation is not certain, the presence of US helicopters near Fao is more difficult to dismiss.[71] The fact that Saddam timed his Fao attack perfectly, striking just as Iranian forces were bracing themselves against the US in the Persian Gulf also indicates possible links with the USN's Operation *Praying Mantis*. Adel Darwish, a London-based Arab journalist who visited Fao and Baghdad in the immediate aftermath of the Iraqi victory stated that "Saddam Hussein was tipped off by the Americans about their willingness to mount their own attack on Iran."[72]

Crippling the Iranian Navy: Operation *Praying Mantis*

Just as Iraq was completing its conquest of Fao, the Iranians were attacked by the USN. The immediate bone of contention was the damage caused to the USN frigate, USS *Samuel Roberts*, by an Iranian mine on April 14. The explosion blasted a 25-ft hole in the hull, flooding and damaging engines, and injured ten US crewmen. The Americans led by Admiral William Crowe, in consultation with Defense Secretary Frank Carlucci, decided to implement a "measured response."

The Americans had been concerned with the activities of the IRIN for some time. Their focus was the Iranian frigate *Sahand* and her sister-ship the *Sabalan*. These ships often attacked merchant ships following Iraqi raids on Iranian shipping. The *Sahand* had actually come to within 23 miles (37km) of USS *Samuel Roberts* when it was damaged on April 14, but halted and turned back. While Crowe and Carlucci hoped to destroy Iranian combat vessels, the Americans must have realized that these actions would benefit Saddam Hussein. Operation *Praying Mantis* consisted of two parts. The first (codenamed Operation *Nimble Archer*) was to strike two militarized sea platforms, the Salman (previously Sassan) and the Sirri-D. These had powerful radars that assisted Iranian military operations in the Persian Gulf. Salman was a base for Pasdaran speedboat attacks, defended by four deadly ZSU-23-2 antiaircraft guns and SA-7 portable SAMs. The Sirri-D was more lightly defended with a single ZSU-23-2 antiaircraft weapon. There was also a third target, a non-military oil platform known as Raksh in the Strait of Hormuz. Part two of Operation *Praying Mantis* depended on how the Iranians responded to Operation *Nimble Archer*.

At 9am on April 18, a massive USN battle group appeared off the Salman, with USN Sea Cobras flying in support. It was an unequal contest. The Americans issued warnings for the Iranian personnel to evacuate, prompting some to do so immediately. Not all complied; some began firing their ZSU-23-2 weapons. These were quickly silenced by the fire of the USS *Merrill*. The survivors evacuated the platform by boat. As the Iranians retired, the platform was pulverized by more heavy naval gunfire.[73] Finally Marines landed from the USS *Trenton* and destroyed the platform with explosives. A number of Iranian F-4s began to approach the US task force during the operation but turned back without engaging the Americans.[74]

Another group of US warships assaulted Sirri-D just 10 minutes after the attack on Salman. Sirri-D's personnel departed after the US warships warned them to leave. The platform was then destroyed with incendiary ammunition, rendering the subsequent landing of USN SEALs unnecessary. Just one hour after Salman had been attacked, Iranian radar at Bandar Abbas detected what appeared to be a E-2C Hawkeye flying just 15 miles (23km) away from the city's shoreline. The Iranians soon realized that the carrier USS *Enterprise* was also nearby. The situation with the Hawkeye was alarming "as the Iranians knew that the Americans passed all available information to Iraq."[75] The IRIAF scrambled five F-4s to chase the Hawkeye away. Just as the aircraft took off, the Iranians realized it was a trap: Iranian listening stations overheard the Hawkeye requesting that four USN F-14s attack and destroy the Iranian fighters. The F-4s immediately disengaged.

The Americans continued to engage the Iranians. After midday, Sea Cobra and Seasprite helicopters of the USS *Sampson* engaged several Iranian speedboats and damaged one. The Iranians claimed to have shot down one US helicopter, but this was dismissed by US officials. Iranian speedboats and a single helicopter then attacked the UAE's Mubarak oilfield and several merchant ships docked there. The USS *Enterprise* sent a group of six to eight A-6E and A-7 aircraft, which disabled three Iranian speedboats.

The IRIN dispatched the Combattante II/Kaman-class *Joshan*, a fast attack vessel towards the destroyed Sirri-D platform. What followed next exemplified the entire engagement: a hopeless contest between a small navy and a superpower. US vessels warned the *Joshan* to halt or risk being sunk. The IRIN had been explicitly ordered to never fire at US vessels, but heightened tensions prompted the *Joshan* to fire a Harpoon missile at the USS *Wainwright*. The missile was led astray by the US warship's firing of chaff. The USS *Simpson* then launched missiles towards the *Joshan*, which managed to deflect one by chaff and evasive measures. The *Joshan*'s crew also fired a SA-7 missile against a Sea Cobra helicopter, claiming a direct hit. The *Joshan* was then hit by more missiles; its engine room exploded which immobilized the vessel. As more missiles slammed into the vessel, it was finally finished off and sunk by huge 127mm naval cannon. The Americans rescued 29 survivors.

The IRIAF scrambled two F-4s to attack those vessels that had sunk the *Joshan*. The USS *Wainwright* warned them to turn back or be destroyed. As the F-4s closed in, USS *Wainwright* fired an antiaircraft missile at the lead aircraft. The F-4 avoided certain destruction by making a sharp dive and evasive action; the missile exploded just behind the aircraft damaging its hydraulics system, wings, left engine and tail. Another missile was fired at the damaged aircraft, which again took evasive measures. The pilot then managed to reach Bandar Abbas and land.

Meanwhile three US warships, USS *O'Brien*, USS *Joseph Strauss* and USS *Jack Williams*, deployed west to attack the Raksh oil platform. The ships were accompanied by helicopters and a platoon of Navy SEALS. While the real US target was the Iranian frigate, *Sabalan*, the Iranians dispatched her sister-ship, the *Sahand*. There had been no major repairs to the *Sahand*'s radar systems with many of its missile launchers in dire need of repairs.

The Americans detected the *Sahand*'s arrival and USS *Jack Williams* warned the ship to stop or be destroyed. Just minutes after the warnings were given, two US A-6Es flew over the *Sahand*. The Iranian ship fired its SAMs and 76mm gun at the aircraft, and also fired an antiship missile towards the US ships. None of these found their target. The USS *Enterprise* sent A-6E and A-7 aircraft which fired missiles and laser-guided bombs at the *Sahand*. These scored direct hits, setting the entire ship ablaze and destroying her hull's integrity. The *Sahand*'s survivors left on the few intact lifeboats.[76]

Rather than cut its terrible losses, the IRIN dispatched what the Americans had been seeking: the *Sabalan*. This sailed out from Bandar Abbas towards the USS *Jack Williams,* which was ordered to "get it."[77] As *Sabalan* closed in, she fired several missiles at the USS *Jack Williams*, and one against a section of A-6E aircraft. None of them achieved a single hit. An A-6E launched a missile against the *Sabalan*, destroying its engine room.[78] The stricken Iranian vessel was now a sitting duck. The Americans could certainly have followed up and sank the *Sabalan* but Crowe and Carlucci ordered the force to stand down. The *Sabalan* was towed back to Bandar Abbas but it was certainly out of the war. *Praying Mantis* had mortally crippled the IRIN, with clear dividends for Saddam. Iran's frigate force had been halved to two vessels, with one fast attack craft, three speedboats and two sea platforms completely destroyed.[79] Iran's ability to intercept Iraq-bound shipping to Saddam-friendly ports had been dealt a heavy blow.

Operation *Tawakalna Al Allah*: Iran expelled from Fish Lake and Shalamcha

With a major portion of their small navy sunk, the Iranians hastily proceeded to coordinate their remaining naval assets with the IRIAF and the Pasdaran. This resulted in a maneuver known as Operation *Zolfaghar*. The real purpose of this exercise was to prepare for the possibility of a massive US assault. The Americans certainly could assault at will and the Iranians could do little to stop them. The American strategy was to keep the Iranians guessing as to their real intentions, and more importantly to distract them from their land war against Iraq. Tehran now had to contemplate the possibility of fighting an unwinnable two-front war. Iran's limited air assets (notably Maverick armed F-4s) were now diverted to Operation *Zolfaghar*. The operation assembled nearly all of Iran's 50 operational naval vessels, marines, commandos, and army units (including airborne brigades). The absence of these professional ground troops and air units from the western (Iraq) front significantly contributed to a new military disaster just days later. Iran's diversion of military planning and assets towards the American colossus in the Persian Gulf again served to promote Iraq's war effort.[80]

The Iraqi assault at Fish Lake on May 25 was concluded at even greater speed than the Fao operation: the 8½ hour battle was over by 6pm. Once again, Iraq had quickly brought overwhelming forces to the combat theater, through its excellent transportation, communications and logistics system. Although precise numbers are difficult to ascertain, the Iraqis were more than capable of quickly assembling up to 200,000 men for military action.[81] The attacking force was composed of Iraq's III and VII Corps, commando units and the Republican Guard. The aim of the offensive was to strike hard and deep towards the rear of Iranian positions to completely destroy their forces at Shalamcha and draw in as much of the IRIAF as possible. The Iraqis opened their assault with a massive artillery barrage, deploying cannon and multiple rocket launchers. Iraqi munitions delivered massive quantities of poison gas onto the Iranian lines.[82] Brazilian Astros II MLRS launchers delivered rockets with deadly accuracy over a distance of 70km.[83] Each of these exploded 150m above the ground to deliver 200 deadly cluster bombs, wreaking havoc inside Iranian lines. The Iraqis had also factored in the weather to maximize the effects of their chemical attacks. With temperatures now soaring at 45 degrees Celsius, the Iranians found it nearly impossible to wear their cumbersome anti-chemical warfare suits and gas masks.[84]

With their barrages now concluded, the Iraqis unleashed their crushing edge in armor. The Iranians were overwhelmed by thousands of Iraqi tanks, against which they could muster at most 100 tanks.[85] A massive fleet of Iraqi aircraft and helicopters supported the powerful Iraqi tank armada. The Iraqi offensive proved unstoppable: five hours into the fighting, Iranian troops began retreating.[86] The retreat appears to have been well organized, because, as at Fao, the Iraqis failed to capture large numbers of prisoners. The Iraqis however, did capture a large haul of abandoned military equipment, including a number of self-propelled guns.

Following the Iranian retreat, the Republican Guard made a determined effort to enter Khuzistan and attack Iranian forces inside Iran. By this time the Iranians had recovered and their defense lines in Iran proved solid. Despite the use of chemical weapons, the Tawakalana Republican Guard Division was solidly beaten on Iranian soil and suffered heavy losses in tanks and personnel.[87] The Guards were pushed back into Iraq by a combination of Iranian antitank weapons, armor, combat helicopters and infantry.

Doomed from the start: Iran's counteroffensive

Iran launched a dramatic air raid against Saddam Hussein's palace at Tikrit on March 3. This raid was conducted by a single F-4, which dropped its munitions onto the gardens just across from Saddam's palace. The raid potently demonstrated to the Iraqi leadership that the IRIAF was far from finished. The plan for the attack must have been meticulous as Iraq by now was fielding 4,000 antiaircraft guns and the world's sixth largest air force.[88]

Rafsanjani ordered Iranian forces to conduct a counteroffensive into Iraq's recently reconquered Shalamcha territory in mid-June. The timing and purpose of this attack suggests that it was partly politically motivated. Iranian morale had taken a beating as a result of the Iraq's victories at Fao and Shalamcha. Rafsanjani most likely wanted to demonstrate, domestically and internationally, that Iran was still capable of taking Iraqi land. If this was the intent, then the consequences of this action only served to embolden Iraq and her allies.

The IRIAF mustered a modest force of eight jets to support Rafsanjani's counteroffensive.[89] The Iraqis had probably been forewarned of this action, most likely by US AWACS or satellites, and prepared a deadly trap. Just as the eight-ship formation prepared to strike, 70 Iraqi combat aircraft surrounded the Iranian jets.[90] The Iraqis had also carefully positioned their SAMs and antiaircraft defenses on the ground, which shot down two Iranian aircraft.[91] At this stage the lead Iranian F-4E fighter engaged larger numbers of MiG-23, shooting one down with itself also being destroyed by the Iraqi fleet. This sacrifice was not in vain as it allowed the remaining four aircraft to extricate themselves from the Iraqi swarm. Of these, two were badly damaged by air-to-air missiles and SAM strikes. Not surprisingly, the Iranians called off a planned second strike.[92] The Iranian ground offensive fared no better. The Iranians claimed to have inflicted 18,000 Iraqi casualties in their drive across Iraqi minefields and defense rings before "voluntarily" withdrawing. Iranian media announcements now resembled Saddam Hussein's "optimistic" speeches following his 1982 defeats in Khuzistan. Iranian casualties, as far as can be verified, were relatively light. They lost around 3,000 men during their attack and lost another 1,000 as they retreated back.[93] Tehran had suffered another defeat as the Iraqis again captured large quantities of Iranian military equipment.

Iraq retakes the Majnoon Islands

The Iraqis were in high spirits. They had defeated the Iranians at Fao and Shalamcha and successfully repelled their counteroffensive. They now struck further north at Mehran on June 19. By now the Iraqis had perfected their chemical "one-two punch." The Iranian front-line was saturated by rapidly dispersing cyanide gas and nerve agents delivered by artillery shells.[94] This allowed Iraqi troops to rapidly secure the area. Longer-lasting mustard gas agents were delivered to the Iranian rear by rockets, artillery, and the IrAF.[95] This prevented the Iranians from counterattacking into Mehran to relieve their comrades. The Iraqis then "officially" handed over Mehran to the National Liberation Army of Iran (NLAI), composed primarily of the Mujaheddin Khalq Organization (MKO, also known as the MEK, Mujaheddin e Khalq). The main Iraqi army then withdrew to Iraq. It is unclear how many Iraqi troops remained to support the MKO, which was easily crushed and thrown back into Iran after three days. The Mehran strike however, had achieved its purpose brilliantly. The Iranian military had been diverted from the new disaster brewing further south where Baghdad proceeded to recapture the last major pockets of Iranian-held territory in the south.

Iraq opened its offensive against the Majnoon island with a massive 600-piece artillery barrage on June 25 in tandem with rocket and air strikes. Chemical bombardments were delivered to Iranian frontal and rear positions. Once again, the emphasis was on overwhelming firepower followed by armored thrusts. This time the Iranians were outnumbered 20-1.[96] Once the barrages were concluded, Republican Guard units landed behind Iranian lines with hovercraft.[97] Another brigade of Iraqi paratroops landed simultaneously inside Iran to the east of the Majnoon. The Iranians were now completely cut off and doomed. There was no sign of any Iranian aircraft or combat helicopters during the Iraqi operations.

The Republican Guard and the Iraqi 3rd Corps now mounted a direct assault to clear the two major islands at Majnoon. The Iraqis launched a massive force of 2,000 tanks to pulverize what was left of the Iranian positions.[98] When the tanks crashed through the Iranian front lines, the Iraqi 3rd Corps (supported by elements of the 6th corps) peeled off to thrust to the Iranian rear (to the east towards Iran) to link up with those Republican Guard already there. The Iraqi offensive was concluded in approximately eight hours. The battle's aftermath resembled Shalamcha: relatively few Iranian prisoners taken (around 2,115), but large stores of heavy military equipment captured.[99]

USS *Vincennes* shoots down an Iranian airliner

The Iranians received another unexpected shock just days after the Iraqi victory at Majnoon. At dawn on July 3, the USS *Vincennes* and the USS *Elmer Montgomery* dispatched helicopters to seek Iranian speedboats. What followed is still mired in controversy but the following sequence of events is generally accepted. The cruisers sank two small Iranian speedboats after they allegedly fired on a US helicopter. Into this tense atmosphere an Iranian Airbus took off from Bandar Abbas airport on a short flight to Dubai. Despite its advanced Aegis computer-radar system, the crew of the USS *Vincennes* mistook the large civilian aircraft for an Iranian F-14. Captain Will Rogers III ordered the ship to shoot down the plane. To their horror, the crew of the *Vincennes* realized that they had just accidentally killed 290 civilians and crew on a passenger airliner. Later investigations revealed earlier complaints within the USN about Captain Rogers' tendency to be "trigger happy."[100]

The disaster prompted the chairman of the Joint Chiefs of Staff, Admiral William Crowe, to make an appearance for the international press. Crowe claimed that the Iranian Airbus had strayed from its designated air corridor and was descending with increasing speed towards the USS *Vincennes*. The aircraft, noted the admiral, ignored several warnings to alter course and return to its designated air corridor. Crowe also showed a map which showed the USS *Vincennes* firmly outside of Iranian territorial waters. The report was essentially the version of events as narrated by Captain Rogers. The "official" version was that Rogers was simply defending his ship from what he mistook to be an Iranian F-14. Vice President George Bush's speech at the UN on July 14, 1988 noted that the USS *Vincennes* was responding to calls made by a merchant ship requesting assistance against Iranian speedboat attacks.

Thanks to the honest reporting and rigorous investigations of John Barry and Roger Charles of *Newsweek Magazine*[101] and Ted Koppel of ABC News' *Nightline*, the ugly truth behind these events finally exploded into the public eye four years later. These investigations verified the following facts: the Iranian Airbus was flying within international air corridors; the Airbus was ascending at the time, not descending as falsely claimed in 1988; there had been no threatened merchant vessel requesting help; the *Vincennes* was operating in Iranian waters. [102] Interestingly, very few reports mentioned that USS *Vincennes*'s real role was to monitor the site of Kuhestak which was being built as a silo for antiship Silkworm missiles, which is why the USS *Vincennes* was sat beneath the air corridor that ran between Bandar Abbas and Dubai.[103]

The Iraqi blitz into Dehloran

The Airbus disaster prompted the Iranian leadership to call for a meeting of the UN Security Council on July 5. Just as the Iranians were reeling from their airliner disaster, Iraq delivered its next blow. Iraqi army operations shifted northwards towards Iranian Luristan. The Iraqi Republican Guard, in concert with the Iraqi 4th Corps, launched a furious attack on 0715 on July 12, 1988. As before, Iraq's massive tank attacks combined with chemical weapons annihilated the Iranian opposition by 1100. In less than four hours, the Iraqis had pummeled their adversaries and penetrated 28 miles (45km) into Iran. The Iranian army had suffered its worst defeat of the entire war. So much Iranian military equipment was captured that it took the Iraqis four days to transport it all to Iraq.[104] Some Western analysts believe that Iran may have lost up to 45–60% of its armor and heavy equipment to Iraq's offensives since Fao.[105] The Iraqis then withdrew into their borders, declaring that they had no territorial ambitions on Iranian territory.

It is remarkable how the Iraqi military had improved after each offensive from Fao to Dehloran. Each succeeding offensive had achieved complete victory in less time and resulted in the capture of large quantities of Iranian equipment. Iraq however, had failed to capture many prisoners. This suggests that the Iranians had been able to extricate many of their personnel after each defeat. Nevertheless, Iran was now tottering on the edge of complete defeat. Saddam Hussein may have seen this as another opportunity to annex as much of Khuzistan as possible.

Dehloran was the last and most deadly of the string of military disasters had befallen the Iranian military. The combination of the Dehloran disaster and the Airbus tragedy shook Iran's upper leadership: they clearly demonstrated Iran's severe military handicaps and the extent of its diplomatic isolation. On Thursday July 14, 1988, just two days after Dehloran, representatives of Iran's military, clerical and political leadership held an emergency session in Tehran to discuss the critical situation facing the country. These agreed that Iran had to unconditionally accept UN ceasefire resolution 598. The next day witnessed a critical meeting of the cabinet, the chairman of the Majlis and Rafsanjani; once again, it was agreed to accept the UN resolution. That same night, a group of Iran's leadership met with Khomeini to inform him of the consensus building towards accepting resolution 598. On Saturday (July 16) the Majles-e Khobregan (assembly of experts) formulated the decree to officially recommend the adoption of the UN resolution to Khomeini.[106] Rafsanjani (speaker of the Majlis, vice-chairman of the Majles-e Khobregan, and commander in acting chief of the military) informed Khomeini of the Khobregan decree. As Iran's supreme leader, Khomeini, had the final say on whether Iran would continue the war or accept the ceasefire. Khomeini gave his consent (apparently in writing) for Resolution 598, allowing Rafsanjani and President Ali Khamnei to formalize Iran's acceptance of the ceasefire. Khamnei gave a letter to UN Secretary General, Perez de Cuellar on July 17 outlining Iran's acceptance of Resolution 598. Final endorsement for the resolution came three days later, by Khomeini himself. Tehran radio conveyed his statement on July 20 in which he officially endorsed Iran's acceptance of UN Resolution 598. The long and bitter war was finally drawing to a close.

Saddam's bid for total victory

Rafsanjani had been appointed as overall commander-in-chief by late May 1988. This proved beneficial as he began examining the reasons for the failures of the Basij at Fao and the Pasdaran and regular army at Shalamcha. His investigation revealed that the military supply system entrusted to the Pasdaran had been severely mismanaged, resulting in the armed forces often not receiving the necessary heavy equipment. Thanks to the stiff US-led arms embargo, Iran already had a severe problem procuring equipment overseas. Iranian tanks that had partaken in the 1987 Basra offensive had yet to be refitted with new engines and gun barrels. The same was true of much of Iranian artillery barrels.

Rafsanjani worked hard to reverse the military's logistics problems. He also worked to increase cooperation between the Pasdaran and the regular army on the battlefield. While these measures needed time to take effect, they proved just enough to stop Saddam's final offensives into Iran.

Saddam wanted to fully exploit his newfound military ascendancy over Iran to secure both banks of the Arvand Rud/Shaat al Arab, one of the original objectives of the 1980 invasion and fully transform recent Iraqi victories into an all-out victory by conquering the Iranians. This would demonstrate to both the domestic Iraqi populace and the wider Arab world that Iraq had indeed won the war. The aim was to completely destroy the Iranian armed forces and permanently capture as much of Khuzistan and western Iran as possible. Given recent Iraqi successes and the use of chemical weapons, an all-out victory seemed assured. At the very least, Saddam calculated that he would gain further leverage over Iran in future negotiations.

The Iraqis opted for three general axes of advance from the northwest, the west, and southwest into Khuzistan.[107] Saddam and the Iraqi high command had evidently failed to appreciate that Iranian forces were rapidly recovering from the shock of their recent defeats. The Iranian high command, aware of Saddam's intentions, opted to see where the main weight of Iraqi thrusts would fall. Having witnessed Iraqi guile, efficient logistics, skillful maneuvering, and rapid strikes, the Iranians were determined not to repeat their recent military mistakes. The euphoria in the Iraqi leadership may have led the Iraqi leadership to discount the IRIAF, which, while outnumbered, was still more than capable of providing an effective defense against invading Iraqi forces. The Iranian army, though battered, remained intact as a fighting force and well prepared for any new Iraqi invasion. Saddam, fully confident that he would fully crush the Iranian military, unleashed his forces in a new invasion of Iran on July 22, 1988.

Iraqi forces attacking into northwest Iran faced fierce resistance. After making some initial gains, the Iraqi army became bogged down. The region's mountainous terrain reduced the effectiveness of armored vehicles, heavy weaponry and aircraft, although combat helicopters proved useful. Iraqis troops and special forces were forced into hand-to-hand combat, with indifferent results. Iranian forces largely contained the Iraqis and pushed many back to the border, although some territory may have remained in Iraqi hands at the onset of the ceasefire. With the blunting of the Iraqi thrust in the northwest, Iran soon witnessed new threats in the center towards Bakhtaran and the southwest in Khuzistan.

The Iraqis had devised an ingenious plan for the central sector; they deployed the NLAI, numbering around 7,000 men and women fighters.[108] The Iraqis supplied the NLAI with cash, training, heavy weaponry and armored vehicles.[109] They also cooperated closely with Massoud Rajavi of the MEK in planning terrorist operations against Iranian civilians and military operations against the Iranian army.[110] The MEK actively cooperated with Saddam's forces as they used chemical weapons against Iranian civilians, as confirmed later by British officials.[111] The Iraqi aim was to have the NLAI thrust into Iran's Kurdistan province and capture its capital Bakhtaran (Kermanshah). The Iraqis hoped that the downfall of Bakhtaran would lead to the overthrow of Tehran's regime.[112] There are reports that Massoud Rajavi was a close friend of Saddam and met with his military intelligence staff on a weekly basis.[113]

The Iraqis opened a furious assault with the now familiar combination of heavy artillery, tanks, aircraft, combat helicopters and assault troops supported by chemical weapons. The Iraqis broke through and supported their NLAI allies' assault into Iran. The border towns of Karand and Eslamabad-e-Gharb were captured on July 26, 1988. Eslamabad-e-Gharb was totally obliterated, alienating the local Kurdish population against the "liberators."[114] Key strongholds along the Tehran–Baghdad highway were also secured, with Iraqi and NLAI forces thrusting 60 miles into Iran. Undeterred by the local population's lack of support, the NLAI and Iraqi forces continued their push towards Bakhtaran, a teeming city of half a million people.

The Iranian high command allowed the NLAI and Iraqi thrust to advance close to Bakhtaran. By now the invasion had penetrated up to 100 miles inside Iran. For a brief moment the highway to Tehran was open. Despite these impressive gains, the Iranian army had prepared a deadly trap. The brunt of the fighting had fallen upon the Iranian Kurds who bought enough time for the Iranian army to organize their counterattack. Up to this point, there had been little sign of Iranian combat helicopters, aircraft or armored vehicles. Then all of a sudden, Iranian F-4s mounted deadly air-to-ground attacks against Iraqi and NLAI forces followed by the deadly TOW-firing antitank helicopters. It is unclear how long the assault took place or how many times these attacks were mounted. What is certain is that they completely stopped the Iraqi and NLAI thrust. The regular army rapidly followed up with attacks by armored vehicles and combat troops. Even as Iranian ground forces encircled Iraqi and NLAI forces, many of the latter's combat vehicles (along with their crews) were already engulfed in flames along the Bakhtaran highway. This scenario was to be replicated on a much larger scale when US F-16s pulverized Iraqi troops retreating from Kuwait in 1991. From what is known, a total of 4,500 NLAI and Iraqis perished in the Iranian counterattacks, including many political and military figures of the MEK.[115] The remnants of Iraqi and NLAI forces announced a "voluntary withdrawal" from Iranian territory on July 29, 2008.[116]

Iran had faced its greatest danger in southern Khuzistan, and it was here that the Iranians concentrated their efforts first. An initial Iraqi thrust from the Shalamcha region was repelled but the Iraqis achieved greater success when their tanks and armored troops rapidly reached the Ahvaz–Khorramshahr highway. Iraqi forces were now punching towards Khorramshahr and Ahvaz for the first time in six years. These thrusts were covered by heavy Iraqi air cover and helicopter attacks.

As Iraqi tanks rolled towards Ahvaz and Khorramshahr, Iranian resistance solidified.[117] Thousands of volunteers arrived from all across Iran, including civil servants, clerics, and even parliament members who took up arms to support the armed forces in Khuzistan. The Iranian army in Khuzistan was already a formidable force. The British *Armed Forces* journal referred to the existence of a huge reserve force of 200,000 troops near Khorramshahr in 1987, known as the Mohammad Corps.[118] This force also included 50,000–60,000 battle-ready regular army troops.[119] The corps had originally been intended as a reserve force for the battle of Basra in 1987, but never used, leaving a powerful strategic reserve in Khuzistan, ready to act in case the Iraqis decided to repeat their 1980 invasion. The Iraqis soon became bogged down in intense hand-to-hand fighting, in which the Iranians gained the upper hand.

Even Iraq's massive tank armada, one of the world's largest, failed to prevail in Khuzistan's flat terrain. Iraqi tanks and artillery were stopped by a combination of Iranian artillery, antitank commandos, and Cobra helicopters.[120] The gigantic Iraqi air force also failed to prevail. Iran's select HAWK, Rapier and other antiaircraft missiles were acting in concert with Iran's few operational aircraft to counterattacking Iraqi aircraft. By July 25, 1988, Iraqi forces had been decisively beaten back and forced to cede 230 square miles of territory that they had wrested earlier from the Iranians.[121] The onset of the ceasefire halted further Iranian counterattacks.

Saddam Hussein and the Iraqi high command had, as in 1980, miscalculated: overestimating their own military capabilities and underestimating their adversaries' ability to resist. This was undoubtedly due to the elation felt by Saddam Hussein, the Iraqi military and civilian leadership following of their victories at Fao, Fish Lake, Majnoon and Dehloran. Believing that he had "won" the war and destroyed the Iranian army and air force, Saddam may have thought that he could finally attain what he had failed to achieve in eight years of war: Iranian territory. But the Iranian military was still intact and very well prepared to fight and repel an Iraqi invasion of Khuzistan. The old maxim of "one fights better in one's own territory" certainly proved itself for the final time in this futile war.

Catastrophic destruction with no winners

While the majority of Western analysts believe that the war had no winners, a select few believe that Iraq emerged as the victor of the war, based on Iraq's overwhelming successes between April and July 1988.[122] Pelletier for example notes that "Tawakalna ala Allah ... resulted in the absolute destruction of Iran's military machine."[123] Cordesman also believes that Iraq was the victor of the war.[124] However, the Pelletier-Cordesman view is selective in that it only focuses on the successful Iraqi offensives that took place before the ceasefire. While Iraq did capture large quantities of Iranian weapons, especially at Dehloran, the conclusion that Iran's war machine had been destroyed appears linear. Had Iran's military been as shattered as Pelletier and Cordesman claim, would it have been able to beat back the Iraqi military's full-scale offensives in late July 1988? It is worth noting that Iraqi firepower and air assets during these operations were far superior to what they had been in 1980. Iranian air defenses and aircraft continued to take a heavy toll of Iraqi aircraft, helicopters and armor right up the ceasefire.

The second factor which highlights the inconclusive nature of the war was the total failure of both Iraq and Iran to attain their objectives. Iraq failed in its original objectives to secure both banks of the Arvand Rud/Shaat al Arab waterway, capture Khuzistan and promote the dissolution of Iran along ethnic-linguistic lines. Iran in turn failed to export its revolution to Iraq or establish an Islamic state modeled on the Tehran's contemporary establishment. The war signaled the defeat of pan-Arabism (which failed to win over Khuzistan's Arab-speakers) just as pan-Islamism failed to win over the Iraqi populace and the wider Arabic and Islamic worlds. The Iran–Iraq War was the ultimate exercise in folly and futility: it was a wasteful calamity that destroyed millions of lives and achieved nothing but destruction. This was a tragic war that should never have happened.

NOTES

Chapter 1

1. As cited in Ettinghausen, 1972, p.1; Farrokh, 2004, pp.276–91.
2. Mackey, 1991, p.67.
3. See discussion by Limbert, 1987, pp.50–5.
4. Arjomand, 2004, p.6.
5. Consult articles in *Encyclopedia Iranica* such as Özgündenli, O., "Persian Manuscripts in Ottoman and Modern Turkish Libraries," and Luther, "Alp Arslân."
6. Lehmann, F., "Zaher ud-Din Babor – Founder of Mughal Empire," *Encyclopaedia Iranica* (online ed.).
7. Frye, 1989, p.236.
8. Newman, 2006, p.18. Technically there were two major invasions, the first one by Ghenghiz Khan in 1219–21, with other by his grandson Hulagu Khan in 1256–60.
9. Price, 2005, p.68; Savory, 1980, p.213.
10. Lewis, 2004, p.46.
11. Savory, 1994, p.246.
12. Limbert, 1987, p.51.
13. Al-Aghānī. *Ab al-Faraj al-Isfahānī*. Vol.4, p.423; See Zarrinkoob, 2000.
14. Clawson, 2005, p.17.
15. Baladhuri, p.417; *Tarikh e Sistan*, p.82; *Tarikh-e Qom*, pp.254–6.
16. Ibid.
17. Momtahen, 1989, p.145.
18. Frye, 1989, p.115.
19. Whittow, 1996, pp.195, 203, 215.
20. Frye, 1989, pp.115, 130.
21. Whittow, 1996, p.195
22. Yarshater, 1985, p.1005.
23. Woodhead, 1983, p.174.
24. For details of these conquests consult Turnbull, 2003a, pp.20–7, and Turnbull, 1980.
25. Mackey, 1998, p.69.
26. Savory, 1994, p.246.
27. Mackey, 1998, p.69.
28. Hawting, 2005, p.153.
29. Savory, 1994, p.246.
30. The topic of Sunni and Shiite factions within Islam is vast and complex, and best examined by theologians and religious historians. Readers are advised to consult Halm, 2007; Lalani, 2000; Lewis, 1994; Momen, 1987; Rogerson, 2007; and Wollaston, 2005.
31. Limbert, 1987, p.69.
32. Black, 2004, p.75.
33. Singh, 2002, p.135.
34. Savory, 1994, p.246; Newman, 2006, pp.9–10.
35. Evidence for this is provided by letters, written by the Ottoman Sultans to the leaders of the Aq Qoyunlu. Examples of Ottoman addresses to the Aq Qoyunlu include *Shahanshah e Iran Khadivajam* (lit. The King of Kings of Iran and Monarch of Persia) and *Soltan Salaten e Iran* (lit. Sultan of Sultans of Iran). Bosworth and Bulliet, 1996, p.275; Uzun Hassan adopted the title of *Padeshah e Iran* (lit. The Monarch of Iran), Van der Leeuw, 2000, p.81.
36. Savory, 1980, p.19.
37. Nicolle, 1990, p.35.
38. Lockhart, 1991, p.377.
39. Ibid.
40. Babinger, 1978, pp.314–5; Savory, 1994, p.44.
41. Kazemzadeh, 1991, p.5.
42. Matini, 1989, p.445.
43. Consult Justin 23.4.13; Strabo XI, 13; Bostock, J. and Riley, H. T., *The Natural History of Pliny* (1890), pp.27–8). See also "Albania, Caucasus" in *Encyclopaedia Brittanica,* 1911; Farrokh, 2004, pp.121–2.
44. Strabo 11.13.1; Thomas, 1977, p.45; Atabaki, 2000, pp.8–9.
45. The continuity of Iranian culture in the post-Seljuk period is witnessed in the continued usage of old Iranian geographical names such as Sahand, Ardabil, Tabriz, and Mianeh, and the continuation of agricultural techniques and settlement patterns. Planhol, 1966, p.305; Planhol, 1960.
46. As noted by Planhol, "Lands of Iran," *Encyclopedia Iranica.*
47. Kazemzadeh, 1950, p.5; Yaqut al-Hamavi, 1866, p.173.
48. By the Ottoman Turkish traveler Evliya Chelebi.
49. Tarverdi and Massoudi, 1971, pp.60, 61, 63; Consult Meyers *Konversations-Lexikon*, Vol.XII, p.873, original German edition, *Persien -Geschichte des neupersischen Reichs*; Savory, *Ebn Bazzazz, Darvis Tawakkoli b. Esmā'il b. Hāji Ardabili.*
50. Tarverdi and Massoudi, 1971, pp. 60, 61, 63.
51. Izady, 1992, pp.137–62.
52. Roemer, 1991, p.198.
53. Matofi, 1999, p.617.
54. Van der Leeuw, 2000, p.198.
55. The Shafii school, the branch closest to the Shia; the Shafii school has often been adopted by Shias masquerading as Sunnis (Roemer, 1001, p.195; Mashkoor, 1999, p.265).
56. See Roemer, 1991, pp.194–200. Shiism is a subject far beyond this text; for an in-depth analysis readers are referred to Savory, 1980, 1987; Melville, 1996; Mazzaoui, 2003; and Newman, 2006.
57. Matofi, 1999, p.618.
58. Krejčí and Krejčová, 1990, p.151.
59. Zarrinkoob, 2002–3, p.658.
60. The issue was Junaid's pro-Shiite ideas which ran counter to Jaafar's Sunnism. Roemer, 1991, p.200. Zarrinkoob, 2002–3, p.658.
61. Roemer, 1991, p.204.
62. Savory, 1980, p.19.
63. Roemer, 1991, p.202.
64. Savory, 1980, p.17; Roemer, 1991, p.202.
65. Zarrinkoob, 2002–3, p.661; Roemer, 1991, p.202.
66. Also known as Halima Begum.
67. Savory, 1980, p.19.
68. Ibid.
69. Zarrinkoob, 2002–3, pp.660–1.
70. Krejčí and Krejčová, 1990, p.152.
71. Savory, 1980, p.18.
72. Krejčí and Krejčová, 1990, p.152.

Chapter 2

1. Savory, 1980, p.20.
2. Ibid., p.21. Zarrinkoob (2002–3, p.552) disagrees.
3. Zarrinkoob, 2002–3, p.552.
4. Savory, 1980, p.21.
5. Âyatollâhi and Haghshenâs, 2003, p.255.
6. Limbert, 1987, p.70. See also Savory, R. M., "Ebn Bazzaz," *Encyclopaedia Iranica*.
7. Roemer, 1991, p.214; Bryer (1975) in the references. Anthony Bryer, "Greeks and Türkmens: The Pontic Exception," *Dumbarton Oaks Papers*, Vol.29, (1975), Appendix II: Genealogy of the Muslim Marriages of the Princesses of Trebizond; Matthee, R., "Georgians in Safavid Adminstration," *Encyclopaedia Iranica*.
8. Halm, 1987, p.75.
9. Minorsky, 1942, p.1053.
10. Doerfer, G., "Azeri Turkish," *Encyclopaedia Iranica*.
11. Newman, 2006, p.19.
12. Roemer, 1991, p.226–7.
13. Safavi, 1962, p.149.
14. Ibid.
15. Savory, 1980, p.25.
16. Matofi, 1999, p.618.
17. Ward, 2009, p.43.
18. Taheri, 1990, p.165.
19. Zarrinkoob, 2002–3, pp.660–1.
20. Matofi, 1999, pp.636, 731; Lockhart, 1991, p.374; Savory, 1980, p.44; *Tarikh-e Rozat ol Safa*, (Original in 1851, Reprinted 1960–1), Vol.IX, p.430; Khorasani, 2010, p.19.
21. Khorasani, 2010, p.19.
22. Matofi, 1999, p.618.
23. Amiri, 1970, pp.31–2.
24. Roemer, 1991, p.211.
25. *Habib ol Seyr*, Vol.IV, pp.456–9
26. Matofi, 1999, p.619.
27. Savory, 1980, p.26.
28. Roemer, 1991, p.212; Matofi, 1999, p.619.
29. The *Tarikh-e Jahan Ara* reports 2,000 dead with the *Leb ol Tavarikh* reporting 8,000 dead. Savory (1980, p.26) agrees with the *Leb ol Tavarikh* estimate; Shokri, 1971, pp.6, 58.
30. For a major account of this battle see Shokri, 1971, pp.58–64.
31. Safavi, 1962, p.146.
32. Krejčí and Krejčová, 1990, p.152.
33. Great Britain Naval Intelligence Division, 1946, p.264.
34. Consult Matini, 1989a, 1989b, and 1992.
35. Savory, 1994, p.248.
36. Roemer, 1991, p.226. See also Savory M. "Ebn Bazzaz," *Encyclopædia Iranica*.
37. Krej í and Krej ová, 1990, p.152. This claim was made later on the basis that the daughter of Yazdegird III had married Imam Ali's youngest son, Hussein. Ismail also claimed descent from these imams.
38. Savory, 1994, p.252. It was completed after Ismail's death.
39. Zarrinkoob, 2002–3, p.668; Savory, 1980, p.30.
40. Axworthy, 2006, p.25.
41. As cited by Jayne, 2004, p.109.
42. Roemer, 1991, pp.218, 227.
43. As described by Lockhart, 1991, pp.579–80.
44. Roemer, 1991, p.218.
45. Matofi, 1999, p.691.
46. Ibid.
47. Ibid., p.620.
48. Shokri, 1971, pp.75–80.
49. Matofi, 1999, p.620.
50. Shokri, 1971, pp.82, 84, 137.
51. Safavi, 1962, p.156.
52. Ibid., pp.164, 168.
53. Shokri, 1971, pp.90–3.
54. Amiri, 1970, p.370.
55. Farrokh, 2007, Ch.13–17.
56. Amiri, 1970, pp.357–61.
57. Ibid.
58. Ibid., pp.365–7; Matofi, 1999, p.622.
59. Amiri, 1970, pp.365–7.
60. Shokri, 1971, pp.517, 519.
61. Roemer, 1991, p.216.
62. McDowall, 2004, p.26.
63. Roemer, 1991, p.216.
64. Zarrinkoob, 2002–3, p.668.
65. Ibid.
66. Roemer, 1991, p.217.
67. Amiri, 1970, pp.325, 429.
68. Shokri, 1971, p.306.
69. Safavi, 1962, pp.225, 240–3.
70. Zarrinkoob, 2002–3, p.668.
71. Consult Briggs, 1829.
72. Krejčí and Krejčová, 1990, p.151.
73. Sicker, 2000, p.189.
74. Savory, 1980, p.37.
75. Zarrinkoob, 2002–3, p.668.
76. Krejčí and Krejčová, 1990, p.151.
77. Newman, 2006, p.20.
78. Ibid., p.20.
79. Roemer, 1991, p.217.
80. Farrokh, 2007, pp.286–7.
81. Ward, 2009, pp.43–4.
82. Lockhart, 1991, p.380.
83. Matofi, 1999, p.626.
84. Ibid., p.627.
85. Lockhart, 1991, p.380, provides a different version of events.
86. Ibid.
87. Matofi, 1999, p.627.
88. Ward, 2009, p.44.
89. Roemer, 1991, p.216.
90. Zarrinkoob, 2002–3, p.670.
91. Jayne, 2004, p.169.
92. Finkel, 2006, p.105.
93. Ibid.
94. McDowall, 2004, p.26.
95. Finkel, 2006, p.105.
96. Kazemzadeh, 1950, p.5.
97. Roemer, 1991, p.224.
98. Özoğlu, 2004, p.48.
99. Taheri, 1990, p.165; Savory, 1980, p.41 (100,000); Zarrinkoob, 2002–3, p.670 (120,000); Creasy, 1877, p.136 (140,000).
100. Finkel, 2006, p.105.
101. Clodfelter, 2008, p.22.
102. Finkel, 2006, p.105.
103. Shokri, 1971, p.489. For more information on Ottoman warfare, readers are referred to Murphey, 1999; and Nicolle, 1987, 1995.
104. Consult Nicolle,1995.
105. Roemer, 1991, p.225.
106. Safavi, 1962, p.354.
107. As cited from Shokri, 1971, p.489.

108. Taheri, 1990, p.165, reports 30,000 with Savory (1980, p.41) citing 40,000.
109. Matofi, 1999, p.628.
110. Shokri, 1971, pp.482–5.
111. Finkel, 2006, p.105.
112. Roemer, 1991, p.224.
113. Ibid.
114. Chase, 2003, p.119.
115. As cited by Savory, 1980, p.41.
116. Holt, Lambton and Lewis, 1977, p.400.
117. Ibid.
118. Savory, 1980, p.41.
119. Chase, 2003, p.119.
120. Matofi, 1999, p.628.
121. Taheri, 1990, p.165.
122. Monshi, 2003, pp.485–6.
123. Savory, 1980, p.42.
124. Holt, Lambton, and Lewis, 1977, p.400.
125. Ghias e Din Khand Mir, *Habib ol Seyr*, Vol.IV, pp.547–8.
126. Malcolm, 1829, p.327. Zarrinkoob, 2002–3, p.670.
127. Ward, 2009, pp.44–5.
128. Matofi, 1999, p.628.
129. Savory, 1980, p.42.
130. Clodfelter, 2008, p.22.
131. *Tarikh-e Rozat ol Safa*, (1851, Reprinted 1960–1), Vol.VIII, p.836.
132. Safavi, 1962, pp.312, 318.
133. Khorasani, 2010, p.19.
134. Falsafi, 1965, Vol.I, pp.175–8.
135. Savory, 1980, p.44.
136. Matofi (1999, p.630) attributes this to the decline in Iranian–Venetian relations before Chaldiran.
137. Jayne, 2004, p.109.
138. Savory, 1980, p.42. Roemer (1991, p.225) cites September 13, 1524 for Selim's arrival at Shiraz.
139. Chase, 2003, p.119.
140. Khorasani, 2010, p.19.
141. Finkel, 2006, p.105.
142. Matofi, 1999, p.631.
143. Mahdavi, 1985, p.21.
144. Newman, 2006, p.21.
145. Bruinessen, 2006, p.71. The Kurds had often been either allies or vassals of those Turkic confederations.
146. Bruinessen, 2006, p.71.
147. Lockhart, 1991, p.380; Matofi, 1999, p.627.
148. Safavi, 1962, pp.209–12.
149. Lockhart, 1991, pp.381–2.
150. Zarrinkoob, 2002–3, p.671.
151. Ibid.
152. Lockhart, 1991, p.382.
153. Zarrinkoob, 2002–3, p.671.
154. Newman, 2006, p.21. For the role of the Mamluks and their military during Selim's conquests, consult Nicolle, 1993.
155. Newman, 2006, p.21.
156. Ibid.
157. Chase, 2003, p.119.
158. Roemer, 1991, p.227.

Chapter 3

1. Amiri, 1970, pp.448–9.
2. Ibid.
3. Ibid.
4. Ibid.
5. Khorasani, 2010, p.20.
6. Ravandi, 1973, Vol.IV, p.693.
7. Pikolosekayev, 1975, p.488.
8. Lockhart, 1991, p.384.
9. Ibid.
10. Ibid.
11. Ibid.
12. *Tarikh-e Rozat ol Safa*, (Original in 1851, Reprinted 1960–1), Vol.VIII, p.151.
13. Shokri (1971, p.609) cites 4,500 with Matofi (1999, p.656) citing 5,000.
14. Shafa, 1969, pp.343–8; Shokri, 1971, p.609.
15. Babaie, 2005a, p.39.
16. The entire description of the armies of Shah Abbas II by Tavernier is provided by Shirani, 1957, pp.256, 278, 548–81, 594, 599–600.
17. Siaghi, 1989, p.7; Abbasi, 1956, Vol.VIII, p.239.
18. Ward, 2009, p.44.
19. Farrokh, 2007, pp.157–8, 168–9.
20. Matofi, 1999, p.659; Shafa, 1969, pp.343–8.
21. Babaie, 2005a, p.39.
22. Consult Shirani (1957).
23. Matofi, 1999, p.672.
24. Siaghi, 1989, p.8.
25. Matofi, 1999, p.658.
26. Pikolosekayev, 1975, pp.525–6.
27. Falsafi, 1965, Vol.I, pp.175–8.
28. Shafa, 1969, pp.343–8.
29. Matofi, 1999, p.658.
30. Siaghi, 1989, p.51.
31. Amiri, 1970, pp.217–8.
32. Ibid.
33. These have been compiled by Shafa, 1969, pp.343–8.
34. *Tarikh-e Rozat ol Safa*, (1851, Reprinted 1960–1), Vol.IX, pp.359, 438.
35. Falsafi, 1965, pp.177–8.
36. *Tarikh-e Rozat ol Safa*, (1851, Reprinted 1960–1), Vol.IX, pp.359, 438.
37. Valle reports these at 20,000 with the *Tazakor o Molook* (compiled by Siaghi) which cites "the Europeans" as reporting 60,000 and a European translator of the Shirley brothers reporting 50,000 (1989, p.51).
38. Consult Shirani, 1957.
39. Ibid.
40. Ibid.
41. Abbasi, 1956, Vol.VIII, pp.214–6.
42. Matofi, 1999, p.667.
43. Siaghi, 1989, p.57.
44. Roemer, 1991, p.291.
45. Siaghi, 1985, p.14.
46. Babaie, 2005a, p.40; Khorasani, 2010, p.21.
47. Matofi, 1999, p.734.
48. Ibid., p.702.
49. Consult Matthee, 1991, pp.394–5.
50. Abbasi, 1956, Vol.VIII, pp.219–22.
51. Matthee, 1991, pp.394–6.
52. Consult Shirani, 1957.
53. Matthee, 1996, p.395.
54. Matofi, 1999, p.672.

55. The entire description of the armies of Shah Safi II/Suleiman by Sanson is provided by Shirani, 1957, p.43–8, 106–7, 137–44, 185–6).

56. Khorasani, 2010, pp.21–2.

57. Amiri, 1970, pp.448–9; Monshi, 2003, Vol.II, p.653.

58. Consult Shirani (1957, pp.43–8, 106–7, 137–44, 185–6).

59. *Tarikh-e Rozat ol Safa*, (1851, reprinted 1960–1), Vol.VIII, p.212.

60. Rajab-Niya, 1955, p.50; Ravandi, 1973, Vol.II, p.398.

61. Babaie, 2005a, p.28.

62. Ravandi, 1973, Vol.II, p.419.

63. Shokri, 1971, p.156.

64. Taghzeli, 1346, Vol.VIII, p.222.

65. The oldest find of the lion and sun representation in Iran has been dated to 1450 BC (Khorasani, 2006, p.320; Nayernuri, 1965, p.78).

66. Mashoun, 2001, pp.77–737.

67. Falsafi, 1965, Vol.II, p.412.

68. Ehsani, 1989, pp.232–4; Khorasani, 2006, p.48.

69. Matofi, 1999, p.720.

70. Abbasi, 1956, Vol.III, pp.93–4. Despite his "Damascene" error Chardin's observations on the Iranian military remain invaluable to military historians. Malcolm, 1991, p.400, notes that Chardin spent ten years in Iran.

71. Shah Abbas I had purchased Indian steel though the offices of European companies established in India.

72. Matofi, 1999, p.721.

73. Abbasi, 1956, Vol.III, p.93–4.

74. Khorasani, 2006, pp.130–40.

75. Ehsani, 1989, p.263.

76. Khorasani, 2006, pp.130–40.

77. Siaghi, 1979, p.52.

78. Pikolosekayev, 1975, pp.541–3.

79. Ehsani, 1989, p.264.

80. Ghirshman, Minorsky, and Sanghvi, 1971, p.149; and Khorasani, 2006, p.619.

81. Khorasani, 2006, pp.727, 737.

82. See publications by Farrokh and Khorasani, 2009, and Khorasani and Farrokh, 2009.

83. Khorasani, 2006, pp.286–315.

84. Abbasi, 1956, Vol.II, p.340.

85. Khorasani, 2006, p.262.

86. Pour-Davood (1969, p.42) citing the *Mehr-Yasht*, verse 131.

87. Khorasani, 2006, p.662.

88. Matofi, 1999, pp.730–1.

89. A variant of this weapon is seen in Khorasani, 2006, p.656.

90. Khorasani, 2006, p.275.

91. Zelter and Rohrer, 1955, p.35.

92. Ibid.

93. Kobylinsky, 2000, p.68.

94. Khorasani, 2006, pp.283–4.

95. Taheri, 1975–8, p.159.

96. Matofi, 1999, p.729.

97. Khorasani, 2006, pp.670, 672.

98. Matofi, 1999, p.728.

99. Khorasani, 2006, pp.270–4.

100. Connell, 1968, p.211.

101. Khorasani, 2006, p.281.

102. Ehsani, 1989, p.258.

103. Juan de Persia, 2004, p.73–4.

104. Khorasani, 2006, p.284.

105. Ibid.

106. Ehsani, 1989, p.256.

107. Khorasani and Chardin have provided detailed descriptions of Iranian martial arts training during the Safavid era: Khorasani, 2006, pp.345–56; Abbasi, 1956, Vol.III, pp.179–84.

108. Abbasi, 1956, Vol.III, p.179.

109. Consult the ancient *Denkard* 8: 26.

110. Consult in-depth discussion by Khorasami, 2006, pp.333–44.

111. The term "Bastan" often refers to "Iran e Bastan" or Ancient Iran/Persia; Kazemini, 1964, p.65.

112. Khorasani, 2006, p.345.

113. There are reports the Pahlavans could wield sticks of up to 9kg; See account of a challenge between a Pahlevan named Darvish Mofred and a hooligan in Kazemini (1964, pp.78–81).

114. Matofi, 1999, p.648.

115. As cited by Matthee, 1991, p.394.

116. Khorasani, 2006, p.351.

117. Kashani, 2003, p.21.

118. Khorasani, 2006, pp.347–9.

119. Abbasi, 1956, Vol.III, pp.179–84.

120. See citations by Wiesehofer (1996, p.92) of Greek sources of the invasion army of Achaemenid Persia during King Xerxes' invasion of Greece in 480 BC.

121. Abbasi, 1956, Vol.III, pp.179–84.

122. Miri, 1970, p.20.

123. Ravandi, 1973, Vol.IV, p.693. For more details on the development of firearms in Iran, readers are encouraged to turn to Rudi Matthee and Manouchehr Khorasani.

124. Matofi, 1999, p.658.

125. Amiri, 1970, pp.448–9; Siaghi, 1979, p.52.

126. Taheri, 1990, p.216.

127. Matthee, 1991, p.391.

128. Ibid.

129. Ravandi, 1973, Vol.IV, p.513.

130. Matthee, 1991, p.391.

131. Lockhart, 1991, p.386.

132. Curzon stated that the Iranians first implemented European methods of cannon manufacturing in 1600, which is consistent with the arrival of the Shirleys.

133. Matofi, 1999, p.659.

134. Lambton, 1953, p.276.

135. Matofi, 1999, p.659.

136. Lambton, 1953, p.276.

137. Savory, 1967, pp.73–81; Lambton, 1991, p.390.

138. Abbasi, 1956, Vol.III, pp.341–2.

139. Siaghi, 1989, p.51.

140. Matofi, 1999, p.660.

141. Ibid., p.734.

142. Matthee, 1991, p.392.

143. Irvine, 2008, p.136; Gommans, 2002, p.128.

144. Khorasani, 2010, p.23.

145. Gommans, 2002, p.128.

146. Consult Shirani, 1957.

147. These new developments and inventions are discussed by Safavi, 1962, p.353.

148. Ravandi, 1973, Vol.IV, p.210.

149. Ibid., Vol.III, p.397.

150. Parizi, 1999, p.151.

151. Siaghi, 1989, p.51.

152. Pikolosekayev, 1975, pp.541, 543.

153. Taheri, 1975–8, p.159.

154. As cited by Matthee, 1991, p.401.

155. Consult Shirani, 1957.

156. See Chardin's extensive discussion on Iranian fortifications and the state of the military during the reign of Shah Safi II/Suleiman in Abbasi (1956, Vol.IV, pp.111, 140, 264–7, 270, 329; Vol.VIII, pp.186, 206–7, 235–6).

157. Matthee, 1991, pp.396–410.

158. Ibid., p.399, table 1.

159. Ibid.

160. Shokri, 1971, p.156; Abbasi, 1956, Vol.V, p.237.

161. Shafa, 1969, pp.343.

162. Abbasi, 1956, Vol.VIII, pp.219–22.

163. Shokri, 1971, pp.142, 550–80.

164. Matofi, 1999, p.712.

165. Falsafi, 1965, Vol.III, pp.124, 177–8, 180.

166. Khorasani, 2010, p.21.

167. Roemer, 1991, p.291.

168. As cited by Curzon, 1892, Vol.II, p.575.

169. Matthee, 1991, p.395.

170. Consult Shirani, 1957.

171. Abbasi, 1956, Vol.VIII, p.224.

172. Ravandi, 1973, Vol.IV, p.156.

173. Abbasi, 1956, Vol.VIII, pp.226–8.

Chapter 4

1. Roemer, 1991, pp.233–4.

2. For a review of invasions of Sassanian Persia from Central Asia consult Farrokh, 2007, pp.201–2, 209–13, 216–8, 255–6.

3. Black, 2004, p.75.

4. Savory, 1994, p.249; Roemer, 1991, p.236. Matofi, 1999, p.632, however, cites a total of six Uzbek attacks.

5. Roemer, 1991, pp.233–6.

6. As cited by Roemer, 1991, p.236.

7. Matofi, 1999, p.632.

8. Roemer, 1991, p.236.

9. Monshi, 2003 (Iskander Beg Torkaman, 1628), Vol.I, pp.54–68.

10. Ibid.

11. Roemer, 1991, p.236.

12. Matofi, 1999, p.632.

13. Ibid.

14. Bokhoor-Tash, 1971, p.48; Ravandi, 1973, Vol.IV, pp.696–7.

15. Roemer, 1991, p.236.

16. Matofi, 1999, p.632; Roemer, 1991, p.236.

17. Newman, 2006, p.27.

18. Roemer, 1991, p.237; Newman, 2006, p.27.

19. Roemer, 1991, p.239.

20. Monshi, 2003 (Iskander Beg Torkaman, 1628), Vol.I, pp. 54–65.

21. Consult Turnbull, 2003, in the references.

22. Roemer rejects this interpretation, 1991, p.248.

23. Izady, 1992, pp.102–3; Matofi, 1999, p.632.

24. Recall that the Tekkelu had been ousted from their position of power in Iran in 1531.

25. Newman, 2006, p.28.

26. Clodfelter, 2008, p.23.

27. Shamim, 1995, pp.20–4.

28. Newman, 2006, p.28; Clodfelter, 2008, p.23.

29. Shamim, 1995, pp.20–4.

30. Roemer, 1991, p.241; Shamim, 1995, pp.20–4.

31. Roemer, 1991, p.245.

32. Newman, 2006, p.28.

33. Clodfelter, 2008, p.23.

34. Roemer, 1991, p.242.

35. Matofi, 1999, p.632.

36. Roemer, 1991, p.242; Newman, 2006, p.28.

37. Matofi, 1999, p.632.

38. Mirkhand, *Tarikh-e Rozat ol Safa*, (Original in 1851, Reprinted 1960–1), Vol.VIII, p.84.

39. Newman, 2006, p.28; Matofi, 1999, p.632.

40. Roemer, 1991, p.243. Newman, 2006, p.28, states that Alghas surrendered to Tahmasp. Matofi, 1999, p.632. In this version of events Alghas and Suleiman developed a serious rift resulting in Alghas being imprisoned and dying shortly afterwards.

41. Krusinski, 1728, p.18.

42. Ibid.

43. Ibid.

44. Ibid.

45. Roemer, 1991, p.243.

46. Clodfelter, 2008, p.23.

47. Roemer, 1991, p.243.

48. Clodfelter, 2008, p.23.

49. Matofi, 1999, p.633.

50. Savory, 1980, p.67; Roemer, 1991, p.248.

51. Savory, 1980, p.67.

52. Ibid.

53. Roemer, 1991, p.248.

54. Ibid.

55. Savory, 1980, p.67.

56. *Ehya ol Molk*, as cited by Matofi, 1999, p.634.

57. Monshi, 2003 (Iskander Beg Torkaman, 1628), Vol.I, p.58.

58. Mirkhand, *Tarikh-e Rozat ol Safa* (1851, Reprinted 1960–1), Vol.VIII, pp.92, 95, 130.

59. Ibid.

60. Roemer, 1991, p.245.

61. Pikolosekayev, 1975, p.489.

62. Ibid.

63. Falsafi, 1965, Vol.I, p.11.

64. Matofi, 1999, p.368.

65. Savory, 1980, p.68.

66. For a full account of these events consult Hinz and Jahandari, 1992, pp.23–41.

67. Savory, 1980, p.68.

68. Newman, 2006, pp.41–9.

69. Savory, 1980, p.69.

70. Hinz and Jahandari, 1992, pp.11, 68.

71. Roemer, 1991, p.252.

72. Roemer, 1991, p.253, notes three accounts of Ismail II's death.

73. Savory, 1980, p.72; Roemer, 1991, p.257.

74. Ravandi, 1873, Vol.II, p.395.

75. Savory, 1980, p.72.

76. Newman, 2006. p.42.

77. Roemer, 1991, p.257.

78. Turnbull, 2003, pp.60–1.

79. Matofi, 1999, p.640, cites 300,000 troops but Savory (1980, p.72) provides a much lower estimate of 100,000.

80. Savory, 1980, p.72.

81. Mirkhand, *Tarikh-e Rozat ol Safa*, (1851, Reprinted 1960–1), Vol.VIII, p.212.

82. Matofi, 1999, p.640.

83. Savory, 1980, p.72.

84. Clodfelter, 2008, p.23.

85. Matofi, 1999, p.640.

86. Matthee, 1991, p.391.
87. Winter, 1991, p.584.
88. Matofi, 1999, p.641.
89. Monshi, 2003 (Iskander Beg Torkaman, 1628), Vol.I, pp.311, 323–9.

Chapter 5

1. Nahavandi and Bomati, 1998, pp.27–8.
2. Savory (1980, p.74).
3. Nahavandi and Bomati, 1998, pp.34–6.
4. Bahl and Syed, 2003, p.84. For an in-depth analysis of the government of Shah Abbas, Savory, 1980, 1987; Melville, 1996; Mazzaoui, 2003; and Newman, 2006, in the references.
5. Kessler and Wong-MingJi, 2009, p.250.
6. This work had been composed by Firdowsi in AD 977–1010.
7. Goodrich, 1896, p.127.
8. As cited from Ravandi, 1973, Vol.II, p.398.
9. Taheri, 1975–8, p.159.
10. Ravandi, 1973, Vol.II, p.409.
11. Roemer, 1991, p.270.
12. Consult Farrokh, 2007, pp.241–3, 261; Singh, 2002, p.227.
13. Bahl and Syed, 2003, p.84; Savory, 1994, p.251.
14. Ibid.
15. Hillenbrand, 1991, pp.775, 779–82.
16. Hattstein and Delius, 2001, p.510; Hillenbrand, 1991, p.808.
17. As noted by Lockhart, 1991, p.384, this had been observed by Vincenzo D'Alessandri.
18. Matofi, 1999, p.663.
19. For Darius the Great's reforms, consult Farrokh, 2007, pp.63–8.
20. Roemer, 1991, pp.269–70.
21. Matofi, 1999, pp.642–3.
22. Savory, 1980, p.81.
23. Ibid., pp.79–80.
24. Farmanfarmaian, 2009, pp.27–34.
25. Muskhelishvili, 1978, pp.17–30; Curtis and Kruszyinski, 2002, pp.50–8; See discussion by Whittow (1996, pp.203–4).
26. Farmanfarmain, 2009, p.24; see also Rayfield, 2000, p.58; Frye, 1977, pp.19, 145.
27. Khanbaghi, 2006, pp.130–1.
28. Savory, 1980, p.68.
29. Juan de Persia, 2004, p.129.
30. Roemer (1991, p.272) reports 20,000 Georgians in Isfahan who assimilated with the Iranian population during the reign of Shah Abbas. For more recent analyses of Iranian Georgians and their history consult Rezvani's 2008 and 2009 articles in the references.
31. See research study by Nasidze, Quinque, Rahmani, Alemohamad, and Stoneking in *Current Biology*, April 4, 2006.
32. Pikolosekayev, 1975, p.511.
33. Newman, 2006, p.52; Matofi, 1999, p.643; Roemer, 1991, p.266.
34. Roemer, 1991, p.267.
35. Newman, 2006, p.52.
36. Matofi, 1999, p.643.
37. Savory, 1980, p.83.
38. Ravandi, 1973, Vol.I, p.699.
39. Monshi, 2003 (Iskander Beg Torkaman, 1628), Vol.I, pp.412, 445.
40. Savory, 1980, p.83.
41. Ibid., p.84.
42. Matofi, 1999, p.643.
43. Savory, 1980, p.83.
44. Ibid., p.84.
45. Shah Abbas reputedly told his men "Attack like men for a valiant death is preferable to life of shame" (as cited by Savory, 1980, p.84).
46. Black, 2004, p.75.
47. Matofi, 1999, p.643; Savory, 1980, p.84.
48. Matofi, 1999, p.643.
49. Ravandi, 1973, p.63.
50. Roemer, 1991, p.267.
51. Ravandi, 1973, p.63.
52. Consult Izady, 1992, p.102.
53. Sardadvar, 1979, pp.120–2, 144.
54. Newman, 2006, p.52.
55. Roemer, 1991, p.267; Newman, 2006, p.52.
56. Monshi, 2003 (Iskander Beg Torkaman, 1628), Vol.II, pp.619, 629.
57. Mirkhand, *Tarikh-e Rozat ol Safa*, (1851, Reprinted 1960–1), Vol.VIII, pp.335–42.
58. Monshi, 2003 (Iskander Beg Torkaman, 1628), Vol.II, pp.619, 629.
59. Mirkhand, *Tarikh-e Rozat ol Safa*, (1851, Reprinted 1960–1), Vol.VIII, pp.335–42.
60. Monshi, 2003 (Iskander Beg Torkaman, 1628), Vol.II, pp.619, 629.
61. Matthee, 1991, p.392.
62. Savory, 1980, p.85; Matofi, 1999, p.646.
63. Pikolosekayev, 1975, p.51.
64. Matofi, 1999, p.646.
65. Savory, 1980, p.85.
66. Bayani, 1974, p.149.
67. Matofi, 1999, p.647.
68. Savory, 1980, p.85.
69. Nahavandi and Bomati, 1998, pp.148–9.
70. Farrokh, 2007, pp.209–13.
71. Abbasi, 1956, Vol.II, p.419. These accounts, and those of Matofi, 1999, p.647, are at variance to those described by Savory, 1980, pp.85–6.
72. Matofi, 1999, p.647; Clodfelter, 2008, p.61; Dupuy and Dupuy, 1977, p.586.
73. Falsafi, 1965, Vol.IV, pp.22–3.
74. Savory, 1980, p.86.
75. Nahavandi and Bomati, 1998, pp.149–50.
76. Savory, 1980, p.86.
77. Ibid.
78. Roemer, 1991, p.267.
79. Matofi, 1999, pp.647–8.
80. Savory, 1980, p.86.
81. Matofi, 1999, p.648.
82. Savory, 1980, p.86.
83. Matofi, 1999, p.702.
84. Ibid., p.648.
85. Ibid.
86. Monshi, 2003 (Iskander Beg Torkaman, 1628), Vol.II, pp.639–45, 654, 681, 683, 687, 697.
87. Matofi, 1999, p.648.
88. Ibid., pp.648–9.
89. Dupuy and Dupuy, 1977, p.586; Clodfelter, 2008, p.61.
90. Dupuy and Dupuy, 1977, p.586.
91. Clodfelter, 2008, p.61.
92. Monshi, 2003 (Iskander Beg Torkaman, 1628), Vol.II, pp.709–15.

93. Matofi, 1999, p.649.
94. Ibid., pp.649–51.
95. Clodfelter (2002, p.60); Izady, 1992, p.102; Roemer, 1991, p.271.
96. Abbasi, 1957 Vol.II, pp.293–4.
97. Roemer, 1991, p.269.
98. Ibid., p.267.
99. Dupuy and Dupuy, 1977, p.586.
100. Ibid.
101. Parizi, 1999, p.224.
102. Roemer, 1991, p.269.
103. The *c.* 50cm tall lion was found in 2000 inside a sepulcher in the Meskheti region of the Georgian republic. A report was submitted by Professor Tsisania Abuladze to the Institute of Manuscripts of the Georgian Academy of Sciences, Tbilisi, Republic of Georgia in 2000.
104. Abuladze, 2000, p.1.
105. Ibid.
106. The Georgian Academy of Sciences examined these documents in collaboration with professors S. Janashi and N. Berdzenishvili.
107. Abuladze, 2000, p.2.
108. Shafa, 1969, pp.343–8.
109. Goodrich, 1896, p.127. Goodrich also reports the Ottoman force as having stood at 100,000 troops.
110. Clodfelter, 2008, p.61.
111. Shafa, 1969, p.343–8.
112. Dupuy and Dupuy, 1977, p.586.
113. Mashkoor, 1999, p.277.
114. Dupuy and Dupuy, 1977, p.586; Clodfelter, 2008, p.61.
115. Ibid.
116. Finkel, 2006, p.205; Cooper, 1979, p.631.
117. Faroqhi, 2006, p.47. Note that the expression "Shia-fy" is used by the author and is not used by Faroqhi.
118. Roemer, 1991, pp.267–8.
119. Savory, 1980, p.89.
120. Roemer, 1991, p.268.
121. An excellent account of these operations is provided by Savory (1980, pp.89–90).
122. Savory, 1980, p.89.
123. Dupuy and Dupuy, 1977, pp.586–7.
124. Savory, 1980, p.90.
125. Dupuy and Dupuy, 1977, p.587.
126. Savory, 1980, p.90.
127. Lockhart, 1991, p.381.
128. For details, consult Wild, *The East India Company: Trade and Conquest from 1600*, 2000.
129. Lockhart, 1991, p.393; Matofi, 1999, p.655.
130. Ibid.
131. Lockhart, 1991, p.393.
132. Matofi, 1999, p.655.
133. Savory, 1980, p.107; Cole, 1987, p.1; Roemer, 1991, p.268.
134. Matofi, 1999, p.655.
135. The Iranians lost up to 7,000 casualties in the failed drive to Qeshm.
136. Lockhart, 1991, p.393; Matofi, 1999, p.656.
137. Sykes (2006, p.277); Matofi, 1999, p.656.
138. Ibid. Statistics for the battle are difficult to verify as Captain Alexander Hamilton, who was in the small British flotilla, reports that 40,000–50,000 Iranian troops landed on the coast of Hormuz, which seems unfeasible given the total number of vessels.

139. Lockhart, 1991, p.393.
140. Roemer, 1991, p.268.
141. Black, 2004, p.75.
142. Tarverdi and Massoudi, 1971, p.54; *Tarikh-e Rozat ol Safa*, (1851, Reprinted 1960–1), Vol.VIII, p.77.
143. Savory, 1980, p.83.
144. Dupuy and Dupuy, 1977, p.587.
145. Eraly, 2000, pp.263–5.
146. Roemer, 1991, p.269.
147. Singh, 2002, p.227.
148. Roemer, 1991, p.277.
149. Ibid.
150. Goodrich, 1896, p.127.
151. Roemer, 1991, p.277.

Chapter 6

1. Roemer, 1991, p.288.
2. Roemer, 1991, p.281, provides an excellent analysis.
3. Roemer re-defines Safil's "generosity" as one of "wild extravagance rather than generosity," 1991, p.280.
4. Roemer, 1991, p.281.
5. Imam Qoli Khan had been murdered two years before Urdubadi. Nearly all of Imam Qoli's sons were also killed.
6. The fact that Ali Pasha, the independent Turkish governor of Basra, refused to get involved in the disorders was of benefit to the Iranians.
7. Roemer, 1991, p.284.
8. Clodfelter, 2008, p.61; Matofi, 1999, p.664.
9. Roemer, 1991, p.284.
10. Ibid.
11. Dupuy and Dupuy, 1977, p.587.
12. Roemer, 1991, p.284.
13. Matofi, 1999, p.664.
14. Isfahani, 1984, pp.86–7.
15. For a full account consult Isfahani, 1984, pp.215–7, 225, 227, 229, 231, 235.
16. Matofi, 1999, pp.665–6.
17. Nicolle, 1987, p.18.
18. Clodfelter, 2008, p.61; Roemer, 1991, p.285.
19. Clodfelter, 2008, p.61.
20. Ibid.
21. Roemer, 1991, p.285.
22. Mahdavi, 1985, pp.104–5.
23. Roemer, 1991, p.295.
24. Architecture: Hillenbrand, 1991, pp.796, 801; Science: Chardin cited by Winter, 1991, p.581; Medicine: Elgood, 1953, p.315. This description may be based on an earlier work by Omar Khayyam (1048–1131).
25. Roemer, 1991, p.302.
26. Ibid., p.283; Matofi, 1999, p.667.
27. Matofi, 1999, p.666.
28. Clodfelter, 2008, p.63.
29. Roemer, 1991, p.299.
30. Dupuy and Dupuy, 1977, p.588; Savory, 1980, p.232.
31. Clodfelter, 2008, p.63.
32. Falsafi, 1965, Vol.IV, p.101.
33. Ibid.
34. He was the son of a Circassian slave woman named Nakihat Khanum. He has been described as "a blonde blue-eyed man of great physical strength" by Roemer, 1991, p.308.

35. The semi-autonomous provinces had now come under central control.
36. Roemer, 1991, p.307.
37. Lockhart, 1991, p.402.
38. Matofi, 1999, p.689.
39. Professor Vladimir Minorsky as cited by Lockhart, 1958, p.22. This is an astute observation as, despite the substantial curbing of their powers, the Qizilbash were still able to exercise their influence, especially with respect to their conservative views on warfare.
40. Lockhart, 1991, p.402.
41. Ibid.
42. Roemer, 1991, pp.307–8.
43. Ibid., p.287.
44. An excellent source on the Uzbek crisis during the time of Shah Safi I is Isfahani's *Kholase ol Seyr*.
45. Isfahani's *Kholase ol Seyr*, 1984, p.41.
46. Ibid., pp.47, 70, 89, 109. Following Zaman Beg's successful campaigns, the numbers of Uzbek military leaders killed were tabulated in government records.
47. Matofi, 1999, p.710; Isfahani, 1984, pp.47, 70, 89, 108.
48. Roemer, 1991, p.287.
49. The entire description of the armies of Shah Abbas II by Tavernier is provided by Shirani, 1957, pp.256, 278, 548–81, 594, 599–600.
50. See research study by Nasidze, Quinque, Rahmani, Alemohamad, and Stoneking, *Current Biology*, April 4, 2006.
51. Mahdavi, 1985, p.117; Duouy and Dupuy, 1977, p.587.
52. Matofi, 1999, p.667.
53. By this time the methods of forced resettlements and deportations had given way to the more "modern" ways of agents providing various inducements (including bribes) for immigration, Roemer, 1991, p.285.
54. Kazemzadeh, 1991, p.314; Roemer, 1991, p.296.
55. Lockhart, 1991, p.402.
56. Yekrangian, 2005, p.19; Dupuy and Dupuy, 1977, p.587.
57. Dupuy and Dupuy, 1977, p.587; Matofi, 1999, p.667. Chardin reports just 2,200 Cossacks, Abbasi, 1956, p.224.
58. Kazemzadeh, 1991, p.314; Abbasi, 1956, Vol.VIII, p.224.
59. Matofi, 1999, p.667.
60. Yekrangian, 2005, p.19.
61. Roemer, 1991, p.309.

Chapter 7

1. Axworthy, 2006, p.29.
2. Ibid.
3. Roemer, 1991, p.311.
4. Axworthy, 2006, p.29; Matofi, 1999, p.676.
5. Roemer, 1991, p.311.
6. Axworthy, 2006, p.29.
7. As cited from Axworthy, 2006, p.30.
8. Savory, 1980, pp.250–1.
9. Axworthy, 2006, p.33.
10. Matofi, 1999, p.677.
11. As cited from Axworthy, 2006, p.35.
12. Axworthy, 2006, p.36.
13. Zarrinkoob, 2002–3, p.735.
14. Matofi, 1999, p.677.
15. Axworthy, 2006, p.42.
16. Lockhart, 1958, p.110.
17. Mashkhoor, 1999, p.283.
18. Ibid.
19. Lockhart, 1958, p.69.
20. See discussion by Lockhart, 1958, pp.434–5, 448, 450, 461–2.
21. Abbasi, 1956, pp.218, 225; Parizi, 1999, p.461.
22. Matofi, 1999, p.690.
23. Abbasi, 1956, Vol.VIII, p.224.
24. Frye, 1989, pp.236; Ibn Battuta, 2004 (first translated and published 1929), p.180.
25. Axworthy, 2006, pp.34–5.
26. Ibid., p.35.
27. Matofi, 1999, p.678.
28. Axworthy, 2006, p.38.
29. Matofi, 1999, p.678.
30. Axworthy, 2006, p.38.
31. Matofi, 1999, p.678.
32. Axworthy, 2006, p.38.
33. Safavi, 1983, p.18.
34. Ibid.
35. Matofi, 1991, p.679.
36. Safavi, 1983, pp.23–4, 28.
37. Ibid.
38. Matofi, 1999, p.679.
39. Axworthy, 2006, p.39.
40. Matofi, 1999, p.679.
41. Matofi (1999, p.679) presents the perspective of Iranian military historiography. Axworthy (2006, pp.42–3) and Lockhart (1958, pp.111–3) suggest that Mahmoud had not been planning for an advance against Isfahan.
42. Lockhart, 1958, p.111.
43. Matofi, 1999, p.679.
44. The *Majma ol Tavarikh*, for example, reports a total of 70,000 Afghan and allied troops, Safavi, 1983, p.56. Matofi, 1999, p.679, summarizing other Iranian historians, estimating 50,000–100,000. Axworthy, 2006, p.42, reports just 10,000 with Lockhart, 1958, p.111, reporting 11,000.
45. Axworthy, 2006, p.39.
46. Matofi, 1999, p.679.
47. Axworthy, 2006, pp.42–3. Lockhart, 1958, p.111.
48. Lockhart, 1958, p.113.
49. Axworthy, 2006, p.44.
50. Shabani, 2005, pp.215.
51. Matofi, 1999, pp.680–1.
52. According to Ravandi, 1973, Vol.IV, p.702, the Safavids could draw on a very large pool of tribal and provincial units. These were composed of the Feili Kurds (12,000 infantry and 12,000 cavalry), Bakhtiaris (8,000 infantry and 2,000 cavalry), Zands and Laks (3,000 cavalry), Mamasani (3,000 cavalry), Mokri (2,000 infantry and 5,000 cavalry), Khorasani Kurds (12,000 cavalry), Jalayer and Jalals (8,000 infantry), and Afghans (10,000 cavalry). Azerbaijanis, Khuzistani Arabs and other contingents from western Iran could provide a total of 13,000 cavalry and 20,000 infantry Tofangchi musketeers.
53. Marvi, 1995, Vol.I, p.27.
54. Axworthy, 2006, p.46.
55. Lockhart, 1958, p.131.
56. Matofi, 1999, p.681.
57. Axworthy, 2006, pp.45; Lockhart, 1958, p.135.
58. Matofi, 1999, p.681 (42,000); Marvi, 1995, Vol.I, p.27 (60,000).
59. Citing Edward Browne, Lockhart, 1958, p.137.
60. Matofi, 1999, p.682.
61. Marvi, 1995, Vol.I, p.27.
62. Matofi, 1999, p.682.
63. Axworthy, 2006, p.51.
64. Matofi, 1999, p.682.

65. Axworthy, 2006, p.52; Lockhart, 1958, p.176.
66. Ibid., p.53.
67. Newman, 2006, p.124; Zarrinkoob, 2002–3, p.738.
68. Axworthy, 2006, p.53.
69. Winter, 1991, p.582; Abivardi, 2001, p.523.
70. Axworthy, 2006, p.55.
71. Zarrinkoobm 2002–3, p.738.
72. Readers are referred to Bain, 2005, pp.368–78, for a discussion of Peter the Great's ambitions in the east, especially Iran.
73. Lockhart, 1958, p.176.
74. Savory, 1980, p.248.
75. Volynsky had urged that the Russians invade but pose as Iran's friend, Bain, 2005, p.375.
76. Savory, 1980, p.126.
77. Dupuy and Dupuy, 1977, p.649.
78. Lockhart, 1958, p.247; Bain, 2005, p.375.
79. Lockhart, 179, p.179.
80. Matofi, 1999, p.683.
81. Bain, 2005, p.376; Lockhart, 179, p.179. More recent Western estimates of Peter's invasion force have been revised to a total of 60,000 troops, Clodfelter, 2008, p.121.
82. Dupuy and Dupuy, 1977, p.649; Clodfelter, 2008, p.121.
83. As cited from Bain, 2005, p.376.
84. Shaw, 1991, p.298.
85. Ibid., p.297.
86. Ibid.
87. Ibid.
88. Lockhart, 1958, p.227.
89. Axworthy, 2006, p.63.
90. *Muhimme Defteri* [lit. "Important Archives"] located in the Prime Ministry Archives, Istanbul], 130, p.360.
91. Muhimme Defteri, 131, p.117.
92. Matofi, 1999, p.686.
93. Shaw, 1991, p.299
94. Lockhart, 1958, pp.260.
95. Shaw, 1991, p.299
96. Dupuy and Dupuy, 1977, p.649; Lockhart, 1958, pp.233–4.
97. Shamim, 1980, pp.14–6.
98. Muhimme Defteri, 132, pp.230, 237; Lockhart, 1958, p.260.
99. Muhimme Defteri, 131, p.190.
100. Axworthy, 2006, p.63.
101. Matofi, 1999, p.686.
102. Lockhart, 1958, p.261; Matofi, 1999, p.686.
103. Lockhart, 1958, p.261.
104. Ibid.
105. Clodfelter, 2008, p.121.
106. Shaw, 1991, p.298.
107. Matofi, 1999, p.686.
108. Shaw, 1991, p.298.
109. Lockhart, 1958, p.263.
110. Matofi, 1999, p.686.
111. Clodfelter, 2008, p.121; Matofi, 1999, p.687.
112. Shaw, 1991, p.299.
113. Clodfelter, 2008, p.121.
114. Muhimme Defteri, 132, p.345; Lockhart, 1958, p.265; Matofi, 1999, p.687.
115. Shaw, 1991, p.299.
116. These hailed from the Kurdish-populated regions of Van and Shahrazur (Shaw, 1991, p.298).
117. Ismail Asim, Kucuk Celebzade, *Asim Tarihi*, 2nd ed., Istanbul, 1787–1808, pp.79–81.
118. Shaw, 1991, p.299.
119. Lockhart, 1958, p.268.
120. Matofi, 1999, p.687.
121. Lockhart, 1958, p.269.
122. Matofi, 1999, p.687.
123. Lockhart, 1958, p.269.
124. Matofi, 1999, p.687.
125. Lockhart, 1958, pp.269–70.
126. Matofi, 1999, p.687.
127. Lockhart, 1958, pp.269–70.
128. Ismail Asim, Kucuk Celebzade, *Asim Tarihi*, 2nd ed., Istanbul, 1787–1808, pp.434–7.
129. Muhimme Defteri, 135, p.145.
130. Shaw, 1991, pp.300–1.
131. Ibid.

Chapter 8

1. The exact date of Nader's birth is a matter of debate. Tucker in the *Encyclopedia Iranica* claims November 1688 as Nader's date of birth, however Axworthy, 2006, p.17, and the *Cambridge History of Iran*, Vol.VII, p.3, argue for August 6, 1689.
2. Zarrinkoob, 2002–3, pp.741–2.
3. Avery, 1991, p.7.
4. Zarrinkoob, 2002–3, p.742.
5. Erdely and Riasanovski, 1997, p.102. See www.ospreypublishing.com/articles/iran_at_war/ for additional information.
6. See www.ospreypublishing.com/articles/iran_at_war/ for additional information.
7. Ibid.
8. Axworthy, 2006, p.39, speculates that Nader may have actually murdered Qorban Ali.
9. See www.ospreypublishing.com/articles/iran_at_war/ for additional information.
10. Axworthy, 2006, p.60.
11. Avery, 1991, p.19.
12. Zarrinkoob 2002–3, p.738.
13. Avery, 1991, p.20.
14. Axworthy, 2006, p.68.
15. Ravandi, 1973, Vol.II, p.432.
16. As noted by Axworthy, 2006, p.67.
17. Zarrinkoob, 2002–3, p.742.
18. Axworthy, 2006, p.67. Matofi, 1999, pp.770 provides a different version of events.
19. Lockhart, 1958, p.306.
20. See www.ospreypublishing.com/articles/iran_at_war/ for additional information.
21. Zarrinkoob, 2002–3, p.741.
22. Lockhart, 1958, p.304.
23. See www.ospreypublishing.com/articles/iran_at_war/ for additional information.
24. Matofi, 1999, p.770.
25. See www.ospreypublishing.com/articles/iran_at_war/ for additional information.
26. Axworthy, 2006, p.70. Matofi, 1999, p.770, disagrees, stating that Nader had fanned the accusations against Fathali and succeeded in having the latter executed by decapitation. Readers are referred to Hedayat, 1960–1, Vol.VIII, p.518, Vol.IX, p.12; Marvi, 1995, Vol.I, p.66.
27. Avery, 1991, p.27.
28. Astrabadi, 1962a, pp.184–95.

Chapter 9

1. Parry and Yapp, 1975, p.24.
2. Axworthy, 2006, p.81.
3. Babaie, 2005, p.42.
4. Matofi, 1999, p.818.
5. Ibid., p.809.
6. Shaabani, 1990, p.165; Marvi, 1995, Vol.I, p.288.
7. Babaie, 2005, p.42; Axworthy, 2006, p.84.
8. Ibid.
9. Hanway, 1753, Vol.IV, p.253; Axworthy, 2006, p.83.
10. See www.ospreypublishing.com/articles/iran_at_war/ for additional information.
11. Shaw, 1991, p.303.
12. Babaie, 2005, p.40.
13. Ibid., pp.42–3.
14. Marvi, Vol.III, p.902.
15. Amiri, 1970, pp.217–8; Farrokh, 2007.
16. Babaie, 2005, p.41.
17. Abraham of Crete (tr. G. A. Bournoutian, 1999), p.116; Axworthy, 2006, p.83.
18. Babaie, 2005, p.41.
19. Amiri, 1970, pp.217–8.
20. Axworthy, 2006, p.197.
21. Venetian travelers in Iran cite only 10,000 men in this unit, Amiri, 1970, pp.217–8.
22. Babaie, 2005, p.42.
23. Axworthy, 2006, p.197.
24. Babaie, 2005, pp.42–3.
25. Amiri, 1970, pp.217–8; Axworthy, 2006, p.197; Matofi, 1999, pp.812–3.
26. Abraham of Crete (tr. G. A. Bournoutian, 1999), p.118.
27. Babaie, 2005, p.41. For additional information, see www.ospreypublishing.com/articles/iran_at_war/
28. Matofi, 1999, p.806.
29. Ravandi, Vol.IV, p.707.
30. Matofi, 1999, p.818.
31. Ravandi, Vol.IV, p.707.
32. Babaie, 2005, p.45.
33. Yekrangian, 2005, p.21.
34. Farrokh, 2007; Matofi, 1999, p.809.
35. Taheri, 1975–8, p.249.
36. Amiri, 1970, pp.217–8.
37. Marvi, Vol.III, p.883.
38. Matofi, 1995, p.816.
39. See www.ospreypublishing.com/articles/iran_at_war/ for additional information.
40. One example is cited by Asad (1914–5), pp.148–9, in which Nader Shah appointed the local Ali Saleh Khan as the head of the Haft Lang Bakhtiaris; Lambton, 1991, p.131.
41. See www.ospreypublishing.com/articles/iran_at_war/ for additional information.
42. Axworthy, 2006, p.111.
43. See www.ospreypublishing.com/articles/iran_at_war/ for additional information.
44. Axworthy, 2006, p.85.
45. Ministry of Culture and Art of Iran, 1974–5, pp.143–52.
46. Axworthy, 2006, pp.85–6.
47. Babaie, 2005, p.45.
48. Matofi, 1999, p.799.
49. Babaie, 2005, p.47.
50. See www.ospreypublishing.com/articles/iran_at_war/ for additional information.
51. Ibid.
52. Matofi, 1999, p.797.
53. Babaie, 2005, p.46.
54. After his capture by Latif Khan, Mohammad Khan Baluch was sent to Isfahan.
55. Matofi, 1999, p.798.
56. See www.ospreypublishing.com/articles/iran_at_war/ for additional information.
57. Babaie, 2005, p.46.

Chapter 10

1. Axworthy, 2006, p.88.
2. Ibid.
3. Axworthy, 2006, p.89.
4. Ibid., p.89.
5. Lockhart, 1958, p.298.
6. Axworthy, 2006, p.89.
7. Lockhart, 1958, p.298.
8. See www.ospreypublishing.com/articles/iran_at_war/ for additional information.
9. Consult Sheikh Hazin, 1831, pp.214–5.
10. Lockhart, 1958, p.298.
11. See www.ospreypublishing.com/articles/iran_at_war/ for additional information.
12. Lockhart, 1958, p.323.
13. Matofi, 1999, p.771.
14. Lockhart, 1958, p.323; Marvi, 1996, Vol.I, pp.85–7; Matofi, 1999, p.772.
15. Lockhart, 1958, p.323.
16. Axworthy, 2006, p.78.
17. As cited by Lockhart, 1958, pp.323–4.
18. See www.ospreypublishing.com/articles/iran_at_war/ for additional information.
19. Lockhart, 1958, p.325.
20. Ibid.
21. Lockhart, 1958, p.326.
22. Axworthy, 2006, p.82.
23. Lockhart, 1958, p.326.
24. See www.ospreypublishing.com/articles/iran_at_war/ for additional information.
25. See www.ospreypublishing.com/articles/iran_at_war/ for additional information.
26. Axworthy, 2006, p.90; According to the reports of William Cockell (resident of the English East India Compnay in Isfahan) and John Geekie (Cockell's assistant). As cited by Lockhart, 1958, p.329.
27. Ibid.
28. Axworthy, 2006, p.90.
29. Lockhart, 1958, p.330.
30. Hanway (as cited by Lockhart, 1958, p.331) (25,000); Fraser, 1842, p.95 (30,000); Otter, 1748, Vol.I, p.307 (50,000).
31. Matofi, 1999, p.772.
32. Axworthy, 2006, p.91.
33. Lockhart, 1958, p.330.
34. Axworthy, 2006, p.93.
35. Lockhart, 1958, p.330.
36. Axworthy, 2006, p.93.
37. Ibid.
38. Lockhart, 1958, p.330.

39. Axworthy, 2006, p.93.
40. Matofi, 1999, p.772.
41. Axworthy, 2006, p.93; Matofi, 1999, p.772.
42. Cockell (as cited by Lockhart, 1958, p.331). See www.ospreypublishing.com/articles/iran_at_war/ for additional information.
43. Lockhart, 1958, p.332.
44. Axworthy, 2006, p.95.
45. See discussion by Lockhart, 1958, p.332, footnote 4, which cites a certain Sheikh Hazin who notes that Ahmad Pasha sent these forces after Ashraf had his peace with the Ottomans.
46. See www.ospreypublishing.com/articles/iran_at_war/ for additional information.
47. Lockhart, 1958, p.333.
48. Axworthy, 2006, p.95.
49. Lockhart, 1958, p.333.
50. Safavi, 1983, p.80; Matofi, 1999, p.773.
51. Matofi (1999, p.773) consulting original Persian sources cites the date of 20 Rabi al-Thani 1142 H. which is calculated as November 12, 1729.
52. Axworthy, 2006, p.96.
53. Lockhart, 1958, p.333.
54. Matofi, 1999, p.774.
55. Axworthy, 2006, p.96.
56. Lockhart, 1958, p.333.
57. Axworthy, 2006, p.97.
58. Lockhart, 1958, p.334.
59. Fraser, 1842, p.100.
60. Axworthy, 2006, p.103.
61. Lockhart, 1958, p.336.
62. Fasai, 1895–6, p.167.
63. Lockhart, 1958, p.339.
64. Marvi, 1995, p.122.

Chapter 11

1. Aktepe, Minir, *Patrona Isyani* (1730), Istanbul: Istanbul University Edebiyat Fakultesi, pp.90–1.
2. Shaw, 1991, p.301.
3. Ibid.; Muhimme Defteri, 136, p.189.
4. Shaw, 1991, p.301.
5. Ibid.
6. Axworthy, 2006, p.107.
7. See www.ospreypublishing.com/articles/iran_at_war/ for additional information.
8. Ibid., p.108.
9. See www.ospreypublishing.com/articles/iran_at_war/ for additional information.
10. Shaw, 1991, p.301; Muhimme Defteri, 136, p.126.
11. Dupuy and Dupuy, 1977, p.649.
12. See www.ospreypublishing.com/articles/iran_at_war/ for additional information.
13. Consult Farrokh, 2007, Ch.17.
14. Matofi, 1999, p.775.
15. Clodfelter, 2008, p.121; Shaw, 1991, p.302.
16. Ibid.
17. Astrabadi, 1962b, p.171.
18. Ibid.
19. Matofi, 1999, p.775.
20. Shaw, 1991, p.302.
21. Subhi, 1783, pp.39–41.
22. Astrabadi, 1962b, pp.173–7.
23. Shaw, 1991, p.302.
24. Matofi, 1999, p.775.
25. Marvi, 1995, Vol.I, p.229.
26. Muhimme Defteri, 138, pp.388, 410.
27. Astrabadi, 1962b, pp.186–90.
28. Axworthy, 2006, p.128.
29. Ibid.
30. Matofi, 1999, p.776.
31. Axworthy, 2006, p.128. see www.ospreypublishing.com/articles/iran_at_war/ for additional information.
32. Axworthy, 2006, p.129.
33. Matofi, 1999, p.776.
34. Farrokh, 2007.
35. Matofi, 1999, p.776.
36. Ibid.
37. Axworthy, 2006, p.129, disputes this and notes that the European was a German engineer.
38. Matofi, 1999, p.776.
39. Axworthy, 2006, p.129. Matofi cites 12,000 having crossed the bridge, while Astrabadi quotes a smaller figure at 4,000 cavalry.
40. Matofi, 1999, p.776.
41. Axworthy, 2006, p.129.
42. Matofi, 1999, p.777; Axworthy, 2006, p.129.
43. Axworthy, 2006, p.130.
44. Ibid.
45. Astrabadi, 1962b, pp.303–4; Marvi, 1995, Vol.I, pp.258–65.
46. Marvi, 1995, Vol.I, p.226.
47. Axworthy, 2006, p.130.
48. Ibid.
49. Matofi, 1999, p.777.
50. Axworthy, 2006, p.130.
51. Matofi, 1999, p.777.
52. Axworthy, 2006, p.131.
53. See www.ospreypublishing.com/articles/iran_at_war/ for additional information.
54. Marvi, 1995, Vol.I, p.288.
55. Ibid. See www.ospreypublishing.com/articles/iran_at_war/ for additional information.
56. Axworthy, 2006, p.132.
57. Matofi, 1999, p.778.
58. See www.ospreypublishing.com/articles/iran_at_war/ for additional information.
59. Matofi, 1999, p.778.
60. Astrabadi, 1962b, p.208.
61. Babaie, 2005, pp.42–3.
62. Marvi, 1995, Vol.I, p.294.
63. Astrabadi, 1962b, p.297.
64. Clodfelter, 2008, p.121. Avery, 1991, p.92, disagrees with the date, citing December 19.
65. Axworthy, 2006, p.141.
66. Dupuy and Dupuy, 1977, p.650.
67. Avery, 1991, p.779.
68. See www.ospreypublishing.com/articles/iran_at_war/ for additional information.
69. Matofi, 1999, p.775.
70. Kazemzadeh, 1991, p.324.
71. Black, 2004, p.80. A number of Russian troops had also been stricken with disease.
72. Kazemzadeh, 1991, p.324.
73. Yekrangain, 2005, p.21.
74. Kazemzadeh, 1991, p.324.

75. Shaw, 1991, p.304.
76. See www.ospreypublishing.com/articles/iran_at_war/ for additional information.
77. Clodfelter, 2008, p.122.
78. Axworthy, 2006, pp.152–3.
79. Kazemzadeh, 1991, p.324; Muhimme Defteri, 140, pp.418–9.
80. Clodfelter, 2008, p.122 (20,000); Matofi, 1999, p.781 (50,000).
81. Consult Matofi, 1999, p.781.
82. For a discussion of the transition of Nader Khan to Shah of Iran, consult Axworthy, 2006, pp.137–174.
83. Matofi, 1999, pp.782.
84. Lambton, 1991, p.131.
85. Clodfelter, 2008, p.122

Chapter 12

1. Tucker, 2006, p.59.
2. Kulke and Rothermund, 2004, p.208.
3. Dupuy, 1986, p.650.
4. Lockhart, 1938, pp.123–4. An excellent study of Iran's financial decrepit state is provided by Matthee, 1999.
5. Dupuy, 1986, p.650.
6. Tucker, 2006, p.60.
7. Ibid.
8. See www.ospreypublishing.com/articles/iran_at_war/ for additional information.
9. Consult Peers, 2006, p.18. For a thorough analysis of the consequences of Alamgir's campaigns, consult Wolpert, 2003.
10. Alam provides an excellent analysis regarding the state of Mughal India's northern tier provinces and their political machinations prior, during, and after Nader's Indian expedition.
11. Consult Steward, 1993 for the political state of the Marathas at the eve of Nader's Indian expedition.
12. Tucker, 2006, p.60.
13. Dupuy, 1986, p.650.
14. Sharma, 1999, p.728, cites September 7, 1738 with Chand (2005, pp.39) only mentioning the month of September 1738. See www.ospreypublishing.com/articles/iran_at_war/ for additional information.
15. Avery, 1991, p.39.
16. Clodfelter, 2008, pp.122; Dupuy and Dupuy, 1977, pp.650.
17. Avery, 1991, p.39.
18. Matofi, 1999, p.787; Avery, 1991, p.39.
19. Note that some references include the following: Astarabadi, 1962a, p.429 (300,000 troops supported by 3,000 cannon and 2,000 elephants); Matofi, 1999, p.787 (200,000 fighting troops accompanied by 100,000–500,000 non-combatants), also noted by Taheri (1975–8). Hariri, 1961, pp.15–6 (citing a doctor at the court of Nader Shah, he estimates 60,000 Iranian combatants at the battle of Karenal); Curzon, 1896 (reprinted 1966), Vol.I, pp.575–6. (200,000 with 160,000 of these present at Delhi, all mounted, figure cited by Curzon from Hanway who witnessed Nader Shah's army on the march). Marvi (as cited by Matofi, 1999, p.787) cites 900,000 troops with Hariri (1961, pp.15–6) providing the highest estimate of 1,400,000 Indian troops.
20. Astrabadi, 1962b. Vol.II, p.710.
21. Hariri, 1961, pp.15–6.
22. Axworthy, 2006, p.196.
23. Ibid. See www.ospreypublishing.com/articles/iran_at_war/ for additional information.
24. Clodfelter (2008, pp.122) cites 50,000 with Dupuy and Dupuy (1977, pp.650) reporting 80,000.

25. Shamim, 1980, pp.56. The women had been recently captured in Kandahar as well as from anti-Nader Turkmen tribes.
26. Axworthy, 2006, p.196.
27. Matofi, 1999, p.787.
28. Qassem Beg Qajar, Jan-Ali Khan Kuklan, and Mohammad Beg Afshar were entrusted the command of the artillery. Consult Matofi, 1999, p.787 and Astarabadi, 1962b. Vol.II, p.710.
29. Axworthy, 2006, p.197, footnote 31. Note that the issue of payment had put a number of Mughal troops in a state of rebellion.
30. Axworthy, 2006, pp.196–7.
31. The right flank was commanded by Mohammad Reza Beg Moghaddam, Ali-Mardan Beg Afshar, Mohammad Reza Khan Afshar, Fathali Khan, and Mozzafar Ali Bayat.
32. Hanway, 1753, pp.369. There is some confusion in the sources as Matofi, 1999, p.822, states that a vessel was fastened to every camel with Hanway stating that one jar was fastened between every two camels.
33. Moghtader, 1939, pp.208–22.
34. Matofi, 1999, p.822.
35. As cited by Hanway (1753, p.369).
36. Matofi, 1999, p.788.
37. Ibid.
38. Ibid.
39. Marvi, 1995, Vol.2, pp.724, 729–30. One example is the case of Janali Kuklan who intercepted and captured a vast supply train hauled by up to 4,000 camels, elephants, horses, etc.
40. See www.ospreypublishing.com/articles/iran_at_war/ for additional information.
41. Farrokh, 2007.
42. Astrabadi, 1962a, pp.452–5; Marvi, 1995, Vol.II, pp.724, 729–30; Matofi, 1999, p.789, Astarabadi, 1962b, p.333. Astrabadi, 1962a, pp.477–80, 739–41. It is known in the West as the Koh-i-Noor diamond.
43. Matofi, 1999, p.789.
44. Farrokh, 2007, pp.270–1.
45. It is possible that the rebellion was also partly sparked by the nobility who had been forced to yield their riches to Nader.
46. Clodfelter, 2008, p.122.
47. Matofi, 1999, p.789.
48. Clodfelter, 2008, p.122.
49. Sarkar, 1973, p.1; Black, 2004, p.4.
50. Panahi-Semnani, 1991.
51. Matofi, 1999, p.792.
52. Marvi, 1995, Vol.II, p.762; Matofi, 1999, p.791. See www.ospreypublishing.com/articles/iran_at_war/ for additional information.
53. Markham, 1874, p.448.
54. Grousset, 1970, p.486.
55. Matofi, 1999, p.791.
56. Consult Astrabadi, 1962b, pp.349–50 for a full list of captured items.
57. Prior to the crossing Nader allowed a number of his war-weary Indian contingents to return home to India.
58. See www.ospreypublishing.com/articles/iran_at_war/ for additional information.
59. Marvi, 1995,Vol.II, pp.791, 799–800, 806, 808.
60. Matofi, 1999, p.792.
61. Avery, 1991, p.43.
62. Yekrangian, 1957, p.225.

Chapter 13

1. Curzon, 1896 (reprinted 1966), Vol.I, pp.135–6.
2. Matofi, 1999, p.792.
3. Hedayati, 1955, Vol.I, p.107.
4. Olson, 1973, pp.21–9.
5. Avery, 1991, p.46.
6. Shaw, 1991, p.308.
7. Avery, 1991, p.44.
8. Matofi, 1999, p.793.
9. Avery, 1991, p.44.
10. Matofi, 1999, p.793.
11. Avery, 1991, p.44.
12. Hariri, 1961, p.16.
13. Avery, 1991, p.44.
14. See www.ospreypublishing.com/articles/iran_at_war/ for additional information.
15. Shaw, 1991, p.308.
16. Avery, 1991, p.46.
17. Shaw, 1991, p.308.
18. Matofi, 1999, p.795. For additional information, see www.ospreypublishing.com/articles/iran_at_war/
19. Ibid.
20. Shaw, 1991, p.308. For additional information, see www.ospreypublishing.com/articles/iran_at_war/
21. Axworthy, 2006, p.325, footnote 19.
22. For an analysis of the dates of Nader Shah's operations in this round of Ottoman–Iranian fighting consult the study by Çiçek, Kuran, İnalcık, Göyünç, and Ortaylı, 2000.
23. Olson, 1973, pp.123–4.
24. Shaw, 1991, p.308.
25. Marvi, Vol.III, p.902; Guest, 1987, p.56.
26. Guest, 1987, p.56.
27. Consult Çiçek, Kuran, nalcık, Göyünç, and Ortaylı, 2000.
28. See www.ospreypublishing.com/articles/iran_at_war/ for additional information.
29. Shaw, 1991, p.309. Shaw quotes primary Ottoman sources.
30. Matofi, 1999, p.796. Matofi quotes primary Iranian sources.
31. See www.ospreypublishing.com/articles/iran_at_war/ for additional information.
32. Shaw, 1991, p.309.
33. Dupuy and Dupuy, 1977, p.650.
34. Clodfelter, 2008, p.122.
35. Axworthy, 2006, p.269.
36. Clodfelter, 2008, p.122.
37. Shaw, 1991, p.309.
38. Clodfelter, 2008, p.122.
39. Ibid.
40. Muhimme Defteri, 151, p.353.
41. See www.ospreypublishing.com/articles/iran_at_war/ for additional information.
42. Black, 2004, p.158.
43. See www.ospreypublishing.com/articles/iran_at_war/ for additional information.
44. As cited by Matofi, 1999, p.807.
45. Ministry of Culture and Art of Iran, 1974–5, p.140.
46. Shafi and Shaabani, 1970, p.242.
47. *Chronicle of the Carmelites in Persia*, 1939, p.650.
48. Axworthy, 2006, p.277.
49. As cited by Matofi, 1999, p.812.
50. Lambton, 1991, p.132. For additional information, see www.ospreypublishing.com/articles/iran_at_war/

Chapter 14

1. Perry, 1991, pp.63; Matofi, 1999, pp.802.
2. An excellent resource for examining the fragmentation and state of the Iranian army until the arrival of Karim Khan Zand is provided by Mirza Mohammad Taghi Golestaneh, a historian who was a contemporary of the Nader Shah era and early Zand era.
3. See www.ospreypublishing.com/articles/iran_at_war/ for additional information.
4. Golestaneh, 1965, pp.134–5.
5. Ibid., p.204.
6. Ibid., pp.27–8, 136, 145.
7. Ibid., p.130.
8. Ibid., p.147.
9. See www.ospreypublishing.com/articles/iran_at_war/ for additional information.
10. Golestaneh, 1965, p.131.
11. Perry, 1991, p.63.
12. Astrabadi, 1962b, pp.425–7.
13. Perry, 1991, p.64.
14. For a thorough discussion of this topic consult Navai, 1965, pp.235–340.
15. Perry, 1991, p.64.
16. Luri dialects still retain much of the ancient Middle Persian (Pahlavi) vocabulary as seen in Kurdish vernaculars today, however the syntax and grammar of Luri are similar to modern-day Persian.
17. See discussion in Farrokh, 2007.
18. Navai, 1965, p.34; Perry, 1991, p.64.
19. Izady, 1992, p.54.
20. Ibid., p.196.
21. For discussion of the arrival of Iranic groups, consult Farrokh 2007.
22. Matofi, 1999, p.835.
23. Golestaneh, 1965, pp.148–9, 159, 168.
24. Perry, 1991, p.65.
25. Ibid., p.76; Mousavi-Isfahani and Nafisi, 1938, pp.15–20.
26. Varahram, 1987, pp.44–5.
27. See www.ospreypublishing.com/articles/iran_at_war/ for additional information.
28. Golestaneh, 1965, p.151.
29. Ibid., p.132.
30. Perry, 1991, p.66.
31. Consult Perry (1991, p.68) for a full narration of these events.
32. See www.ospreypublishing.com/articles/iran_at_war/ for additional information.
33. See www.ospreypublishing.com/articles/iran_at_war/ for additional information.
34. Matofi, 1991, p.836, states that Mohammad Hassan Khan was defeated but Perry states that "the Qajars refused battle and retired straight to Astarabad," 1991, p.68.
35. Ibid.
36. Golestaneh, 1965, p.204.
37. Saravi and Tabatabai-Majd, 1992, p.40.
38. See www.ospreypublishing.com/articles/iran_at_war/ for additional information.
39. Perry, 1991, p.68.
40. Golestaneh, 1965, pp.208–10.
41. Ibid.
42. See www.ospreypublishing.com/articles/iran_at_war/ for additional information.

43. Golestaneh, 1965, p.214; Saravi and Tabatabai-Majd, 1992, p.32.
44. Golestaneh, 1965, pp.205–15.
45. Perry, 1991, p.69.
46. Perry has suggested that the pretender may have been insane, uncooperative, or nervous, which obliged Ali Mardan Khan to prevent him from being seen by incoming contingents (1991, p.69). Denial of direct access and audience with the Safavid pretender resulted in many potential allies melting away from Ali Mardan's army.
47. Perry, 1991, pp.70, 72.
48. See www.ospreypublishing.com/articles/iran_at_war/ for additional information.
49. See www.ospreypublishing.com/articles/iran_at_war/ for additional information.
50. Matofi, 1999, p.804.
51. Gmelin and Floor, 2007, p.71.
52. Perry, 1991, pp.72–3.
53. See www.ospreypublishing.com/articles/iran_at_war/ for additional information.
54. See www.ospreypublishing.com/articles/iran_at_war/ for additional information.
55. Matofi, 1999, p.858.
56. See www.ospreypublishing.com/articles/iran_at_war/ for additional information.
57. Perry, 1991, p.73.
58. After leaving Isfahan, Azad Khan stopped first in Kashan.
59. Perry, 1991, p.74.
60. See www.ospreypublishing.com/articles/iran_at_war/ for additional information.
61. Ghaffari-Kashani and Tabatabai, 1990, pp.50–2. See www.ospreypublishing.com/articles/iran_at_war/ for additional information.
62. Perry, 1991, p.75.
63. Ghaffari-Kashani and Tabatabai, 1990, pp.50–2.
64. Perry, 1991, p.75.
65. Ibid.; Ghaffari-Kashani and Tabatabai, 1990, pp.50–2.
66. Tapper, 1997, p.111.
67. Matofi, 1999, p.839.
68. Ibid.; Perry, 1991, p.75
69. Matofi, 1999, p.839.
70. Perry, 1991, p.75.
71. Tapper, 1997, p.111.
72. Perry, 1991, p.75.
73. Tapper, 1997, p.111. Tapper notes that Mohammad Hassan Khan Qajar was hoping for the support of the Shahsevan tribes, Kazem Khan of Qara-Dagh, Hussein-Ali Khan of Qobbeh, and Panah-Khan Javanshir of Qara-Bagh,
74. Ibid.
75. Matofi, 1999, p.839; Tapper, 1997, p.111.
76. Ghaffari-Kashani and Tabatabai, 1990, pp.50–2.
77. Matofi, 1999, p.839.
78. See www.ospreypublishing.com/articles/iran_at_war/ for additional information.
79. Perry, 1991, p.75.
80. Tapper, 1997, p.111.
81. Perry, 1991, p.76.
82. Matofi, 1991, p.840.
83. Perry, 1991, p.76.
84. Matofi, 1999, p.840.
85. Perry, 1991, p.76.
86. Navai, 1965, p.149.
87. Perry, 1991, p.76; Matofi, 1999, p.840.
88. Perry, 1991, p.76.
89. Matofi, 1999, p.840.
90. Perry, 1991, p.76.
91. Ghaffari-Kashani and Tabatabai, 1990, pp.87–8, 91.
92. Tapper, 1997, p.112.
93. Perry, 1991, p.77.
94. Ibid.
95. Matofi, 1999, p.841; Perry, 1991, p.77.
96. See www.ospreypublishing.com/articles/iran_at_war/ for additional information.
97. Perry, 1991, p.77.
98. Matofi, 1999, p.841; Perry, 1991, p.77.
99. Perry, 1991, p.77.
100. Ibid., p.78.
101. See www.ospreypublishing.com/articles/iran_at_war/ for additional information.
102. Ghaffari-Kashani and Tabatabai, 1990, pp.163–9,172 .
103. Shahbaz Khan transferred his allegiance to Karim Khan.
104. Perry, 1991, p.78. For additional information see www.ospreypublishing.com/articles/iran_at_war/
105. Navai, 1965, p.92; Perry, 1991, p.78.

Chapter 15

1. See www.ospreypublishing.com/articles/iran_at_war/ for additional information.
2. Perry, 1991, p.83.
3. Ibid., p.84.
4. See www.ospreypublishing.com/articles/iran_at_war/ for additional information.
5. Perry, 2008, "Karim Khan Zand," *Encyclopedia Iranica*.
6. This occurred right on the edge of the Zarde Kuh hills.
7. Perry, 1991, p.80.
8. Ibid., p.81.
9. See www.ospreypublishing.com/articles/iran_at_war/ for additional information.
10. Matofi, 1999, p.845.
11. See www.ospreypublishing.com/articles/iran_at_war/ for additional information.
12. Perry, 1991, p.99.
13. See www.ospreypublishing.com/articles/iran_at_war/ for additional information.
14. Perry, 1991, p.78; Matofi, p.860.
15. Mousavi-Isfahani and Nafisi, 1938, pp.272, 131, 138; Ghaffari-Kashani and Tabatabai, 1990, pp.365–8; Varahram, 1987, pp.138–44; Navai, 1965, pp.185, 191–2, 241; Hedayati, 1955, pp.94–101.
16. Herodotus, *The Histories*, I:106; IV:112; Farrokh, 2007, pp.29–31.
17. Mousavi-Isfahani and Nafisi, 1938, pp.272, 131, 138; Ghaffari-Kashani and Tabatabai, 1990, pp.365–8; Varahram, 1987, pp.138–44; Navai, 1965, pp.185, 191–2, 241; Hedayati, 1955, pp.94–101.
18. Ibid.
19. See discussion by Hambly, 1991a, p.112.
20. Perry, 1991, p.85.
21. Ibid., p.86.
22. Tapper, 1997, p.119.
23. This action earned Hussein Qoli the infamous title of "*Jahansuz Shah*" (lit. the Shah who burns the world).
24. Hassan Khan had earlier yielded his post at Astrabad precisely due to fears of being attacked.

25. See www.ospreypublishing.com/articles/iran_at_war/ for additional information.
26. Hambly, 1991a, p.113.

Chapter 16

1. Perry, 1991, p.68.
2. See www.ospreypublishing.com/articles/iran_at_war/ for additional information.
3. Matofi, 1999, p.853.
4. Perry, 1991, p.91, and Abdullah, 2001, p.54, report 30,000 while Matofi, 1999, p.843, reports 60,000 troops.
5. Babaie, 2005, pp.47–8.
6. Matofi, 1999, pp.859–60.
7. Ibid., p.859.
8. Ibid., p.853.
9. Ibid., p.853.
10. Comte de Ferrières-Sauveboeuf, 1789, pp.121–4.
11. Babaie, 2005, p.50.
12. As cited by Babaie, 2005, p.49.
13. For a full discussion see Farrokh, 2007.
14. Ibid.
15. Matofi, 1991, p.854.
16. Babaie, 2005, p.48.
17. Matofi, 1991, p.854.
18. Ibid.
19. Babaie, 2005, p.48.
20. Ibid.
21. Matofi, 1991, p.859.
22. Babaie, 2005, p.508. For additional information see www.ospreypublishing.com/articles/iran_at_war/
23. Perry, 1991, pp.99–100.
24. As cited by Matofi, 1999, p.858.
25. Perry, 1991, p.100.
26. It was surrounded by a deep water-ditch.
27. Amiri, 1970, pp.217–8.
28. Saravi and Tabatabai, 1992, p.40.
29. As cited by Matofi, 1999, p.855.
30. As cited by Babaie, 2005, p.50.
31. See report by Khorasani, 2010. Persian Firepower: Artillery. *Classic Arms and Militaria*, Vol.XVI Issue 1, pp.19–25.
32. Varahram, 1987, p.142.
33. As cited by Babaie, 2005, p.52.
34. Kazemzadeh, 1991, p.325.

Chapter 17

1. Matofi, 1999, p.861.
2. Hassan, 2005, p.21.
3. Amini, 1999, p.35.
4. Perry, 2006, p.64.
5. Hassan, 2005, p.20.
6. Matofi, 1999, p.862.
7. The Governor of Basra reputedly "begged" Kniphausen to return after having "refunded" his fine, Perry, 1991, p.87.
8. For an excellent overview of these quarrels consult "Mir Muhanna and the Dutch" in Perry, 2006.
9. Matofi, 1999, p.862.
10. Apparently Karim Khan had been convinced to release Mir Muhanna due to negotiating efforts of the latter's relatives.
11. The force was led by Amir Guna Khan Afshar.
12. Matofi, 1999, p.862; Hassan, 2005, p.21.

13. See also Chaqueri, 2001, p.36.
14. Lorimor, 1986, p.1815. The British East India Company promised to assist by the end of May 1765, an action which pleased the Zands in Shiraz.
15. Matofi, 1999, p.862.
16. Hassan, 2005, p.21.
17. Slot, 1999, p.109; Library Information and Research Service, 2006, p.376.
18. Perry, 1991, p.88.
19. Kelly, 1968, pp.52. The British East India Company had used just one combat vessel against Mir Muhanna.
20. Lorimor, 1986, p.1804.
21. Perry, 2006, p.112.
22. Matofi, 1999, p.864.
23. Ibid., p.863.
24. Ibid.
25. Hassan, 2005, p.21.
26. Hedayati, 1955, p.240.
27. Varahram, 1987, p.67–70.
28. Perry, 1991, p.89–90.
29. See www.ospreypublishing.com/articles/iran_at_war/ for additional information.
30. Perry, 1991, p.89.
31. Serjeant and Bidwell, 2005, p.95.
32. Consult Allen, *International Journal of Middle East Studies*, May 1983.
33. Potter, 2008, p.129.
34. See www.ospreypublishing.com/articles/iran_at_war/ for additional information.
35. Matofi, 1999, p.862.
36. Abdullah, 2001, p.54.
37. Perry, 1991, p.91.
38. Abdullah, 2001, p.54.
39. Matofi, 1999, p.843.
40. For a full account of the military operations against Basra consult Moussavi-Isfahani and Nafisi (1938, pp.132–4, 138, 186, 188–210) and Kashani and Tabatabai, 1990 (pp.323–7, 330, 336); Perry, 1991, p.91.
41. Perry, 1991, p.91; Abdullah, 2001, p.54; Matofi, 1999, p.843.
42. See www.ospreypublishing.com/articles/iran_at_war/ for additional information.
43. Perry, 1991, pp.90, 91.
44. Potter, 2008, p.127.
45. Perry, 1991, pp.90, 91.
46. Matofi, 1999, p.843.
47. Perry, 1991, p.91.
48. Abdullah, 2001, p.54.
49. See www.ospreypublishing.com/articles/iran_at_war/ for additional information.
50. Serjeant and Bidwell, 2005, p.95.
51. Ibid., p.96; Matofi cites Ghaffari as reporting 12,000 men, while the former believes that only 2,000 Omani fighters arrived (1999, p.844).
52. Matofi, 1999, p.844; Serjeant and Bidwell, 2005, p.96.
53. Perry, 1991, p.91.
54. Serjeant and Bidwell, 2005, p.96.
55. See www.ospreypublishing.com/articles/iran_at_war/ for additional information.
56. Perry, 1991, p.92.
57. Ibid., (April 16); Abdullah, 2001, p.54 (April 20).
58. Serjeant and Bidwell, 2005, p.96.

59. Matofi, 1999, p.844.
60. Moussavi-Isfahani and Nafisi, 1938, pp.188–210.
61. Abdullah, 2001, p.55.
62. As cited by Izady, 1992, p.54.
63. Perry, 1991, p.92.
64. Abdullah, 2001, p.55; Perry, 1991, p.92.
65. Ingram, 1995, p.34.
66. Choueiri, 2005, p.231.

Chapter 18

1. Matofi, 1999, p.848.
2. Perry, 1991, p.93.
3. Matofi, 1999, p.845.
4. Ibid.
5. Ibid.
6. Narvand, 1975, Vol.I, pp.32–33, 35.
7. Ghaffari-Kashani and Tabatabaie, 1990, pp.599, 611, 620.
8. Perry, 1991, p.93.
9. Matofi, 1999, p.845.
10. Perry, 1991, p.94.
11. Ibid., p.95.
12. Ibid.
13. Consult Floor, 2007.
14. Potter, 2008, p.128.
15. Perry, 1991, p.95.
16. Landen, 1967, p.24; Potter, 2008, p.128.
17. Ibid.
18. Potter, 2008, p.127.
19. Kazemzadeh, 1991, p.326.
20. Comte de Ferrières-Sauveboeuf, 1789, Vol.II, pp.202–3.
21. Kazemzadeh, 1991, p.325.

Chapter 19

1. Pelliot, 1949, pp.203–4; Suleiman Effendi, 1881, p.214.
2. Lambton, 1987, p.1.
3. Hambly, 1991a, pp.104–5; Zarrinkoob, 2002–3, p.770.
4. Lambton, 1987, p.1.
5. Consult Hassan Beg Rumlu, *Ahsan ol Tavareekh*.
6. Monshi, 2003, Vol.I, p.140, Vol.II, p.1085; Lambton, 1987, p.2; Zarrinkoob, 2002–3, p.771; Matofi, 1999, p.870; Hambly, 1991a, p.106.
7. Matofi, 1999, p.870; Hambly, 1991a, p.106); Lambton, 1987, pp.2–3. A number of tribes were present alongside the Quyunlu and the Develu.
8. Consult Reza Qoli Khan Hedayat, *Fihrist ol Tavareekh*; Lambton, 1987, p.3.
9. For more information on Mohammad Khan, readers are referred to Mohammad Taghi Saravi, *Tarikhe Mohammadi* [*The History of Mohammad*], Lambton, Hambly, and Farmanfarmaian.
10. Zarrinkoob, 2002–3, p.778.
11. Daniel and Mahdi, 2006, p.24; Rostam ol Hokma, 1973, p.338.
12. Sykes, 1936, p.385.
13. Ward, 2009, p.62.
14. Axeworthy, 2006, p.144.
15. Zarrinkoob, 2002–3, p.779; Yekrangian, 2005, p.27.
16. Zarrinkoob, 2002–3, p.779.
17. Yekrangian, 2005, p.27.
18. Perry, 1991, p.93.

19. See www.ospreypublishing.com/articles/iran_at_war/ for additional information.
20. Akin, 1980, p.37. In exchange, the Russians would recognize Ali Morad Khan's rule over the rest of Iran.
21. Akin, 1980, p.37, also notes that Ali Morad Khan had developed second thoughts about his proposed alliance with the Russians.
22. Lambton, 1987, p.10.
23. Yekrangian, 2005, p.30.
24. Hambly, 1991a, p.136.
25. Ibid.
26. Note reference by Hambly, 1991a, p.115, to the role of the Mazandarani Tofanchis from 1779 onward.
27. Yekrangian, 2005, p.30. Tehran did not have any military barracks at this time obliging Agha Mohammad Khan to place his troops in the *Ordu* camps during his tenure in the city.
28. Yekrangian, 2005, p.30.
29. As cited by Hambly, 1991a, p.135.
30. Nafisi, 2004, p.73.
31. As cited by Hambly, 1991a, p.135.
32. See discussion by Ward, 2009, p.64.
33. Yekrangian, 2005, p.30.
34. Hambly, 1991a, p.136.
35. Ibid.
36. Nicolle.
39. Artemi, p.205.
38. Hambly, 1991a, p.137.
39. Ibid.
40. Hambly, 1991a, p.116.
41. Kazemzadeh, 1991, p.326.
42. Ibid. See www.ospreypublishing.com/articles/iran_at_war/ for additional information.
43. Ibid.
44. Hedayat, 1960–1, Vol.IX, p.187.
45. See www.ospreypublishing.com/articles/iran_at_war/ for additional information.
46. Matofi, 1999, p.848.
47. Hambly, 1991a, p.117.
48. See www.ospreypublishing.com/articles/iran_at_war/ for additional information.
49. Hambly, 1991a, p.116.
50. Ibid., p.117.
51. Perry, 1991, p.94.
52. For a full account of these events consult Narvand, 1975, Vol.I, p.107. For a detailed account of the Jaafar Khan Zand's career in 1785–9 see also Narvand, 1975, pp.107–14), Mousavi-Isfahani and Nafisi, 1938, pp.241–62, and Ghaffari-Kashani and Tabatabai, 1990, pp.680–2.
53. Hambly, 1991a, p.118.
54. Matofi, 1999, p.849.
55. Hambly, 1991a, p.118.
56. See www.ospreypublishing.com/articles/iran_at_war/ for additional information.
57. See www.ospreypublishing.com/articles/iran_at_war/ for additional information.
58. Hambly, 1991a, p.120.
59. Ibid., p.121.
60. Ibid.
61. See www.ospreypublishing.com/articles/iran_at_war/ for additional information.
62. Hambly, 1991a, p.122.
63. See www.ospreypublishing.com/articles/iran_at_war/ for additional information.

64. Perry, 1991, p.94.

65. Hambly, 1991a, p.122.

66. Ibid.

67. See www.ospreypublishing.com/articles/iran_at_war/ for additional information.

68. Consult also Hedayat (with collaboration of Navai and Mahdas), 1994, pp.312–6 and Narvand, 1975, Vol.I, pp.235–40.

69. The Qajar army first besieged Abarkouh with inconclusive results and then marched to Nayriz.

70. See www.ospreypublishing.com/articles/iran_at_war/ for additional information.

71. Hambly, 1991, p.126.

72. Matofi, 1999, p.851.

73. See www.ospreypublishing.com/articles/iran_at_war/ for additional information.

74. Hedayat, 1960-1961, Vol.IX, pp.254–9.

75. Narvand, 1975, Vol.I, pp.268–9.

76. Keddie, and Richard, 2006, p.37.

77. Hambly, 1991, p.125.

78. For all full account of these events consult Saravi and Tabatabaie, 1992, pp.247-254 and Mousavi-Isfahani and Nafisi, 1938, pp.374–92.

79. Pirnia and Ashtiani, 2003, p.655; Consult the pages cited for Saravi and Tabatabaie and Mousavi-Isfahani and Nafisi.

80. Pirnia and Ashtiani, 2003, p.655.

81. Hambly 1991b, p.146; Kazemzadeh, 1991, p.328.

82. Price, 2005, p.88.

83. Hambly, 1991a, p.127.

84. Zarrinkoob, 2002–3, pp.775–6.

85. See www.ospreypublishing.com/articles/iran_at_war/ for additional information.

86. Matofi, 1999, p.871.

87. See www.ospreypublishing.com/articles/iran_at_war/ for additional information.

88. Hambly, 1991a, p.126.

89. Ibid.

90. Yekrangian, 2005, p.28.

91. Tapper, 1997, p.122.

92. Hambly, 1991a, p.128.

93. As cited in Yekrangian, 2005, p.28 and Hambly, 1991a, pp.127–8.

94. Hambly, 1991a, p.128.

95. Tapper, 1997, p.122.

96. Matofi, 1999, p.871; Hambly, 1991a, p.128.

97. Ibid; Zarrinkoob, 2002–3, p.776.

98. Yekrangian, 2005, p.29.

99. Matofi, 1999, p.871. The Kura is the ancient Cyrus River as cited by the Greeks (see Allen, 1971, pp.8 and Gachechiladze, 1995, p.18).

100. Yekrangian, 2005, p.29.

101. Vance, and Azari, 1961, p.66 (15,000); Yekrangian, 2005, p.29 (50,000).

102. Matofi, 1999, p.871.

103. Tapper, 1997, p.122.

104. Ibid.

105. Ibid.

106. Hedayat, 1960–1, Vol.IX, p.242.

107. See www.ospreypublishing.com/articles/iran_at_war/ for additional information.

108. Hambly, 1991a, p.129.

109. Matofi, 1999, p.871.

110. Lambton, 1987, p.10.

111. Momen, 1987, p.309; Bournoutian, 1992; p.8; Hovannisian, 2004, p.83; Daniel and Mahdi, 2006, p.24.

112. Hambly, 1991a, p.129.

113. Tapper, 1997, p.122; Hambly, 1991a, p.129.

114. Zarrinkoob, 2002–3, p.776. For further information see www.ospreypublishing.com/articles/iran_at_war/

115. Hambly, 1991a, p.130.

116. Matofi, 1999, p.873.

117. Hambly, 1991a, p.130.

118. Matofi, 1999, p.873.

119. Yekrangian, 2005, p.29.

120. Zarrinkoob, 2002–3, p.776. Shahrokh and his family were sent by Agha Mohammad to Mazandaran but Shahrokh died at Damghan, aged 63, as a result of the severity of his tortures.

121. Matofi, 1999, p.873.

122. Hambly, 1991a, p.129.

123. Yekrangian, 2005, p.29; Houtsma, 2004, p.761; Watson, 1988, p.61.

124. Kazemzadeh, 1991, p.129.

125. Zarrinkoob, 2002–3, p.776.

126. Kazemzadeh, 1991, p.129.

127. Hambly, 1991a, p.132.

128. Consult Bournoutian, "Ebrauhem Kalel Khan Javaunsher," *Encyclopedia Iranica.*

129. Hambly, 1991a, p.132.

130. Tapper, 1997, p.123.

131. Yekrangian, 2005, p.30.

132. Matofi, 1991, p.873.

133. Tapper, 1997, p.123.

134. Hambly, 1991a, p.132.

135. Zarrinkoob, 2002–3, p.777.

136. Tapper, 1997, p.123.

137. Hambly, 1991a, p.132.

138. Ibid., p.133.

139. Zarrinkoob, 2002–3, p.780.

140. Hambly, 1991a, p.133.

141. Ibid.

142. Zarrinkoob, 2002–3, p.777.

143. Hambly, 1991a, p.133.

144. Zarrinkoob, 2002–3, p.780.

145. Tapper, 1997, p.124.

Chapter 20

1. Gardane as cited by The Iranian Armed Forces Command, 1963; pp.64, 66, and Haghighat, 1989, p.175. See references for Gardane's own account of his mission to Iran (1865); Joubert as cited by Ravandi, 1973, p.719; Malcolm as cited by Matofi, 1999, p.900; Stoddart as cited by Ravandi, 1973, p.50. Fabvier as cited by Nafisi, 2004, pp.206–11.

2. Matofi, 1999, p.900; Ravandi, 1973, p.50.

3. Haghighat, 1989, p.175; Matofi, 1999, p.900.

4. Ravandi, 1973, p.50.

5. Cronin, 2008, p.52.

6. Ibid.; Morier, 1812, pp.242–3.

7. Hambly, 1991a, p.136.

8. Cronin, 2008, p.52.

9. Matofi, 1999, p.908.

10. Matofi, 1999, p.900; Cronin, 2008, p.52.

11. Nafisi, 2004, p.206.

12. Haghighat, 1989, p.175.
13. See www.ospreypublishing.com/articles/iran_at_war/ for additional information.
14. Amini, 1999, p.69.
15. Matofi, 1999, p.900.
16. The Iranian Armed Forces Command, 1963, p.64.
17. Thornton, 1995, pp.16–17, 42–47.
18. Sir Malcolm in Matofi, 1999, p.901, notes that royal units were never disbanded.
19. Sir Malcolm cited in Matofi, 1999, p.901.
20. Thornton, 1995, pp.16–17, 42–47.
21. Amiri, 1970, pp.217–8.
22. The Iranian Armed Forces Command, 1963, p.66.
23. 1,550: Stoddard in Ravandi, 1973, p.50; 2,500: Gardane in Haghighat, 1989, p.175; 150: Fabvier in Nafisi, 2004, p.211.
24. Hambly, 1991a, p.136.
25. 20: Malcolm in Matofi, 1999, p.900; 60: Stoddard in Ravandi, 1973, pp.50.
26. The Iranian Armed Forces Command, 1963; p.66.
27. Nafisi, 2004, pp.210–1.
28. M. M. Khorasani, 2010. "Persian Firepower: Artillery" *Classic Arms and Militaria*, Vol.XVI/1, pp.19–25.
29. Ibid.
30. Nafisi, 2004, p.211.
31. Matofi, 1999, p.907.
32. The Iranian Armed Forces Command, 1963, pp.4–5; Atkin, 1980, pp.106–7.
33. Cronin, 2008, p.54.
34. Wright, 1977, p.4.
35. See www.ospreypublishing.com/articles/iran_at_war/ for additional information.
36. See www.ospreypublishing.com/articles/iran_at_war/ for additional information.
37. Kibovskii and Yegorov, 1996, p.20.
38. Eskandari-Qajar, 2007, p.35.
39. Wright, 1977.
40. Ibid,
41. Lambton, 1987, p.22.
42. Cronin, 2008, p.59.
43. Wright, 1977, p.56.
44. Matofi, 1999, p.920.
45. Wright, 1977, p.57.
46. Ibid.
47. The Iranian Armed Forces Command, 1963, p.266. See www.ospreypublishing.com/articles/iran_at_war/ for additional information.
48. Matofi, 1999, p.905.
49. Ravandi, 1973, p.49.
50. Cronin, 2008, p.54.
51. The Iranian Armed Forces Command, 1963; p.7.
52. Hedayat, 1851, Vol.IX, pp.336–9.
53. See discussion by Mohyi, 1969, pp.165–76.
54. Ravandi, 1973, p.726.
55. Nafisi, 2004, p.119.
56. Matofi, 1999, p.907.
57. Ibid., p.908.
58. See www.ospreypublishing.com/articles/iran_at_war/ for additional information.
59. Consult Ralston, 1990.
60. As cited by Cronin, 2008, p.54.
61. Cronin, 2008, p.53.
62. Ibid.
63. See www.ospreypublishing.com/articles/iran_at_war/ for additional information.
64. Lambton, 1991.
65. Matofi, 1999, p.920.
66. Ravandi, 1973, p.719.
67. See www.ospreypublishing.com/articles/iran_at_war/ for additional information.
68. See www.ospreypublishing.com/articles/iran_at_war/ for additional information.
69. See www.ospreypublishing.com/articles/iran_at_war/ for additional information.
70. See www.ospreypublishing.com/articles/iran_at_war/ for additional information.
71. See www.ospreypublishing.com/articles/iran_at_war/ for additional information.
72. Matofi, 1999, p.901.
73. Ravandi, 1973, p.50.
74. Matofi, 1999, pp.900–1; Ravandi, 1973, p.50. See www.ospreypublishing.com/articles/iran_at_war/ for additional information.
75. See www.ospreypublishing.com/articles/iran_at_war/ for additional information.
76. See www.ospreypublishing.com/articles/iran_at_war/ for additional information.
77. Cronin, 2008, p.53. For additional information see www.ospreypublishing.com/articles/iran_at_war/
78. Hedayat, 1994, p.361.
79. Matofi, 1999, p.918.
80. See www.ospreypublishing.com/articles/iran_at_war/ for additional information.

Chapter 21

1. See www.ospreypublishing.com/articles/iran_at_war/ for additional information.
2. See www.ospreypublishing.com/articles/iran_at_war/ for additional information.
3. Hedayat, 1994, pp.427–8.
4. Hambly, 1991b, p.146.
5. See www.ospreypublishing.com/articles/iran_at_war/ for additional information.
6. Kazemzadeh, 1991, pp.329–30.
7. As cited in Kazemzadeh, 1991, p.330. See www.ospreypublishing.com/articles/iran_at_war/ for additional information.
8. Atkin, 1980, p.59.
9. Andreeva, 2007, p.14.
10 Cohen, 1996, p.50.
11. Andreeva, 2007, p.15.
12. Kazemzadeh, 1991, p.327.
13. Atkin, 1980, p.64.
14. See www.ospreypublishing.com/articles/iran_at_war/ for additional information.
15. Kazemzadeh, 1991, p.351.
16. Atkin, 1980, p.55.
17. See www.ospreypublishing.com/articles/iran_at_war/ for additional information.
18. Matofi, 1999, p.885.
19. Clodfelter, 2002, p.229.
20. Dupuy and Dupuy, 1986, p.779. For additional information see www.ospreypublishing.com/articles/iran_at_war/
21. Wieczynski, 1976, p.233.
22. Tapper, 1997, p.152.

23. Singh, 2002, p.410; Gvosdev, 2000, p.106.
24. Daniel, 2001, p.102.
25. Matofi, 1999, p.885.
26. Hovannisian, 2004, p.100.
27. Holding, 2006, p.82.
28. Hambly, 1991b, p.146.
29. Shamim, 1995, p.86.
30. Matofi, 1999, p.885.
31. See www.ospreypublishing.com/articles/iran_at_war/ for additional information.
32. Nafisi, 2004, p.243.
33. Matofi, 1999, p.885.
34. Nafisi, 2004, p.243; Kazemzadeh, 1991, p.332; Holding, 2006, p.82.
35. Gvosdev, 2000, p.106.
36. Ibid.
37. Mikaberidze, 2005, p.203.
38. Matofi, 1999, p.885.
39. Ibid., p.886.
40. See www.ospreypublishing.com/articles/iran_at_war/ for additional information.
41. See www.ospreypublishing.com/articles/iran_at_war/ for additional information.
42. Bournoutian, "Ebrauhem Kalel Khan Javaunsher" in Encyclopedia Iranica; Rau, 2008, p.16.
43. Mostashari, 2006, p.144.
44. Ibid.
45. Tapper, 1997, p.16.
46. See www.ospreypublishing.com/articles/iran_at_war/ for additional information.
47 Matofi, 1999, p.887.
48. Ibid.
49. See www.ospreypublishing.com/articles/iran_at_war/ for additional information.
50. Matofi, 1999, p.887.
51. Atkin, 1980, p.79.
52. Ibid.
53. See www.ospreypublishing.com/articles/iran_at_war/ for additional information.
54. Rywkin, 1988, p.176.
55. See www.ospreypublishing.com/articles/iran_at_war/ for additional information.
56. Rywkin, 1988, p.176.
57. Bournoutian, "Ebrauhem Kalel Khan Javaunsher," in Encyclopedia Iranica.
58. Ibid.
59. Atkin, 1980, p.88.
60. See www.ospreypublishing.com/articles/iran_at_war/ for additional information.
61. Eskandari-Qajar, 2008, p.35.
62. Matofi, 1999, p.889.
63. See www.ospreypublishing.com/articles/iran_at_war/ for additional information.
64. Matofi, 1999, p.889.
65. Amini, 1999, p.165.
66. Tapper, 1997, p.157.
67. Dubrovin, N., 1886–8, Vol.4–6.81. Lambton, 1987, p.20.
68. Matofi, 1999, p.889.
69. Hedayat, 1960-1961, Vol.IX, pp.438–95.
70. Tapper, 1997, p.157.
71. Matofi, 1999, p.889.
72. Williamson, 2008, p.94.
73. Atkin, 1980, p.117.
74. Tapper, 1997, p.157.
75. Ibid.
76. Hedayat, 1960–1, Vol.IX, pp.89–90.
77. Kazemzadeh, 1991, p.334; Ward, 2006, p.75, reports just 5000 Iranian troops with 2,500 becoming casualties.
78. Lambton, 1987, p.19.
79. Matofi, 1999, p.889.
80. Dupuy and Dupuy, 1986, p.779; Kazemzadeh, 1991, p.334.
81. Vance and Azari, 1961, p.117; Wright, 1977, p.53.
82. Kazemzadeh, 1991, p.334.
83. Singh, 2002, p.410.
84. Lankaran was the capital of the Talysh Khanate.
85. Ward, 2009, p.76.
86. Ibid.
87. Clodfelter, 2002, p.229.
88. Matofi, 1999, p.890.
89. Sicker, 2000, p.117; Matofi, 1999, p.890.
90. Lambton, 1987, p.119.
91. Ibid., p.19.
92. Sicker, 2000, p.117.
93. Ministry of Culture and Art of Iran, 1971, pp.127–8.
94. Lambton, 1987, p.120.
95. Ibid., p.119.
96. Farrokh, 2007.
97. "Persians" includes speakers of all closely related and mutually intelligible dialects, notably the Tats, who are predominantly Jewish.
98. Matofi, 1999, p.890.
99. Kazemzadeh, 1991, p.354.
100. Mostashari, 2006, p.19.
101. Kazemzadeh, 1991, p.355.
102. Ibid., p.354.
103. See www.ospreypublishing.com/articles/iran_at_war/ for additional information.
104. Kazemzadeh, 1991, p.336; Atkin, 1980, p.157.
105. King, 2008, pp.49–50.
106. Wright, 1977, pp.53–4.
107. Atkin, 1980, p.157.
108. Ibid.
109. Ibid.
110. Wieczynski. 1976, p.235; Guthrie, 1843, p.527.
111. Matofi, 1999, p.892.
112. Ibid.
113. Ibid.
114. Ibid.
115. Atkin, 1980, p.158.
116. Matofi, 1999, p.892.
117. Vance and Azari, 1961, p.148–9.
118. See www.ospreypublishing.com/articles/iran_at_war/ for additional information.
119. See www.ospreypublishing.com/articles/iran_at_war/ for additional information.
120. Hedayat, 1960–1, Vol.IX, pp.680–9.
121. Walker, 1990, p.46.
122. Hedayat, 1960–1, Vol.IX, p.663.
123. Ibid.
124. Baddeley, 1908, p.167; Barratt, 1972, p.386.
125. Asiatic Intelligence, 1827, p.620; Allison, 1854, p.258; Baddeley, 1908, p.167.
126. Asiatic Intelligence, 1827, p.619.

127. Hedayat, 1960–1, Vol.IX, pp.649, 671; Some Western sources contradict these reports by describing the majority of these engagements as decisive defeats for Iranian forces.

128. Allison 1854, p.258, reports a total of 1,200 Russians killed, with Baddeley, 1908, p.168, reporting 1,154. Baddeley, 1908, p.168, reports 400 Iranians as having been killed with Allison citing 2,000 Iranian dead.

129. Allison, 1854, pp.86–7; Baddeley, 1908, p.169; Hovanissian, 2004, p.112.

130. Allison, 1854, p.87.

131. Walker, 1990, p.46.

132. Baddeley, 1908, p.169. Hassan Qajar had been captured by the Russians, after the fall of Yerevan.

133. Shamim, 1995, p.101; Clodfelter, 2002, pp.230. Marand had fallen to the Russians as early as October 2. The Russians had even taken Urmia and Ardabil by early January against virtually no opposition.

134. Shamim, 1995, p.101.

135. Kazemzadeh, 1991, p.338.

136. Matofi, 1999, p.895.

137. Ibid.

138. Ministry of Culture and Art of Iran, 1971, p.139.

139. Kazemzadeh, 1991, p.338.

140. See www.ospreypublishing.com/articles/iran_at_war/ for additional information.

Chapter 22

1. Ravandi, 1973, Vol.II, p.500.

2. Lambton, 1987, p.23.

3. Thornton, 1995, p.47.

4. Wright, 1977, pp.56–7. Rawlinson had deciphered much of the ancient script at the site of Bisitun from the time of Darius the Great; Matofi, 1999, p.920; Kaye, 1857, p.137. See www.ospreypublishing.com/articles/iran_at_war/ for additional information.

5. See www.ospreypublishing.com/articles/iran_at_war/ for additional information.

6. The assembly took place after the conclusion of the Treaty of Golestan on September 24, 1813.

7. Farwell, 2001, p.643.

8. Clodfelter, 2008, p.231; Dupuy and Dupuy, 1977, p.779.

9. Hambly, 1991b, p.163.

10. Matofi, 1999, p.898.

11. Ibid.; Hedayat, 1960–1, Vol.IX, p.558, has provided a detailed account of the subsequent events.

12. See www.ospreypublishing.com/articles/iran_at_war/ for additional information.

13. Matofi, 1999, p.898; Kazemzadeh, 1991, p.340.

14. Hedayat has provided detailed accounts of the Qajar pacification campaign: Hedayat, 1960–1, Vol.X, p.211–2.

15. Vance and Azari, 1961, p.203.

16. See www.ospreypublishing.com/articles/iran_at_war/ for additional information.

17. See www.ospreypublishing.com/articles/iran_at_war/ for additional information.

18. Hedayat, 1960–1, Vol.X, p.209; Ward, 2009, p.77. See www.ospreypublishing.com/articles/iran_at_war/ for additional information.

19. Elgood, 1991, p.539.

20. See www.ospreypublishing.com/articles/iran_at_war/ for additional information.

21. See www.ospreypublishing.com/articles/iran_at_war/ for additional information.

22. Balfour,1885, p.188.

23. Lambton, 1987, p.23. Cronin, 2008, p.62, provies an excellent overview of the trials and challenges of the British military mission until their complete departure from Iran in 1838.

24. Kelly, 1968, p.293.

25. Wright, 1977, p.58; Andreeva, 2007, p.16.

26. Vance and Azari, 1961, p.204.

27. Tanner, 2009, p.135; Wright, 1977, p.58; Matofi, 1999, p.916.

28. Adamiyat, 1984, p.287.

29. Institute for Research and Studies of Culture, 1992, pp.211–4; Tanner, 2009, p.135; Cronin, 2008, p.59.

30. Hedayat, 1960–1, Vol.X, p.269. The map has survived to the present and is housed at the Military Museum of Saadabad in Tehran.

31. Hedayat, 1960–1, Vol.X, pp.231–4.

32. Institute for Research and Studies of Culture, 1992, pp.211–4.

33. Ward, 2009, p.78.

34. See www.ospreypublishing.com/articles/iran_at_war/ for additional information.

35. Vance and Azari, 1961, p.205.

36. Wright, 1977, p.58.

37. According to Mirza Taqhi Khan "No one can rule in Iran except with British approval" as cited by Matofi, 1999, p.917.

38. See detailed discussion by Etehadiye, 1976, pp.70–6, 79–91.

39. Andreeva, 2007, p.71.

40. Matofi, 1999, p.918; Kelly, 1968, pp.297; Wright, 1977, pp.58–9.

41. Ibid.

42. Mahdavi, 1985, p.252.

43. Wright, 1977, p.59.

44. Shamim, 1995, p.149.

45. Yekrangian, 2005, p.69.

46. Shamim, 1995, pp.151–2.

47. Yekrangian, 2005, p.69.

48. Shamim, 1995, p.151.

49. Yekrangian, 2005, p.69.

50. Hiro, 1990, p.8.

51. See www.ospreypublishing.com/articles/iran_at_war/ for additional information.

52. Shamim, 1995, p.117; Matofi, 1999, p.890.

53. Shamim, 1995, p.118.

54. Shaw, 1977, p.16.

55. Williamson, 2008, pp.92–3.

56. Ibid., p.93.

57. As cited by Hambly, 1991b, p.150.

58. Hambly, 1991b, p.171.

59. As cited by Hambly, 1991b, p.172.

60. Williamson, 2008, p.92.

61. Ibid.

62. Williamson, 2008, p.93.

63. See www.ospreypublishing.com/articles/iran_at_war/ for additional information.

64. Shamim, 1995, p.118.

65. Matofi, 1999, p.890.

66. Shamim, 1995, p.118.

67. Ibid.

68. See www.ospreypublishing.com/articles/iran_at_war/ for additional information.

69. Yekrangian, 2005, p.56.

70. Lambton, 1987, p.20; Shamim, 1995, p.119.

71. Matofi, 1999, p.891;Hedayat, 1960–1, Vol.. IX, pp.608–11.

72. Williamson, 2008, p.96, cites 40,000–60,000 Ottoman troops with Shamim, 1995, p.119, citing 70,000.

73. Williamson, 2008, pp.95–6.

74. See www.ospreypublishing.com/articles/iran_at_war/ for additional information.

75. Matofi, 1999, p.891; Shamim, 1995, p.120.

76. Abdolghani, 1984, p.5.

77. Ibid., pp.5–6.

78. Lambton, 1987, p.20.

79. Matofi, 1999, p.919.

80. Lambton, 1987, p.20.

81. Ibid; Matofi, 1999, p.919.

82. Mashkoor, 1999, p.344.

83. Ghareeb, 1990, p.25.

84. Shamim, 1995, p.216.

85. Ibid.

86. Lambton, 1987, p.20.

87. Ibid., p.21.

88. King, 1987, p.6.

89. Hiro, 1990, p.8.

90. Hambly, 1991b, p.145.

91. Ibid.

92. Greaves, 1991, p.394.

93. Matofi, 1999, p.918.

94. Mahdavi, 1985, p.266.

Chapter 23

1. Matofi, 1999, p.923.

2. Consult Tahmasbpour, 2008.

3. Zarrinkoob, 2002–3, p.813; Hervai and Fekri, 1993, pp.25–49.

4. Zarrinkoob, 2002–3, p.813.

5. Matofi, 1999, p.924.

6. Zarrinkoob, 2002–3, p.813.

7. For the history of the Bahai movement, readers are referred to Smith, 2008, and Momen, 2007.

8. Dumper and Stanley, 2006, p.341.

9. Afaqi and Jasion, 2004, p.69.

10. Mackey, 1996, p.132.

11. Ibid.

12. Matofi, 1999, p.924.

13. Daniel, 2001, p.108.

14. Mashkoor, 1999, p.347. Hutter, 2005, pp.737–40.

15. Ghani, 2000, p.3.

16. See www.ospreypublishing.com/articles/iran_at_war/ for additional information.

17. Matofi, 1999, p.935.

18. Keddie, 1991, p.182; Matofi, 1999, p.936.

19. See www.ospreypublishing.com/articles/iran_at_war/ for additional information.

20. Babaie, 2005a, p.57.

21. Adamiyat, 1984, pp.172–219, 295, 297.

22. Abrahamian, 1982, p.54.

23. Daniel, 2001, p.110.

24. Lambton, 1987, p.23.

25. Cronin, 2008, p.61.

26. Yekrangian, 2005, p.70; Adamiyat, 1984, p.734.

27. Cronin, 2008, p.61.

28. Babaie, 2005a, p.57; Matofi, 1999, p.939.

29. Adamiyat, 1984, pp.290–7; Yekrangian, 2005, p.74; Matofi, 1999, p.939.

30. Adamiyat, 1984, pp.292–9.

31. Daniel, 2001, p.110; Matofi, 1999, p.938.

32. Ward, 2009, p.81.

33. Abrahamian, 1982, p.54.

34. Daniel, 2001, p.110.

35. Amanat, 1997, p.161.

36. Daniel, 2001, p.111.

37. Abrahamian, 1982, p.54.

38. Matofi, 1999, p.936.

39. Daniel, 2001, p.111.

40. Browne, 1910, p.xvi.

41. Keddie, 1991, p.182; Ghani, 2000, p.4.

42. Kelly, 1968, p.454; Wright, 1977, p.59.

43. Ibid.

44. Kazemzadeh, 1991, p.141.

45. Kelly, 1968, p.455.

46. Shamim, 1995, p.230.

47. Kazemzadeh, 1991, p.141; Kelly, 1968, p.456.

48. Kelly, 1968, p.459.

49. Wright, 1977, p.23. For additional information see www.ospreypublishing.com/articles/iran_at_war/

50. Greaves, 1991, p.394.

51. Kelly, 1968, p.461.

52. Ibid., p.459.

53. Razi, 1957–8, p.521. Sicker, 2000, p.154, notes Shahzadeh Mohammad Yusef was favorable to the Qajars at this time.

54. Kelly, 1968, p.459.

55. Matofi, 1999, p.924.

56. Ward, 2009, p.78.

57. See www.ospreypublishing.com/articles/iran_at_war/ for additional information.

58. Shiels, 2003, p.185; Sykes, 2006, p.452.

59. Ward, 2009, p.78.

60. Lee, 1996, p.251; For a full account of the mobilization of the army and all the details of the Herat campaign, consult Hedayat, Vol.X, pp.67–9.

61. See www.ospreypublishing.com/articles/iran_at_war/ for additional information.

62. See www.ospreypublishing.com/articles/iran_at_war/ for additional information.

63. Kelly, 1968, p.463.

64. Ibid., p.465.

65. As cited by Kelly (1968, p.465) from British government archives outlining the communication of Lord Clarendon (the British foreign secretary) to the Sadr e Azam on July 11, 1856.

66. Kelly, 1968, p.472.

67. Matofi, 1999, p.928. Kelly (1968, pp.469, 472) however reports 5,700 men (including infantry, light cavalry and artillery) being ferried by a total of 45 vessels, with eight of these being combat steamers.

68. Kelly, 1968, p.427.

69. Matofi, 1999, p.928; Haghighat, 1989, pp.925–57.

70. Matofi, 1999, p.928.

71. Kelly, 1968, p.473; Shamim, 1995, p.234.

72. It is unclear whether the Ottomans openly cooperated with the British in this case or that they were simply unable to prevent the British from engaging in these activities.

73. Hedayat, 1960–1, Vol.X, pp.819–45.

74. Kelly, 1968, p.473.

75. Shamim, 1995, p.234.

76. Kelly, 1968, p.473.

77. Hedayat, 1960–1, Vol.X, pp.819–45.

78. Matofi, 1999, p.928.
79. Ibid.
80. Kelly, 1968, p.473.
81. Ibid.
82. Sykes, 2006, p.452.
83. See www.ospreypublishing.com/articles/iran_at_war/ for additional information.
84. Kelly, 1968, p.480.
85. Matofi, 1999, p.928.
86. Wright, 1977, p.60; Kelly, 1968, p.482.
87. Wright, 1977, p.60.
88. Hedayat, 1960–1, Vol.X, pp.72–43.
89. Matofi, 1999, p.929.
90. Ibid.
91. Kelly, 1968, p.482.
92. Wright, 1977, p.60.
93. Matofi, 1999, p.929.
94. Kelly, 1968, p.494.
95. Matofi, 1999, p.929.
96. See www.ospreypublishing.com/articles/iran_at_war/ for additional information.
97. Vance and Azari, 1961, pp.290–303.
98. Ibid. Kelly, 1968, p.485, claims 200 Iranian dead.
99. Shamim, 1995, p.238.
100. Ibid.
101. Matofi, 1999, p.931.
102. Mahdavi, 1985, p.275.
103. Razi, 1957–8, p.522; Lambton, 1987, p.21.
104. Shamim, 1995, pp.239–40.
105. Karsh, 2007, p.125.
106. Ibid.
107. Wright, 1977, p.61.
108. Lambton, 1987, p.21.
109. Razi, 1957–8, p.523.
110. See www.ospreypublishing.com/articles/iran_at_war/ for additional information.
111. Shamin, 1995, p.254.
112. Kazemzadeh, 1991, p.141.
113. Lambton, 1987, p.21.
114. Ibid.
115. Matofi, 1999, p.932.
116. For further sources on the Qajar army, see Lord Nathaniel Curzon, 1892, Heravi and Fekri, Mahdavi.
117. Curzon, 1892, p.590.
118. Ibid.
119. Matofi, 1999, p.949.
120. Consult Heravi and Fekri, 1993, pp.50–1 and Ravandi, 1973, pp.728, 738.
121. Vance and Azari, 1961, pp.24–5.
122. Matofi, 1999, p.957.
123. Ward, 2009, p.72.
124. Ibid.
125. Matofi, 1999, p.960; Cronin, 2008, p.64.
126. Tousi, 1988, pp.211–2, 215.
127. Curzon, 1892, pp.589–90.
128. Vance and Azari, 1961, pp.24–5.
129. De Gobineau, 1905, pp.109–14.
130. Ibid.
131. Ward, 2009, pp.69–71.
132. Cronin, 2008, pp.66–7.
133. Ibid.
134. Tousi, 1988, pp.218–9; Abdollah, 1974, p.149.
135. Ward, 2008, p.73.
136. Ibid.
137. Curzon, 1892, pp.67, 592. For additional information see www.ospreypublishing.com/articles/iran_at_war/
138. Cronin, 2008, p.62.
139. Matofi, 1999, p.958.
140. Cronin, 2008, pp.62–3.
141. Lambton, 1987, p.23.
142. Etemadolsaltaneh, 1971, pp.207, 461.
143. See www.ospreypublishing.com/articles/iran_at_war/ for additional information.
144. Matofi, 1999, p.961.
145. Ward, 2009, p.82.
146. Fernier, 1982, p.44.
147. See www.ospreypublishing.com/articles/iran_at_war/ for additional information.
148. Cronin, 2008, p.68.
149. Hiro, 2000, p.16; Ward, 2009, p.83.
150. Cronin, 2008, p.68; Lambton, 1987, pp.23–4.
151. Padgin, 2009, p.477.
152. Herrman, 2006, p.26.
153. Ewans, Pottinger, Macdonald-Kinneir, von Meyendorf, De Lacy Evans and MacNeill, 2002, p.10.
154. Rejendra and Kaplan, 2003, p.22.
155. Padgin, 2009, p.477.
156. Milani, 1994, p.25.
157. Ewans, Pottinger, Macdonald-Kinneir, von Meyendorf, De Lacy Evans and MacNeill, 2002, p.10; Adelson, 1995, pp.57–8, 65, 67.
158. See www.ospreypublishing.com/articles/iran_at_war/ for additional information.
159. Wright, 1977, p.95.
160. Shamim, 1995, p.250.
161. Wright, 1977, p.101.
162. See www.ospreypublishing.com/articles/iran_at_war/ for additional information.
163. Telegraph: Greaves, 1991, p.483; Keddie, 2006, p.64; Postage: Matofi, 1999, p.934; Russia however imposed two moratoriums on railway building in Iran, preventing expansion between 1890 and 1910. Davenport-Hines and Jones, 2003, p.36.
164. Ward, 2009, p.64.
165. Potter, 2008, p.141.
166. Ibid., p.132.
167. Ibid.
168. Ward, 2009, p.66.
169. Matofi, 1999, p.989.
170. Ward, 2009, p.66.
171. Matofi, 1999, pp.991–2.
172. Potter, 2008, p.133.
173. See www.ospreypublishing.com/articles/iran_at_war/ for additional information.
174. Potter, 2008, p.138.
175. Ibid.
176. Curzon, 1892, p.406.
177. Ibid.
178. See www.ospreypublishing.com/articles/iran_at_war/ for additional information.
179. Marschall, 2003, p.129.
180. Potter, 2008, p.141.
181. Marschall, 2003, p.129.

182. Ibid.
183. Ibid.
184. Standish, 1998, pp.149–77.
185. Kelly, 1968, p.458.
186. Potter, 2008, p.132.
187. Bruinessen, 2006, p.72.
188. See www.ospreypublishing.com/articles/iran_at_war/ for additional information.
189. Yekrangian, 2005, p.325.
190. Ibid.
191. Zarrinkoob, 2002-2003, p.814.
192. Bruinessen, 2006, p.82.
193. Bruinessen, 1992, pp.328–9.
194. Bruinessen, 2006, p.82.
195. Joseph, 1961, p.109.
196. Ward, 2009, p.86.
197. Zarrinkoob, 2002–3, p.814; Ward, 2009, p.86) disputes this by stating that the Kurdish rebels had already departed before the arrival of the Iranian army. For additional information see www.ospreypublishing.com/articles/iran_at_war/
198. Whittow, 1996, p.203–4; See translation of Dasxuranci by Dowsett, 1961, pp.110–3 and translation of Sebeos by Macler, pp.98–9; consult Farmanfarmian's publication on the subject in the *Journal of Persianate Studies* (see references); Zenkowsky, 1960, p.10.
199. Zenkowsky, 1960, p.94.
200. Altstadt, 1992, pp.52–6.
201. Kushner, 1977, p.12; Zenkowsky, p.94, 297; Swietochowski, 1995, p.29.
202. Mulla Nasrredin is the name of a satirical-comical character highly popular in Turkey, Iran, the Republic of Azerbaijan as well as the Georgian republic; Zenkowsky, 1960, p.95; The cartoons published by the *Mulla Nasrredin* papers provides evidence of consistent anti-Iranian and anti-Islamic imagery. A number of these cartoons are now posted on the official website of the Republic of Azerbaijan: www.azer.com.
203. Swietochowski, 1995, p.29; See report by the Unrepresented Nations and Peoples organization on the history of the Talysh in history to the present day in the ROA: www.unpo.org/member_profile.php?id=65
204. See www.ospreypublishing.com/articles/iran_at_war/ for additional information.
205. Ward, 2009, p.83.
206. Ibid.
207. O'Shea, 2004, p.96.
208. Ibid.

Chapter 24

1. Lambton, 1987, p.307.
2. Cronin, 2008, pp.68–9; Ward, 2009, p.83.
3. See www.ospreypublishing.com/articles/iran_at_war/ for additional information.
4. Consult Cantwill-Smith, 1957, p.49.
5. Afary, 1996, p.33.
6. Destrée-Donckier de Donceel, 1974, pp.2–3; Afary, 1996, p.33.
7. Consult Edward Browne and Cosroe Chaqueri in references.
8. Lambton, 1987, p.314.
9   Adelson, 1995, p.59.
10. Cleveland, 1999, p.142.
11. Shuster, 1912, p.20.
12. Afary, 1996, p.33.
13. Ibid., p.54.

14. See www.ospreypublishing.com/articles/iran_at_war/ for additional information.
15. Cronin, 2008, p.69.
16. Ibid., p.70.
17. Cleveland, 1999, p.142.
18. Shuster 1912, pp.21–2. See www.ospreypublishing.com/articles/iran_at_war/ for additional information.
19. Kazemzadeh, 1991, p.343.
20. Keddie, 2006, p.69.
21. Adelson, 1995, p.61.
22. Keddie, 2006, pp.69–70.
23. Chaqueri, 2000, p.102.
24. Adelson, 1995, p.61.
25. Keddie, 2006, p.69.
26. Shuster, 1912, p.30.
27. Chaqueri, 2000, p.100.
28. Ibid., p.101.
29. Shuster, 1912, p.31.
30. Ibid., 37–9.
31. Ibid., p.24.
32. Van Bruinessen, 2006, p.70.
33. Ibid.; Afary, 1996, p.140.
34. Ward, 2009, p.83; Hiro, 2000, p.16.
35. Ward, 2009, p.85.
36. Cronin, 2008, p.69.
37. Shamim, 2005, p.504; Shuster, 1912, p.31; Chaqueri, 2000, p.102.
38. Ward, 2009, p.83.
39. Cronin, 1997, p.61.
40. Cronin, 1997, p.60.
41. Afary, 1996, p.141.
42. Shuster, 1912, p.34.
43. Chaqueri, 2000, p.102.
44. Shuster, 1912, p.34.
45. Cronin, 1997, p.61.
46. Keddie, 2006, p.70.
47. Ibid.
48. Chaqueri, 2000, p.102.
49. Afary, 1996, p.223.
50. Chaqueri, 2000, p.159.
51. Ibid., p.102.
52. Price, 2005, p.148.
53. Afary, 1996, p.223.
54. Shafaq, 2008, p.9.
55. Shuster, 1912, p.37.
56. Bosworth, 2007, p.496.
57. Keddie, 2006, p.70; Daniel and Mahdi, 2006, pp.27–8.
58. Ibid.
59. Chaqueri, 2000, p.104.
60. Ward, 2009, p.100.
61. Ibid.
62. Gaunt, Bet-şawoce and Donef, 2006, p.91.
63. Ward, 2009, p.100.
64. Browne, 1914, p.316.
65. Shuster, 1912, p.37.
66. Ward, 2009, p.100.
67. Ibid.
68. Ibid.
69. Browne, 1914, p.316.
70. Shuster, 1912, p.37.

71. Cronin.1997, p.81; Browne, 1914, p.316.
72. Afary, 1996.
73. Ibid.
74. Afary, 1996, p.292.
75. Cronin, 1997, p.61.
76. Ibid., p.62.
77. Shamim, 1995, p.572.
78. Holt, Lambton and Lewis, 1977, p.598.
79. Shamim, 1995, p.574.
80. Ibid., pp.572–3.
81. Ibid., p.573.
82. Ward, 2009, p.104.
83. Holt, Lambton and Lewis, 1977, p.598.
84. Shamim, 1995, p.574.
85. Ward, 2009, p.104.
86. Ibid.
87. Shamim, 1995, p.575.
88. Adelson, 1995, p.96.
89. Keddie, 1991, p.206.
90. Ibid.
91. Ward, 2009, p.101.
92. Shuster, 1912, pp.97–104, 106, 120, 154–5, 351.
93. Cronin, 2008, p.70.
94. Shuster, 1912, p.157; Adelson, 1995, p.96; Daniel and Mahdi, 2006, pp.27–8.
95. Adelson, 1995, p.96.
96. Shuster, 1912, p.157.
97. Afary, 1996, pp.329–30. Shuster claims the date as November 17, 1911.
98. Browne, 1910, p.333.
99. Ibid.; Adelson, 1995, p.96; Keddie, 1991, p.206.
100. Price. 2005, pp.153. Shuster, 1912, pp.183–9.
101. Afary, 1996, p.331.
102. Shuster, 1912, pp.177, 180.
103. Yekrangian, 2005, p.138.
104. Browne, 1912, p.333.
105. Shuster, 1912, p.179.
106. Yekrangian, 2005, p.138.
107. Shuster, 1912, p.183.
108. See www.ospreypublishing.com/articles/iran_at_war/ for additional information.
109. Hershlag, 1980, p.161.
110. Berberian, 2001, p.173.
111. Gallagher, 2006, p.21.
112. Chaqueri, 2001, p.105; Shuster, 1912, p.201.
113. As cited by Shuster, 1912, pp.201, 202–23.
114. Edward Browne, *The Reign of Terror at Tabriz*, as cited by Chaqueri, 2001, p.105.
115. Shuster, 1912, p.203.

Chapter 25

1. Matofi, 1999, p.998.
2. Unit for the Publication of Documents-Office of International Political Studies, 1991, p.92.
3. Afaz ol Molk, 1982, pp.72, 250.
4. Ward, 2009, p.87.
5. Bina, 1959, pp.81–2; Matofi, 1999, p.997.
6. Ward, 2009, p.86.
7. Cronin, 2008, p.71; Ward, 2009, p.105.
8. Yekrangian, 2005, p.157.
9. Matofi, 1999, pp.1082–3.
10. Yekrangian, 2005, pp.134.
11. Babaie, 2005b, pp.98–110; Yekrangian, 2005, pp.221–32; Matofi, 1999, pp.1082–3.
12. Ward, 2009, p.102. Iranian Gendarmerie units, personnel and equipment at the eve of the First World War: Yusef Abad had 140 gendarmes and 450 cavalry; Bagh e Shah had 1,450 gendarmes and 500 cavalry; Shiraz had 2,622 gendarmes, 845 cavalry, one machinegun group and an artillery unit; Kerman had 200 gendarmes and two machinegun groups; Ghazvin had 700 gendarmes and 250 cavalry; and Isfahan had 500 gendarmes and 250 cavalry. Data on numbers of personnel and equipment for machinegun and artillery units not available. Babaie, 2005b, pp. 98–110; Yekrangian, 2005, pp.221–32; Matofi, 1999, pp.1082–3.
13. Cronin, 1997, p.64.
14. Ibid., p.63.
15. Ibid., p.64.
16. Ibid.
17. Tehran's factories could produce 1,000 rifles per month, gunpowder and ammunition; Tabriz produced unknown quantities of 3-pounder cannon; Shiraz, Isafan, Khansar, Galpayegan and Mashad could produce each 1,000 rifles per month; Shahsavar mainly produced ammunition. The facilities may have been a part of the production centres in Babolsar. The inventory of Rasht's armament production centers are not known.
18. This facility was able to produce up to 10,000 cartridges daily but in practice only half that number was produced, Ward, 2009, p.87, partly due to poor management; Matofi, 2004, p.960.
19. Heravi and Fekri, 1993, p.149.
20. Ibid., p.161.
21. Babaie, 2005, p.20.
22. Nicolle, 1994. p.36
23. In one notable engagement, Pesyan led a contingent of the Gendarmerie and Melliyun (nationalist) fighters at Hamadan (just below northwest Iran) to defeat and repel a force of Persian Cossacks.
24. Ward, 2009, p.115.
25. Heravi and Fekri, p.149.
26. These were christened as the *Mazandran*, *Azerbaijan*, *Gilan* and *Khorasan*. They were powered by coal but later converted to petroleum.
27. Ward, 2009, p.112.
28. Ibid., p.110.
29. Van Bruinessen, 2006, p.70.
30. Bruinessen, 2006, p.70.
31. O'Shea, 2004, p.96.
32. Gilak, 1992, pp.10–3; Fakhrai, 1977, pp.146, 250–1; Fakhrai, 1982, p.40; Dailami, 2006, p.143.
33. Kasravi, 2005, p.712.
34. For a complete account consult Miroshnikov in references; Dailami, 2006, p.144.
35. Ward, 2009, p.114
36. Dailami, 2006, p.146; 10,000 was cited by Turkish diplomat Ubeydollah Effendi in his correspondence with Mirza Kuchik Khan, the leader of the Jangali movement. Consult British Foreign Office documents FO248/1203.
37. Dailami, 2006, p.146.
38. Kasravi, 2005, pp.712–3.
39. Ward, 2009, p.113.
40. Cronin, 1997, p.77.

41. Ibid., p.66. The British had originally mooted the idea of a British-led indigenous force to protect British interests in Iran in 1902.
42. Matofi, 1999, p.1020; Mahdavi, 1985, pp.345–8.
43. Ward, 2009, p.118.
44. Baratov had landed with fresh troops at Bandar Anzali on November 12, 1915.
45. Hinterhoff, 1984, pp.1153–7.
46. Ward, 2009, pp.115–6.
47. Hinterhoff, 1984, pp.1153–7.
48. Ward, 2009, p.116.
49. O'Shea, 2004, p.96.
50. Ward, 2009, p.116.
51. O'Shea, 2004, p.96.
52. Ward, 2009, p.117.
53. Ibid.
54. Ibid.
55. Tucker and Roberts, 2005, p.2005.
56. Burg and Purcell, 2004, p.102.
57. Shermer,1973, p.148.
58. Yekrangian, 1995, p.164.
59. Ward, 2009, p.117.
60. Ibid.
61. Ibid.
62. Yekrangian, 1995, p.164.
63. Tucker and Roberts, 2005, p.2005.
64. Matofi, 1999, p.1020.
65. Dailami, 2006, p.139.
66. Shermer,1973, p.148.
67. Ward, 2009, p.120.
68. Matofi, 1999, p.1021; October 24–25 in the Julian calendar. Shermer, 1973, pp.175–80.
69. Cronin, 1997, pp.68–9.
70. Matofi, 1999, p.1021.
71. Ward, 2009, p.122.
72. Ward, 2009, p.121.
73. Dailami, 2006, p.150.
74. Ibid.
75. Valenta, 1974, pp.231–5.
76. These were Fritz Wedig and Wilhelm von Paschen.
77. Kasravi, 1995, p.691.
78. Ward, 2009, p.122.
79. Cronin, 1997, p.77.
80. Kasravi, 1995, p.691.
81. Ibid.
82. Ward, 2009, p.123.
83. Kasravi, 1995, p.692.
84. Ward, 2009, p.123.
85. Kasravi, 1995, p.692.
86. Majd, 2003, pp.191, 225–34.
87. Ward, 2009, p.123.
88. German sources report Kuchik Khan's forces as having been defeated by August 1918, Dailami, 2006, p.155.
89. British forces may have worked out an accord with the Armenian nationalists of Baku, Zurrer, 1978, p.65.
90. Ottoman forces had been making a determined thrust towards Baku since early May 1918.
91. Numbers of escaped Austro-Hungarians POWs had also found refuge in Gilan.
92. Dailami, 2006, p.152.
93. Cronin, 1997, p.77.
94. Ibid.
95. Keddie, 1991, p.209.
96. Turkaman, 1991, pp.474–5.
97. The letter and number of others by Turks and Germans were discovered by British forces in 1919 in Kuchik's home (see Dailami, 2006, footnote 44, p.210).
98. Dailami, 2006, p.147.
99. Ibid.
100. Ibid., pp.147–8.
101. Bayat, 1990, pp.275–7.
102. Dailami, 2006, p.152.
103. Wratislaw, 1924, pp.213–4, 229–32
104. This suggestion was made by Ubeydollah Effendi in his correspondence with Mirza Kuchik Khan. Consult British Foreign Office documents FO248/1203.
105. Zurrer, 1978, pp.105–10.
106. Nicolle, 1994.
107. Dailami, 2008, pp.148, 154.
108. Dailami, 2006, p.154.
109. Consult British Foreign Office documents FO248/1203 with respect to correspondence between the Northern Persia Force to Kuchik Khan on November 9, 1918.
110. Atabaki, 2000, p.11.
111. Consult British Foreign Office documents FO248/1203 with respect to Qazvin dated October 25, 1918. See also Dailami, 2006, p.154.
112. Greaves, 1991, p.412; Fernier and Bamberg, 1994, pp.27–8.
113. Mortom, 2006. p.8; Adelson, 1995, p.97; Bostock and Jones, p.3.
114. Adelson, 1995, pp.97–8.
115. Farmanfarmaian and Farmanfarmaian, 2005, p.89; Nersesian, 2006, p.121.
116. Farmanfarmaian and Farmanfarmaian, 2005, p.89.
117. Ibid.; Adelson, 1995, p.97.
118. Foran, 1994, p.63.
119. Dailami, 2006, p.148; Erteshadiyyeh, 1992, p.43.
120. Sabahi, 1990, p.11.
121. Khazal had been in contact with the British in 1902, 1907, Sabahi, 1990, p.11; Ward, 2009, p.138.
122. Ward, 2009, p.138; Price, 2005, p.160.
123. As noted by Adelson, "Given the weakness of the government in Tehran, APOC [Anglo-Persian Oil Company] simply negotiated with Arab chiefs in Khuzistan and arranged for Bakhtiyari tribal leaders to guard the company facilities," 1995, p.97.
124. Price, 2005, p.160. Nevertheless, the attribution of separatism to Khazal has been challenged as his letters to the Qajars and other Iranian political leaders revealed him to be a supporter of the Iranian state and the Constitutional movement which he had not participated in.
125. Ibid.
126. Consult Hopkirk, 1994.
127. Ward, 2009, p.110.
128. Yekrangian, 1995, p.162.
129. Ibid.
130. Olson, 1984, p.71.
131. Mousavian, 2008, p.13.
132. Hopkirk, 1994.
133. Yekrangian, 1995, p.165.
134. Hopkirk, 2001, p.106.
135. Ibid., pp.107–8; The British however did capture Wassmuss' luggage which they sent to the British India Office in London.
136. Hopkirk, 2001, pp.107–8.
137. Ibid., p.110.

138. Oberling, *"Kamsa,"* Encyclopedia Iranica, 2004.

139. Ward, 2009, p.111.

140. Hopkirk, 2001, p.113; Mousavian, 2008, p.13.

141. Yekrangian, 1995, p.165.

142. Ibid., p.164.

143. Ward, 2009, p.111.

144. Yekrangian, 1995, p.166.

145. Cronin, 2008, p.72.

146. Yekrangian, 1995, p.166.

147. Ward, 2009, p.112.

148. Ibid., p.118.

149. Yekrangian, 1995, p.167.

150. Ibid.

151. Ibid.

152. Ward, 2009, p.118.

153. Yekrangian, 1995, pp.167–8.

154. Ward, 2009, pp.123–4.

Chapter 26

1. Ward, 2009, pp.123–4; Katouzian, 2006, Chapters 4–5.

2. Cronin, 2008, pp.75.

3. Ibid.

4. Holt, Lambton and Lewis, 1977, pp.599.

5. Olson,1984, pp.72–73.

6. Keddie, 1991, p.209.

7. Shamim, 1995, pp.632-633.

8. Zirinsky, 1994, pp.50.

9. Shamim, 1995, pp.632.

10. Ibid., pp.633.

11. See Khiyabani as cited by Shamim, 1995, p.634.

12. Documents of the FO 248/1278. Khiyabani met Major C. J. Edmonds of Norperforce on May 1, 1922; Ghani, 2000, p.103.

13. Shamim, 1995, p.635.

14. Kasravi, 2005, p.763; Shamim, 1995, p.636.

15. Khiyabani was in fact arrested and exiled by the Ottoman occupation forces. Zirinsky,1994, p.50; Atabaki, 2000, pp.45–6; Katouzian, 2006, pp.110, 203–4, note 44 on pp.203–4.

16. The main proponents of this name change were the local Turkic and non-Turkic Muslim elites as well as Ottoman pan-Turk activists (Matini, 1989, p.445) and ex-Ottoman officers who had fought in the Caucasus. For a study of Ottoman military operations and personnel in the Caucasus and Iran during the First World War, consult Nicolle, 1994, pp.37, 39–40.

17. Matini, 1989, p.452.

18. Atabaki, 2006, p.132; Kasravi, 1998, p.756.

19. Ibid.

20. Azari, 1983, p.299.

21. Swietochowski, 1995, p.69.

22. Ward, 2009, p.83.

23. Shamim, 1995, pp.636–7.

24. Kasravi, 2005, p.766.

25. Shamim, 1995, p.637.

26. Zirinsky, 1994, p.50.

27. Ibid..

28. Shamim, 1995, p.637.

29. Kasravi, 2005, p.763; Shamim, 1995, pp.636–7, 632; Katouzian, 2003, p.222.

30. Shamim, 1995, p.636.

31. Tapper, 1997, p.272.

32. Ibid.

33. He was born in the village of Alasht in 1878.

34. This was an Imperial officers' order established by Nasser e Din Shah in 1870. The neshan e Aqdas distinction was dissolved after the overthrown of the Qajar government in 1925.

35. A full account of the removal of Russian officers from senior positions of command is provided by Babaie, 2005a, pp.236–42; Graham, 1979, p.54.

36. Cronin, 1997, p.83.

37. Ibid., p.84.

38. Cronin, 1997, pp.84–5.

39. Ward, 2009, p.129.

40. Matofi, 1999, p.1042.

41. Tafrashi, 1985, pp.217–8.

42. This was relayed by a situation report to the British War Office on December 8, 1920.

43. See discussion by Ullman, 1972, p.384.

44. Cronin, 2008, p.76.

45. Ibid.

46. Ibid.

47. Abrahamian, 1982, p.117; Ansari, 2003, pp.26–31; Wright, 1977, pp.180–4; Babaie, 2005a, p.178.

48. Granmayeh, 2004, p.18.

49. Shamim, 1995, p.649.

50. Granmayeh, 2004, p.18.

51. Kazemzadeh, 1991, p.347.

52. Granmayeh, 2004, p.18.

53. Shamim, 1995, p.649.

54. Kazemzadeh, 1991, p.347.

55. Shamim, 1995, p.650.

56. Ibid., p.649.

57. As cited by Kazemzadeh, 1991, p.347.

58. Potter, 2008, p.141.

59. Kasravi, 2005, p.725.

60. Arfa, 1966, p.56.

61. Ibid., pp.63–4.

62. Natali, 2005, p.119.

63. Ibid.

64. Kasravi, 2005, p.725.

65. Van Brunessen, 2006, p.87.

66. Arfa, 1966, p.56.

67. Yekrangian, 2005, pp.325; British and Foreign State Papers by the Great Britain Foreign Office Foreign and Commonwealth Office (Published by HMSO, 1868); see especially p.11.

68. Romano, 2006, p.223.

69. Kasravi, 2005, p.724.

70. Gaunt, Bet-şawoce and Donef, 2006, p.91.

71. Bruinessen, 2006, p.82; Ahmad, 1994, p.61; Gaunt, Bet- awoce and Donef, 2006, p.91.

72. Russia was in control of parts of Iranian Kurdistan at the time O'Shea, 2004, p.96.

73. *The New York Times*, July 10, 1922; Jwaideh, 2006, p.141.

74. McDowall, 2004, p.464.

75. Arfa, 1966, p.56.

76. Gaunt, Bet-şawoce and Donef, 2006, p.91.

77. O'Shea, 2004, p.96.

78. Sanasarian, 2000, p.178.

79. Joseph, 1961, p.147.

80. Sanasarian, 2000, pp.178.

81. Arfa, 1966, pp.56. Kasravi (2005, pp.726) reports the meeting as having taken place between Sardar Fateh the governor of Rezaieh who had arrived from Tabriz the previous month.

82. Kasravi, 2005, pp.726. Kasravi characterized this appeal as "humiliating behavior."
83. Iranian sources are contradictory as to who actually sent the package, Yekrangian, 2005, p.325; Kasravi, 2005, p.724.
84. Yekrangian, 2005, p.325.
85. Kasravi, 2005, p.726.
86. Yekrangian, 2005, p.325; According to Arfa, 1966, p.57, frightened Qajar authorities sent two people under escort to Simko alleging that they were the ones responsible for the attempt on his life. Simko executed the two men and their entire escort upon their arrival at Chehreeqh.
87. Kasravi, 2005, pp.727–32.
88. Arfa, 1966, p.57.
89. Kasravi, 2005, p.732.
90. Ibid.
91. Kasravi, 2005, p.740.
92. There is a large discrepancy between two primary sources of this event, Kasravi and Arfa. Kasravi (2005, pp.740) states that resistance broke in just two hours and not two days as reported by Arfa, 1966, p.57.
93. Arfa, 1966, p.57.
94. Yekrangian, 2005, p.325. He was also known as "Salar Nizam"; his failed campaigns occurred during the administration of Ayn o Dowleh.
95. Kasravi, 2005, pp.741–2.
96. Arfa, 1966, pp.57–8. This occurred at Deilamghan. Kasravi, 2005, p.742.
97. Arfa, 1966, p.58.
98. Ibid.
99. Kasravi, 2005, p.742.
100. Arfa, 1966, pp.58.
101. Ibid., pp.59–60.
102. Yekrangian, 2005, p.326.
103. Van Bruinessen 2006, p.89.
104. Yekrangian, 2005, pp.325–6.
105. Van Bruinessen, 2006, p.89.
106. Yekrangian, 2005, p.326.
107. Arfa, 1966, p.58.
108. Yekrangian, 2005, p.326.
109. Arfa, 1966, p.58; Yekrangian, 2005, p.326.
110. Arfa, 1966, p.61; Yekrangian, 2005, p.326.
111. Yekrangian, 2005, p.326.
112. Arfa, 1966, p.61.
113. Yekrangian, 2005, pp.326–7.
114. Van Bruinessen, 2006, p.90.
115. Ibid.
116. Arfa, 1966, p.61.
117. Jahanbani's operations in Salams and Shapur had been supported by the partisans led by Morad Khan and a mixed detachment from Qazvin.
118. Yekrangian, 2005, pp.329–30.
119. The Azerbaijan force was composed of the infantry regiment of Azerbaijan, Azerbaijani cavalry units, and mountain troops.
120. Yekrangian, 2005, p.330.
121. Arfa, 1966, p.62.
122. Yekrangian, 2005, p.330.
123. Arfa, 1966, p.62.
124. Ibid. The 1,000 who remained with Simko were Shikak Kurds.
125. Van Bruinessen, 2006, p.93.
126. Ibid.
127. Zirinsky, 1994, p.50.
128. Much of the roots of this party was with Iranian immigrants based in Baku.
129. While an Iranian, Ehsan ollah Khan, was nominally in charge, it was the Russians under the person of Soviet Commissar Abukov who were in control.
130. Abrahamian, 1982, pp.116–7.
131. Mackie, 1996, p.167.
132. Price, 2005, p.160.
133. Foran, 1994, p.63.
134. Cottam, 1964.
135. Yekrangian, 2005, p.333.
136. Ibid.
137. Ward, 2009, pp.138.
138. Yekrangian, 2005, pp.334.
139. Price, 2005, pp.160.
140. Bahar, 1982, p.150.
141. Mackey, 1996, p.168.
142. Ibid., p.166.
143. Holt, Lambton and Lewis, 1977, p.601; Schulze, 2002, p.84.
144. Zarrinkoob, 2002–3, p.866; Holt, Lambton and Lewis, 1977, p.601.
145. Zarrinkoob, 2002–3, p.866.
146. Mackey, 1998, p.169.
147. Schulze, 2002, p.84.
148. Keddie and Richard, 1981, p.91; Graham, 1979, p.54; Mackey, 1998, p.169.
149. Mackey, 1998, p.169.
150. Elwell-Sutton, 1978, p.24.
151. Keddie and Richard, 1981, pp.91.
152. Yekrangian, 2005, pp.331.
153. Shamim, 1995, p.658.
154. Ibid., pp.660-661.
155. Yekrangian, 2005, pp.332.
156. Pesyan's body was transported on top of a large cannon towards the burial grounds. The funeral was arranged by Pesyan's surviving men and his other followers.
157. Yekrangian, 2005, p.333.
158. Ward, 2009, p.139.
159. Yekrangian, 2005, p.325.
160. Ibid., p.326; Setad e Bozorg e Arteshdaran, 1963, p.82.
161. Yekrangian, 2005, p.358.
162. The entire telegram is cited by Yekrangian 2005, p.358.
163. Yekrangian, 2005, p.360.
164. Ibid., p.361.
165. Ibid., p.343.

Chapter 27

1. Swietochowski, 1995, p.27.
2. Ibid.
3. Ibid.
4. Atabaki, 2000, p.56.
5. The most vivid example of this was a poem by "Aref" that appeared in the Iranian magazine Iranshahr (The Iranian realm). Atabaki, 2000, p.55.
6. Ayandeh, vol 1, number 1, 1925, pp.5–6.
7. Babaie, 2005a, p.295.
8. Ward, 2009, p.134.
9. Mohammadi, 2003, p.191.
10. Ghirshman, Minorsky, and Sanghvi, 1971, p.190.
11. Ward, 2009, pp.136; Pollack, 2002, p.33.
12. Cockcroft 1989, pp.40.

13. British Central Office of Information, 1948, p.92.
14. Pollack, 2002, p.33.
15. Ibid.
16. Perl, 2007, p.23.
17. Keddie, 2007, p.87.
18. Milani, 2008, pp.199–220.
19. Hunter and Malik, 2005, p.264.
20. Abrahamian, 1982, p.146; Pollack, 2002, p.34.
21. Ibid.
22. Ward, 2009, p.150.
23. Pollack, 2002, p.33; Farmanfarmaian, 2005, p.113.
24. Wright, 2001, p.45.
25. Ward, 2009, p.140; Zabih, 1988, p.84.
26. Pollack, 2002, p.36.
27. Arjomand, 1988, p.64.
28. Saikal, 1991, p.434.
29. Babaie, 2005a, p.249.
30. Cronin, 1997, p.38; Babaie, 2005a, pp.250–2.
31. Babaie, 2005a, p.178. The British demanded 2 million Lira compensation, and seeing that the Iranian government lacked the funds to pay, the British destroyed much of the SPR's ammunition and equipment as well as taking stocks of these with them out of Iran.
32. Cronin, 1997, p.38.
33. Ibid., Babaie, 2005a, pp.254–7; Yekrangian, 2005, pp.256–8.
34. Yekrangian, 2005, Fig.3.
35. Matofi, 1999, p.1044.
36. Ibid., p.1045.
37. Ward, 2009, p.142.
38. Matofi, 1999, p.1045.
39. Setad e Bozorg e Arteshdaran, 1963, Matofi, 1999, pp.1044–57.
40. Cronin, 1997, pp.38–9; Matofi, 1999, pp.1044–57; Majd, 2001; pp.286–91; Ward, 2009, p.142).
41. Cronin, 1997, p.38.
42. Ibid.
43. Cronin, 1997, p.44.
44. Ward, 2009, pp.141–2; Yekrangian, 2005, p.369.
45. Matofi, 1999, pp.1053–55.
46. Ward, 2009, p.148.
47. Setad e Bozorg e Arteshdaran, 1963, p.132.
48. Imperial Iranian Army, 1976, Vol.I, p.55; Matofi, 1999, p.1045.
49. Setad e Bozorg e Arteshdaran, 1963, pp.89–96. Babaie, 2005b, pp.66–7; Majd, 2001, p.302; Ward, 2009, p.154; British Central Office of Information, 1948, p.67.
50. Yekrangian, 2005, p.369.
51. Ward, 2009, p.154.
52. The airbases of Mashad, Ahvaz, and Tabriz became operational by August 1934, March 1937, and June 1939 respectively .
53. Ward, 2009, p.154.
54. Babaie, 2005a, p.277.
55. Cooper and Bishop, 2000, p.11.
56. This entailed working alongside Italian naval advisors to appropriate ships suitable for Iran's naval needs. Italian naval advisors were in Iran, 1928–33.
57. These were christened as the *Gilan, Mazandaran* and *Azerbaijan*. These were each armed with a 75mm cannon.
58. By the mid-1930s the headquarters for the Caspian coastal guard was based at Bandar Anzali.
59. Setad e Bozorg e Arteshdaran, 1963, pp.81–86.

Chapter 28

1. Brown, 2003, p.79.
2. Mousavian, 2008, p.14.
3. Avery, 1965, p.326.
4. Mousavian, 2008, p.15.
5. Avery, 1965, p.326.
6. Mckenzie, 1951, p.584.
7. Mousavian, 2008, p.15.
8. Avery, 1965, p.326.
9. Mousavian, 2008, p.15.
10. Avery, 1965, p.326.
11. This meant that as AIOC's revenues decreased (due to its support of London in the war), Iran's percentage of those profits also declined. Farmanfarmaian, 2005, p.132.
12. Ibid.
13. Cooper and Bishop. 2000, p.11.
14. Mackenzie, 1951, p.129.
15. Stewart, 1988, p.73.
16. Saracoglu as cited by Stewart, 1988, p.73; Farmanfarmaian, 2005, p.132; Saikal, 1991, p.434.
17. Cronin, 1997, p.59.
18. Hirszowicz, 1966, p.126.
19. Stewart, 1988, p.76.
20. An excellent source for these events is provided by Lyman, 2006, pp.63–8; Hirszowicz, 1966, pp.148–9.
21. Hirszowicz, 1966, p.169.
22. Mackenzie, 1951, p.129; Hirszowicz, 1966, p.208.
23. The Nessah Educational and Cultural Center and The Council of Iranian-American Jewish Organizations in the United States sponsored a Holocaust commemoration event at the National Defence University in Washington D.C., on April 18, 2004, honouring the role of Mr. Sardari in saving Jews from being slaughtered by the Nazis. Sardari was honoured as the "Schindler of Iran."
24. "Abdol Hossein Sardari (1895–1981)," *Holocaust Encyclopaedia*.
25. Ibid.
26. As summarized by Roxanne Farmanfarmaian who noted "It wasn't that the Iranians were pro-German, it was that they were anti-British and anti-Russian."
27. Cronin, 1997, p.59.
28. Elm, 1994, p.43.
29. Saikal, 1991, p.434.
30. Stewart, 1988, p.78.
31. Ibid.
32. Afkhami, 2008, p.73.
33. Ibid.
34. Afkhami, 2008, p.73.
35. Cronin, 1997, p.83.
36. Ward, 2009, p.147; Yekrangian, 2005, p.373.
37. British Central Office of Information, 1948, p.62; Cronin, 1997, p.83.
38. Ibid.
39. Much of this can again be traced to problems with military conservatism which did much to hinder the development of a focused military doctrine.
40. Ward, 2009, p.143.
41. Yekrangian, 1995, p.406.
42. Ansari, 2003, pp.84-85.
43. Interview with Dr. Ahmad Tahami, August 15, 2001 in which he presented a personal diary from one of his relatives who

had fought against the Soviets in August 1941. The diary dated August 26, 1941 noted that "we were firing with our rifles and machineguns at the Russians but were running out of ammunition. When a supply column arrived we were horrified to see that it was stocked with the wrong ammunition originally destined for the southern sector." Yekrangian, 1995, p.369–70.

44. Ward, 2009, p.142; Yekrangian, 2005, p.370.
45. Ward, 2009, p.142.
46. As cited in Cronin, 1997, p.44.
47. Yekrangian, 2005, p.372.
48. Ward, 2009, p.143.
49. Kuznetsov, p.45.
50. Stewart, 1988, p.83. Kozlov's army was composed of the 6th Tank Division, 63rd (Georgian) Mountain Infantry Division, 76th (Armenian) Mountain Infantry Division, the 24th Cavalry Division, the 54th Tank Division, the 236th Infantry Division and a squadron of the 7th Independent Armored Train Battalion.
51. Ward, 2009, p.162.
52. Stewart, 1988, p.83.
53. Ibid.
54. Jones and Idriess, 1952, p.196.
55. Stewart, 1988, p.135.
56. Yekranigian, 2005, p.381.
57. Yekranigian, 2005, pp.380–1.
58. Ward, 2009, p.162.
59. The soldiers dug foxholes to face the Soviets.
60. Ward, 2009, p.165.
61. Stewart, 1988, p.134.
62. Ward, 2009, p.162.
63. Stewart, 1988, p.134.
64. Ward, 2009, p.163.
65. Stewart, 1988, p.134.
66. Ward, 2009, p.163; Yekranigian, 2005, p.382.
67. Yekranigian, 2005, p.381.
68. Stewart, 1988, p.149.
69. Ward, 2009, p.165; Stewart, 1988, p.135.
70. Ward, 2008, p.163; Yekranigian, 2005, p.382.
71. Ward, 2009, pp.163–4.
72. Yekranigian, 2005, p.382. The explosives were from the 3rd Division.
73. Ward, 2009, p.165.
74. Sheibani and his pilots had flown out of Tabriz just in time as the Russian 44th Army was pouring towards Zanjan from recently occupied Astara. Two of the planes crashed, but their pilots survived and made their way to Tehran.
75. Yekranigian, 2005, p.383.
76. Stewart, 1988, p.82; Yekranigian, 2005, p.415.
77. Stewart, 1988, p.82.
78. The 30-ton gunboats were the *Sefid-rood*, *Gorgan*, and *Babolsar* and the two other vessles were the *Shahsavar* and the *Nahang* (Babaie, 2005a, p.294; Yekranigian, 2005, p.415).
79. Stewart, 1988, p.149.
80. Ibid.
81. Ward, 2009, p.165, only identifies machineguns but Yekrangian, 2005; p.415, identified these craft having 47mm cannon as well.
82. Yekranigian, 2005, p.421.
83. Babaie, 2005a, p.294.
84. These had arrived from Rasht after its fall to Soviet troops.
85. Stewart, 1988, p.179. Captain Daftary's sailors were also forcibly lined up and placed under guard.

86. Stewart, 1988, p.179.
87. Ibid.
88. Yekranigian, 2005, p.377.
89. One was in Bojnurd and another close to the Afghan border at Torbat e Jam.
90. Stewart, 1988, p.163.
91. Ward, 2009, p.167.
92. Stewart, 1988, p.170.
93. Yekranigian, 2005, p.380.
94. "Situation in Iran," *Supplement to the London Gazette* of August 13, 1946 – published on August 14, 1946, pp.4097.
95. Yekranigian, 2005, pp.419.
96. Ibid.
97. Iranian sources claim that the British captured three German vessels with two German and three Italian vessels scuttled by their crews, Yekranigian, 2005, p.419; Mackenzie claims that only one of the eight was scuttled, 1951, pp.134. This is corroborated by the British Central Office of Information, 1948, pp.66-67, and Ward, 2009, pp.156.
98. Stewart, 1988, pp.112–3.
99. Mackenzie, 1951, p.134. These were 40 German and 60 Italian prisoners.
100. Stewart (1988, p.111) and Ward (2009, p.156) identify the *Shahbaz* as the *Karkas* (presumably *Charkas*) with Yekrangian (2005, pp.419) reporting the vessels at Bandar Shapur as the *Simurgh* and *Shahbaz*. This must be incorrect as the *Simurgh* was in Khorramshahr area at the time.
101. Yekranigian, 2005, p.419.
102. Mackenzie, 1951, p.134.
103. Stewart, 1988, pp.112–3; Ward, 2009, p.156.
104. British Central Office of Information, 1948, p.67.
105. Yekranigian, 2005, p.419.
106. Yekranigan, 2005, p.419.
107. Ward, 2009, pp.156; Yekranigian, 2005, p.419; Stewart, 1988, p.107.
108. Yekranigian, 2005, pp.419; Ward, 2009, p.156. Stewart notes that many of the crew were killed with Milanian severely woulded; a few survivors then made it shore (1988, p.107).
109. Stewart, 1988, p.107.
110. Ward, 2009, p.156.
111. British Central Office of Information, 1948, p.65.
112. Stewart, 1988, p.115.
113. Ward, 2009, p.157.
114. The Sikhs who broke into the office building of BP were dissuaded from further shooting by BP personnel.
115. Mackenzie, 1951, p.131. Stewart, 1988, p.117.
116. Ward, 2009, p.157.
117. Stewart, 1988, p.118.
118. Ward, 2009, p.157.
119. Ibid.
120. Stewart, 1988, p.118.
121. Stewart, 1988, p.119.
122. Ibid.
123. Ward, 2009, p.157.
124. Stewart, 1988, p.120.
125. Ibid., p.121.
126. Ward, 2009, p.158.
127. Stewart, 1988, p.154.
128. British Central Office of Information, 1948, p.66.
129. Stewart, 1988, p.128.
130. Mackenzie, 1951, p.132.
131. Prasad, 1957, pp.291, 335–6; Stewart, 1988, p.123; Ward, 2009, pp.158-9.

132. Stewart, 1988, p.125.
133. Ward, 2009, p.167.
134. Ibid., p.159.
135. Stewart, 1988, p.155.
136. Ward, 2009, p.157, speculates that the two biplanes may have been on a reconnaissance mission.
137. Arfa,1964, p.298.
138. Stewart, 1988, p.173.
139. Mackenzie, 1951, p.133.
140. Ward, 2009, p.160.
141. Mackenzie, 1951, p.135.
142. Stewart, 1988, p.129.
143. British Central Office of Information, 1948, p.68.
144. Stewart, 1988, p.131.
145. British Central Office of Information, 1948, p.68.
146. Ward, 2009, p.161.
147. Stewart, 1988, p.157.
148. British Central Office of Information, 1948, p.69; Mackenzie, 1951, p.135.
149. Stewart, 1988, p.177.
150. Saikal, 1991, p.434.
151. Mckensize, 1951, p.137.
152. Arfa, 1964, pp.299–300.
153. Arfa, 1964.
154. Mackenzie, 1951, p.130.
155. Ward, 2009, p.167.
156. Colonel M. A., a veteran of the 3rd Tabriz Division, claimed that an antiaircraft gun unit based near Mianeh, in Iranian Azerbaijan refused to surrender and continued to hold out until it was finally destroyed by Soviet troops. Personal Communication, July 20, 2009.
157. Babaie, 2005b, p.67.
158. Ibid., p.68.
159. Cooper and Bishop, 2000, pp.12–3.
160. Ibid. Vassiq crashed into the Caspian with Shishtari crashing into the northern Iranian forests.
161. Saikal, 1991, p.434.
162. Elm, 1994, p.43.
163. Ward, 2009, p.176.
164. Fardust, 1998, p.57. Interestingly, Fardust opines that Churchill's statement was really intended to show that Joseph Stalin was critically dependent on US military supplies.
165. Elm, 1994, p.43.
166. Pollack, 2002, p.43; Farmanfarmaian, 2005, pp.148.
167. Pollack, 2002, p.43.
168. Stewart, 1988, p.195.
169. Louis, 2004, p.168.
170. Fardust, 1998, p.57.

Chapter 29

1. Lenczowski, 1980, p.183.
2. Roosevelt, 1947, pp.253; Ward, 2009, p.181.
3. Churchill, 1950, pp.476–7.
4. Yevgorova, 1996, p.2.
5. Ibid., p.3.
6. Roosevelt, 1947, p.258; Sicker, 2001, p.165. Roosevelt actually uses the term "puppet states."
7. As cited by Dzhirkvelov, 1987, p.66.
8. Roosevelt, 1947, p.251. According to Nader Paymai, an Iranian cultural activists of Azerbaijani origin, the late Haydar Aliev (1923–2003) who was president of the Republic of Azerbaijan (1993–2003) was one of the Soviet communist agents operating in Iran at the time (personal communication, May 20, 2008).
9. The title of these particular organizations had the word "*Iran*" removed, one example being the "*Anjoman-e Farhangiy-e Kurdistan va Shoravi*" (Kurdistan-Soviet Cultural Relations Society).
10. Yegorova, 1996.
11. An excellent Dissertation on the topic is that Abrahamian, E., *Social Basis of Iranian Politics, The Tudeh Party (1941–1953)*, Columbia University as well as Eskandari's 4-volume publication "*Khaterat.* [Memoirs],"1988.
12. As cited by Atabaki, 2000, pp.72, 208.
13. This was done through a series of articles. Consult *Rahbar* No.402, October 13, 1944 and No.411, October 24, 1944.
14. Eskandari, 1988, Vol.II, pp.84–6.
15. See discussion by Atabkai, 2000, pp.99–128; Roosevelt, 1947, p.253.
16. Yegorova, 1996, pp.9–11.
17. Ibid., p.10.
18. Baghirov was the Communist leader of the Soviet SSR in 1932–53.
19. George Kerman cited by Ramazani, 1971, p.401–2.
20. Kolarz, 1952, p.245.
21. As cited by Behrooz, 2000, p.158.
22. Bartold, VV., *Sochineniia, Tom II, Chast I, Izdatelstvo Vostochnoi Literary*, 1963 p.217.
23. Roosevelt, 1947, p.251.
24. Roosevelt, 1947, p.262.
25. Ward, 2009, p.171.
26. Consult discussion by Atabaki, 2000, pp.99–128.
27. Central Intelligence Agency Report, June 4, 1947, p.6. Ward however estimates the initial number of Soviet troops to have been 30,000, 2009, p.181.
28. Ramazani, 1974, p.407
29. Rossow, 1956, p.18.
30. Ramazani, 1971, p.412.
31. Rossow, 1956, p.17.
32. Ramazani, 1971, p.412.
33. Ibid., p.408
34. Roosvelt, 1947, p.256.
35. Arfa, 1966, p.96; Ramazani, 1971, p.413.
36. Arfa, 1966, p.90.
37. Ibid., pp.81–2.
38. Ward, 2009, p.182.
39. Ramazani, 1971, p.413.
40. Atabaki, 2000, p.112.
41. For a detailed compendium of these particular developments consult Pesyan, 1948–49, pp.126–48.
42. Ramazani, 1971, p.413; Pesyan, 1948–49, pp.126–48.
43. Leffler and Painter, 2005, p.102.
44. Ward, 2009, p.182.
45. "Underground army in Azerbaijan Fights Autonomous regime, Official Says," *New York Times*, January 9, 1946.
46. Arfa, 1966, p.101.
47. Izady, 1992, p.66.
48. Roosevelt, 1947, pp.251.
49. The Soviets had first turned to Qaraney Rais ol Ashair, Amir Khan Sharifi, and Amir Asad the chiefs of the Mamesh, Shikak and Dehbokri tribes respectively but had not obtained their cooperation. Amir Asad had been in charge of the local Gendarmerie by the Iranian government.
50. Roosevelt, 1947, p.262.

51. Ibid., p.254.
52. Ibid., pp.254.
53. Arfa, 1966, p.78.
54. Ibid., p.79 cites 3,000 with Ward citing 1,000.
55. Roosevelt, 1947, p.256.
56. Ibid.
57. Arfa, 1966, p.79.
58. Ibid.
59. Ramazani, 1971, p.408.
60. As cited by Roosevelt, 1947, p.257; see also Chailand, 1992, p.129.
61. Ramazani, 1971, p.408.
62. Roosevelt, 1947, pp.263–4, 265–6. Numbers of these Kurds fled to Tehran.
63. Chailand, 1992, p.129; Ward, 2009, p.182.
64. Roosevelt, 1947, p.258.
65. Arfa, 1964, pp.352–6.
66. Ward (2009, p.183) notes that Stalin had pushed another 15 brigades, heavy guns, motorized troops and hundreds of tanks into Soviet occupied Iranian territory before making his next move towards Tehran.
67. For a full account of these events consult, "Russians at Karaj," *New York Times*, March 14, 1946..
68. Truman later claimed that he had issued the Russians with an "ultimatum" to withdraw but no actual records of this have surfaced as of yet, Ward, 2009, p.173; Mihalkanin, 2004, p.7.
69. Mihalkanin, 2004, p.7.
70. Sicker, 2001, p.165.
71. Arfa, 1966, p.95.
72. Hume, 1994, p.17.
73. Daniel, 2001, p.147.
74. Arfa, 1966, p.96.
75. Sicker, 2001, p.165; Qavam cited by Hume, 1994, p.17.
76. Heravi and Key, 1999, pp.110–1.
77. As cited by Yegorova, 1996, p.24.
78. Ibid.
79. Stalin as cited by Yegorova, 1996, p.23.
80. Arfa, 1966, pp.94–5.
81. As cited by Elm, 1994, p.47.
82. Daniel, 2001, p.147.
83. Elm, 1994, p.47.
84. Louis, 1984, p.57. Jahanshahlu-Afshar, 2006, pp.99–100.
85. Ward, 2009, p.184.
86. Arfa, 1966, p.95.
87. Ward, 2009, p.184.
88. Central Intelligence Agency Report, June 4, 1947, p.6.
89. MG noted in a personal interview (May 25, 2009) that a very small number of Greek communists were brought by the Soviets into Iranian Azarbaijan to undertake in these operations. These later attempted to stop the Iranian army from entering Azarbaijan in 1946.
90. Arfa, 1966, p.97.
91. Heravi and key, 1999, p.111.
92. This was to have become the *Lashkar e Azerbaijan* (Lit. Army Division of Azerbaijan).
93. Arfa, 1966, p.97; Roosevelt, 1947, p.266.
94. Arfa, 1966, p.97.
95. Ibid.
96. Arfa, 1967, p.97. Arfa breaks down the forces as follows: 22 infantry battalions, 4 cavalry regiments, 2 mountain and 2 field batteries, 3 light tank companies (30 tanks), and support forces equipped with mortars, antitank guns, etc.
97. Babaie, 2005 (Air Force), p.207.
98. Roosevelt, 1947, p.266.
99. Ward, 2009, p.185.
100. Babaie, 2005 (Air Force), pp.207.
101. Roosevelt, 1947, p.267; Gregorian, 2003, p.23.
102. Atabaki, 2000, p.176. Ward, 2009, p.185.
103. Mafinezam, and Mehrabi, 2007, p.24.
104. Ramazani, 1971, p.413.
105. Jahanshahlu-Afshar, 2006, pp.97, 151.
106. Roosevelt, 1947, p.264.
107. See discussion by Atabaki, 2000, p.167, footnote 127 on p.226); Jahanshahlu-Afshar, 2006, pp.150–1, 205. Kolarz, 1952, p.247.
108. Tafreshiyan, 1980, pp.71–2; Mafinezam, and Mehrabi, 2007, p.57.
109. Jahanshahlu-Afshar, 2006, p.202; Atabaki, 2000, pp.218–9; Swietochowski, 1995, p.164.
110. Swietochowski notes that Baghirov made threatening gestures to Pishevari during the meeting: "Baghirov ... taking off his glasses, wiped his forehead in a gesture that seemed to express his wish to wipe Pishevari off the face of the earth," Swietochowski, 1995, p.164.
111. Arfa, 1966, pp.95.
112. Roosevelt, 1947, p.266.
113. Arfa, 1966, p.95.
114. Roosevelt, 1947, p.268.
115. These arrived at Naqadeh by December 15, 1946.
116. Heravi and Kay, 1999, pp.111.
117. Roosevelt, 1947, p.257.
118. Roosevelt, 1947, p.264.
119. Arfa, 1966, p.86.
120. Ibid., p.101.

Chapter 30

1. Ward, 2009. p.170.
2. The Shah attended military schools at the primary and secondary levels and was to graduate from the military academy as a second lieutenant. He had served as the chief Inspector of the Army until he became shah.
3. Ward, 2009. p.171.
4. Motter, 1952, pp.464–5, 470.
5. Ward, 2009. p.172.
6. Motter, 1952, p.465.
7. Ward, 2009. p.174.
8. Saikal, 1991, p.437.
9. Ward, 2009. p.175.
10. Babaie, 2005b, p.209.
11. Ibid., p.210.
12. Ibid., pp.408–9. The agreement had been signed between Mahmoud Jaam, the Iranian minister of war and George Allen, the US ambassador to Iran at the time.
13. Ibid., p.213.
14. Rubin, 1981, pp.41–2.
15. Consult the Princeton Seminars May 15–16 1954, the Dean Acheson Papers in the Harry S. Truman Library.
16. Babaie, 2005b, p.213.
17. Elm, 1994, p.97.
18. Abrahamian, 1982, pp.314–21.
19. Afkhami, 2008, p.116; Pollack, 2002, p.52; Ward, 2009, p.186.
20. Abrahamian, 1982, p.317.
21. Pollack, 2002, p.52.
22. Ward, 2009, p.186.

23. Katouzian, 2004, p.4.
24. Diba, 1960, pp.60–2. Mossadegh was officially arrested on July 26, 1940 and transferred to house arrest to his home at Ahmad-Abad on November 3, 1940.
25. Mafinezam, and Mehrabi, 2007, p.24.
26. Ibid.
27. Elm, 1994, p.97.
28. Louis, 1984, p.633.
29. Saikal, 1980, p.38.
30. Elm, 1994, p.49. The AIOC had 60,000 Iranian employees.
31. Ibid.. Louis, 1984, pp.638–40.
32. Elm, 1994, pp.98–9.
33. As cited by Elm, 1994, p.99.
34. The Supplemental Agreement would have increased the royalties to from roughly 15% to 20% of the original 1933 agreement, Louis, 1984, p.641.
35. Mackey, 1997, p.198.
36. Louis, 1984, pp.642–3.
37. Babaie, 2005b, p.214.
38. Ward, 2009, p.186.
39. Babaie, 2005b, p.214.
40. Louis, 1984, pp.649–51.
41. Ibid., pp.646–7, 650, 656.
42. Mackey, 1997, pp.198–9.
43. Ibid., p.199.
44. Saikal, 1980, pp.38–9; Kinzer, 2003, p.88; Farsoun, 1985, p.80; Voli, 1994, p.286; Esposito, 2010, p.31.
45. Ward (2009, p.187)provides a brief discussion of the Shah's desire to retain control over the military.
46. Elm, 1994, p.99. Mexico had nationalized its indiginous US assets.
47. Abrahamian, 1982, p.268.
48. Louis, 1984, p.676; Mackey, 1997, p.199.
49. Katouzian, 2004, p.2.
50. Ibid., pp.5–6.
51. Louis, 1984, p.675.
52. Ibid.
53. As cited and analyzed by Louis, 1984, pp.675–6.
54. Louis, 1984, pp.673–5.
55. With India's independence, the British could no longer rely on Indian troops for an invasion of Iran's southwest as they had in August 1941.
56. Abrahamian, 1982, p.268.
57. Ibid., pp.268–70. Abrahamian also notes that Mossadegh did not enjoy the same level of support in the provincial areas
58. Ibid., pp.268–9; Ward, 2009, p.187.
59. This was partly due to the dismissal of the General Fazlollah Zahedi by the shah a year before. Zahedi had been arrested by the British in 1943 when he was minister of the interior after his security forces shot thirty protestors. This may partly explain why many army commanders were reluctant to become engaged in a violent confrontation with pro-Mossadegh protestors.
60. Ward, 2009, p.187.
61. Ibid.
62. Louis, 2004, p.169; See discussion by Richelson (1997, p.249) regarding the CIA effort to recruit these troops for the cause of the shah against Mossadegh.
63. Ward, 2009, pp.187–8; Richelson, 1997, p.249.
64. Kinzer, 2003, pp.150–1.
65. For an in-depth insight into the British role in the crisis consult Kinzer, 2003, pp.62-118.
66. Abrahamian, 1993, p.119.
67. Louis, 2004, p.168.
68. Ward, 2009, p.188.
69. Dean Acheson (the US Secretary of State) clearly stated that British policies were "destructive and determined on a rule or ruin policy in Iran" (Sarkal, 1980, p.42).
70. As cited by Milani, 2008, p.236.
71. "No Traction for Proposal to name Street after Mossadegh," Tehran Times, April 10, 2009.
72. Gasiorowski and Byrne, 2004, p.125.
73. Richelson, 1997, p.249.
74. Louis, 2004, p.168.
75. Richelson, 1997, p.249.
76. "Flaming Oil At The UN," New York Times, October 1, 1951.
77. Teddy Roosevelt was to acknowledge as such as by stating "The British motivation was to recover the AIOC... we were not concerned with that but with the obvious threat of a Russian takeover." (Richelson, 1997, p.249).
78. Abrahamian, 1982, p.320.
79. Ibid.
80. As cited by Louis, 2004, p.170.
81. Richelson, 1997, p.249.
82. "Kermit Roosevelt, Leader of CIA Coup in Iran, Dies at 84," New York Times, June 11, 2000.
83. Ibid.
84. Ward, 2009, p.188.
85. Louis, 2004, p.170.
86. Poulson, 2006, p.172.
87. Louis, 2004, p.170.
88. Majd, 2002, p.29.
89. Ward, 2009, p.189.
90. Richelson, 1997, p.249.
91. Poulson, 2006, p.172.
92. Ward, 2009, p.189.
93. Spencer, 2004, p.1959.
94. Richelson, 1997, p.249; Ward, 2009, p.189.
95. Ward, 2009, pp.168–9.
96. Hertz, 2003, p.88.
97. Louis, 1984, p.680.
98. Mackey, 1998, p.208.

Chapter 31

1. American University (Washington, D.C.), Foreign Areas Studies Division, US. Army, 1964, pp.599, 1978 (3rd Edition), p.404; Babaie, 2005a, pp.326, 368; Cooper and Bishop, 2000, p.25.
2. Ward, 2009, p.196.
3. Babaie, 2005b, p.220.
4. Ledeen and Lewis, 1982, p.38.
5. Ibid.
6. Sreedhar, 1985, p.8.
7. Ibid.; Ward, 2009, p.196.
8. Saikal, 1991, p.449.
9. Babaie, 2005a, p.364.
10. Sreedhar, 1985, p.9.
11. Babaie, 2005a, p.364.
12. Personal interview with the late Colonel Hedayat Behzadi on March 15, 1998. Hedayat told the author that "there are three fundamentals for the tank's survival on the battlefield: firepower, armoured protection and mobility ... the Chieftain tanks delivered to us were excellent in terms of armour and firepower but deficient in mobility ... many of us were concerned about its ability to manoeuvre against the highly mobile Soviet made

tanks, especially in the flat terrain of the southwest in Khuzistan … our US-made M-60s and newer model Chieftains were our most reliable machines overall and their engines never gave us the same level of trouble that the Chieftains did." Behzadi had been retired by the shah from the Iranian Army by 1976. O'Ballance, 1988, p.74; Dunstan, 2003, pp.14–5.

13. O'Ballance, 1988, p.74.
14. Babaie, 2005a, p.363.
15. SORECOM, 1979, p.42.
16. Consult Ripley, *Osprey's Desert Storm Special 1: Land Power: The Coalition and Iraqi Armies.*
17. Cooper and Bishop, 2000, pp.46–7.
18. Ibid., p.29.
19. Gansler, 1986, p.214.
20. Babaie, 2005a, p.368.
21. Ward, 2009, p.197.
22. Cooper and Bishop, 2000; p.38; Sreedhar, 1985, p.9.
23. Jenkins, 1997, pp.22–4.
24. Cooper and Bishop, 2004, p.17.
25. Cooper and Bishop, 2000, p.33.
26. Babaie, 2005a, p.322; Babaie, 2005b, p.253; Cooper and Bishop, 2000; pp.20–4, 33, 38; Sreedhar, 1985, p.9.
27. Cooper and Bishop, 2000, p.38.
28. Babaie, 2005b, p.440.
29. Ward, 2009, p.198.
30. Ibid; American University: Foreign Areas Studies Division, 1978 (3rd Edition), p.404.
31. *Shipping World and Shipbuilder*, 1978, Vol.171, p.538.
32. *Shipbuilding and Marine Engineering International*, 1977, Vol.100, p.99.
33. Babaie, 2005a, p.253; Babaie, 2005b, p.325.
34. Lenczowski, 1978, p.425.
35. Babaie, 2005a, p.317.
36. Ibid., pp.317–8.
37. Ward, 2009, p.192.
38. Ibid.
39. Saikal, 1991, pp.447, 449.
40. Ibid., p.446.
41. Babaie, 2005b, p.223.
42. Cottrell, 1978. p.399.
43. Ward, 2009, p.193.
44. More difficult to substantiate are alleged Western nuclear plans to deter a Soviet attack across Iran towards the oilfields of Khuzistan in Iran and the Persian Gulf region. An Iranian diplomat who had served in the Shah's regime noted that "while no specific documents were shown to us, there were rumors in the Iranian ministries of Foreign Affairs and Defense that the US military had made clear through private channels to the Soviets that if they broke through Iranian defenses in the north, they seriously consider deploying nuclear weapons" (Personal interview with 35-year veteran diplomat of the Pahlavi government's Ministry of Foreign Affairs of Iran, Dr. N. P. on September 4, 2008). While this statement cannot be independently verified, it is certainly plausible.
45. Chegnizadeh, 1997, pp.248–9.
46. Hiro, 1987, p.351.
47. Kapur, 1990, p.14.
48. *Far Eastern Economic Review*, 1973, Vols.79–80.
49. Kapur, 1990, p.14.
50. Zabih, 1988, p.106.
51. Ibid.
52. Mobley, 2003, pp.107–8.
53. Ibid., p.108.
54. Ibid.
55. Readers are cautioned that the role of Bahrain and its historical links with Iran are an important issue. See Mojtahed-Zadeh, "Bahrain: the land of political movements," in *Rahavard*, a Persian Journal of Iranian Studies, Vol.XI/39, 1995.
56. As cited by Mojtahed-Zadeh, 2007, pp.342.
57. Hoveida as cited by Mojtahed-Zadeh, 2007, p.342.
58. Mobley, 2003, pp.108; Mojtahed-Zadeh, 2007, p.342.
59. For a full account of these proceedings consult Mojtahed-Zadeh, 2007, pp.345–4.
60. Mojtahed-Zadeh, 2007, pp.344–5; Ismail and Ismail, 1984, p.307.
61. Pelletiere, 1992, p.30.
62. Hiro, 1990, p.14.
63. Cordesman, 2003, p.82.
64. Brown and Snyder, 1985, p.154.
65. Hiro, 1990, p.15.
66. Al-Azhary, 1984, p.2.
67. Miller and Myloroie, 1990, p.108.
68. Munro, 2006, p.4.
69. Hiro, 1990, p.15.
70. Glassner, 1998, p.29.
71. Ghareeb, 1990, p.26.
72. Shofield, 2004, pp.43-44.
73. Karsh, 2002, p.8.
74. Ghareeb, 1990, p.26.
75. Ibid., p.27.
76. Ibid.
77. Rajaee, 1993, pp.111–2.
78. Interestingly Ghassem was of mixed Faili Shia Kurd-Sunni Arab descent. He worked hard at granting the Kurds equal rights in the Iraqi constitution and reconciling Kurds and Arabs within a single united Iraqi state.
79. Tucker, 1987, p.319.
80. Abdul Salem Aref, who leaned towards pan-Arabism, had been Ghassem's second in command. Aref had assumed the posts of Deputy Prime Minister, Deputy Coomander in Chief of the Armed Forces and Minister of the interior during Ghassem's tenure.
81. Pollack, 2002c, p.8. "A Tyrant 40 years in the Making," *New York Times*, March 14, 2003.
82. Ibid.
83. Arfa, 1966, p.106.
84. Al-Bakr tried to reconcile the party but in vain.
85. Pollack, 2002c, p.9.
86. "A Tyrant 40 years in the Making," *New York Times*, March 14, 2003; Pollack, 2002c, p.9.
87. Ibid.
88. Shofield, 2004, p.53.
89. Karsh, 2002, p.8.
90. Shofield, 1993, p.114.
91. Mafinezam and Mehrabi, 2007, p.31.
92. Parsi, 2007, p.53.
93. Hiro, 2003, p.51.
94. Ibid.
95. Mafinezam and Mehrabi, 2007, p.32.
96. Abdulghani, 1984, p.52.
97. Tucker, 1987, p.319.
98. Cooper and Bishop, 2000, p.61.
99. Mafinezam and Mehrabi, 2007, p.32.
100. See reports in *Le Figaro* (December 17, 1974) and *The Washington* Post (December 17, 1974).

101. Cashman and Robinson, 2007, p.275.
102. Tehrani, 1993, p.13.
103. Cooper and Bishop, 2000, p.62.
104. Tehrani, 1993, p.13.
105. Abdulghani, 1984, p.153.
106. Ghareeb, 1990, p.29.
107. King, 1987, p.7.
108. Romano, 2006, p.196.
109. Ibid.; Marcus, 2007, p.33.
110. Abdulghani, 1984, p.153.
111. Ibid.
112. Although not yet nominally president of Iraq, by 1979 Saddam Hussein was the undisputed leader of Iraq.
113. Cooper and Bishop, 2000, p.62.
114. Ibid.
115. Ibid.
116. Mafinezam and Mehrabi, 2007, p.32.
117. China later withdrew its support for the rebels when she opened diplomatic relations with Iran.
118. Ward, 2009, p.203.
119. Allen and Rigsbee, 2000, p.72.
120. Behrooz, 2000, p.63.
121. Cooper and Bishop, 2000, p.44.
122. For a full account of the support given to the rebels consult Peterson, 1978, pp.187–92.
123. Helms, 2005, p.146.
124. Allen and Rigsbee, 2000, p.70.
125. The first Phantoms to arrive were four F-4Ds stationed at Oman's Bait al-Falaj air base and Sultan Qaboos Air Academy.
126. These were the AB205 and AB206 types.
127. Townsend, 1977, p.105.
128. Ward, 2009, p.204.
129. Allen and Rigsbee, 2000, p.72.
130. Ibid.
131. Ward, 2009, p.204.
132. Townsend, 1977, p.105.
133. Allen and Rigsbee, 2000, p.72.
134. Cooper and Bishop, 2000, p.44.
135. Ibid.
136. Ward, 2009, p.204.
137. Townsend, 1977, p.105; Helms, 2005, p.146.
138. Garver, 2006, p.42.
139. Garver, 2006, pp.42–3
140. Hiro, 1987, p.351.
141. Alagappa, 2008, p.305.
142. Harrison, "Pakistan's Baluch insurgency," *Le Monde Diplomatique*, October 2006.
143. Consult presentation by Selig S. Harrison (Director of the Asia Program, Center for International Policy) entitled "The Baluch," Baluchistan International Conference, Washington, DC, November 21, 2009.
144. Wirsing, 1991, p.105.
145. Cooper and Bishop, 2000, p.30.
146. Bamford, 1982, p.198.
147. "Two Iranian helicopters shot down by Russian air defence personnel," *The Times* [London, England], July 18, 1978.
148. Cooper and Bishop, 2000, p.41.
149. Jenkins, 1997, p.24; Cooper and Bishop, 2004, pp.16–7.
150. Cooper and Bishop, 2004, p.17.
151. As cited by Zabih, 1988, p.10.
152. Consult USAF Aeronautical Systems Division and Hughes Aircraft Company, US DoD, Washington Archives II, MF89

#47T. See declassified extracts of a report outlining the deployment of the AGM-65 in combat in 1972–79.
153. Personal Communication, December 18, 2009.
154. Personal Communication, March 15, 1998.
155. Mirfakhrai, 1984, pp.190–1.
156. Ward, 2009, p.205.
157. Ibid. Iranian infantry were also described as "trigger-happy."
158. Zabih, 1988, p.10. Consult also the interview with the Shah in *Newsweek*, November 14, 1977.
159. Zabih, 1988, p.11.
160. Ibid., p.12.
161. Babaie, 2005a, pp.364–5.
162. Cooper and Bishop, 2000, p.47.
163. Ibid. The Iranians often complained that American servicemen often stayed beyond their contract dates to obtain higher pay and as many other privileges as possible.
164. Babaie, 2005a, pp.364–5. Cooper and Bishop (2004, p.19) note of Iran's KC-707 air tanker fleet which was mostly flown by US pilots under contract. After the revolution and the onset of the Iran–Iraq War, Iran was only able to fly 6 of these.
165. Cooper and Bishop, 2000, p.46.
166. Babaie, 2005b, p.243.
167. Ibid., p.365.
168. Zabih, 1988, p.107.
169. Mirfakhrai, 1984, pp.230–40, 249–50, 258–9; Ward, 2009, pp.209.
170. Mafinezam and Mehrabi, 2007, p.28.
171. Colonel Behzadi noted that after submitting his report about the problems with the Iranian armored corps mobility and logistics, he was summoned by the shah who told him of his dislike of the report. Behzadi was then retired from the Iranian army in 1976. Personal interview on March 15, 1998.
172. Ward, 2009, p.209.
173. Saikal, 1991, p.289; On the popular TV program *60 Minutes* on October 24, 1976, CBS reporter Wallace read quotes from a CIA profile of the shah describing him as a "dangerous megalomaniac … likely to pursue his own aims in disregard of US interests … an uncertain ally." A full transcript of the CBS interview between Michael Wallace and the shah on October 24, 1976 is available online. Treasury Secretary William Simon described the shah as a "nut … irresponsible and reckless," Mafinezam and Mehrabi, 2007, p.25.
174. Cooper and Bishop, 2000, p.47.
175. Karsh, 1996, p.100; Portions of the French interview with the shah made circa 1975–76 are available online.
176. *Newsweek*, May 21, 1973, p.21.
177. D'Souza, 2008, p.206. Ball as cited by Little, 2003, p.225.
178. Perl, 2007, p.25.
179. Amnesty International report cited in Beirne and Messerschmidt, 1999, p.417.
180. Interview with the BBC on January 28, 1974, full transcript online; Another interview with Mike Wallace, *Shah's Message to the Blue Eyed People,* full transcript online.
181. Mafinezam and Mehrabi, 2007, p.26.

Chapter 32

1. Mafinezam and Mehrabi, 2007, pp.32–3.
2. Ward, 2009, pp.190–1.
3. Beirne and Messerschmidt, 1999, p.416.
4. Melman and Javedanfar, 2008, p.154.
5. Babaie, 2005a, pp.356–7.
6. Ibid., p.356.

7. "SAVAK: Like the CIA," *TIME Magazine*, February 19, 1979; Babaie, 2005a, p.357.

8. Mackey, 1998, p.213.

9. Dorman and Farhang, 1988, p.171.

10. Mackey, 1998, p.221.

11. Parsa, 2000, p.134.

12. Mackey, 1998, p.221.

13. Davari, 2005, p.37.

14. Mackey, 1998, p.226 (85); Beirne and Messerschmidt, 1999, p.417 (6,000).

15. Hiro, 1987, p.48.

16. Mackey, 1998, p.227.

17. Hiro, 1987, p.48.

18. Parsa, 2000, p.134.

19. The vote passed by a margin of 71 (pro) to 61 (against) in the Majlis in October 1964.

20. Davari, 2005, p.37; Hiro, 1987, p.48.

21. Del Testa, Lemoine, and Strickland, 2001, p.100; Moin, 1999, p.139.

22. One notable case is the arrest of Hojjat ol Islam Mohammad Reza Saidi in May 1971, who died in SAVAK custody.

23. Mackey, 1998, p.267.

24. Dzhirkvelov, 1987, p.51.

25. Ibid., p.215.

26. Ward, 2009, p.194.

27. Dzhirkvelov, 1987, p.179.

28. Mafinezam and Mehrabi, 2007, pp.2–3.

29. Behrooz, 2000, p.40.

30. Ibid., p.41. the leader of the movement Bahman Qashqai was executed after giving himself up to government forces.

31. Abrahamian, 1982, p.480; Behrooz (2000, p.52) however reports 13 attackers.

32. Behrooz, 2000, p.52.

33. Ward, 2009, p.212

34. Ibid., p.211.

35. Behrooz, 2000, p.62.

36. Ibid.

37. Sazman e Azadibakhshe Khalqhaye Iran (The Organization for the Liberation of the Peoples of Iran), Gorouhe Luristan (the Luristan Group), Sazmane Armane Khalq (The Organization for the People's Ideal), Gorouhe Etehade Kommonistha (the Group for the Union of the Communists), Partiye Demokrate Kurdistan (the Kurdish Democratic Party), Gorouhe Toofan (the Toofan or Storm Group), and the Hezbe Tudeh (Tudeh Party).

38. Gorouhe Shii'ane Rastin (The True Shiite Group) based in Hamadan, Gorouhe Allaho Akbar (the Allaho Akbar Group) based in Isfahan, Gorouhe Al-Fajr (Al Fajr Group) based in Zahedan and Gorouhe Abu Zarr (The Abu Zarr Group) based in Nahavand.

39. Abrahamian, 1982, p.489.

40. Ronczkowski, 2003, p.187.

41. The Marxist branch was to name itself as the Paykar Group following the Iranian revolution.

42. Mackey, 1998, p.303.

43. Hiro, 1987, p.145.

44. Ward, 2009, p.212.

45. Abrahamian, 1982, p.489. Of the 341 total, 177 were killed in combat, 91 by execution (some without trials, some by secret tribunals or similar), 42 by torture by SAVAK, 9 shot while attempting to flee, 7 committing suicide to avoid capture, with 15 arrested and never seen again.

46. Afkhami, 2008, p.398; Bill, 1989, p.181.

47. Bakhash, 1985, p.9.

48. *New York Times*, September 21, 1972.

49. "SAVAK: Like the CIA," *TIME Magazine*, February 19, 1979) "Torture in Iran," *Sunday Times*, January 19, 1975. *New York Times*, September 21, 1972). Abrahamian, 1999, pp.107–8.

50. Afkhami, 2008, p.387.

51. Ibid., p.385.

52. Interested readers in such are referred studies of researchers such as Saikal (1991), Foran (1994), Mackey (1998), Kurzman (2004) and especially the publications of Dr. Jalal Matini, Chief Editor of the *Iranshenasi* peer-reviewed journals (readers are encouraged to consult articles in this publication that have been in print since the early 1980s); Dr. Homa Katouzian, Chief Editor of the peer-reviewed *Iranian Studies* journal (readers are encouraged to consult this journal for all matters relating to Iranian cultural, historical and social developments); and Dr. Abbas Milani, Hamid and Christina Moghadam Director of Iranian Studies at Stanford University, a research fellow and co-director of the Iran Democracy Project at the Hoover Institution.

53. Saikal, 1991, p.289.

54. Graham, 1979, p.237.

55. See detailed discussion by Mackey, 1998, pp.251–2.

56. Mackey, 1998, p.252.

57. Zabih, 1988, p.106.

58. Saikal, 1991, p.288. With respect to the shortage of technical personnel, Iranians felt that training programs could be effectively utilized to make up for these shortfalls.

59. The article described Khomeini as having forged his Iranian nationality, claiming that he was of Indian descent. The actual author of that article remains unknown or anonymous.

60. Kurzman, 2004, p.37, cites a list recently produced by the Iranian government's *Center for Documents on the Islamic Revolution*; Ward, 2009, p.213.

61. Kurzman, 2004, p.46, reports 13 dead according to current Iranian government documents, with the opposition at the time having reported up to 500 killed.

62. Joseph Kraft, "Letter from Tehran," *The New Yorker*, December 18, 1978.

63. Fischer, 2003, pp.194–202.

64. There is the *Khatm* ceremony of burial, followed by mourning 3 days after burial, 7 days after burial, 40 days after burial (*Arbain*) and one year after burial. Note that in Islam the deceased must be buried the same day they passed away.

65. Farmanfarmain, 2005, p.441; Mottahedeh, 2000, p.374.

66. Pahlavi, 2005, pp.280–1.

67. Willett, 2004, p.61; *The Intercontinental Press/Inprecor*, Vol.16, 1978.

68. Vance, 1983, p.326.

69. Ward, 2009, p.215; D'Souza, 2008, p.207. This may have partly to do with the US State Department's Human Rights Officer, Patricia Derian, who had consistently demanded that Jimmy Carter cut all ties to the shah. D'Souza, 2008, p.207.

70. Pollack, 2002a, p.130 (5,000); Sick, 1985, p.50 (20,000).

71. Personal communication with a shopkeeper who witnessed events, January 10, 2010. Also reported by Sick, 1985, p.50.

72. The eyewitness mentioned that he had not been aware of the martial law.

73. The eyewitness survived by diving into one of open street waterways running beside the sidewalks.

74. Zakir, 1988, p.163 (58); Shawcross, 1989, p.21; Pollack, 2002a, p.130; May, Zelikow and Lundberg, 2007, p.118 (all claim hundreds); Taheri, 1985, p.223 (thousands, these numbers were quoted by the opposition).

75. Sick, 1985, p.51.

76. Shawcross, 1989, p.24.

77. Harney, 1998, p.16.

78. Graham, 1979, p.237.

79. Ibid.

80. Moin, 1999, p.189.

81. Personal communication, Fereydoun Farrokh, December 11, 2009. Farrokh was a career diplomat in Iran's Ministry of Foreign Affairs (1950–79) and Iran's first ambassador to (former) East Germany.

82. This event greatly distressed the shah who reputedly admonished Oveissi.

83. Ward, 2009, p.214.

84. Kurzman 2004, p.108.

85. Arjomand, 1988, pp.111–5.; Keddie, 2000, pp.255–6.

86. Sullivan, 1981, pp.17–8.

87. As cited by Kamrava, 1990, p.43.

88. Zabih, 1988, p.13.

89. Ibid,, p.107.

90. Consult Hickman, 1981.

91. Afkhami, 2008, p.487. One of the most dramatic incidents was on December 11, 1978, when a corporal and a private opened fire from opposite sides of the Imperial Guard's mess hall killing 13 and wounding 36 before being gunned down.

92. Zabih, 1988, p.107.

93. Hickman, 1982, p.7.

94. Ward, 2009, pp.216–8.

95. The scale of desertions in Mashad for example, forced the local division to disband by December.

96. Kamrava, 1990, p.90.

97. Reynolds, 2001, p.389.

98. Examples of such sentiments among US officials can be seen in Andrew Young (US ambassador to the UN) describing the Ayatollah as a "saint" (Seliktar, 2000, p.121) or William Sullivan (US ambassador to Iran) who referred to him as the "second Gandhi of Asia" (Ganji, 2002, p.68).

99. Farmanfarmaian, 2005, pp.43–4.

100. As cited by Zabih, 1988, p.95.

101. Afkhami, 2008, p.483.

102. Kamrava, 1990, p.37.

103. Ganji, 2002, p.24.

104. Hoveida had loyally served as the shah's prime minster from January 27, 1965–August 7, 1977. Kamrava (1990, p.37) reports that the shah had been persuaded by some of his advisors to execute Hoveida but was dissuaded from doing so by the minister of justice.

105. This is a religious time as it is the first month of the Muslim calendar during which fighting is banned. Muharram is the most holy of the muslim months with the exception of Ramadan.

106. Hiro, 1987, p.84.

107. Ibid.

108. Fischer, 2003, p.205.

109. Abrahamian, 1982, pp.521–2. Estimates vary with Hiro (1987, p.84) citing 300,000 to one million.

110. Kurzman, 2004, pp.121–2.

111. Fischer, 2003, p.205.

112. Azhari had suffered a heart attack on December 20, 1978 and resigned his post as prime minster on December 31, 1978.

113. By late 1977 Bakhtiar had become the deputy chief of the outlawed National Front. Bakhtiar became the head of the Iran Party which was the largest group within the National Front. He was expelled from the National Front for accepting the post of prime minster.

114. Zabih, 1988, p.95.

115. The three of these had resigned in early January but as nobody was there to replace them, the generals stayed at their posts.

116. Consult Mirfakhrai's 1984 dissertation, p.338.

117. Foran, 1994, p.171; Little, 2003, p.225.

118. Foran, 1994, p.171.

119. Arjomand, 1988, p.129; Afkhami, 2008, p.487; Seliktar, 2000, p.115.

120. Sick, 1985, p.132.

121. Foran, 1994, p.171; Zabih, 1988, p.94.

122. Sick, 1985, p.132.

123. Zabih, 1988, p.95; Kurzman, 2004, p.157; Ward, 2009, pp.219–20.

124. Zabih, 1988, p.99.

125. A massive rebuttal was printed by Qarabaqhi and a whole host of other Iranian commanders in a special issue of the *Artesh-e Raha-i-Bakhsh-e Iran* [The Liberation Army of Iran] in December 1986 in Paris, France.

126. Ward, 2009, p.221.

127. This was noted by Qarabaqhi in a special issue of the *Artesh-e Raha-i-Bakhsh-e Iran* [The Liberation Army of Iran] in December 1986 in Paris, France.

128. Ward, 2009, p.221.

129. Huyser, 1986, p.1.

130. Zabih, 1982, pp.44–5.

131. "Shah says US General Helped Force him to Leave," *The Day* (New London, Connecticut), December 11, 1979. During his trial in early April by a revolutionary court, Air Force Lieutenant-General Amir Hossein Rabii stated of the shah "I realized what a hollow man I was working for when Americans such as Huyser could lead him out of the country by the nose " (as cited in *New York Times* report "Tehran Announces 4 More Executions," April 9, 1979).

132. Amuzegar, 1991, p.256.

133. Keddie and Richard, 2000, p.234.

134. Saikal, 1991, p.456.

135. Ward, 2009, p.221.

136. Afkhami, 2008, p.534.

137. Arjomand, 1988, p.131.

138. Steinmetz, 1994, p.62.

139. Zabih, 1988, p.97.

140. Ward, 2009, p.221.

141. Zabih, 1988, p.101. These allegations were later dismissed by Qarabaqhi in exile who also denied that he had been involved in any plans for a coup, in a special issue of the *Artesh-e Raha-i-Bakhsh-e Iran* [The Liberation Army of Iran] in December 1986 in Paris, France.

142. Zabih, 1988, p.58.

143. Abrahamian, 1989, p.40. See also *"Dastan-e Enghelab"* [The Story of the Revolution], comments of The Joint Chief of Staff, General Qarabaghi BBC World Service Report, Persian Service.

144. Abrahamian, 1989, p.40.

145. Zabih, 1988, p.64.

146. Ward, 2009, p.222.

147. Zabih, 1988, p.64.

148. Ward, 2009, p.221.

149. Zabih, 1988, p.64.

150. Babalie, 2005a, pp.322–3.

151. Ibid., p.323; Ward, 2009, pp.221–2.

152. Zabih, 1988, pp.69–70.

153. Babalie, 2005a, p.323.

154. Zabih, 1988, p.71. It is also noteworthy that Qarabaghi did not confirm the details of Bakhtiar's later reports regarding the bombing request or Rabii's objections to this.

452 IRAN AT WAR

155. Ward, 2009, p.225.
156. Babalie, 2005a, p.323.There is also an interesting narration of events by General Rabie himself in post-revolutionary newspaper, the *Ayandegan* of February–March 1979.
157. Ward, 2009, pp.224–5.
158. "Iranian Rebels Take Command," *The Age* (official Australian newspaper), February 14, 1979.
159. Ward, 2009, p.225.
160. Despite heavy police protection, Bakhtiar, and his secretary, Soroush Katibeh, were assassinated by three men in his home on 7 August 7, 1991.
161. Ward, 2009, p.225.
162. Zabih, 1988, pp.152–3, Footnote 24 (p.162).
163. Zabih, 1982, p.200.
164. Ibid., p.85.
165. Behrooz, 2000, pp108, 112.
166. Zabih, 1982, p.201.
167. "Kurds said to repel 400 Iranian troops from Rebel Center," *New York Times*, September 3, 1979. "Kurdish Rebels Flee Stronghold as Iranians drive through Lines," *New York Times*, September 4, 1979.
168. Ward, 2009, p.231.
169. Cooper and Bishop, 2000, pp.63–70.
170. Ward, 2009, pp.232. "Kurds and Iran's troops reported in Major Battle," *New York Times*, August 31, 1980.
171. "Heavy Fighting by Iran and Iraqi-Backed Kurds Reported," *New York Times*, December 31, 1980.
172. University of Tel Aviv, Soviet and Slavic Series, Vols.2–5, p.71.
173. Behrooz, 2000, pp.110, 113.
174. Ward, 2004, p.226.
175. Ward, 2009, p.235.
176. Emadi, 2001, p.69.
177. Tarock, 1998, p.81.
178. Ibid.
179. Ward, 2009, p.226.
180. Emadi, 2001, p.69.
181. Ward, 2009, p.235.
182. Emadi, 2001, p.69.
183. "Turkomens battle Iranian Forces in New Outbreak of Tribal Separatism," *New York Times*, March 28, 1979.
184. "Iran Reports Cease-Fire with Turkomen Rebels after 8 Days of Fighting," *New York Times*, April 3, 1979.
185. Al-Azhary, 1984, p.2.
186. Miller and Myloroie, 1990, p.107.
187. Ward, 2009, p.233.
188. See "Iran Declares State of Emergency in Baluchistan as Fight Continues," *New York Times*, December 23, 1979 and "For Now, the Baluchis Hold Their Fire," *New York Times*, December 25, 1979.
189. See discussion by Mackey, 1998, p.233.
190. Hiro, 1987, p.118.
191. Ward, 2009, p.234; "Rebels in Azerbaijan Bar Governor from Gaining Access to Statehouse," *New York Times*, December 9, 1979; "Fighting Breaks Out for Tabriz Station: 3 Reported Killed," *New York Times*, December 10, 1979.
192. Ward, 2009, p.234.
193. Hiro, 1987, pp.139–43.
194. Cooper and Bishop, 2000, p.49.
195. For a full perspective by the Islamic Republic of the planning of the coup and intended bombing targets, consult the Institute of Political Studies and Research's "*Koodetayeh Nojeh [The Coup d'etat of Nojeh]*." Another report from the perspective of a handful of some members of the Nojeh coup

who escaped from Iran is available on the widely consulted the Iranian.com news and report outlet, entitled "*Anatomy of a Coup*" (July 23, 2004). URL: www.iranian.com/History/2004/July/Nojeh/index.html
196. Schahgaldian, Barkhordarian, United States. Office of the Under Secretary of Defense for Policy, Rand Corporation, 1987, p.23.
197. Scott, 2008, p.316; Institute of Political Studies and Researcher, 1985, pp.1–9); "Anatomy of a Coup," Iranian.com, July 23, 2004).
198. Cooper and Bishop, 2000, p.49.
199. It is claimed that these were to be clothed like the Pasdaran with their green bandanas featuring the words "*Ya Vatan*" [Oh Nation/Motherland].
200. Wehrey, Green, Nichiporuk, 2008, p.27; Cooper and Bishop, 2000, p.49.
201. "The Lone Assassin," *Washington Post*, August 25, 1996; Cooper and Bishop, 2000, p.49.
202. Consult also Mark Bowden, "Among the Hostage-takers," *The Atlantic*, December 2004; Scott Macleod, "Radicals Reborn," *TIME Magazine*, November 15, 1999.
203. Mackey, 1998, p.295.
204. Mafinezam, and Mehrabi, 2007, p.36.
205. Bowden, 2006, pp.40, 47.
206. Ward, 2009, pp.236–7; Bowden, 2006, pp.127–8.
207. Ward, 2009, pp.236–7.
208. One example is Ibrahim Yazdi who had forced the withdrawal of Leftists who had overrun the US embassy and seized its personnel (including US Ambassador Sullivan) in February 1979 (see Pollack, 2002a, p.153).
209. Ward, 2009, p.236.
210. Cooper and Bishop, 2000, p.64.
211. O'Ballance,1988, p.22.
212. Palmer and Palmer, 2007, p.75.
213. It is also worth noting that prior to the hostage crisis, the Americans had earmarked almost 300 million USD worth of military equipment to be immediately shipped to Iran in case the Soviet Union invaded.
214. Mafinezam and Mehrabi, 2007, p.36. The authors appear to also link the Iran–Iraq War to the hostage crisis.
215. Ibid.
216. Amirahmadi, 1993, pp.257; Venter, 2005, p.61.

Chapter 33

1. Cooper and Bishop, 2000, p.47–8.
2. Ibid.
3. Chubin and Tripp, 1988, pp.23–4.
4. Brown and Snyder, 1985, p.154.
5. Karsh, 2002, p.9.
6. Cooper and Bishop, 2000, p.65. Iraq claimed 115 square miles (300 square kilometers) in the Zain ol Qaws area. Iranian forces also lost control of Sayf e Saad (also in Iranian Kurdistan) to invading Iraqi forces. Baghdad again claimed the region as Iraqi under the auspices of the 1975 treaty.
7. Abdulghani, 1984, p.201.
8. Chubin and Tripp, 1988, p.29.
9. Cooper and Bishop, 2000, p.66.
10. Pipes, 1983, pp.7–8 offers an excellent rebuttal.
11. Al-Khalil, 1989, p.264.
12. Consult Halliday, F. (1996). *Arabs and Persians*. Cahiers d'etudes sur la Mediterranee Orientale et le monde Turco-Iranien, no.22, July–December. Report is available at: www.ceri-sciencespo.com/publica/cemoti/textes22/halliday.pdf

13. Souresrafil, 1989, p.27.
14. Al-Khalil, 1989, p.198.
15. The overall ideological aims of the pan-Islamism are to "eliminate their borders and unify as one state" (as cited from Pipes, 1983, p.6).
16. Staudenmaier, 1983, p.28; Khadduri, 1988, p.65.
17. Al-Azhary, 1984, pp.1–.
18. Cockburn, 2008, p.44.
19. Al-Khalil, 1989, p.265.
20. Hiro, 1990, p.108.
21. Aburish, 2000, p.123.
22. Al-Khalil, 1989, p.264.
23. Iran is host to 8,000 historical sites and monuments. For full report consult Hojjat, 1993, pp.41–6.
24. Sreedhar, 1985, p.11.
25. Wright, 1980–1, pp.276–85.
26. Sreedhar, 1985, p.11.
27. Wright, 1980-1981, p.286.
28. Miller and Mylroie, 1990, p.109.
29. Halloran, R. "British in 1950, Helped Map Iraqi Invasion of Iran," *New York Times*, October 16, 1980.
30. Pelletiere, 1991, p.xiii.
31. Zaloga, 1984, p.29; Hiro, 1990, pp.44.
32. The Nojeh purges in particular had significantly weakened Iran's 92nd Armored Division in the critical Khuzistan theater. Ward, 2009, p.241.
33. Dishon, D., Legum, C., and Shaked, H. (1983). *Middle East Contemporary Survey: Vol.V 1980–1.* (New York: Holmes and Meier), pp.26–7.
34. Retired Iranian Colonel F. Farzaneh (a pseudonym) noted in an interview with the author (October 6, 2008) that many Iranian tanks went into combat "completely blind," perhaps due to incomplete refits during and after the Revolution.
35. Ibid.
36. Tucker, 1988, p.226.
37. Sreedhar, 1984, p.96.
38. Hiro, 1990, p.44.
39. Ibid., p.40.
40. The first air-to-air victory was scored by Iranian F-14s which shot down an Iraqi helicopter supporting Iraqi troops in Zain ol Qows on September 7.
41. Cooper and Bishop, 2000, pp.65, 66, 67.
42. Ibid., p.68.
43. Phythian, 1997, p.291.
44. An editorial in the *Washington Post* dated June 4, 1980 as cited in Fayazmanesh, 2008, p.15.
45. Carter, 1995, pp.516; Brzezinski labeled the Iranian claims of his complicity with Saddam as "*lunatic assertions*" (see *Washington Post*, April 1, 1980) and "*absolutely false*" (see Brzezinski's letter to the editors of the *Wall Street Journal*, July 3, 1991 regarding his retort to Bani-Sadr's 1991 book).
46. Tarock, 1998, p.215; Jokic, 2003, p.124; Healy, 1989, p.98; Downing and Beck, 2003, p.141; Flippin, 2003, p.237; Lando, 2007, p.53; Ralph, 2006, p.264.
47. Hiro, 1990, p.38.
48. Palmer and Palmer, 2007, p.75.
49. King, 1987, p.33.
50. Graz, 1992, p.37; Hiro, 1987, p.167; Fayazmanesh, 2008, p.22; Timmerman, 1991, p.78; Hussein, 1985, p.172; Ward, 2009, p.241; Pelletiere, 1992, pp.34–5; Miller and Mylroie, 1990, p.109.
51. Hiro, 1987, p.167.
52. O'Ballance, 1988, p.207.
53. Hiro, 1990, p.43.
54. Zabih, 1988, p.169.
55. Ripley, 1991, p.6; Miller and Mylroie, 1990, p.109.
56. Pelletiere, 1992, p.35.
57. Sridhar, 1985, p.11.
58. Wagner, 1983, p.63; Pelletiere, 1992, p.36.
59. Grummon, 1982, p.23.
60. IRIAF aircraft were fitted with bombs, rockets, Electronic Countermeasure (ECM) pods, and the deadly Maverick air-to-ground TV guided missiles. As air-to-air combat was envisaged, Sparrow and sidewinder missiles were fitted with each of the F-14s being given a load of four Phoenix missiles.
61. 14 Boeing 707-3J9C and 4 Boeing 747-2J9C tankers.
62. These included new Iraqi bases at Al-Tallil, Mosul and Shoabah, as well as Kut, Baghdad's Al-Rasheed and Al-Dadjil and Al-Bakr (to Baghdad's north).
63. Cooper and Bishop, 2003, pp.25–8.
64. O'Ballance, 1988, p.33.
65. Hiro, 1990, p.40.
66. Grummon, 1982, p.13.
67. As events were to soon show, Iranian aircraft proved more than capable of air combat and ground support.
68. Hiro, 1990, p.43.
69. "Farhad," an Iranian Kurdish activist, noted to the author (on October 13, 2008) a group of 20 or so Kurds held up an Iraqi column in one pass for 10–15 days. The reason the Kurds, including autonomists, fought the Iraqis was attributed to the racialist pan-Arabist rhetoric aimed against ancient Iranian history and culture, a domain which the Kurds share with their Iranian kin, the Persians, Rashtis, the Turkic-speaking Azarbaijanis, etc. "Farhad" mentioned that in a televised interview with the western press in Qasr-e Shirin, Iraqi troops tore up symbols of ancient Iran in front of the resident Kurdish population. The Kurds were not won over by Saddam Hussein's anti-Iranian rhetoric.
70. Sreedhar, 1985, p.10.
71. O'Ballance, 1988, p.35.
72. Sreedhar, 1985, p.10.
73. Hiro, 1990, p.41.
74. Sreedhar, 1986, p.11.
75. Grumman, 1982, p.17.
76. Cooper and Bishop, 2000, pp.94–5.
77. O'Ballance, 1988, p.36; Hiro, 1990, p.43.
78. As reported by eyewitness accounts of former Ahvaz residents "Shaheen" and "Tarek" to the author in an interview on October 10, 2008.
79. Grummon, 1982, p.23.
80. Bishop and Cooper, 2003, p.26. It would appear that one of the F-4 attacked the Iraqi ground forces with the other F-4 possibly acting as an escort against possible IrAF interceptors.
81. Bishop and Cooper, 2003, p.31.
82. Copper and Bishop, 2000, p.94.
83. O'Ballance, 1988, p.37.
84. Tucker, 1988, p.225.
85. Zabih, 1988, p.173.
86. Hiro, 1990, p.45.
87. Zabih, 1988, p.173. Estimates however do vary as some sources cite 1,500 Iraqi dead and 2,000 wounded; Cooper and Bishop, 2000, p.103.
88. Hiro, 1990, p.45.
89. Tucker, 1988, p.225.
90. Ibid.
91. Hiro, 1990, p.46.

92. These included raids against antiaircraft SA-6 sites in Shalamcha, the dropping of deadly cluster bombs and the firing of Maverick air to ground missiles. Even Saddam's home city, Tikrit, was bombed by Iranian aircraft.

93. The Iraqi helicopters were then attacked by the Iranian Cobras shooting one down with a TOW missile Other helicopter "dogfights" reported include the duel on November 7, 1980 between two Cobras and two Iraqi Mi-25s in which the latter were destroyed by TOW and 20mm gunfire.

94. Islamic Republic of Iran Navy (IRIN)

95. The Iraqi vessels apparently used the metal structures of the rigs as cover to mask them from Iranian radar.

96. These were two Phantoms and one Sea King helicopter.

97. The stricken aircraft was a MiG-23. The *Paykan* had fired its deadly 76 mm Otto Melara gun rounds into the MiG-23s wing, forcing it crash into the Persian Gulf.

98. Cooper and Bishop, 2000, p.108.

99. Another dogfight later however resulted in the downing of one Phantom and one MiG-23 respectively.

100. Dishon, D., Legum, C., and Shaked, H. (1983). *Middle East Contemporary Survey: Vol. V 1980–1*. New York: Holmes and Meier, p.601.

101. Zabih, 1988, p.172.

102. Tucker, 1988, p.226. The Iraqis however claimed to have destroyed 270 tanks. Zabih (1988, pp.173) cites 30 captured tanks with Hiro (1990, pp.48) citing 100.

103. Dunstan, 2003, pp.14–5.

104. O'Ballance, 1988, p.74.

105. Rottman, 1993, p.48.

106. *Marine Corps Gazette*, February 1982, p.49; Cooper and Bishop, 2000, p.115.

107. See *New York Times*, March 2, 1981.

108. King, 1987, p.10; See also *International Herald Tribune*, March 17, 1981.

109. See *Washington Post*, April 19, 1981.

110. Grummon, 1982, p.19.

111. Cooper and Bishop. 2000, pp.118–9.

112. Cooper and Bishop, 2000, p.120.

113. Nevertheless, the Iranian raid could have been more successful according to veteran IRIAF pilot Captain "S. K." "some of the less experienced pilots began to chatter over our radios when they saw Iraqi SAMs flying into their midst – this compromised the efficiency of the attack by distracting the team leaders and wasting a number of precious seconds. This meant that the methodical nature of the attack plan became transformed into a series of spectacular bombing runs and strafing passes" (Interview with author, October 28, 2008).

Chapter 34

1. Mackie, 1998, p.321.

2. The Cobras were apparently trying to "entice" Iraqi jets into the open. Just as the Iraqi jets (presumably MiG-21s) arrived to kill the Cobras, Iranian jets intervened resulting in an air-to-air battle in which the outcome remains unknown.

3. Zabih, 1988, p.173.

4. Some Iranian officers even reported rumors among some troops in June 1981 that Bani Sadr may have been attempting to keep the regular army and the Pasdaran-Basij from cooperating with each other (Interview with Colonel A. B. on July 2, 2007). A. B., who fought in the Susangerd battles in January 1981, noted that "Bani Sadr appeared to favor the regular army over the Pasdaran-Basij, and in public appearances one would always see him escorted by regular army troops. This was provocative and led to the impression that he was attempting to spark conflict between us

[the army] and the Pasdaran. Relations at the time were not as constructive as could be – and Bani Sadr certainly did not help. One thing is certain: when Bani Sadr left, we and the Pasdaran began to cooperate much better against the Iraqis and finally pushed them out of our lands."

5. Cooper and Bishop, 2000, p.126; Hiro, 1990, p.52.

6. The IRIAF had resorted to using F-5 Tigers as bombers and F-4 Phantoms as fighter escorts. This measure was necessary given the inferiority of the F-5 against the MiG-23 in dogfights.

7. Hiro, 1990, p.53.

8. Cooper and Bishop, 2000, p.127. The aircraft involved in these missions were F-5Es.

9. Ibid.

10. Veteran solider Shahram T., who fought in the 92nd Armored Division to lift the siege of Abadan noted in an interview to the author on May 22, 2008 that "the Iraqis fought very hard to stay across the Karun River – when the fighting was over one could see hundreds of bodies of dead Iranian troops."

11. Cordesman, 1984, p.670.

12. The Iraqis also suffered 3,000 injured.

13. Tucker, 1988, p.226.

14. Ibid.

15. Hiro, 1990, p.55.

16. Cooper and Bishop, 2000, p.130.

17. Hiro, 1990, p.56.

18. Pelletiere, 1992, p.42.

19. Cooper and Bishop, 2000, p.130.

20. Hiro, 1990, pp.56.

21. Cooper and Bishop, 2000, p.131; Hiro, 1990, p.56.

22. Tucker, 1988, p.226.

23. Al-Samarrai, V., *Devastation at the Eastern Gates*, p.81. Vafiq Al-Samarrai was a lieutenant in the Iraqi army.

24. Iraq however did claim that a MiG-21MF armed with an indigenously designed 4 barrel Gatling-type gun had managed to down an F-14 (possibly March 22–23). This was not verified by independent military sources. There were no other reports of this type of gun appeared throughout the Iran–Iraq War and the succeeding Iraqi wars with the west.

25. Babaie, 2005, p.327.

26. Hiro, 1990, p.56.

27. The Iraqis only managed to down two F-5Es by April 3.

28. *The New York Times*, March 30, 1982; *The New York Times*, April 1, 1982; *The Economist*, April 24, 1982.

29. Miller and Mylroie, 1990, p.113.

30. Hiro, 1990, p.56. During the course of the Nowruz offensives, the Iranians did lose 4,000 troops and another 6,000 were captured by the Iraqis.

31. Miller and Mylroie, 1990, p.114.

32. The archives of the Iraqi News Agency, March 29, 1982.

33. Hiro, 1990, pp.63–4.

34. Cooper and Bishop, 2000, p.132; Babaie, 2005, p.328.

35. Babaie, 2005, p.328. These new Iraqi Mirages were equipped with the deadly Matra Super 530F-1 medium range antiaircraft missiles.

36. Cooper and Bishop, 2000, p.131. F-14As shot down two Iraqi MiG-23s and an F-4 downed an MiG-21. The Iraqis also lost three of their MiG-21s to technical problems or friendly fire.

37. Hiro, 1990, p.59.

38. Cooper and Bishop, 2000, p.134. In the West, the world record for this type of transport is incorrectly attributed to the EL AL airlift of 1,200 Ethiopian Jews in a single night.

39. Ibid., p.132.

40. Hiro, 1990, p.59; Cooper and Bishop, 2000, pp.132–3, 136.
41. The Gazelle and Mi-25 were armed with the HOT and AT-6 antitank missiles respectively.
42. Hiro, 1990, p.39. Cooper and Bishop, 2000, p.133.
43. O'Ballance, 1988, p.85.
44. Hiro, 1990, p.60.
45. This had been made possible, thanks to Delfani's earlier RF-4E mission which had obtained valuable aerial photo intelligence on occupied Khorramshahr's supply dumps, defense systems, communication networks and bridges.
46. Pelletiere, 1992, p.42.
47. Miller and Mylroie, 1990, p.114.
48. Interview by author with J. N. on August 31, 2008. J. N. was one of the Pasdaran troops who entered Khorramshahr. He reported that "we heard an Iraqi helicopter trying to take off – our captain shouted orders to aim or weapons at it – some of us were now using captured Iraqi AK-47s, and the rest of us had the G-3 … we all fired at once – the poor chopper was aloft for only perhaps 150 meters or so – then smoke began coughing out of its main rotor…the chopper slowly landed back down – we rushed to where it crash landed – the occupants were injured but still alive – we pulled out the pilot and a number of Iraqi officers, I think they were staff planners as they were carrying maps and documents."
49. *New York Times*, May 29, 1982.
50. Ripley, 1991, p.9.
51. Mackie, 1998, p.321.
52. O'Ballance, 1988, p.95.
53. Bengio, 1982, p.28.
54. Zaloga, 1993b, p.40.
55. Middleton, D., New Iraqi Strategy is Seen in War with Iran, *New York Times*, October 31, 1982, pp.6.
56. By now the French had stationed 400 technicians in Iraq to build up Iraq's air defenses and defenses.
57. Cooper and Bishop, 2003, pp.66–7.

Chapter 35

1. O'Ballance, 1988, p.94.
2. Pelletiere, 1992, pp.63–4.
3. Hiro, 1990, p.87.
4. Zabih, 1988, p.181.
5. A full tabulation of Iraqi prisoners is given in the *Kayhan Newspaper* (Tehran edition) prints of July 14 and 15, YEAR.
6. See *Financial Times*, August 16, 1982; Hiro, 1990, p.88.
7. O'Ballance, 1988, p.95.
8. Zabih, 1988, p.181.
9. Ripley, 1991, p.8.
10. Hiro, 1990, p.87.
11. Cooper and Bishop, 2003, pp.67–8. A second F-4 was crippled and was pursued by MiG-23s and Su-22s but two F-14A interceptors shot down one MiG-23 and Su-22 respectively allowing the F-4 to escape.
12. Cooper and Bishop, 2003, p.69.
13. O'Ballance, 1988, p.98.
14. Hiro, 1990, p.91.
15. As reported in *Kayhan Newspaper* (Tehran edition), October 11 and 12, YEAR.
16. Zabih, 1988, p.181.
17. O'Ballance, 1990, p.102.
18. Sreedhar, 1985, p.105.
19. Hiro, 1990, p.92.
20. Cooper and Bishop, 2000, p.147.
21. Zabih, 1988, p.181.
22. Rasheed was the commanding officer of the Fourth Army Corps and was also a member of the Army General Staff. Mohsen was the assistant commanding officer as well as being the Iraqi army's spokesman.
23. Cooper and Bishop, 2004, p.45.
24. Hiro, 1990, pp.95.
25. Tucker, 1988, p.225.
26. Hiro, 1990, p.95; Zabih, 1988, p.185.
27. Zabih, 1988, p.185.
28. By this time the SCIRI was led by Ayatollah Mohammad-Bagher Al-Hakim. The latter was being groomed to become Iraq's supreme leader (like Ayatollah Khomeini) once the Baathist government in Baghdad was overthrown.
29. Cooper and Bishop, 2000, p.156.
30. Full coverage of this offensive was provided the Iranian weekly *El-Ahram* of August 12, 1983.
31. Ripley, 1991, p.9. The Guards managed to seal the breach that had developed in the Iraqi lines.
32. Zabih, 1988, p.186.
33. Consult *BBC Summary of World Broadcasts*, November 1 and 12, 1983.
34. Karsh, 2002, p.53.
35. Ripley, 1991, p.8.
36. Cordesman, 1987, p.65.
37. Tucker, 1988, p.225; Earthwatch Institute-Australia, Action Research, 1969, p.106; Farouk-Slugett and Slugett, 1987, p.181; Rajesh, 1984, p.138; Rottman, 1993, p.48.
38. Cordesman, 1987, p.65.
39. Cooper and Bishop, 2000, p.165.
40. *Financial Times*, February 7, 1984.
41. *Newsweek*, April 1981, p.16.
42. *Guardian*, April 9, 1985.
43. Tucker, 1988, p.225.
44. Ward, 2009, p.264.
45. Hiro, 1990, p.103.
46. Ibid.
47. Personal interviews with two veterans of the Pasdaran (T. S. and S. R.) on September 23, 2008, who had been in the Majnoon assault in February 23–25, 1984.
48. Hiro, 1990, p.103.
49. The Iraqis mounted 100 air sorties versus Tehran's 10.
50. Hiro, 1990, p.104.
51. Ibid., p.105. This was reported by the *Sunday Times*, March 18, 1984. There are references to earlier uses by of mustard gas by the Iraqis in *Jane's Defense Quarterly* on January 25, 1984.
52. See report in *Sunday Times*, March 11, 1984.
53. See report in *Sunday Times*, April 29, 1984.
54. Ibid.
55. O'Ballance, 1988, p.160.
56. An enthusiastic proponent of a "Final Offensive" was none other than Hojat ol Islam Rafsanjani.
57. O'Ballance, 1988, p.161.
58. The Shah had installed RPG-7 plants in Iran and these were producing ample supplies of the weapons. Like Iran, Iraq also produced copies of the Soviet-designed RPG-7.
59. O'Ballance, 1988, p.162.
60. The Iraqis responded in kind on Tehran, however both sides refrained from attacking each other's cities as a result of a UN sponsored "aerial ceasefire" with respect to metropolitan centers.
61. The Iranians also targeted Basra for punishing artillery strikes on March 10, possibly in preparation for Badr.
62. O'Ballance, 1988, p.162.
63. Ibid., p.163.

456 IRAN AT WAR

64. Ibid.

65. Ibid., p.162.

66. Ibid., p.164.

67. Veterans M. T. and K. I. were interviewed by the author on October 1, 2008.

68. Ibid.

69. Cooper and Bishop, 2000, p.180.

70. Saivetz, 1989, p.36; Herbet E. Denton, "Iraq's Apparent Goading of Iran Nearly backfired," *Washington Post*, March 25, 1985, pp.A1, A6.

71. Saivetz, 1989, p.58.

72. Some of these actions witnessed cooperation between the Iraqi navy and air force such as the raid in April 1983 when Super Frelons, escorted by fighters and followed by Iraqi missile boats attacked Iranian ships, but actions like these were often countered by the IRIN and aircraft.

73. *International Security Yearbook*, 1984, p.148.

74. Pollack, 1992, p.216.

75. Pfaltzgraff, 1988, p.240.

76. Western officials at the time officially claimed that Iran was not capable of flying its Tomcats and the Dassault Company claimed that only one of the planes had been damaged due to "training."

77. The American journal *AW and ST*, September 30, 1985 issue reported that three of the Super Etendards had been returned by Iraq intact with another aircraft damaged due to a landing exercise. The fate of the fifth aircraft has not been specified. Fredriksen, 2001, pp.81.

78. Cordesman, 1987, p.81, reports Kharq Island's defences as having Hawk antiaircraft missiles and effective low altitude antiaircraft batteries in 1985.

79. Cordesman, 1987, p.44.

80. Karsh, 2002, pp.74–5.

Chapter 36

1. Cooper and Bishop, 2000, p.194.

2. Tucker, 1988, p.225.

3. Zaloga, 1993b, pp.38–40.

4. Ripley, 1991, p.9.

5. Supplies did arrive from Israel, notably air to air and ground to air missiles, but many of these had often passed their shelf-life and often unreliable in combat.

6. *Nuclear Non-Proliferation and US National Security*, Hearings before the Committee on Governmental Affairs, US Senate February 25, 1987, p.57; Cooper and Bishop, 2000, p.192.

7. Tucker, 1988, p.226.

8. These were the Iraqi 1st and 5th Mechanized Divisions.

9. Cooper and Bishop, 2000, p.197.

10. Ripley, 1991, p.9.

11. Cooper and Bishop, 2000, p.199.

12. Tucker, 1988, p.226.

13. Cooper and Bishop, 2000, p.201.

14. On February 16 alone, repositioned Hawk missile batteries shot down a MiG-23 with F-14A Tomcats shooting down five more Iraqi aircraft (including two supersonic TU-22s).

15. Cooper and Bishop, 2000, p.205.

16. Tucker, 1988, p.226.

17. It is possible that the Iraqis may have been concerned that the F-5s could have been "doubling up" as bait for Iraqi interceptors which would be then targeted by F-14As and Hawk missiles.

18. Data regarding Egyptian–Iranian air-to-air engagements are harder to obtain, as the Iranians never "officially" admitted to the existence of the advanced Egyptian Mirage fighters amongst the Iraqis.

19. Interview with Fao veteran "Farzin" on January 20, 2009.

20. After the Iran–Iraq War, the Iraqi ambassador to the US, Al-Mashat made the same allegations and noted that the US had deliberately provided false intelligence to the Iraqis.

21. Evidently no Iranian interceptors had appeared, but two Iraqi aircraft were shot down by the Iranians on the platform.

22. Pelletiere, 1992, p.103.

23. Hiro, 1990, p.172.

24. Tucker, 1988, p.226.

25. Phythian, 1997, pp.19–93.

26. Rottman, 1993, p.50.

27. Cooper and Bishop, 2000, p.221.

28. For a summary of these views consult articles on the subject in the Israeli newspaper, *Ha'aaretz*, November 21, 1986.

29. Amirahmadi, 1993, p.177.

30. *Washington Post*, December 7, 1986.

31. Cordesman, 1987, p.30; Consult also the *New York Times*, February 2, 1987.

32. Cooper and Bishop, 2004, p.191.

33. Braybrook, 1991, p.6–8. Note that 5,166 of the antitank missiles were of the HOT series.

34. Consult Ranstorp (1997) and especially the links between the TWA flight 847 hijacking on June 1985 and the Iranian links to the Lebanese hijackers on p.95.

35. Cordesman, 1987, p.158.

36. Ward, 2009, p.277.

37. Cooper and Bishop, 2000, p.232.

38. Hiro, 1990, pp.180.

39. *New Scientist*, January 17, 1985, p.10.

40. O'Ballance, 1988, p.194.

41. Hiro, 1990, p.181.

42. Ibid.

43. See *New York Times*, September 26 and October 12, 1987.

44. Cooper and Bishop, 2000, p.236. The Iranians could only field 60 fighters versus Iraq's total of 600 combat jets.

45. Cooper and Bishop, 2004, p.70.

46. Brown and Snyder, 1985, p.147, make reference to the Soviet build-up along Iran's borders during the Iran–Iraq War.

47. O'Ballance, 1988, p.198.

48. Tucker, 1987, p.321.

49. The regular army opposed this offensive and refused to support it. This explains why the offensive lacked support by regular army helicopters, tanks, and had no proper air cover.

50. *The Guardian*, May 2, 1987.

51. Iraqi fighters and bombers often rapidly turned back when they detected F-14As. Exceptions were the MiG-25 which tried to use its speed to advantage when encountering the F-14A.

52. During Iraq's bombing runs in January-February 1987, 3,050 Iranian civilians were killed.

53. Cordesman, 1997, p.46.

Chapter 37

1. Hiro, 1990, p.195.

2. Phythian, 1997, pp.111, 113.

3. Rottman, 1993, p.48.

4. Braybrook, 1991, p.5.

5. Tarock, 1998, p.175.

6. These explanations may not be far-fetched as the Soviet economy was in dire need of reform as indicated by Gorbachev's coining of the need for "*Glasnost*" (transparency,

openness) and *"Perestroika"* (reference to the need to restructure the Soviet economy). The need for western goodwill, especially economic and political support was seen as increasingly paramount.

7. The US wanted to push an arms embargo against Iran this through the United Nations Security Council (Consult Joyner, 1990, p.144; Hiro, 1991, p.229-230).

8. Cooper and Bishop, 2000, p.273; Braybrook, 1991, p.9.

9. Braybrook, 1991, p.11.

10. Cooper and Bishop, 2000, p.265.

11. Ibid., p.209.

12. Ibid., p.229; Tarock, 1998, p.174; Margolis, *Toronto Sun*, Sunday, January 19, 2004.

13. Joe Stork and Martha Wenger, 1984, "US Ready to Intervene in the Gulf War," *Middle East Research and Information Project (MERIP)*, no.s 125–6, July-September, pp.44–8; specific citation from pp.47–8.

14. Consult *Financial Times*, November 14, 1992.

15. This list is only partial. For the entire inventory of military gear shipped by Britain to Iraq consult House of Commons Trade and Industry Committee's *Exports to Iraq: Memoranda of Evidence*, July 17, 1991, pp.43–8.

16. Phythian, 1997, p.100.

17. Ibid., p.79.

18. Stockman-Shomron, 1984, p.321.

19. Phythian, 1997, p.99; House of Commons Trade and Industry Committee's *Exports to Iraq: Evidence of Christopher Cowley*, March 13, 1992, p.189; Cooper and Bishop, 2000, p.265.

20. Ripley, 1991, p.62.

21. Cooper and Bishop, 2000, p.222–33, and footnote 371).

22. Ibid., p.231.

23. Cooper and Bishop, 2004, pp.63, 73; Cooper and Bishop, 2000, pp.176, 255.

24. Briganti, 1990, p.33; Bruce, 1990, p.30; Cordesman and Wagner, 1990, pp.162, 400.

25. Consult *Financial Times*, November 14, 1992.

26. Braybrook, 1991, p.12–3.

27. Hiro, 1990, p.158.

28. Ibid., p.195.

29. Rottman, 1995, p.49.

30. Ibid.; Zaloga, 1993b, p.20; Zaloga, 1994, p.34.

31. Cooper and Bishop, 2000, p.265.

32. Tarock, 1998, p.175.

33. The missile was also developed with North Korean assistance. It was known as the Badr 2000 in Egypt and Iraq. The missile was known as the Condor II in Argentina.

34. See Bowman's report to US Congress in references; Consult also Howard, Sawyer and McCaffrey (2003) in references.

35. Rottman, 1993, p.49.

36. Associated Press, January 18, 1998; See also report by the Austrian Red Cross Accord, "Iraq: Treatment of prisoners of war during the Iran–Iraq War," Query response a-6973 of 16 October 2009, pp.7–8.

37. See reports in the *Daily Telegraph* (May 28, 1988), *The Independent* (August 2, 1988) and *The Guardian* (October 6, 1988).

38. See reports in the *Independent*, September 23, 1987, and The *Middle east Economic Digest*, November 21, 187, p.12. Hiro, 1990, p.195.

39. Cooper and Bishop, 2000, p.259.

40. It was Ardestani who organized the installation of engine repair facilities by arranging to have these taken out storage from the former shah's warehouses. These were then set up in bases and workshops throughout Iran.

41. "IRIAF: 75th Anniversary review," *World Air Power Journal*, Vol.39 Winter 1999, pp.28–37; *Air Forces Monthly* (December 2002 Issue, pp.30–3); Nadimi, F., 2000, *Air Forces Monthly Special: Classic Aircraft Series Number 1*, "Combat over Iraq," pp.77, 79.

42. While these were not yet the equal of their predecessors in the in the 1970s, they were trained by combat veterans who had experience flying F-4, F-5 and F-14 aircraft against western (i.e. Mirage F-1) and Soviet (i.e. MiG) aircraft. These proved more than capable against the best Iraqi pilots.

43. Cooper and Bishop, 2000, p.257, footnote 413.

44. As cited in Hiro, 1990, p.207.

45. Tarock, 1998, p.175.

46. See *Keesing's Record of World Events*, September 1988, pp.36. Keesing's news archives available online at: www.keesings.com

47. Freedman, 1991, p.56.

48. Bermudez, 1991, pp.132–5.

49. Ripley, 1991, p.14.

50. If successful, this would deprive Iraq of one of its major sources of electricity.

51. This operation had very meager helicopter support at just seven machines (only one was a TOW-firing Cobra).

52. Ripley, 1991, p.9.

53. Karsh, 2002, pp.76–8.

54. Cordesman, 1999, p.534.

55. Statements such as these caused some consternation among the Iranian intelligentsia, duly expressed by the chair of the London-based Soudavar Foundation, Fatema Soudavar Farmanfarmaian, who wrote in 2002 that "some of us [Iranians] remember how the United States insisted that it was Iran, not Iraq, that was using poisonous chemicals against Kurds, and so strong was that propaganda that most believed it, even after Flavio Cotti of the International Red Cross publicly corrected the record." Fatema Soudavar Farmanfarmain, "Defending our Turf," June 5, 2002, Iranian.com. Available at: http://www.iranian.com/Opinion/2002/June/Farman/

56. Hilterman, 2007, p.215.

57. Rottman, 1993, p.48.

58. Hiro, 1990, p.203.

59. Ripley, 1991, p.10.

60. Pelletiere, 1992, p.142.

61. Cooper and Bishop, 2000, p.265; Hiro, 1990, p.203. The agents used were either nerve agents or cyanide gas.

62. Hiro, 1990, p.203.

63. Cooper and Bishop, 2000, p.267, Footnote 429 on p.279.

64. Laffin, 1989, p.107.

65. Cooper and Bishop, 2000, p.267.

66. Patrick E, Tyler, "Rout of Iran from Fao still puzzling to West," *Washington Post*, May 3, 1988, p.A-20; Cooper and Bishop, 2000, p.267.

67. These air strikes temporarily held back a number of Iraqi attacks, allowing a number of surviving troops in Fao to escape.

68. The Iranians had built silos at Fao for their Silkworms. These silos were empty by the time the Iraqi forces had arrived.

69. Karsh, 2002, p.57.

70. Iranian listening posts are claimed to have intercepted the (non-Arabic?) communications of these helicopters, however they stopped short of stating that the crews were communicating in English.

71. Cooper and Bishop, 2000, p.273.

72. See *The Middle East*, June 1988, p.6; also quoted in Hiro, 1990, p.204. Cooper and Bishop, 2000, p.273.

73. These were 127mm cannon.

74. Cooper and Bishop, 2000, p.268.

75. Ibid., p.269.

76. This version of events is disputed by the Iranians. Captain Shahrokhfar, who had survived the attack later claimed that the US aircraft continued to target himself and his men with gunfire and rockets even as they had abandoned their doomed ship. These claims were never corroborated by the US Navy.

77. Hiro, 1990, p.204.

78. Consult *The Times*, April 19, 1988 and *Middle East Economic Digest*, April 29, 1988, p.20.

79. Hiro, 1990, p.204.

80. Ibid., p.207.

81. Pelletiere, 1992, p.142.

82. Hiro, 1990, p.206; Cooper and Bishop, 2000, p.273.

83. Hiro, 1990, p.206.

84. "Aslan" A. a veteran combat engineer who survived the battle noted that "temperatures were around 45–46 degrees C which made the wearing of these clumsy suits useless – it was simply impossible to wear these in these hot temperatures."

85. Pelletiere, 1992, p.142.

86. Patrick E, Tyler, "Iraq dislodges Iranians from outside Basrah," *Washington Post*, May 26, 1988, p.A–14.

87. Cooper and Bishop, 2000, p.275.

88. Braybrook, 1991, p.9–51.

89. These were four F-5s and one F-4D escorted by three F-4Es.

90. These were organized in three formations.

91. These were F-5s.

92. Cooper and Bishop, 2000, p.275.

93. Ibid.

94. Hiro, 1990, p.209.

95. Ibid.

96. Pelletier, 1992, p.144.

97. Ripley, 1991, p.9.

98. Hiro, 1990, p.210.

99. Pelletier (1990, p.149) bases his estimates on radio broadcasts and reports on June 26–27, 1988.

100. Barry and Charles, 1992, p.30. In June 1988, Captain Robert Hattan (of the frigate USS *Sides*) had complained to higher authorities that Rogers was too provocative in his actions vis a vis the IRIN.

101. Barry, J., and Charles, R., "Sea of Lies," *Newsweek*, July 13, pp.29–33, 36–9, 1992.

102. Barry and Charles, 1992, pp.38–9.

103. Hiro, 1990, p.211.

104. Pelletier, 1992, p.144.

105. Cordesman, 1999, p.23.

106. Also known as Majles-e Khebregan-e Rahbari (assembly of experts of the leadership).This is a popularly elected permanent body of constitutional experts; these are all clerics.

107. Hiro, 1990, p.246.

108. Ibid.

109. Video footage uncovered by US troops after the fall of Iraq shows a meeting between MKO staff and Iraqi intelligence personnel in the Jalalzadeh building in Baghdad in 1986 in which the transfer of Iraqi funds for the MKO's operations are being discussed. Footage available online.

110. Video footage uncovered after the fall of Iraq to US forces shows a meeting between the MKO and Iraqi military intelligence staff in which intelligence is provided on Pasdaran positions along the Bahmanshir River in Iran, and in which MKO staff in Iraq are planning terrorist bombings in Iran in coordination with the operations of the Iraqi armed forces. Footage available online.

111. Costigan and Gold, 2007, p.68. British officials later reported that the MKO had provided support for Saddam Hussein's chemical and biological weapons programs against Iranian civilians. This was reported to the SkyNews network by British government official, Baroness Emma Nicholson who noted of secret video footage that was handed to her after the US conquest of Iraq. The report shows footage of very large sums of cash being given by Iraqi security forces to MKO officials to help fund their terrorist activities. Footage available online.

112. Hiro, 1990, p.246.

113. Evidence is provided of a rare 1986 film footage by the MKO organization that shows Massoud Rajavi meeting Saddam meeting as well as Tarek Aziz. Footage is available online. Video footage uncovered after the fall of Iraq, shows a meeting between Rajavi and the Iraqi military intelligence staff (headed by General Saber) in the Mokhaberat (Iraqi intelligence) building in Baghdad. Footage available online.

114. Hiro, 1990, p.246. Many of the town's population of 15,000 were killed, wounded, or made homeless.

115. As reported in *The Independent* (July 27 and 30 1988) and *Guardian* (July 27, 30, and September 5, 1988); Hiro, 1990, p.247.

116. Ibid.

117. The Iraqi air force also launched new raids against Bushehr and Bandar Abbas on July 19, 2008, again inflicting heavy damage to infrastructure and personnel. This time Iraq lost two jets to Iranian fighters and another to HAWK ground-to-air missiles (consult Cooper and Bishop, 2000, p.276).

118. Tucker, 1987, p.323.

119. Ibid.

120. Iranian military industries had succeeded in adapting a number of artillery pieces for antitank warfare.

121. Hiro, 1990, p.246.

122. See for example Zwier and Weltig, 2005, p.17; Hiro, 2003, p.44; Tarock, 1998, p.211; Ripley, 1991, p.8.

123. Pelletier, 1992, p.141.

124. Cordesman, 2002, p.23

BIBLIOGRAPHY

Abbasi, M. (1956). *Siyahnameye Chardin [The Travelogues of Chardin]* (10 volumes). Tehran: Amir Kabir.

Abbasi, M. R., and Badiee, P. (1993). *Gozaresh-haye Ozaye Siyasi va Ejtemaie Velayat-e Ahd-e Nasseri [Reports on the Political and Social situation of the Districts/Regions in the times of Nasser e Din Shah].* Tehran: Entesharat-e Pazhoheshgah-e Asnad (Sazman-e Asnad-e melliye Iran).

Abdulghani, J. M. (1984). *Iraq and Iran: The Years of Crisis.* Sydney, Australia: Croom Helm.

Abdollah, S. (Translated from Russian original, Russian author unknown, in 1974). *Gozareshe Iran az yek Sayyah-e Russi [A Report of Iran from a Russian Traveler].* Tehran: Ketabkhaneye Tahori.

Abdullah, Th. (2001). *Merchants, Mamluks and Murder.* SUNY Press.

Abdullaeva, F. I. (2007). "What's in a Safina?" in A. A. Seyid-Gohrab and S. McGlinn (eds.), *A Treasury from Tabriz: the Great Il-Khanid Compendium,* pp.46–68. Amsterdam: Rozenberg Publishers.

Abiverdi, C. (2001). *Iranian Entomology: an Introduction, Volume 1.* Springer.

Abraham of Crete (translated by G. A. Bournoutian 1999). *The Chronicle of Abraham of Crete.* Costa Mesa:-.

Abrahamian, E. (1982). *Iran Between Two Revolutions.* Princeton University Press.

Abrahamian, E. (1999). *Tortured Confessions: Prisons and Public Recantations in Modern Iran.* University of California Press.

Abrahamian, E. (2008). *History of Modern Iran.* New York: Columbia University Press.

Abrahamian, E. (1989). *Political Islam: The Iranian Mojahedin.* I. B. Taurus.

Aburish, S. (2000). *Saddam Hussein: The Politics of Revenge.* London: Bloomsbury.

Adamiyat, F. (1984). *Amir Kabir va Iran [Amir Kabir and Iran].* Tehran: Sherkat-e Sahamiye Entesharat-e Kharazmi.

Adamiyat, F., and Nategh, H. (1977). *Afkare Ejtemaie va Siyasi va Eghtesadi dar Asare Montasher Nashodeye Dorran e Qajar [The Social, Political and Economic Thoughts/Intellectual Currents in the Unpublished Works of the Qajar Era].* Tehran: Agah.

Adams, C. J. (1972). *Iranian Civilization and Culture: Essays in Honor of the 2500th Anniversary of the Founding of the Persian Empire.* McGill University Institute of Islamic Studies.

Adelson, R. (1995). *London and the Invention of the Middle East: Money, Power, and War 1902-1922.* Yale University Press.

Afaqi, S., and Jasion, J. T. (2004). *Tahirih In History: Perspectives On Qurratu'l-'Ayn From East And West.* Kalimat Press.

Afary, J. (1996). *The Iranian Constitutional Revolution, 1906–1911: Grassroots Democracy.* Columbia University Press.

Afaz ol Molk, M. G. K. (1982). *Afzal ol Tavareekh.* Tehran: Nashre Tarikhe Iran.

Afkhami, G. R. (2008). *The Life and Times of the Shah.* University of California Press.

Ahmad, K. M. (1992). *Kurdistan during the First World War.* London: Saqi.

Akin, M. (1980). *Russia and Iran: 1780–1828.* University of Minnisota Press.

Al-Azhary, (1984). *The Iran–Iraq War: An Historical, Economic and Political Analysis.* London: Croom Helm.

Al-Qasimi, S. B. M. (1999). *Power Struggles and Trade in the Gulf.* Great Britain: University of Exeter Press.

Alagappa, M. (2008). *The Long Shadows: Nuclear Weapons and Security in 21st Century Asia.* Stanford University Press.

Al-Khalil, S. (1989). *Republic of Fear: The Inside Story of Saddam's Iraq.* Los Angeles, California: pantheon Books.

Alam, M (1986). *The Crisis of Empire in Mughal North India: Awadh and the Punjab 1707–1748.* Dehli: Oxford University Press.

Allen, W. E. D. (1971). *History of the Georgian People.* Routledge and Kegan Paul.

Allen, C. H. (1982). The state of Masqat in the Gulf and East Africa 1785–1829. *International Journal of Middle East Studies, 14*(2), May, 117–27.

Allen, C. H., and Rigsbee, W. L. (2003). *Oman under Qaboss: From Coup to Constitution 1970 to 1996.* Routledge.

Allen, L. (2005). *The Persian Empire: A History.* London.

Allen, C. (2006). *God's Terrorists: The Wahhabi Cult and the Hidden Roots of Modern Jihad.* Charles, London: Abacus.

Allison, Sir A. (1854). *History of Europe from the Fall of Napoleon in 1815 to the Accession of Louis Napoleon, in 1852, Volume 3.* Edinburgh and London: William Blackwood and Sons.

Amanat, A. (1997). *Pivot of the Universe: Nasir al-Din Shah Qajar and the Iranian Monarchy.* IB. Taurus Publishers.

Amini, D. M. (1942). *Az Sevvom ta Bist-o-Panjom e Shahrivar [From August 25 to -].* Tehran:-.

Amini, I. (1999). *Napoleon and Persia: Franco-Persian relations under the First Empire.* Mage Publishers.

Amiri, M. (1970). *Safarnameye Venezian dar Iran [The Travelogues of the Venetians in Persia].* Tehran: Entesharat-e Kharazmi.

Amiri, M. (translation from English original, 1988). *Safarnameye Sir Austin Henry Layard (Majerahaye Avalliyyeh dar Iran) [The Travelogues of Sir Austin Henry Layard (Early Travels in Persia)].* Tehran: Vahid.

Amirahmadi, H. (1993). *The United States and the Middle East: Search for New Perspectives.* New York: State University of New York Press.

Amuzegar, J. (1991). *The Dynamics of the Iranian Revolution: The Pahlavi's Triumph and Tragedy.* SUNY Press.

Andreeva, Y. (2007). *Russian and Iran in the Great Game: Travelogues and Orientalism.* London: Routledge.

Andronikashvili, M. (1966). *Narkvevebi Iranul-Kartul enobrivi Urtiertobidan [Essays on Iranian-Georgian linguistic contacts].* Tbilisi.

Ansari, A. (2003). *Modern Iran since 1921: The Pahlavis and After*. Longman.

Arfa, H. (1964). *Under Five Shahs*. New York: Morrow.

Arfa, H. (1966). *The Kurds: A Historical and Political Study*. London: Oxford University Press.

Arjomand, S. A. (1988). *The Turban for the Crown: The Islamic Revolution in Iran*. Oxford University Press.

Arjomand, S. A. (2004). *Studies on Persianate Societies*.

Arnold, S. T. W. et al. (ed.). *E. J. Brill's First Encyclopaedia of Islam*. Brill.

Asad, S. (1914). *Tarikh-e Bakhtiari [The History of the Bakhtiars]*. Tehran.

Asiatic Intelligence (1827). Persia, *The Asiatic Journal and Monthy Register for British India nd its Dependencies*, Volume XXIV, July–December 1827, pp.619–620, London: Parbury Allen and Co.

Astrabadi, M. M. K. (reprinted 1962a). *Darre-ye Naderi: Tarikh-e Asr e Nader Shah*. Tehran: Tehran University Press.

Astrabadi, M. M. K. (reprinted 1962b). *Tarikh-e- Jahangosha-ye Naderi*. Tehran: Anjoman e Asar e Melli.

Atabaki, T. (2000). *Azerbaijan: Ethnicity and the Struggle for Power in Iran*. IB Taurus.

Atabaki, T. (2001). Recasting Oneself, Rejecting the Other: Pan-Turkism and Iranian Nationalism. In Van Schendel, W. (Ed.), *Identity Politics in Central Asia and the Muslim World: Nationalism, Ethnicity and Labour in the Twentieth Century*, pp.65–84. London: I. B. Tauris.

Atkin, M. (1980). *Russia and Iran 1780–1828*. University of Minnesota Press.

Avery, P. (1965). *Modern Iran*. New York: Frederick A. Praeger Publishers.

Avery, P. (1991). Nader Shah and the Afsharid Legacy. In P., Avery, G. Hamfly, and C. Melville (ed. s), *The Cambridge History of Iran Volume 7: From Nader Shah to the Islamic Republic*, pp.3–62, Cambridge: Cambridge University Press.

Avery, P. (2008). Prologue: the Dream of Empire. In R. Farmanfarmaian, R. (Ed.), *Qajar Persia: Implications Past and Present*, pp.13–17. Routledge.

Ayatollahi, H., and Haghshenas, Sh. (2003). *The Book of Iran: The History of Iranian Art. Teheran* : Center for International Cultural Studies.

Axworthy, M. (2006). *The Sword of Persia: Nadir Shah from Tribal warrior to Conquering Tyrant*. I. B. Taurus Publishers.

Azari, A. (1983). *Qiyam e Sheikh Mohammad e Khiyabani dar Tabriz [The Rebellion of Sheikh Mohammd Khiyabani in Tabriz]*. Tehran, Iran: Safi'alishah.

Azimzadeh, I. (2007). *Tokens of God*. Los Angeles: Ketab Corp.

Babaie, S. (2004). *Slaves of the Shah: New Elites of Safavid Iran*. I. B. Taurus.

Babaie, A. (2005a). *Tarikh e Artesh e Iran [The History of the Iranian Army]*. Tehran: Iman Publications.

Babaie, A. (2005b). *Tarikh e Neeroye Havayee Iran [The History of the Iranian Air Force]*. Tehran: Iman Publications.

Babinger, F. (1978, ed. by William C. Hickman, trans. by Ralph Manheim). *Mehmed the Conqueror and his Time*. Princeton University Press.

Baddeley, J. F. (1908). *The Russian Conquest of the Caucasus*. Reprinted by Routledge (1999).

Bahar, M. T. (1982). *Tarikh e Mokhtasar e Ahzab e Siyasi ye Iran [A Brief History of the Political Parties in Iran]*. Tehran: Amir Kabir Publications.

Bahl, T., and Syed, M. H. (2003). *Encyclopedia of the Muslim World*. Anmol Publications.

Bain, R. (originally 1095, reprinted 2005). *The First Romanovs*. Kessinger Publishing.

Bakhash, S. (1985). *Reign of the Ayatollahs: Iran and the Islamic Revolution*. IB Taurus.

Balfour, E. (1885). *The Eyclopaedia of India and of Eastern and Southern Asia: Commercial, Industrial and Scientific*. London: Bernard Quaritch.

Bamdad, M. (1968). *Tarikh-e Rejal-e Iran: Jeld-e Yek ta Shesh [The History of the Royalty of Iran: Volumes I–VI]*. Tehran: Ketabforoosheye Zevar.

Bamford, J. (1982). *The Puzzle Palace*. London: Sidewick and Jackson.

Bani-Sadr, A. (1991). *My Turn to Speak: Iran, the Revolution and Secret Deals with the US*.

Barratt, G. R. (1972). A Note on the Russian Conquest of Armenia (1827). *The Slavonic and East European Review*, Vol. 50 (No. 120), pp.386–409.

Barthold V. V. (1963). *Sochineniaa*. Moscow: Izdatelstvo Vostochnoi Literarury.

Bayani, J. (1974). *Tarikh-e Nezamiye Iran (Janghay-e Dorrey-e Safaviye) [The Military History of Iran (The Wars of the Safavid Era)]*. Tehran: Entesharat-e Setad Bozorg-e Arteshdaran.

Bayat, K. (1990). *Iran va Jang Jahani e Avaal: Asnad e Vezarat e Dakheleh [Iran and World War One: Documents from the Ministry of the Interior]*. Tehran: Sazman e Asnad e Melli.

Bayat, M. (1991). *Iran's First Revolution: Shiism and the Constitutional Revolution: 1905–1909*. Oxford University Press.

Becker, S. (2004). *Russian's Protectorates in Central Asia: Bukhara and Khiva 1853–1924*. Routledge.

Beizai-Kashani, H. P. (2003). *Tarikh-e Varzesh-e Bastani-ye Iran: Zoorkhaneh [The History of the Ancient Sports of Iran: the Zoorkhaneh]*. Tehran: Entesharat-e Savvar.

Berberian, H. (2001). *Armenians And The Iranian Constitutional Revolution Of 1905–1911: The Love For Freedom Has No Fatherland*. Westview Press.

Beeman, W. (2006). *The Great Satan versus the Mad Mullahs: How the United States and Iran Demonize each Other*. Greenwood Publishing Group.

Behrooz, M. (2000). *Rebels with a Cause: The Failure of the Left in Iran*. I. B. Taurus.

Bengio, O. (1984). *Middle East Contemporary Survey: Volume VI (1981–1982)*. New York: Holmes and Meier Publishing Inc.

Bermudez, J. S., (1991). Iraqi missile operations during "Desert Storm". Jane's Soviet Intelligence Review, March, 131–135.

Beirne, P., and Messerschmidt, J. W. (1999). *Criminology (3rd Edition)*. Westview Press.

Bill, J. A. (1989). *The Eagle and the Lion: The Tragedy of American-Iranian Relations*. Yale University Press.

Bina, A. A. (1959). *Tarikh-e Siyasi va Diplomasi-ye Iran: (Jeld-e Aval) Az Golanabad ta Torkamanchay [The political and Diplomatic History of Iran: (Volume I) From Golanabad to Torkamanchay]*. Tehran: Tehran University Press.

Black, J. (2004). *Rethinking Military History*. London and New York: Routledge.

Blucher, W. (Translated from German original "*Zeitwende in Iran: Erlebnisse und Beobachtungen* (1949)" to Persian by K. Jahandari in 1984). *The Travelogues of Blucher*. Tehran: Sherkate Sahami Entesharate Kharazmi.

Bokhoor-Tash, N. (1971). *Estrategiy-e Nezamiy-e Iran [The Military Strategy of Iran]*. Tehran: Chapkhaneye Zohreh.

Bonakarian, M. (2006). *Britain and the Iranian Constitutional Revolution of 1906–1911: Foreign Policy, Imperialism, and Dissent*. Syracuse University Press.

Bostock, F., and Jones, G. (1989). *Planning and power in Iran: Ebtehaj and economic development under the Shah*. Routledge.

Bosworth, C. E., and Bulliet, R. (1996). *The New Islamic Dynasties: A Chronological and Genealogical Manual*. Columbia University Press.

Bosworth, C. E., (2007). *Historic Cities of the Islamic World*. Brill.

Boucharlat, R. and Razmjou, S. (2005). In Search of the Lost Median Art. *Iranica Antiqua*, Volume 28, pp.271–314.

Bournoutian, G. A. (1992). *The Khanate of Erevan under Qajar Rule 1795–1828*. Mazda Publishers.

Bournoutian, G. A. (1999). *History of the Wars: (1721–1736)*. Mazda Publishers.

Bowden, (2006). *Guests of the Ayatollah: he First Battle in America's War with Militant Islam*. New York: Atlantic Monthly Press.

Bowman, S. R. (1999). *Chemical Weapons Convention: Issues for Congress: Issue Brief 94029*. Washington, Congressional Research Service, January 12.

Bradley, M. (2008). *Iran: Open hearts in a Closed Land*. Great Britain, Sparkford: J. H. Haynes and Co.

Briganti, G. (1990). Iraqi air power: less than meets the eye. *Defense News*, August edition.

Briggs, J. (1829). *History of the Rise of the Mahomedan Power in India Till the Year A. D. 1612*. London, Printed for Longman, Rees, Orme, Brown, and Green.

British Central Office of Information (1948). *PAIFORCE: The Official Story of the Persia and Iraq Command 1941–1946*. London: HMSO..

Brown, C. (2003). *Diplomacy in the Middle East: The International Relations of Regional and Outside Powers*. I. B. Taurus.

Brown, B., and Snyder, W. P. (1985). *The Regionalization of Warfare: The Falkland Islands, Lebanon, and the Iran–Iraq Conflict*. Transaction Publishers.

Browne, E. G. (1910, reprinted 1995). *The Persian Revolution of 1905–1909*. Cambridge University Press.

Browne, E. G., and (1914, reprinted 1983). *The Press and Poetry of Modern Persia: Partly Based on the Manuscript Work of Mirza Muhammad Ali Khan Tarbiyat of Tabriz*. Cambridge University Press.

Broyles, M. (2007). *Mahmoud Ahmadinejad: President of Iran*. Rosen Publishing.

Bruce, N. (1990). Planes against Brawn. *Time Magazine*, August 20 edition.

Bryer, A. (1975). Greeks and Türkmens: The Pontic Exception. *Dumbarton Oaks Papers, Vol. 29*, Appendix II – Genealogy of the Muslim Marriages of the Princesses of Trebizond.

Brummell, P. (2006). *Turkmenistan*. Bradt.

Burg, D. F., and Purcell, L. E. (2004). *Almanac of World War I*. University Press of Kentucky.

Burke, A. (2008). *Lonely Planet: Iran (5th Edition)*. Lonely Planet Publications.

Canby, S. (2002). *The Golden age of Persian Art*. British Museum Press.

Carter, J. (1995). *Keeping Faith: Memoirs of a President*. Fayetteville, AR: University of Arkansas Press.

Chardin, J. (1983). *Voyage de Paris à Ispahan I: De Paris à Tiflis*. Paris.

Cashman, G., Robinson, L. C. (2007). *An Introduction to the Causes of War: Patterns of Interstate Conflict from World War One to Iraq*. Rowman and Littlefield.

Chailand, G. (1992). *A People without a Country: the Kurds and Kurdistan*. Zed Publications.

Chand, H. (2005). *History of Medieval India*. New Delhi: Anmol Publications.

Chaqueri, C. (2001). *Origins of Social Democracy on Iran*. Seattle, Washington: University of Washington Press.

Chase, K. W. (2003). *Firearms: a global history to 1700*. Cambridge University Press.

Chegnizadeh, G. (1997). *Persian Military Modernization: 1921–1979*. PhD Dissertation, Department of Political Science, University of Bradford.

Christensen, A. (1941). *Essai sur la démonologie iranienne [An Essay/Survey regarding Iranian Demonology]*. Copenhagen.

Chronicle of the Carmelites in Persia and the Papal Mission of the Seventeenth and Eighteenth Centuries (2 Volumes) (1939). London: Eyre and Spottiswoode.

Chubin, Sh., and Tripp, C. (1988). *Iran and Iraq at War*. London: IB Taurus.

Churchill, R. (1967). *The Young Statesman, Volume 2, 1901–1914*. London: Houghton Mifflin.

Çiçek, K., Kuran, E., nalcık, H.,Göyünç, N., Ortaylı, I. (2000). *The Great Ottoman-Turkish Civilisation*. Yeni Türkiye.

Cleveland, W. L. (1999). *A History of the Middle East*. Boulder, CO: Westview Press.

Clodfelter, M. (2002). *Warfare and Armed Conflicts: A Statistical Reference to Casualty and Other Figures, 1500–2000*. Jefferson NC: McFarland and Company.

Cockburn, P. (2008). *Muqtada: Muqtada Al-Sadr, the Shia Revival, and the Struggle for Iraq*. New York: Simon and Schuster.

Cockcroft, J. (1989). *Mohammad Reza Pahlavi Shah of Iran*. Chelsea House Publishing.

Cohen, A. (1996). *Russian Imperialism: Development and Crisis*. Westport, Connecticut: Praeger.

Cole, J. R. I. (1987). Rival Empires of Trade and Imami Shiism in Eastern Arabia, 1300–1800. *Journal of Middle Eastern Studies, 19*, 177–204.

Comte de Ferrieres-Sauveboeuf (1789). *Memoires Historiques, Politques et Geographique des Voyages du Comte de Ferrieres-Sauveboeuf en Turquie, en Perse et en Arabie, depuis 1782 jusqu'en 1789*. Paris: Buisson.

Connell, E. (translated into Persian in 1968 by H. Taheri). *Honar-e Islami [The Islamic Arts]*. Entesharate daneshgahe Tehran.

Cooper, J. P. (1979). *The New Cambridge Modern History, Volume IV: The Decline of Spain and the Thirty Years War, 1609–48/59*. Cambridge University Press.

Cooper, T. and Bishop, F. (2000). *Iran–Iraq War in the Air 1980–1988*. Atglen, PA: Shiffer military History.

Cooper, T. and Bishop, F. (2004). *Iranian F-14 Tomcat Units in Combat*. Oxford: Osprey Publishing.

Costigan, S. S., and Gold, D. (2007). *Terrornomics*. United Kingdom: Ashgate Publishing.

Cottrell, A. J. (1978). Iran's armed forces under the Pahlavi dynasty. In G. Lenczowski (ed.), *Iran Under the Pahlavis*, pp.389–432, Stanford University: Hoover Institution Press.

Cordesman, A. H. (1984). *The Gulf and the Search for Strategic Stability: Saudi Arabia, the Military balance in the gulf, and trends in the Arab-Israeli Military Balance*. Boulder, Colorado: Westview Press.

Cordesman, A. H. (1999). *Iraq and the War of Sanctions: Conventional Threats and Weapons of Mass Destruction*. Praeger Publishers.

Cordesman, A. H. (1999b). *Iran's Military Forces in Transition: Conventional Threats and Weapons of Mass Destruction*. Greenwood Publishing Group.

Cordesman, A. H. (2002). *Iran's Military Capabilities in 2002: A Dynamic Net Assessment*. Center for Strategic and International Studies.

Cordesman, A. H. (2003). *Saudi Arabia enters the Twenty-First Century*. Greenwood Publishing Group.

Cordesman, A. H. and Kleiber, M. (2007). *Iran's Military Forces and Warfighting Capabilities: The Threat in the Northern Gulf.* Greenwood Publishing Group.

Cordesman, A. H., and Wagner, A. R. (1990). *The Lessons of Modern War: Volume III: The Afghan and Falklands Conflicts*. London, England: Mansell Publishing Limited.

Cottam, R. W. (1964). *Nationalism in Iran*. Pittsburgh: University of Pittsburgh Press.

Craig, S. (2000). *Sports and Games of the Ancients*. Greenwood Publishing Group.

Creasy, S. E. S. (1877). *History of the Ottoman Turks*. New York, H. Holt and Company.

Cronin, S. (1997). *The Army and the creation of the Pahlavi State in Iran, 1910–1926*. London: I. B. Tauris.

Cronin, S. (2008). Building a mew army: military reform in the Qajar era. In R. Farmanfarmaian (ed.), *War and Peace in Qajar Persia: Implications Past and Present*, London: Routlidge, pp.47–87.

Curtis, J., and Kruszynnski, M. (2002). *Ancient Caucasian and Related Material in the British Museum*. London: British Museum Occasional Paper no. 121).

Curatola, G., and Scarcia, G. (2007). *The Art and Architecture of Persia*. Abbeville Press.

Curzon, G. N. (1892). *Persia and the Persian Question (2 Volumes)*. London: Longmans, Green and Company.

Custos, Dominicus (1600–1602). *Atrium Heroicum Caesarum*. Augsburg: M. Manger, J. Praetorius.

D'Souza, D. (2008). *The Enemy at Home: The Cultural left and its Responsibility for 9/11*. Random House of Canada.

Dailami, P. (2006). The populists of Rasht: Pan-Islamism and the role of the Central Powers. In Atabaki, T. (Ed.), *Iran and the First World War: Battleground of the Great Powers*, London: I. B. Tauris, pp.137–162.

Daniel, E. L. (2001). *The History of Iran*. Greenwood Publishing Group.

Daniel, E. L., and Mahdi, A. A. (2006). *The Culture and Customs of Iran*. Greenwood Publishing Group.

Davari, M. T. (2005). *The Political Thought of Ayatullah Murtaza Mutahhari: An Iranian*. Routledge.

Davenport-Hines, R. P. T., and Jones, G. (2003). *British Businesses in Asia since 1860*. Cambridge University Press.

De Gobineau, C. (Translated from French original in 1905 to Persian by Z. Mansouri n. d). *Se Sal dar Iran [Three years in Iran]*. Tehran: Entesharate Farrokhi.

DeFronzo, J. (1996). *Revolutions and Revolutionary Movements*. Westview Press.

Del Testa, D. W., Lemoine, F., Strickland, J. (2001). *Government Leaders, Military Rulers, and Political Activists*. Greenwood Publishing Group.

Destrée-Donckier de Donceel, A. (Translated from French original to Persian by N. Mafi in 1974). *Mostakhdemine Belgiki dar Khedmate Dolate Iran [Belgian Employees in the Service of the Iranian Government]*. Tehran: Nashre Tarikh-e Iran.

Diakonov, I. M. (1985a). Media. In I., Gershevitch (Ed.), *Cambridge History of Iran: Vol. 2 The Median and Achaemenean Periods*, Great Britain, Cambridge University Press, pp.36–148.

Diakonov, I. M. (1985b). Elam. In I., Gershevitch (Ed.), *Cambridge History of Iran: Vol. 2 The Median and Achaemenean Periods*, Great Britain, Cambridge University Press, pp.1–24.

Diba, F. (1986). *Mohammad Mossadegh: Political Autobiography*. London and New York: Routledge.

Dodgeon, M. H. and Lieu, S. M. C. (1991). *The Roman Eastern Frontier and the Persian Wars (AD 226–363)*. London and New York: Routledge.

Dorman, W. A., and Farhang, M. (1988). *The US Press and Iran: Foreign Policy and the Journalism of Deference*. University of California Press.

Downing, M., Beck, S. and BBC (2003). *Battle for Iraq: BBC News Correspondents on the War against Saddam*. Johns Hopkins University Press.

Dumper, M. R. T. and Stanley, B. E. (2006). *Cities of the Middle East and North Africa: A Historical Encyclopedia*. ABC-CLIO.

Dunstan, S. (2003). *Chieftain Main Battle Tank 1965–2003*. Oxford: Osprey Publishing.

Dupuy, R. E., Dupuy, T. N. (1986). *The Encyclopedia of Military History: From 3500 B. C. to the Present*. Harper and Row.

Dzhirkvelov, I. (1987). *Secret Servant: My Life with the KGB and the Soviet Elite*. New York: Simon and Shuster.

Eagleton, W. (1963). *The Kurdish Republic of Mahabad 1946*. Oxford University Press.

Earthwatch Institute-Australia, Action Research (1969). *Annual Review*. Great Britain, Institute for Defense Studies and Analyses and Earthwatch Institute-Australia.

Edwardes, S. M., Garrett, H. L. O. (1950). *Mughal Rule in India*. Netcong, New Jersey: Atlantic Publishers and Distributers.

Ehsani, M. T. (1989). *Haft Hezar Sal Honar-e Felezkari dar Iran [Seven Thousand Years of the Art/Craft of Metalworking in Iran]*. Tehran: Entesharate Elmi va Farhangi.

Elgood, C. (1953). Persian carpets. In A. J. Arberry (Ed.), *The Legacy of Persia*, Oxford: Clarendon Press. pp.292–317.

Elgood, C. (Translated from English original into Persian by B. Farghani, 1991). *Tarikhe Pezeshkiye Iran [The Medical History of Persia]*. Tehran: Amir Kabir.

Elm, M. (1994). *Oil, Power, and Principle: Iran's Oil Nationalization and Its Aftermath*. Syracuse University Press.

Elwell-Sutton, L. P. (1978). Reza Shah the Great: Founder of the Pahlavi Dynasty. In G. Lenczowski (Ed.), *Iran under the Pahlavis*, Stanford: Hoover Institute Press, pp.1–50.

Emadi, H. (2001). *Politics of the Dispossessed: Superpowers and Developments in the Middle East*. Greenwood Publishing Group.

Eraly, A. (2000). *The Mughal Throne*. London: Phoenix.

Erdely, S., and Riasanovski, V. A. (1997). *The Uralic and Altaic Series*. Routledge.

Erteshadiyyeh, M. (1992). *Azhab e Siyasee dar Majles e Sevom [Political Parties in the Third Majlis]*. Tehran: Nashr e Tarikh e Iran.

Eskandari, I. (1988). *Khaterat [Memoirs]*, 2 volumes Paris: Hezb e Demokrat e Mardom e Iran.

Eskandari-Qajar. M. M. (2008). Between Scylla and Charybdis: policy making under conditions of constraint in early Qajar Persia. In R. Farmanfarmaian, R. (Ed.), *Qajar Persia: Implications Past and Present*, pp.21–46. Routledge.

Esposito, J. L. (2010). *The Future of Islam*. Oxford University Press.

Ettehadiye, M. (1976). *Ghooshei az Ravabete Kharejeeye Iran (1200–1280 HG) [A Sketch/Overview of Iran's Foreign Relations (1821–1901 AD)]*. Tehran: Agah.

Etemadolsaltaneh, M. H. K. (1970). *Sadr ol Tavareekh*. Tehran: Entesharate Vahid.

Etemadolsaltaneh, M. H. K. (1971). *Rooznameye Khaterate Etemadolsaltaneh [The Newspaper/Journal of the Memoirs of Etemadolsaltaneh]*. Tehran: Amir Kabir.

Etemadsaltaneh, M. H. K. (r. 1995). *Chehel Sal Tarikhe Iran [Forty years of Iranian History]*. Tehran: Asat.

Ettinghausen, (1972). *From Byzantium to Sasanian Iran and the Islamic world : Three Modes of Artistic Influence*. Leiden Brill.

Ewans, M., Pottinger, H., Macdonald-Kinneir, J., von Meyendorf, G., De Lacy Evans, G., MacNeill, J. (2002). *The Great Game: Britain and Russia in Central Asia: Part I*. Routledge.

Fakhrai, I. (1977). *Gilan dar Jonbesh e Mashrootiyat [Gilan in the Constitutional Movement]*. Tehran: Jibi.

Fakhrai, I. (1982). *Sardar e Jangal [The commander of the forest]*. Tehran: Javidan.

Falola, T., and Genova, A. (2006). *The Politics of the Global Oil Industry: an Introduction*. Greenwood Publishing Group.

Falsafi, N. (1965). *Zendeganiye Shah Abbas Avval [The Life and Times of Shah Abbas the First] (6 Volumes)*. Tehran University.

Fardust, H. (1998, translated by A. A. Dareini). *The Rise and Fall of the Pahlavi Dynasty: Memoirs of former General Fardust*. Motilal Banarsidass.

Farmanfarmaian, R. (2005). *Blood and Oil: a Prince's Memoir of Iran, from the Shah to the Ayatollah* . Random House of Canada.

Farmanfarmaian, R. (Ed.) (2008). *Qajar Persia: Implications Past and Present*. Routledge.

Farmanfarmaian, F. S. (2009). Georgia and Iran: Three Millennia of Cultural Relations An Overview. *Journal of Persianate Studies*, Volume 2 (1), pp.1–43.

Farouk-Slugett, M., and Slugett, P. (1987). *Iraq since 1958: From Revolution to Dictatorship*.Routledge.

Faroqhi, S. (2006). *The Cambridge History of Turkey: The Later Ottoman Empire, 1603–1839*. Cambridge University Press.

Farrokh, K. and Khorasani, M. M. (2009). Arms, Armor and Tactics of Sassanian Savaran. *Journal of the Iranian Studies*. Faculty of Literature and Humanities. Shahid Bahonar University of Kerman. Volume 8, Number 15, Spring 2009, pp.288–305.

Farsoun, S. K. (1985). *Arab Society: Continuity and Change*. Routledge.

Farwell, W. (2001). *The Encyclopedia of Nineteenth-Century Land Warfare*. W. W. Norton.

Fasai, Hassan Ibn (1895–1896). *Fars Name e Nassiri [The Book of Fars of Nassiri]*. Tehran.

Fayazmanesh, S. (2008). *The United States and Iran: Sanctions, Wars and the Policy of Dual Containment*. Routledge Publishers.

Fernier, R. W. (1982). *History of the British Petroleum Company: Volume I the Developing Years 1901–1932*. Cambridge: Cambridge University Press.

Fernier, R. W., and Bamberg, J. H. (1994). *The History of the British Petroleum Company*. Cambridge University Press.

Feuvrier, J. B. (Translated from French by A. Iqbal-Ashtiani in 1989). *Se Sal dar Darbare Iran [Three years in the Court of Iran]*. Tehran: Donyaye Ketab.

Finkel, C. (2006). *Osman's dream: the story of the Ottoman Empire, 1300–1923*. Perseus Books Group.

Fischer, M. M. J. (2003). *Iran: From Religious Dispute to Revolution*. University of Wisconsin Press.

Flippin, R. (2003). *The Best American Political Writing*. Thunder's Mouth Press.

Floor, W. (2007). *The Rise of the Gulf Arabs: The Politics of Trade on the Persian Littoral*. Washington, D. C. : Mage Publishers.

Foran, J. (1994). *A Century of Revolution: Social Movements in Iran*. University of Minnisota Press.

Fraser, J. (1842). *The History of Nader Shah Formerly called Thamas Kuli Khan, the Present Emperor of Persia*. London: A. Millar.

Fredrikson, J. C, and Boyne, W. J. (2001). *Warbirds II: International Warbirds: An Illustrated Guide to World Military Aircraft, 1914–2000*. ABC-Clio.

Freedman, R. O. (1991). *The Middle East from the Iran-Contra Affair to Intifada*, New York: Syracuse University Press.

Freedman, R. O. (2009). *A Choice of Enemies: America Confronts the Middle East*. Public Affairs.

Frye, R. N. (1996). *The Heritage of Central Asia: from Antiquity to the Turkish Expansion*. Markus Wiener Publishers.

Frye, R. N. (1984). *The History of Ancient Iran*. C. H. Beck Verlag.

Frye, R. (1989). *The Golden Age of Persia: Arabs in the East*. London: Weidenfeld and Nicolson.

Gachechiladze, R. G. (1995). *The New Georgia*. Blackwell.

Gardane, C. A. (Translated from French 1865 original to Persian by A. E. Ashtiani in 1931, reprinted 1990). *Mission du General Gardane en Perse [The Mission of General Gardane in Persia]*. Bethesda, MD: Ibex Publications.

Garver, J. W. (2006). *China and Iran: Ancient Partners in a Post-Imperial World*. University of Washington Press.

Gaunt, D., Bet- awoce, J., and Donef, R. (2006). *Massacres, Resistance, Protectors: Muslim-Christian Relations in Eastern Anatolia in World War One*. Gorgias Press LLC.

Ganji, M. (2002). *Defying the Revolution: from a Minister to the Shah to a Leader of Resistance*. Greenwood Publishing Group.

Ganji, B. (2006). *Politics of Confrontation: The Foreign Policy of the USA and Revolutionary Iran*. Palgrave Macmillan.

Gansler, J. S. (1986). *The Defense Industry*. The M. I. T. Press.

Gasiorowski, M. J., and N. R. Keddie (1990). *Neither East nor West: Iran, the United States and the Soviet Union*. Yale University Press.

Ghani, C. (2000). *Iran and the rise of Reza Shah: from Qajar collapse to Pahlavi rule*. IB Taurus.

Ghareeb, E. (1990). The roots of crisis: Iraq and Iran. In C. C. Joyner (Ed.), *The Persian Gulf War: Lessons for Strategy, Law, and Diplomacy*, New York: greenwood Press, pp.21–38.

Ghirshman, R. (1962). *Iran: Parthians and Sassanians*. London: Thames and Hudson.

Ghirshman, R. (1964). *The Art of Ancient Iran (Volume I)*. New York: Golden Press.

Ghirshman, R., Minorsky, V., and Sanghvi, R. (1971), *Persia: The Immortal Kingdom*. London, England: Published by Orient Commerce Establishment.

Gilak, M. A. (1992). *Tarikh e Enghelab e Jangal [The History of the Revolution in the Forest]*. Rasht, Gilan: Gilakan.

Gilanshah, A., and Homayoun, E. (1961). *Yeksad o Panjah sal Saltanat dar Iran [150 Years of Monarchy in Iran]*. Tehran.

Golestaneh, A. M. A. (1965). *Majmal ol Tavareekh: Tarikh-e Vaghaye 35 sal baad az Nader Shah*. Tehran: Ketabkhaneye Ibn Sina.

Gommans, J. J. L. (2002). *Mughal Warfare: Indian Frontiers and Highroads to Empire: 1500–1700*. Routledge.

Goel, R. G., and Goel, V. (1988). *Encyclopaedia of Sports and Games*. Vikas Publishing House.

Graham, R. (1979). *Iran: the Illusion of Power*. Croom Helm Ltd.

Grammar, M. (2003). *Muslim Resistance to the Tsar: Shamil and the Conquest of Chechnia and Daghestan*.

Granmayeh, A. (2004). Legal History of the Caspian Sea, in Aldis, A. (Ed.), *The Caspian: Politics, Energy and Security*, pp.17–47. Routledge.

Graf, D. F., Hirsch, S. W., Gleason, K., and Krefter, F. (1992). *A Soaring Spirit 600–400 BC*. Time-Life Books.

Graz, L. (1993). *The Turbulent Gulf: People, Politics and Power*. Palgrave Macmillan.

Great Britain Naval Intelligence Division (1946). *Persia*. Oxford: *Its* Geographical Handbook Series.

Greaves, R. (1991). Iranian relations with Great Britain and British India 1798–1921. In P. Avery, G. Hambly, and C. Melville (ed. s), *Cambridge History of Iran Volume 7: From Nader Shah to the Islamic Republic*, Cambridge: Cambridge University Press, pp.374–425.

Gregorian, V. (2003). *The Road to Home: My Life and Times*. Simon and Schuster.

Goodrich, S. G. (1896). *A history of all Nations, from the Earliest Periods to the Present*. New York and Auburn, Miller, Orton and Mulligan.

Greatrex, G. and Lieu, S. M. C. (2002). *The Roman Eastern Frontier and the Persian Wars*. London and New York: Routledge.

Grummon, S. R. (1982). *The Iran–Iraq War: Islam Embattled. New York*: Praeger Publishers.

Grousset, R. (1970). *The Empire of the Steppes: A History of Central Asia*. Rutgers University Press.

Guest, J. S. (1987). *The Yezidis: A Study in Survival*. Routledge Kegan and Paul.

Guthrie, W. (1843). A new Geographical, Historical, and Commercial Grammar.

Guzel, H. C. Oguz, C., Karatay, O., and Ocak, M. (2002). *The Turks: Ottomans (2 volumes)*. Ankara: Yeni Turkiye.

Gvakharia, A. (1995). On the History of Persian-Georgian Contacts. *Proceedings of the Second European Conference of Iranian Studies*, edited by B. G. Fragner et al. Rome.

Gveseliani, (2008). The Notion of Iranian xvar nah in Post-Achaemenid Georgian Kingship.Journal of Persianate Studies 1, pp.174–182.

Gvosdev, N. K. (2000). *Imperial policies and perspectives towards Georgia, 1760–1819*. Pelgrave-Macmillan.

Haghighat, A. (1989). *Tarikh-e Nehzathay-e Fekriy-e Iranian dar Dorre-ye Qajariyeh: Bakhsh-e Dovom [A History of the Intellectual Movements of the Qajar Era-Part Two]*. Tehran: Sherkat-e Moalefan va Motarjeman-e Iran.

Halm, H. (2007). *The Shi'ites: A Short History*. Markus Wiener Publications.

Hambly, G. R. G. (1991a). Agha Mohammad Khna and the establishment of the Qajar dynasty. In P. Avery, G. Hambly, and C. Melville (ed. s), *Cambridge History of Iran Volume 7: From Nader Shah to the Islamic Republic*, Cambridge: Cambridge University Press, pp.104–143.

Hambly, G. R. G. (1991b). Iran during the reigns of Fathali Shah and Mohammad Shah. In P. Avery, G. Hambly, and C. Melville (ed. s), *Cambridge History of Iran Volume 7: From Nader Shah to the Islamic Republic*, Cambridge: Cambridge University Press, pp.144–173.

Hamblin, W. (1986). Sassanian military science and its transmission to the Arabs. *BRISMES Proceedings of the 1986 International Conference on Middle Eastern Studies*, 99–106.

Hansman, J. (1985). Anshan in the Median and Achaemenen periods. In I., Gershevitch (Ed.), *Cambridge History of Iran: Vol. 2 The Median and Achaemenean Periods*, Great Britain, Cambridge University Press, pp.25–35.

Hanway, J. (1753). *An Historical Account of the British Trade over the Caspian Sea…to which are added the Revolutions in Persia during the present Century, with the particular history of the great Usurper Nadir Kouli (Four Volumes)*. London.

Harding, S. A. (Translated from English original to Persian in 1974). *Khaterate Siyasi e Sir Arthur Harding [The Political memoirs of Sir Arthur Harding]*. Tehran: Markaz-e Nashr-e Daneshgahi.

Hariri, A. A. (1961). *Nameh-ha-ye Tabib-e Nader Shah*. Tehran: Anjoman e Asar e Melli.

Harney, D. (1998). *The Priest and the King: An eyewitness Account of the Iranian Revolution*. IB Taurus Publishers.

Harris, (2007). *The Indian Mutiny*. Wordsworth Editions.

Hattstein, M., and Delius, P. (2001). *Islam Art and Architecture*. Konemann.

Hawting, (2005). *Muslims, Mongols and Crusaders: Key Papers from SOAS*. Routledge.

Hazin, M. A. Sheikh (1831; edition of text by F. C. Balfour). *Tadhikirat al-Ahwal []*. London.

Healy, K. (1989). *Rajiv Ghandi: The Years of Power*. Vikas Publishing House.

Hedayat (Mokhber ol Saltaneh), M. (1965). *Khaterat va Khatarat [Memoirs/Memories and Dangers]*. Tehran: Ketabfoorooshiye Zavar.

Hedayat (Mokhber ol Saltaneh), M., and Soti, M. A. (1984). *Gozaresh-e Iran (Qajar va Mashrootiye) [The Report of iran: Qajars and the Constitutionalists]*. Tehran: Noghreh.

Hedayat, R. Gh. (reprinted 1994; with the supervision of Navai, A., and Mahdas, M. H.). *Fihrist ol Tavareekh []*. Tehran: The Social Sciences and Cultural Studies Research Center.

Hedayati, H. (1955). *Tarikh-e Zandiyeh [History of the Zands]*. Tehran: Tehran University Press.

Heinz Halm, H. (1987, Translated by J. Watson and M. Hill). *Shi'a Islam*. Columbia University Press.

Helms, C. M. (2005). *Iraq: Eastern Flank of the Arab World*. Brookings Institution Press.

Heravi, M. Y. R. and Fekri, M. A. (1993). *Eyn ol Vagheye*. Tehran: Entesharat va Amoozeshe Enghelabe Eslami.

Heravi. M., and Kay, K. K. (1999). *Iranian-American Diplomacy*. Ibex Publishers.

Herrman, A. (2008). *Gandhi and Churchill: the Epic Rivalry that Destroyed an Empire and Forged our Age*. Random House Canada.

Hershlag, Z. Y. (1980). *Introduction to the Modern Economic History of the Middle East*. Brill.

Herrmann, G. (1977). *The Iranian Revival*. Elsevier-Phaedon.

Hertz, N. (2003). *The Silent Takeover: Global Capitalism and the Death of Democracy*. HarperCollins.

Hickman, (1982). *Ravaged and Reborn: The Iranian Army 1982*. The Brookings Institution.

Ho, Y., Scott, R. H., Wong, K. I., and Chan, A. K. K. (1991). *The Hong Kong Financial System*.

Hobhouse, P., Hunningher, E., and Harpur, J. (2004). *Gardens of Persia*. Kales Press.

Hewson, R. H. (1982). Ethno-History and the Armenian Influence upon the Caucasian Albanians. In Samuelian, T. (Ed.), *Classical Armenian Culture: Influences and Creativity.*, pp.27–40. Chicago.

Hewson, R. (2001). *Armenia: A Historical Atlas*. The University of Chicago Press.

Hicks, J. (1975). *The Persians*. New York: Time-Life Books.

Hillenbrand, R. (1991). Safavid Architecture. In P. Jackson and L. Lockhart (ed. s), *The Cambridge History of Iran Volume 6: The Timurid and Safavid Periods*, pp.759–842, Cambridge: Cambridge University Press.

Hilterman, J. R. (2007). *A Poisonous Affair: America, Iraq, and the Gassing of Halabja*. Cambridge University Press.

Hinterhoff, E. (1984). *Persia: The Stepping Stone To India*. Marshall Cavendish Illustrated Encyclopedia of World War I, Volume IV. New York: Marshall Cavendish Corporation.

Hinz, W, and Jahandari, K. (1992). *Shah Ismail-e Dovom-e Safavi [Shah ismail II Safavid]*. Tehran: Entesharat-e Elmi va Farhangi.

Hiro, D. (1987). *Iran under the Ayatollahs*. Routledge.

Hiro, D. (1990). *The Longest War: The Iran–Iraq Military Conflict*. London, England: Paladin.

Hiro, D. (2003). *Desert Shield to Desert Storm: The Second Gulf War*. Author's Choice press.

Hirszowicz, (1966). *The Third Reich and the Arab East*. London, England: Routledge.

Hodgson, M. G. S. (1974). *The Venture of Islam (3 volumes)*. University of Chicago Press.

Hojjat, M. (1993). Cultural identity in danger. In (F. Rajaee, Ed.), in. *The Iran–Iraq War: The Politics of Aggression*, Miami, Florida: University Press of Florida, pp.41–46.

Holding, N. (2006). *Armenia with Nagorno Karabagh*. Bradt Travel Guides.

Holt, P. M., Lambton A. K. S., and Lewis, B. (1977). *Cambridge History of Islam: part I*. Cambridge University press.

Hopkirk, P. (1994). *Like Hidden Fire: The Plot to Bring Down the British Empire*. New York: Kodansha Globe.

Hopkirk, P. (2001). *On Secret Service east of Constantinople: the Plot to Bring down the British Empire*. Oxford University Press.

Hovannisian, R. G. (2004). *The Armenian People from Ancient to Modern Times*. Palgrave-Macmillan.

Howard, R. D., Sawyer, R. L., McCaffrey, B. R. (2003). *Terrorism and Counterterrorism: Understanding the New Security Environment*. McGraw-Hill.

Hughes, L. (2002). *Norman Schwartzkopf: Hero with a Heart*. Backprint Publications.

Hume, C. R. (1994). *The United nations, Iran, and Iraq*. Indiana University Press.

Hume-Griffith, M. E. (2008). *Behind the Veil in Persia and Turkish Arabia*. Das Press.

Hunter, S. T. (1995). Greater Azerbaijan: Myth or Reality? In M. R. Djalali (ed.), *Le Caucase post-Sovietique: La Transition dons le Conflicts*. Brussels: Bruylent and Paris, pp.115–142.

Hunter, S. T., and Malik, H. (2005). *Modernization, Democracy and Islam*. Greenwood Publishing Group.

Hussein, A. (1985). *Islamic Iran: Revolution and Counter-Revolution*. New York: St. Martin's Press.

Hutter, M. (2005). Bah ' s. In L. Jones, (Ed.), *Encyclopedia of Religion 2 (2nd ed.)*, Detroit: Macmillan Reference, pp.737–740.

HSBC Bank (2009). *HSBC: A Brief History*. London: HSBC Publications.

Huyser, R. E. (1986). *Mission to Tehran*. New York: Harper and Row.

Ibn Battuta (first translated and published 1929, reprinted 2004). *Travels in Asia and Africa 1325–1354*. Routledge.

Imperial Iranian Army (1967). *Mahnameye Nirooye Shahanshahi (Shomareye 2) [(Number 2)]*. Tehran: Enteshrate Ravabete Omoomiye Artesh.

Imperial Iranian Army (1969). *Mahnameye Nirooye Shahanshahi (Shomareye 3–3) [(Numbers 3–4)]*. Tehran: Enteshrate Ravabete Omoomiye Artesh.

Imperial Iranian Army (1969). *Mahnameye Nirooye Zameeniye Shahanshahi (Shomareye 15–17) [(Numbers 15–17)]*. Tehran: Enteshrate Ravabete Omoomiye Artesh.

Imperial Iranian Army (1976). *Shashanshiye Pahlavi: Nashreeye Yek, Farvardin [The Pahlavi Monarchy: First Publication, March–April]*. Tehran: Nirooye Zamaniye Shahanshahi.

Ingram, E. (1992). *Britain's Persian Connection 1798–1828: Prelude to the Great Game in Asia*. Oxford: Clarendon press.

Ingram, E. (1995). *Empire-Building and Empire-Builders*. Routledge.

International Security Yearbook (1984). *International Security Yearbook*. Georgetown University Center for Strategic and International Studies. St. Martin's Press.

Institute for Research and Studies of Culture (1992). *Farmanha va Raghamhaye Dorreye Qajar: Jeld-e Yek (1211–1260 H. G.) []*. Tehran: Moasseye Pazhohesh va Motaleat-e Farhangi (The Institute for Research and Studies of Culture).

Institute of Political Studies and Researcher (1985, 3rd ed.). *Koodetayeh Nojeh [The Coup d'etat of Nojeh]*. Tehran: Islamic Revolutionary Documents Center.

Iran Photo Foundation (1988). *A Photo Report on: the Chemical massacre in Halanbja by Iranian Photographers*. Tehran: Iran Photo Foundation.

Irvine, W. (2008). *The Army of the Indian Moghuls: Its Organization and Administration*. Yoakum Press.

Isfahani, M. M. B. Kh. (1984). *Kholase ol Seyr (Tarikh-e Roozegar Shah Safi Safavi)*. Tehran: Entesharat-e Elmi.

Ismael, T. Y., and Ismael, J. S. (1994). *The Gulf War and the new World Order: International Relations of the Middle East.* University Press of Florida.

Ivanov, M. S. (Translation from Russian original to Persian by K. Ansari, 1978). *The Constitutional Revolution of Iran.* Tehran: Amir Kabir.

Izady, M. (1992). *The Kurds: A Concise History and Fact Book.* Taylor and Francis.

Jahanshahlu-Afshar, N. (2006; compiled and edited by Nader Paymai). *Ma va Biganegan: Khaterate Siyasiye Dr. Bosratollah Jahanshalu-Afshar [Us and the Foreigners: The Political Memoirs of Dr. Bosratollah Jahanshalu-Afshar].* Tehran: Entesharate Samarqand.

Jangali, I. (1979). *Qiyam e Jangal [The Revolt of the Forest].* Tehran: Javidan.

Jayne, K. G. (2004). *Vasco Da Gama and His Successors 1460 to 1580.* Kessinger Publishing.

Jenkins, D. R. . (1997). *Grumman F-14 Tomcat: Leading US Navy Fleet Fighter.* Midland Publishing Limited.

Jouannin, J. M. (1840). *Turquie: L'Univers, Histoire et Description de tous les Peuples [Turkey: The Universe, History and Description of all the Peoples].* Paris.

Jokic, A. (2003). *Lessons of Kosovo: The Dangers of Humanitarian Intervention.* Broadview Press.

Jones, T. M., and Idriess, J. L. (1952). *Silent Service: Action Stories of the Anzac Navy.* Sydney: Angus and Robertson.

Joseph, J. (1961). *The Nestorians and their Neighbors: A study of Western Influence on their Relations.* Princeton University Press.

Juan de Persia (2004). *Don Juan of Persia,* Routledge,

Jwaideh, W. (2006). *The Kurdish National Movement: its Origins and Development.* Syracuse University Press.

Kamrava, M (1990). *Revolution in Iran: Roots of Turmoil.* Routledge.

Kapur, A. (1990). *Diplomatic Ideas and practices of Asian States.* Brill.

Karabaghi, M. J. J. (1845, reprinted 1950 with M. Adigozel-bek). *Karabakh-Name.* Baku.

Karsh, E. (1996). *Between War and Peace: Dilemmas of Israeli Security.* Routledge

Karsh, E. (2002). *The Iran–Iraq War 1980–1988.* Osprey Publishing.

Karsh, E. (2007). *Islamic Imperialism: A History.* Yale University Press.

Kashani, M. H. M., Etehadiye, M., and Saadvandian, S. (1983). *Vagheate Etefaghiye dar Roozegar (Vaghaye, Tarikh va Asnade Dorre Mashrootiyeh) (Do Jeld) [The Eventful occurrences of the times (Events, History and Documents of the Constitutional Era) (2 Volumes)].* Tehran: Nashre Tarikhe Iran.

Kasravi, A. (). *Tarikh-e Pansad Saley-e Khuzestan [The Five Hundred Year History of Khuzestan].* Tehran:-.

Kasravi, A. (reprinted 1999). *Tarikh-e Mashrooteye Iran [The History of the Constitutional Movement of Iran].* Tehran: Sedaye Moasser.

Kasravi, A. (Reprinted 2005; Orginally printed 1934–1940). *Tarikh-e Hejdah Saleye Azarbaijan [The Eighteen Year History of Azarbaijan: Remnant of the History of the Iranian Constitutional Revolution].* Tehran: Entesharat-e Majod.

Katouzian, H. (2006). *State and Society in Iran: The Eclipse of the Qajars and the Emergence of the Pahlavis.* I. B. Taurus.

Katouzian, H. (2004). Mosaddeq's Government in Iranian History: Arbitrary Rule, Democracy, and the 1953 Coup.In M. J. Gasiorowski and M. Byrne (Ed. s), *Mohammad Mossadegh and the 1953 Coup in Iran,* Syracuse University Press, pp.1–26.

Katouzian, H. (2003). *Iranian History and Politics: the Dialectic of State and Society.* Routledge.

Kaye, J. W. (1857). *History of the War in Afghanistan.* London: Richard Bently.

Kazemi, M., Alborz, M., and Vaziri, A. (1976). *Tarikhe Panjah Saleye Neeroye Zameeneye Shahanshahiye Iran [The Fifty Year History of the Land Forces of the Imperial Iranian Army].* Tehran: Published by the Imperial Iranian Army.

Kazemini, (1964). *Nagsh-e- Pahlevanan va Nehzat-e Ayyari dar Tarikh-e Ejtemai va Hayat Siyasi-e Mellat-e Iran [The Role of Pahlevanan and the Movement of Ayyan in the Social History and Political Settings of the People of Iran].* Tehran: Chapkhaneye Bank-e Melli-e Iran.

Kazemzadeh, F. (1950). *The Struggle for Transcaucasia.* New York: Philosophical Library.

Kazemzadeh, F. (1991). Iranian relations with Russia and the Soviet Union, to 1921. In P., Avery, G. Hamfly, and C. Melville (ed. s), *The Cambridge History of Iran Volume 7: From Nader Shah to the Islamic Republic,* pp.314–349, Cambridge: Cambridge University Press.

Keddie, N. R. (1966). *Religion and Rebellion Iran: The Tobacco Protest of 1891–1892.* Routledge.

Keddie, N. R. (1991). Iran under the Later Qajars 1848–1922. In P., Avery, G. Hamfly, and C. Melville (ed. s), *The Cambridge History of Iran Volume 7: From Nader Shah to the Islamic Republic,* pp.174–212, Cambridge: Cambridge University Press.

Keddie, N. R., and Richard, Y. (2000). *Modern Iran: Roots and Results of Revolution.* Yale University Press.

Keddie, N. R. (2007). *Women in the Middle East: Past and Present.* Princeton University Press.

Keegan, J. (1979). *World Armies.* New York: Macmillan Press.

Kashani, A. Gh., and Tabatabai, Gh. (1990). *Golshan Morad (Tarikh-e Zandiye).* Tehran: Zarrin.

Keddie, N. R., and Richard, Y. (1981). *Roots of Revolution; An Interpretive History of Modern Iran.* Yale University Press.

Keddie, N. R. (1999). *Qajar Iran and the Rise of Reza Khan 1796–1925.* Mazda Publishers.

Keddie, N. R. (2006). *Modern Iran: Roots and Results of Revolution.* Yale University Press.

Kelly, J. B. (1968). *Britain and the Persian Gulf: 1795–1880.* Oxford: Clarendon Press.

Kessler, E. H., and Wong-MingJi, D. J. (2009). *Cultural Mythology and Global Leadership.*Edward Elgar Publishing.

Khadduri, M. (1988). *The Gulf War.* Oxford: Oxford University Press.

Khanbaghi, A. (2006). *The Fire, the Star and the Cross: Minority Religions in Medieval and Early Modern Iran.* IB Tauris.

Khorasani, M. M. (2006). *Arms and Armor from Iran: The Bronze Age to the End of the Qajar Period.* Legat Verlag.

Khorasani, M. M. (2009a). Las Técnicas de la Esgrima Persa. *Revista de Artes Marciales Asidticas.* Volumen 204, Número 1, pp.20–49.

Khorasani, M. M. (2009b). Persian Firearms Part Four: Pistols and Gun Accessories in Iran. *Classic Arms and Militaria,* Vol.XVI/5, pp.35–40.

Khorasani, M. M. (2009c). Persian Firearms Part Three: The Percussion Cap Lock. *Classic Arms and Militaria,* Volume XVI Issue 3, pp.18–23.

Khorasani, M. M. (2009d). Persian Firearms Part Two: The Flintlock. *Classic Arms and Militaria,* Volume XVI Issue 2, pp.22–26.

Khorasani, M. M. (2009e). Persian Firearms Part One: The Matchlocks. *Classic Arms and Militaria,* Volume XVI Issue 1, pp.42–47.

Khorasani, M. M. (2010). Persian Firepower: Artillery. *Classic Arms and Militaria,* Volume XVI Issue 1, pp.19–25.

Khoury, D. R. (2002). *State and Provincial Society in the Ottoman Empire*. Cambridge University Press.

King, C. (2008). *The Ghost of Freedom: A History of the Caucasus*. Oxford University Press.

King, R. (1987). *The Adelphi papers 219: The Iran–Iraq War: The Political Implications*. London: The International Institute for Strategic Studies.

Kibovskii, A. andYegorov, V. (1996; translated by Mark Conrad 1998). The Persian Regular Army of the First Half of the Nineteenth Century. *Tseikhgauz*, pp.20–25.

Kinzer, S. (2003). *All the Shah's Men*. Wiley.

Kobylinsky, L. (2000). Persian and Indo-Persian arms. In A. R. Chodynski (ed.), *Persian and Indo-Persian Arms and Armour of 16th to 19th Century from Polish Collections*, Malbok: Museum Zamkowe w Malborku, pp.57–74.

Kolarz, W. (1952). *Russia and her Colonies*. London, England: G. Philip.

Krej í, J., and Krej ová, A. (1990). *Before the European Challenge: The Great Civilizations of Asia and the Middle East*. SUNY Press.

Kreyenbroek, P. G., and Sperl, S. (1992). *The Kurds: A Contemporary Overview*. Routledge.

Krusinski, Juda Thaddaeus (1728). *The History of the Revolution of Persia*. London: Originally Printed by S. Aris for J. Pemberton, 1728 and then printed for J. Osborne in 1740.

Kulke, H. and Rothermund, D. (2004). *A History of India*. Routledge.

Kurzman, C. (2004). *The Unthinkable Revolution in Iran*, Harvard University Press.

Kuznetsov, - (). *Tolbukhin*.

Laffin, J. (1989). *The World in Conflict 1989*. Oxford: Brassey's.

Lalani, A. R. (2000). *Early Shi'i Thought: The Teachings of Imam Muhammad Al-Baqir*. I. B. Tauris.

Lambton, A. K. S. (1953). *Persian Grammar: Including Key* . Cambridge University Press.

Lambton, A. K. S. (1969, reprinted 1991, I. B. Taurus Publishers). *Landlord and Peasant in Persia: A Study of Land tenure and Land*. Oxford: Oxford University Press.

Lambton, A. K. S. (1987). *Qajar Persia*. London: I. B. Tauris.

Landen, R. G. (1967). *Oman since 1856: Disruptive Modernization in a Traditional Arab Society*. Princeton: Princeton University Press.

Lando, B. (2007). *Web of Deceit: The History of Western Complicity in Iraq, from Churchill to Kennedy to George W. Bush*. Michigan: University of Michigan Press.

Lang, D. M. (1962), *A Modern History of Georgia*. London: Weidenfeld and Nicolson.

Lang, D. M. (1966). *The Georgians*. New York and Washington.

Ledeen, M., and Lewis, W. (1982). *Debacle: The American failure in Iran*. New York: Vintage Books.

Lee, J. L. (1996). *The Ancient Supremacy: Bukhara, Afghanistan and the Battle for Balkh: 1731–1901*. Brill.

Leffler, M. P., and Painter, D. S. (2005). *Origins of the Cold War: an International history*. Routledge.

Lewis, B. (ed.) (1994), *The World of Islam: Faith, People and Culture*, Thames and Hudson.

Lewis, B. (2004). *From Babel to Dragomans: Interpreting the Middle* East. Oxford University Press.

Lenczowski, G. (1980). *The Middle East in World Affairs*. Ithaca: Cornell University Press.

Limbert, J. W. (1987). *Iran at War with History*. Croom Helm.

Little, D. (2003). *American Orientalism: the United States and the Middle East since 1945* . IB Taurus.

Lockhart, L. (1938). *Nadir Shah: A Critical Study based Mainly upon Contemporary Sources*. London: Luzac.

Lockhart, L. (1958). *The fall of the Safavi dynasty and the Afghan occupation of Persia*. Cambridge, England: Cambridge University Press.

Lockhart, L. (1991). European contacts with Persia, 1350–1736. In P. Jackson and L. Lockhart (ed. s), *The Cambridge History of Iran Volume 6: The Timurid and Safavid Periods*, pp.373–409, Cambridge: Cambridge University Press.

Louis, Wm., R. (1984). *The British Empire in the Middle East*. Oxford: Clarendon Press.

Louis, Wm., R. (2004). Britain and the overthrow of the Mossadegh government. In M. J. Gasiorowski and M. Byrne (Ed. s), *Mohammad Mossadegh and the 1953 Coup in Iran*, Syracuse University Press, pp.126–177.

Library Information and Research Service (2006). *The Middle East*. Library Information and Research Service.

Lorimor, J. G. (1986). *Gazetteer of the Persian Gulf, Oman and Central Arabia (6 Volumes)*. Buckinghamshire, England: Archive Editions.

Lyman, R. (2006). *Iraq 1941: The Battles for Basra, Habbaniya, Fallujah and Baghdad*. Oxford: Osprey Publishing.

Mackey, S. (1998). *The Iranians: Persia, Islam and the Soul of a Nation*. New York: The Penguin Group.

Mackenzie, C. (1951). *Eastern Epic: Volume I: September 1939–March 1943 Defence*. London: Chatto and Windus.

Mafi, H. M. (1974). *Moghadamate Mashrootiyat [The background to the Constitutional Movement]*. Tehran: Entesharate Elmi.

Mafinezam, A., and Mehrabi, A. (2007). *Iran and its Place Among Nations*. Greenwood Publishing Group.

Mahdavi, A. H. (1985). *Tarikh-e Ravabete Kharejeeye Iran az Ebtedaye Dowran-e Safaviye ta payan-e Jang-e- Jahaniye Dovom*. Tehran: Amir Kabir.

Majd, M. G. (2001). *Great Britain and Reza Shah: The Plunder of Iran 1921–1941*. University Press of Florida.

Majd, M. G. (2003). *Persia in World War I and its Conquest by Great Britain*. University Press of America

Makki, H. (1991). *Zendeganiye Siyasiye Ahmad Shah [The Political Life of Ahmad Shah]*. Tehran: Amir Kabir.

Malcolm, S. J. (1829). *The History of Persia: From the most Early Period to the Present Time*. London, Murray.

Marcus, A. (2007). *Blood and belief: the PKK and the Kurdish fight for independence*. New York University Press.

Markham, C. R. (1874). *A General Sketch of the History of Persia*. London: Longmans, Green, and Company.

Marr, N. Y. (1897). *Khiton gospogen v kniinikh legendakh armian, gruzin i siriicev [God's tunic and Armenian, Georgian, and Syrian legend]*. St. Petersburg: Sbornik statei uchenikov Professora Barona Victora Romanovicha Rozena.

Marschall, C. (2003). *Iran's Persian Gulf policy: from Khomeini to Khatami*. Routledge.

Martin, V. (2008). Social networks and border conflicts: the First Herat War 1838–1841. In R. Farmanfarmaian (ed.), *War and Peace in Qajar Persia: Implications Past and Present*, London: Routlidge, pp.110–122.

Marvi, M. H. (1995). *Alam-ara-ye Naderi (3 volumes)*. Tehran: Elm.

Marzban, P. (1995). Honare Iran [The Arts of Iran]. Tehran: Nashre Farzan.

Mashkoor, M. J. (1999). *Tarikhe Iran Zamin az Roozegar Bastan ta Ghajarieh*. Tehran: Oshraghi.

Mashoun, H. (2001). *Tarikh-e Moosighiye Iran [The History of the Music of Iran]*. Tehran: Farhange Nashre Now.

Masoudi, A, H. A. H. (Translated by A. G. Payande in 1370). *Masrvaz Al-Zahab*. Tehran, Iran: Ali Farhangi Publishers.

Matini, J. (1989a). Persian artistic and literary pieces in the Saudi Arabian exhibition. *Iranshenasi: A Journal of Iranian Studies*, I (2), pp.390–404.

Matini, Jalal. (1989b). Azerbaijan Koja Ast? [Where is Azerbaijan?]. *Iranshenasi: A Journal of Iranian Studies*, I (3), pp.443–462.

Matini, Jalal. (1992). Nazaree be naghshe-ha-ye ghadeeme-ye Iran [An examination of the ancient maps of Iran]. *Iranshenasi: A Journal of Iranian Studies*, IV(2), pp.269–302.

Matofi, A. (1995). *Astarabad va Gorgan dar Bastar-e Tarikh-e Iran [Astarbad and Gorgan in the Context of the History of Iran]*. Derakhshesh.

Matofi, A. (1999). *Tarikh e Chahar Hezar Saleye Artesh e Iran: Jled e Dovoom [The Four Thousand Year History of the Iranian Army: Volume Two]*. Tehran: Iman Publications.

Matthee, R. P. (1991). *The Politics of Trade in Safavid Iran*. Cambridge: Cambridge University Press.

Matthee, R. P. (1996). Unwalled cities and restless nomads: Firearms and artillery in Safavid Iran. In C. Melville, (ed.), *Safavid Persia: The History and Politics of an Islamic Society*. I. B. Taurus, pp.389–416.

Mazzaoui, M. (ed.) (2003). *Safavid Iran and her Neighbors*. Salt Lake City: University of Utah Press.

May, E. R., Zelikow, P., and Lundberg, K. (2007). *Dealing with Dictators: Dilemmas of U. S. diplomacy and Intelligence Analysis 1945–1990*. The MIT Press.

McDowall, D. (2004). *A Modern History of the Kurds*. I. B. Taurus.

Muskhelishvili, D. L. (1978). K voprosu o svyazyakh Tsentral'nogo Zakavkaz'ya s Peredinim Vostokom v Ranneantichnuyu Epokhu [On the links of Central Transcaucasia with the Near East in the early ancient period]. In O. D. Lordkipanidze (ed.), *Sakatvelos arkheolgiis sakitkhebi* [Questions of Georgian archaeology] I, Tbilisi, pp.17–30.

Melman, Y., and Javedanfar, M. (2008). *The Nuclear Sphinx of Tehran*. Basic Books.

Melville, C. (ed.) (1996). *Safavid Persia: The History and Politics of an Islamic Society*. I. B. Taurus.

Melville, Ch. (2007). Qadi Baidawi's Nizam al-tawarikh in the Safina-yi Tabriz: An early witness of the text. In A. A. Seyed-Gohrab and S. McGlinn (Eds.), *The Treasury of Tabriz: The Great Il-Khanid Compendium* (pp.91–102). Amsterdam: Rozenberg Publishers.

Mikaberidze, A. (2005). *The Russian Officer Corps in the Revolutionary and Napoleonic Wars: 1795–1815*. Spellmount Publishers.

Mihalkanin, E. S. (2004). *American statesmen: secretaries of state from John Jay to Colin Powell*. Greenwood Publishing Group.

Milani, M. M. (1994). *The Making of Iran's Islamic Revolution: from Monarchy to Islamic Republic*. Westview Press.

Milani, A. (2008). *Eminent Persians: the Men and Women who made Modern Iran 1941–1979*. Syracuse University Press.

Miller, J., and Mylroie, L. (1990). *Saddam Hussein and the Crisis in the Gulf*. New York: Times Books.

Miller, F. P., Vandome, A. F., and McBrewster, J. (2009). *Sassanid Empire: Fall of Sassanids, Muslim Conquest of Persia, Sassanid Army, Sassanid Music, Sassanid architecture, Sassanid Church, Sasanian Family Tree*. Alphascript Publishing.

Ministry of Culture and Art of Iran (1971). *Majmoo-ey-e Ahd-e namehay-e Tarikhi-ye Iran (az Ahd-e Hakhamaneshi ta ahd-e Pahlavi) [A Collection of the Historical Treaties of Iran (From thje Achaemenid to the Pahlavi eras)]* . Tehran: Ministry of Culture and Art of Iran.

Ministry of Culture and Art of Iran (1974–1975). *Aeen-e Keshvardari-e Iranian*. Tehran: Ministry of Culture and Art of Iran.

Minorsky, (1942). The Poetry of Shah Ismail. *Bulletin of the School of Oriental and African Studies*, 10 (4), pp.1006–1053.

Mirfakhrai, H. (1984). *Imperial Iranian armed forces and the revolution of 1978–1979*. PhD Dissertation, Department of Political Science, State University of New York, Buffalo.

Mirii, H. (1970). *Ayneye Pahlevan Name [The Mirror of the Book of the Pahlavan]*. Tehran: Mihan.

Mirkhand, (Volumes I–VII), and Hedayat, R. Gh. (Volumes VIII–X) (Original in 1851, Reprinted 1960–1961). *Tarikh-e Rozat ol Safa [-]*. Tehran: Entesharat-e Ketabfooroshiye Khayyam, Markazi va Pirooz.

Miroshnikov, L. E. (1978). *Iran dar Jang e Jahani e Aval [Iran in the First World War]*. Tehran: Farzaneh Publications.

Mobley, R. (2003). Deterring Iran, 1968–71: the Royal Navy, Iran, and the disputed Persian Gulf islands. *Naval War College Review, October*, pp.107–119.

Moghtader, Gh. (1939). *Tarikh-e Nezamiye Iran [The Military History of Iran]*. Tehran: Chapkhaneye Fardin va Baradar.

Mohammadi, A. (2003). *Iran Encountering Globalization: Problems and Prospects*. Routledge.

Mohyi, J. (translation from French original to Persian, 1969). *Safarnameye de Ville (Sarhang Gaspar de Ville) [The Travelogues of De Ville (Colonel Gaspar de Ville)-Second print] – Chapp-e Dovom*. Tehran: Gutenberg.

Moin, M. (ed.) (1963). *Borhan Qate*. Tehran: Ibn Sina Books.

Moin, B. (1999). *Khomeini: the Life of the Ayatollah*. IB Taurus.

Mojtahed-Zadeh, P. (2007). *Boundary Politics and International Boundaries of Iran: A Study of the Origin, Evolution and Implications of the Boundaries of Modern Iran*. Universal Publishers.

Molavi, A. (2005). *The Soul of Iran*. Norton.

Momen, M. (1987). *An Introduction to Shii Islam: The History and Doctrines of Twelver Shiism*. Yale University Press.

Momen, M. (2007). The Bahá'í Faith, in C. H. Partridge (ed.), *New Lion Handbook: The World's Religions (3rd ed.)*, Oxford, UK: Lion Hudson.

Momeni, H. (1973). *Dowlat-e Nader Shah Afshar*. Tehran: Tehran University Press.

Monshi, I. B. (first published 1628, reprinted 1955–56, 1971, 2003 under Iskander Beg Torkaman). *Tarikh-e Alam Araye Abbasi*. Tehran: Amir Kabir.

Monshi, M. A. (reprinted 1977). *Safarnamye Rokn ol Dowleh [The Travelogues of Rokn ol Dowleh]*. Tehran: Sahar.

Morier, J. (1812). *A Journey through Persia, Armenia, Asia Minor to Constantinople, in the years 1808 to 1809*. London: Longman.

Morse, C. (2003). *The Nazi Connection to Islamic Terrorism*. Universe.

Morton, M. Q. (2006). *In the Heart of the Desert: The Story of an Exploration Geologist and the Search for Oil in the Middle East*. Green Mountain Press.

Mostashari, F. (2006). *On the Religious Frontier: Tsarist Russia and Islam in the Caucasus*. I. B. Tauris.

Mottahedeh, R. P. (2000). *The Mantle of the Prophet: Religion and Politics in Iran*. Oxford: Oneworld.

Motter, T. H. V. (1952). *The Persian Corridor and Aid to Russia*. Office of the Chief of Military History.

Moukbil Bey, M. (1928). *La Campagne en Perse 1514 [The Campaign in Persia 1514]*. Paris:-.

Mousavi-Isfahani. M. M. S., and Nafisi, S. (1938). *Tarikh-e Giti Gosha*. Tehran: Iqbal Publishers.

Mousavian, S. H. (2008). *Iran-Europe Relations: Challenges and Opportunities*. Routledge.

Motarjem, A. (translation from French originally during the reign of Nasser e Din Shah in 19th century) (reprinted 1977). *Safarnameye Tukestan va Iran: Henri Moser [The Travelogues of Turkestan and Iran: Henri Moser] – Chapp-e Dovom*. Tehran: Sahar.

Mowat, C. L. (1968). *The new Cambridge Modern History Volume XII: The Shifting Balance of World Forces, 1898–1945*. Cambridge University Press.

Munro, A. (2006). *Arab Storm: Politics and Diplomacy Behind the Gulf War*. IB Taurus.

Murphey, R. (1999). *Ottoman Warfare, 1500–1700*. Routledge.

Nafisi, S. (2004). *Tarikh-e Ejtemaee va Siasi-ye Iran Dar Dore-ye Moaser Az Saltanat-e Ghajar Ta Saranjam-e Fathali Shah* (2 Volumes). Tehran: Asatir.

Nafisi, S. (2005). *Babak-e Khorramdin*. Tehran: Attar.

Nahavandi, H., and Bomati, Y. (1998). *Shah Abbas, Empereur de Perse (1587–1629)*. Perrin, Paris.

Najmol-Molk, H. A. and Siaghi, M. D. (1962). *Safarnamey-e Khuzestan [The Travel Accounts of Khuzestan]*. Tehran: Moassesey-e Matbooati-ye Elmi.

Narvand, - (1975). *Ghoroob-e Khandan-e Zand [The Dusk/Decline of the Zand Clan/Dynasty]*. Tehran: Chapkhanye Etehad.

Nasidze, I., Quinque, D., Rahmani, M., Alemohamad, S. Y., Stoneking, M. (2006). Concomitant Replacement of Language and mtDNA in South Caspian Populations. *Current Biology*, 16, 668–673.

Natali, D. (2005). *The Kurds and the State: Evolving National Identity in Iraq, Turkey, and Iran*. Syracuse University Press

Navai, A. H. (1965). *Karim Khan Zand*. Tehran: Ketabkhaneye Ibn Sina.

Navai, A. H. (1977). *Fathe Tehran [The Conquest of Tehran]*. Tehran: Entesharat-e Babak.

Nayernuri, H. (1965). *Tarikhcheye Beyraq e Iran va Shir o Khorshid [A History of the Banner of Iran and the Lion and the Sun]*. Tehran: Entesharat e Motalleat va Tahghighat e Ejtema.

Nersesian, R. L. (2006). *Energy for the 21st Century: A Comprehensive Guide to Conventional and Alternative Sources*. M. E. Sharpe.

Newman, A. J. (2006). *Safavid Iran: rebirth of a Persian Empire*. I. B. Taurus.

Nicolle, D. (1995). *The Janissaries*. London, England: Osprey Elite Series.

Nicolle, D. (1993). *The Mamluks 1250–1517*. London, England: Osprey Men at Arms Series.

Nicolle, D. (1990). *The Age of Tamerlane*. London, England: Osprey Men at Arms Series.

Nicolle, D. (1987). *Armies of the Ottoman Turks 1300–1774*. London, England: Osprey Men at Arms Series.

Nikitine, B. and Sloan, E. B. (1923). The tale of Suto and Tato: Kurdish text with translation and notes. *Bulletin of the School of Oriental Studies*, 3(1), pp.69–106.

O'Ballance, E. (1988). *The Gulf War*. Brassey's.

Olson, R. W. (1973). *The Siege of Mosul: War and Revolution in the Ottoman Empire, 1720–1743*. Indianapolis, Indiana: Indiana University.

Olson, W. J. (1984). *Anglo-Iranian relations during World War I*. Routledge.

O'Shea, M. T. (2004). *Trapped between the Map and Reality: Geography and Perceptions of Kurdistan*. Routledge.

Otter, J. (1748). *Voyage en Turquie et la Perse [Voyage to Turkey and Persia]* (Volume I). Strasbourg and Paris.

Özo lu, H. (2004). *Kurdish Notables and the Ottoman Stat: Evolving Identities, Competing Loyalties, and Shifting Boundaries*. SUNY Press.

Padgin, A. (2009). *World's at War: 2,500 year Struggle between East and West*. Random House of Canada.

Pahlavi, F. (2005). *An Enduring Love: My Life with the Shah: A Memoir*. Hyperion – Miramax.

Palmer, M., and Palmer, P. (2007). *Islamic Extremism: Causes, Diversity, Challenges*. Rowman and Littlefield Publishers.

Panahi-Semnani, M. A. (1991). *Nader Shah: Baztab-e Hamase va Faje-eye Milli [Nader Shah: A reflection of the and the National Tragedy]*. Tehran: Ketab-e Nemoon-e.

Parizi, M. (1999). *Siasat va Eghtesad dar Asre Safavi [Policy and Economics during the Safavid Era]*. Tehran: Safi Alishah.

Parsa, M. (2000). *States, Ideologies and Social Revolutions: A Comparative Analysis of Iran*. Cambridge University Press.

Parsi, T. (2007). *Treacherous Alliance: the secret dealings of Israel, Iran, and the United States*. Yale University Press.

Parry, V. J., and Yapp, M. E. (1975). *War, Technology and Society in the Middle East*. London:-.

Peacock, L. (1986). *F-14 Tomcat*. London, England: Osprey Publishing.

Peers, D. M. (2006). *India under Colonial Rule*. Pearson Longman.

Pelletiere, S. C. (1992). *The Iran–Iraq War: Chaos in a Vacuum*. London, England: Praeger.

Pelliot, P. (1949). *Notes sur l'Histoire de la Horde d'Or [Notes on the History of the Golden Horde]*. Paris: Adrien-Maisonneuve.

Perry, J. R. (2006). *Karim Khan Zand*. Oneworld Publications.

Perl, L. (2007). *Theocracy*. Benchmark Books.

Pesyan, N. (1948–1949). *Marg Bood Bazgasht ham Bood [Death it was and the Return it Was]*. Tehran:-.

Peterson, J. E. (1978). *Oman in the Twentieth Century: political Foundations of an Emerging State*. Taylor and Francis

Page, M. E., and Sonnenburg, P. M. (2003). *Colonialism: An International Social, Cultural, Political Encyclopedia*. ABC-Clio.

Pfaltzgraff, R. L. (1988). *Emerging Doctrines and Technologies: Implications for Global and Regional Political-military Balances*. Published by Lexington Books, 1988

Pikolosekayev, [Translated to Persian by K. Keshavarz] (1975). *Tarikh-e Iran az Doran Bastan ta Payan-e Sadeye Hejdah Miladi*. Tehran: Payam.

Pipes, D. (1983). A border adrift: Origins of the conflict. In E. Tahir-Kheli and S. Ayubi (Ed. s), *The Iran–Iraq War: New Weapons Old Conflicts*, New York: Praeger, pp.3–25.

Pirnia, H., and Ashtiani, A. E. (2003). *Tarikh-e Iran [History of Iran/Persia]*. Tehran: -.

Pollack, K. M. (2002a). *The Persian Puzzle: The Conflict between Iran and America*. Random House of Canada.

Pollack, K. M. (2002b). *Arabs at War: Military Effectiveness 1948–1991*. University of Nebraska Press.

Pollack, K. M. (2002c). *The Threatening Storm: The case for Invading Iraq*. Random House of Canada.

Pope, A. A. (1945). *Masterpieces of Persian Art*. New York: The Dryden Press.

Porada, E. (1965). *The Art of Ancient Iran: Pre-Islamic Cultures*. New York: Crown Publishers.

Porada, E. (1991). Classic Achaemenean architecture and sculpture. In I., Gershevitch (Ed.), *Cambridge History of Iran: Vol. 2 The Median and Achaemenean Periods*, Great Britain, Cambridge University Press, pp.793–827.

Potter, L. G. (2008). The consolidation of Iran's frontier on the Persian Gulf in the nineteenth century. In R. Farmanfarmaian (ed.), *War and Peace in Qajar Persia: Implications Past and Present*, London: Routledge, pp.126–148.

Poulson, S. C. (2006). *Social Movements in Twentieth Century Iran: Culture, Ideology and Modelizing Frameworks*. Lexington Books.

Pour-Davood, I. (1949). *Zeen Abzar [Armament]*. Tehran: Chapkhaneye Arteshe Shahanshahi.

Prasad, B. (1957). *Campaign in Western Asia*. Calcutta: Official History of the Indian Armed Forces in the Second World War –1939–45.

Price, M. (2005). *Iran's Diverse Peoples: A Reference Sourcebook*. Santa Barbara, California: ABC-CLIO.

Pyankov, I. V. (1965). "Istoriya Persii Ktesiya I Sredneaziatskie Satrapii Achemenidov vo Konste V. B. do N. E". *Vestnik Drevnej Istorii*, 2, pp.35–50.

Qassem, A. S. (2009). *Afghanistan's Political Stability: A Dream Unrealized*. Ashgate Publishing.

Raeen, I. (1971). *Darynavardiyeh Iranian (Do jeld) [The Seafaring of the Iranians (Two Volumes)]*. Tehran: Chapkhaneye Ziba.

Rahman, M. (2007). *Khoda Hafez Vs Allah Hafez and Other Critical Essays*. Bangladesh: The University Press.

Radtke, B. (2007). Die mystischen schriften der Safina-yi Tabriz. In A. A. Seyed-Gohrab and S. McGlinn (Eds.), *The Treasury of Tabriz: The Great Il-Khanid Compendium* (pp.257–279). Amsterdam: Rozenberg Publishers.

Reza Rajab-Niya, R. (1955). Sazman-e Edari-ye Hokumat-e Safavi [The Administrative Organization of the Safavid State]. Tehran.

Rezazadeh, M. R. (1973). *Guyesh e Azari [The Azari Dialect]*. Tehran, Iran: Anjuman Farhang Iran Bastan publishers.

Rajaee, F. (1993). *The Iran–Iraq War: The Politics of Aggression*. Miami, Florida: University Press of Florida.

Ralph, D. (2006). In Zerembka (Ed.), *The Hidden History of 9-11-2001*, JAI Press.

Ralston, D. B. (1990). *Importing the European Army: The Introduction of European Military Techniques and Institutions into the Extra-European World, 1600–1814*. Chicago: University of Chicago Press.

Ramazani, R. K. (1971). The Autonomous Republic of Azerbaijan and the Kurdish People's Republic: Their Rise and Fall. *Studies on the Soviet Union*, 11 (4), pp.401–427.

Ranstorp, M. (1997). *Hizb'allah in Lebanon : The Politics of the Western Hostage Crisis*. New York, St. Martins Press.

Rau, J. (2008). *The Nagorno-karabakh conflict between Armenia and Azerbaijan. A brief historical outline*. Berlin: Verlag-Koester.

Ravandi, M. (1973). *Tarikh Ejtemaie Iran [Social History of Iran] (8 Volumes)*. Tehran: Gilan Press.

Ravasani, Sh. (n. d.). *Dolat va Hokoomat dar Iran [Government and Governance in Iran]*. Tehran: Nashe Shaam.

Rawlinson, (1875). *England and Russia in the East: A Series of Papers on the Political and Geographical Condition of Central Asia*. London: John Murray.

Rayfield, M. (2000). *The Literature of Georgia: A History*. Richmond.

Razi, A. (1957–1958). *Tarikh-e Kamel-e Iran [The Complete History of Iran]*. Tehran: Eqbal.

Reich, B. (1990). *Political Leaders of the Contemporary Middle East and North Africa: A Biographical Dictionary*. Greenwood Publishing Group.

Renfrew, C. (1994). World linguistic diversity. *Scientific American*, 270 (1), pp.116–120, 122–123.

Reynolds, D. (2001). *One World Divisible: A Global History Since 1945*. W. W. Norton.

Rezvani. B. (2008). The Islamization and Ethnogenesis of the Fereydani Georgians. *Nationalities Papers*, 36 (4), 593–623.

Rezvani. B. (2009). Iranian Georgians: Prerequistes for a Research. *Iran and the Caucasus*, 13, 197–204.

Rajendra, R., and Kaplan, G. T. (2003). *Iran*. Marshall Cavendish.

Richards, J. F. (1996). The Mughul Empire. Cambridge University Press.

Richelson, J. T. (1997). *A Century of Spies: Intelligence in the Twentieth Century*. Oxford University Press.

Roemer, H. R. (1991). The Safavid Period. In P. Jackson and L. Lockhart (ed. s), *The Cambridge History of Iran Volume 6: The Timurid and Safavid Periods*, pp.189–347, Cambridge: Cambridge University Press.

Rogerson, B. (2007). *The Heirs of Muhammad: Islam's First Century and the Origins of the Sunni Shia split*. Overlook Press.

Romano, D. (2006). *The Kurdish Nationalist Movement: Opportunity, Mobilization, and Identity*. Cambridge University Press.

Romlu, H. B. (reprinted in 2005). *Ahsan ol Tavarikh [(3 Volumes)]*. Tehran: Bongahe Tarjome va Nashre Ketab reprinted by Asatir.

Ronczkowski, M. (2003). *Terrorism and Organized Hate Crime*. CRC Press.

Roosevelt Jr., A. (1947). The Kurdish republic of Mahabad. *The Middle East Journal*, I(3), pp.247–269.

Rossow, R. (1956). The battle of Azerbaijan. *The Middle east Journal*, X(1).

Rostam ol-Hokma, M. H. (1800; reprinted 1973). *Rostam ol Tavarikh*. Tehran: Amir Kabir.

Rubin, B. (1981). *Paved with Good Intentions: The American Experience and Iran*. Penguin Books.

Rywkin, M. (1988). *Russian Colonial Expansion to 1917*.

Sabahi, H. (1990). *British Policy in Persia: 1918–1925*. London, England: Frank Cass.

Sackville-West, V. (1953). Persian carpets. In A. J. Arberry (Ed.), *The Legacy of Persia*, Oxford, Clarendon Press, pp.259–291.

Safavi, R. (1962). *Zendeganiye Shah Ismail e Safavi [The Life and Times of Shah Ismail the Safavid]*. Tehran: Ketbaforoushiye Khayyam.

Safavi, M. M. K. M. (1983). *Majma ol Tavareekh: Tareekh e Engheraz-e Selseley-e Safaviye ta sal-e 1207 Hejri*. Tehran: Ketabforooshiy-e Tehoori.

Saikal, A. (1980). *The Rise and Fall of the Shah: 1941–1979*. Princeton: Princeton University Press.

Saivetz, C. (1989). *The Soviet Union and the Gulf in the 1980s*. Boulder, Colorado: Westview Press.

Sakao lu, N. (2008). *Bu Mülkün kadın Sultanları: Vâlide Sultanlar, Hâtunlar, Hasekiler, kadınefendiler, Sultanefendiler*. O lak Yayıncılık.

Sanasarian, E. (2000). *Religious Minorities in Iran*. Cambridge University Press.

Saravi. M. F. T., and Tabatabai-Majd, Gh. (1992). *Tarikh-e Mohammadi [The History of Muhammad]*. Tehran: Amir Kabir.

Sardadvar, H. (1979). *Tazakoreye Joghrafiyaieh Tarikhiye Iran* [Notes on the geographical History of Iran], Tehran: Entesharate Toos.

Sarkar, J. (1973). *Nadir Shah in India*. Published by Naya Prokash.

Savory, R. M. (1967). The Sherley myth. *Iran, Journal of the British Institute of Persian Studies*, V, 73–81.

Savory, R. M. (1980). *Iran under the Safavids*. Cambridge University Press.

Savory, R. M. (1987). *Studies on the History of Safavid Iran*. London: Varorium Reprints.

Savory, R. M. (1994). Land of the Lion and the Sun, in Lewis, B. (ed.), *The World of Islam: Faith, People and Culture*, Thames and Hudson, pp.245–271.

Schahgaldian, N., Barkhordarian, G., United States. Office of the Under Secretary of Defense for Policy, Rand Corporation (1987). *The Iranian Military Under the Islamic Republic*. Rand Corporation.

Schulze, R. (2002). *A Modern History of the Islamic World*. NYU Press.

Sciolino, E. (2000). *Persian Mirror*. Touchstone.

Scott, P. D. (2008). *The Road to 9/11: Wealth, Empire and the Future of America*. University of California Press.

Seliktar, O. (2000). *Failing the Crystal Ball Test: The Carter Administration and the Fundamentalist Revolution in Iran*. Greenwood Publishing Group.

Setad e Bozorg e Arteshdaran [The Iranian Armed Forces Command] (1963). *Tarikh e Artesh e Novin e Iran [The History of the New Iranian Army]*. Tehran: Chapkhaney e Artesh.

Seton-Watson, H. (1988). *The Russian Empire 1801–1917*. Oxford University Press.

Shabani, R. (1990). *Tarikh Ejtemaie Iran dar Asr-e Afshariye [Social History of Iran during the Afsharid Period (2 volumes)]*. Tehran.

Shabani, R. (2005). *Iranian History at a Glance*. United Kingdom: Alhoda.

Shafi, M., and Shaabani, R. (1970). *Tarikh-e Nader Shahi*. Tehran: Bonyad-e Farhang-e Iran.

Shamim, A. A. (1995). *Iran dar Dorrey-e Saltanat-e Qajar (Chapp-e Sheshom) [Iran during the Qajar Monarchy Era* (6th ed.)]. Tehran: Moddaber.

Shamim, A. A. (1980). *Az Nader ta Koodetaye Reza Khan Mir Panj*. Tehran: Moddaber.

Shamim, A. A. (2005). *Iran dar Dorre ye Saltanat e Qajar [Iran during the Era of the Qajar Dynasty]*. Tehran: Entesharat e Zaryab.

Sharma, R. C. (1984). *Perspectives on the Iran–Iraq Conflict*. New Delhi: Rajesh Publications.

Sharma, S. R. (1999). *Mughal Empire in India: A Systematic Study including Source Material (Volume 3)*. New Delhi: Atlantic Publishers and Distributors.

Sharma, S. (2007). Wandering Quatrains and Women Poets in the Khulasat al-asharr fi al-rubayat. In A. A. Seyed-Gohrab and S. McGlinn (Eds.), *The Treasury of Tabriz: The Great Il-Khanid Compendium* (pp.153–169). Amsterdam: Rozenberg Publishers.

Shaw, S. (1991). Iranian relations with the Ottoman Empire in the Eighteenth and Nineteenth centuries. In P. Avery, G. Hambly, and C. Melville (ed. s), *Cambridge History of Iran Volume 7: From Nader Shah to the Islamic Republic*, Cambridge: Cambridge University Press, pp.297–313.

Shaw, E. K. (1977). History of the Ottoman Empire and modern Turkey (Volume 2).

Shawcross, W. (1989). *The Shah's Last Ride*. Touchstone Books

Shermer, D. (1973). *World War One*. London, England: Octopus Books.

Shofield, R. N. (1993). *Kuwait and Iraq: Historical Claims and Territorial Disputes*. London: Royal Institute of International Affairs.

Shofield, R. N. (2004). Position, function and symbol: the Shaat al Arab dispute in perspective. In L. G., Potter and G. G. Sick (Ed. s), *Iran, Iraq and the Legacies of War*, New York: Palgrave Macmillan, pp.29–70.

Shafa, Sh. (1969). *Safarnamey Pietro Della Valle-Ghesmat e Marbood be Iran [The Travelogues of Pietro Della Valle- The Section pertaining to Iran]*. Tehran: Bongah e Tarjome va Nashr e Ketab.

Shiels, S. (2004). *Stan Shiels on Centrifugal Pumps: Collected Articles from "World Pumps" Magazine*. Elsevier Science.

Shirani, H. (1957). *Safarnamye Jean baptiste Tavernier (Chape Dovvom) [The Travelogues of Jean baptiste Tavernier] (Second Edition)*. Tehran.

Shokri, Y. (1971). *Alam Araye Safavi []*. Tehran: Bonyade Farhange Iran.

Siaghi, M. D. (1989). *Tazakor ol Molook (Sazman e Edari e Hokoomat-e Safavi)*. Tehran: Amir Kabir.

Sick, G. (1985). *All Fall Down: America's Encounter with Iran*. IB Taurus.

Sicker, M. (2000). *The Islamic World in Decline:from the Treaty of Karlowitz to the Disintegration of the Ottoman Empire*. Greenwood Publishing Group.

Sicker, M. (2001). *The Middle East in the Twentieth Century*. Greenwood Publishing Group.

Singh, N. K. (2002). *International Encyclopaedia of Islamic Dynasties*. New Dehli: Anmol Publications.

Shuster, W. M. (1912). *The Strangling of Persia*. London: T. Fisher Unwin.

Slot, B. J. (1991). *The Origins of Kuwait*. Brill.

Smith, P. (2008). *An Introduction to the Bahai Faith*. Cambridge University Press.

Souresrafil, B. (1989). *The Iran–Iraq War*. Plainview, New York: Guinan Company Inc.

Spencer, W. (2004). *The United States and Iran*. Fitzhenry and Whiteside.

Spuler, B., and Marcinkowski, M. I. (2003). *Persian historiography and geography : Bertold Spuler on major works produced in Iran, the Caucasus, Central Asia, India and Early Ottoman Turke*y. Singapore : Pustaka Nasional.

Sreedhar (1985). *Iraq-Iraq War*. New Dehli, India: ABC Publishing House.

Staudenmaier, W. O. (1983). A strategic analysis. In E. Tahir-Kheli and S. Ayubi (Ed. s), *The Iran–Iraq War: New Weapons Old Conflicts*, New York: Praeger, pp.27–50.

Standish, J. F. (1998). *Persia and the Gulf: Retrospect and Prospect*. Richmond: Curzon Press.

Steinmetz, S. (1994). *Democratic Transition and Human Rights*. SUNY Press.

Steward, G. (1993). *The Marathas: 1600–1818*. Cambridge: Cambridge University Press.

Stewart, R. A. (1988). *Sunrise at Abadan: The British and Soviet Invasion of Iran, 1941*. New York: Praeger.

Stockman-Shomron, I. (1984). *Israel, Middle East and the Great Powers*. Transaction Books.

Strabo (translated 1924, ed. H. L. Jones). *Geographica*. Tufts University.

Stronach, D. (1991). Pasargardae. In I., Gershevitch (Ed.), *Cambridge History of Iran: Vol. 2 The Median and Achaemenean Periods*, Great Britain, Cambridge University Press, pp.838–855.

Subhi, M. (1783). *Tarih i Subhi [The History of Subhi]*. Istanbul:-.

Subrahmanyam, S. (1997). *The Career and Legend of Vasco da Gama*. Cambridge University Press.

Suleiman Effendi (1881). *Lughat e Chaqhatai (Chaqhatai Vocabulary)*. Istanbul.

Sullivan, W. H. (1981). *Mission to Tehran*. W. W. Norton.

Swietochowski, T. (1995). *Russia and Azerbaijan: A Borderland in Transition*. New York: Columbia University Press.

Sykes, C. (1936). *Wassmuss: The German Lawrence*. New York: Longmans, Green and Co.

Sykes, P. M. (2006). *A History of Persia*. Hesperides Press.

Tadnell, C. (1999). *Imperial Form: From Achaemenid Iran to Augustan Rome (A History of Architecture #3)*. Ellipsis Arts.

Tafrashi, M. S. Q. (1983). *Nazm o Nazeemeh dar Dorre Qajar []*. Tehran: Farhangsara.

Tafreshiyan, A. (1980). *Qiaym e Afsaran e Khorasan* [The Rebellion of the Officers of Khorasan]. Tehran: Elm Publications.

Taghzeli, N. (1967). *Safarnameye Sanson [The Travelogues of Sanson]*. Tehran.

Taheri, A. (1975–1978). *Tarikh-e Ravabet-e Bazargani va Siyasi-ye Iran va Inglis [The history of the Mercantile and Political relationship between Iran and England] (2 volumes)*. Tehran: Anjoman e Asar e Melli.

Taheri, A. (1985). *The Spirit of Allah*. Hutchinson.

Taheri, A. (1990). *Tarikh-e Siyasi va Ejtemaie ye Iran az Marg-e Timur ta Marg-e Shah Abbas [The political and Social history of Iran from the Death of Timur to the Death of Shah Abbas]*. Tehran: Sherkat-e Sahami e Ketabhay-e Jibi.

Tahmasbpour, M. R. (2008). *Nasser-od-din: The photographer King*. Tehran: Nashr-e Tarikh-e Iran.

Talbert, R. J. A. (2000). *Barrington atlas of the Greek and Roman world: Map-by-map Directory*. Princeton, NJ: Princeton University Press.

Tanner, (2009). *Afghanistan: A Military History from Alexander the Great to the War against the Taliban*. De Capo Press.

Tapper, R. (1997). *The Frontier Nomads of Iran: A Political and Social History of the Shahsevan*. Cambridge University Press.

Tarock, A. (1998). *The superpowers' involvement in the Iran–Iraq War*. Commack, New York: Nova Science Publishers, Inc.

Tarverdi, R, and A. Massoudi, A. (1971). *The land of Kings*, Tehran: Rahnama Publications.

Tehrani, I. A. (1993). Iraqi attitudes and the interpretation of the 1975 agreement. In (Ed.) F. Rajaee, *The Iran–Iraq War: The Politics of Aggression*, Miami: University Press of Florida, pp.2–23.

Timmerman, K. R. (1991). *The Death Lobby: How the West Armed Iraq*. Houghton-Mifflin Company.

Timmerman, K. R. (2004). *The French Betrayal of America*. Houghton-Mifflin Company.

Thomas, G. (1977). *The Languages and Literatures of the Non-Russian Peoples of the Soviet Union*. Canada Council, McMaster University Interdepartmental Committee on Communist and East European Affairs.

Thornton, L. (Translation from French original to Persian by M. Navai, 1995). *Images de Perse: Le Voyage du Colonel F. Colombari a la cour du Chah de Perse de 1833 a 1848 [The Images of Persia: The Travel of Colonel F. Colmbari to the Court of the Shah of Persia in 1833 to 1848]*. Tehran: Daftar-e Pezhoheshhay-e Farhangi.

Tourkin, S. (2007). Astronomical and astrological works in the 'Safine-ye Tabriz. In A. A. Seyed-Gohrab and S. McGlinn (Eds.), *The Treasury of Tabriz: The Great Il-Khanid Compendium* (pp.185–205). Amsterdam: Rozenberg Publishers.

Tousi, R. R. (1988). The Persian army 1880–1907. *Middle Eastern Studies*, 24(2), pp.206–229.

Townsend, J. (1977). *Oman: The Making of a Modern State*. London: Croom Helm.

Tripp, C. (2002). *The History of Iraq*. Cambridge University Press.

Tucker, A. R. (1987). Armies of the Gulf War. *Armed Forces*, July, pp.319–323.

Tucker, A. R. (1988). Armored warfare in the Gulf. *Armed Forces*, May, pp.223–226.

Tucker, E. S. (2006). *Nader Shah's Quest for Legitimacy in Post-Safavid Iran*. Miami: University Press of Florida.

Tucker, S., and Roberts, P. N. (2005). *Encyclopedia of World War One*. ABC-CLIO.

Turkaman, M (Ed.) (1991). *Asnadi darbareye Hojoom e Eenglis va Rous be Iran [Documents pertaining to the Assault of the British and the Russians against Iran]*. Tehran: Motale-ate Siyasi.

Turnbull, S. (1980). *The Mongols*. Osprey Publishing.

Turnbull, S. (2003a). *Ghengiz Khan and the Mongol Conquests 1190–1400*. Osprey Publishing.

Turnbull, S. (2003). *The Ottoman Empire 1326–1699*. Osprey Publishing.

Ullman, R. (1972). *The Anglo-Soviet Accord: Volume 3 of Anglo-Soviet relations 1917–1921*. Princeton: Princeton University Press.

Unit for the Publication of Documents-Office of International Political Studies (1991). *Nehzat e Mashroote dar Iran (bar Payeye Asnad e Vezarate Omoor e Khareje) [The Constitutional Movement of Iran (based on the Documents of the Ministry of Foreign Affairs)]*. Tehran: Dafter e Motaleate Siyasiye Bein ol Melali [Office of International Political Studies].

Valenta, J. (1974). The treaty of Brest Litovsk. History of World War One. Tayloer, A. J. P. (Ed.), *History of World War One*, London: Octopus Books, pp.231–235.

Van Beek, G. V. (1987). "Arches and vaults in the ancient Near East". *Scientific American*, July, pp.78–85.

Van Bruinessen, M. V. (2006). A Kurdish warlord on the Turkish-Persian frontier in the early twentieth century: Isma'il Aqa Simko. In Atabaki, T. (Ed.), *Iran and the First World War: Battleground of the Great Powers*, London: I. B. Tauris, pp.69–93.

Van Bruninessen, M. V. (1992). *Agha, Shaikh and State: The Social and Political Structures of Kurdistan*. London, England: Zed Books.

Van der Leeuw, C. (2000). *Azerbaijan: A Quest for Identity*. Palgrave Macmillan.

Vance, C. (1983). *Hard Choices. Critical years in US Foreign Policy*. Simon and Schuster.

Vance, R. G., Azari, A. (1961). *Tarikh-e Qajar az Ebteday-e Gharn-e 11 ta 1858 miladi*. Tehran.

Varahram, Gh. (1987). *Tarikh-e Siyasi va Ejtemai Iran dar Aasr-e Zand [The Political and Social History of Iran during the Zand Era]*. Tehran: Enteshart-e Moin.

Varahram, Gh. (1988). *Nezame Siyasi va Sazmanhaye Ejtemaeeye Iran dar Asr Qajar [The Political Establishment and Social organizations during the Qajar Era]*. Tehran: Entesharate Moin.

Venter, A. J. (2005). *Iran's Nuclear Option: Tehran's Quest for the Atom Bomb*. Casemate Publishers and Book Distributors

Volli, J. O. (1994). *Islam, Continuity and Change in the Modern World*. Syracuse University Press.

Von Kotzebue, M. (Translated from French original into Persian by M. Hedayat, 1969). *Mosaferat be Iran [Travel to Iran]*. Tehran: Amir Kabir.

Wagner, J. (1983). Fighting armies antagonisms in the Middle East, a combat assessment. In R. Gabriel (Ed.), Fighting Armies, Westport, Connecticut: Greenwood Press, pp.-.

Walker, C. J. (1990). *Armenia: the Survival of a Nation*. Palgrave Macmillan.

Ward, S. R. (2009). *Immortal: A Military History of Iran and its Armed Forces*. Georgetown University Press.

Wehrey, F., Green, J. D., Nichiporuk, B. (2008). *The Rise of the Pasdaran: Assessing the Domestic roles of Iran's Islamic Revolutionary Guards Corps*.

Wertheim, E. (2007). *The Naval Institute Guide to Combat Fleets of the World*. US Naval Institute Press.

Whittow, M. (1996). *The Making of Byzantium: 600–1025*. Berkley: University of California Press.

Wieczynski, J. L. (ed.) (1976). *The Modern Encyclopedia of Russian and Soviet history, Volume 14*. Academic International Press.

Wiesehofer, J. (Translated by Azizeh Azodi, 1996). *Ancient Persia: From 550 BC to 650 AD*. London: I. B. Taurus Publishers.

Wilcox, P. (1986). *Rome's Enemies: Parthians and Sassanid Persians*. Oxford: Osprey Publishing.

Wild, A. (2000). *The East India Company: Trade and Conquest from 1600*. The Lyons Press.

Wilkinson-Latham, C., and Embleton, G. (1977). *The Indian Mutiny (Men at Arms 67)*. Osprey Publishing.

Willet, E. (2004). *Ayatollah Khomeini*. The Rosen Publishing Group.

Williamson, G. (2008). The Turko-Persian War 1821–1823. In R. Farmanfarmaian (ed.), *War and Peace in Qajar Persia: Implications Past and Present*, London: Routledge, pp.88–109.

Winter, H. J. J. (1991). Persian Science in Safavid Times. In P. Jackson and L. Lockhart (ed. s), *The Cambridge History of Iran Volume 6: The Timurid and Safavid Periods*, pp.581–614, Cambridge: Cambridge University Press.

Wirsing, R. (1991). *Pakistan's Military under Zia, 1977–1988*. Palgrave-Macmillan.

Wolpert, S. A. (2003). *A New History of India*. Oxford: Oxford University Press.

Woodhead C., (1983), An Experiment in Official Historiography: The Post of Sehnameci in the Ottoman Empire, c. 1555-1605. *Wiener Zeitschrift für die Kunde des Morgenlandes, 75*.

Wollaston, A. N. (2005). *The Sunnis and Shias*. Kessinger Publishing.

Wratislaw, A. C. (1924). *A Consul in the East*. Edinburgh and London: Blackwoods.

Wright, D. (1980–1981). The implications of the Iran–Iraq War. *Foreign Affairs*, Winter, 59, pp.275–303.

Wright, D. (1977). *The English amongst the Persians*. London: I. B. Taurus.

Wright, R. B. (2001). *The Last Great Revolution*. Random House of Canada.

Yagut Al-Hamavi (Edited by Wustenfeld, F., 1866). *Kitab Mu'jam al-Buldan*. Leipzig, Germany: Bruckhaus.

Yekrangiyan, M. H. (1957). *Golgun-kafanan, Gushei az Tarikh-e Nezami-ye Iran*. Tehran: Mohammad Ali Elmi.

Yekrangian, M. H. (2005). *Seyrey dar Tarikh e Artesh e Iran: Az Aghaz ta Payan Shahreevar e 1320 [A Survey of the History of the Iranian Army: From the Beginning to September 1941]*. Tehran: Khojaste Press.

Yevgorova, N. I. (1996). *The "Iran Crisis" of 1945–1946: A View from the Russian Archives*. Washington, D. C.: Woodrow Wilson International Center for Scholars, Cold War International History Project, Working Paper No. 15.

Zabih, S. (1982). *Iran since the Revolution*. Croom Helm Ltd.

Zabih, S. (1988). *The Iranian Military in Revolution and War*. New York: Routledge.

Zakir, N. A. (1988). *Notes on Iran: Aryamehr to the Ayatollahs*. Karachi, Pakistan: Royal Book Company.

Zaloga, S. J. (1984). Hind overpowering or underrated? *Air International*, May, pp.-.

Zarevand (1926, translated from Armenian to English by V. N. Dadrian 1971). *United and Independent Turania*. Leiden: E. J. Brill.

Zarrinkoob, A. (2002–2003). *Roozegaran: Tarikh-e Iran az Aghaz ta Soghoot Saltanat-e Pahlavi [The Epocjs/Times Past: The Hisotry of Iran from its Origins until the Downfall of the Pahlavi Regime]*. Tehran: Chapkhany-e Meharat.

Zekaa, Y., Shushtari, M. A. E., and Ghaem-Maghami, J. (1970). *Pishineye San va Rezhe dar Iran*. Tehran: Entesharate Vezarate Farhang va Honar.

Zelter, R. and Rohrer, E. F. (1955). *Orientalische Sammlung Henri Moser- Chrlottenfeis Beschreibender der Waffen Sammlung*. Bern: Kommissionsverlag von KJ.

Zenkowsky, S. A. (1960). *Pan-Turkism and Islam in Russia*. Cambridge: Harvard University Press.

Zirinsky, M. F. (1994). The rise of Reza Khan. In J. Foran (Ed.), *A Century of Revolution: Social Movements in Iran*, pp 44–77. University of Minnesota Press.

Zurrer, W. (1978). *Kaukasien, 1918–1921: Der Kampf der Gorssmachte um die Landbrucke zwischen Schwarzem und Caspischen Meer [The Caucasus 1918–1921: The Battle of the Great Powers in the Land-bridge between the Black and Caspian Seas]*. Dusseldorf: Droste-Verlag.

Zwier, L. J., and Weltig, M. S. (2005). *The Persian Gulf and Iraqi Wars*. Lerner Publishing Group.

INDEX